Study Guide with Language Development Guide

for

Coon's

Psychology
A Modular Approach to Mind and Behavior

Study Guide with Language Development Guide

for

Coon's

Psychology
A Modular Approach to Mind and Behavior

Tenth Edition

Study Guide by
Thuy Karafa
Ferris State University

Language Development Guide by
Robert Moore
Marshalltown Community College

THOMSON
✳
WADSWORTH

Australia • Brazil • Canada • Mexico • Singapore • Spain • United Kingdom • United States

Printed in the United States of America
1 2 3 4 5 6 7 09 08 07 06 05

Printer: Globus Printing

ISBN 0-495-03114-3

Credit image: (c) Masterfile/Daryl Benson

Thomson Higher Education
10 Davis Drive
Belmont, CA 94002-3098
USA

For more information about our products, contact us at:
Thomson Learning Academic Resource Center
1-800-423-0563

For permission to use material from this text or product, submit a request online at
http://www.thomsonrights.com.
Any additional questions about permissions can be submitted by email to **thomsonrights@thomson.com.**

TABLE OF CONTENTS

Study Guide

Language Development Guide

Introduction
HOW TO USE THIS STUDY GUIDE

This *Study Guide* for *Psychology: A Modular Approach to Mind and Behavior, Tenth Edition* is designed to help you learn more, study efficiently, and get better grades. The exercises in this guide are closely coordinated with text chapters so that you can practice and review what you have read.

Each *Study Guide* chapter contains the following sections:

- ✗ **Chapter Overview**
- ✗ **Learning Objectives**
- ✗ **Recite and Review**
- ✗ **Connections**
- ✗ **Check Your Memory**
- ✗ **Final Survey and Review**
- ✗ **Mastery Test**
- ✗ **Answers**

A brief description of each section follows, along with suggestions for using them.

Chapter Overview

The Chapter Overview is a highly focused summary of major ideas in the text. By boiling chapters down to their essence, the Chapter Overview will give you a framework to build on as you learn additional ideas, concepts, and facts. Before you work on any other sections of this guide, read the Chapter Overview. In fact, it would be a good idea to re-read the Chapter Overview each time you use the *Study Guide*.

Learning Objectives

The Learning Objectives will show you, in detail, if you have mastered a reading assignment. To use them, you may want to write brief responses for each objective after you finish reading a chapter of the text. As an alternative, you may want to just read the Learning Objectives, pausing after each to see if you can respond in your own words. Then, after you have completed all of the other exercises in the *Study Guide* you can return to the Learning Objectives. At that time, you can either respond verbally or in writing. In either case, give special attention to any objectives you can't complete.

Recite and Review

This section will give you a chance to review major terms and concepts. Recite and Review is organized with the same Survey Questions found in the textbook chapters. This exercise will help you actively process information, so that it becomes more meaningful. Recite and Review also gives you a chance to practice recalling ideas from your reading, after you've closed the book.

As you work through Recite and Review, don't worry if you can't fill in all of the blanks. All of the answers are listed at the end of each *Study Guide* chapter. Filling in missing terms with the help of the answer key will focus your attention on gaps in your knowledge. That way, you can add new information to what you *were* able to remember. Page numbers are provided for each section of Recite and Review so you can return to the text to clarify any points that you missed.

Connections

This section contains matching-type items. It will help you build associations between related terms, facts, concepts, and ideas. Where appropriate, art is reproduced from the text so that you can match to images, rather than words. This is a good way to add links to your memory networks. Again, answers are listed at the end of the chapter.

Check Your Memory

The true-false statements in Check Your Memory highlight facts and details that you may have overlooked when you read the text. It's easy to fool yourself about how much you are remembering as you read. If you answered wrong for any of the items in Check Your Memory, you should return to the textbook to find out why. Page numbers listed for each group of items will make it easy for you to locate the relevant information in the textbook.

Final Survey and Review

This exercise might seem like a repeat of the Recite and Review section, but it's not. This time, you must supply a different set of more difficult terms and concepts to complete the review. The Final Survey and Review challenges you to consolidate your earlier learning and to master key concepts from the text. The Final Survey and Review is not a test. Don't be upset if you can't fill in some of the blanks. But do give missing ideas extra practice when you check your answers. Indeed, try to learn more each time you complete a *Study Guide* exercise, check your answers, or return to the text for review and clarification.

Mastery Test

The multiple-choice items of the Mastery Test are at least as difficult as those found on typical in-class tests. If you do well on the Mastery Test, you can be confident that you are prepared for in-class tests. On the other hand, a low score is a clear signal that further study and review are needed. However, don't expect to always get perfect scores on the Mastery Tests. In some cases, the questions cover information that was not reviewed in any of the preceding *Study Guide* sections. The Mastery Tests are designed to continue the learning process, as well as to give you feedback about your progress.

Answers

Answers for all of the preceding exercises are listed at the end of each *Study Guide* chapter. Answers for the Mastery Test include page numbers so you can locate the source of the question in the textbook.

A Five-Day Study Plan

There is no single "best" way to use this guide. Getting the most out of the *Study Guide* depends greatly on your personal learning style and study habits. Nevertheless, as a starting point, you might want to give the following plan a try.

Days 1 and 2   Read the assigned chapter in the textbook. As you do, be sure to make use of the Knowledge Builders and all the steps of the SQ4R method described in the textbook.

Day 3   Review the textbook chapter and any notes you made as you read it. Read the Chapter Overview in the *Study Guide* and read the Learning Objectives. Now do the Recite and Review section.

Day 4   Read the margin definitions in the textbook and the Chapter Overview in the *Study Guide*. Do the Connections and Check Your Memory sections of the *Study Guide*. Return to the textbook and make sure you understand why any items you missed were wrong.

Day 5   Review the textbook chapter and any notes you made as you read it. Read the Chapter Overview in the *Study Guide*. Then do the Final Survey and Review section, and check your answers. Return to the textbook and clarify any items you missed. Now take the Mastery Test. If you miss any questions, review appropriate sections of the textbook again. To really consolidate your learning, say or write responses to all of the Learning Objectives.

Summary

The close ties between *Psychology: A Modular Approach to Mind and Behavior* and the *Study Guide with Language Development Guide* make it possible for the *Study Guide* to be used in a variety of ways. You may prefer to turn to the *Study Guide* for practice and review after you have completed a reading assignment, as suggested in the Five-Day Plan. Or, you might find it more helpful to treat the *Study Guide* as a reading companion. In that case, you would complete appropriate *Study Guide* sections from each type of exercise as you progress through the text. In any event, it is nearly certain that if you use the *Study Guide* conscientiously, you will retain more, learn more efficiently, and perform better on tests. I hope you enjoy your journey into the fascinating realm of human behavior.

Introduction to
LANGUAGE DEVELOPMENT GUIDE

The *Language Development Guide* has been developed to help you master the material in your textbook, *Psychology: A Modular Approach to Mind and Behavior*, Tenth Edition. Each chapter of your text contains many idioms, special phrases, historical and cultural allusions, and challenging vocabulary that might be unfamiliar to you. In this guide, you will find simple definitions for these words and phrases.

Keep the guide open beside your textbook as you read each chapter. When you come to a word or phrase that is unfamiliar, look for the definition in the guide. To make it easy to use, the guide has been divided into manageable sections that correspond to sections in your textbook. In addition, the number of the page on which it appears in your text precedes each defined word or phrase.

PART I:

Study Guide

INTRODUCING PSYCHOLOGY AND RESEARCH METHODS

CHAPTER OVERVIEW

Psychology is the scientific study of behavior and mental processes. Psychology's goals are to describe, understand, predict, and control behavior. Psychologists answer questions about behavior by applying the scientific method and gathering empirical evidence. Psychologists may research such topics as development, learning, personality, sensation and perception, biopsychology, cognition, gender, social influence, culture, and evolution.

Psychology grew out of philosophy. The first psychological laboratory was established by Wilhelm Wundt, who studied conscious experience. The first school of thought in psychology was structuralism, a kind of "mental chemistry." Structuralism was followed by the rise of functionalism, behaviorism, Gestalt psychology, psychoanalytic psychology, and humanistic psychology. Five main streams of thought in modern psychology are behaviorism, humanism, the psychodynamic approach, biopsychology, and cognitive psychology.

The training of psychologists differs from that of psychiatrists, psychoanalysts, counselors, and social workers. Nearly 30 percent of all psychologists are employed full-time at colleges or universities. Some psychologists conduct basic research while others do applied research. Clinical and counseling psychologists specialize in doing psychotherapy. Other specialties are industrial-organizational, educational, consumer, school, developmental, engineering, medical, environmental, forensic, psychometric, and experimental psychology.

Scientific investigation involves observing, defining a problem, proposing a hypothesis, gathering evidence/testing the hypothesis, publishing results, and forming a theory.

Many psychological investigations begin with naturalistic observation, which is informative despite its limitations. In the correlational method, the strength of the relationship between two measures is investigated. Correlations allow predictions, but they do not demonstrate cause-and-effect connections.

Experiments show whether an independent variable has an effect on a dependent variable. This allows cause-and-effect connections to be identified. In an experiment, only participants in the experimental group are exposed to the independent variable. To control for placebo effects, a single-blind experiment is implemented, and to control for experimenter effects, a double-blind experiment is implemented.

The clinical method employs detailed case studies of single individuals such as the four Genain sisters who all became schizophrenic before age 25. In the survey method, people in a representative sample are asked a series of questions. This provides information on the behavior of large groups of people.

A key element of critical thinking is an ability to weigh the evidence bearing on a claim and to evaluate the quality of that evidence through careful comparisons, analyses, critiques, and syntheses.

Belief in various pseudo-psychologies is based in part on uncritical acceptance, the fallacy of positive instances, and the Barnum effect.

Information in the popular media varies greatly in quality and accuracy. It is wise to approach such information with skepticism regarding the source of information, uncontrolled observation, correlation and causation, inferences, oversimplification, single examples, and unrepeatable results.

LEARNING OBJECTIVES

To demonstrate mastery of this chapter, you should be able to:

1. List two reasons for studying psychology.

2. Define "psychology."

3. Define the term "behavior" and differentiate overt from covert behavior.

4. Explain the term "empirical evidence" and give an example of it.

5. Explain the term "scientific observation."

6. Give two reasons why the study of some topics in psychology is difficult.

7. Write a brief summary of each of the following areas of specialization in psychology: a. developmental b. learning c. personality d. sensation and perception e. comparative f. biopsychology g. psychology of gender h. social i. cultural j. evolutionary k. cognitive

8. Explain why animals are used in research and define the term "animal model" in your discussion.

9. Explain the four goals of psychology.

10. Explain the sentence "Psychology has a long past but a short history."

11. Describe the school of psychology known as structuralism, including: a. where and when it was established b. who established it (the "father" of psychology) c. the focus of its study d. research method and its drawback e. goal f. who took structuralism to the United States

12. Describe the functionalist school of psychology, including: a. its founder b. its goal c. major interests d. impact on modern psychology

13. Describe behaviorism, including: a. its founder b. why its founder could not accept structuralism or functionalism c. its emphasis d. Skinner's contributions and his concept of a "designed culture" e. its application in therapy

14. Describe the view of cognitive behaviorism.

15. Describe the Gestalt school of psychology, including: a. who founded it b. its goal c. its slogan d. areas of interest

16. Describe the contribution of women in the early history of psychology, and contrast the representation of women in psychology then and now. Name the first woman to receive her doctorate in psychology.

17. Describe the psychoanalytic school of psychology, including: a. who founded it b. its major emphasis c. the concept of repression d. the method of psychotherapy

18. Describe the humanistic school of psychology, including: a. how its approach differs from psychoanalytic and behavioristic thought b. who its major representatives are c. its position on "free will" (as contrasted with determinism) d. its focus on psychological needs e. its stress on subjective factors rather than the scientific approach f. the concept of self-actualization

19. Describe the eclectic approach.

20. List and briefly describe the five major perspectives in modern psychology.

21. Briefly describe biopsychology and cognitive psychology.

22. Describe the field known as "positive psychology."

23. Describe how an appreciation of cultural relativity and human diversity might enrich the understanding of psychology.

24. Characterize the differences in training, emphasis, and/or expertise among psychologists, psychiatrists, psychoanalysts, counselors, and psychiatric social workers. Describe the roles of clinical and counseling psychologists, and define the term "scientist-practitioner model."

25. List three points in the professional ethics code for psychologists established by the APA.

26. Identify the largest areas of specialization among psychologists. Name the major sources of employment for psychologists.

27. Differentiate basic from applied research.

The following objective is related to the material in the "Discovering Psychology" section of the text.

28. Identify other occupations that training in psychology can help you succeed in.

29. Explain the problem with using common sense as a source of information.

30. List the six steps of the scientific method.

31. Define the term "hypothesis" and be able to identify one. Explain what an operational definition is.

32. Explain the purpose of theory building and the importance of publication.

33. Describe the technique of naturalistic observation including both the advantages and limitations of this method. Explain what the "observer bias," the "observer effect," and the "anthropomorphic fallacy" are, and how they can lead to problems in psychological research.

34. Describe what a correlational study is, and list any advantages and disadvantages of this method. Explain what a correlation coefficient is, how it is expressed, what it means, and why it does not demonstrate causation.

35. List and describe the three essential variables of the experimental method.

36. Explain the nature and purpose for the control group and the experimental group in an experiment.

37. Explain the purpose of randomly assigning subjects to either the control or the experimental group.

38. Identify the advantages and disadvantages of the experimental method.

39. Explain what a placebo is, how effective it is, how it probably works, and what its purpose in an experiment is.

40. Explain what single-blind and double-blind experimental arrangements are.

41. Explain the nature of the experimenter effect and how it is related to the self-fulfilling prophecy.

The following objective is related to the material in the "Critical Thinking" section of the text.

42. List and describe three areas of ethical concern in psychological experiments, and explain the position of the APA in terms of ethical guidelines.

43. Briefly describe the clinical method of research, including advantages and disadvantages. Give an example of a case in which the clinical method would be used.

44. Briefly describe the survey method of investigation, including the importance of a representative sample, and an advantage and a disadvantage of the method. Define the terms "representative sample," "population," and "courtesy bias."

45. Define the term "critical thinking." Describe each of the four principles which form the foundation of critical thinking.

46. Briefly describe each of the following pseudo-psychologies: a. palmistry b. phrenology c. graphology d. astrology

47. List and explain the three reasons why pseudo-psychologies continue to thrive even though they have no scientific basis.

48. List seven suggestions that your author gives to help you become a more critical reader of psychological information in the popular press.

RECITE AND REVIEW

MODULE 1.1

Survey Questions: What is psychology? What are its goals? Pages 14-17

Psychology is both a science and a [1] _____ .

Psychology is defined as the scientific study of behavior and [2] _____ processes.

Psychologists study overt and covert [3] _____ .

Psychologists seek empirical [4] _____ based on scientific observation.

Scientific observation is [5] _____ so that it answers questions about the world.

Answering psychological questions requires a valid research [6] _____ .

Developmental psychologists study the course of human [7] _____ .

Learning theorists study how and why [8] _____ occurs.

Personality [9] _____ study personality traits and dynamics.

Sensation and perception psychologists study the [10] _____ organs and perception.

Comparative psychologists study different species, especially [11] _____ .

Biopsychologists study the connection between biological processes and [12] _____ .

Gender psychologists study differences between [13] _____ and [14] _____ .

Social psychologists study [15] _____ behavior.

Cultural psychologists study the ways that culture affects [16] _____ .

Evolutionary psychologists are interested in patterns of behavior that were shaped by [17] _____ .

Other species are used as [18] _____ models in psychological research to discover principles that apply to human behavior.

Psychology's goals are to describe, [19] _____ , predict, and control behavior.

MODULE 1.2

Survey Question: How did psychology emerge as a field of knowledge? Pages 19-23

Historically, psychology is an outgrowth of philosophy, the study of [20] _____ , reality, and human nature.

The first psychological [21] _____ was established in Germany by Wilhelm Wundt.

Wundt tried to apply scientific methods to the study of conscious [22] _____ .

Functionalism was concerned with how the mind helps us [23] _____ to our environments.

Behaviorism was launched by John B. [24] _____ .

Behaviorists objectively study the relationship between stimuli and [25] _____ .

The modern behaviorist B. F. Skinner believed that most behavior is controlled by [26] _____ reinforcers.

Cognitive behaviorism combines [27] _____ , reinforcement, and environmental influences to explain behavior.

Gestalt psychology emphasizes the study of [28] _____ units, not pieces.

According to the Gestalt view, in psychology the whole is often [29] _____ than the sum of its parts.

The psychoanalytic approach emphasized the [30] _____ origins of behavior.

Psychoanalytic psychology, developed by Austrian physician Sigmund [31] _____ , is an early psychodynamic approach.

Alfred Adler and Karen Horney are two well-known [32] _____ who revised part of Freud's theory by placing less emphasis on sex and aggression.

Humanistic psychology emphasizes free will, subjective experience, human potentials, and personal [33] _____ .

Psychologically, humanists believe that self-[34] _____ and self-evaluation are important elements of personal adjustment.

Humanists also emphasize a capacity for self-actualization—the full development of personal [35] _____ .

Positive psychology focuses on topics that relate to [36] _____ human functioning.

MODULE 1.3

Survey Question: What are the major trends and specialties in psychology? Pages 24-30

Five main streams of thought in modern psychology are behaviorism, [37] _____ , the psychodynamic approach, biopsychology, and cognitive psychology.

Much of contemporary psychology is an eclectic [38] _____ of the best features of various viewpoints.

To fully understand behavior, psychologists must be aware of human [39] _____ as well as human universals.

Our behavior is greatly affected by cultural [40] _____ and by social norms ([41] _____ that define acceptable behavior).

Psychologists who treat emotional problems specialize in [42] _____ or counseling psychology.

Psychiatrists typically use both [43] _____ and psychotherapy to treat emotional problems.

Freudian psychoanlysis is a specific type of [44] _____ .

Both counselors and psychiatric social workers have [45] _____ degrees.

Some major [46] _____ in psychology are clinical, counseling, industrial-organizational, educational, consumer, school, developmental, engineering, medical, environmental, forensic, psychometric, and experimental psychology.

Scientific research in psychology may be either [47] _____ or applied.

MODULE 1.4

Survey Questions: Why is the scientific method important to psychologists? How do psychologists collect information? Pages 31-36

Scientific investigation in psychology is based on reliable evidence, accurate description and [48] _____ , precise definition, controlled observation, and repeatable results.

Six elements of a scientific method involve observing, defining a [49] _____ , proposing a hypothesis, gathering evidence/testing the hypothesis, publishing [50] _____ , and forming a theory.

To be scientifically [51] _____ a hypothesis must be testable.

Psychological concepts are given operational [52] _____ so that they can be observed.

A [53] _____ is a system of ideas that interrelates facts and concepts.

Published research reports usually include the following sections: an [54] _____ , an introduction, a methods section, a [55] _____ section, and a final discussion.

The tools of psychological research include naturalistic observation, the correlational method, the experimental method, the [56] _____ method, and the survey method.

Naturalistic observation refers to actively observing behavior in [57] _____ settings.

Two problems with naturalistic studies are the effects of the observer on the observed (the observer [58] _____) and [59] _____ bias.

The anthropomorphic fallacy is the error of attributing human qualities to [60] _____ .

Problems with naturalistic studies can be minimized by keeping careful observational [61] _____ .

In the correlational method, the [62] _____ between two traits, responses, or events is measured.

Correlation coefficients range from +1.00 to −1.00. A correlation of [63] _____ indicates that there is no relationship between two measures.

Correlations of +1.00 and −1.00 reveal that [64] _____ relationships exist between two measures.

The closer a correlation coefficient is to plus or [65] _____ 1.00, the stronger the measured relationship is.

A positive correlation shows that [66] _____ in one measure correspond to increases in a second measure.

In a negative correlation, [67] _____ in one measure correspond to decreases in a second measure.

Correlations allow us to make [68] _____ , but correlation does not demonstrate causation.

MODULE 1.5

Survey Question: How is an experiment performed? Pages 37-40

[69] _____ -and-effect relationships in psychology are best identified by doing a controlled experiment.

In an experiment, conditions that might affect behavior are intentionally [70] _____ . Then changes in behavior are observed and recorded.

In an experiment, a variable is any condition that can [71] _____ and that might affect the outcome of the experiment (the behavior of subjects).

Experimental conditions that are intentionally varied are called [72] _____ variables.

[73] _____ variables measure the results of the experiment.

Extraneous variables are conditions that a researcher wishes to [74] _____ from affecting the outcome of the experiment.

Extraneous variables are controlled by making sure that they are the same for all [75] _____ in an experiment.

Subjects exposed to the independent variable are in the experimental [76] _____ . Those not exposed to the independent variable form the control [77] _____ .

Extraneous variables that involve personal [78] _____ , such as age or intelligence, can be controlled by randomly assigning subjects to the experimental and control groups.

If all extraneous variables are [79] _____ for the experimental group and the control group, any differences in behavior must be caused by differences in the independent variable.

Experiments involving drugs must control for the placebo [80] _____ .

In a single-[81] _____ study, subjects don't know if they are getting a drug or a placebo. In a double-[82] _____ study, neither experimenters nor subjects know who is receiving a real drug.

Researchers must minimize the experimenter effect (the tendency for people to do what is [83] _____ of them).

In many situations, the experimenter effect leads to self-fulfilling [84] _____ .

MODULE 1.6

Survey Question: What other research methods do psychologists use? Pages 42-44

Clinical psychologists frequently gain information from [85] _____ studies.

Case studies may be thought of as [86] _____ clinical tests.

In the survey method, information about large populations is gained by asking people in a representative [87] _____ a series of carefully worded questions.

Even though samples from [88] _____ -based research are not representative, advantages of it are the low cost and easy access to large groups.

The value of surveys is lowered when the sample is biased and when replies to questions are [89] _____ because of [90] _____ (a tendency to give socially desirable answers).

Survey Question: What is critical thinking? Pages 44-45

Critical thinking is the ability to [91] _____ , compare, analyze, critique, and synthesize information.

In psychology, [92] _____ thinking skills help evaluate claims about human behavior.

Critical thinking involves a willingness to [93] _____ evaluate [94] _____ .

Scientific observations usually provide the highest-quality [95] _____ about various claims.

Survey Question: How does psychology differ from false explanations of behavior? Pages 45-48

Palmistry, phrenology, graphology, and astrology are [96] _____ systems or pseudo-psychologies.

Belief in pseudo-psychologies is encouraged by uncritical acceptance, the fallacy of positive instances, and the [97] _____ effect, named after a famous showman who had "something for everyone."

PSYCHOLOGY IN ACTION

Survey Question: How good is psychological information found in the popular media? Pages 49-50

[98] _____ and critical thinking are called for when evaluating claims in the popular media.

You should be on guard for [99] _____ or biased sources of information in the media.

Many claims in the media are based on unscientific observations that lack control [100] _____ .

In the popular media, a failure to distinguish between correlation and [101] _____ is common.

Inferences and opinions may be reported as if they were [102] _____ observations.

Single cases, unusual [103] _____ , and testimonials are frequently reported as if they were valid generalizations.

CONNECTIONS

MODULE 1.1

1. _____ biopsychology
2. _____ psychology
3. _____ personality theorist
4. _____ empirical evidence
5. _____ covert behavior
6. _____ scientific observation
7. _____ EEG
8. _____ comparative psychology
9. _____ description
10. _____ understanding
11. _____ control

a. mental activities
b. brain waves
c. systematic observation
d. animal behavior
e. detailed record
f. human and animal behavior
g. "why" questions
h. brain and behavior
i. direct observation
j. traits, dynamics, individual differences
k. influencing behavior

MODULE 1.2

1. _____ Alfred Adler
2. _____ Wundt
3. _____ Titchener
4. _____ James
5. _____ Darwin
6. _____ Skinner
7. _____ Maslow
8. _____ Freud
9. _____ Pavlov
10. _____ Wertheimer
11. _____ Ladd-Franklin

a. father of psychology
b. psychoanalysis
c. natural selection
d. behaviorism
e. neo-Freudian
f. functionalism
g. color vision
h. introspection
i. self-actualization
j. Gestalt
k. conditioned responses

MODULE 1.3

1. _____ ethics
2. _____ psychiatrist
3. _____ psychologist
4. _____ social psychologist
5. _____ counseling psychologist
6. _____ school psychologist
7. _____ applied research
8. _____ positive psychology
9. _____ behavioristic view
10. _____ psychodynamic view
11. _____ cognitive view
12. _____ humanistic view

a. internal forces
b. environmental forces
c. marital consultant
d. solves practical problems
e. information processing
f. investigates attitudes and persuasion
g. Ph.D., Psy.D., Ed.D.
h. D.
i. professional code of conduct
j. self-image
k. optimal behavior
l. conducts psychological testing

MODULE 1.4

1. _____ observer effect
2. _____ hypothesis
3. _____ operational definition
4. _____ Clever Hans
5. _____ single-blind experiment
6. _____ correlational study
7. _____ correlation of +3.5
8. _____ scientific method

a. tentative explanation
b. placebo effect control
c. specific procedures
d. related traits, behaviors
e. math error
f. head signals
g. behavioral change due to awareness
h. controlled observation

MODULE 1.5

1. _____ identify causes of behavior
2. _____ independent variable
3. _____ dependent variable
4. _____ extraneous variables
5. _____ control group
6. _____ random assignment to groups

a. done by using chance
b. excluded by experimenter
c. reference for comparison
d. experimental method
e. varied by experimenter
f. effect on behavior

MODULE 1.6

1. _____ survey method
2. _____ placebos
3. _____ pseudo-psychology
4. _____ case studies
5. _____ valid sample
6. _____ courtesy bias
7. _____ ethical research

a. public polling techniques
b. participation is voluntary
c. clinical method
d. representative of population
e. inaccurate answers
f. astrology
g. sugar pills

CHECK YOUR MEMORY

MODULE 1.1

Survey Questions: What is psychology? What are its goals? Pages 14-17

1. Psychology can best be described as a profession, not a science.
   TRUE or FALSE

2. Psychology is defined as the scientific study of human behavior.
   TRUE or FALSE

3. Although it is a covert activity, dreaming is a behavior.
   TRUE or FALSE

4. The term *empirical evidence* refers to the opinion of an acknowledged authority.
   TRUE or FALSE

5. The term *data* refers to a systematic procedure for answering scientific questions.
   TRUE or FALSE

6. Naming and classifying are the heart of psychology's second goal, understanding behavior.
   TRUE or FALSE

7. Cognitive psychologists are interested in researching memory, reasoning, and problem solving.
   TRUE or FALSE

8. Animal models are used to discover principles that can be applied to animals only.
   TRUE or FALSE

MODULE 1.2

Survey Question: How did psychology emerge as a field of knowledge? Pages 19-23

9. In 1879, Wundt established a lab to study the philosophy of behavior.
   TRUE or FALSE

10. Wundt used introspection to study conscious experiences.
    TRUE or FALSE

11. Edward Titchener is best known for promoting functionalism in America.
    TRUE or FALSE

12. The functionalists were influenced by the ideas of Charles Darwin.
    TRUE or FALSE

13. Behaviorists define psychology as the study of conscious experience.
    TRUE or FALSE

14. Watson used Pavlov's concept of conditioned responses to explain most behavior.
    TRUE or FALSE

15. The "Skinner Box" is used primarily to study learning in animals.
    TRUE or FALSE

16. Cognitive behaviorism combines thinking and Gestalt principles to explain human behavior.
    TRUE or FALSE

17. Margaret Washburn was the first woman in America to be awarded a Ph.D. in psychology.
    TRUE or FALSE

18. Mary Calkins did early research on memory.
    TRUE or FALSE

19. According to Freud, repressed thoughts are held out of awareness, in the unconscious.
    TRUE or FALSE

20. Carl Jung and Erik Erikson were two neo-Freudians who firmly believed in Freud's psychodynamic theory.
    TRUE or FALSE

21. Humanists generally reject the determinism of the behavioristic and psychodynamic approaches.
    TRUE or FALSE

MODULE 1.3

Survey Question: What are the major trends and specialties in psychology? Pages 24-30

22. The five major perspectives in psychology today are behaviorism, humanism, functionalism, biopsychology, and cognitive psychology.
    TRUE or FALSE

23. Believing that human's behaviors are controlled by rewards, B. F. Skinner invented the "Skinner box" to study animals' responses.
    TRUE or FALSE

24. "The whole is greater than the sum of its parts" is a slogan of structuralism.
TRUE or FALSE

25. Mary Calkins was the first woman president of the American Psychological Association in 1905.
TRUE or FALSE

26. Freud's psychodynamic theory of personality focused on the unconscious thoughts, impulses, and desires with the exception of sex and aggression since they describe negative views of human behavior.
TRUE or FALSE

27. Humanism offers a positive, philosophical view of human nature.
TRUE or FALSE

28. The cognitive view explains behavior in terms of information processing.
TRUE or FALSE

29. Positive psychology focuses on the negative aspects of the self in order to achieve one's happiness and well-being.
TRUE or FALSE

30. To understand behavior, psychologists must be aware of the cultural relativity of standards for evaluating behavior.
TRUE or FALSE

31. Most psychologists work in private practice.
TRUE or FALSE

32. The differences between clinical and counseling psychology are beginning to fade.
TRUE or FALSE

33. To enter the profession of psychology today you would need to earn a doctorate degree.
TRUE or FALSE

34. The Psy.D. degree emphasizes scientific research skills.
TRUE or FALSE

35. More than half of all psychologists specialize in clinical or counseling psychology.
TRUE or FALSE

36. Clinical psychologists must be licensed to practice legally.
TRUE or FALSE

37. Over 40 percent of all psychologists are employed by the military.
TRUE or FALSE

38. Studying ways to improve the memories of eyewitnesses to crimes would be an example of applied research.
TRUE or FALSE

MODULE 1.4

Survey Questions: Why is the scientific method important to psychologists? How do psychologists collect information? Pages 31-36

39. The scientific method involves testing a proposition by systematic observation.
    TRUE or FALSE

40. An operational definition states the exact hypothesis used to represent a concept.
    TRUE or FALSE

41. Clever Hans couldn't do math problems when his owner left the room.
    TRUE or FALSE

42. Operational definitions link concepts with concrete observations.
    TRUE or FALSE

43. Most research reports begin with an abstract.
    TRUE or FALSE

44. Jane Goodall's study of chimpanzees made use of the clinical method.
    TRUE or FALSE

45. Concealing the observer helps reduce the observer effect.
    TRUE or FALSE

46. Anthropomorphic error refers to attributing animals' behaviors, thoughts, emotions, and motives to humans.
    TRUE or FALSE

47. A correlation coefficient of +.100 indicates a perfect positive relationship.
    TRUE or FALSE

48. Strong relationships produce positive correlation coefficients; weak relationships produce negative correlations.
    TRUE or FALSE

49. Perfect correlations demonstrate that a causal relationship exists.
    TRUE or FALSE

50. The best way to identify cause-and-effect relationships is to perform a case study.
    TRUE or FALSE

MODULE 1.5

Survey Question: How is an experiment performed? Pages 37-40

51. Extraneous variables are those that are varied by the experimenter.
    TRUE or FALSE

52. Independent variables are suspected causes for differences in behavior.
TRUE or FALSE

53. In an experiment to test whether hunger affects memory, hunger is the dependent variable.
TRUE or FALSE

54. Independent variables are randomly assigned to the experimental and control groups.
TRUE or FALSE

55. A person who takes a drug may be influenced by his or her expectations about the drug's effects.
TRUE or FALSE

56. Placebos appear to reduce pain because they cause a release of endogenous dexedrine.
TRUE or FALSE

57. In a single-blind experiment, the experimenter remains blind as to whether she or he is administering a drug.
TRUE or FALSE

58. Subjects in psychology experiments can be very sensitive to hints about what is expected of them.
TRUE or FALSE

59. The use of deception, invasion of privacy, and risk of harming subjects are some areas of ethical concerns in psychology.
TRUE or FALSE

60. It is easier and more accessible to use animals in research since guidelines for animals are more lenient than guidelines for humans.
TRUE or FALSE

MODULE 1.6

Survey Question: What other research methods do psychologists use? Pages 42-44

61. Phineas Gage is remembered as the first psychologist to do a case study.
TRUE or FALSE

62. Case studies may be inconclusive because they lack formal control groups.
TRUE or FALSE

63. The case study of the four Genain sisters who developed schizophrenia by the age of 25 is an example of environmental (nature) influence.
TRUE or FALSE

64. Representative samples are often obtained by randomly selecting people to study.
TRUE or FALSE

65. Representative sampling is an advantage of web-based research.
TRUE or FALSE

66. A tendency to give socially desirable answers to questions can lower the accuracy of surveys.
   TRUE or FALSE

Survey Question: What is critical thinking? Pages 44-45

67. Critical thinking is the ability to make good use of intuition and mental imagery.
   TRUE or FALSE

68. Critical thinkers actively evaluate claims, ideas, and propositions.
   TRUE or FALSE

69. A key element of critical thinking is evaluating the quality of evidence related to a claim.
   TRUE or FALSE

70. Critical thinkers recognize that the opinions of experts and authorities should be respected without question.
   TRUE or FALSE

Survey Question: How does psychology differ from false explanations of behavior? Pages 45-48

71. Pseudo-scientists test their concepts by gathering data.
   TRUE or FALSE

72. Phrenologists believe that lines on the hands reveal personality traits.
   TRUE or FALSE

73. Graphology is only valid if a large enough sample of handwriting is analyzed.
   TRUE or FALSE

74. Astrological charts consisting of positive traits tend to be perceived as "accurate" or true, even if they are not.
   TRUE or FALSE

75. The Barnum effect refers to our tendency to remember things that confirm our expectations.
   TRUE or FALSE

PSYCHOLOGY IN ACTION

Survey Question: How good is psychological information found in the popular media? Pages 49-50

76. The existence of dermo-optical perception (sixth sense) was confirmed by recent experiments.
   TRUE or FALSE

77. Psychological courses and services offered for profit may be misrepresented, just as some other products are.

TRUE or FALSE

78. At least some psychic ability is necessary to perform as a stage mentalist.

TRUE or FALSE

79. Successful fire walking requires neurolinguistic programming.

TRUE or FALSE

80. Violent crime rises and falls with lunar cycles.

TRUE or FALSE

81. If you see a person crying, you must infer that he or she is sad.

TRUE or FALSE

82. Individual cases and specific examples tell us nothing about what is true in general.

TRUE or FALSE

FINAL SURVEY AND REVIEW

MODULE 1.1

Survey Questions: What is psychology? What are its goals? Pages 14-17

Psychology is both a [1] _____ and a [2] _____ .

Psychology is defined as the scientific study of [3] _____ and [4] _____ .

Psychologists study both overt and [5] _____ behavior.

Psychologists seek [6] _____ evidence based on scientific observation. They settle disputes by collecting [7] _____ .

[8] _____ observation is structured and systematic.

Answering psychological questions requires a valid [9] _____ .

[10] _____ psychologists study the course of human development.

Learning [11] _____ study how and why learning occurs.

[12] _____ theorists study personality traits and dynamics.

[13] _____ and perception psychologists study the sense organs and perception.

[14] _____ psychologists study different species, especially animals.

[15] _____ study biological processes and behavior.

[16] _____ psychologists study differences between males and females.

Social psychologists study [17] _____ .

[18] _____ psychologists study the ways that culture affects behavior.

[19] _____ psychologists are interested in patterns of behavior that were shaped by natural selection.

Other species are used as [20] _____ in psychological research to discover principles that apply to human behavior.

Psychology's goals are to describe, understand, [21] _____ , and [22] _____ behavior.

MODULE 1.2

Survey Question: How did psychology emerge as a field of knowledge? Pages 19-23

Historically, psychology is an outgrowth of [23] _____ .

The first psychological laboratory was established in Germany by [24] _____ .

His goal was to apply scientific methods to the study of [25] _____ .

The first school of thought in psychology was [26] _____ , a kind of "mental chemistry."

[27] _____ was concerned with how the mind helps us adapt to our environments. William

[28] _____ was one of its proponents.

[29] _____ was launched by John B. Watson, who wanted to study the relationship between

[30] _____ and responses.

The modern behaviorist B. F. [31] _____ believed that most behavior is controlled by positive

[32] _____ .

[33] _____ behaviorism combines thinking and environmental influences to explain behavior.

[34] _____ psychology emphasizes the study of whole experiences, not elements or pieces.

According to Max [35] _____ and other [36] _____ psychologists, the whole is often greater than the [37] _____ of its parts.

The [38] _____ approach emphasizes the unconscious origins of behavior.

The Austrian physician, Sigmund [39] _____ , developed a psychodynamic system called

[40] _____ .

[41] _____ and Karen Horney are two well-known neo-Freudians who had revised part of Freud's theory by placing less emphasis on sex and aggression.

[42] _____ psychology emphasizes free will, subjective experience, human [43] _____ , and personal growth.

Psychologically, humanists believe that [44] _____ , self-evaluation, and one's

[45] _____ of reference are important elements of personal adjustment.

Humanists also emphasize a capacity for [46] _____ —the full development of personal potential.

[47] _____ psychology focuses on topics that relate to optimal human functioning.

MODULE 1.3

Survey Question: What are the major trends and specialties in psychology? Pages 24-30

Five main streams of thought in modern psychology are [48] _____ , [49] _____ , the

psychodynamic approach, [50] _____ , and cognitive psychology.

Much of contemporary psychology is an [51] _____ blend of the best features of various

viewpoints.

To fully understand behavior, psychologists must be aware of human [52] _____ , as reflected

in personal and [53] _____ differences.

Our behavior is greatly affected by [54] _____ values and by social [55] _____

(rules that define acceptable behavior).

Psychologists who treat emotional problems specialize in [56] _____ or [57] _____

psychology.

[58] _____ are medical doctors who typically use both drugs and [59] _____ to

treat emotional problems.

Freudian [60] _____ is a specific type of psychotherapy.

Both counselors and [61] _____ workers have Master's degrees.

[62] _____ psychologists specialize in the growth of children; [63] _____ psychologists

help design machinery; [64] _____ psychologists study classroom dynamics.

Scientific research in psychology may be either basic or [65] _____ .

MODULE 1.4

Survey Questions: Why is the scientific method important to psychologists? How do psychologists
collect information? Pages 31-36

Scientific investigation in psychology is based on reliable [66] _____ , accurate description and

[67] _____ , precise definition, controlled observation, and repeatable results.

The scientific method involves observing, defining a problem, proposing a [68] _____ , gathering

evidence/testing the hypothesis, publishing results, and forming a [69] _____ .

To be [70] _____ valid a hypothesis must be [71] _____ .

Psychological concepts are given [72] _____ definitions so that they can be observed. Such definitions state the exact [73] _____ used to represent a concept.

A [74] _____ is a system of ideas that interrelates facts and concepts. In general, good [75] _____ summarize existing [76] _____ , explain them, and guide further research.

The results of scientific studies are [77] _____ in professional [78] _____ so they will be publicly available.

The tools of psychological research include naturalistic observation, the correlational method, the [79] _____ method, the clinical method, and the [80] _____ method.

Naturalistic observation refers to actively observing behavior in [81] _____ , which are the typical [82] _____ in which people and animals live.

Two problems with naturalistic observation are the effects of the observer on the [83] _____ and observer [84] _____ .

The [85] _____ fallacy is the error of attributing human qualities to animals.

Problems with naturalistic observation can be minimized by keeping careful [86] _____ .

In the [87] _____ method, the strength of the relationship between two traits, responses, or events is measured.

Correlation [88] _____ range from +1.00 to −1.00.

A correlation of [89] _____ indicates that there is no relationship between two measures.

Correlations of +1.00 and −1.00 reveal that [90] _____ relationships exist between two measures.

The [91] _____ a correlation coefficient is to plus or minus 1.00, the stronger the measured relationship is.

A [92] _____ correlation or relationship shows that increases in one measure correspond to increases in a second measure.

In a negative correlation, [93] _____ in one measure correspond to [94] _____ in a second measure.

Correlations allow prediction, but correlation does not demonstrate [95] _____ .

MODULE 1.5

Survey Question: How is an experiment performed? Pages 37-40

Cause-and-effect relationships in psychology are best identified by doing a [96] _____ .

In an experiment, conditions that might affect behavior are intentionally varied. Then changes in behavior are [97] _____ and [98] _____ .

In an experiment a [99] _____ is any condition that can change and that might affect the outcome of the experiment.

Experimental conditions that are intentionally varied are called [100] _____ variables; they are potential [101] _____ of changes in behavior.

[102] _____ variables measure the results of the experiment; they reveal any [103] _____ on behavior.

[104] _____ variables are conditions that a researcher wishes to prevent from affecting the [105] _____ of the experiment.

Extraneous variables are [106] _____ by making sure that they are the same for all subjects in an experiment.

Subjects exposed to the independent variable are in the [107] _____ group. Those not exposed to the independent variable form the [108] _____ group.

Extraneous variables that involve [109] _____ characteristics, such as age or intelligence, can be controlled by [110] _____ assigning subjects to the experimental and control groups.

If all extraneous variables are identical for the experimental group and the control group, any differences in behavior must be caused by differences in the [111] _____ variable

Experiments involving drugs must control for the [112] _____ effect.

In a [113] _____ study, subjects don't know if they are getting a drug or a placebo. In a [114] _____ study, neither experimenters nor subjects know who is receiving a real drug.

Researchers must also minimize the [115] _____ (the tendency for people to do what is expected of them).

In many situations, the experimenter effect leads to [116] _____ prophecies.

MODULE 1.6

Survey Question: What other research methods do psychologists use? Pages 42-44

Clinical psychologists frequently gain information from [117] _____ , which focus on all aspects of a single [118] _____ .

Case studies may be thought of as natural [119] _____ of the effects of brain tumors, accidental poisonings, and other unusual conditions.

In the survey method, information about large [120] _____ is gained by asking people in a [121] _____ sample a series of carefully worded questions.

Web-based research is not representative even though it provides a large sample of people's responses.

The value of surveys is lowered when the sample is [122] _____ and when replies to [123] _____ are inaccurate or untruthful.

Survey Question: What is critical thinking? Pages 44-45

Critical thinking is the ability to evaluate, compare, analyze, [124] _____ , and [125] _____ information.

In psychology, critical thinking skills help [126] _____ claims about human behavior.

Critical thinking involves evaluating the quality of the [127] _____ used to support various claims.

[128] _____ observations usually provide the highest-quality evidence about various claims.

Survey Question: How does psychology differ from false explanations of behavior? Pages 45-48

Palmistry, [129] _____ , graphology, and astrology are [130] _____ -psychologies.

Belief in false psychologies is encouraged by [131] _____ acceptance, the fallacy of [132] _____ instances, and the [133] _____ effect.

PSYCHOLOGY IN ACTION

Survey Question: How good is psychological information found in the popular media? Pages 49-50

[134] _____ and [135] _____ thinking are called for when evaluating claims in the popular media.

You should be on guard for unreliable or [136] _____ sources of information in the media.

Many claims in the media are based on unscientific observations that lack [137] _____ groups.

[138] _____ does not demonstrate causation. In the popular media, a failure to distinguish between [139] _____ and causation is common.

Inferences and opinions may be reported as if they were objective [140] _____ .

Single [141] _____ , unusual examples, and testimonials are frequently reported as if they were valid [142] _____ .

MASTERY TEST

1. Data in psychology are typically gathered to answer questions about
   a. clinical problems
   b. human groups
   c. human cognition
   d. overt or covert behavior

2. Who among the following would most likely study the behavior of gorillas?
   a. developmental psychologist
   b. comparative psychologist
   c. environmental psychologist
   d. forensic psychologist

3. An engineering psychologist helps redesign an airplane to make it safer to fly. The psychologist's work reflects which of psychology's goals?
   a. understanding
   b. control
   c. prediction
   d. description

4. Who among the following placed the greatest emphasis on introspection?
   a. Watson
   b. Wertheimer
   c. Washburn
   d. Wundt

5. Which pair of persons had the most similar ideas?
   a. Titchener—Skinner
   b. James—Darwin
   c. Watson—Rogers
   d. Wertheimer—Maslow

6. The behaviorist definition of psychology clearly places great emphasis on
   a. overt behavior
   b. conscious experience
   c. psychodynamic responses
   d. introspective analysis

7. As a profession, psychology is fully open to men and women, a fact that began with the success of
   a. O'Sullivan-Calkins
   b. Tyler-James
   c. Ladd-Franklin
   d. Neal-Collins

8. The idea that threatening thoughts are sometimes repressed would be of most interest to a
    a. structuralist
    b. psychoanalyst
    c. humanist
    d. Gestaltist

9. "A neutral, reductionistic, mechanistic view of human nature." This best describes which viewpoint?
    a. psychodynamic
    b. cognitive
    c. psychoanalytic
    d. biopsychological

10. Which of the following professional titles usually requires a doctorate degree?
    a. psychologist
    b. psychiatric social worker
    c. counselor
    d. all of the preceding

11. Who among the following is most likely to treat the physical causes of psychological problems?
    a. scientist-practitioner
    b. psychoanalyst
    c. forensic psychologist
    d. psychiatrist

12. More than half of all psychologists specialize in what branches of psychology?
    a. counseling and comparative
    b. applied and counseling
    c. psychodynamic and clinical
    d. counseling and clinical

13. When critically evaluating claims about behavior it is important to also evaluate
    a. the source of anecdotal evidence
    b. the credentials of an authority
    c. the quality of the evidence
    d. the strength of one's intuition

14. Which of the following pairs is most different?
    a. pseudo-psychology—critical thinking
    b. graphology—pseudo-psychology
    c. palmistry—phrenology
    d. psychology—empirical evidence

15. The German anatomy teacher Franz Gall popularized
    a. palmistry
    b. phrenology
    c. graphology
    d. astrology

16. A tendency to believe flattering descriptions of oneself is called
    a. the Barnum effect
    b. the astrologer's dilemma
    c. the fallacy of positive instances
    d. uncritical acceptance

17. Descriptions of personality that contain both sides of several personal dimensions tend to create
    a. an illusion of accuracy
    b. disbelief and rejection
    c. the astrologer's dilemma
    d. a system similar to phrenology

18. Appreciating an orchestra playing Mozart's fifth symphony more than a musician playing a solo on a clarinet reflects _____ psychology.
    a. Gestalt
    b. cognitive
    c. behavioral
    d. biopsychology

19. If an entire population is surveyed, it becomes unnecessary to obtain a
    a. control group
    b. random comparison
    c. random sample
    d. control variable

20. Control groups are most often used in
    a. naturalistic observation
    b. the clinical method
    c. parascience
    d. experiments

21. Concealing the observer can be used to minimize the
    a. observer bias effect
    b. double-blind effect
    c. observer effect
    d. effects of extraneous correlations

22. A psychologist studying lowland gorillas should be careful to avoid the
    a. anthropomorphic error
    b. Gestalt fallacy
    c. psychodynamic fallacy
    d. fallacy of positive instances

23. Testing the hypothesis that frustration encourages aggression would require
    a. a field study
    b. operational definitions
    c. adult subjects
    d. perfect correlations

24. In experiments involving drugs, experimenters remain unaware of who received placebos in a
    _____ arrangement.
    a. zero-blind
    b. single-blind
    c. double-blind
    d. control-blind

25. The idea that Clever Hans's owner might be signaling him was an informal
    a. research hypothesis
    b. self-fulfilling prophecy
    c. operational definition
    d. dependent variable

26. In psychology, the _____ variable is a suspected cause of differences in
    _____.
    a. independent, the control group
    b. dependent, the experimenter effect
    c. independent, behavior
    d. dependent, correlations

27. A person who is observed crying may not be sad. This suggests that it is important to distinguish between
    a. individual cases and generalizations
    b. correlation and causation
    c. control groups and experimental groups
    d. observation and inference

28. In an experiment on the effects of hunger on the reading scores of elementary school children,
    reading scores are the
    a. control variable
    b. independent variable
    c. dependent variable
    d. reference variable

29. Which of the following correlation coefficients indicates a perfect relationship?
    a. 1.00
    b. 100.0
    c. −1
    d. both a and c

30. Jane Goodall's studies of chimpanzees in Tanzania are good examples of
    a. field experiments
    b. experimental control
    c. correlational studies
    d. naturalistic observation

31. To equalize the intelligence of members of the experimental group and the control group in an experiment, you could use
    a. extraneous control
    b. random assignment
    c. independent control
    d. subject replication

32. Which method would most likely be used to study the effects of tumors in the frontal lobes of the brain?
    a. sampling method
    b. correlational method
    c. clinical method
    d. experimental method

33. An in-depth study on the life history of the four Genain sisters, who by the age of 25 had developed schizophrenia, is an example of
    a. survey method
    b. correlational method
    c. scientific method
    d. clinical method

34. The fact that all four identical Genain sisters developed schizophrenia and were in and out of mental hospitals by the age of 25 suggests that their disorder was influenced by
    a. only environmental conditions
    b. nature
    c. heredity
    d. both a and b

35. The release of endorphins by the pituitary gland helps explain the
    a. experimenter effect
    b. placebo effect
    c. multiple-personality effect
    d. gender-bias effect

36. Cause is to effect as _____ variable is to _____ variable.
    a. extraneous, dependent
    b. dependent, independent
    c. independent, extraneous
    d. independent, dependent

37. The specific procedures used to gather data are described in which section of a research report?
    a. introduction
    b. abstract
    c. method
    d. discussion

38. Which of the following correlations demonstrates a cause-effect relationship?
    a. .980
    b. 1.00
    c. .50
    d. none of the preceding

SOLUTIONS

RECITE AND REVIEW

MODULE 1.1

1. profession
2. mental
3. behavior
4. evidence
5. planned or structured
6. method
7. development

8. learning
9. theorists
10. sense (or sensory)
11. animals
12. behavior
13. males
14. females

15. social
16. behavior
17. evolution
18. animal
19. understand

MODULE 1.2

20. knowledge
21. laboratory
22. experience
23. adapt
24. Watson
25. responses
26. positive

27. thinking
28. whole
29. greater
30. unconscious
31. Freud
32. neo-Freudians
33. growth

34. image
35. potentials
36. optimal

MODULE 1.3

37. humanism
38. blend
39. diversity (or differences)
40. values

41. rules
42. clinical
43. drugs
44. psychotherapy

45. Master's
46. specialties
47. basic

MODULE 1.4

48. measurement
49. problem
50. results
51. valid (or useful)
52. definitions
53. theory
54. abstract
55. results

56. clinical
57. natural
58. effect
59. observer
60. animals
61. records
62. correlation (or relationship)
63. zero

64. perfect
65. minus
66. increases
67. increases
68. predictions

MODULE 1.5

69. Cause
70. varied
71. change
72. independent
73. Dependent
74. prevent

75. subjects
76. group
77. group
78. characteristics
79. identical
80. effect

81. blind
82. blind
83. expected
84. prophecies

MODULE 1.6

85. case
86. natural

87. sample
88. web

89. untruthful (or inaccurate)
90. courtesy bias

91. evaluate
92. critical

93. actively
94. ideas

95. evidence

96. false

97. Barnum

PSYCHOLOGY IN ACTION

98. Skepticism
99. unreliable (or inaccurate)

100. groups
101. causation

102. valid (or scientific)
103. examples

CONNECTIONS

MODULE 1.1

1. h
2. f
3. j
4. i

5. a
6. c
7. b
8. d

9. e
10. g
11. k

MODULE 1.2

1. e
2. a
3. h
4. f

5. c
6. d
7. i
8. b

9. k
10. j
11. g

MODULE 1.3

1. i
2. h
3. g
4. f

5. c
6. l
7. d
8. k

9. b
10. a
11. e
12. j

MODULE 1.4

1. g
2. a
3. c

4. f
5. b
6. d

7. e
8. h

MODULE 1.5

1. d

| 2. e | 4. b | 6. a |
| 3. f | 5. c | |

MODULE 1.6

1. a	4. c	7. b
2. g	5. d	
3. f	6. e	

CHECK YOUR MEMORY

MODULE 1.1

1. F	4. F	7. T
2. F	5. F	8. F
3. T	6. F	

MODULE 1.2

9. F	14. T	19. T
10. T	15. T	20. F
11. F	16. F	21. T
12. T	17. T	
13. F	18. T	

MODULE 1.3

22. F	29. F	36. T
23. T	30. T	37. F
24. F	31. F	38. T
25. T	32. T	
26. F	33. F	
27. T	34. F	
28. T	35. T	

MODULE 1.4

39. T	43. T	47. F
40. F	44. F	48. F
41. F	45. T	49. F
42. T	46. F	50. F

MODULE 1.5

51. F	55. T	59. T
52. T	56. F	60. F
53. F	57. F	
54. F	58. T	

MODULE 1.6
61. F

62. T	64. T	66. T
63. F	65. F	

67. F	69. T	
68. T	70. F	

71. F	73. F	75. F
72. F	74. T	

PSYCHOLOGY IN ACTION

76. F	79. F	82. T
77. T	80. F	
78. F	81. F	

FINAL SURVEY AND REVIEW

MODULE 1.1

1. science
2. profession
3. behavior
4. mental processes
5. covert
6. empirical
7. data
8. Scientific
9. research method
10. Developmental
11. theorists
12. Personality
13. Sensation
14. Comparative
15. Biopsychologists
16. Gender
17. social behavior
18. Cultural
19. Evolutionary
20. animal models
21. predict
22. control

MODULE 1.2

23. philosophy
24. Wilhelm Wundt
25. conscious experience
26. structuralism
27. Functionalism
28. James
29. Behaviorism
30. stimuli
31. Skinner
32. reinforcers
33. Cognitive
34. Gestalt
35. Wertheimer
36. Gestalt
37. sum
38. psychoanalytic (or psychodynamic)
39. Freud
40. psychoanalysis
41. Alfred Adler
42. Humanistic
43. potentials
44. self-image
45. frame
46. self-actualization
47. Positive

MODULE 1.3

48. behaviorism
49. humanism
50. biopsychology
51. eclectic
52. diversity
53. cultural
54. cultural
55. norms
56. clinical
57. counseling
58. Psychiatrists
59. psychotherapy

60. psychoanalysis
61. psychiatric social
62. Developmental
63. engineering
64. educational
65. applied

MODULE 1.4

66. evidence
67. measurement
68. hypothesis
69. theory
70. scientifically
71. testable
72. operational
73. procedures
74. theory
75. theories
76. observations

77. published
78. journals
79. experimental
80. survey
81. natural settings
82. environments
83. observed
84. bias
85. anthropomorphic
86. observational records
87. correlational

88. coefficients
89. zero
90. perfect
91. closer
92. positive
93. increases
94. decreases
95. causation

MODULE 1.5

96. controlled experiment
97. observed
98. recorded
99. variable
100. independent
101. causes
102. Dependent
103. effects

104. Extraneous
105. outcome
106. controlled
107. experimental
108. control
109. personal
110. randomly
111. independent

112. placebo
113. single-blind
114. double-blind
115. experimenter effect
116. self-fulfilling

MODULE 1.6

117. case studies
118. subject
119. clinical tests

120. populations
121. representative
122. biased

123. questions

124. critique
125. synthesize

126. evaluate
127. evidence

128. Scientific

129. phrenology
130. pseudo

131. uncritical
132. positive

133. Barnum

PSYCHOLOGY IN ACTION

134. Skepticism
135. critical
136. biased

137. control
138. Correlation
139. correlation

140. observations
141. cases
142. generalizations

MASTERY TEST

1. D, (p. 14)
2. B, (p. 15)
3. B, (p. 17)
4. D, (p. 19)
5. B, (p. 20)
6. A, (p. 20)
7. C, (p. 22)
8. B, (p. 22)
9. D, (p. 24)
10. A, (p. 27)
11. D, (p. 27)
12. D, (p. 27)
13. C, (p. 44)

14. A, (p. 45)
15. B, (p. 45-46)
16. D, (p. 46)
17. A, (p. 47)
18. A, (p. 21)
19. C, (p. 43)
20. D, (p. 37)
21. C, (p. 34)
22. A, (p. 34)
23. B, (p. 31-32)
24. C, (p. 40)
25. A, (p. 32)
26. C, (p. 37)

27. D, (p. 50)
28. C, (p. 37)
29. D, (p. 35)
30. D, (p. 33)
31. B, (p. 38)
32. C, (p. 42)
33. D, (p.42)
34. C, (p. 42)
35. B, (p. 39)
36. D, (p. 37-38)
37. C, (p. 33)
38. D, (p. 35)

BRAIN AND BEHAVIOR

CHAPTER OVERVIEW

The brain and nervous system are made up of networks of neurons. Nerve impulses are basically electrical. Communication between neurons is chemical in that neurons release neurotransmitters that affect other neurons. Rather than merely carrying messages, neuropeptides regulate the activity of neurons in the brain.

The nervous system includes the central nervous system (CNS), consisting of the brain and spinal cord, and the peripheral nervous system (PNS). The PNS includes the somatic system and the autonomic system, with its sympathetic and parasympathetic branches.

Conventional brain research relies on dissection, staining, ablation, deep lesioning, electrical recording, electrical stimulation, micro-electrode recording, EEG recording, and clinical studies. Newer methods such as a PET scan and MRI scan make use of computer-enhanced images of the brain and its activities.

The left and right cerebral hemispheres have different specialized abilities. The left hemisphere processes information sequentially while the right processes information simultaneously and holistically.

The brain is subdivided into the forebrain, midbrain, and hindbrain. The subcortex includes important brain structures at all three levels. These are: the medulla ("vegetative" functions), the cerebellum (coordination), the reticular formation (sensory and motor messages and arousal), the thalamus (sensory information), and the hypothalamus (basic motives). The limbic system is related to emotion. The cerebral cortex of the forebrain is divided into several lobes. The basic functions of the lobes are as follows: occipital lobes—vision; parietal lobes—bodily sensation; temporal lobes—hearing and language; frontal lobes—motor control, speech, and abstract thought. Association areas of the cortex are related to complex abilities such as language, memory, and problem solving.

The endocrine system provides chemical communication in the body through the release of hormones into the bloodstream.

Hand dominance ranges from strongly left- to strongly right-handed, with mixed handedness and ambidexterity in between. In general, the left-handed are less strongly lateralized in brain function than are right-handed persons.

LEARNING OBJECTIVES

To demonstrate mastery of this chapter, you should be able to:

1. Name the basic unit of the nervous system, state what it is specifically designed to do, and list and describe its four parts.

2. Explain how a nerve impulse (action potential) occurs and how it is an all-or-nothing event, and how a cell returns to its resting state after the nerve cell impulse passes. Define "ions," "ion channels," and "negative after-potential."

3. Describe the difference between the nature of a nerve impulse and the nature of the communication between neurons.

4. Explain how nerve impulses are carried from one neuron to another at the synapse.

5. Explain what determines whether a neuron will trigger an action potential in another neuron.

6. Explain the function of neuropeptides.

7. Describe the effect of myelin on the speed of the nerve impulse.

8. Differentiate a nerve from a neuron.

9. Describe the process of neurogenesis and its connection to brain repair.

10. Explain what determines whether or not a neuron or a nerve will regenerate. Briefly describe the progress in generating regrowth of brain and spinal cord neurons.

11. Chart the various subparts of the human nervous system and generally explain their functions.

12. Differentiate between the two branches of the autonomic nervous system.

13. Explain the mechanism of the reflex arc.

14. List and describe five techniques for studying the brain. Briefly describe how EEG works.

15. Describe each of the four scanning techniques for studying the entire brain as it functions.

The following two objectives are related to the material in the "Discovering Psychology" section of the text.

16. Describe an example of how to test your reaction time, which would demonstrate how the brain requires a few seconds to process sensory information before sending a response signal.

17. Explain how this activity will start before you are consciously aware of it.

18. Describe the main difference between the brains of lower and higher animals. Name what appears to be the foundation of human intellectual superiority.

19. Describe the main difference between the brains of people who score high versus low on mental tests.

20. Define the term "hemispheres" and explain the function of the corpus callosum. Describe the problem known as spatial neglect.

21. Explain how and why a brain is "split" and describe what the resulting effects are.

22. Differentiate the abilities of the two hemispheres of the cerebral cortex. Describe what is known about their working together as well as how they process information.

23. Describe the function(s) of each of the following: a. occipital lobes b. parietal lobes (include the somatosensory areas) c. temporal lobes d. frontal lobes (include the motor cortex) e. associative areas (include Broca's and Wernicke's areas)

24. Explain the relationship between the size of the various parts of the somatosensory and motor areas of the cortex and the degree of sensitivity or importance of the corresponding body parts.

25. Describe the cause and effect of the disorder aphasia.

The following objective is related to the "Human Diversity" section of the text.

26. Explain how male and female brains tend to differ in ways that can affect speech and language and whether they use both left and right hemispheres equally to process language. Are there gender differences in this process and in the recovery from aphasia?

27. List and be able to recognize the three areas of the subcortex.

28. Explain the function of the following parts of two of the three areas of the subcortex: a. Hindbrain (brainstem) i. pons ii. medulla iii. cerebellum iv. reticular formation b. Forebrain i. thalamus ii. hypothalamus

29. Name the structures that comprise the limbic system and explain its function (include a description of the function of the amygdala and the hippocampus).

30. Briefly describe the significance of "pleasure" and "aversive" areas in the limbic system.

31. List six basic functions of the brain.

32. Briefly describe the research of Bakay and Kennedy with cortical stimulation in paralyzed persons.

33. Briefly explain the purpose of the endocrine system. Describe the action of hormones in the body.

34. Describe the effect that the following glands have on the body and behavior: a. pituitary (include a description of giantism, hypopituitary dwarfism, and acromegaly) b. pineal c. thyroid (include a description of hyperthyroidism and hypothyroidism) d. adrenal medulla e. adrenal cortex (include a description of virilism, premature puberty, and the problems of anabolic steroids)

35. Describe the relationship among handedness, brain dominance, and speech. Describe the element of handedness that appears to be inherited.

36. Explain how a person can determine which hemisphere is dominant.

37. State the incidence of left-handedness and discuss the relative advantages and/or disadvantages of being right-handed versus left-handed.

RECITE AND REVIEW

MODULE 2.1

Survey Question: How do nerve cells operate and communicate? Pages 54-58

The [1] _____ and nervous system are made up of linked nerve cells called [2] _____ , which pass information from one to another through synapses.

The brain consists of approximately [3] _____ neurons, which form a [4] _____ network to produce thought, intelligence, and consciousness.

The basic conducting fibers of neurons are [5] _____ , but dendrites (a receiving area), the soma (the cell body and also a receiving area), and [6] _____ terminals (the branching ends of a neuron) are also involved in communication.

A [7] _____ refers to an inactive neuron's electrical charge (-60 to -70 millivolts).

The firing of an action potential ([8] _____) is basically electrical, whereas communication between neurons is chemical.

An action potential occurs when the [9] _____ potential is altered enough to reach the threshold for firing. At that point, sodium [10] _____ flow into the axon, through [11] _____ channels.

After each action potential, the neuron has a brief [12] _____ after-potential. Next, potassium ions flow out of the [13] _____ , restoring the resting potential.

The [14] _____ potential is an all-or-nothing event.

Experiencing and reacting to events in the environment lag slightly behind the actual occurrences of the events because [15] _____ takes time.

Neurons release neurotransmitters at the synapse. These cross to [16] _____ sites on the receiving cell, causing it to be excited or inhibited. For example, the transmitter chemical acetylcholine activates [17] _____ .

Some neurotransmitters act to [18] _____ (move it closer to firing) the next neuron, and some neurotransmitters act to inhibit (make firing less likely) the next neuron.

Disturbances of any neurotransmitters found in the brain can have serious consequences, such as too [19] _____ can cause muscle tremors of Parkinson's disease or too [20] _____ can cause schizophrenic symptoms.

Chemicals called neuropeptides do not carry messages directly. Instead, they [21] _____ the activity of other neurons.

Opiate-like neural regulators called enkephalins and endorphins are released in the brain to relieve [22] _____ and stress.

[23] _____ may help explain how some women who suffer from severe premenstrual pain and distress have unusually low endorphin levels.

Survey Question: What are the functions of major parts of the nervous system? Pages 58-62

Nerves are made of large bundles of [24] _____ and dendrites. Neurons and nerves in the peripheral nervous system can often regenerate; damage in the central nervous system is usually [25] _____ , unless a repair is attempted by grafting or implanting healthy tissue.

Axons are coated with a fatty layer called [26] _____ , which helps nerve impulses move faster down the axons. [27] _____ also wraps around axons, but it forms a "tunnel" so damaged fibers can repair themselves.

With the discovery of [28] _____ (the production of new brain cells), scientists hope that some brain-damaged cells can be repaired by nudging immature brain cells to develop into particular types of neurons to cure such disease as Parkinson's disease.

The nervous system can be divided into the [29] _____ nervous system (the [30] _____ and spinal cord) and the peripheral nervous system.

The CNS includes the somatic ([31] _____) and autonomic ([32] _____) nervous systems.

The autonomic system has two divisions: the sympathetic (emergency, activating) [33] _____ and the parasympathetic (sustaining, conserving) [34] _____ .

Thirty-one pairs of spinal [35] _____ leave the spinal cord. Twelve pairs of cranial [36] _____ leave the brain directly. Together, they carry sensory and motor messages between the brain and the body.

The simplest [37] _____ is a reflex arc, which involves a sensory neuron, a connector neuron, and a [38] _____ neuron.

Survey Question: How do we know how the brain works? Pages 62-64

Conventional brain research relies on dissection, staining, ablation, deep lesioning, electrical recording,

[39] _____ stimulation, micro-electrode recording, EEG recording, and [40] _____

studies.

Computer-enhanced techniques are providing three-dimensional [41] _____ of the living human

brain and its [42] _____ . Examples of such techniques are CT scans, MRI scans, and PET scans.

The [43] _____ scan produces images of the brain by using X-rays, the [44] _____

scan produces images of the brain by using a magnetic field, and the [45] _____ scan produces

images of the brain as well as the activities of the brain by detecting positrons emitted by a weak

radioactive glucose in the brain.

MODULE 2.2

Survey Question: How is the brain organized and what do its higher structures do? Why are the brain's
association areas important? What happens when they are injured? Pages 66-72

The human [46] _____ is marked by advanced corticalization, or enlargement of the cerebral

[47] _____ , which covers the outside surface of the cerebrum.

Using a PET scan, Haier and colleagues found that intelligence is related to [48] _____ : A

less efficient brain works much harder than a more efficient brain.

The [49] _____ cerebral hemisphere contains speech or language "centers" in most people. It

also specializes in [50] _____ , calculating, judging time and rhythm, and ordering complex

movements.

The [51] _____ hemisphere is largely nonverbal. It excels at spatial and perceptual skills,

visualization, and recognition of [52] _____ , faces, and melodies.

"Split brains" have been created by [53] _____ the corpus callosum. The split-brain individual

shows a remarkable degree of independence between the right and left [54] _____ .

Another way to summarize specialization in the brain is to say that the [55] _____ hemisphere is

good at analysis and processing information sequentially; the [56] _____ hemisphere processes

information simultaneously and holistically.

The most basic functions of the lobes of the cerebral cortex are as follows: occipital lobes—[57] _____ ; parietal lobes—bodily sensation; temporal lobes—[58] _____ and language; frontal lobes—motor control, speech, and abstract thought.

Association areas on the cortex are neither [59] _____ nor [60] _____ in function. They are related to more complex skills such as language, memory, recognition, and problem solving.

Damage to either Broca's area or Wernicke's area causes [61] _____ and language problems known as aphasias.

Damage to Broca's area causes problems with [62] _____ and pronunciation. Damage to Wernicke's area causes problems with the [63] _____ of words.

MODULE 2.3

Survey Question: What kinds of behaviors are controlled by the subcortex? Pages 74-77

All of the brain areas below the [64] _____ are called the subcortex.

The medulla contains centers essential for reflex control of [65] _____ [66] _____ , breathing, and other "vegetative" functions.

The cerebellum maintains [67] _____ , posture, and muscle tone.

The [68] _____ lies inside the medulla and the brainstem, influences [69] _____ , and does not mature until [70] _____ . It also directs sensory and motor messages, and part of it, known as the RAS, acts as an [71] _____ system for the cerebral cortex.

The thalamus carries [72] _____ information to the cortex. The hypothalamus exerts powerful control over eating, drinking, sleep cycles, body temperature, and other basic [73] _____ and behaviors.

The limbic system is strongly related to [74] _____ and motivated behavior. It also contains distinct reward and punishment areas.

A part of the limbic system called the amygdala is related to [75] _____ . An area known as the hippocampus is important for forming [76] _____ .

Survey Question: Does the glandular system affect behavior? Pages 77-80

The endocrine system provides [77] _____ communication in the body through the release of [78] _____ into the bloodstream. Endocrine glands influence moods, behavior, and even personality.

Many of the endocrine glands are influenced by the pituitary (the "[79] _____ gland"), which is in turn influenced by the hypothalamus.

The pituitary supplies [80] _____ hormone. Too little GH causes [81] _____ ; too much causes giantism or acromegaly.

Body rhythms and [82] _____ cycles are influenced by melatonin, secreted by the pineal gland.

The thyroid gland regulates [83] _____ . Hyperthyroidism refers to an overactive thyroid gland; hypothyroidism to an underactive thyroid.

The adrenal glands supply [84] _____ and norepinephrine to activate the body. They also regulate salt balance and responses to stress, and they are a secondary source of [85] _____ hormones.

Most drugs like anabolic steroids are synthetic versions of [86] _____ .

PSYCHOLOGY IN ACTION

Survey Question: How do right- and left-handed individuals differ? Pages 81-84

Hand dominance ranges from strongly left- to strongly right-handed, with [87] _____ handedness and ambidexterity in between.

Ninety percent of the population is basically [88] _____ -handed, 10 percent [89] _____ -handed.

The vast majority of people are right-handed and therefore [90] _____ brain dominant for motor skills. Ninety-seven percent of right-handed persons and 68 percent of the left-handed also produce [91] _____ from the left hemisphere.

[92] _____ people in the past were forced to [93] _____ as right-handed people; therefore, there are fewer left-handed older people living than right-handed older people.

In general, the [94] _____ -handed are less strongly lateralized in brain function than are [95] _____ -handed persons.

CONNECTIONS

MODULE 2.1

1. _____ soma
2. _____ neurilemma
3. _____ axon collateral
4. _____ myelin
5. _____ dendrites
6. _____ axon terminals
7. _____ axon

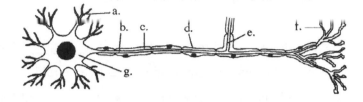

1. _____ spinal cord
2. _____ autonomic system
3. _____ parasympathetic branch
4. _____ peripheral nervous system
5. _____ sympathetic branch
6. _____ brain
7. _____ somatic system

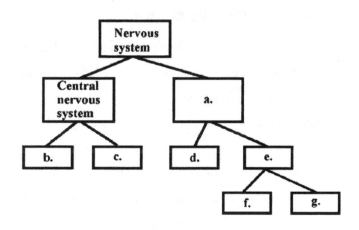

1. _____ CT scan
2. _____ EEG
3. _____ deep lesioning
4. _____ PET scan
5. _____ ablation

a. brain waves
b. radioactive glucose
c. surgery
d. electrode
e. computerized X-rays

MODULE 2.2

1. _____ Wernicke's area
2. _____ temporal lobe
3. _____ cerebellum
4. _____ Broca's area
5. _____ parietal lobe
6. _____ frontal lobe
7. _____ occipital lobe

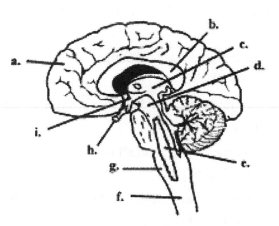

MODULE 2.3

1. _____ midbrain
2. _____ reticular formation
3. _____ cerebrum
4. _____ medulla
5. _____ hypothalamus
6. _____ corpus callosum
7. _____ pituitary
8. _____ spinal cord
9. _____ thalamus

1. _____ amygdala
2. _____ pituitary
3. _____ thalamus
4. _____ hippocampus
5. _____ pineal gland
6. _____ thyroid gland
7. _____ adrenal glands
8. _____ testes

a. testosterone
b. metabolism
c. growth hormone
d. epinephrine
e. melatonin
f. memory formation
g. sensory switching station
h. fear producing

CHECK YOUR MEMORY

MODULE 2.1

Survey Question: How do nerve cells operate and communicate? Pages 54-58

1. The dendrites receive incoming information from the neurilemma.
   TRUE or FALSE

2. Human axons may be up to a meter long.
   TRUE or FALSE

3. The resting potential is about plus 70 millivolts.
   TRUE or FALSE

4. The interior of the axon becomes positive during an action potential.
   TRUE or FALSE

5. The action potential is an all-or-nothing event.
   TRUE or FALSE

6. The negative after-potential is due to an inward flow of potassium ions.
   TRUE or FALSE

7. Nerve impulses travel faster in axons surrounded by myelin.
   TRUE or FALSE

8. Neurotransmitters activate other neurons; neuropeptides activate muscles and glands.
   TRUE or FALSE

9. Enkephalins are neuropeptides.
   TRUE or FALSE

10. Neuropeptides regulate the activity of other neurons.
    TRUE or FALSE

11. Many drugs imitate, duplicate, or block neurotransmitters to excite or inhibit an action potential.
    TRUE or FALSE

Survey Question: What are the functions of major parts of the nervous system? Pages 58-62

12. The neurilemma helps damaged nerve cell fibers regenerate after an injury.
    TRUE or FALSE

13. Neurons in the brain and spinal cord can sometimes be repaired by neurogenesis.
    TRUE or FALSE

14. The word *autonomic* means "self-limiting."
    TRUE or FALSE

15. The parsympathetic branch quiets the body and returns it to a lower level of arousal.
    TRUE or FALSE

16. The sympathetic system generally controls voluntary behavior.
    TRUE or FALSE

17. Thirty-one cranial nerves leave the brain directly.
    TRUE or FALSE

18. "Fight-or-flight" emergency reactions are produced by the autonomic nervous system.
    TRUE or FALSE

19. Activity in the parasympathetic system increases heart rate and respiration.
    TRUE or FALSE

20. In a reflex arc, motor neurons carry messages to effector cells.
    TRUE or FALSE

Survey Question: How do we know how the brain works? Pages 62-64

21. Deep lesioning in the brain is usually done surgically.
    TRUE or FALSE

22. Micro-electrodes are needed in order to record from single neurons.
    TRUE or FALSE

23. CT scans form "maps" of brain activity.
    TRUE or FALSE

24. Electroencephalography records waves of electrical activity produced by the brain.
    TRUE or FALSE

25. Radioactive glucose is used to make PET scans.

    TRUE or FALSE

MODULE 2.2

Survey Question: How is the brain organized and what do its higher structures do? Why are the brain's association areas important? What happens when they are injured? Pages 66-72

26. Elephants have brain-body ratios similar to those of humans.

    TRUE or FALSE

27. The corpus callosum connects the right and left brain hemispheres.

    TRUE or FALSE

28. The cerebellum makes up a large part of the cerebral cortex.

    TRUE or FALSE

29. Much of the cerebral cortex is made up of gray matter.

    TRUE or FALSE

30. Damage to the left cerebral hemisphere usually causes spatial neglect.

    TRUE or FALSE

31. In general, smart brains tend to be the hardest-working brains.

    TRUE or FALSE

32. The right half of the brain mainly controls left body areas.

    TRUE or FALSE

33. Roger Sperry won a Nobel Prize for his work on corticalization.

    TRUE or FALSE

34. According to Richard Haier, a less efficient brain works harder and still accomplishes less than a more efficient brain because a less efficient brain uses less glucose to process information.

    TRUE or FALSE

35. Cutting the reticular formation produces a "split brain."

    TRUE or FALSE

36. Information from the right side of vision is sent directly to the right cerebral hemisphere.

    TRUE or FALSE

37. The right hemisphere tends to be good at speaking, writing, and math.

    TRUE or FALSE

38. The left hemisphere is mainly involved with analysis.

    TRUE or FALSE

39. Both brain hemispheres are normally active at all times.
    TRUE or FALSE

40. The motor cortex is found on the occipital lobes.
    TRUE or FALSE

41. The somatosensory area is located on the parietal lobes.
    TRUE or FALSE

42. Electrically stimulating the motor cortex causes movement in various parts of the body.
    TRUE or FALSE

43. Large parts of the lobes of the brain are made up of association cortex.
    TRUE or FALSE

44. Damage to either brain hemisphere usually causes an aphasia.
    TRUE or FALSE

45. A person with Broca's aphasia might say "pear" when shown an apple.
    TRUE or FALSE

46. Damage to Wernicke's area causes the condition known as spatial neglect.
    TRUE or FALSE

47. Women are much more likely than men to use both cerebral hemispheres for language processing.
    TRUE or FALSE

MODULE 2.3

Survey Question: What kinds of behaviors are controlled by the subcortex? Pages 74-77

48. The cerebrum makes up much of the medulla.
    TRUE or FALSE

49. Injury to the medulla may affect breathing.
    TRUE or FALSE

50. Injury to the cerebellum affects attention and wakefulness.
    TRUE or FALSE

51. The reticular formation is the switching station for sensory messages and is fully developed at birth.
    TRUE or FALSE

52. Smell is the only major sense that does not pass through the thalamus.
    TRUE or FALSE

53. Stimulating various parts of the limbic system can produce rage, fear, pleasure, or arousal.
    TRUE or FALSE

54. The hippocampus is associated with hunger and eating.
TRUE or FALSE

Survey Question: Does the glandular system affect behavior? Pages 77-80

55. Androgens ("male" hormones) are related to the sex drive in both men and women.
TRUE or FALSE

56. Hormones secreted during times of high emotion tend to increase memory loss.
TRUE or FALSE

57. After watching violent scenes, men had high levels of testosterone in their bloodstream.
TRUE or FALSE

58. "Normal short" children grow faster when given synthetic growth hormone, but their final height is not taller.
TRUE or FALSE

59. Activity of the pituitary is influenced by the hypothalamus.
TRUE or FALSE

60. A person who is slow, sleepy, and overweight could be suffering from hypothyroidism.
TRUE or FALSE

61. Virilism and premature puberty may be caused by problems with the adrenal glands.
TRUE or FALSE

62. Steroid drugs may cause sexual impotence and breast enlargement in males.
TRUE or FALSE

63. There is much evidence to support that steroids do improve performance, which is why all major sports organizations ban the use of steroids.
TRUE or FALSE

PSYCHOLOGY IN ACTION

Survey Question: How do right- and left-handed individuals differ? Pages 81-84

64. Left-handers have an advantage in fencing, boxing, and baseball.
TRUE or FALSE

65. Most left-handed persons produce speech from their right hemispheres.
TRUE or FALSE

66. Left- or right-handedness is inherited from one's parents.
TRUE or FALSE

67. On average, left-handed persons die at younger ages than right-handed persons do.
    TRUE or FALSE

FINAL SURVEY AND REVIEW

MODULE 2.1

Survey Question: How do nerve cells operate and communicate? Pages 54-58

The brain and nervous system are made up of linked nerve cells called [1] _____ , which pass information from one to another through [2] _____ .

The brain consists of approximately 100 billion neurons, which form a [3] _____ to produce thought, intelligence, and consciousness.

The basic conducting fibers of neurons are axons, but [4] _____ (a receiving area), the [5] _____ (the cell body and also a receiving area), and axon terminals (the branching ends of an axon) are also involved in communication.

A resting potential refers to an electrical charge (-60 to -70 millivolts) of an [6] _____ .

The firing of an [7] _____ [8] _____ (nerve impulse) is basically electrical, whereas communication between neurons is chemical.

An action potential occurs when the resting potential is altered enough to reach the [9] _____ for firing. At that point, [10] _____ ions flow into the axon, through ion channels.

After each action potential, the neuron has a brief negative [11] _____ . Next, [12] _____ ions flow out of the axon, restoring the resting potential.

The action potential is an [13] _____ event.

Because [14] _____ takes time, our response to events in the environment lags slightly behind the actual occurrence of those events.

In chemical synapses, neurons release [15] _____ . These cross to receptor sites on the receiving cell, causing it to be excited or inhibited. For example, the transmitter chemical [16] _____ activates muscles.

Some neurotransmitters act to excite the receiving neuron by increasing its ability to [17] _____ an action potential, and some neurotransmitters act to inhibit the receiving neuron by [18] _____ its ability to fire.

Disturbances of any neurotransmitters found in the brain can have serious consequences, such as too little dopamine can cause muscle tremors of [19] _____ or too much dopamine can cause [20] _____ .

Chemicals called [21] _____ do not carry messages directly. Instead, they regulate the activity of other neurons.

Opiate-like neural regulators called enkephalins and [22] _____ are released in the brain to relieve pain and stress.

Brain regulators may help explain how some women who suffer from severe premenstrual pain and distress have unusually [23] _____ levels.

Survey Question: What are the functions of major parts of the nervous system? Pages 58-62

[24] _____ are made of axons and associated tissues. Neurons and nerves in the [25] _____ nervous system can often regenerate; damage in the [26] _____ nervous system is usually permanent.

Axons are coated with a fatty layer called myelin, which helps nerve impulses move [27] _____ down the axons. Neurilemma also wraps around axons, but it forms a "tunnel" so damaged fibers can [28] _____ themselves.

With the discovery of [29] _____ , scientists hope that some brain-damaged cells can be repaired by nudging immature brain cells to develop into particular types of [30] _____ to cure such disease as Parkinson's disease.

The nervous system can be divided into the [31] _____ nervous system (the brain and [32] _____ [33] _____) and the peripheral nervous system.

The CNS includes the [34] _____ (bodily) and [35] _____ (involuntary) nervous systems.

The autonomic system has two divisions: the [36] _____ (emergency, activating) branch and the [37] _____ (sustaining, conserving) branch.

Thirty-one pairs of [38] _____ nerves leave the spinal cord. Twelve pairs of [39] _____ nerves leave the brain directly. Together, these nerves carry sensory and [40] _____ messages between the brain and the body.

The simplest behavior is a [41] _____ [42] _____ , which involves a sensory neuron, a [43] _____ neuron, and a [44] _____ neuron.

Survey Question: How do we know how the brain works? Pages 62-64

Conventional brain research relies on [45] _____ (separation into parts), staining, ablation, deep lesioning, electrical recording, electrical [46] _____ , micro-electrode recording, EEG recording, and clinical studies.

Computer-enhanced techniques are providing three-dimensional images of the living human brain and its activities. Examples of such techniques are CT scans, [47] _____ scans, and [48] _____ scans, which record brain activity.

The CT scan produces images of the brain by using [49] _____ , the MRI scan produces images of the brain by using a [50] _____ , and the PET scan produces images of the brain as well as the activities of the brain by detecting positrons emitted by a weak [51] _____ in the brain.

MODULE 2.2

Survey Question: How is the brain organized and what do its higher structures do? Why are the brain's association areas important? What happens when they are injured? Pages 66-72

The human brain is marked by advanced [52] _____ , or enlargement of the cerebral cortex, which covers the outside surface of the [53] _____ .

Using a PET scan, Haier and colleagues found that intelligence is related to brain efficiency: A [54] _____ efficient brain works much harder than a [55] _____ efficient brain.

The right cerebral [56] _____ contains speech or language "centers" in most people. It also specializes in writing, calculating, judging time and rhythm, and ordering complex [57] _____ .

The left hemisphere is largely nonverbal. It excels at [58] _____ and perceptual skills, visualization, and recognition of patterns, [59] _____ , and melodies.

"Split brains" have been created by cutting the [60] _____ [61] _____ . The split-brain individual shows a remarkable degree of independence between the right and left [62] _____ .

Another way to summarize specialization in the brain is to say that the left hemisphere is good at [63] _____ and processing information sequentially; the right hemisphere processes information [64] _____ and holistically.

The most basic functions of the lobes of the cerebral [65] _____ are as follows: occipital lobes—vision; parietal lobes—bodily [66] _____ ; temporal lobes—hearing and language; frontal lobes—motor control, [67] _____ , and abstract thought.

Association areas on the cortex are neither [68] _____ nor [69] _____ in function. They are related to more complex skills such as [70] _____ , memory, recognition, and problem solving. Damage to either Broca's area or Wernicke's area causes speech and language problems known as [71] _____ .

Damage to [72] _____ area causes problems with speech and pronunciation. Damage to [73] _____ area causes problems with the meaning of words.

MODULE 2.3

Survey Question: What kinds of behaviors are controlled by the subcortex? Pages 74-77

All of the brain areas below the cortex are called the [74] _____ .

The [75] _____ contains centers essential for reflex control of heart rate, breathing, and other "vegetative" functions.

The [76] _____ maintains coordination, posture, and muscle tone.

The [77] _____ lies inside the medulla and the brainstem, influences attention, and does not mature until adolescence. It also directs sensory and motor messages, and part of it, known as the RAS, acts as an activating system for the [78] _____ [79] _____ .

The [80] _____ carries sensory information to the cortex. The [81] _____ exerts powerful control over eating, drinking, sleep cycles, body temperature, and other basic motives and behaviors.

The [82] _____ system is strongly related to emotion and motivation. It also contains distinct [83] _____ and punishment areas.

A part of the limbic system called the [84] _____ is related to fear. An area known as the [85] _____ is important for forming lasting memories.

Survey Question: Does the glandular system affect behavior? Pages 77-80

The [86] _____ system provides chemical communication in the body through the release of hormones into the [87] _____ .

Many of the endocrine glands are influenced by the [88] _____ (the "master gland"), which is in turn influenced by the [89] _____ .

The [90] _____ supplies growth hormone. Too little GH causes dwarfism; too much causes giantism or [91] _____ .

Body rhythms and sleep cycles are influenced by [92] _____ , secreted by the [93] _____ gland.

The thyroid gland regulates metabolism. Hyperthyroidism refers to an [94] _____ thyroid gland; hypothyroidism to an [95] _____ thyroid.

The [96] _____ glands supply epinephrine and norepinephrine to activate the body. They also regulate salt balance, responses to [97] _____ , and they are a secondary source of sex hormones. Most drugs like anabolic steroids are [98] _____ versions of testosterone.

PSYCHOLOGY IN ACTION

Survey Question: How do right- and left-handed individuals differ? Pages 81-84

[99] _____ [100] _____ ranges from strongly left- to strongly right-handed, with mixed handedness and [101] _____ in between.

[102] _____ percent of the population is basically right-handed, [103] _____ percent left-handed.

The vast majority of people are [104] _____ -handed and therefore [105] _____ brain dominant for motor skills. Ninety-seven percent of right-handed persons and 68 percent of the left-handed produce speech from the [106] _____ hemisphere.

Left-handed people in the past were forced to [107] _____ as [108] _____ -handed people; therefore, there are fewer left-handed older people living than right-handed older people.

In general, the left-handed are less strongly [109] _____ in brain function than are right-handed persons.

MASTERY TEST

1. At times of emergency, anger, or fear, what part of the nervous system becomes more active?
   a. corpus callosum of the forebrain
   b. sympathetic branch of the ANS
   c. parasympathetic branch of the PNS
   d. Broca's area

2. The highest and largest brain area in humans is the
   a. cerebrum
   b. cerebellum
   c. frontal lobes
   d. gray matter of the callosum

3. A tumor in which brain area would most likely cause blind spots in vision?
   a. occipital lobe
   b. temporal lobe
   c. somatosensory area
   d. association cortex

4. Neurotransmitters are found primarily in
   a. the spinal cord
   b. the neurilemma
   c. synapses
   d. motor neurons

5. Enkephalins are an example of
   a. acetylcholine blockers
   b. neuropeptides
   c. receptor sites
   d. adrenal hormones

6. Electrically stimulating a portion of which brain area would produce movements in the body?
   a. occipital lobe
   b. frontal lobe
   c. parietal lobe
   d. temporal lobe

7. When a neuron reaches its threshold, a(an) _____ occurs.
   a. volume potential
   b. ion potential
   c. action potential
   d. dendrite potential

8. A person's ability to work as a commercial artist would be most impaired by damage to the
   a. left temporal lobe
   b. right cerebral hemisphere
   c. left cerebral hemisphere
   d. frontal association cortex

9. ESB will most likely produce anger if it is applied somewhere in the
   a. association cortex
   b. limbic system
   c. parasympathetic branch
   d. reticular activating system

10. Information in neurons usually flows in what order?
    a. soma, dendrites, axon
    b. dendrites, soma, axon
    c. dendrites, myelin, axon terminals
    d. axon, soma, axon terminals

11. Regulating the activity of other neurons is most characteristic of
    a. neuropeptides
    b. acetylcholine
    c. reflex arcs
    d. resting potentials

12. Nerve impulses occur when _____ rush into the axon.
    a. sodium ions
    b. potassium ions
    c. negative charges
    d. neurotransmitters

13. Attempts to repair brain injuries by injecting immature neurons into the damaged area make use of the recently discovered existence of
    a. myelin
    b. neurogenesis
    c. neuropeptides
    d. corticalization

14. Negative after-potentials are caused by the outward flow of _____ from the axon.
    a. negative charges
    b. potassium ions
    c. neurotransmitters
    d. sodium ions

15. A person who says "bife" for bike and "seep" for sleep probably suffers from
    a. Broca's aphasia
    b. Wernicke's aphasia
    c. spatial neglect
    d. the condition known as "mind blindness"

16. Damage to which part of the limbic system would most likely impair memory?
    a. thalamus
    b. hypothalamus
    c. amygdala
    d. hippocampus

17. Changes in heart rate, blood pressure, digestion, and sweating are controlled by the
    a. thoracic nerves
    b. parietal lobes
    c. somatic system
    d. autonomic system

18. In which of the following pairs are both structures part of the forebrain?
    a. medulla, hypothalamus
    b. cerebrum, cerebellum
    c. medulla, thalamus
    d. cerebrum, thalamus

19. Which of the following is a specialized type of X-ray?
    a. PET scan
    b. CT scan
    c. MRI scan
    d. EEG scan

20. Which two problems are associated with the pituitary gland?
    a. dwarfism, acromegaly
    b. virilism, acromegaly
    c. mental retardation, dwarfism
    d. giantism, premature puberty

21. The cerebral hemispheres are interconnected by the
    a. reticular system
    b. cerebellum
    c. cerebrum
    d. corpus callosum

22. Damage to which of the following would most likely make it difficult for a person to play catch with a ball?
    a. reticular formation
    b. limbic system
    c. cerebellum
    d. association cortex

23. Speech, language, calculation, and analysis are special skills of the
    a. right cerebral hemisphere
    b. limbic system
    c. left cerebral hemisphere
    d. right somatosensory area

24. The usual flow of information in a reflex arc is
    a. cranial nerve, connector neuron, spinal nerve
    b. sensory neuron, connector neuron, motor neuron
    c. effector cell, interneuron, connector neuron
    d. sensory neuron, connector neuron, reflex neuron

25. A person will "hear" a series of sounds when which area of the cortex is electrically stimulated?
    a. frontal lobe
    b. parietal lobe
    c. occipital lobe
    d. temporal lobe

26. Which of the following pairs contains the "master gland" and its master?
    a. pineal—thalamus
    b. thyroid—RAS
    c. pituitary—hypothalamus
    d. adrenal—cortex

27. Many basic motives and emotions are influenced by the
    a. thalamus
    b. hypothalamus
    c. corpus callosum
    d. cerebellum

28. Both surgical ablation and _____ remove brain tissue.
    a. the MEG technique
    b. tomography
    c. micro-electrode sampling
    d. deep lesioning

29. Which of the following techniques requires access to the interior of the brain?
    a. micro-electrode recording
    b. EEG recordings
    c. PET scanning
    d. functional MRI

30. Which of the following statements about handedness is FALSE?
    a. Handedness is directly inherited from one's parents.
    b. A majority of left-handers produce speech from the left hemisphere.
    c. The left-handed are less lateralized than the right-handed.
    d. Left-handedness is an advantage in boxing and fencing.

31. Scott was challenged to catch a dollar bill as fast as he could with his thumb and index finger as it fell between them. Scott was successful one time out of five trials. Which statement best explains why Scott failed to catch the dollar bill?
    a. Scott's injury to the temporal lobe has caused him to not see when the dollar bill falls.
    b. This simple yet common test signifies that Scott has serious cognitive deficits and must seek a specialist immediately.
    c. From the time Scott processes the information to when his brain tells the muscles to grab the dollar bill, the dollar bill has already slipped by.
    d. none of the above

32. People with Parkinson's disease lack or have very little of the neurotransmitter _____.
    a. dopamine
    b. endorphins
    c. epinephrine
    d. serotonin

33. While walking in the woods, Whitney got distracted and accidentally walked into a tree branch and now she cannot see out of her left eye. With the discovery of _____, her doctors hope that in the near future, they can repair the damaged neurons in her eyes by grafting immature brain cells to replace the damaged ones.
    a. deep lesioning
    b. neurogenesis
    c. electrical stimulation of the brain (ESB)
    d. fMRI

34. Which statement correctly reflects the findings of Haier and his colleagues on the relationship between intelligence and brain efficiency?
    a. A less efficient brain works much harder than a more efficient brain.
    b. A more efficient brain works much harder than a less efficient brain.
    c. A less efficient brain uses less glucose when processing information.
    d. A more efficient brain uses more glucose when processing information.

SOLUTIONS

RECITE AND REVIEW

MODULE 2.1

1. brain
2. neurons
3. 100 billion
4. communication
5. axons
6. axon
7. resting potential
8. nerve impulse
9. resting
10. ions
11. ion
12. negative
13. axon
14. action
15. neural processing
16. receptor
17. muscles
18. excite
19. little dopamine
20. much dopamine
21. regulate
22. pain
23. Brain regulators

24. axons
25. permanent
26. myelin
27. Neurilemma
28. neurogenesis
29. central
30. brain
31. bodily
32. involuntary
33. branch
34. branch
35. nerves
36. nerves
37. behavior
38. motor

39. electrical
40. clinical
41. images
42. activity
43. CT
44. MRI
45. PET

MODULE 2.2

46. brain
47. cortex
48. brain efficiency
49. left
50. writing
51. right
52. patterns
53. cutting
54. hemispheres
55. left
56. right
57. vision
58. hearing
59. sensory
60. motor
61. speech
62. grammar
63. meaning

MODULE 2.3

64. cortex
65. heart
66. rate
67. coordination
68. reticular formation
69. attention
70. adolescence
71. activating
72. sensory
73. motives
74. emotion
75. fear
76. memories

77. chemical

78. hormones	81. dwarfism	84. epinephrine
79. master	82. sleep	85. sex
80. growth	83. metabolism	86. testosterone

PSYCHOLOGY IN ACTION

87. mixed	90. left	93. masquerade
88. right	91. speech	94. left
89. left	92. Left-handed	95. right

CONNECTIONS

MODULE 2.1

1. g	4. c	7. b
2. d	5. a	
3. e	6. f	

1. c or b	4. a	7. d
2. e	5. f or g	
3. f or g	6. c or b	

1. e	3. d	5. c
2. a	4. b	

MODULE 2.2

1. d	4. b	7. e
2. g	5. c	
3. f	6. a	

MODULE 2.3

1. d	4. g	7. h
2. e	5. i	8. f
3. a	6. b	9. c

1. h	4. f	7. d
2. c	5. e	8. a
3. g	6. b	

CHECK YOUR MEMORY

MODULE 2.1

1. F

2. T	6. F	10. T
3. F	7. T	11. T
4. T	8. F	
5. T	9. T	

12. T	15. T	18. T
13. T	16. F	19. F
14. F	17. F	20. T

21. F	23. F	25. T
22. T	24. T	

MODULE 2.2

26. F	34. F	42. T
27. T	35. F	43. T
28. F	36. F	44. F
29. T	37. F	45. F
30. F	38. T	46. F
31. F	39. T	47. T
32. T	40. F	
33. F	41. T	

MODULE 2.3

48. F	51. F	54. F
49. T	52. T	
50. F	53. T	

55. T	58. T	61. T
56. F	59. T	62. T
57. T	60. T	63. F

PSYCHOLOGY IN ACTION

64. F	66. F
65. F	67. F

FINAL SURVEY AND REVIEW

MODULE 2.1

1. neurons	4. dendrites	7. action
2. synapses	5. soma	8. potential
3. communication network	6. inactive neuron	9. threshold

Chapter 2

10. sodium
11. after-potential
12. potassium
13. all-or-nothing
14. neural processing
15. neurotransmitters

16. acetylcholine
17. fire
18. reducing
19. Parkinson's disease
20. schizophrenia
21. neuropeptides

22. endorphins
23. low endorphin

24. Nerves
25. peripheral
26. central
27. faster
28. repair
29. neurogenesis
30. neurons
31. central

32. spinal
33. cord
34. somatic
35. autonomic
36. sympathetic
37. parasympathetic
38. spinal
39. cranial

40. motor
41. reflex
42. arc
43. connector
44. motor

45. dissection
46. stimulation
47. MRI

48. PET
49. X-rays
50. magnetic field

51. radioactive glucose

MODULE 2.2

52. corticalization
53. cerebrum
54. less
55. more
56. hemisphere
57. movements
58. spatial
59. faces

60. corpus
61. callosum
62. hemispheres
63. analysis
64. simultaneously
65. cortex
66. sensation
67. speech

68. sensory
69. motor
70. language
71. aphasias
72. Broca's
73. Wernicke's

MODULE 2.3

74. subcortex
75. medulla
76. cerebellum
77. reticular formation

78. cerebral
79. cortex
80. thalamus
81. hypothalamus

82. limbic
83. reward
84. amygdala
85. hippocampus

86. endocrine
87. bloodstream
88. pituitary
89. hypothalamus
90. pituitary

91. acromegaly
92. melatonin
93. pineal
94. overactive
95. underactive

96. adrenal
97. stress
98. synthetic

PSYCHOLOGY IN ACTION

99. Hand
100. dominance
101. ambidexterity
102. Ninety

103. 10
104. right
105. left
106. left

107. masquerade
108. right
109. lateralized

MASTERY TEST

1. B, (p. 60)
2. A, (p. 66)
3. A, (p. 70)
4. C, (p. 57)
5. B, (p. 58)
6. B, (p. 70)
7. C, (p. 55)
8. B, (p. 68)
9. B, (p. 75)
10. B, (p. 54)
11. A, (p. 58)
12. A, (p. 55)

13. B, (p. 59)
14. B, (p. 56)
15. A, (p. 70-71)
16. D, (p. 76)
17. D, (p. 60)
18. D, (p. 74)
19. B, (p. 63)
20. A, (p. 78)
21. D, (p. 67)
22. C, (p. 74)
23. C, (p. 68)
24. B, (p. 61)

25. D, (p. 70)
26. C, (p. 78)
27. B, (p. 74-75)
28. D, (p. 62)
29. A, (p. 62)
30. A, (p. 82)
31. C, (p. 57)
32. A, (p. 58)
33. B, (p. 59)
34. A, (p. 66-67)

CHILD DEVELOPMENT

CHAPTER OVERVIEW

Heredity affects personal characteristics, including temperament, and it organizes the human growth sequence. Environmental influences can have especially lasting effects during sensitive periods in development. Prenatal development is affected by diseases, drugs, radiation, or the mother's diet and health. Early perceptual, intellectual, and emotional deprivation seriously retards development. Deliberate enrichment of the environment has a beneficial effect on early development.

Most psychologists accept that heredity and environment are inseparable and interacting forces. A child's developmental level reflects heredity, environment, and the effects of the child's own behavior.

Human newborns have adaptive reflexes, are capable of learning, and have visual preferences, especially for familiar faces. Maturation underlies the orderly sequence of motor, cognitive, language, and emotional development.

Emotional attachment of infants to their caregivers is a critical event in social development. For optimal development, emotional attachment between infants and their caregivers must occur during the infant's first year. Three types of emotional attachments include secure, insecure-avoidant, and insecure-ambivalent.

Caregiving styles affect social, emotional, and intellectual development. Optimal caregiving includes proactive involvement, a good fit between the temperaments of parent and child, and responsiveness to a child's needs and signals. Three major parenting styles are authoritarian, permissive, and authoritative (effective). Effective parental discipline tends to emphasize child management techniques rather than power assertion or withdrawal of love. Parents who use authoritative parenting techniques encourage resiliency in their children, teach them to monitor their emotions, and use positive coping skills. The debate on whether parents should spank their children depends on whether the spanking was followed by supportive parenting techniques. Along with harsh parenting techniques, frequent or severe spanking may emotionally damage the child.

Language development is based on a biological predisposition, which is augmented by learning. Language acquisition begins with prelanguage communication between parent and child and progresses to telegraphic speech.

Jean Piaget theorized that children go through a series of cognitive stages as they develop intellectually. Learning principles provide an alternate explanation, which does not assume that cognitive development occurs in stages. Lev Vygotsky's sociocultural theory says that cognitive gains occur primarily in a child's zone of proximal development. Adults who engage in the scaffolding of a child's intellectual growth also impart cultural values and beliefs to the child.

Responsibility, mutual respect, consistency, love, encouragement, and clear communication are features of effective parenting. Effective parenting also utilizes I-messages and logical consequences when trying to manage children's behaviors and get them to accept responsibility for their actions.

LEARNING OBJECTIVES

To demonstrate mastery of this chapter, you should be able to:

1. Define developmental psychology and name its principal focus.

2. Define the terms "nature" and "nurture" as they relate to human development. Define the terms "heredity" and "conception."

3. Define or describe each of the following terms: a. chromosome b. gene c. polygenic d. dominant gene e. recessive gene

4. Briefly describe the human growth sequence.

5. Characterize the three types of children according to temperament and explain how these temperamental differences influence development.

6. Discuss the concept of sensitive periods and the effects of early environmental experiences.

7. Distinguish between congenital and genetic disorders.

8. Describe the relationship between the blood supplies of the mother and her developing child. Discuss the effect of teratogens on the unborn child, including the effects of drugs, alcohol (include a description of fetal alcohol syndrome), and tobacco.

9. Describe how prenatal risks can be minimized.

10. Briefly describe the two most important differences in the brain of a newborn and the brain of an adult.

11. Briefly discuss the impact of poverty on children's IQ and behavior.

12. Review the research demonstrating the benefits of enriched environments

13. Briefly discuss the "Mozart effect" and the problems surrounding the original research.

14. Describe the apparent outcome of the nature-nurture debate. List the three factors that combine to determine a person's developmental level.

15. Name and describe four adaptive reflexes of a neonate.

16. Describe the intellectual capabilities and the sensory preferences of a neonate.

17. Discuss the concept of maturation and define the terms "cephalocaudal" and "proximodistal."

18. Discuss the concept of readiness. Include in your answer the outcome of forcing a child to learn skills too early.

19. With respect to maturation, describe the course of emotional development.

20. Explain how there is an interplay between the emotions of infants and adults. Include the concept of the social smile.

21. Explain the concepts of self-awareness and social referencing.

22. Discuss the importance of emotional attachment, including the concept of separation anxiety. Include in your answer a differentiation of Ainsworth's attachment types as well as the key to secure attachments.

23. Discuss the effects of day care on attachment.

24. Discuss the importance of children's play, including the concepts of solitary play and cooperative play.

25. Discuss the importance of affectional needs.

The following objective is related to the material in the "Discovering Psychology" section of the text.

26. Discuss how our first attachments continue to affect us as adults. Describe the three attachment styles that adults tend to exhibit.

27. Discuss how maternal influences affect a child's competence by describing the two types of caregiving styles observed in the White and Watts' (1973) study.

28. Briefly describe the three ingredients that promote optimal caregiving.

29. Discuss the importance of paternal influences in child development. Compare these influences to maternal ones.

30. Compare and contrast the following three parenting styles and their effects on children: a. authoritarian b. overly permissive c. authoritative

31. Briefly describe some of the differences in child-rearing practices of the four ethnic groups listed in this section, and the conclusion that can be drawn from these differences.

32. Give a brief description of each of the following types of discipline and describe their effects on children a. power assertion b. withdrawal of love c. management techniques (include the concept of self-esteem)

33. Briefly describe how discipline affects a child's self-esteem.

34. Describe ways to encourage resilience in children.

The following objective is related to the material in the "Using Psychology" section of the text.

35. Briefly describe the drawbacks of spanking children as a primary form of discipline.

36. List and briefly describe the five stages of language acquisition.

37. Briefly discuss the concept of the "terrible twos."

38. Describe what a "language dance" is and explain why children probably do it.

39. Explain Noam Chomsky's concept of biological predisposition and briefly describe the typical language patterns that appear to be innate.

40. Define the term psycholinguist. Describe the role of learning in the acquisition of language.

41. Explain how parents can communicate with infants before the infants can talk. Include the ideas of signals, turn taking, and motherese (parentese).

42. Explain how a child's intelligence and thinking differ from an adult's. Explain the concept of transformations.

43. List (in order) and briefly describe Piaget's four stages of cognitive development. Include an explanation of assimilation and accommodation.

44. Describe the methods of encouraging intellectual development in children in each of Piaget's cognitive stages.

45. Briefly describe the dangers of forced teaching.

46. Describe the research which indicates that Piaget may have underestimated infant cognitive abilities.

47. Describe the sociocultural theory of Leo Vygotsky and define the terms "zone of proximal development" and "scaffolding."

48. Name the two most important areas of effective parent-child relationships.

49. Discuss the importance of using consistent discipline in childrearing.

50. List seven guidelines that should be followed if physical punishment is used in disciplining children.

51. List the four basic ingredients (Dinkmeyer & McKay) of a positive parent-child relationship.

52. Describe four important aspects of communication between parents and children, including what Dr. Thomas Gordon calls an "I" message.

53. Describe the use of natural and logical consequences to correct children's misbehavior.

RECITE AND REVIEW

MODULE 3.1

Survey Question: How do heredity and environment affect development? Pages 88-93

Developmental psychology is the study of progressive changes in [1] _____ and abilities, from [2] _____ to [3] _____ .

The nature-nurture debate concerns the relative contributions to development of heredity

([4] _____) and environment ([5] _____).

Hereditary instructions are carried by [6] _____ (deoxyribonucleic acid) in the form of chromosomes and [7] _____ in each cell of the body.

Most characteristics are polygenic (influenced by a combination of [8] _____) and reflect the combined effects of dominant and recessive [9] _____ .

Heredity organizes the general human growth sequence—the general pattern of [10] _____ from birth to death.

Heredity also influences differences in temperament (the physical core of [11] _____). Most infants fall into one of three temperament categories: easy children, [12] _____ children, and slow-to-warm-up children

Environment refers to all [13] _____ conditions that affect development.

A variety of sensitive periods (times of increased [14] _____ to environmental influences) exist in development.

Prenatal development is subject to [15] _____ influences in the form of diseases, drugs, radiation, or the mother's diet and health.

Prenatal damage to the fetus may cause congenital problems, or [16] _____ . In contrast, genetic problems are inherited from one's parents.

Fetal alcohol syndrome ([17] _____) is the result of heavy [18] _____ during pregnancy, which causes the infant to have [19] _____ birth weight, a small head, and [20] _____ malformations.

Exposure to any forms of teratogens such as radiation, [21] _____ , and pesticides during pregnancy is likely to cause [22] _____ .

Compared to an adult brain, newborn babies have neurons with [23] _____ dendrites and [24] _____ . These neurons grow rapidly, making millions of connections as the newborns interact with their environment in the first three years.

To promote successful pregnancies, mothers should eat [25] _____ food, avoid teratogens, and [26] _____ .

Early perceptual, intellectual, and emotional deprivation seriously retards [27] _____ .

Poverty greatly increases the likelihood that children will experience various forms of [28] _____ .

Deliberate enrichment of the [29] _____ in infancy and early childhood has a beneficial effect on development.

Ultimately, most psychologists accept that [30] _____ and environment are inseparable and interacting forces.

A child's developmental level (current state of development) reflects heredity, environment, and the effects of the child's [31] _____ .

MODULE 3.2

Survey Questions: What can newborn babies do? What influence does maturation have on early development? Pages 95-99

The human [32] _____ (newborn) has a number of [33] _____ reflexes, including the grasping, rooting, sucking, and Moro reflexes.

Newborns begin to [34] _____ immediately, and they imitate adults.

Tests in a looking chamber reveal a number of [35] _____ preferences in the newborn. The neonate is drawn to complex, [36] _____ , curved, and brightly lighted designs.

Infants prefer human face patterns, especially [37] _____ . In later infancy, interest in the unfamiliar emerges.

Maturation of the body and nervous system underlies the orderly [38] _____ of motor, cognitive, language, and emotional development.

While the rate of maturation varies from child to child, the [39] _____ is nearly universal.

The development of [40] _____ control (motor development) is cephalocaudal (from head to toe) and proximodistal (from the [41] _____ of the body to the extremities).

Many early [42] _____ are subject to the principle of readiness.

Emotional development begins with a capacity for [43] _____ excitement. After that, the first pleasant and unpleasant emotions develop.

Some psychologists believe that basic emotional expressions arc [44] _____ and that some appear as early as two and a half months of age.

By two to three months, babies display a social smile when other [45] _____ are nearby.

MODULE 3.3

Survey Question: Of what significance is a child's emotional bond with parents? Pages 101-104

[46] _____ development refers to the emergence of self-awareness and forming relationships with parents and others.

Self-awareness (consciousness of oneself as a person) and [47] _____ referencing (obtaining guidance from others) are elements of early [48] _____ development.

For optimal development in human infants, the development of an emotional attachment to their primary [49] _____ is a critical early event that must occur during the [50] _____ (within the first year) of infancy.

Infant attachment is reflected by [51] _____ anxiety (distress when infants are away from parents). The quality of attachment can be classified as [52] _____ , insecure-avoidant, or insecure-ambivalent.

Having a secure attachment style tends to promote caring, [53] _____ , and understanding in adulthood while having an avoidant attachment style tends to promote [54] _____ toward intimacy and commitment to others. An ambivalent attachment style tends to promote [55] _____ feelings about love and friendship in adulthood.

The relationship between quality of attachment and the type of caregiving that is provided appears to be [56] _____ in all cultures.

High-quality day care does not [57] _____ children; high-quality care can, in fact, accelerate some areas of development.

Some characteristics of high-quality day care include having a [58] _____ number of children per caregiver, trained caregivers, an overall group size of [59] _____ children, and minimal staff turnover.

A child's [60] _____ development is also affected by playing with other children. For example, cooperative [61] _____ is a major step toward participation in social life outside the family.

An infant's affectional [62] _____ are every bit as important as more obvious needs for physical care.

MODULE 3.4

Survey Question: How important are parenting styles? Pages 105-109

Caregiving styles (patterns of parental care) have a substantial impact on emotional and intellectual [63] _____ .

Maternal influences (the effects [64] _____ have on their children) tend to center on caregiving.

Super mothers are mothers who go out of their way to provide [65] _____ experiences and encourage [66] _____ in their children.

Optimal caregiving includes proactive maternal [67] _____ , a good fit between the temperaments of parent and child, and responsiveness to a child's needs and [68] _____ .

Paternal influences differ in their impact because [69] _____ tend to function as a playmate for the infant.

Authoritarian parents enforce rigid [70] _____ and demand strict obedience to [71] _____ .

Overly permissive parents give little [72] _____ and don't hold children accountable for their actions.

Authoritative ([73] _____) parents supply firm and consistent guidance, combined with love and affection.

Caregiving styles among various ethnic groups tend to reflect each culture's [74] _____ and [75] _____ . For example, fathers in Arab American families tend to be strong authority figures, demanding absolute obedience.

Effective child [76] _____ is based on a consistent framework of guidelines for acceptable behavior.

Good discipline tends to emphasize child management techniques (especially communication) rather than [77] _____ assertion or withdrawal of [78] _____ .

While using supportive parenting techniques, spanking a child [79] _____ seem to show signs of long-term effects. However, if the spanking is severe, frequent, or paired with a harsh parenting technique, spanking may [80] _____ damage a child.

[81] _____ techniques tend to produce the highest levels of self-esteem in children.

An [82] _____ (effective) style of parenting encourages children to manage their emotions and use [83] _____ coping skills to be [84] _____ (able to bounce back after bad experiences), capable, and successful adults.

MODULE 3.5

Survey Question: How do children acquire language? Pages 111-113

Language development proceeds from control of [85] _____ , to cooing, then babbling, the use of single words, and then to telegraphic [86] _____ .

The patterns of early speech suggest a [87] _____ predisposition to acquire language.

Psycholinguists (psychologists who study [88] _____) believe that innate language predispositions are augmented by [89] _____ .

Prelanguage communication between parent and child involves shared rhythms, nonverbal [90] _____ , and turn-taking.

Parents help children learn language by using distinctive caretaker [91] _____ or parentese.

MODULE 3.6

Survey Question: How do children learn to think? Pages 115-120

The intellects of children are [92] _____ abstract than those of adults. Jean Piaget theorized that [93] _____ growth occurs through a combination of assimilation and accommodation.

Piaget also held that children go through a fixed series of cognitive [94] _____ .

These are: sensorimotor (0-2), preoperational (2-7), [95] _____ operational (7-11), and formal [96] _____ (11-adult).

Object permanence (the ability to understand that [97] _____ continue to [98] _____ when they are out of sight) emerges during the [99] _____ stage while conservation (the ability to understand that mass, weight, and volume remain [100] _____ when the shape of objects changes) emerges during the [101] _____ stage.

Unlike the preoperational stage of development, when children exhibit [102] _____ , children in the formal operational stage of development are less egocentric and can think [103] _____ , hypothetically, and theoretically.

Learning theorists dispute the idea that cognitive development occurs in [104] _____ . Recent studies suggest infants are capable of levels of thinking beyond that observed by [105] _____ .

A one-step-ahead strategy that takes into account the child's level of [106] _____ development helps adapt instruction to a child's needs.

According to the sociocultural theory of Russian scholar Lev Vygotsky, a child's interactions with others are most likely to aid [107] _____ development if they they take place within the child's [108] _____ of proximal [109] _____ .

Adults help children learn how to think by scaffolding, or [110] _____ , their attempts to solve problems or discover principles.

During their collaborations with adults, children learn important cultural [111] _____ and values.

PSYCHOLOGY IN ACTION

Survey Question: How do effective parents discipline their children? Pages 122-125

Responsibility, mutual [112] _____ , consistency, love, encouragement, and clear [113] _____ are features of effective parenting.

When disciplining children, consistent discipline (maintaining a [114] _____ rule of conduct) fosters security and [115] _____ , whereas inconsistent discipline fosters insecurity and [116] _____ .

Much misbehavior can be managed by use of [117] _____ and by applying [118] _____ and logical consequences to children's behavior.

I-messages focus on the behavior you [119] _____ , and you-messages focus on children's [120] _____ .

CONNECTIONS

MODULE 3.1

1. _____ gene
2. _____ senescence
3. _____ congenital problems
4. _____ heredity
5. _____ sensitive period
6. _____ environment
7. _____ enrichment
8. _____ prenatal period
9. _____ FAS
10. _____ temperament

a. DNA area
b. old age
c. nature
d. nurture
e. conception to birth
f. prenatal alcohol exposure
g. magnified environmental impact
h. personality characteristics
i. "birth defects"
j. stimulating environment

MODULE 3.2

1. _____ grasping reflex
2. _____ rooting reflex
3. _____ Moro reflex
4. _____ neonate
5. _____ readiness
6. _____ motor development
7. _____ familiar faces
8. _____ maturation

a. rapid motor learning
b. palm grip
c. startled embrace
d. food search
e. control of muscles and movement
f. newborn infant
g. physical growth
h. preferred pattern

Chapter 3

MODULE 3.3

1. _____ secure attachment	a. love and attention
2. _____ insecure-avoidant	b. social development
3. _____ affectional needs	c. anxious emotional bond
4. _____ separation anxiety	d. positive emotional bond
5. _____ resilient	e. emotional distress
6. _____ social referencing	f. observing reactions of others
7. _____ cooperative play	g. trained caregivers
8. _____ high-quality day care	h. bouncing back after hardship

MODULE 3.4

1. _____ super mother	a. proactive educational interactions
2. _____ Asian-American families	b. strict obedience
3. _____ optimal caregiving	c. caregiving style
4. _____ paternal influence	d. firm and consistent guidance
5. _____ management techniques	e. little guidance
6. _____ authoritative style	f. playmates
7. _____ authoritarian style	g. bounce back from hardship
8. _____ permissive style	h. interdependence
9. _____ power assertion	i. produce high self-esteem
10. _____ resilience	j. show of force

MODULE 3.5

1. _____ biological predisposition	a. vowel sounds
2. _____ cooing	b. vowels and consonants
3. _____ babbling	c. caretaker speech
4. _____ telegraphic speech	d. "Mama gone."
5. _____ turn-taking	e. hereditary readiness for language
6. _____ Noam Chomsky	f. psycholinguists
7. _____ parentese	g. conversational style of communication

MODULE 3.6

1.	_____ assimilation	a.	changing existing mental patterns
2.	_____ accommodation	b.	egocentricism
3.	_____ sensorimotor stage	c.	applying mental patterns
4.	_____ preoperational stage	d.	abstract principles
5.	_____ concrete operations	e.	"Will you kids please stop yelling or go outside and play"
6.	_____ formal operations		
7.	_____ hothousing	f.	conservation
8.	_____ scaffolding	g.	object permanence
9.	_____ I-message	h.	skilled support for learning
10.	_____ Piaget	i.	forced teaching
		j.	stage theory of cognitive development

CHECK YOUR MEMORY

MODULE 3.1

Survey Question: How do heredity and environment affect development? Pages 88-93

1. Developmental psychology is the study of progressive changes in behavior and abilities during childhood.
    TRUE or FALSE

2. Each cell in the human body (except sperm cells and ova) contains 23 chromosomes.
    TRUE or FALSE

3. The order of organic bases in DNA acts as a genetic code.
    TRUE or FALSE

4. Two brown-eyed parents cannot have a blue-eyed child.
    TRUE or FALSE

5. Identical twins have identical genes.
    TRUE or FALSE

6. More children have a slow-to-warm-up temperament than a difficult temperament.
    TRUE or FALSE

7. The sensitive period during which German measles can damage the fetus occurs near the end of pregnancy.
    TRUE or FALSE

8. Teratogens are substances capable of causing birth defects.
    TRUE or FALSE

9. An infant damaged by exposure to X-rays during the prenatal period suffers from a genetic problem.
   TRUE or FALSE

10. Many drugs can reach the fetus within the intrauterine environment.
    TRUE or FALSE

11. To prevent FAS, the best advice to pregnant women is to get plenty of rest, vitamins, and good nutrition.
    TRUE or FALSE

12. Prepared childbirth tends to reduce the need for pain medications during birth.
    TRUE or FALSE

13. Poverty is associated with retarded emotional and intellectual development.
    TRUE or FALSE

14. In animals, enriched environments can actually increase brain size and weight.
    TRUE or FALSE

15. There is evidence that the "Mozart effect" might just be based on the fact that college students were more alert or in a better mood after listening to music.
    TRUE or FALSE

16. Factors that influence developmental levels are heredity, environment, and parental discipline.
    TRUE or FALSE

MODULE 3.2

Survey Questions: What can newborn babies do? What influence does maturation have on early development? Pages 95-99

17. The Moro reflex helps infants hold on to objects placed in their hands.
    TRUE or FALSE

18. As early as nine weeks of age, infants can imitate actions a full day after seeing them.
    TRUE or FALSE

19. Three-day-old infants will pay an equal amount of attention to a person who is gazing at them as well as a person who is not looking at them.
    TRUE or FALSE

20. Three-day-old infants prefer to look at simple colored backgrounds rather than more complex patterns.
    TRUE or FALSE

21. After age two, familiar faces begin to hold great interest for infants.
    TRUE or FALSE

22. Most infants learn to stand alone before they begin crawling.
    TRUE or FALSE

23. Motor development follows a top-down, center-outward pattern.
    TRUE or FALSE

24. Toilet training should begin soon after a child is one year old.
    TRUE or FALSE

25. Anger and fear are the first two emotions to emerge in infancy.
    TRUE or FALSE

26. An infant's social smile appears within one month after birth.
    TRUE or FALSE

MODULE 3.3

Survey Question: Of what significance is a child's emotional bond with parents? Pages 101-104

27. Most infants have to be 15 weeks old before they can recognize themselves on videotape.
    TRUE or FALSE

28. Securely attached infants turn away from their mother when she returns after a period of separation.
    TRUE or FALSE

29. A small number of children per caregiver is desirable in day care settings.
    TRUE or FALSE

30. Children who spend too much time in poor-quality day care tend to be insecure and aggressive.
    TRUE or FALSE

31. Children typically first begin to engage in cooperative play around age four or five.
    TRUE or FALSE

MODULE 3.4

Survey Question: How important are parenting styles? Pages 105-109

32. Early patterns of competence are well established by the time a child reaches age three.
    TRUE or FALSE

33. The "zookeeper" mother provides poor physical, emotional, and intellectual care for her child.
    TRUE or FALSE

34. The goodness of fit between parents and children refers mainly to the compatibility of their temperaments.
    TRUE or FALSE

35. Responsive parents are sensitive to a child's feelings, need, rhythms, and signals.
    TRUE or FALSE

36. Fathers typically spend about half their time in caregiving and half playing with the baby.

    TRUE or FALSE

37. Paternal play tends to be more physically arousing for infants than maternal play is.

    TRUE or FALSE

38. Since mothers spend more time caring for infants, mothers are more important than fathers.

    TRUE or FALSE

39. Authoritarian parents view children as having adult-like responsibilities.

    TRUE or FALSE

40. Permissive parents basically give their children the message "Do it because I say so."

    TRUE or FALSE

41. The children of authoritarian parents tend to be independent, assertive, and inquiring.

    TRUE or FALSE

42. Asian cultures tend to be group-oriented and they emphasize interdependence among individuals.

    TRUE or FALSE

43. As a means of child discipline, power assertion refers to rejecting a child.

    TRUE or FALSE

44. Severely punished children tend to be defiant and aggressive.

    TRUE or FALSE

45. Punishment is most effective when it is given immediately after a disapproved act.

    TRUE or FALSE

46. Spanking, even if it is backed up with a supportive parenting technique, is still emotionally damaging to most children.

    TRUE or FALSE

47. An authoritarian style of parenting is necessary since encouraging resiliency in children is challenging and difficult for most parents and children.

    TRUE or FALSE

MODULE 3.5

Survey Question: How do children acquire language? Pages 111-113

48. The single-word stage begins at about six months of age.

    TRUE or FALSE

49. "That red ball mine" is an example of telegraphic speech.

    TRUE or FALSE

50. Noam Chomsky believes that basic language patterns are innate.
    TRUE or FALSE

51. The "terrible twos" refers to the two-word stage of language development.
    TRUE or FALSE

52. The "I'm going to get you" game is an example of prelanguage communication.
    TRUE or FALSE

53. Parentese is spoken in higher pitched tones with a musical inflection.
    TRUE or FALSE

54. Motherese or parentese language used by mothers and fathers to talk to their infants does more harm than good to their infants' language development.
    TRUE or FALSE

MODULE 3.6

Survey Question: How do children learn to think? Pages 115-120

55. According to Piaget, children first learn to make transformations at about age three.
    TRUE or FALSE

56. Assimilation refers to modifying existing ideas to fit new situations or demands.
    TRUE or FALSE

57. Cognitive development during the sensorimotor stage is mostly nonverbal.
    TRUE or FALSE

58. Reversibility of thoughts and the concept of conservation both appear during the concrete operational stage.
    TRUE or FALSE

59. Three-year-old children are surprisingly good at understanding what other people are thinking.
    TRUE or FALSE

60. An understanding of hypothetical possibilities develops during the preoperational stage.
    TRUE or FALSE

61. Playing peekaboo is a good way to establish the permanence of objects for children in the sensorimotor stage.
    TRUE or FALSE

62. Contrary to what Piaget observed, infants as young as three months of age show signs of object permanence.
    TRUE or FALSE

63. Hothousing or the forced teaching of children to learn reading or math is encouraged to accelerate their intellectual development and to prevent apathy.

TRUE or FALSE

64. A criticism of Piaget's theory of cognitive development is that he underestimated the impact of cultural influence on children's mental development.

TRUE or FALSE

65. Vygotsky's key insight was that children's thinking develops through dialogues with more capable persons.

TRUE or FALSE

66. Learning experiences are most helpful when they take place outside of a child's zone of proximal development.

TRUE or FALSE

67. Scaffolding is like setting up temporary bridges to help children move into new mental territory.

TRUE or FALSE

68. Vygotsky empasized that children use adults to learn about their culture and society.

TRUE or FALSE

PSYCHOLOGY IN ACTION

Survey Question: How do effective parents discipline their children? Pages 122-125

69. Consistency of child discipline is more important than whether limits on children's behavior are strict or lenient.

TRUE or FALSE

70. Encouragement means giving recognition for effort and improvement.

TRUE or FALSE

71. Logical consequences should be stated as you-messages.

TRUE or FALSE

FINAL SURVEY AND REVIEW

MODULE 3.1

Survey Question: How do heredity and environment affect development? Pages 88-93

[1] _____ psychology is the study of [2] _____ changes in behavior and abilities, from birth to death.

The nature-nurture debate concerns the relative contributions to development of [3] _____ (nature) and [4] _____ (nurture).

Hereditary instructions are carried by DNA ([5] _____ acid) in the form of [6] _____ ("colored bodies") and genes in every cell.

Most characteristics are [7] _____ (influenced by a combination of genes) and reflect the combined effects of dominant and [8] _____ genes.

Heredity organizes the general human [9] _____ [10] _____ —the general pattern of physical development from birth to death.

Heredity also influences differences in [11] _____ (the physical foundations of personality).

Most infants fall into one of three categories: [12] _____ children, difficult children, and [13] _____ children.

[14] _____ refers to all external conditions that affect development.

A variety of [15] _____ [16] _____ (times of increased sensitivity to environmental influences) exist in development.

During pregnancy, [17] _____ development is subject to environmental influences in the form of diseases, [18] _____ , [19] _____ , or the mother's diet and health.

Prenatal damage to the fetus may cause [20] _____ problems, or birth defects. In contrast, [21] _____ problems are inherited from one's parents.

[22] _____ (FAS) is the result of heavy drinking during [23] _____ , which causes the infant to have [24] _____ birth weight, a small head, and [25] _____ malformations.

Exposure to any forms of [26] _____ such as radiation, lead, and pesticides during pregnancy will likely cause [27] _____ .

Compared to an adult brain, newborn babies have neurons with fewer [28] _____ and [29] _____ . These neurons grow rapidly, making millions of connections as the newborns interact with their environment in the first three years.

To promote successful pregnancies, mothers should eat [30] _____ food, avoid [31] _____ , and exercise.

Early perceptual and intellectual [32] _____ seriously retards development.

[33] _____ greatly increases the likelihood that children will experience various forms of deprivation.

Deliberate [34] _____ of the environment in infancy and early childhood has a beneficial effect on development.

Ultimately, most psychologists accept that heredity and environment are inseparable and [35] _____ forces.

A child's [36] _____ [37] _____ (current state of development) reflects heredity, environment, and the effects of the child's own behavior.

MODULE 3.2

Survey Questions: What can newborn babies do? What influence does maturation have on early development? Pages 95-99

The human neonate (newborn) has a number of adaptive reflexes, including the [38] _____ , rooting, [39] _____ , and [40] _____ reflexes.

Newborns begin to learn immediately, and they [41] _____ (mimic) adults.

Tests in a [42] _____ [43] _____ reveal a number of visual preferences in the newborn.

The neonate is drawn to [44] _____ , circular, curved, and brightly lighted designs.

Infants prefer [45] _____ [46] _____ patterns, especially familiar faces. In later infancy, interest in the [47] _____ emerges.

[48] _____ of the body and [49] _____ [50] _____ underlies the orderly sequence of motor, cognitive, language, and emotional development.

While the [51] _____ of maturation varies from child to child, the order is nearly [52] _____ .

The development of muscular control ([53] _____ development) is [54] _____ (from head to toe) and [55] _____ (from the center of the body to the extremities).

Many early skills are subject to the principle of [56] _____ .

Emotional development begins with a capacity for general [57] _____ . After that, the first [58] _____ and [59] _____ emotions develop.

Some psychologists believe that basic [60] _____ expressions are innate and that some appear as early as two and a half [61] _____ of age.

By two to three months, babies display a [62] _____ smile when other people are nearby.

MODULE 3.3

Survey Question: Of what significance is a child's emotional bond with parents? Pages 101-104

Social development refers to the emergence of self-[63] _____ and forming [64] _____ with parents and others.

[65] _____ (consciousness of oneself as a person) and social [66] _____ (obtaining guidance from others) are elements of early social development.

For optimal development in human infants, the development of an emotional attachment to their primary [67] _____ is a critical early event that must occur during the [68] _____ (within the first year) of infancy.

Emotional [69] _____ of human infants to their caregivers is a critical early event.

Infant attachment is reflected by separation [70] _____ (distress when infants are away from parents).

The quality of attachment can be classified as secure, insecure-[71] _____ , or insecure-[72] _____ .

Having a [73] _____ attachment style tends to promote caring, supportiveness, and understanding while having an [74] _____ attachment style tends to promote resistance toward intimacy and commitment to others. An [75] _____ attachment style tends to promote mixed feelings about love and friendship.

The relationship between quality of attachment and the type of [76] _____ that is provided appears to be [77] _____ in all cultures.

[78] _____ day care does not harm children; excellent care can, in fact, [79] _____ some areas of development.

Some characteristics of high-quality day care include having a [80] _____ number of children per caregiver, trained caregivers, an overall group size of [81] _____ children, and minimal [82] _____ turnover.

A child's social development is also affected by playing with other children. For example, [83] _____ play is a major step toward participation in social life outside the family.

An infant's [84] _____ needs are every bit as important as more obvious needs for physical care.

MODULE 3.4

Survey Question: How important are parenting styles? Pages 105-109

[85] _____ [86] _____ (patterns of parental care) have a substantial impact on emotional and intellectual development.

[87] _____ influences (the effects mothers have on their children) tend to center on [88] _____ .

[89] _____ are mothers who go out of their way to provide educational experiences and encourage [90] _____ in their children.

Optimal caregiving includes [91] _____ maternal involvement, a good fit between the [92] _____ of parent and child, and responsiveness to a child's needs and signals.

[93] _____ influences differ in their impact because fathers tend to function as a [94] _____ for the infant.

[95] _____ parents enforce rigid rules and demand strict obedience to authority.

Overly [96] _____ parents give little guidance and don't hold children accountable for their actions.

[97] _____ (effective) parents supply firm and consistent guidance, combined with love and affection.

Caregiving styles among various ethnic groups tend to reflect each culture's [98] _____ . For example, fathers in Arab-American families tend to be strong [99] _____ figures, demanding absolute obedience.

Effective child discipline is based on consistent parental [100] _____ concerning acceptable behavior.

Good discipline tends to emphasize child [101] _____ techniques (especially communication) rather than power [102] _____ or withdrawal of love.

While using supportive parenting techniques, spanking a child [103] _____ seem to show signs of long-term effects. However, if spanking is severe, frequent, or paired with a harsh parenting technique, spanking may [104] _____ damage a child.

Management techniques tend to produce the highest levels of [105] _____ in children.

An [106] _____ style of parenting encourages children to manage their emotions and use [107] _____ coping skills to be [108] _____ (able to bounce back after bad experiences), capable, and successful adults.

MODULE 3.5

Survey Question: How do children acquire language? Pages 111-113

Language development proceeds from control of crying, to [109] _____ , then

[110] _____ , the use of single words, and then to [111] _____ speech (two-word

sentences).

The patterns of early speech suggest a biological [112] _____ to acquire language.

[113] _____ (psychologists who study language) believe that innate language predispositions

are augmented by learning.

[114] _____ communication between parent and child involves shared rhythms, nonverbal

signals, and [115] _____ -taking.

Parents help children learn language by using distinctive caretaker speech or [116] _____ .

MODULE 3.6

Survey Question: How do children learn to think? Pages 115-120

The intellects of children are less [117] _____ than those of adults. Jean Piaget theorized that

cognitive growth occurs through a combination of [118] _____ and accommodation.

Piaget also held that children go through a fixed series of [119] _____ stages.

The stages are: [120] _____ (0-2), [121] _____ (2-7), concrete operational (7-11), and

formal operations (11-adult).

[122] _____ (the ability to understand that objects continue to exist when they are out of sight)

emerges during the [123] _____ stage while [124] _____ (the ability to understand

that mass, weight, and volume remain unchanged when the shape of objects changes) emerges during the

[125] _____ stage.

Unlike the preoperational stage of development, when children exhibit egocentrism, children in the

[126] _____ stage of development are less egocentric and can think abstractly, hypothetically,

and theoretically.

[127] _____ theorists dispute the idea that cognitive development occurs in stages. Recent studies

suggest infants are capable of levels of [128] _____ beyond that observed by Piaget.

A [129] _____ strategy that takes into account the child's level of cognitive development

helps adapt instruction to a child's needs.

According to the [130] _____ theory of Russian scholar Lev [131] _____ , a child's interactions with others are most likely to aid cognitive development if they take place within the child's zone of [132] _____ development.

Adults help children learn how to think by [133] _____ , or supporting, their attempts to solve problems or discover principles.

During their collaborations with others, children learn important [134] _____ beliefs and values.

PSYCHOLOGY IN ACTION

Survey Question: How do effective parents discipline their children? Pages 122-125

Responsibility, mutual respect, [135] _____ , love, [136] _____ , and clear communication are features of effective parenting.

When disciplining children, [137] _____ discipline (maintaining a stable rule of conduct) fosters security and [138] _____ , whereas [139] _____ discipline fosters insecurity and unpredictability.

Much misbehavior can be managed by use of I-messages and by applying natural and [140] _____ [141] _____ to children's behavior.

MASTERY TEST

1. The universal patterns of the human growth sequence can be attributed to
   a. recessive genes
   b. environment
   c. polygenic imprinting
   d. heredity

2. Exaggerated or musical voice inflections are characteristic of
   a. prelanguage turn-taking
   b. parentese
   c. telegraphic speech
   d. prompting and expansion

3. The emotion most clearly expressed by newborn infants is
   a. joy
   b. fear
   c. anger
   d. excitement

4. Explaining things abstractly or symbolically to a child becomes most effective during which stage of cognitive development?
   a. postconventional
   b. formal operations
   c. preoperational
   d. post intuitive

5. An infant startled by a loud noise will typically display
   a. a Moro reflex
   b. a rooting reflex
   c. a Meltzoff reflex
   d. an imprinting reflex

6. If one identical twin has a Y chromosome, the other must have a
   a. recessive chromosome
   b. sex-linked trait
   c. dominant chromosome
   d. Y chromosome

7. Ideas about Piaget's stages and the cognitive abilities of infants are challenged by infants' reactions to
   a. hypothetical possibilities
   b. impossible events
   c. turn-taking
   d. separation anxiety

8. The type of play that is observed first in most children is called
   a. selective play
   b. secure play
   c. solitary play
   d. social play

9. The largest percentage of children display what type of temperament?
   a. easy
   b. difficult
   c. slow-to-warm-up
   d. generic

10. Which of the following is a congenital problem?
    a. FAS
    b. sickle-cell anemia
    c. hemophilia
    d. muscular dystrophy

11. A child might begin to question the idea that Santa Claus's sack could carry millions of toys when the child has grasped the concept of
    a. assimilation
    b. egocentricism
    c. conservation
    d. reversibility of permanence

12. In most areas of development, heredity and environment are
    a. independent
    b. interacting
    c. conflicting
    d. responsible for temperament

13. Children who grow up in poverty run a high risk of
    a. insecure scaffolding
    b. hospitalism
    c. deprivation
    d. colostrum

14. By definition, a trait that is controlled by a dominant gene cannot be
    a. eugenic
    b. hereditary
    c. carried by DNA
    d. polygenic

15. _____ development proceeds head-down and center-outward.
    a. Cognitive
    b. Motor
    c. Prelanguage
    d. Preoperational

16. You could test for _____ by videotaping a child and then letting the child see the video on television.
    a. social referencing
    b. self-awareness
    c. the quality of attachment
    d. the degree of readiness

17. After age two, infants become much more interested in
    a. bonding
    b. nonverbal communication
    c. familiar voices
    d. unfamiliar faces

18. According to Piaget, one of the major developments during the sensorimotor stage is emergence of the concept of
    a. assimilation
    b. accommodation
    c. object permanence
    d. transformation

19. Poverty is to deprivation as early childhood stimulation is to
    a. imprinting
    b. enrichment
    c. responsiveness
    d. assimilation

20. Which principle is most relevant to the timing of toilet training?
    a. readiness
    b. sensitive periods
    c. nonverbal signals
    d. assimilation

21. High self-esteem is most often a product of what style of child discipline?
    a. power assertion
    b. child management
    c. withdrawal of love
    d. the natural consequences method

22. Consonants first enter a child's language when the child begins
    a. babbling
    b. cooing
    c. the single-word stage
    d. turn-taking

23. Physically arousing play is typically an element of
    a. the zookeeper mother's caregiving style
    b. paternal influences
    c. proactive maternal involvement
    d. secure attachment

24. Insecure attachment is revealed by
    a. separation anxiety
    b. seeking to be near the mother after separation
    c. turning away from the mother after separation
    d. social referencing

25. A healthy balance between the rights of parents and their children is characteristic of
    a. authoritarian parenting
    b. permissive parenting
    c. authoritative parenting
    d. consistent parenting

26. Studies of infant imitation
    a. are conducted in a looking chamber
    b. confirm that infants mimic adult facial gestures
    c. show that self-awareness precedes imitation
    d. are used to assess the quality of infant attachment

27. Threatening, accusing, bossing, and lecturing children is most characteristic of
    a. PET
    b. you-messages
    c. applying natural consequences
    d. management techniques

28. According to Vygotsky, children learn important cultural beliefs and values when adults provide
    _____ to help them gain new ideas and skills.
    a. scaffolding
    b. proactive nurturance
    c. imprinting stimuli
    d. parentese

29. One thing that all forms of effective child discipline have in common is that they
    a. are consistent
    b. make use of punishment
    c. involve temporary withdrawal of love
    d. emphasize you-messages

30. A major problem with using the "Mozart effect" as a basis for promoting intellectual development in babies is that the original research was done on
    a. laboratory animals
    b. mentally retarded infants
    c. children in the concrete operations stage
    d. college students

31. The intellectual development of babies begins as young as _____ when they start to pay more attention to a person who is looking directly at them than someone who is looking away from them.
    a. Two to five days old
    b. two to five weeks old
    c. two to five months old
    d. two years old

32. Children who are securely attached to their parents tend to _____ when they interact with others.
    a. be anxious and remote
    b. be resilient and curious
    c. dislike direct physical contact
    d. lack social skills

33. Which statement correctly states the relationship between sensitive caregiving and secure attachment when applied cross-culturally?
    a. There is no relationship between the two variables in any culture.
    b. A minimal relationship can be found only in the United States.
    c. A relationship between the two variables can be found in all cultures.
    d. A relationship between the two variables can be found in all cultures if both biological parents raised the child.

34. To provide optimal care for children, caregivers
    a. must get involved proactively in educating children
    b. must respond to children's feelings and needs
    c. and children temperaments should match closely to each other
    d. all the preceding

35. The debate on the issue of the effectiveness of spanking suggests that
    a. frequent spanking may lead to an increase in aggression in children
    b. spanking stops the bad behavior from occurring again in the future
    c. when coupled with harsh parenting, frequent spanking leads to more problem behaviors
    d. both a and c

36. Parents who use a(an) _____ form of parenting tend to teach their children to manage and control their emotions and to use positive coping skills.
    a. authoritative
    b. authoritarian
    c. overly permissive
    d. power assertion

SOLUTIONS

RECITE AND REVIEW

MODULE 3.1

1. behavior
2. birth
3. death
4. nature
5. nurture
6. DNA
7. genes
8. genes
9. genes
10. physical development
11. personality
12. difficult
13. external
14. sensitivity
15. environmental
16. birth defects
17. FAS
18. drinking
19. low
20. facial
21. lead
22. birth defects
23. force
24. synapses
25. nutritious
26. exercise
27. development
28. deprivation
29. environment
30. heredity
31. own behavior

MODULE 3.2

32. neonate
33. adaptive
34. learn
35. visual
36. circular
37. familiar faces
38. sequence
39. order
40. muscular
41. center
42. skills
43. general
44. innate
45. people

MODULE 3.3

46. Social
47. social
48. social
49. caregivers
50. sensitive period
51. separation
52. secure
53. supportiveness
54. resistance
55. mixed
56. universal
57. harm
58. small
59. 12 to 15
60. social
61. play
62. needs

MODULE 3.4

63. development
64. mothers
65. educational
66. initiative
67. involvement
68. preferences
69. fathers
70. rules
71. authority
72. guidance
73. effective
74. customs
75. beliefs
76. discipline
77. power
78. love
79. does not
80. emotionally
81. Management
82. authoritative
83. positive
84. resilient

MODULE 3.5

85. crying

86. speech
87. biological
88. language
89. learning
90. signals
91. speech

MODULE 3.6

92. less
93. intellectual
94. stages
95. concrete
96. operations
97. objects
98. exist
99. sensorimotor
100. unchanged
101. concrete operational
102. egocentrism
103. abstractly
104. stages
105. Piaget
106. cognitive
107. cognitive
108. zone
109. development
110. supporting
111. beliefs

PSYCHOLOGY IN ACTION

112. respect
113. communication
114. stable
115. stability
116. unpredictability
117. I-messages
118. natural
119. object
120. characteristics

CONNECTIONS

MODULE 3.1

1. a
2. b
3. i
4. c
5. g
6. d
7. j
8. e
9. f
10. h

MODULE 3.2

1. b
2. d
3. c
4. f
5. a
6. e
7. h
8. g

MODULE 3.3

1. d
2. c
3. a
4. e
5. h
6. f
7. b
8. g

MODULE 3.4

1. c
2. h
3. a
4. f
5. i
6. d
7. b
8. e
9. j
10. g

MODULE 3.5

1. e
2. a
3. b

4. d
5. g

6. f
7. c

MODULE 3.6

1. c
2. a
3. g
4. b

5. f
6. d
7. i
8. h

9. e
10. j

CHECK YOUR MEMORY

MODULE 3.1

1. F
2. F
3. T
4. F
5. T
6. T

7. F
8. T
9. F
10. T
11. F
12. T

13. T
14. T
15. T
16. F

MODULE 3.2

17. F
18. F
19. F
20. F

21. F
22. F
23. T
24. F

25. F
26. F

MODULE 3.3

27. F
28. F

29. T
30. T

31. T

MODULE 3.4

32. T
33. F
34. T
35. T
36. F
37. T

38. F
39. T
40. F
41. F
42. T
43. F

44. T
45. T
46. F
47. F

MODULE 3.5

48. F
49. F
50. T

51. F
52. T
53. T

54. F

MODULE 3.6

55. F

56. F

57. T

58. T	62. T	66. F
59. F	63. F	67. T
60. F	64. T	68. T
61. T	65. T	

PSYCHOLOGY IN ACTION

69. T	70. T	71. F

FINAL SURVEY AND REVIEW

MODULE 3.1

1. Developmental
2. progressive
3. heredity
4. environment
5. deoxyribonucleic
6. chromosomes
7. polygenic
8. recessive
9. growth
10. sequence
11. temperament
12. easy
13. slow-to-warm-up

14. Environment
15. sensitive
16. periods
17. prenatal
18. drugs
19. radiation
20. congenital
21. genetic
22. Fetal alcohol syndrome
23. pregnancy
24. low
25. facial
26. teratogens

27. birth defects
28. dendrites
29. synapses
30. nutritious
31. teratogens
32. deprivation
33. Poverty
34. enrichment
35. interacting
36. developmental
37. level

MODULE 3.2

38. grasping
39. sucking
40. Moro
41. imitate
42. looking
43. chamber
44. complex
45. human
46. face

47. unfamiliar
48. Maturation
49. nervous
50. system
51. rate
52. universal
53. motor
54. cephalocaudal
55. proximodistal

56. readiness
57. excitement
58. pleasant
59. unpleasant
60. emotional
61. months
62. social

MODULE 3.3

63. awareness
64. relationships
65. Self-awareness
66. referencing
67. caregivers
68. sensitive period
69. attachment
70. anxiety
71. avoidant

72. ambivalent
73. secure
74. avoidant
75. ambivalent
76. caregiving
77. universal
78. High-quality
79. accelerate
80. small

81. 12 to 15
82. staff
83. cooperative
84. affectional

MODULE 3.4

85. Caregiving
86. styles
87. Maternal
88. caregiving
89. Super mothers
90. initiative
91. proactive
92. temperaments
93. Paternal

94. playmate
95. Authoritarian
96. permissive
97. Authoritative
98. beliefs
99. authority
100. guidance
101. management
102. assertion

103. does not
104. emotionally
105. self-esteem
106. authoritative
107. positive
108. resilient

MODULE 3.5

109. cooing
110. babbling
111. telegraphic

112. predisposition
113. Psycholinguists
114. Prelanguage

115. turn
116. parentese

MODULE 3.6

117. abstract
118. assimilation
119. cognitive
120. sensorimotor
121. preoperational
122. Object permanence

123. sensorimotor
124. conservation
125. concrete operational
126. formal operational
127. Learning
128. thinking

129. one-step-ahead
130. sociocultural
131. Vygotsky
132. proximal
133. scaffolding
134. cultural

PSYCHOLOGY IN ACTION

135. consistency
136. encouragement
137. consistent

138. stability
139. inconsistent
140. logical

141. consequences

MASTERY TEST

1. D, (p. 88)
2. B, (p. 113)
3. D, (p. 98)
4. B, (p. 117)
5. A, (p. 95)
6. D, (p. 90)
7. B, (p. 118)
8. C, (p. 103)
9. A, (p. 88)
10. A, (p. 91)
11. C, (p. 116)
12. B, (p. 93)

13. C, (p. 92)
14. D, (p. 88)
15. B, (p. 98)
16. B, (p. 101)
17. D, (p. 97)
18. C, (p. 116)
19. B, (p. 87)
20. A, (p. 98)
21. B, (p. 108)
22. A, (p. 111)
23. B, (p. 105-106)
24. C, (p. 102)

25. C, (p. 106)
26. B, (p. 96)
27. B, (p. 124)
28. A, (p. 119-120)
29. A, (p. 122)
30. D, (p. 93)
31. A, (p. 95)
32. B, (p. 102)
33. C, (p. 102)
34. D, (p. 105)
35. D, (p. 109)
36. A, (p. 108-109)

FROM BIRTH TO DEATH: LIFE-SPAN DEVELOPMENT

CHAPTER OVERVIEW

Life-span psychologists study continuity and change in behavior as well as tasks, challenges, milestones, and problems throughout life. According to Erikson, each life stage provokes a different psychosocial dilemma.

Childhood problems such as sleep disturbances, fear of the dark, sibling rivalry, and clinging to mothers are normal processes of growing up. These problems can provide opportunities for children to learn and develop skills. However, serious problems in childhood include toilet training, feeding disturbances, speech disturbances, learning disorders, and attention-deficit hyperactivity disorder. Childhood autism and child abuse are examples of the more severe problems that can occur. Behavior modification programs can reduce an autistic child's maladaptive behaviors. Parents who are under tremendous stress and believe in physical punishment are likely to abuse their children. Both emotional and physical abuse can leave long-lasting emotional scars on children.

Adolescence is culturally defined; puberty is a biological event. Early maturation is beneficial mostly for boys; its effects are mixed for girls. Adolescent identity formation is accelerated by cognitive development and influenced by parents and peer groups. As adolescents prolong their identity explorations into the college years, their emerging adulthood has been extended into their mid-20s.

Moral development bridges childhood, adolescence, and early adulthood. Lawrence Kohlberg believed that moral development occurs in stages. Some psychologists question whether moral development is based only on a sense of justice. Caring for others also appears to be important.

Adult development is marked by events that range from escaping parental dominance in the late teens to a noticeable acceptance of one's lot in life during the 50s. Some people experience a midlife crisis, but this is not universal. Adjustment to later middle age is sometimes complicated by menopause and the climacteric. Biological aging begins between 25 and 30, but peak performance in specific pursuits may come at any point in life. Intellectual declines due to aging are limited. Life expectancy can be increased by carefully monitoring one's activity level, one's emotional state, what one consumes, and having parents who are over the age of 75. Two major theories of successful aging are disengagement and activity. Activity theory appears to apply to more people. It seems seniors who have a positive outlook on aging tend to live seven and a half years longer than seniors who have a negative outlook. Ageism is especially damaging to older people.

Impending death and bereavement both produce a series of typical emotional reactions. New approaches to death include the hospice movement and living wills.

Subjective well-being (happiness) is a combination of general life satisfaction and positive emotions. People with extraverted and optimistic personalities tend to be happy. Making progress toward your goals is associated with happiness, especially if the goals express your personal interests and values.

LEARNING OBJECTIVES

To demonstrate mastery of this chapter, you should be able to:

1. Define the terms "developmental tasks," "developmental milestones" and "life-span perspective."

2. Describe the term "psychosocial dilemma" and explain, according to Erikson, how the resolution of the psychosocial dilemmas affects a person's adjustment to life.

3. State the nature of the psychosocial crisis and the nature of an adequate or inadequate outcome for each of Erikson's eight life stages. Match each crisis with the corresponding age.

4. Discuss the positive and negative aspects of stress on a developing child.

5. List and describe (where applicable) nine "normal" childhood problems.

6. Give a brief description of the following childhood disorders and their possible causes: a. enuresis b. encopresis c. overeating d. anorexia nervosa e. pica f. delayed speech g. stuttering

7. Describe what the label "learning disorder" includes. Briefly describe dyslexia, including its possible cause.

8. Describe the following disorders in terms of symptoms, causes, and treatments: a. ADHD (also explain what relationship sugar has to ADHD and the controversy surrounding the use of Ritalin for treatment of ADHD) b. autism (include a definition of echolalia)

9. Describe the characteristics of abusive parents and the conditions likely to foster abusive behavior.

10. Describe what can be done to prevent child abuse.

11. Define and differentiate the terms "adolescence" and "puberty," and list the three most widely accepted criteria for adult status in North America.

12. Discuss the advantages and disadvantages of early and late puberty for males and females.

13. Explain why Elkind believes that our society is rushing adolescents and what he feels the net effect will be.

14. Briefly discuss the impact of ethnic heritage on identity formation. Describe the interactions between an adolescent and his/her parents as identity formation occurs.

15. Discuss the importance of imaginary audiences to adolescents.

16. Describe the importance of the peer group in identity formation, including the danger of foreclosure.

17. Briefly describe each of Kohlberg's three levels of moral development as well as their respective stages.

18. Describe how Kohlberg's moral development levels are distributed among the population.

19. Explain Gilligan's argument against Kohlberg's system of moral development. Describe the current status of the argument.

20. Generally describe the pattern of adult life stages proposed by Roger Gould.

21. Describe what a midlife crisis is and how it can be both a danger and an opportunity. Explain how the midlife transition is different for women as opposed to men.

22. Distinguish menopause from the male climacteric and describe the typical reactions to each.

23. Briefly discuss the empty nest syndrome and the different effects of this syndrome on mothers who work at home versus mothers who work outside the home.

24. List six elements of well-being during adulthood.

25. Describe what is meant by the term "biological aging." Include the terms "gerontologist" and "fluid and crystallized abilities" in your answer.

The following objective is related to the "Discovering Psychology" section of the text.

26. Differentiate the concepts of "maximum life span" and "life expectancy." Describe the difference in life expectancy in the 1800s as compared to today. List at least five factors that add to life expectancy and five that subtract from life expectancy.

27. Describe the disengagement theory and the activity theory of aging.

28. Describe Baltes' view of selective optimization with compensation.

29. Outline the characteristics of ageism. List four significant myths of aging, and relate them to the concept of ageism.

30. Explain how fears about death might be expressed as a denial of death.

31. Explain the purpose or intent of a living will.

32. List and briefly characterize the five emotional reactions typically experienced by people facing death.

33. Explain how knowledge of the reactions to coping with death is important.

34. Describe what generally happens during a near death experience (NDE), how it can be explained in two different ways, and how an NDE can change a person's life.

35. Describe the purpose of a hospice.

36. Discuss the general characteristics of the process of bereavement. Explain how suppression of the grieving process is related to later problems.

37. Define the term "subjective well-being."

38. List five characteristics of a satisfied life.

39. Briefly discuss the relationship of positive and negative emotional experiences to happiness.

40. Briefly discuss the way in which perception, interpretation, and management of events is related to happiness.

41. List and briefly discuss eight personal factors related to overall happiness.

42. Discuss the connection between one's goals in life and happiness. Include a discussion of the findings of McGregor and Little.

RECITE AND REVIEW

MODULE 4.1

Survey Question: What are the typical tasks and dilemmas through the life span? Pages 130-132

Life-span psychologists study continuity and [1] _____ over the life span.

They are also interested in [2] _____ milestones, or prominent landmarks in personal development.

According to Erik Erikson, each life stage provokes a specific psychosocial [3] _____ .

During childhood these are: trust versus mistrust, autonomy versus [4] _____ and doubt, initiative versus [5] _____ , and industry versus [6] _____ .

In [7] _____ , identity versus role confusion is the principal dilemma.

In young adulthood we face the dilemma of intimacy versus [8] _____ . Later, generativity versus [9] _____ becomes prominent.

Old age is a time when the dilemma of integrity versus [10] _____ must be faced.

In addition, each life stage requires successful mastery of certain [11] _____ tasks (personal changes required for optimal development).

MODULE 4.2

Survey Question: What are some of the more serious childhood problems? Pages 134-139

Few children grow up without experiencing some of the normal problems of childhood, including negativism, clinging, specific fears, sleep [12] _____ , general dissatisfaction, regression, sibling [13] _____ , and rebellion.

[14] _____ parents or parents in blended families should give children who are coping with [15] _____ extra attention to reduce the risk of developing problems in school, [16] _____ , and depression.

Major areas of difficulty in childhood are [17] _____ [18] _____ (including enuresis and encopresis) and [19] _____ disturbances, such as overeating, anorexia nervosa (self-starvation), and pica (eating nonfood substances).

Other problems include [20] _____ disturbances (delayed speech, stuttering); [21] _____ disorders, including dyslexia (an inability to read with understanding); and attention-deficit hyperactivity [22] _____ (ADHD).

Childhood [23] _____ is a severe problem involving mutism, sensory disturbances, tantrums, and a lack of responsiveness to other people.

Some cases of autism are being treated successfully with [24] _____ modification.

Child abuse (physically or emotionally [25] _____ a child) is a major problem. Roughly [26] _____ percent of all abused children become abusive adults. Emotional support and therapy can help break the cycle of abuse.

Factors that increase the risk of child abuse include parental [27] _____ and the belief in [28] _____ .

Parents who inflict [29] _____ abuse by neglect, humiliation, intimidation, or terror may leave long-lasting [30] _____ scars on their children.

It is recommended that if parents feel the urge to [31] _____ their children, they should sit down, close their eyes, and vividly [32] _____ themselves in a [33] _____ place.

MODULE 4.3

Survey Question: Why is adolescent development especially challenging? Pages 140-143

Adolescence is a culturally defined [34] _____ status. Puberty is a [35] _____ event.

On average, the peak growth spurt during puberty occurs earlier for [36] _____ than for [37] _____ .

Early maturation is beneficial mostly for [38] _____ ; its effects are mixed for [39] _____ .

Establishing a clear sense of personal identity is a major task of [40] _____ . One danger of [41] _____ maturation is premature identity formation.

Adolescent identity formation is accelerated by cognitive development and influenced by [42] _____ and peer groups (age mates).

David Elkind believes that adolescents today do not show traditional signs of [43] _____ (visible signs that indicate a person's social status such as a driver's license) and have become self-conscious and preoccupied with imaginary [44] _____ (imagined viewers).

By taking pride in their ethnic heritage, teenagers from different ethnic groups have [45] _____ self-esteem, a better self-image, and a stronger ethnic [46] _____ when compared to teens who do not take pride in their ethnic identity.

As more people enroll in colleges and delay starting a family, the period of [47] _____ adulthood for adolescents has been pushed back from the late teens to the [48] _____

Survey Question: How do we develop morals and values? Pages 143-145

Lawrence Kohlberg theorized that [49] _____ development passes through a series of stages revealed by [50] _____ reasoning about [51] _____ dilemmas.

Kohlberg identified preconventional, conventional, and postconventional levels of moral [52] _____ .

Some psychologists have questioned whether measures of moral development should be based only on a morality of [53] _____ . Adults appear to base moral choices on either [54] _____ or caring, depending on the situation.

[55] _____ can be described as combining justice and caring (reason and emotion) when making the best moral judgment.

MODULE 4.4

Survey Question: What happens psychologically during adulthood? Pages 147-150

Certain relatively consistent events mark [56] _____ [57] _____ in our society.

In order these are: [58] _____ from parental dominance, leaving the [59] _____ , building a workable life, a crisis of questions, a crisis of urgency, attaining stability, and mellowing.

Contrary to popular belief, people who are in their early adulthood seem to experience more [60] _____ feelings than people who are in their early 40s or older. Older adults are more likely to feel [61] _____ , secure, self-confident, and [62] _____ .

A midlife crisis affects many people in the 37-41 age range, but this is by no means [63] _____ .

A transition period during midlife can provide individuals with opportunities for personal growth or make "[64] _____ corrections" as it allows individuals to [65] _____ their identities, their goals, and prepare for old age.

Adjustment to later middle age is sometimes complicated for [66] _____ by menopause and for [67] _____ by a climacteric.

Some doctors are using hormones to treat [68] _____ , which can reduce levels of [69] _____ in men leading to a decrease in sex drive, alertness, bone density, and strength.

Experts have questioned the value of using hormone [70] _____ therapy (HRT) for both men and women for treating symptoms of normal [71] _____ processes.

When the last child leaves home, women who define themselves as traditional [72] _____ may become [73] _____ (the empty-nest syndrome).

Well-being at midlife is related to self-acceptance, positive relationships, autonomy, mastery, a [74] _____ in life, and continued personal [75] _____ .

Survey Question: What are the psychological challenges of aging? Pages 150-155

The elderly are the [76] _____ -growing segment of society in North America.

Biological [77] _____ begins between 25 and 30, but peak performance in specific pursuits may come at various points throughout life.

The length of human lives is limited by the [78] _____ life span. [79] _____ expectancy (the average number of years people live) is much shorter.

Intellectual declines associated with aging are limited, at least through one's [80] _____ . This is especially true of individuals who remain mentally [81] _____ .

The greatest losses occur for fluid abilities (which require [82] _____ or rapid learning); crystallized abilities (stored up [83] _____ and skills) show much less decline and may actually improve.

Maintaining a low-fat diet, exercising daily, eating fruits and vegetables, and not smoking are ways in which one can [84] _____ one's life expectancy between one to [85] _____ years for each factor.

Gerontologists (those who study [86] _____) have proposed the disengagement theory of successful [87] _____ . It holds that withdrawal from society is necessary and desirable in old age.

The activity theory states that optimal adjustment to aging is tied to continuing [88] _____ and involvement. The activity theory applies to more people than disengagement does.

For individuals who are over 50, having a [89] _____ outlook on aging by believing that they do not lose "pep" as they get older may [90] _____ their life expectancy by seven years.

Ageism refers to prejudice, discrimination, and stereotyping on the basis of [91] _____ . It affects people of all ages but is especially damaging to [92] _____ people.

People who work in fields that require speed and skill often reach their [93] _____ performance between the ages of 30 and 50. To maintain [94] _____ levels of [95] _____ as they age, individuals should practice their skills on a regular basis.

MODULE 4.5

Survey Question: How do people typically react to death and bereavement? Pages 157-161

Older people fear the circumstances of [96] _____ more than the fact that it will occur.

Typical emotional reactions to impending death are denial, [97] _____ , bargaining, [98] _____ , and acceptance.

A living will may help a person ensure that his or her life will not be artificially prolonged during a [99] _____ illness.

Near-death [100] _____ (NDEs) frequently result in significant changes in personality, [101] _____ , and life goals.

One approach to death is the hospice movement, which is devoted to providing humane care to persons who are [102] _____ .

Bereavement also brings forth a typical series of [103] _____ reactions.

Initial shock is followed by pangs of [104] _____ . Later, apathy, dejection, and depression may occur. Eventually, grief moves toward [105] _____ , an acceptance of the loss.

Grief [106] _____ helps people adapt to their loss and integrate changes into their lives.

It is recommended that bereaved individuals grieve at their own pace and [107] _____ their emotions and [108] _____ thoughts after the death of a loved one.

PSYCHOLOGY IN ACTION

Survey Question: What factors contribute most to a happy and fulfilling life? Pages 162-164

Subjective well-being ([109] _____) occurs when [110] _____ emotions outnumber [111] _____ emotions and a person is satisfied with his or her life.

Happiness is only mildly related to [112] _____ , education, marriage, religion, age, sex, and work. However, people who have an extraverted, optimistic [113] _____ do tend to be happier.

People who are making progress toward their long-term [114] _____ tend to be happier. This is especially true if the [115] _____ have integrity and personal meaning.

CONNECTIONS

MODULE 4.1

1. _____	Erik Erikson	a. received praises versus lacking support
2. _____	optimal development	b. self-control versus inadequacy
3. _____	developmental milestones	c. love versus insecurity
4. _____	trust versus mistrust	d. freedom to choose versus criticism
5. _____	developmental task	e. psychosocial dilemmas
6. _____	autonomy versus shame and doubt	f. mastered developmental tasks
7. _____	initiative versus guilt	g. notable events or marker
8. _____	industry versus inferiority	h. skills to be attained

MODULE 4.2

1. _____	overprotection	a. hyperactive
2. _____	regression	b. "soiling"
3. _____	enuresis	c. reading disorder
4. _____	encopresis	d. shaken baby
5. _____	pica	e. "smother love"
6. _____	dyslexia	f. bed-wetting
7. _____	echolalia	g. eating disorder
8. _____	ADHD	h. infantile behavior
9. _____	child abuse	i. autism symptom
10. _____	emotional abuse	j. humiliate and intimidate

MODULE 4.3

1. _____	adolescence	a. moral dilemmas
2. _____	puberty	b. status or role clue
3. _____	social marker	c. social contract/individual principles
4. _____	imaginary audiences	d. good boy or girl/respect for authority
5. _____	emerging adulthood	e. avoiding punishment or seeking pleasure
6. _____	Kohlberg	f. sexual maturation
7. _____	preconventional	g. mid 20s
8. _____	conventional	h. cultural status
9. _____	postconventional	i. imagined viewers
10. _____	identity	j. teen's task

MODULE 4.4

1. _____ "empty nest"		a.	common prejudice
2. _____ climacteric		b.	life change
3. _____ transition period		c.	reduced testosterone levels
4. _____ menopause		d.	significant physical change
5. _____ andropause		e.	adult development
6. _____ Roger Gould		f.	daily exercise and low-fat diet
7. _____ compensation and optimization		g.	children leave
8. _____ ageism		h.	expert on aging
9. _____ gerontologist		i.	successful aging
10. _____ increased life expectancy		j.	end of menstruation

MODULE 4.5

1. _____ hospice		a.	intense sorrow
2. _____ living will		b.	expert on death
3. _____ thanatologist		c.	clinical death
4. _____ good life		d.	happiness and meaningful goals
5. _____ Elizabeth Kübler-Ross		e.	care for dying
6. _____ NDE		f.	acceptance of loss
7. _____ bargaining		g.	general life satisfaction
8. _____ subjective well-being		h.	avoid heroic measures
9. _____ grief		i.	reactions to dying
10. _____ resolution		j.	reaction to impending death

CHECK YOUR MEMORY

MODULE 4.1

Survey Question: What are the typical tasks and dilemmas through the life span? Pages 130-132

1. Learning to read in childhood and establishing a vocation as an adult are typical life stages.
   TRUE or FALSE

2. Psychosocial dilemmas occur when a person is in conflict with his or her social world.
   TRUE or FALSE

3. Initiative versus guilt is the first psychosocial dilemma a child faces.
   TRUE or FALSE

4. Answering the question "Who am I?" is a primary task during adolescence.
   TRUE or FALSE

5. Generativity is expressed through taking an interest in the next generation.
TRUE or FALSE

MODULE 4.2

Survey Question: What are some of the more serious childhood problems? Pages 134-139

6. It is best for parents to protect children from all stressful stimulation as much as possible.
TRUE or FALSE

7. Clinging is one of the more serious problems of childhood.
TRUE or FALSE

8. Supportive and affectionate fathers tend to minimize sibling rivalry.
TRUE or FALSE

9. Toilet training is typically completed by age three or earlier.
TRUE or FALSE

10. A child who eats mud, buttons, or rubber bands suffers from enuresis nervosa.
TRUE or FALSE

11. Stuttering is more common among girls than boys.
TRUE or FALSE

12. Autism can be described as "word blindness."
TRUE or FALSE

13. ADHD affects five times as many boys as girls and may be partly hereditary.
TRUE or FALSE

14. Eating too much sugar is one of the main causes of hyperactivity in children.
TRUE or FALSE

15. The first signs of autism often appear in infancy, when autistic children may be extremely aloof and withdrawn.
TRUE or FALSE

16. Ritalin is used primarily to treat delayed speech.
TRUE or FALSE

17. The risk of committing child abuse is highest for young parents.
TRUE or FALSE

18. Abusive mothers tend to believe that their children are intentionally annoying them.
TRUE or FALSE

19. One-third of abused children become abusive adults.
TRUE or FALSE

20. Parents Anonymous is an organization for parents who have autistic children.

    TRUE or FALSE

21. Nearly 25 percent of all American parents have spanked their children with an object.

    TRUE or FALSE

22. Although it is illegal for people to hit other adults, prisoners, and even animals, it is not illegal for American parents to spank their children.

    TRUE or FALSE

23. It is illegal for parents to physically punish their children in any country.

    TRUE or FALSE

MODULE 4.3

Survey Question: Why is adolescent development especially challenging? Pages 140-143

24. The length of adolescence varies in different cultures.

    TRUE or FALSE

25. The average onset of puberty is age 12 for boys and age 14 for girls.

    TRUE or FALSE

26. Early maturation tends to enhance self-image for boys.

    TRUE or FALSE

27. Early-maturing girls tend to date sooner and are more likely to get into trouble.

    TRUE or FALSE

28. Because adolescence is such a turbulent stage for teenagers, permissive parenting techniques remain the best approach for parents to use.

    TRUE or FALSE

29. David Elkind believes that today's adolescents should be "hurried into adulthood" to maximize their potentials.

    TRUE or FALSE

30. By taking pride in their ethnic heritage, teenagers from different ethnic groups have reduced self-esteem, a negative self-image, and a weakened ethnic identity.

    TRUE or FALSE

31. The term *imaginary audience* refers to adolescent peer groups and the influence they have on personal identity.

    TRUE or FALSE

32. Being able to think about hypothetical possibilities helps adolescents in their search for identity.

    TRUE or FALSE

33. Increased conflict with parents tends to occur early in adolescence.
    TRUE or FALSE

34. Early maturation can contribute to adopting a foreclosed identity.
    TRUE or FALSE

Survey Question: How do we develop morals and values? Pages 143-145

35. Lawrence Kohlberg used moral dilemmas to assess children's levels of moral development.
    TRUE or FALSE

36. At the preconventional level, moral decisions are guided by the consequences of actions, such as punishment or pleasure.
    TRUE or FALSE

37. The traditional morality of authority defines moral behavior in the preconventional stage.
    TRUE or FALSE

38. Most adults function at the conventional level of moral reasoning.
    TRUE or FALSE

39. All children will achieve Kohlberg's conventional level of moral development, and approximately 80 percent of all adults will achieve the postconventional level of morality.
    TRUE or FALSE

40. Both men and women may use justice or caring as a basis for making moral judgments.
    TRUE or FALSE

MODULE 4.4

Survey Question: What happens psychologically during adulthood? Pages 147-150

41. According to Gould, building a workable life is the predominant activity between ages 16 to 18.
    TRUE or FALSE

42. A crisis of urgency tends to hit people around the age of 30.
    TRUE or FALSE

43. Maintaining good health is a prominent goal among the elderly.
    TRUE or FALSE

44. Levinson places the midlife transition in the 40-55 age range.
    TRUE or FALSE

45. Only a small minority of the men studied by Levinson experienced any instability or urgency at midlife.
    TRUE or FALSE

46. During the midlife transition, women are less likely than men to define success in terms of a key event.
TRUE or FALSE

47. Wealth is one of the primary sources of happiness in adulthood.
TRUE or FALSE

48. Over half of all women have serious emotional problems during menopause.
TRUE or FALSE

49. After the climacteric has occurred, men become infertile.
TRUE or FALSE

50. Andropause is a hormone that can increase women's sex drive, alertness, bone density, and strength.
TRUE or FALSE

51. Having a sense of purpose in life is one element of well-being during adulthood.
TRUE or FALSE

Survey Question: What are the psychological challenges of aging? Pages 150-155

52. By the year 2020, one out of every five North Americans will be over age 65.
TRUE or FALSE

53. Peak functioning in most physical capacities occurs between ages 25 and 30.
TRUE or FALSE

54. The maximum human life span is around 120 years.
TRUE or FALSE

55. Life expectancy has increased dramatically in the last 200 years.
TRUE or FALSE

56. Being exposed to secondhand smoke, drinking three alcoholic beverages per day, and having little exercise may reduce one's life expectancy from three to nine years.
TRUE or FALSE

57. Crystallized abilities are the first to decline as a person ages.
TRUE or FALSE

58. Perceptual speed declines steadily after age 25.
TRUE or FALSE

59. For many people, successful aging requires a combination of activity and disengagement.
TRUE or FALSE

60. To remain active and happy in old age, people should use the strategy of selective optimization with compensation by finding ways to continue to perform well on certain tasks to reduce age-related losses.
TRUE or FALSE

61. Research found that for people over 50, having a positive outlook about aging does not increase their life expectancy.
TRUE or FALSE

62. Ageism refers to prejudice and discrimination toward the elderly.
TRUE or FALSE

63. Few elderly persons become senile or suffer from mental decay.
TRUE or FALSE

MODULE 4.5

Survey Question: How do people typically react to death and bereavement? Pages 157-161

64. Most of the deaths portrayed on television are homicides.
TRUE or FALSE

65. A living will is not legally binding in most states in the United States.
TRUE or FALSE

66. The "Why me" reaction to impending death is an expression of anger.
TRUE or FALSE

67. Trying to be "good" in order to live longer is characteristic of the denial reaction to impending death.
TRUE or FALSE

68. It is best to go through all the stages of dying described by Kübler-Ross in the correct order.
TRUE or FALSE

69. To help reduce the feeling of isolation, Kirsti Dyer suggests that family members or friends should try to be respectful, genuine, aware of nonverbal cues, or just be there for the dying person.
TRUE or FALSE

70. Medical explanations of NDEs attribute them to brain activities caused by oxygen starvation and a certain area in the brain that when stimulated produces out-of-body experiences.
TRUE or FALSE

71. Hospice care can be provided at home as well as in medical centers.
TRUE or FALSE

72. Hospice programs are designed to avoid the use of painkilling drugs.
TRUE or FALSE

73. Bereaved persons should work through their grief as quickly as possible.
TRUE or FALSE

PSYCHOLOGY IN ACTION

Survey Question: What factors contribute most to a happy and fulfilling life? Pages 162-164

74. Subjective well-being is primarily a matter of having relatively few negative emotions.
    TRUE or FALSE

75. Subjective well-being is affected by many factors such as our goals, choices, emotions, values, and personality.
    TRUE or FALSE

76. A person who agrees that "The conditions of my life are excellent" would probably score high in life satisfaction.
    TRUE or FALSE

77. Wealthier people are generally happier people.
    TRUE or FALSE

78. Life satisfaction and happiness generally decline with increasing age.
    TRUE or FALSE

79. You are likely to be happy if you are making progress on smaller goals that relate to long-term life goals.
    TRUE or FALSE

80. Usually, a good life is one that is happy and meaningful.
    TRUE or FALSE

FINAL SURVEY AND REVIEW

MODULE 4.1

Survey Question: What are the typical tasks and dilemmas through the life span? Pages 130-132

[1] _____ psychologists study [2] _____ and change from birth to death.

They are also interested in developmental [3] _____ , or prominent landmarks in personal development.

According to Erik [4] _____ , each life stage provokes a specific [5] _____ dilemma.

During childhood these are: [6] _____ versus mistrust, [7] _____ versus shame and doubt, initiative versus guilt, and [8] _____ versus inferiority.

In adolescence, [9] _____ versus [10] _____ confusion is the principal dilemma.

In young adulthood we face the dilemma of [11] _____ versus isolation. Later, [12] _____ versus stagnation becomes prominent.

Old age is a time when the dilemma of [13] _____ versus despair must be faced.

In addition, each life stage requires successful mastery of certain developmental [14] _____

(personal changes required for optimal development).

MODULE 4.2

Survey Question: What are some of the more serious childhood problems? Pages 134-139

Few children grow up without experiencing some of the normal problems of childhood, including

[15] _____ , [16] _____ , specific [17] _____ , sleep disturbances, general

dissatisfaction, regression, sibling rivalry, and rebellion.

[18] _____ [19] _____ or parents in blended families should give [20] _____

who are coping with [21] _____ extra attention to reduce the risk of developing problems

in school, [22] _____ , and depression.

Major areas of difficulty in childhood are toilet training (including [23] _____ and

[24] _____) and feeding disturbances, such as overeating, anorexia nervosa (self-starvation), and

[25] _____ (eating nonfood substances).

Other problems include speech disturbances (delayed speech, [26] _____); learning

disorders, including [27] _____ (an inability to read with understanding); and attention-deficit

[28] _____ disorder (ADHD).

Childhood autism is a severe problem involving [29] _____ (failure to speak), sensory

disturbances, tantrums, and a lack of responsiveness to [30] _____ [31] _____ .

Some cases of autism are being treated successfully with behavior [32] _____ .

[33] _____ [34] _____ (physically or emotionally harming a child) is a major problem.

Roughly 30 percent of all abused children become abusive [35] _____ . Emotional support

and therapy can help break the cycle of abuse.

Factors that increase the risk of child abuse include parental [36] _____ and the belief in

[37] _____ .

Parents who inflict [38] _____ by neglect, humiliation, intimidation, or terror may leave

long-lasting emotional scars on their children.

It is recommended that if parents feel the urge to [39] _____ their children, they should sit down,

close their eyes, and vividly imagine themselves in a [40] _____ place.

MODULE 4.3

Survey Question: Why is adolescent development especially challenging? Pages 140-143

[41] _____ is a culturally defined social status. [42] _____ is a biological event.

On average, the peak [43] _____ spurt during [44] _____ occurs earlier for girls than for boys.

Early [45] _____ is beneficial mostly for boys; its effects are mixed for girls.

Establishing a clear sense of personal [46] _____ is a major task of adolescence. One danger of early maturation is premature [47] _____ formation.

Adolescent identity formation is accelerated by [48] _____ development and influenced by parents and [49] _____ groups (age mates).

David Elkind believes that adolescents today do not show traditional signs of [50] _____ (visible signs that indicate a person's social status such as a driver's license) and have become self-conscious and preoccupied with [51] _____ audiences (imagined viewers).

By taking pride in their ethnic heritage, teenagers from different ethnic groups have [52] _____ self-esteem, a better self-image, and a stronger ethnic [53] _____ when compared to teens who do not take pride in their ethnic identity

As more people enroll in colleges and delay starting a family, the period of [54] _____ [55] _____ for adolescence has been pushed back from the late teens to the mid-20s.

Survey Question: How do we develop morals and values? Pages 143-145

Lawrence Kohlberg theorized that moral development passes through a series of stages revealed by moral [56] _____ about moral [57] _____ .

Kohlberg identified [58] _____ , conventional, and postconventional levels of moral reasoning.

Some psychologists have questioned whether measures of moral development should be based only on a morality of justice. Adults appear to base moral choices on either justice or [59] _____ , depending on the [60] _____ .

Wisdom can be described as combining [61] _____ and [62] _____ (reason and emotion) when making the best moral judgment.

MODULE 4.4

Survey Question: What happens psychologically during adulthood? Pages 147-150

Certain relatively [63] _____ events mark adult development in our society.

In order these are: escape from parental [64] _____ , leaving the family, building a workable life,

a crisis of [65] _____ , a crisis of [66] _____ , attaining stability, and mellowing.

Contrary to popular belief, people who are in their early adulthood seem to experience more

[67] _____ feelings than people who are in their early 40s or older. [68] _____ adults

are more likely to feel happy, secure, self-confident, and at peace.

A [69] _____ [70] _____ affects many people in the 37-41 age range, but this is

by no means universal.

A [71] _____ during midlife can provide individuals with opportunities for personal growth

or make "midcourse corrections" as it allows individuals to [72] _____ their identities, their

goals, and prepare for old age.

Adjustment to later middle age is sometimes complicated for women by menopause and for men by a

[73] _____ .

Some doctors are using hormones to treat [74] _____ , which can reduce levels of

[75] _____ in men leading to a decrease in sex drive, alertness, bone density, and strength.

Experts have questioned the value of using [76] _____ therapy (HRT) for both men and women

for treating symptoms of normal aging.

When the last child leaves home, women who define themselves as traditional mothers may become

depressed (the [77] _____ -[78] _____ [79] _____).

Well-being at midlife is related to self-[80] _____ , positive relationships, [81] _____ ,

mastery, a purpose in life, and continued personal growth.

Survey Question: What are the psychological challenges of aging? Pages 150-155

The [82] _____ are the fastest-growing segment of society in North America.

Biological aging begins between 25 and 30, but [83] _____ [84] _____ in specific

pursuits may come at various points throughout life.

The length of human lives is limited by the maximum [85] _____ [86] _____ . Life

[87] _____ (the average number of years people live) is much shorter.

[88] _____ declines associated with aging are limited, at least through one's 70s. This is especially true of individuals who remain mentally active.

The greatest losses occur for [89] _____ abilities (which require speed or rapid learning);

[90] _____ abilities (stored up knowledge and skills) show much less decline and may actually improve

Maintaining a low-fat diet, exercising daily, eating fruits and vegetables, and not smoking are ways in which one can increase one's [91] _____ between one to three years for each factor.

[92] _____ (those who study aging) have proposed the [93] _____ theory of successful aging. It holds that withdrawal from society is necessary and desirable in old age.

The [94] _____ theory states that optimal adjustment to aging is tied to continuing action and involvement. This theory applies to more people than withdrawal from society does.

For individuals who are over 50, having a [95] _____ outlook on aging by believing that they do not lose "pep" as they get older may increase their life expectancy by [96] _____ years.

[97] _____ refers to prejudice, discrimination, and stereotyping on the basis of age. It affects people of all ages but is especially damaging to older people.

People who work in fields that require speed and skill often reach their peak performance between the ages of 30 and 50. To maintain high levels of [98] _____ as they age, individuals should practice their skills on a regular basis.

MODULE 4.5

Survey Question: How do people typically react to death and bereavement? Pages 157-161

Older people fear the [99] _____ of death more than the fact that it will occur.

Typical emotional reactions to impending death are [100] _____ , anger, [101] _____ , depression, and acceptance.

A [102] _____ [103] _____ may help a person ensure that his or her life will not be artificially prolonged during a terminal illness.

[104] _____ experiences (NDEs) frequently result in significant changes in personality, values, and life goals.

One approach to death is the [105] _____ movement, which is devoted to providing humane care to persons who are dying.

[106] _____ also brings forth a typical series of grief reactions.

Initial [107] _____ is followed by [108] _____ of grief. Later, apathy, dejection, and [109] _____ may occur. Eventually, grief moves toward resolution, an acceptance of the loss. [110] _____ work helps people adapt to their loss and [111] _____ changes into their lives.

It is recommended that bereaved individuals grieve at their own pace and [112] _____ their emotions and [113] _____ thoughts after the death of a loved one.

PSYCHOLOGY IN ACTION

Survey Question: What factors contribute most to a happy and fulfilling life? Pages 162-164

[114] _____ [115] _____ (happiness) occurs when positive emotions outnumber negative emotions and a person is satisfied with his or her life.

Happiness is only mildly related to wealth, education, marriage, religion, age, sex, and work. However, people with [116] _____ , optimistic personalities do tend to be happier.

People who are making progress toward their long-term goals tend to be happier. This is especially true if the goals have [117] _____ and personal [118] _____ .

MASTERY TEST

1. According to Erikson, a conflict between trust and mistrust is characteristic of
   a. infancy
   b. adolescence
   c. marriage
   d. old age

2. Identity formation during adolescence is aided by
   a. cognitive development
   b. attaining the preoperational stage
   c. emotional bargaining
   d. you-messages from parents

3. Which of the following is not a normal, relatively mild childhood problem?
   a. negativism
   b. clinging
   c. sibling rivalry
   d. delayed speech

4. Infancy, childhood, adolescence, and young adulthood are
   a. developmental tasks
   b. life stages
   c. psychosocial dilemmas
   d. biologically defined social statuses

5. Premature identity formation is one of the risks of early
   a. generativity
   b. preoccupation with imaginary audiences
   c. trust-mistrust resolution
   d. puberty

6. The thought, "It's all a mistake" would most likely occur as part of which reaction to impending death?
   a. anger
   b. freezing up
   c. denial
   d. bargaining

7. The choice of whether to use justice or caring to make moral decisions depends on the
   _____ a person faces.
   a. situation
   b. punishment
   c. level of authority
   d. exchange

8. Which of the following is a correct match?
   a. enuresis—eating disorder
   b. anorexia—speech disturbance
   c. dyslexia—learning disorder
   d. pica—autism

9. According to Erikson, the first dilemma a newborn infant must resolve is
   a. independence versus dependence
   b. initiative versus guilt
   c. trust versus mistrust
   d. attachment versus confusion

10. Seeking approval and upholding law, order, and authority are characteristics of what stage of moral development?
    a. preconventional
    b. conventional
    c. postconventional
    d. postformal

11. An inability to read with understanding defines the problem formally known as
    a. ADHD
    b. dyslexia
    c. NDE
    d. echolalia

12. For both boys and girls, a growth spurt corresponds with
    a. adolescence
    b. puberty
    c. cognitive maturation
    d. less prestige with peers

13. Autonomy, environmental mastery, a purpose in life, and continued personal growth help maintain well-being in old age. This observation supports the _____ theory of successful aging.
    a. disengagement
    b. reengagement
    c. activity
    d. reactivation

14. Research on well-being suggests that a good life is one that combines happiness and
    a. financial success
    b. educational achievement
    c. an introverted personality
    d. achieving meaningful goals

15. According to Erikson, developing a sense of integrity is a special challenge in
    a. adolescence
    b. young adulthood
    c. middle adulthood
    d. late adulthood

16. The event for males that is most comparable to menopause in women is the
    a. climacteric
    b. midlife crisis
    c. generativity transition
    d. genophase

17. Grief following bereavement typically begins with _____ and ends with _____.
    a. anger, disengagement
    b. dejection, disengagement
    c. isolation, depression
    d. shock, resolution

18. Physicians typically use the stimulant drug Ritalin to control
    a. oncoprosis
    b. echolalia
    c. ADHD
    d. anorexia nervosa

19. The smallest number of Levinson's subjects experienced midlife as a(an)
    a. last chance
    b. period of serious decline
    c. time to start over
    d. escape from dominance

20. According to Erikson, a dilemma concerning _____ usually follows one that focuses on identity.
    a. trust
    b. industry
    c. initiative
    d. intimacy

21. Which combination would lead to the highest risk of child abuse?
    a. young parent, high income, child over three years
    b. young parent, low income, abused as a child
    c. older parent, low income, child over three years
    d. older parent, high income, abused as a child

22. Foreclosed identity formation is a special risk for
    a. late maturing boys
    b. adolescents
    c. the elementary school years
    d. the preoperational stage

23. Oxygen deprivation in the brain best accounts for which element of an NDE?
    a. the tunnel of light
    b. the pangs of grief
    c. the period of depression
    d. the life review and personality changes

24. People who have many positive emotional experiences and relatively few negative experiences usually rate high in
    a. generativity
    b. moral reasoning
    c. subjective well-being
    d. crystallized abilities

25. Overprotective parenting ignores the fact that _____ is a normal part of life.
    a. rebellion
    b. punishment
    c. rejection
    d. stress

26. Ivar Lovaas has successfully used _____ to treat _____.
    a. Ritalin, echolalia
    b. operant shaping, dyslexia
    c. restricted sugar diets, ADHD
    d. behavior modification, autism

27. Skills that rely on fluid abilities could be expected to show declines beginning in
    a. adolescence
    b. young adulthood
    c. middle adulthood
    d. late adulthood

28. Which of the following is a common myth about old age?
    a. Most elderly persons are isolated and neglected.
    b. A large percentage of the elderly suffer from senility.
    c. A majority of the elderly are dissastified with their lives.
    d. All the preceding are myths.

29. Gould's study of adult development found that a crisis of _____ is common between the ages of 35 and 43.
    a. urgency
    b. questions
    c. dominance
    d. stability

30. With respect to aging, it is least possible to modify which of the following?
    a. life expectancy
    b. crystallized abilities
    c. mental abilities
    d. maximum life span

31. Which of the following statement about physical abuse is true?
    a. It is illegal for teachers to spank a child in several states in America.
    b. It is illegal for parents to physically punish their children in 11 countries.
    c. It is legal for parents to spank their children in the United States.
    d. All the above are true.

32. A period of _____ has been extended from the late teens to the mid 20s because young people are _____.
    a. emerging adulthood, prolonging their identity exploration
    b. emerging adolescence, actively exploring their love and worldviews
    c. puberty, immature and irresponsible
    d. none of the above

33. Kohlberg believed that moral development typically begins _____ and continues into adulthood with ___ percent of adults achieving postconventional morality.
    a. at the onset of puberty, 50
    b. in childhood, 20
    c. in early adolescence, 40
    d. in late adolescence, 80

34. A national survey reported that _____ are more likely to say they often feel happy, truly alive, and peaceful than _____.
    a. young adults, older adults
    b. older adults, young adults
    c. adolescents, older adults
    d. adolescents, young adults

35. Hormone replacement therapy has reduced symptoms caused by menopause and andropause; however, some experts have suggested that it might not be a good idea to treat _____ as a medical problem.
    a. psychological processes
    b. behavioral conditions
    c. biological conditions
    d. normal aging

36. Hormone replacement therapy has been used to treat
    a. women who experience menopause
    b. men who experience menopause
    c. men who experience andropause
    d. both women and men who experience menopause and andropause

37. To increase one's life expectancy up to nine years, one should do the following
    a. exercise daily
    b. do not smoke
    c. stay in a happy marriage
    d. all the preceding

38. Seniors' attitude about aging is positively correlated to their life expectancy. This statement suggests that
    a. a positive outlook on life increases life's expectancy
    b. as people age, their attitude on their life's expectancy increases
    c. aging causes life's expectancy to increase
    d. none of the above

SOLUTIONS

RECITE AND REVIEW

MODULE 4.1

1. change
2. developmental
3. dilemma
4. shame
5. guilt
6. inferiority
7. adolescence
8. isolation
9. stagnation
10. despair
11. developmental

MODULE 4.2

12. disturbances
13. rivalry
14. Single
15. divorce
16. drugs
17. toilet
18. training
19. feeding
20. speech
21. learning
22. disorder
23. autism
24. behavior
25. harming
26. 30
27. stress
28. physical punishment
29. emotional
30. emotional
31. strike
32. imagine
33. pleasant

MODULE 4.3

34. social
35. biological
36. girls
37. boys
38. boys
39. girls
40. adolescence
41. early
42. parents
43. social markers
44. audiences
45. higher
46. identity
47. emerging
48. mid 20s

49. moral
50. moral
51. moral
52. reasoning
53. justice
54. justice
55. Wisdom

MODULE 4.4

56. adult
57. development
58. escape
59. family
60. negative
61. happy
62. at peace
63. universal
64. midcourse
65. reevaluate
66. women
67. men
68. andropause
69. testosterone
70. replacement
71. aging
72. mothers
73. depressed
74. purpose
75. growth

76. fastest

77. aging
78. maximum
79. Life
80. 70s
81. active
82. speed
83. knowledge

84. increase
85. three
86. aging
87. aging
88. activity
89. positive
90. increase

91. age
92. older
93. peak
94. high
95. performance

MODULE 4.5

96. death
97. anger
98. depression
99. terminal
100. experiences

101. values
102. dying
103. grief
104. grief
105. resolution

106. work
107. restrict
108. upsetting

PSYCHOLOGY IN ACTION

109. happiness
110. positive
111. negative

112. wealth
113. personality
114. goals

115. goals

CONNECTIONS

MODULE 4.1

1. e
2. f
3. g

4. c
5. h
6. b

7. d
8. a

MODULE 4.2

1. e
2. h
3. f
4. b

5. g
6. c
7. i
8. a

9. d
10. j

MODULE 4.3

1. h
2. f
3. b
4. i

5. g
6. a
7. e
8. d

9. c
10. j

MODULE 4.4

1. g
2. d
3. b
4. j

5. c
6. e
7. i
8. a

9. h
10. f

MODULE 4.5

1. e
2. h
3. b
4. d
5. i
6. c
7. j
8. g
9. a
10. f

CHECK YOUR MEMORY

MODULE 4.1

1. F
2. T
3. F
4. T
5. T

MODULE 4.2

6. F
7. F
8. T
9. T
10. F
11. F
12. F
13. T
14. F
15. T
16. F
17. T
18. T
19. T
20. F
21. T
22. T
23. F

MODULE 4.3

24. T
25. F
26. T
27. T
28. F
29. F
30. F
31. F
32. T
33. T
34. T

35. T
36. T
37. F
38. T
39. F
40. T

MODULE 4.4

41. F
42. F
43. T
44. F
45. F
46. T
47. F
48. F
49. F
50. F
51. T

52. T
53. T
54. T
55. T
56. T
57. F
58. T
59. T
60. T
61. F
62. F
63. T

MODULE 4.5

64. T

65. T	68. F	71. T
66. T	69. T	72. F
67. F	70. T	73. F

PSYCHOLOGY IN ACTION

74. F	77. F	80. T
75. T	78. F	
76. T	79. T	

FINAL SURVEY AND REVIEW

MODULE 4.1

1. Life-span
2. continuity
3. milestones
4. Erikson
5. psychosocial
6. trust
7. autonomy
8. industry
9. identity
10. role
11. intimacy
12. generativity
13. integrity
14. tasks

MODULE 4.2

15. negativism
16. clinging
17. fears
18. Single
19. parents
20. children
21. divorce
22. drugs
23. enuresis
24. encopresis
25. pica
26. stuttering
27. dyslexia
28. hyperactivity
29. mutism
30. other
31. people
32. modification
33. Child
34. abuse
35. adults
36. stress
37. physical punishment
38. emotional abuse
39. strike
40. pleasant

MODULE 4.3

41. Adolescence
42. Puberty
43. growth
44. puberty
45. maturation
46. identity
47. identity
48. cognitive
49. peer
50. social markers
51. imaginary
52. higher
53. identity
54. emerging
55. adulthood

56. reasoning
57. dilemmas
58. preconventional
59. caring
60. situation
61. justice
62. caring

MODULE 4.4

63. consistent

64. dominance
65. questions
66. urgency
67. negative
68. Older
69. midlife

70. crisis
71. transition period
72. reevaluate
73. climacteric
74. andropause
75. testosterone

76. hormone replacement
77. empty
78. nest
79. syndrome
80. acceptance
81. autonomy

82. elderly
83. peak
84. performance
85. life
86. span
87. expectancy
88. Intellectual

89. fluid
90. crystallized
91. life expectancy
92. Gerontologists
93. disengagement
94. activity
95. positive

96. 7
97. Ageism
98. performance

MODULE 4.5

99. circumstances
100. denial
101. bargaining
102. living
103. will

104. Near-death
105. hospice
106. Bereavement
107. shock
108. pangs

109. depression
110. Grief
111. integrate
112. restrict
113. upsetting

PSYCHOLOGY IN ACTION

114. Subjective
115. well-being

116. extraverted
117. integrity

118. meaning

MASTERY TEST

1. A, (p. 130)
2. A, (p. 142)
3. D, (p. 134)
4. B, (p. 130)
5. D, (p. 141)
6. C, (p. 157)
7. A, (p. 145)
8. C, (p. 136)
9. C, (p. 130)
10. B, (p. 144)
11. B, (p. 136)
12. B, (p. 140)
13. C, (p. 153)
14. D, (p. 163)

15. D, (p. 132)
16. A, (p. 149)
17. D, (p. 159-160)
18. C, (p. 136)
19. C, (p. 148)
20. D, (p. 132)
21. B, (p. 137)
22. B, (p. 143)
23. A, (p. 160)
24. C, (p. 162)
25. D, (p. 134)
26. D, (p. 137)
27. B, (p. 151-152)
28. D, (p. 154-155)

29. A, (p. 147)
30. D, (p. 151)
31. D, (p. 139)
32. A, (p. 143)
33. B, (p. 145)
34. B, (p. 147)
35. D, (p. 149)
36. D, (p. 149)
37. D, (p. 152)
38. A, (p. 151)

SENSATION AND PERCEPTION

CHAPTER OVERVIEW

Sensory systems collect, select, transduce, analyze, and code information from the environment and send it to the brain.

Vision and visual problems can be partly understood by viewing the eyes as optical systems. However, the visual system also analyzes light stimuli to identify patterns and basic visual features. Color sensations are explained by the trichromatic theory (in the retina) and the opponent-process theory (for the rest of the visual system). Common vision defects are myopia, hyperopia, presbyopia, and astigmatism.

The inner ear is a sensory mechanism for transducing sound waves in the air into nerve impulses. The frequency and place theories of hearing explain how sound information is coded. Cochlear implants allow people with nerve deafness to hear human voices again. Other types of deafness are conduction deafness and stimulation deafness (e.g., hunter's notch).

Olfaction is based on receptors that respond to gaseous molecules in the air. The lock-and-key theory and the locations of olfactory receptors activated by different scents explain how various odors are coded. Taste is another chemical sense. A lock-and-key match between dissolved molecules and taste receptors also explains many taste sensations.

The somesthetic, or bodily, senses include the skin senses, the kinesthetic senses, and the vestibular senses.

Our awareness of sensory information is altered by sensory adaptation, selective attention, and sensory gating. Counterirritation can be used to reduce or block an agonizing pain by applying a hot-water bottle to the body.

Perception involves organizing sensations into meaningful patterns. Visual perceptions are stabilized by size, shape, and brightness constancies. The most basic perceptual pattern (in vision) is figure-ground organization. Sensations tend to be organized on the basis of nearness, similarity, continuity, closure, contiguity, and common region.

Depth perception depends on accommodation, convergence, retinal disparity, and various pictorial cues. The pictorial cues include linear perspective, relative size, light and shadow, overlap, texture gradients, aerial haze, and relative motion.

Learning, in the form of perceptual habits, influences perceptions. Perceptions are also greatly affected by attention, motives, values, and expectations (perceptual sets). Perceptual learning can explain why illusions occur, but it cannot explain hallucinations. Hallucinations are different than sane hallucinations. People who experience sane hallucinations actually process stimuli from the environment. When we narrow our focus too much to one event, we may experience inattentional blindness to other stimuli.

Parapsychology is the study of purported psi phenomena, including clairvoyance, telepathy, precognition, and psychokinesis. The bulk of the evidence to date is against the existence of extrasensory perception. Stage ESP is based on deception and tricks.

Because perceptions are reconstructions of events, eyewitness testimony can be unreliable. Perceptual accuracy can be improved by reality testing, dishabituation, actively paying attention, breaking perceptual habits, using broad frames of reference, and being aware of perceptual sets.

LEARNING OBJECTIVES

To demonstrate mastery of this chapter, you should be able to:

1. Explain how our senses act as a data reduction system by selecting, analyzing, and condensing incoming information.

2. Explain how sensory receptors act as biological transducers. Define sensory coding.

3. Explain the concept of sensory localization including the idea behind the statement, "Seeing does not take place in the eyes."

4. Define "sensation" and "perception."

5. Describe hue, saturation, and brightness in terms of their representation in the visual spectrum.

6. Briefly compare the structure of the eye to a camera and explain the process of accommodation.

7. Describe the following four conditions: a. hyperopia b. myopia c. astigmatism d. presbyopia

8. Describe the location and explain the functions of the following parts of the eye: a. lens b. retina c. cornea d. rods (including sensitivity to light) e. cones f. blind spot g. fovea

9. Discuss peripheral vision. Include the structures responsible for it and how this type of vision affects night vision.

10. Discuss the following theories of color vision: a. trichromatic theory b. opponent-process theory

11. Describe color blindness and color weakness.

12. Briefly describe the process of dark adaptation including the function of rhodopsin in night vision and night blindness. Explain how dark adaptation can be speeded up.

The following objective is related to the material in the "Discovering Psychology" section of the text.

13. Explain the purpose of the Ishihara test.

14. Describe the process by which sound travels and what psychological dimensions correspond to the physical ones.

15. Describe the location and explain the function(s) of the following parts of the ear: a. pinna b. tympanic membrane (eardrum) c. auditory ossicles d. cochlea e. oval window f. hair cells g. organ of Corti h. stereocilia

16. Briefly explain how the sense of hearing works by tracing an incoming stimulus from the time it strikes the tympanic membrane until it is sent to the brain.

17. Describe the frequency and the place theories of hearing.

18. List and describe the three general types of deafness.

19. Describe how cochlear implants can help overcome deafness.

20. Describe the factors that determine whether hearing loss will occur from stimulation deafness.

21. Describe the sense of olfaction (smell) including: a. its nature b. how it works c. a description of the condition anosmia d. a description of the lock-and-key theory

22. Describe the sense of gustation (taste) including: a. its nature b. the four basic taste sensations c. the tastes to which humans are most and least sensitive d. how the vast number of flavors is explained e. how it works

23. List the three somesthetic senses and be able to describe the function of each.

24. List and be able to recognize the five different sensations produced by the skin receptors.

25. Explain why certain areas of the body are more sensitive to touch than other areas.

26. List the numbers of nerve endings for each of the following: temperature, touch and pressure, and pain.

27. Name and describe the two different pain systems in the body.

28. List and describe three ways to reduce pain.

29. Name and describe the functions of the structures responsible for the vestibular sense.

30. Explain how the sensory conflict theory explains motion sickness.

31. Describe sensory adaptation, selective attention, and sensory gating, and explain how they keep sensory events from reaching consciousness. Include a discussion of the gate control theory of pain.

32. List and describe three characteristics of a stimulus that can make it attention getting.

33. Explain the concept of counterirritation as it relates to pain control. List at least three "common" counterirritation techniques, and explain how these techniques and acupuncture are related to sensory gating.

34. Describe the visual abilities of a person who has just had his or her sight restored.

35. Describe the following constancies: a. size b. shape c. brightness

36. Give examples of the following as they relate to the organization of perception: a. figure-ground (include the concept of reversible figures) b. nearness c. similarity d. continuation e. closure (include the concept of illusory figures) f. contiguity g. common region

37. Explain the meaning of a perceptual hypothesis.

38. Define and give an example of an "ambiguous stimulus."

39. Define "depth perception."

40. Describe two techniques for investigating depth perception, and describe the end results of studies with each technique.

41. Describe the following cues for depth perception and indicate in each case whether the cue is monocular or binocular: a. accommodation b. convergence c. retinal disparity

42. Describe the following two-dimensional, monocular, pictorial depth cues: a. linear perspective b. relative size c. height in the picture plane d. light and shadow e. overlap (interposition) f. texture gradients g. aerial perspective h. relative motion (motion parallax)

43. Describe the phenomenon of the moon illusion. Include in your explanation the apparent-distance hypothesis.

44. Define "perceptual reconstructions," "perceptual learning," and "perceptual habits" and explain how they affect perception.

45. Explain how the Ames room poses problems for perceptual organization and for a person's perceptual habits.

46. Describe the research which demonstrates the brain's sensitivity to perceptual features in the environment.

47. Differentiate between an illusion and a hallucination.

48. Describe the Müller-Lyer illusion and explain how perceptual habits may account for this illusion.

49. Explain and give experimental evidence of how motives may alter attention and perception.

50. Explain what bottom-up and top-down processing are.

51. Explain how perceptual expectancies may influence perception.

52. Define the terms "extrasensory perception," "psi phenomenon," and "parapsychology."

53. Describe the following psychic abilities: a. clairvoyance b. telepathy c. precognition d. psychokinesis

54. Describe the research with Zener Cards and explain why most psychologists remain skeptical about psi abilities.

55. Describe the concept of stage ESP.

56. Explain why eyewitness testimony can be inaccurate, including the concept of weapon focus.

57. Explain what the term "reality testing" means.

58. Explain Maslow's concept of perceptual awareness and discuss how attention affects perception.

59. List seven ways to become a better "eyewitness" to life.

RECITE AND REVIEW

MODULE 5.1

Survey Question: In general, how do sensory systems function? Pages 168-169

Sensory organs transduce physical energies into [1] _____ impulses.

The senses act as [2] _____ reduction systems that select, [3] _____ , and filter sensory information.

A good example of sensory analysis is the identification of basic [4] _____ features in a stimulus pattern.

In fact, many sensory systems act as feature [5] _____ .

Phosphenes and visual pop-out are examples of feature detection and [6] _____ coding in action.

Sensory response can be partially understood in terms of [7] _____ localization in the brain. That is, the area of the brain [8] _____ ultimately determines which type of sensory experience we have.

[9] _____ refers to the information brought in by the senses, and [10] _____ refers to the process by which the brain organizes and interprets the information into meaningful patterns.

Survey Question: How is vision accomplished? Pages 169-175

The [11] _____ spectrum consists of electromagnetic radiation in a narrow range.

The electromagnetic spectrum ranges from violet, with a [12] _____ of 400 nanometers, to red, with a [13] _____ of 700 nanometers.

Hue refers to a color's name, which corresponds to its [14] _____ . Saturated or "pure" colors come from a [15] _____ band of wavelengths. Brightness corresponds to the amplitude of light waves.

The eye is in some ways like a camera. At its back lies an array of photoreceptors, called [16] _____ and [17] _____ , that make up a light-sensitive layer called the retina.

[18] _____ theory was unable to explain why people experience [19] _____ or visual sensations that persist after a color stimulus is removed.

Vision is focused by the [20] _____ of the cornea and lens and by changes in the [21] _____ of the lens, called accommodation.

Four common visual defects, correctable with glasses, are myopia ([22] _____), hyperopia (farsightedness), presbyopia (loss of [23] _____), and astigmatism (in which portions of vision are out of focus).

In the retina, the [24] _____ specialize in night vision, black-and-white reception, and motion detection.

The [25] _____ , found exclusively in the fovea and otherwise toward the middle of the eye, specialize in [26] _____ vision, acuity (perception of fine detail), and daylight vision.

The [27] _____ supply much of our peripheral vision. Loss of peripheral vision is called tunnel vision.

In the [28] _____ , color vision is explained by the trichromatic theory. The theory says that three types of [29] _____ exist, each most sensitive to either red, green, or blue light.

Three types of light-sensitive visual pigments are found in the [30] _____ , each pigment most sensitive to either red, green, or blue light.

Beyond the retina, the visual system analyzes colors into [31] _____ messages. According to the opponent-process theory, color information can be coded as either red or green, yellow or blue, and [32] _____ [33] _____ [34] _____ messages.

[35] _____ color blindness is rare, but 8 percent of males and 1 percent of females are red-green color blind or color weak.

The Ishihara test is used to detect [36] _____ [37] _____ .

Dark adaptation, an [38] _____ in sensitivity to light, is caused by increased concentrations of visual pigments in the [39] _____ and the [40] _____ .

Most dark adaptation is the result of increased rhodopsin concentrations in the [41] _____ .

MODULE 5.2

Survey Question: What are the mechanisms of hearing? Pages 177-180

Sound waves are the stimulus for hearing. Sound travels as waves of compression ([42] _____) and rarefaction ([43] _____) in the air.

The [44] _____ of a sound corresponds to the frequency of sound waves. Loudness corresponds to the amplitude ([45] _____) of sound waves.

Sound waves are transduced by the [46] _____ , auditory ossicles, oval window, cochlea, and ultimately, the [47] _____ cells in the organ of Corti.

The frequency theory says that the [48] _____ of nerve impulses in the auditory nerves matches the [49] _____ of incoming sounds (up to 4,000 hertz).

Place theory says that [50] _____ tones register near the base of the cochlea and [51] _____ tones near its tip.

Three basic types of deafness are [52] _____ deafness, conduction deafness, and stimulation deafness.

Conduction deafness can often be overcome with a hearing aid. [53] _____ deafness can sometimes be alleviated by cochlear implants.

Stimulation deafness can be prevented by avoiding excessive exposure to [54] _____ sounds. Sounds above 120 decibels pose an immediate danger to hearing.

Survey Question: How do the chemical senses operate? Pages 180-181

Olfaction ([55] _____) and gustation ([56] _____) are chemical senses responsive to airborne or liquefied molecules.

The lock-and-key theory partially explains smell. In addition, the [57] _____ of the olfactory receptors in the nose helps identify various scents.

The top outside edges of the tongue are responsive to sweet, salty, sour, and [58] _____ tastes. It is suspected that a fifth taste quality called umami also exists.

Taste also appears to be based in part on lock-and-key [59] _____ of molecule shapes.

Chemical senses of [60] _____ and [61] _____ operate together to allow us to experience the flavor of food.

MODULE 5.3

Survey Question: What are the somesthetic senses and why are they important? Pages 183-185

The somesthetic senses include the [62] _____ senses, vestibular senses, and kinesthetic senses (receptors that detect muscle and joint positioning).

The skin senses include touch, [63] _____ , pain, cold, and warmth. Sensitivity to each is related to the [64] _____ of receptors found in an area of skin.

Distinctions can be made between warning system pain and [65] _____ system pain.

Telling soldiers that they are relieved from combat [66] _____ their anxiety level, which desensitized them to their wounds. It seems unpleasant emotions increase pain level, and [67] _____ emotions decrease pain level.

Pain can be reduced by [68] _____ anxiety and redirecting attention to stimuli other than the pain stimulus.

Feeling that you have control over a stimulus tends to [69] _____ the amount of pain you experience.

Various forms of motion sickness are related to messages received from the vestibular system, which senses gravity and [70] _____ movement.

The otolith organs detect the pull of [71] _____ and rapid head movements.

The movement of [72] _____ within the semicircular canals, and the movement of the [73] _____ , detects head movement and positioning.

According to sensory conflict theory, motion sickness is caused by a [74] _____ of visual, kinesthetic, and vestibular sensations. Motion sickness can be avoided by minimizing sensory conflict.

Survey Question: Why are we more aware of some sensations than others? Pages 186-188

Incoming sensations are affected by sensory adaptation (a [75] _____ in the number of nerve impulses sent).

Selective attention (selection and diversion of messages in the brain) and sensory [76] _____ (blocking or alteration of messages flowing toward the brain) also alter sensations.

Selective gating of pain messages apparently takes place in the [77] _____ [78] _____ .

Gate control theory proposes an explanation for many pain phenomena.

[79] _____ is used by pain clinics to reduce people's experiences of [80] _____ by introducing an additional, less intense pain signal such as a mild electrical current to the brain through the fast nerve fiber.

MODULE 5.4

Survey Question: How do perceptual constancies affect our perceptions? Pages 189-190

Perception is the process of assembling sensations into [81] _____ that provide a usable mental [82] _____ of the world.

In vision, the retinal [83] _____ changes from moment to moment, but the external world appears stable and undistorted because of [84] _____ constancies.

In size and shape [85] _____ , the perceived sizes and shapes of objects remain the same even though their retinal images change size and shape. The apparent brightness of objects remains stable (a property called brightness constancy) because each reflects a [86] _____ proportion of light. Perceptual constancies are partly native ([87] _____) and partly empirical ([88] _____).

Survey Question: What basic principles do we use to group sensations into meaningful patterns? Pages 190-192

The most basic organization of sensations is a division into figure and ground ([89] _____ and [90] _____). Reversible figures, however, allow figure-ground organization to be reversed.

A number of factors, identified by the Gestalt psychologists, contribute to the [91] _____ of sensations. These are nearness, [92] _____ , continuity, closure, contiguity, [93] _____ region, and combinations of the preceding.

Stimuli near one another tend to be perceptually [94] _____ together. So, too, do stimuli that are similar in [95] _____ . Continuity refers to the fact that perceptions tend to be organized as simple, uninterrupted patterns.

Closure is the tendency to [96] _____ a broken or incomplete pattern. Contiguity refers to nearness in [97] _____ and space. Stimuli that fall in a defined area, or common region, also tend to be grouped together.

A perceptual organization may be thought of as a [98] _____ held until evidence contradicts it. Camouflage patterns disrupt perceptual [99] _____ , especially figure-ground perceptions. Perceptual organization shifts for ambiguous [100] _____ , which may have more than one interpretation. An example is Necker's [101] _____ . Impossible figures resist stable organization altogether.

MODULE 5.5

Survey Question: How is it possible to see depth and judge distance? Pages 194-199

[102] _____ perception is the ability to perceive three-dimensional space and judge distances. Depth perception is present in basic form soon after [103] _____ as shown by testing with the visual cliff and other methods. As soon as infants become active [104] _____ , they refuse to cross the visual cliff.

[105] _____ (one eye) and [106] _____ (two eyes) cues are depth cues in the environment that help us perceive and judge distance and depth.

Depth perception depends on the muscular cues of accommodation (bending of the [107] _____) and convergence (inward movement of the [108] _____).

A number of pictorial [109] _____ , which will work in [110] _____ paintings, drawings, and photographs, also underlie normal depth perception.

Some pictorial cues are: linear perspective (the apparent convergence of [111] _____ [112] _____), relative size (more distant objects appear [113] _____), height in the [114] _____ plane, light and shadow (shadings of light), and overlap or interposition (one object overlaps another).

Additional pictorial cues include: texture gradients (textures become [115] _____ in the distance), aerial haze (loss of color and detail at great distances), and relative [116] _____ or [117] _____ parallax (differences in the apparent movement of objects when a viewer is moving).

All the pictorial cues are monocular depth cues (only [118] _____ [119] _____ is needed to make use of them).

The moon illusion refers to the fact that the moon appears [120] _____ near the horizon than it does when overhead.

The moon illusion appears to be explained by the apparent [121] _____ hypothesis, which emphasizes the greater number of depth cues present when the moon is on the [122] _____ .

Stereoscopic vision ([123] _____ sight) relies on retinal disparity to determine the depth of objects that are within 50 feet of us.

MODULE 5.6

Survey Question: How are our perceptions altered by learning, expectations, and motives? Pages 200-205

Organizing and interpreting sensations is greatly influenced by learned perceptual [124] _____ .

An example is the Ames room, which looks rectangular but is actually distorted so that objects in the room appear to change [125] _____ .

Sensitivity to perceptual [126] _____ is also partly learned. Studies of inverted vision show that even the most basic organization is subject to a degree of change.

Illusions are often related to perceptual [127] _____ . One of the most familiar of all illusions, the Müller-Lyer illusion, seems to be related to perceptual learning based on experience with box-shaped [128] _____ and rooms.

People who have lost touch with reality may experience [129] _____ that involve auditory, visual, touch, smell, or taste sensations created by the brain without proper environmental input.

"[130] _____ hallucinations" are created by the brain to interpret sensory input received by partially [131] _____ individuals who "see" objects appearing and disappearing in front of their eyes.

[132] _____ blindness refers to people's inability to [133] _____ a stimulus that is right in front of their eyes because they were too busy focusing on another stimulus.

Linear perspective, [134] _____ invariance relationships, and mislocating the endpoints of the [135] _____ also contribute to the Müller-Lyer illusion.

Personal motives and [136] _____ often alter perceptions by changing the evaluation of what is seen or by altering attention to specific details.

Perceptions may be based on [137] _____ or bottom-up processing of information.

In bottom-up processing, perceptions begin with the organization of low-level [138] _____ . In top-down processing, previous knowledge is used to rapidly [139] _____ sensory information.

Attention, prior experience, suggestion, and motives combine in various ways to create perceptual sets, or [140] _____ . A perceptual set is a readiness to perceive in a particular way, induced by strong expectations.

Perceptual categories (or [141] _____) of people impact our perception of their behaviors.

MODULE 5.7

Survey Question: Is extrasensory perception possible? Pages 207-209

Parapsychology is the study of purported [142] _____ phenomena, including clairvoyance (perceiving events at a distance), [143] _____ ("mind reading"), precognition (perceiving future events), and psychokinesis (mentally influencing inanimate objects).

Clairvoyance, telepathy, and precognition are purported types of extrasensory [144] _____ .

Research in parapsychology remains controversial owing to a variety of problems. [145] _____ and after-the-fact reinterpretation are problems with "natural" ESP episodes.

With no evidence supporting the existence of ESP, psychologists strongly suggest that people be
[146] _____ of those who claim to have [147] _____ abilities. For example, the owner of
the "Miss Cleo" TV-psychic operation made $1 billion from people who believed "Miss Cleo" was a psychic.
Many studies of ESP overlook the impact of statistically unusual outcomes that are no more than runs of
[148] _____ .

The bulk of the evidence to date is [149] _____ the existence of ESP. Very few positive results in
ESP research have been replicated ([150] _____) by independent scientists.

Stage ESP is based on [151] _____ and tricks.

PSYCHOLOGY IN ACTION

Survey Question: How can I learn to perceive events more accurately? Page 211-213

Perceptions are a reconstruction of events. This is one reason why eyewitness testimony is surprisingly
[152] _____ .

In many crimes, eyewitness accuracy is further damaged by weapon [153] _____ . Similar
factors, such as observer stress, brief exposure times, cross-racial inaccuracies, and the wording of
questions, can [154] _____ eyewitness accuracy.

Perceptual accuracy is enhanced by reality [155] _____ , dishabituation, and conscious efforts to
pay [156] _____ .

It is also valuable to break perceptual habits, to [157] _____ frames of reference, to beware of
perceptual sets, and to be aware of the ways in which motives and emotions influence perceptions.

CONNECTIONS

MODULE 5.1

1. _____ ciliary muscle
2. _____ iris
3. _____ cornea
4. _____ blind spot
5. _____ lens
6. _____ fovea
7. _____ retinal veins
8. _____ optic nerve
9. _____ aqueous humor
10. _____ pupil
11. _____ retina

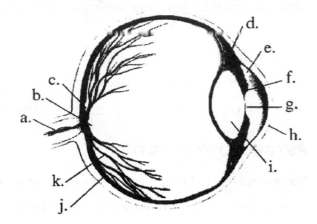

1. _____ transducer
2. _____ cones
3. _____ rods
4. _____ afterimages
5. _____ sensation
6. _____ trichromatic theory
7. _____ opponent process theory
8. _____ accommodation
9. _____ perception

a. sensory impression
b. analyze colors in either-or messages
c. convert energy into neural impulse
d. lens modification
e. receptors for dim light
f. receptors for colors
g. three types of cones
h. interpreting sensory input
i. seeing images after stimuli are gone

MODULE 5.2

1. _____ vestibular system
2. _____ cochlea
3. _____ round window
4. _____ auditory canal
5. _____ stapes
6. _____ auditory nerve
7. _____ incus
8. _____ oval window
9. _____ malleus
10. _____ tympanic membrane

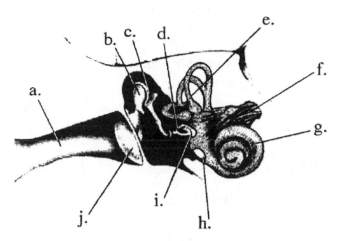

1. _____ frequency theory
2. _____ place theory
3. _____ taste buds
4. _____ auditory ossicles
5. _____ unami
6. _____ organ of corti
7. _____ gustatory
8. _____ olfactory

a. "brothy"
b. matching the speed of incoming frequency
c. contains hair cells
d. malleus, incus, and stapes
e. sense of smell
f. sense of taste
g. taste receptors
h. location of sound processing

MODULE 5.3

1. _____ counterirritation
2. _____ kinesthetic
3. _____ semicircular canals
4. _____ selective attention
5. _____ vestibular
6. _____ gate control theory
7. _____ sensory conflict theory

a. body movement
b. sense of balance
c. organs of balance
d. explains motion sickness
e. pain processing
f. applying ice packs to skin
g. bottle neck filtration

MODULE 5.4

1. _____ continuity
2. _____ common region
3. _____ closure
4. _____ nearness
5. _____ reversible figure
6. _____ similarity

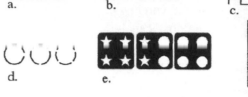

MODULE 5.5

1. _____ texture gradients
2. _____ stereoscopic vision
3. _____ convergence
4. _____ light and shadow
5. _____ relative size
6. _____ overlap
7. _____ retinal disparity
8. _____ linear perspective

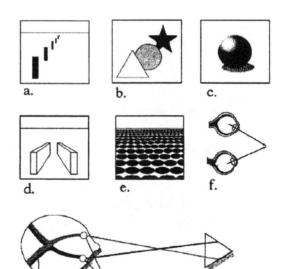

1. _____ binocular depth cue
2. _____ monocular depth cue
3. _____ mismatch
4. _____ visual cliff
5. _____ ponzo illusion

a. infant depth perception
b. convergence
c. stereoscopic vision
d. moon illusion
e. accommodation

MODULE 5.6

1.	_____ Zulu	a.	diminished Müller-Lyer illusion
2.	_____ illusions	b.	perceptual expectancy
3.	_____ top-down	c.	imaginary sensation
4.	_____ bottom-up	d.	surrender to experience
5.	_____ perceptual awareness	e.	misleading perception of real sensations
6.	_____ hallucination	f.	low-level features
7.	_____ sane hallucination	g.	partially blinded perception of images

MODULE 5.7

1.	_____ Zener cards	a.	run of luck
2.	_____ telepathy	b.	study of ESP
3.	_____ parapsychology	c.	mind reader
4.	_____ psychokinesis	d.	clairvoyance test
5.	_____ psychic fraud	e.	"Miss Cleo"
6.	_____ decline effect	f.	ability to move objects

CHECK YOUR MEMORY

MODULE 5.1

Survey Question: In general, how do sensory systems function? Pages 168-169

1. The electromagnetic spectrum includes ultraviolet light and radio waves.
   TRUE or FALSE

2. Each sensory organ is sensitive to a select range of physical energies.
   TRUE or FALSE

3. The artificial vision system described in the text is based on electrodes implanted in the retina.
   TRUE or FALSE

4. The retina responds to pressure as well as light.
   TRUE or FALSE

Survey Question: How is vision accomplished? Pages 169-175

5. A nanometer is one-millionth of a meter.
   TRUE or FALSE

6. The lens of the eye is about the size and thickness of a postage stamp.

   TRUE or FALSE

7. The functions of a human eye have often been compared to a camera with the retina as the layer of film.

   TRUE or FALSE

8. Farsightedness is corrected with a convex lens.

   TRUE or FALSE

9. The myopic eye is longer than normal.

   TRUE or FALSE

10. There are more rods than cones in the eyes.

    TRUE or FALSE

11. The blind spot is the point where the optic nerve leaves the eye.

    TRUE or FALSE

12. Vision rated at 20/200 is better than average.

    TRUE or FALSE

13. If your vision is 20/12 like Gordon Cooper, an American astronaut, you would be able to see eight feet farther than someone who has 20/20 vision.

    TRUE or FALSE

14. Blue emergency lights and taxiway lights are used because at night they are more visible to the cones.

    TRUE or FALSE

15. The trichromatic theory of color vision says that black and white are produced by the rods.

    TRUE or FALSE

16. According to the opponent-process theory it is impossible to have a reddish green or yellowish blue.

    TRUE or FALSE

17. Yellow-blue color weakness is very rare.

    TRUE or FALSE

18. In the United States and Canada, stoplights are always on the bottom of traffic signals.

    TRUE or FALSE

19. Complete dark adaptation takes about 12 minutes.

    TRUE or FALSE

20. Dark adaptation can be preserved by working in an area lit with red light.

    TRUE or FALSE

MODULE 5.2

Survey Question: What are the mechanisms of hearing? Pages 177-180

21. Sound cannot travel in a vacuum.
TRUE or FALSE

22. The visible, external portion of the ear is the malleus.
TRUE or FALSE

23. The hair cells are part of the organ of Corti.
TRUE or FALSE

24. Hunter's notch occurs when the auditory ossicles are damaged by the sound of gunfire.
TRUE or FALSE

25. Cochlear implants stimulate the auditory nerve directly.
TRUE or FALSE

26. Deaf children can learn spoken language close to a normal rate if they have cochlear implants before the age of two.
TRUE or FALSE

27. A 40-decibel sound could be described as quiet.
TRUE or FALSE

28. A 100-decibel sound can damage hearing in less than eight hours.
TRUE or FALSE

29. Every 20 decibels increases sound energy by a factor of 10.
TRUE or FALSE

Survey Question: How do the chemical senses operate? Pages 180-181

30. At least 300 different types of olfactory receptors exist.
TRUE or FALSE

31. Etherish odors smell like garlic.
TRUE or FALSE

32. Flavors are greatly influenced by odor as well as taste.
TRUE or FALSE

33. Taste buds are found throughout the mouth, not just on the tongue.
TRUE or FALSE

34. Umami is a pleasant "brothy" taste.
TRUE or FALSE

MODULE 5.3

Survey Question: What are the somesthetic senses and why are they important? Pages 183-185

35. Vibration is one of the five basic skin sensations.
    TRUE or FALSE

36. Areas of the skin that have high concentrations of pain receptors are no more sensitive to pain than other areas of the body.
    TRUE or FALSE

37. Small nerve fibers generally carry warning-system pain messages.
    TRUE or FALSE

38. High levels of anxiety tend to amplify the amount of pain a person experiences.
    TRUE or FALSE

39. The level of pain people experience is related to their emotions: Unpleasant emotions increase pain while pleasant emotions decrease pain.
    TRUE or FALSE

40. As a means of reducing pain, hot-water bottles are an example of counterirritation.
    TRUE or FALSE

41. The semicircular canals are especially sensitive to the pull of gravity.
    TRUE or FALSE

42. Motion sickness is believed to be related to the body's reactions to being poisoned.
    TRUE or FALSE

Survey Question: Why are we more aware of some sensations than others? Pages 186-188

43. If you wear a ring, you are rarely aware of it because of sensory gating.
    TRUE or FALSE

44. The "seat-of-your-pants" phenomenon is related to selective attention.
    TRUE or FALSE

45. Attention is related to contrast or changes in stimulation.
    TRUE or FALSE

46. Mild electrical stimulation of the skin can block reminding system pain.
    TRUE or FALSE

47. Mild electrical stimulation of the skin causes a release of endorphins in free nerve endings.
    TRUE or FALSE

MODULE 5.4

Survey Question: How do perceptual constancies affect our perceptions? Pages 189-190

48. Perception involves selecting, organizing, and integrating sensory information.
TRUE or FALSE

49. Some perceptual abilities must be learned after sight is restored to the previously blind.
TRUE or FALSE

50. Newborn babies show some evidence of size constancy.
TRUE or FALSE

51. Houses and cars look like toys from a low-flying airplane because of shape constancy.
TRUE or FALSE

52. Brightness constancy does not apply to objects illuminated by different amounts of light.
TRUE or FALSE

Survey Question: What basic principles do we use to group sensations into meaningful patterns? Pages 190-192

53. Basic figure-ground organization is learned at about age two.
TRUE or FALSE

54. Contiguity refers to our tendency to see lines as continuous.
TRUE or FALSE

55. Common region refers to the tendency to see stimuli that are close together as one unit.
TRUE or FALSE

56. Necker's cube and the "three-pronged widget" are impossible figures.
TRUE or FALSE

MODULE 5.5

Survey Question: How is it possible to see depth and judge distance? Pages 194-199

57. Depth perception is partly learned and partly innate.
TRUE or FALSE

58. Human depth perception typically emerges at about four months of age.
TRUE or FALSE

59. Most infants, when coaxed by their mothers, will crawl across the visual cliff.
TRUE or FALSE

60. Accommodation and convergence are muscular depth cues.

    TRUE or FALSE

61. Accommodation acts as a depth cue primarily for distances greater than four feet from the eyes.

    TRUE or FALSE

62. Convergence acts as a depth cue primarily for distances less than four feet from the eyes.

    TRUE or FALSE

63. With one eye closed, the pictorial depth cues no longer provide information about depth and distance.

    TRUE or FALSE

64. Changing the image size of an object implies that its distance from the viewer has changed too.

    TRUE or FALSE

65. In a drawing, the closer an object is to the horizon line, the nearer it appears to be to the viewer.

    TRUE or FALSE

66. Aerial perspective is most powerful when the air is exceptionally clear.

    TRUE or FALSE

67. When an observer is moving forward, objects beyond the observer's point of fixation appear to move forward too.

    TRUE or FALSE

68. The moon's image is magnified by the dense atmosphere near the horizon.

    TRUE or FALSE

69. More depth cues are present when the moon is viewed near the horizon.

    TRUE or FALSE

MODULE 5.6

Survey Question: How are our perceptions altered by learning, expectations, and motives? Pages 200-205

70. The Ames room is primarily used to test the effects of inverted vision.

    TRUE or FALSE

71. Cats that grow up surrounded by horizontal stripes are unusually sensitive to vertical stripes when they reach maturity.

    TRUE or FALSE

72. Hearing voices when no one is speaking is an example of a perceptual illusion.

    TRUE or FALSE

73. Seeing images appearing and disappearing because one is partially blind can be described as "sane hallucination."

    TRUE or FALSE

74. According to Richard Gregory, the arrowhead-tipped line in the Müller-Lyer illusion looks like the outside corner of a building.
    TRUE or FALSE

75. Zulus rarely see round shapes and therefore fail to experience the Müller-Lyer illusion.
    TRUE or FALSE

76. Failing to see a pedestrian crossing a street because one is busy using a cell phone while driving is referred to as attentional blindness.
    TRUE or FALSE

77. Analyzing information into small features and then building a recognizable pattern is called top-up processing.
    TRUE or FALSE

78. Perceptual sets are frequently created by suggestion.
    TRUE or FALSE

79. Labels and categories have been shown to have little real effect on perceptions.
    TRUE or FALSE

MODULE 5.7

Survey Question: Is extrasensory perception possible? Pages 207-209

80. Uri Geller was one of the first researchers in parapsychology to use the Zener cards.
    TRUE or FALSE

81. Psychokinesis is classified as a psi event but not a form of ESP.
    TRUE or FALSE

82. Prophetic dreams are regarded as a form of precognition.
    TRUE or FALSE

83. Strange coincidences are strong evidence for the existence of ESP.
    TRUE or FALSE

84. The Zener cards eliminated the possibility of fraud and "leakage" of information in ESP experiments.
    TRUE or FALSE

85. "Miss Cleo" is one of the few people who truly have psychic abilities.
    TRUE or FALSE

86. "Psi missing" is perhaps the best current evidence for ESP.
    TRUE or FALSE

87. Stage ESP relies on deception, sleight of hand, and patented gadgets to entertain the audience.
    TRUE or FALSE

88. Belief in psi events has declined among parapsychologists in recent years.
TRUE or FALSE

89. A skeptic of psi means that a person is unconvinced and is against the idea that psi exists.
TRUE or FALSE

PSYCHOLOGY IN ACTION

Survey Question: How can I learn to perceive events more accurately? Page 211-213

90. In many ways we see what we believe as well as believe what we see.
TRUE or FALSE

91. The more confident an eyewitness is about the accuracy of his or her testimony, the more likely it is to be accurate.
TRUE or FALSE

92. The testimony of crime victims is generally more accurate than the testimony of bystanders.
TRUE or FALSE

93. Police officers and other trained observers are more accurate eyewitnesses than the average person.
TRUE or FALSE

94. Victims tend to not notice detail information such as the appearance of their attacker because they fall prey to weapon focus.
TRUE or FALSE

95. Reality testing is the process Abraham Maslow described as a "surrender" to experience.
TRUE or FALSE

96. Perceptually, Zen masters have been shown to habituate more rapidly than the average person.
TRUE or FALSE

FINAL SURVEY AND REVIEW

MODULE 5.1

Survey question: In general, how do sensory systems function? Pages 168-169

Sensory organs [1] _____ physical energies into nerve impulses.

The senses act as data [2] _____ systems that select, analyze, and [3] _____ sensory information.

A good example of [4] _____ [5] _____ is the identification of basic perceptual features in a stimulus pattern.

In fact, many sensory systems act as [6] _____ detectors.

[7] _____ and visual pop-out are examples of feature detection and sensory [8] _____ in action.

Sensory response can be partially understood in terms of sensory [9] _____ in the brain. That is, the [10] _____ of the brain activated ultimately determines which type of sensory experience we have.

[11] _____ refers to the information brought in by the senses, and [12] _____ refers to the process by which the brain organizes and interprets the information into meaningful patterns.

Survey Question: How is vision accomplished? Pages 169-175

The visible spectrum consists of [13] _____ radiation in a narrow range.

The visible spectrum ranges from violet, with a wavelength of [14] _____ [15] _____ , to red, with a wavelength of [16] _____ [17] _____ .

[18] _____ refers to a color's name, which corresponds to its wavelength. Saturated or "pure" colors come from a narrow band of wavelengths. Brightness corresponds to the [19] _____ of light waves.

The eye is in some ways like a camera. At its back lies an array of [20] _____ , called rods and cones, that make up a light-sensitive layer called the [21] _____ .

[22] _____ theory was unable to explain why people experience [23] _____ or visual sensations that persist after a color stimulus is removed.

Vision is focused by the shape of the [24] _____ and lens and by changes in the shape of the lens, called [25] _____ .

Four common visual defects, correctable with glasses, are [26] _____ (nearsightedness), hyperopia (farsightedness), presbyopia (loss of accommodation), and [27] _____ (in which portions of vision are out of focus).

In the retina, the rods specialize in night vision, black-and-white reception, and [28] _____ detection.

The cones, found exclusively in the [29] _____ and otherwise toward the middle of the eye, specialize in color vision, [30] _____ (perception of fine detail), and daylight vision.

The rods supply much of our [31] _____ vision. Loss of [32] _____ vision is called tunnel vision.

In the retina, color vision is explained by the [33] _____ theory. The theory says that three types of cones exist, each most sensitive to either red, green, or blue light.

Three types of light-sensitive visual [34] _____ are found in the cones, each most sensitive to either red, green, or blue light.

Beyond the retina, the visual system analyzes colors into either or messages. According to the [35] _____ theory, color information can be coded as either [36] _____ [37] _____ , yellow or blue, and black or white messages.

Total color blindness is rare, but 8 percent of males and 1 percent of females are [38] _____ color blind or color weak.

The [39] _____ test is used to detect color blindness.

Dark adaptation, an increase in sensitivity to light, is caused by increased concentrations of [40] _____ in the rods and the cones.

Most dark adaptation is the result of increased [41] _____ concentrations in the rods.

MODULE 5.2

Survey Question: What are the mechanisms of hearing? Pages 177-180

Sound waves are the stimulus for hearing. Sound travels as waves of [42] _____ (peaks) and [43] _____ (valleys) in the air.

The pitch of a sound corresponds to the [44] _____ of sound waves. Loudness corresponds to the [45] _____ (height) of sound waves.

Sound waves are transduced by the eardrum, auditory [46] _____ , oval window, cochlea, and ultimately, the hair cells in the organ of [47] _____ .

The frequency theory says that the frequency of nerve impulses in the [48] _____ [49] _____ matches the frequency of incoming sounds (up to 4,000 hertz).

Place theory says that high tones register near the [50] _____ of the cochlea and low tones near its [51] _____ .

Three basic types of deafness are nerve deafness, conduction deafness, and [52] _____ deafness.

Conduction deafness can often be overcome with a hearing aid. Nerve deafness can sometimes be alleviated by [53] _____ implants.

Stimulation deafness can be prevented by avoiding excessive exposure to loud sounds. Sounds above [54] _____ [55] _____ pose an immediate danger to hearing.

Survey Question: How do the chemical senses operate? Pages 180-181

[56] _____ (smell) and [57] _____ (taste) are chemical senses responsive to airborne or liquefied molecules.

The [58] _____ theory partially explains smell. In addition, the location of the olfactory receptors in the nose helps identify various scents.

The top outside edges of the tongue are responsive to [59] _____ , [60] _____ , [61] _____ , and bitter tastes. It is suspected that a fifth taste quality called [62] _____ also exists.

Taste also appears to be based in part on lock-and-key coding of [63] _____ shapes.

Chemical senses of [64] _____ and [65] _____ operate together to allow us to experience the flavor of food.

MODULE 5.3

Survey Question: What are the somesthetic senses and why are they important? Pages 183-185

The somesthetic senses include the skin senses, vestibular senses, and [66] _____ senses (receptors that detect muscle and joint positioning).

The skin senses include touch, pressure, [67] _____ , cold, and warmth. Sensitivity to each is related to the number of [68] _____ found in an area of skin.

Distinctions can be made between [69] _____ system pain and [70] _____ system pain.

Telling soldiers that they are relieved from combat reduced their [71] _____ level, which desensitized them to their wounds. It seems [72] _____ emotions increase pain level, and [73] _____ emotions decrease pain level.

Pain can be reduced by lowering anxiety and redirecting [74] _____ to stimuli other than the pain stimulus.

Feeling that you have [75] _____ over a stimulus tends to reduce the amount of pain you experience.

Various forms of motion sickness are related to messages received from the [76] _____ system, which senses gravity and head movement.

The [77] _____ organs detect the pull of gravity and rapid head movements.

The movement of fluid within the [78] _____ canals, and the movement of the crista, detects head movement and positioning.

According to [79] _____ [80] _____ theory, motion sickness is caused by a mismatch of visual, kinesthetic, and vestibular sensations. Motion sickness can be avoided by minimizing sensory conflict

Survey Question: Why are we more aware of some sensations than others? Pages 186-188

Incoming sensations are affected by sensory [81] _____ (a decrease in the number of nerve impulses sent).

Selective [82] _____ (selection and diversion of messages in the brain) and sensory gating (blocking or alteration of messages flowing toward the brain) also alter sensations.

Selective gating of pain messages apparently takes place in the spinal cord. [83] _____

[84] _____ theory proposes an explanation for many pain phenomena.

[85] _____ is used by pain clinics to reduce people's experiences of [86] _____ by introducing an additional, less intense pain signal such as a mild electrical current to the brain through the fast nerve fiber.

MODULE 5.4

Survey Question: How do perceptual constancies affect our perceptions? Pages 189-190

Perception is the process of assembling [87] _____ into patterns that provide a usable [88] _____ [89] _____ of the world.

In vision, the [90] _____ image changes from moment to moment, but the external world appears stable and undistorted because of perceptual [91] _____ .

In size and shape constancy, the perceived sizes and shapes of objects remain the same even though their retinal images change size and shape. The apparent [92] _____ of objects remains stable (a property called brightness constancy) because each reflects a constant [93] _____ of [94] _____ .

Perceptual constancies are partly [95] _____ (inborn) and partly [96] _____ (learned).

Survey Question: What basic principles do we use to group sensations into meaningful patterns? Pages 190-192

The most basic organization of sensations is a division into [97] _____ and [98] _____ (object and background).

A number of factors, identified by the [99] _____ psychologists, contribute to the organization of sensations. These are [100] _____ , similarity, continuity, [101] _____ , contiguity, common region, and combinations of the preceding.

Stimuli near one another tend to be perceptually grouped together. So, too, do stimuli that are similar in appearance. [102] _____ refers to the fact that perceptions tend to be organized as simple, uninterrupted patterns.

[103] _____ refers to nearness in time and space. Stimuli that fall in a defined area, or common region, also tend to be grouped together.

A perceptual organization may be thought of as a hypothesis held until evidence contradicts it.

[104] _____ patterns disrupt perceptual organization, especially figure-ground perceptions.

Perceptual organization shifts for [105] _____ stimuli, which may have more than one interpretation. An example is [106] _____ cube. Impossible [107] _____ resist stable organization altogether.

MODULE 5.5

Survey Question: How is it possible to see depth and judge distance? Pages 194-199

Depth perception is the ability to perceive [108] _____ space and judge distances.

Depth perception is present in basic form soon after birth as shown by testing with the [109] _____ [110] _____ and other methods. As soon as infants become active crawlers, they refuse to cross the deep side of the [111] _____ [112] _____ .

[113] _____ (one eye) and [114] _____ (two eyes) cues are depth cues in the environment that help us perceive and judge distance and depth.

Depth perception depends on the muscular cues of [115] _____ (bending of the lens) and [116] _____ (inward movement of the eyes).

A number of [117] _____ cues, which will work in flat paintings, drawings, and photographs, also underlie normal depth perception.

Some of these cues are: [118] _____ [119] _____ (the apparent convergence of parallel lines), relative size (more distant objects appear smaller), height in the picture plane, light and shadow (shadings of light), and overlap or [120] _____ (one object overlaps another).

Additional pictorial cues include: texture [121] _____ (textures become finer in the distance), aerial haze (loss of color and detail at great distances), and relative motion or motion [122] _____ (differences in the apparent movement of objects when a viewer is moving).

All the pictorial cues are [123] _____ depth cues (only one eye is needed to make use of them).

The moon illusion refers to the fact that the moon appears larger near the [124] _____ .

The moon illusion appears to be explained by the [125] _____ [126] _____ hypothesis, which emphasizes the greater number of depth [127] _____ present when the moon is on the horizon.

[128] _____ (three-dimensional sight) relies on retinal disparity to determine the depth of objects that are within 50 feet of us.

MODULE 5.6

Survey Question: How are our perceptions altered by learning, expectations, and motives? Pages 200-205

Organizing and interpreting sensations is greatly influenced by learned [129] _____ [130] _____ . An example is the [131] _____ room, which looks rectangular but is actually distorted so that objects in the room appear to change size.

Sensitivity to perceptual features is also partly learned. Studies of [132] _____ vision show that even the most basic organization is subject to a degree of change.

Illusions are often related to perceptual habits. One of the most familiar of all illusions, the [133] _____ illusion, involves two equal-length lines tipped with arrowheads and Vs. This illusion seems to be related to perceptual learning based on experience with box-shaped buildings and rooms.

People who have lost touch with [134] _____ may experience hallucinations that involve auditory, [135] _____ , touch, smell, or taste sensations created by the brain without proper environmental input. "[136] _____ hallucinations" are created by the brain to interpret sensory input received by partially blind individuals who "see" objects appearing and disappearing in front of their eyes.

[137] _____ blindness refers to people's inability to detect a stimulus that is right in front of their eyes because they were too busy focusing on another stimulus or activity.

Linear perspective, size-distance [138] _____ relationships, and mislocating the

[139] _____ of the lines also contribute to the Müller-Lyer illusion.

Personal [140] _____ and values often alter perceptions by changing the evaluation of what is

seen or by altering attention to specific details.

Perceptions may be based on top-down or bottom-up [141] _____ of information.

[142] _____ perceptions begin with the organization of low-level features. In

[143] _____ processing, previous knowledge is used to rapidly organize sensory information.

Attention, prior experience, suggestion, and motives combine in various ways to create [144] _____

[145] _____ , or expectancies. A [146] _____ [147] _____ is a readiness to

perceive in a particular way, induced by strong expectations.

[148] _____ categories (or labels) of people impact our perception of their behaviors.

MODULE 5.7

Survey Question: Is extrasensory perception possible? Pages 207-209

[149] _____ is the study of purported psi phenomena, including clairvoyance (perceiving

events at a distance), telepathy ("mind reading"), [150] _____ (perceiving future events), and

psychokinesis (mentally influencing inanimate objects).

Clairvoyance, telepathy, and precognition are purported types of [151] _____ perception.

Research in parapsychology remains controversial owing to a variety of problems. Coincidence and

after-the-fact [152] _____ are problems with "natural" ESP episodes.

With no evidence supporting the existence of ESP, psychologists strongly suggest that people be

[153] _____ of those who claim to have [154] _____ abilities. For example, the owner of

the "Miss Cleo" TV-psychic operation made $1 billion from people who believed "Miss Cleo" was a psychic.

Many studies of ESP overlook the impact of [155] _____ unusual outcomes that are no more

than runs of luck.

The bulk of the evidence to date is against the existence of ESP. Very few positive results in ESP research

have been [156] _____ (repeated) by independent scientists.

[157] _____ ESP is based on deception and tricks.

PSYCHOLOGY IN ACTION

Survey Question: How can I learn to perceive events more accurately? Page 211-213

Perception is an active [158] _____ of events. This is one reason why eyewitness testimony is surprisingly inaccurate.

In many crimes, eyewitness accuracy is further damaged by [159] _____ focus. Similar factors, such as observer [160] _____ , brief exposure times, cross-racial inaccuracies, and the wording of questions, can lower eyewitness accuracy.

Perceptual accuracy is enhanced by reality testing, [161] _____ , and conscious efforts to pay attention.

It is also valuable to break [162] _____ [163] _____ , to broaden frames of reference, to beware of perceptual sets, and to be aware of the ways in which motives and emotions influence perceptions.

MASTERY TEST

1. Sensory conflict theory attributes motion sickness to mismatches between what three systems?
   a. olfaction, kinesthesis, and audition
   b. vision, kinesthesis, and the vestibular system
   c. kinesthesis, audition, and the somesthetic system
   d. vision, gustation, and the skin senses

2. Which of the following types of color blindness is most common?
   a. yellow-blue, male
   b. yellow-blue, female
   c. red-green, female
   d. red-green, male

3. Which of the following does not belong with the others?
   a. Pacinian corpuscle
   b. Merkle's disk
   c. organ of Corti
   d. free nerve endings

4. Which theory of color vision best explains the fact that we do not see yellowish blue?
   a. trichromatic
   b. chromatic gating
   c. Ishihara hypothesis
   d. opponent process

5. Dark adaptation is closely related to concentrations of _____ in the _____.
   a. retinal, aqueous humor
   b. photopsin, cones
   c. rhodopsin, rods
   d. photons, optic nerve

6. Sensory analysis tends to extract perceptual _____ from stimulus patterns.
   a. features
   b. thresholds
   c. transducers
   d. amplitudes

7. Which pair of terms is most closely related?
   a. hyperopia—color blindness
   b. astigmatism—presbyopia
   c. myopia—astigmatism
   d. hyperopia—presbyopia

8. The painkilling effects of acupuncture are partly explained by the _____ theory.
   a. lock-and-key
   b. gate control
   c. opponent-process
   d. frequency

9. According to the _____ theory of hearing, low tones cause the greatest movement near the _____ of the cochlea.
   a. place, outer tip
   b. frequency, outer tip
   c. place, base
   d. frequency, base

10. Which of the following best represents the concept of a transducer?
    a. translating English into Spanish
    b. copying a computer file from one floppy disk to another
    c. speaking into a telephone receiver
    d. turning water into ice

11. Rods and cones are to vision as _____ are to hearing.
    a. auditory ossicles
    b. vibrations
    c. pinnas
    d. hair cells

12. Which two dimensions of color are related to the wavelength of electromagnetic energy?
    a. hue and saturation
    b. saturation and brightness
    c. brightness and hue
    d. brightness and amplitude

13. The existence of the blind spot is explained by a lack of
    a. rhodopsin
    b. peripheral vision
    c. photoreceptors
    d. activity in the fovea

14. In vision, a loss of accommodation is most associated with aging of the
    a. iris
    b. fovea
    c. lens
    d. cornea

15. Visual acuity and color vision are provided by the _____ found in large numbers in the _____ of the eye.
    a. cones, fovea
    b. cones, periphery
    c. rods, fovea
    d. rods, periphery

16. The Ames room creates a conflict between
    a. horizontal features and vertical features
    b. attention and habituation
    c. top-down and bottom-up processing
    d. shape constancy and size constancy

17. Weapon focus tends to lower eyewitness accuracy because it affects
    a. selective attention
    b. the adaptation level
    c. perceptions of contiguity
    d. dishabituation

18. The fact that American tourists in London tend to look in the wrong direction before stepping into crosswalks is based on
    a. sensory localization
    b. perceptual habits
    c. sensory gating
    d. unconscious transference

19. Size constancy
    a. emerges at about four months of age
    b. is affected by experience with seeing objects of various sizes
    c. requires that objects be illuminated by light of the same intensity
    d. all the preceding

20. Which of the following cues would be of greatest help to a person trying to thread a needle?
    a. light and shadow
    b. texture gradients
    c. linear perspective
    d. overlap

21. Size-distance invariances contribute to which of the following?
    a. Müller-Lyer illusion
    b. the stroboscopic illusion
    c. perceptual hallucinations
    d. changes in perceptual sets

22. The visual cliff is used primarily to test infant
    a. size constancy
    b. figure-ground perception
    c. depth perception
    d. adaptation to spatial distortions

23. Which of the following organizational principles is based on nearness in time and space?
    a. continuity
    b. closure
    c. contiguity
    d. size constancy

24. Which of the following is both a muscular and a monocular depth cue?
    a. convergence
    b. relative motion
    c. aerial perspective
    d. accommodation

25. A previously blind person has just had her sight restored. Which of the following perceptual experiences is she most likely to have?
    a. perceptual set
    b. size constancy
    c. linear perspective
    d. figure-ground

26. An artist manages to portray a face with just a few unconnected lines. Apparently the artist has capitalized on
    a. closure
    b. contiguity
    c. the reversible figure effect
    d. the principle of camouflage

27. The most basic source of stereoscopic vision is
    a. accommodation
    b. retinal disparity
    c. convergence
    d. stroboscopic motion

28. Necker's cube is a good example of
    a. an ambiguous stimulus
    b. an impossible figure
    c. camouflage
    d. a binocular depth cue

29. Skeptics regard the decline effect as evidence that _____ occurred in an ESP test.
    a. replication
    b. cheating
    c. a run of luck
    d. leakage

30. Which of the following is a binocular depth cue?
    a. accommodation
    b. convergence
    c. linear perspective
    d. motion parallax

31. Ambiguous stimuli allow us to hold more than one perceptual
    a. gradient
    b. parallax
    c. constancy
    d. hypothesis

32. Increased perceptual awareness is especially associated with
    a. dishabituation
    b. unconscious transference
    c. high levels of stress
    d. stimulus repetition without variation

33. Joan, failing to see a pedestrian crossing the street because she is too busy using a cell phone, is an example of
    a. inattentional blindness
    b. attentional blindness
    c. perceptual habits
    d. apparent-distance hypothesis

34. Standing eight feet farther away than Jacob who has 20/20 vision, Paul is able to identity the furry animal as a mouse. An optometrist might conclude that Paul has a better-than-average acuity and he has _____ vision.
    a. 20/8
    b. 20/18
    c. 20/12
    d. 20/80

35. Children who are born deaf have a good chance at learning spoken language at an almost normal rate if they receive cochlear implants before they reach the age of
    a. 2
    b. 9
    c. 12
    d. 16

36. Telling wounded soldiers that they are relieved of their duty to reduce anxiety and increase pleasant emotions has _____ their pain perception.
    a. increased
    b. decreased
    c. no effect on
    d. little effect on

37. Chloe screams out loud saying "insects are crawling everywhere!" when none are present, and Hilda, who is partially blind, claims that people are disappearing and appearing in front of her eyes. Chloe is experiencing _____ because she is seeing objects that are not present in her environment, and Hilda is experiencing _____ since her brain in trying to seek meaningful patterns from her sensory input.
    a. hallucinations, "sane hallucinations"
    b. hallucinations, inattentional blindess
    c. illusions, extrasensory perception (ESP)
    d. none of the above

SOLUTIONS

RECITE AND REVIEW

MODULE 5.1

1. nerve
2. data
3. analyze
4. perceptual

5. detectors
6. sensory
7. sensory
8. activated

9. Sensation
10. perception

11. visible
12. wavelength
13. wavelength
14. wavelength
15. narrow
16. rods
17. cones
18. Trichromatic
19. afterimages
20. shape
21. shape

22. nearsightedness
23. accommodation
24. rods
25. cones
26. color
27. rods
28. retina
29. cones
30. cones
31. either-or
32. black

33. or
34. white
35. Total
36. color
37. blindness
38. increase
39. rods
40. cones
41. rods

MODULE 5.2

42. peaks
43. valleys
44. pitch
45. height
46. eardrum

47. hair
48. frequency
49. frequency
50. high
51. low

52. nerve
53. Nerve
54. loud

55. smell
56. taste
57. location

58. bitter
59. coding
60. smell

61. taste

MODULE 5.3

62. skin
63. pressure
64. number
65. reminding
66. reduced

67. pleasant
68. lowering
69. reduce
70. head
71. gravity

72. fluid
73. crista
74. mismatch

75. reduction or decrease

76. gating
77. spinal

78. cord
79. Counterirritation

80. pain

MODULE 5.4

81. patterns
82. model
83. image

84. perceptual
85. constancy
86. constant

87. inborn
88. learned

89. object
90. background
91. organization
92. similarity
93. common

94. grouped
95. appearance
96. complete
97. time
98. hypothesis

99. organization
100. stimuli
101. cube

MODULE 5.5

102. Depth
103. birth
104. crawlers
105. Monocular
106. binocular
107. lens
108. eyes
109. cues

110. flat
111. parallel
112. lines
113. smaller
114. picture
115. finer
116. motion
117. motion

118. one
119. eye
120. larger
121. distance
122. horizon
123. three-dimensional

MODULE 5.6

124. habits
125. size
126. features
127. habits
128. buildings
129. hallucinations

130. Sane
131. blind
132. Inattentional
133. detect
134. size-distance
135. lines

136. values
137. top-down
138. features
139. organize
140. expectancies
141. labels

MODULE 5.7

142. psi
143. telepathy
144. perception
145. Coincidence

146. skeptical
147. psychic
148. luck
149. against

150. repeated
151. deception

PSYCHOLOGY IN ACTION

152. inaccurate
153. focus

154. lower
155. testing

156. attention
157. broaden

CONNECTIONS

MODULE 5.1

1. d
2. f
3. h
4. b

5. i
6. c
7. k
8. a

9. e
10. g
11. j

---

1. c
2. f
3. e

4. i
5. a
6. g

7. b
8. d
9. h

MODULE 5.2

1. e
2. g
3. h
4. a

5. d
6. f
7. c
8. i

9. b
10. j

---

1. b
2. h
3. g

4. d
5. a
6. c

7. f
8. e

MODULE 5.3

1. f
2. a
3. c

4. g
5. b
6. e

7. d

MODULE 5.4

1. c
2. e

3. d
4. a

5. f
6. b

MODULE 5.5

1. e
2. g
3. f

4. c
5. a
6. b

7. h
8. d

---

1. b
2. e

3. c
4. a

5. d

MODULE 5.6

1. a

2. e	4. f	6. c
3. b	5. d	7. g

MODULE 5.7

1. d	3. b	5. e
2. c	4. f	6. a

CHECK YOUR MEMORY

MODULE 5.1

1. T	3. F
2. T	4. T

5. F	11. T	17. T
6. F	12. F	18. F
7. T	13. T	19. F
8. T	14. F	20. T
9. T	15. T	
10. T	16. T	

MODULE 5.2

21. T	24. F	27. T
22. F	25. T	28. T
23. T	26. T	29. T

30. T	32. T	34. T
31. F	33. T	

MODULE 5.3

35. F	38. T	41. F
36. F	39. T	42. T
37. F	40. T	

43. F	45. T	47. F
44. T	46. T	

MODULE 5.4
48. T

49. T	51. F
50. T	52. T

53. F	55. T
54. F	56. F

MODULE 5.5

57. T	62. F	67. T
58. T	63. F	68. F
59. F	64. T	69. T
60. T	65. F	
61. F	66. F	

MODULE 5.6

70. F	74. T	78. T
71. F	75. F	79. F
72. F	76. F	
73. T	77. F	

MODULE 5.7

80. F	84. F	88. T
81. T	85. F	89. F
82. T	86. F	
83. F	87. T	

PSYCHOLOGY IN ACTION

90. T	93. F	96. F
91. F	94. T	
92. F	95. F	

FINAL SURVEY AND REVIEW

MODULE 5.1

1. transduce	5. analysis	9. localization
2. reduction	6. feature	10. area
3. filter	7. Phosphenes	11. Sensation
4. sensory	8. coding	12. perception

13. electromagnetic	17. nanometers	21. retina
14. 400	18. Hue	22. Trichromatic
15. nanometers	19. amplitude	23. afterimages
16. 700	20. photoreceptors	24. cornea

25. accommodation
26. myopia
27. astigmatism
28. motion
29. fovea
30. acuity
31. peripheral

32. peripheral
33. trichromatic
34. pigments
35. opponent-process
36. red or
37. green
38. red-green

39. Ishihara
40. visual pigments
41. rhodopsin

MODULE 5.2

42. compression
43. rarefaction
44. frequency
45. amplitude
46. ossicles
47. Corti

48. auditory
49. nerves
50. base
51. tip
52. stimulation
53. cochlear

54. 120
55. decibels

56. Olfaction
57. gustation
58. lock-and-key
59. sweet

60. salty
61. sour
62. umami
63. molecule

64. smell
65. taste

MODULE 5.3

66. kinesthetic
67. pain
68. receptors
69. warning
70. reminding

71. anxiety
72. unpleasant
73. pleasant
74. attention
75. control

76. vestibular
77. otolith
78. semicircular
79. sensory
80. conflict

81. adaptation
82. attention

83. Gate
84. control

85. Counterirritation
86. pain

MODULE 5.4

87. sensations
88. mental
89. model
90. retinal

91. constancies
92. brightness
93. proportion
94. light

95. native
96. empirical

97. figure
98. ground
99. Gestalt
100. nearness
101. closure

102. Closure
103. Contiguity
104. Camouflage
105. ambiguous
106. Necker's

107. figures

MODULE 5.5

108. three-dimensional
109. visual
110. cliff
111. visual
112. cliff
113. Monocular
114. binocular
115. accommodation

116. convergence
117. pictorial
118. linear
119. perspective
120. interposition
121. gradients
122. parallax
123. monocular

124. horizon
125. apparent
126. distance
127. cues
128. Stereoscopic vision

MODULE 5.6

129. perceptual
130. habits
131. Ames
132. inverted
133. Müller-Lyer
134. reality
135. visual
136. Sane

137. Inattentional
138. invariance
139. end-points
140. motives
141. processing
142. Bottom-up
143. top-down
144. perceptual

145. sets
146. perceptual
147. set
148. Perceptual

MODULE 5.7

149. Parapsychology
150. precognition
151. extrasensory

152. reinterpretation
153. skeptical
154. psychic

155. statistically
156. replicated
157. Stage

PSYCHOLOGY IN ACTION

158. reconstruction
159. weapon

160. stress
161. dishabituation

162. perceptual
163. habits

MASTERY TEST

1. B, (p. 185)
2. D, (p. 173)
3. C, (p. 183)
4. D, (p. 172)
5. C, (p. 175)
6. A, (p. 168)
7. D, (p. 170)
8. B, (p. 187)
9. A, (p. 177-178)
10. C, (p. 168)
11. D, (p. 177)
12. A, (p. 169)

13. C, (p. 171)
14. C, (p. 169)
15. A, (p. 171)
16. D, (p. 201)
17. A, (p. 211)
18. B, (p. 200)
19. B, (p. 189-190)
20. D, (p. 197)
21. A, (p. 203)
22. C, (p. 194)
23. C, (p. 192)
24. D, (p. 194)

25. D, (p. 190)
26. A, (p. 192)
27. B, (p. 195)
28. A, (p. 192)
29. C, (p. 208)
30. B, (p. 194)
31. D, (p. 192)
32. A, (p. 213)
33. A, (p. 203)
34. C, (p. 171)
35. A, (p. 179)
36. B, (p. 184)
37. A, (p. 202)

STATES OF CONSCIOUSNESS

CHAPTER OVERVIEW

Consciousness consists of everything you are aware of at a given instant. Altered states of consciousness (ASCs) differ significantly from normal waking consciousness. Many conditions produce ASCs, which frequently have culturally defined meanings.

Sleep is an innate biological rhythm characterized by changes in consciousness and brain activity. People who deprive themselves of sleep may experience sleep-deprivation psychosis. Hypersomnia is a common problem that adolescents have due to lack of sleep. Brain-wave patterns and sleep behaviors define four stages of sleep. The two most basic forms of sleep are rapid eye movement (REM) sleep and nonrapid eye movement (NREM) sleep. Dreams and nightmares occur primarily in REM sleep. Sleepwalking, sleeptalking, and night terrors are NREM events. Insomnia and other sleep disturbances are common but generally treatable. REM rebound occurs when one is deprived of REM sleep the night before. Dreaming is emotionally restorative, and it may help form adaptive memories. The psychodynamic view portrays dreams as a form of wish fulfillment; the activation-synthesis hypothesis says that dreaming is a physiological process with little meaning.

Hypnosis is characterized by narrowed attention and increased openness to suggestion. People vary in hypnotic susceptibility. Most hypnotic phenomena are related to the basic suggestion effect. Hypnosis can relieve pain and it has other useful effects, but it is not magic. Stage hypnotists simulate hypnosis in order to entertain. Similar to hypnotic suggestion, one might mentally "move" an object by using autosuggestion.

Meditation can be used to alter consciousness, promote relaxation, and reduce stress. Two types of meditations are concentrative and receptive. The state of mindfulness (nonjudgmental awareness of current experiences) can be achieved through receptive meditation. Three benefits of meditation are its ability to interrupt anxious thoughts, to elicit the relaxation response, and to improve physical health. Sensory deprivation refers to any major reduction in external stimulation. Sensory deprivation also produces deep relaxation and a variety of perceptual effects. It can be used to help people enhance creative thinking and to change bad habits.

Psychoactive drugs are substances that alter consciousness by blocking or mimicking neurotransmitters' activities in the brain. Most can be placed on a scale ranging from stimulation to depression, although some drugs are better classified as hallucinogens. The potential for abuse is high for drugs that lead to physical dependence, but psychological dependence can also be a serious problem. Drug abuse is often a symptom, rather than a cause, of personal maladjustment. It is supported by the immediate pleasure but delayed consequences associated with many psychoactive drugs and by cultural values that encourage drug abuse.

Various strategies, ranging from literal to highly symbolic, can be used to reveal the meanings of dreams. Dreaming—especially lucid dreaming—can be a source of creativity, and it may be used for problem solving and personal growth.

LEARNING OBJECTIVES

To demonstrate mastery of this chapter, you should be able to:

1. Define "consciousness" and explain what waking consciousness is.

2. Define and describe "altered state of consciousness." Include a description of the meaning and uses of altered states of consciousness in other cultures.

3. Describe the limitations of sleep learning.

4. Define the term"biological rhythm" and explain its relationship to sleep.

5. Define and describe the term "microsleep."

6. Describe the general effects of two or three days of sleep deprivation. Name and describe the condition that occurs when a person is deprived of sleep for a longer period of time. Discuss teenage sleep deprivation.

7. Explain what circadian rhythms are and what bodily functions are related to them.

8. State how long the average sleep-waking cycle is. Explain how we tie our sleep rhythms to a 24-hour day.

9. Describe the normal range of sleep needs. Describe how the aging process affects sleep.

10. Explain how and why shift work and jet lag may adversely affect a person. Explain how the direction of travel (or of rotating shifts) affects rhythms and how to minimize the effects of shifting one's rhythms.

11. Describe how the brain's systems and chemistry promote sleep.

12. Briefly describe each of the four stages of sleep. Include a description of the brain waves associated with each and those associated with wakefulness.

13. Describe the cyclical nature of the sleep stages.

14. Name and differentiate the two basic states of sleep. Explain how the relative amounts of each of these two sleep states can be influenced by events of the day.

15. State the total of REM a person experiences per night on average. State how long dreams usually last at various times during the sleep cycle.

16. List the physiological changes that occur during REM sleep, including a description of REM behavior disorder.

17. List and briefly describe the 12 sleep disorders that are found in the DSM-IV.

18. Define "insomnia." Describe the effects of nonprescription and prescription drugs on insomnia.

19. List and describe the characteristics and treatment of the three types of insomnia.

20. List and briefly describe six behavioral remedies that can be used to combat insomnia.

21. Characterize the following major sleep disturbances of NREM sleep: a. somnambulism b. sleeptalking c. night terrors (include a differentiation between night terrors and nightmares) d. sleep apnea (include a description of SIDS)

22. Describe William Dement's studies and his findings, including the concept of "REM rebound."

23. Describe the probable value of REM sleep.

24. Explain Calvin Hall's view of dreams.

25. Explain how Freud viewed dreams and present the evidence against his view.

26. Describe the activation-synthesis hypothesis concerning dreaming.

27. Give the general definition of hypnosis and then describe how it is that the general definition is not accepted by all psychologists.

28. Trace the history of hypnosis from Mesmer through its use today.

29. State the proportion of people who can be hypnotized.

30. Explain how a person's hypnotic susceptibility can be determined. Include a brief description of the dimensions of the Stanford Hypnotic Susceptibility Scale.

31. List the four common factors in all hypnotic techniques.

The following objective is related to material in the "Discovering Psychology" section of the text.

32. Explain why all hypnosis may really be self-hypnosis and explain how this autosuggestion (self-hypnosis) works.

33. Explain what the basic suggestion effect is and describe how this view of hypnosis differs from that portrayed in movies.

34. Explain how hypnosis can affect: a. strength b. memory c. amnesia d. pain relief e. age regression f. sensory changes

35. Using the five characteristics of the stage setting outlined in the chapter, explain how a stage hypnotist gets people to perform the way they do in front of an audience.

36. Name and describe the two major forms of meditation.

37. Describe the relaxation response.

38. Describe what is known about the effects of meditation.

39. Explain what sensory deprivation is. Include a discussion of the positive and negative effects of this procedure.

40. Define the term "psychoactive drug."

41. Differentiate physical dependence from psychological dependence.

42. Describe the following frequently abused drugs in terms of their effects, possible medical uses, side effects or long term symptoms, organic damage potential, and potential for physical and/or psychological dependence: a. amphetamines (include the term "amphetamine psychosis") b. cocaine (include the three signs of abuse) c. MDMA d. caffeine (include the term "caffeinism") e. nicotine f. barbiturates g. GHB h. tranquilizers (include the concept of drug interaction) i. alcohol (include the concept of binge drinking) j. hallucinogens (include marijuana).

43. Compare the efficacy of quitting smoking "cold turkey" versus cutting down or smoking low-tar cigarettes.

44. List and explain the three phases in the development of a drinking problem.

45. Generally describe the treatment process for alcoholism. Name the form of therapy that has probably been the most successful.

46. Explain why drug abuse is such a common problem.

47. List and describe the four processes identified by Freud that disguise the hidden meaning of dreams.

48. Contrast Hall's and Cartwright's views of dream interpretation.

49. List the eight steps for remembering dreams.

50. Explain how Perls viewed dreams and how he suggested that people interpret them.

51. Describe how one could use dreams to aid in problem solving. Include a description of lucid dreams and how they have been used in the problem solving process.

RECITE AND REVIEW

MODULE 6.1

Survey Question: What is an altered state of consciousness? Page 218

States of [1] _____ that differ from normal, alert, [2] _____ consciousness are called altered states of consciousness (ASCs).

ASCs involve distinct shifts in the quality and [3] _____ of mental activity.

Altered states are especially associated with [4] _____ and [5] _____ , hypnosis, meditation, [6] _____ deprivation, and psychoactive drugs.

Cultural conditioning greatly affects what altered states a person recognizes, seeks, considers

[7] _____ , and attains.

Survey Question: What are the effects of sleep loss or changes in sleep patterns? Pages 219-222

Sleep is an innate biological [8] _____ essential for [9] _____ .

Higher animals and people deprived of sleep experience [10] _____ microsleeps.

Moderate sleep loss mainly affects alertness and self-motivated performance on [11] _____ or boring tasks.

Extended sleep [12] _____ can (somewhat rarely) produce a [13] _____ sleep-deprivation psychosis, marked by confusion, delusions, and possibly hallucinations.

[14] _____ change during puberty increases adolescents' need for [15] _____ , which many lack since they tend to stay up late and get up early for school. This pattern causes them to experience hypersomnia (excessive daytime [16] _____).

The "storm and stress" that adolescents experience may, in part, be caused by [17] _____ of sleep.

Circadian [18] _____ within the body are closely tied to sleep, activity levels, and energy cycles.

Sleep patterns show some flexibility, but seven to eight hours remains average. The unscheduled human sleep-waking cycle averages [19] _____ hours and [20] _____ minutes, but cycles of [21] _____ and [22] _____ tailor it to 24-hour days.

The amount of daily sleep [23] _____ steadily from birth to old age and switches from multiple sleep-wake cycles to once-a-day sleep periods.

Adapting to [24] _____ or [25] _____ sleep cycles is difficult and inefficient for most people.

Time zone travel and [26] _____ work can cause jet lag, a serious disruption of [27] _____ and bodily rhythms.

If you are flying east, it is best to [28] _____ early in the day. If you are flying west, it is better to [29] _____ late in the day. If you anticipate a major change in [30] _____ rhythms, it helps to preadapt to the new [31] _____ .

Survey Question: Are there different stages of sleep? Pages 222-224

Sleepiness is associated with the accumulation of a sleep hormone in the [32] _____ and spinal cord.

Sleep depends on which of [33] _____ opposed sleep and waking systems in the [34] _____ is dominant at any given moment.

Sleep occurs in [35] _____ stages defined by changes in behavior and brain [36] _____ recorded with an electroencephalograph (EEG).

Stage 1, [37] _____ sleep, has small, irregular brain waves. In stage 2, [38] _____ spindles appear. [39] _____ waves appear in stage 3. Stage 4, or deep sleep, is marked by almost pure delta waves.

Sleepers [40] _____ between stages 1 and 4 (passing through stages 2 and 3) several times each night.

There are two basic sleep states, rapid eye [41] _____ (REM) sleep and non-REM (NREM) sleep. REM sleep is much more strongly associated with [42] _____ than non-REM sleep.

[43] _____ and REMs occur mainly during stage 1 sleep but usually not during the first stage 1 period.

Dreaming is accompanied by sexual and [44] _____ arousal but relaxation of the skeletal [45] _____ . People who move about violently while asleep may suffer from [46] _____ behavior disorder.

A day of [47] _____ exertion generally leads to an increase in NREM sleep, which allows our body to recover from bodily fatigue. A day of [48] _____ would lead to an increase in REM sleep.

MODULE 6.2

Survey Question: What are the cause of sleep disorders and unusual sleep events? Pages 226-229

Insomnia, which is difficulty in getting to sleep or staying asleep, may be [49] _____ or chronic.

When insomnia is treated with drugs, sleep quality is often [50] _____ , and drug-dependency [51] _____ may develop.

The amino acid tryptophan, found in bread, pasta, and other foods, helps promote [52] _____ .

Behavioral approaches to managing insomnia such as relaxation, sleep restriction, [53] _____ control, and paradoxical [54] _____ are quite effective.

[55] _____ (somnambulism) and sleeptalking occur during NREM sleep in stages 3 and 4.

Night terrors occur in [56] _____ sleep, whereas nightmares occur in [57] _____ sleep.

Nightmares can be eliminated by the method called imagery [58] _____ .

During sleep apnea, people repeatedly stop [59] _____ . Apnea is suspected as one cause of [60] _____ infant death syndrome (SIDS).

The first [61] _____ months are critical for babies who are at risk for SIDS. Other factors include the baby being a [62] _____ , breathing through an open [63] _____ , having a mother who is a [64] _____ , and having a crib that contains soft objects such as a pillow and quilts.

The phrase "[65] _____ to sleep" refers to the safest position for most babies: their [66] _____ .

Survey Question: Do dreams have meaning? Pages 229-230

People will experience REM [67] _____ if they are deprived of REM sleep the night before.

People deprived of REM sleep showed an urgent need to [68] _____ and mental disturbances the next day. However, total sleep loss seems to be more important than loss of a single sleep [69] _____ .

One of the more important functions of REM sleep appears to be the processing of adaptive [70] _____ .

Calvin Hall found that most dream content is about [71] _____ settings, people, and actions.

Dreams more often involve negative [72] _____ than positive [73] _____ .

The Freudian, or psychodynamic, view is that dreams express unconscious [74] _____ , frequently hidden by dream symbols.

Allan Hobson and Robert McCarley's [75] _____ -synthesis model portrays dreaming as a physiological process. The brain, they say, creates dreams to explain [76] _____ and motor messages that occur during REM sleep.

MODULE 6.3

Survey Questions: How is hypnosis done and what are its limitations? Pages 232-234

Hypnosis is an altered state characterized by narrowed attention and [77] _____ suggestibility.

In the 1700s, Franz Mesmer (whose name is the basis for the term *mesmerize*) practiced "[78] _____ magnetism," which was actually a demonstration of the power of [79] _____ .

The term [80] _____ was first used by James Braid, an English doctor.

People vary in hypnotic susceptibility; [81] _____ out of 10 can be hypnotized, as revealed by scores on the Stanford Hypnotic Susceptibility [82] _____ .

The core of hypnosis is the [83] _____ suggestion effect—a tendency to carry out suggested actions as if they were involuntary. However, a hypnotized person will not perform behaviors that he or she deems to be [84] _____ or repulsive.

Mentally moving an object back and forth, such as a ring that is dangling from a string you are holding, is the result of [85] _____ (your own suggestive power made your hand move in small increments).

Hypnosis appears capable of producing relaxation, controlling [86] _____ , and altering perceptions.

Stage hypnotism takes advantage of typical stage behavior, [87] _____ suggestibility, responsive subjects, disinhibition, and [88] _____ to simulate hypnosis.

Survey Questions: What is meditation? Does it have any benefits? Pages 235-237

Meditation refers to mental exercises that are used to alter [89] _____ .

In receptive meditation, attention is [90] _____ to include an awareness of one's entire moment-by-moment experience, which is more [91] _____ to achieve than the concentrative meditation where attention is focused on a [92] _____ object or thought.

Three major benefits of meditation are its ability to interrupt anxious thoughts, elicit the relaxation response (the pattern of changes that occur in the body at times of deep [93] _____), and improve physical health.

Sensory deprivation takes place when there is a major reduction in the amount or variety of sensory [94] _____ available to a person.

Prolonged sensory deprivation is stressful and disruptive, leading to [95] _____ distortions.

Brief or mild sensory deprivation can enhance sensory sensitivity and induce deep [96] _____ .

Sensory deprivation also appears to aid the breaking of long-standing [97] _____ and promotes creative thinking. This effect is the basis for Restricted Environmental Stimulation Therapy (REST).

People who use receptive meditation seek to achieve the [98] _____ state involving being open-minded, nonjudgmental, and [99] _____ of their current experience.

[100] _____ has been shown to [101] _____ levels of stress and increase perceived well-being among cancer patients.

MODULE 6.4

Survey Question: What are the effects of the more commonly used psychoactive drugs? Pages 238-251

A psychoactive drug is a substance that affects the brain in ways that [102] _____ consciousness.

Drugs alter the activities in the brain by [103] _____ and blocking neurotransmitters ([104] _____ that carry messages between neurons) to produce feelings of pleasure.

Most psychoactive drugs can be placed on a scale ranging from stimulation to [105] _____ .

Some, however, are best described as hallucinogens (drugs that alter [106] _____ impressions).

Drugs may cause a physical dependence ([107] _____) or a psychological dependence or both. The physically addicting drugs are alcohol, amphetamines, barbiturates, cocaine, codeine, GHB, heroin, methadone, morphine, tobacco, and tranquilizers. All psychoactive drugs can lead to [108] _____ dependence.

Prolonged use of a drug can lead to drug tolerance (a [109] _____ response to a drug) whereby the abuser must [110] _____ the amount of a drug to receive the same desired effect.

Stimulant drugs are readily abused because of the period of [111] _____ that often follows stimulation. The greatest risks are associated with amphetamines, cocaine, MDMA, and nicotine, but even [112] _____ can be a problem.

Amphetamines, known as "bennies," "dex," "go," and "[113] _____ ," are synthetic stimulants that produce a rapid drug [114] _____ . Abusers typically go on binges that last for several days until they "[115] _____ ," suffering from [116] _____ , confusion, depression, uncontrolled irritability, and aggression.

Methamphetamine, known as "[117] _____ ," "speed," "meth," or "crystal," is cheaply produced in labs and can be snorted, [118] _____ , or eaten.

Repeated use of amphetamine can cause brain damage and amphetamine [119] _____ .

Amphetamine psychosis can cause the abuser to act on their delusions and risk [120] _____ -injury or injury to [121] _____ .

Signs of cocaine abuse are: compulsive use, loss of [122] _____ , and a disregard for [123] _____ .

MDMA or "[124] _____ ," which is similar to amphetamine, has been linked with numerous deaths and with mental impairment.

Users of MDMA are likely to risk an [125] _____ in body temperature, liver damage, and unsafe sex. In addition, [126] _____ brain cells may be damaged, which could increase levels of anxiety or depression.

Caffeine can be found in coffee, [127] _____ , soft drinks, and chocolate. It stimulates the brain by [128] _____ chemicals that inhibit nerve activities.

[129] _____ includes the added risk of lung cancer, heart disease, and other health problems.

The smoking of cigarettes releases carcinogens ([130] _____ -causing substances) in the air, which expose people to [131] _____ smoke and places them at risk for developing lung cancer.

Barbiturates are [132] _____ drugs whose overdose level is close to the intoxication dosage, making them dangerous drugs. Common street names for barbiturates are "downers," "[133] _____ heavens," "[134] _____ hearts," "goofballs," "[135] _____ ladies," and "rainbows." Mixing barbiturates and alcohol may result in a fatal [136] _____ interaction (in which the joint effect of two drugs exceeds the effects of adding one drug's effects to the other's)

The depressant drug [137] _____ (gamma-hydroxybuyrate) can cause coma, breathing failure, and death in relatively low doses. GHB is commonly called "goop," "scoop," "max," or "[138] _____ Home Boy."

Benzodiazepine tranquilizers, such as [139] _____ , are used to lower anxiety. When abused, they have a strong [140] _____ potential.

[141] _____ , a tranquilizer, also known as "roofies" and the "[142] _____ -rape drug," is odorless and tasteless and is sometimes used to spike drinks.

Every year in the United States, 75,000 people die of [143] _____ -related deaths. Binge drinking (having [144] _____ or more drinks in a short time) is responsible for 14,000 college student deaths a year.

Alcohol is the most heavily abused drug in common use today. The development of a drinking problem is usually marked by an [145] _____ phase of increasing consumption, a crucial phase, in which a [146] _____ drink can set off a chain reaction, and a chronic phase, in which a person lives to drink and drinks to live.

People who undergo detoxification (the [147] _____ of poison) often experience unpleasant symptoms of drug [148] _____ .

Marijuana ("pot," "herb," and "[149] _____ ") is a hallucinogen that is subjected to an [150] _____ pattern similar to alcohol. Studies have linked chronic marijuana use with memory impairment, lung cancer, reproductive problems, immune system disorders, and other health problems.

[151] _____ , the main active chemical in marijuana, accumulates in the cerebral cortex and reproductive organs.

Potential problems caused by frequent marijuana use are short-term [152] _____ loss and a decline in learning, [153] _____ , and thinking abilities. In addition, people who smoke [154] _____ or more joints a week tend to score four points lower on IQ tests.

Drug abuse is related to personal and social maladjustment, attempts to cope, and the [155] _____ reinforcing qualities of psychoactive drugs.

PSYCHOLOGY IN ACTION

Survey Question: How are dreams used to promote personal understanding? Pages 253-255

Freud held that the meaning of dreams is [156] _____ by four dream [157] _____ he called condensation, displacement, symbolization, and secondary elaboration.

Calvin Hall emphasizes the setting, cast, [158] _____ , and emotions of a dream.

Rosalind Cartwright's view of dreams as feeling statements and Fritz Perls's technique of [159] _____ for dream elements are also helpful.

Dreams may be used for [160] _____ problem solving, especially when dream control is achieved through lucid dreaming (a dream in which the dreamer feels capable of normal thought and action).

CONNECTIONS

MODULE 6.1

1. _____ Randy Gardner
2. _____ short sleep cycles
3. _____ alpha waves
4. _____ long sleepers
5. _____ hypnic jerk
6. _____ sleep spindles
7. _____ REM sleep
8. _____ beta waves
9. _____ circadian rhythms
10. _____ severe sleep loss

a. over nine hours
b. infancy
c. reflex muscle contraction
d. awake, alert
e. relaxed
f. sleep deprivation
g. sexual arousal
h. biological clocks
i. sleep-deprivation psychosis
j. stage 2 of sleep

MODULE 6.2

1. _____ hypersomnia
2. _____ narcolepsy
3. _____ apnea
4. _____ stimulus control
5. _____ SIDS
6. _____ tryptophan
7. _____ dream symbols
8. _____ sleep drunkenness
9. _____ REM behavior disorder
10. _____ sleepwalking

a. interrupted breathing
b. slow awakening
c. excessive sleepiness
d. violent actions
e. sudden daytime REM sleep
f. fatal to infants
g. sleep-inducing foods
h. unconscious meanings
i. occurs in NREM
j. remedy for insommia

MODULE 6.3

1. _____ mesmerize
2. _____ pain relief
3. _____ REST
4. _____ mantra
5. _____ autosuggestion

a. flotation tank
b. hypnotize
c. self-hypnosis
d. hypnosis effect
e. meditation word

MODULE 6.4

1. _____ anhedonia
2. _____ drug tolerance
3. _____ amphetamine
4. _____ nicotine
5. _____ carcinogen
6. _____ Sigmund Freud
7. _____ MDMA
8. _____ barbiturate
9. _____ AA
10. _____ alcohol treatment
11. _____ lucid dream
12. _____ THC

a. dangerous stimulant
b. cancer agent
c. addiction
d. sedative
e. hallucinogen
f. detoxification
g. loss of pleasure
h. stimulant
i. self-help group
j. insecticide
k. awake during REM
l. dream processes

CHECK YOUR MEMORY

MODULE 6.1

Survey Question: What is an altered state of consciousness? Page 198

1. The quality and pattern of mental activity change during an ASC.

   TRUE or FALSE

2. All people experience at least some ASCs.

   TRUE or FALSE

3. Both sensory overload and monotonous stimulation can produce ASCs.

   TRUE or FALSE

4. Almost every known religion has accepted some ASCs as desirable.

   TRUE or FALSE

Survey Question: What are the effects of sleep loss or changes in sleep patterns? Pages 219-222

5. Through sleep learning it is possible to master a foreign language.
    TRUE or FALSE

6. A total inability to sleep results in death.
    TRUE or FALSE

7. Even after extended sleep loss, most symptoms are removed by a single night's sleep.
    TRUE or FALSE

8. Hallucinations and delusions are the most common reaction to extended sleep deprivation.
    TRUE or FALSE

9. Physical changes during puberty increase adolescents' need for sleep.
    TRUE or FALSE

10. Without scheduled light and dark periods, human sleep rhythms would drift into unusual patterns.
    TRUE or FALSE

11. The average human sleep-wake cycle lasts 23 hours and 10 minutes.
    TRUE or FALSE

12. Short sleepers are defined as those who average less than five hours of sleep per night.
    TRUE or FALSE

13. Shortened sleep cycles, such as three hours of sleep to six hours awake, are more efficient than sleeping once a day.
    TRUE or FALSE

Survey Question: Are there different stages of sleep? Pages 222-224

14. Sleep is promoted by a chemical that accumulates in the bloodstream.
    TRUE or FALSE

15. Body temperature drops as a person falls asleep.
    TRUE or FALSE

16. A hypnic jerk is a sign of serious problems.
    TRUE or FALSE

17. Delta waves typically first appear in stage 2 sleep.
    TRUE or FALSE

18. About 45 percent of awakenings during REM periods produce reports of dreams.
    TRUE or FALSE

19. REM sleep occurs mainly in stages 3 and 4.
    TRUE or FALSE

20. REM sleep increases when a person is subjected to daytime stress.
    TRUE or FALSE

21. The average dream only lasts three to four minutes.
    TRUE or FALSE

22. Most people change positions in bed during REM sleep.
    TRUE or FALSE

23. REM behavior disorder causes people to briefly fall asleep and become paralyzed during the day.
    TRUE or FALSE

MODULE 6.2

Survey Question: What are the cause of sleep disorders and unusual sleep events? Pages 226-229

24. Bread, pasta, pretzels, cookies, and cereals all contain melatonin.
    TRUE or FALSE

25. Caffeine, alcohol, and tobacco can all contribute to insomnia.
    TRUE or FALSE

26. The two most effective behavioral treatments for insomnia are sleep restriction and stimulus control.
    TRUE or FALSE

27. Sleepwalking occurs during NREM periods, sleeptalking during REM periods.
    TRUE or FALSE

28. People who have NREM night terrors usually can remember very little afterward.
    TRUE or FALSE

29. Imagery rehearsal is an effective way to treat recurrent nightmares.
    TRUE or FALSE

30. REM sleep appears to help the brain process memories formed during the day.
    TRUE or FALSE

31. People who take barbiturate sleeping pills may develop drug-dependency insomnia.
    TRUE or FALSE

32. Newborn babies spend eight or nine hours a day in REM sleep.
    TRUE or FALSE

33. Sleep apnea does not increase the risk of having a heart attack. This is only a myth.
    TRUE or FALSE

Survey Question: Do dreams have meaning? Pages 229-230

34. REM rebound refers to people having more REM sleep when they do not get enough REM sleep the night before.
TRUE or FALSE

35. People report feeling more negative emotions when they are awakened during REM sleep.
TRUE or FALSE

36. The favorite dream setting is outdoors.
TRUE or FALSE

37. Pleasant emotions are more common in dreams than unpleasant emotions.
TRUE or FALSE

38. According to Freud, dreams represent thoughts and wishes expressed as images.
TRUE or FALSE

39. The activation-synthesis hypothesis emphasizes the unconscious meanings of dream symbols.
TRUE or FALSE

40. The activation-synthesis hypothesis does believe that dreams are created from memories or past experiences.
TRUE or FALSE

MODULE 6.3

Survey Questions: How is hypnosis done and what are its limitations? Pages 232-234

41. The Greek word *hypnos* means "magnetism."
TRUE or FALSE

42. Only about 4 people out of 10 can be hypnotized.
TRUE or FALSE

43. The "finger-lock" is an example of animal magnetism.
TRUE or FALSE

44. Physical strength cannot be increased with hypnosis.
TRUE or FALSE

45. Hypnosis is better at changing subjective experiences than behaviors.
TRUE or FALSE

46. Stage hypnotists look for responsive volunteers who will cooperate and not spoil the show.
TRUE or FALSE

47. Autosuggestion is used by people who believe they have psychic abilities.
    TRUE or FALSE

48. Hypnosis is not a valuable tool since its main purpose is entertainment.
    TRUE or FALSE

Survey Questions: What is meditation? Does it have any benefits? Pages 235-237

49. Receptive meditation is typically harder to do than concentrative meditation.
    TRUE or FALSE

50. A mantra is used as a focus for attention during receptive meditation.
    TRUE or FALSE

51. Herbert Benson states that the physical benefits of meditation are based on evoking the body's relaxation response.
    TRUE or FALSE

52. The harder you try to meditate, the more likely you are to succeed.
    TRUE or FALSE

53. People who use receptive meditation are trying to achieve the state of mindfulness.
    TRUE or FALSE

54. Similar to hypnosis, mindfulness does not have any health benefits.
    TRUE or FALSE

55. Sensory deprivation is almost always unpleasant, and it usually causes distorted perceptions.
    TRUE or FALSE

56. Prolonged sensory deprivation produces deep relaxation.
    TRUE or FALSE

57. REST is a form of brainwashing used during the Vietnam War.
    TRUE or FALSE

MODULE 6.4

Survey Question: What are the effects of the more commonly used psychoactive drugs? Pages 238-251

58. Abuse of any psychoactive drug can produce physical dependence.
    TRUE or FALSE

59. People who believe they have used too many drugs and feel they need to reduce their drug use are in need of professional help.
    TRUE or FALSE

60. Amphetamines are used to treat narcolepsy and hyperactivity.
    TRUE or FALSE

61. Amphetamine is more rapidly metabolized by the body than cocaine.
    TRUE or FALSE

62. Ecstasy and amphetamine reduce the production of neurotransmitters in the brain.
    TRUE or FALSE

63. Cocaine ("coke" or "snow") produces feelings of alertness, euphoria, well-being, powerfulness, boundless energy, and pleasure.
    TRUE or FALSE

64. MDMA is chemically similar to amphetamine.
    TRUE or FALSE

65. MDMA is widely used by college students (1 in 20 students have tried Ecstasy).
    TRUE or FALSE

66. Disregarding consequences is a sign of cocaine abuse.
    TRUE or FALSE

67. Caffeine can increase the risk of miscarriage during pregnancy.
    TRUE or FALSE

68. Unlike other drugs, caffeine does not cause dependency or side effects.
    TRUE or FALSE

69. Twenty-five cigarettes could be fatal for a nonsmoker.
    TRUE or FALSE

70. Regular use of nicotine leads to drug tolerance and often to physical addiction.
    TRUE or FALSE

71. Every cigarette reduces a smoker's life expectancy by seven minutes.
    TRUE or FALSE

72. Secondary smoke only causes harm to the person who smokes, not those around them.
    TRUE or FALSE

73. In order to stop smoking, tapering off is generally more successful than quitting abruptly.
    TRUE or FALSE

74. One of the most effective ways to stop smoking is to schedule the number of cigarettes smoked each day.
    TRUE or FALSE

75. There have been no known deaths caused by barbiturate overdoses.
    TRUE or FALSE

76. GHB, a hallucinogen, can be easily purchased over the Internet.
    TRUE or FALSE

77. Drinking alone is a serious sign of alcohol abuse.
    TRUE or FALSE

78. To pace alcohol intake, you should limit drinking primarily to the first hour of a social event or party.
    TRUE or FALSE

79. Over 80 percent of fraternity and sorority members in the United States have engaged in binge drinking.
    TRUE or FALSE

80. Alcoholics Anonymous (AA) and Secular Organizations for Sobriety are organizations that seek to make money from drug abusers.
    TRUE or FALSE

81. Hallucinogens generally affect brain transmitter systems.
    TRUE or FALSE

82. THC receptors are found in large numbers in the cerebellum of the brain.
    TRUE or FALSE

83. People who smoke marijuana on a regular basis report that they are satisfied with their lives, earn more money, and are healthier than nonusers at the age of 29.
    TRUE or FALSE

84. Pregnant mothers who use marijuana may increase the risk that their babies will have trouble succeeding in goal-oriented tasks.
    TRUE or FALSE

85. Drug abuse is frequently part of a general pattern of personal maladjustment.
    TRUE or FALSE

86. The negative consequences of drug use typically follow long after the drug has been taken.
    TRUE or FALSE

PSYCHOLOGY IN ACTION

Survey Question: How are dreams used to promote personal understanding? Pages 253-255

87. Displacement refers to representing two or more people with a single dream image.
    TRUE or FALSE

88. Secondary elaboration is the tendency to make a dream more logical when remembering it.
    TRUE or FALSE

89. According to Calvin Hall, the overall emotional tone of a dream is the key to its meaning.
    TRUE or FALSE

90. Alcohol decreases REM sleep.
    TRUE or FALSE

91. It is basically impossible to solve daytime problems in dreams.
    TRUE or FALSE

92. Lucid dreams either occur or they don't; there is no way to increase their frequency.
    TRUE or FALSE

FINAL SURVEY AND REVIEW

MODULE 6.1

Survey Question: What is an altered state of consciousness? Page 218

States of awareness that differ from normal, alert, waking [1] _____ are called altered states of

[2] _____ (ASCs).

ASCs involve distinct shifts in the quality and pattern of [3] _____ [4] _____ .

Altered states are especially associated with sleep and dreaming, [5] _____ , meditation, sensory

[6] _____ , and psychoactive drugs.

[7] _____ conditioning greatly affects what altered states a person recognizes, seeks, considers

normal, and attains.

Survey Question: What are the effects of sleep loss or changes in sleep patterns? Pages 219-222

Sleep is an [8] _____ [9] _____ rhythm essential for survival.

Higher animals and people deprived of sleep experience involuntary [10] _____ (a brief shift to

sleep patterns in the brain).

Moderate sleep loss mainly affects [11] _____ and self-motivated performance on routine

or boring tasks.

Extended sleep loss can (somewhat rarely) produce a temporary sleep-deprivation [12] _____ ,

marked by confusion, [13] _____ , and possibly hallucinations.

[14] _____ change during puberty increases adolescents' need for sleep, which many lack

since they tend to stay up late and get up early for school. This pattern causes them to experience

[15] _____ (excessive daytime sleepiness).

The "storm and stress" that adolescents experience may, in part, be caused by [16] _____ of sleep.

[17] _____ rhythms within the body are closely tied to sleep, activity levels, and energy cycles. Sleep patterns show some flexibility, but seven to eight hours remains average. The unscheduled human [18] _____ [19] _____ averages 24 hours and 10 minutes, but cycles of light and dark tailor it to 24-hour days.

The amount of daily sleep decreases steadily from birth to [20] _____ [21] _____ and switches from [22] _____ sleep-wake cycles to once-a-day sleep periods.

Adapting to shorter or longer [23] _____ [24] _____ is difficult and inefficient for most people.

Time zone travel and shift work can cause [25] _____ [26] _____ , a serious disruption of sleep and [27] _____ [28] _____ .

If you are flying east, it is best to travel [29] _____ in the day. If you are flying west, it is better to travel [30] _____ in the day. If you anticipate a major change in sleep rhythms, it helps to [31] _____ to the new schedule.

Survey Question: Are there different stages of sleep? Pages 222-224

Sleepiness is associated with the accumulation of a sleep [32] _____ in the brain and [33] _____ [34] _____ .

Sleep depends on which of two [35] _____ sleep and waking [36] _____ in the brain is dominant at any given moment.

Sleep occurs in four stages defined by changes in behavior and brain waves recorded with an [37] _____ (EEG).

Stage 1, light sleep, has small, irregular brain waves. In stage 2, sleep [38] _____ appear. Delta waves appear in stage 3. Stage 4, or deep sleep, is marked by almost pure [39] _____ [40] _____ .

Sleepers alternate between stages [41] _____ and [42] _____ (passing through stages [43] _____ and [44] _____) several times each night.

There are two basic sleep states, [45] _____ [46] _____ movement (REM) sleep and non-REM (NREM) sleep.

[47] _____ sleep is much more strongly associated with dreaming than [48] _____ sleep.

Dreams and REMs occur mainly during [49] _____ [50] _____ sleep but usually not during the first [51] _____ [52] _____ period.

Dreaming is accompanied by sexual and emotional [53] _____ but [54] _____ of the skeletal muscles. People who move about violently while asleep may suffer from REM behavior [55] _____ .

A day of physical exertion generally leads to an increase in [56] _____ sleep, which allows our body to recover from bodily fatigue. A day of stress would lead to an increase in [57] _____ sleep.

MODULE 6.2

Survey Question: What are the cause of sleep disorders and unusual sleep events? Pages 226-229

Insomnia, which is difficulty in getting to sleep or staying asleep, may be temporary or [58] _____ .

When insomnia is treated with drugs, sleep quality is often lowered, and drug- [59] _____ insomnia may develop.

The amino acid [60] _____ , found in bread, pasta, and other foods, helps promote sleep.

Behavioral approaches to managing insomnia such as relaxation, sleep [61] _____ , stimulus control, and [62] _____ intention are quite effective.

Sleepwalking ([63] _____) and sleeptalking occur during [64] _____ sleep in stages 3 and 4.

Night terrors occur in [65] _____ sleep, whereas nightmares occur in [66] _____ sleep.

Nightmares can be eliminated by the method called [67] _____ [68] _____ .

During sleep [69] _____ , people repeatedly stop breathing. [70] _____ is suspected as one cause of sudden [71] _____ [72] _____ syndrome.

The first [73] _____ months are critical for babies who are at risk for SIDS. Other factors include the baby being a [74] _____ , breathing through an open [75] _____ , having a mother who is a [76] _____ , and having a crib that contains soft objects such as a pillow and quilts.

The phrase "[77] _____ to sleep" refers to the safest position for most babies: their [78] _____ .

Survey Question: Do dreams have meaning? Pages 229-230

People will experience [79] _____ if they are deprived of REM sleep the night before.

People deprived of [80] _____ sleep showed an urgent need to dream and [81] _____ disturbances the next day. However, the [82] _____ amount of sleep loss seems to be more important than loss of a single sleep stage.

One of the more important functions of [83] _____ [84] _____ appears to be the processing of adaptive memories.

Calvin [85] _____ found that most dream content is about familiar settings, people, and actions.

Dreams more often involve [86] _____ emotions than [87] _____ emotions.

The Freudian, or [88] _____ , view is that dreams express unconscious wishes, frequently hidden by dream [89] _____ .

Allan Hobson and Robert McCarley's activation-[90] _____ model portrays dreaming as a physiological process. The brain, they say, creates dreams to explain sensory and [91] _____ messages that occur during REM sleep.

MODULE 6.3

Survey Questions: How is hypnosis done and what are its limitations? Pages 232-234

Hypnosis is an altered state characterized by narrowed attention and increased [92] _____ .

In the 1700s, Franz [93] _____ (whose name is the basis for the term [94] _____) practiced "animal magnetism," which was actually a demonstration of the power of suggestion.

The term *hypnosis* was first used by James [95] _____ , an English doctor.

People vary in hypnotic susceptibility; 8 out of 10 can be hypnotized, as revealed by scores on the [96] _____ Hypnotic Susceptibility Scale.

The core of hypnosis is the basic [97] _____ effect—a tendency to carry out suggested actions as if they were [98] _____ . However, a hypnotized person will not perform behaviors that he or she deems to be [99] _____ or a repulsive act.

Mentally moving an object back and forth, such as a ring that is dangling from a string you are holding, is the result of [100] _____ (your own suggestive power made your hand move in small increments).

Hypnosis appears capable of producing [101] _____ , controlling pain, and altering perceptions.

[102] _____ [103] _____ takes advantage of typical stage behavior, waking suggestibility, responsive subjects, disinhibition, and deception to [104] _____ hypnosis.

Survey Questions: What is meditation? Does it have any benefits? Pages 235-237

[105] _____ refers to mental exercises that are used to alter consciousness.

In [106] _____ meditation, attention is broadened to include an awareness of one's entire moment-by-moment experience. In [107] _____ meditation, attention is focused on a single object or thought.

Three major benefits of meditation are its ability to interrupt anxious thoughts, its ability to elicit the [108] _____ [109] _____ (the pattern of changes that occur in the body at times of deep relaxation), and improve physical health.

Sensory deprivation takes place when there is a major reduction in the amount or variety of [110] _____ [111] _____ available to a person.

[112] _____ sensory deprivation is stressful and disruptive, leading to perceptual distortions.

Brief or mild sensory [113] _____ can induce deep [114] _____ .

Sensory deprivation also appears to aid the breaking of long-standing habits and promotes creative thinking. This effect is the basis for [115] _____ [116] _____ Stimulation Therapy (REST).

People who use [117] _____ meditation seek to achieve the mindfulness state involving being open-minded, non[118] _____ , and aware of their current experience.

[119] _____ has been shown to [120] _____ levels of stress and increase a sense of well-being for cancer patients.

MODULE 6.4

Survey Question: What are the effects of the more commonly used psychoactive drugs? Pages 238-251

A psychoactive drug is a substance that affects the brain in ways that alter [121] _____ .

Drugs alter the activities in the brain by mimicking and blocking [122] _____ (chemicals that carry messages between neurons) to produce feelings of pleasure.

Most psychoactive drugs can be placed on a scale ranging from [123] _____ to [124] _____ . Some, however, are best described as [125] _____ (drugs that alter sensory impressions).

Drugs may cause a physical [126] _____ (addiction) or a psychological [127] _____ or both.

The [128] _____ [129] _____ drugs are alcohol, amphetamines, barbiturates, cocaine, codeine, GHB, heroin, methadone, morphine, tobacco, and tranquilizers. All psychoactive drugs can lead to psychological dependence.

Prolonged use of a drug can lead to drug [130] _____ (a reduced response to a drug) whereby the abuser must [131] _____ the amount of a drug to receive the same desired effect

Stimulant drugs are readily abused because of the period of depression that often follows stimulation. The greatest risks are associated with amphetamines, [132] _____ , MDMA, and nicotine, but even caffeine can be a problem.

[133] _____ , known as "bennies," "dex," "go," and "uppers," are synthetic stimulants that produce a rapid drug [134] _____ .

[135] _____ , known as "crank," "speed," "meth," or "crystal," is cheaply produced in labs and can be snorted, injected, or eaten.

Repeated use of amphetamine can cause brain damage and amphetamine [136] _____ .

Amphetamine psychosis can cause the abuser to act on their delusions and risk [137] _____ -injury or injury to others.

Signs of cocaine abuse are: compulsive use, loss of [138] _____ , and the disregard for [139] _____ .

MDMA or "Ecstasy," which is similar to [140] _____ , has been linked with numerous deaths and with [141] _____ impairment.

Users of MDMA are likely to risk an [142] _____ in body temperature, liver damage, and unsafe sex. [143] _____ brain cells may be damaged, which could increase anxiety level or lead to depression.

[144] _____ can be found in coffee, tea, soft drinks, and chocolate. It stimulates the brain by [145] _____ chemicals that inhibit nerve activities.

Nicotine (smoking) includes the added risk of [146] _____ [147] _____ , heart disease, and other health problems.

The smoking of cigarettes releases [148] _____ (cancer-causing substances) in the air, which expose people to secondhand smoke and places them at risk for developing lung cancer.

Barbiturates are depressant drugs whose overdose level is close to the intoxication dosage, making them dangerous drugs. Common street names for [149] _____ are "downers," "blue heavens," "purple hearts," "goofballs," "pink ladies," and "rainbows."

Mixing barbiturates and [150] _____ may result in a fatal drug [151] _____ (in which the joint effect of two drugs exceeds the effects of adding one drug's effects to the other's).

The [152] _____ drug GHB ([153] _____) can cause coma, breathing failure, and death in relatively low doses. [154] _____ is commonly called "goop," "scoop," "max," or "Georgia Home Boy."

[155] _____ tranquilizers, such as Valium, are used to lower anxiety. When abused, they have a strong addictive potential.

[156] _____ , a tranquilizer, also known as "roofies" and the "date-rape drug," is odorless and tasteless and is sometimes used to spike drinks.

Every year in the United States, 75,000 people die of [157] _____ -related deaths.

[158] _____ drinking (having five or more drinks in a short time) is responsible for 14,000 college student deaths a year.

[159] _____ is the most heavily abused drug in common use today. The development of a drinking problem is usually marked by an initial phase of increasing consumption, a [160] _____ phase, in which a single drink can set off a chain reaction, and a chronic phase, in which a person lives to drink and drinks to live.

People who undergo [161] _____ (the removal of poison) often experience unpleasant symptoms of drug [162] _____ .

Marijuana is a [163] _____ subject to an abuse pattern similar to alcohol. Studies have linked chronic marijuana use with memory impairment, [164] _____ cancer, reproductive problems, immune system disorders, and other health problems.

[165] _____ , the main active chemical in marijuana, accumulates in the [166] _____ cortex and reproductive organs.

Potential problems caused by frequent marijuana use are short-term [167] _____ loss and decline in learning, [168] _____ , and thinking abilities. In addition, people who smoke five or more joints a week tend to score four points [169] _____ on IQ tests.

Drug abuse is related to personal and social [170] _____ , attempts to cope, and the immediate reinforcing qualities of psychoactive drugs.

PSYCHOLOGY IN ACTION

Survey Question: How are dreams used to promote personal understanding? Pages 253-255

Freud held that the meaning of dreams is hidden by the dream processes he called [171] _____ ,

displacement, symbolization, and [172] _____ elaboration.

Calvin Hall emphasized the [173] _____ , [174] _____ , plot, and emotions of a dream.

Rosalind Cartwright's view of dreams as [175] _____ statements and Fritz [176] _____

technique of speaking for dream elements are also helpful.

Dreams may be used for creative problem solving, especially when dream control is achieved through

[177] _____ dreaming (a dream in which the dreamer feels capable of normal thought and action).

MASTERY TEST

1. Delirium, Ecstasy, and daydreaming all have in common the fact that they are
    a. forms of normal waking consciousness
    b. caused by sensory deprivation
    c. perceived as subjectively real
    d. ASCs

2. The street drug GHB is
    a. chemically similar to morphine
    b. a depressant
    c. capable of raising body temperature to dangerous levels
    d. a common cause of sleep-deprivation psychosis

3. Which of the following does not belong with the others?
    a. nicotine
    b. caffeine
    c. cocaine
    d. codeine

4. Sleep spindles usually first appear in stage _____, whereas delta waves first appear in stage

    _____.
    a. 1, 2
    b. 2, 3
    c. 3, 4
    d. 1, 4

5. Which of the following is NOT one of the dream processes described by Freud?
   a. condensation
   b. illumination
   c. displacement
   d. symbolization

6. Which of the following most clearly occurs under hypnosis?
   a. unusual strength
   b. memory enhancement
   c. pain relief
   d. age regression

7. Alcohol, amphetamines, cocaine, and marijuana have in common the fact that they are all
   a. physically addicting
   b. psychoactive
   c. stimulants
   d. hallucinogens

8. Emotional arousal, blood pressure changes, and sexual arousal all primarily occur during
   a. REM sleep
   b. NREM sleep
   c. delta sleep
   d. stage 4 sleep

9. The REST technique makes use of
   a. sensory deprivation
   b. hypodynamic imagery
   c. hallucinogens
   d. a CPAP mask

10. Mesmerism, hypnosis, hypnotic susceptibility scales, and stage hypnotism all rely in part on
    a. disinhibition
    b. rapid eye movements
    c. suggestibility
    d. imagery rehearsal

11. Shortened sleep-waking cycles overlook the fact that sleep
    a. must match a 3 to 1 ratio of time awake and time asleep
    b. is an innate biological rhythm
    c. is caused by a sleep-promoting substance in the blood
    d. cycles cannot be altered by external factors

12. Morning drinking appears during the _____ phase in the development of a drinking problem.
    a. initial
    b. crucial
    c. chronic
    d. rebound

13. Which of the following statements about sleep is true?
    a. Learning math or a foreign language can be accomplished during sleep.
    b. Some people can learn to do without sleep.
    c. Calvin Hall had hallucinations during a sleep-deprivation experiment.
    d. Randy Gardner slept for 14 hours after ending his sleep-deprivation.

14. Amphetamine is very similar in effects to
    a. narcotics and tranquilizers
    b. methaqualone
    c. codeine
    d. cocaine

15. Microsleeps would most likely occur
    a. in stage 4 sleep
    b. in a 3 to 1 ratio to microawakenings
    c. in conjunction with delusions and hallucinations
    d. during sleep-deprivation

16. Adolescents who abuse drugs tend to be
    a. suffering from brain dysfunctions
    b. high in self-esteem but unrealistic about consequences
    c. maladjusted and impulsive
    d. similar in most respects to nonabusers

17. Sleepwalking, sleeptalking, and severe nightmares all have in common the fact that they
    a. are REM events
    b. are NREM events
    c. are sleep disorders
    d. can be controlled with imagery rehearsal

18. In its milder forms, sensory deprivation sometimes produces
    a. cataplectic images
    b. deep relaxation
    c. tryptophanic images
    d. REM symbolizations

19. The basic suggestion effect is closely related to
    a. hypnosis
    b. sensory enhancement after sensory deprivation
    c. hypersomnia
    d. the frequency of dreaming during REM sleep

20. A person who feels awake and capable of normal action while sleeping has experienced
    a. lucid dreaming
    b. the basic suggestion effect
    c. sleep drunkenness
    d. REM rebound

21. Which of the following is a hallucinogen?
    a. LSD
    b. THC
    c. "magic mushroom"
    d. all the preceding

22. The two most basic states of sleep are
    a. stage 1 sleep and stage 4 sleep
    b. REM sleep and NREM sleep
    c. alpha sleep and delta sleep
    d. alpha sleep and hypnic sleep

23. A mantra would most commonly be used in
    a. Perls's method of dream interpretation
    b. sensory deprivation research
    c. inducing hypnosis
    d. concentrative meditation

24. Learning to use a computer would most likely be slowed if you were _____ each night.
    a. deprived of a half hour of NREM sleep
    b. allowed to engage in extra REM sleep
    c. prevented from dreaming
    d. awakened three times at random

25. By definition, compulsive drug use involves
    a. dependence
    b. experimentation
    c. repeated overdoses
    d. anhedonia

26. A particularly dangerous drug interaction occurs when _____ and _____ are combined.
    a. alcohol, amphetamine
    b. barbiturates, nicotine
    c. alcohol, barbiturates
    d. amphetamine, codeine

27. Narcolepsy is an example of
    a. a night terror
    b. a sleep disorder
    c. a tranquilizer
    d. an addictive drug

28. Sleep restriction and stimulus control techniques would most likely be used to treat
    a. insomnia
    b. narcolepsy
    c. sleepwalking
    d. REM behavior disorder

29. In addition to the nicotine they contain, cigarettes release
    a. dopamine
    b. tryptophan
    c. noradrenaline
    d. carcinogens

30. Disguised dream symbols are to psychodynamic dream theory as sensory and motor messages are to
    a. the Freudian theory of dreams
    b. the activation-synthesis hypothesis
    c. Fritz Perls's methods of dream interpretation
    d. paradoxical intention

31. Which is the most frequently used drug in North America?
    a. caffeine
    b. nicotine
    c. marijuana
    d. cocaine

32. Joan is 14 years old and is experiencing _____ throughout the day because she tends to stay up late and gets up early.
    a. insomnia
    b. narcolepsy
    c. hypersomnia
    d. none of the above

33. Gene was awakened throughout the night for a sleep study and did not receive enough REM sleep. The next night, he was allowed to sleep without interruption. Gene would be likely to experience
    a. insomnia
    b. REM rebound
    c. sleepwaking disorder
    d. REM behavior disorder

34. Holding a string with a ring attached, Eric mentally made the ring swing back and forth. Eric used _____, which means that as he thought about moving the ring, he made micromuscular movements with his fingers to move the string.
    a. autosuggestion
    b. telekinesis
    c. hypnotic susceptibility
    d. all the above

35. To achieve a state of mindfulness and reduce her levels of distress, Carla used _____ meditation to widen her awareness of her thoughts, emotions, and sensations without reaction or forming an opinion of them.
    a. suggestive
    b. concentrative
    c. focus
    d. receptive

36. Nicotine and opiates stimulate the brain by _____ neurotransmitters.
    a. mimicking
    b. blocking
    c. suppressing
    d. eliminating

SOLUTIONS

RECITE AND REVIEW

MODULE 6.1

1. awareness
2. waking
3. pattern

4. sleep
5. dreaming
6. sensory

7. normal

8. rhythm
9. survival
10. involuntary
11. routine
12. loss
13. temporary
14. Physical
15. sleep
16. sleepiness

17. lack
18. rhythms
19. 24
20. 10
21. light
22. dark
23. decreases
24. shorter
25. longer

26. shift
27. sleep
28. travel
29. travel
30. sleep
31. schedule

32. brain
33. two
34. brain
35. four
36. waves
37. light
38. sleep

39. Delta
40. alternate
41. movement
42. dreaming
43. Dreaming
44. emotional
45. muscles

46. REM
47. physical
48. stress

MODULE 6.2

49. temporary
50. lowered
51. insomnia
52. sleep
53. stimulus
54. intention

55. Sleepwalking
56. NREM
57. REM
58. rehearsal
59. breathing
60. sudden

61. six
62. preemie
63. mouth
64. teenager
65. *Back*
66. backs

67. rebound
68. dream
69. stage
70. memories

71. familiar
72. emotions
73. emotions
74. wishes

75. activation
76. sensory

MODULE 6.3

77. increased

78. animal
79. suggestion
80. *hypnosis*
81. 8

82. Scale
83. basic
84. immoral
85. autosuggestion

86. pain
87. waking
88. deception

89. consciousness
90. widened
91. difficult
92. single
93. relaxation

94. stimulation
95. perceptual
96. relaxation
97. habits
98. mindfulness

99. aware
100. Mindfulness
101. reduce

MODULE 6.4

102. alter (affect or change)
103. mimicking
104. chemicals
105. depression
106. sensory
107. addiction
108. psychological
109. reduced
110. increase
111. depression
112. caffeine
113. uppers
114. tolerance
115. crash
116. fatigue
117. crank
118. injected
119. psychosis

120. self
121. others
122. control
123. consequences
124. Ecstasy
125. increase
126. serotonergic
127. tea
128. blocking
129. Nicotine (or Smoking)
130. cancer
131. second-hand
132. depressant
133. blue
134. purple
135. pink
136. drug
137. GHB

138. Georgia
139. Valium
140. addictive
141. Rohypnol
142. date
143. alcohol
144. five
145. initial
146. single
147. removal
148. withdrawal
149. weed
150. abuse
151. THC
152. memory
153. attention
154. five
155. immediate

PSYCHOLOGY IN ACTION

156. hidden
157. processes

158. plot
159. speaking

160. creative

CONNECTIONS

MODULE 6.1

1. i
2. b
3. e
4. a

5. c
6. j
7. g
8. d

9. h
10. f

MODULE 6.2

1. c

2. e	5. f	8. b
3. a	6. g	9. d
4. j	7. h	10. i

MODULE 6.3

1. b	3. a	5. c
2. d	4. e	

MODULE 6.4

1. g	5. b	9. i
2. c	6. l	10. f
3. h	7. a	11. k
4. j	8. d	12. e

CHECK YOUR MEMORY

MODULE 6.1

1. T	3. T	
2. T	4. T	

5. F	8. F	11. F
6. T	9. T	12. T
7. T	10. T	13. F

14. F	18. F	22. F
15. T	19. F	23. F
16. F	20. T	
17. F	21. F	

MODULE 6.2

24. F	28. T	32. T
25. T	29. T	33. F
26. T	30. T	
27. F	31. T	

34. T	37. F	40. T
35. F	38. T	
36. F	39. F	

MODULE 6.3
41. F

42. F	45. T	48. F
43. F	46. T	
44. T	47. F	

49. T	52. F	55. F
50. F	53. T	56. F
51. T	54. F	57. F

MODULE 6.4

58. F	68. F	78. T
59. T	69. T	79. T
60. T	70. T	80. F
61. F	71. T	81. T
62. F	72. F	82. F
63. T	73. T	83. F
64. T	74. T	84. T
65. T	75. F	85. T
66. T	76. F	86. T
67. T	77. T	

PSYCHOLOGY IN ACTION

87. F	89. F	91. F
88. T	90. T	92. F

FINAL SURVEY AND REVIEW

MODULE 6.1

1. consciousness	4. activity	7. Cultural
2. consciousness	5. hypnosis	
3. mental	6. deprivation	

8. innate	17. Circadian	26. lag
9. biological	18. sleep-waking	27. bodily
10. microsleeps	19. cycle	28. rhythms
11. alertness	20. old	29. early
12. psychosis	21. age	30. late
13. delusions	22. multiple	31. preadapt
14. Physical	23. sleep	
15. hypersomnia	24. cycles	
16. lack	25. jet	

32. hormone

33. spinal
34. cord
35. opposed
36. systems
37. electroencephalograph
38. spindles
39. delta
40. waves
41. 1

42. 4
43. 2
44. 3
45. rapid
46. eye
47. REM
48. non-REM
49. stage
50. 1

51. stage
52. 1
53. arousal
54. relaxation
55. disorder
56. NREM
57. REM

MODULE 6.2

58. chronic
59. dependency
60. tryptophan
61. restriction
62. paradoxical
63. somnambulism
64. NREM
65. NREM

66. REM
67. imagery
68. rehearsal
69. apnea
70. Apnea
71. infant
72. death
73. six

74. preemie
75. mouth
76. teenager
77. *Back*
78. backs

79. REM rebound
80. REM
81. mental
82. total
83. REM

84. sleep
85. Hall
86. negative
87. positive
88. psychodynamic

89. symbols
90. synthesis
91. motor

MODULE 6.3

92. suggestibility
93. Mesmer
94. *mesmerize*
95. Braid
96. Stanford

97. suggestion
98. involuntary
99. immoral
100. autosuggestion
101. relaxation

102. Stage
103. hypnotism
104. simulate

105. Meditation
106. receptive
107. concentrative
108. relaxation
109. response
110. sensory

111. stimulation
112. Prolonged
113. deprivation
114. relaxation
115. Restricted
116. Environmental

117. receptive
118. judgmental
119. Mindfulness
120. reduce

MODULE 6.4

121. consciousness
122. neurotransmitters
123. stimulation

124. depression
125. hallucinogens
126. dependence

127. dependence
128. physically
129. addicting

130. tolerance
131. increase
132. cocaine
133. Amphetamines
134. tolerance
135. Methamphetamine
136. psychosis
137. self
138. control
139. consequences
140. amphetamine
141. mental
142. increase
143. Serotonergic

144. Caffeine
145. blocking
146. lung
147. cancer
148. carcinogens
149. barbiturates
150. alcohol
151. interaction
152. depressant
153. gamma-hydroxybuyrate
154. GHB
155. Benzodiazepine
156. Rohypnol
157. alcohol

158. Binge
159. Alcohol
160. crucial
161. detoxification
162. withdrawal
163. hallucinogen
164. lung
165. THC
166. cerebral
167. memory
168. attention
169. lower
170. maladjustment

PSYCHOLOGY IN ACTION

171. condensation
172. secondary
173. setting

174. cast
175. feeling
176. Perls's

177. lucid

MASTERY TEST

1. D, (p. 218)
2. B, (p. 245)
3. D, (p. 239)
4. B, (p. 224)
5. B, (p. 253)
6. C, (p. 234)
7. B, (p. 238)
8. A, (p. 224)
9. A, (p. 236)
10. C, (p. 232-233)
11. B, (p. 221)
12. A, (p. 247-248)

13. D, (p. 220)
14. D, (p. 240)
15. D, (p. 219)
16. C, (p. 251)
17. C, (p. 227-228)
18. B, (p. 236)
19. A, (p. 233)
20. A, (p. 255)
21. D, (p. 249)
22. B, (p. 224)
23. D, (p. 235)
24. C, (p. 229)

25. A, (p. 239)
26. C, (p. 246)
27. B, (p. 226)
28. A, (p. 227)
29. D, (p. 244)
30. B, (p. 230)
31. A, (p. 242)
32. C, (p. 226)
33. B, (p. 229)
34. A, (p. 233)
35. D, (p. 235)
36. A, (p. 238)

CONDITIONING AND LEARNING

CHAPTER OVERVIEW

Learning is a relatively permanent change in behavior due to experience. Two basic forms of learning are classical conditioning and operant conditioning.

Classical conditioning is also called respondent or Pavlovian conditioning. Classical conditioning occurs when a neutral stimulus is associated with an unconditioned stimulus (which reliably elicits an unconditioned response). After many pairings of the NS and the US, the NS becomes a conditioned stimulus that elicits a conditioned response. Learning is reinforced during acquisition of a response. Withdrawing reinforcement leads to extinction (although some spontaneous recovery of conditioning may occur). It is apparent that stimulus generalization has occurred when a stimulus similar to the CS also elicits a learned response. In stimulus discrimination, people or animals learn to respond differently to two similar stimuli. Conditioning often involves simple reflex responses, but emotional conditioning is also possible.

In operant conditioning (or instrumental learning), the consequences that follow a response alter the probability that it will be made again. Positive and negative reinforcers increase responding, punishment suppresses responding, and nonreinforcement leads to extinction. Various types of reinforcers and different patterns of giving reinforcers greatly affect operant learning. Four types of schedules of partial reinforcements are fixed ratio, variable ratio, fixed interval, and variable interval. Fix ratio produces a high response rate while variable interval produces a slow and steady response rate; it has a strong resistance to extinction. Informational feedback (knowledge of results) also facilitates learning and performance. Antecedent stimuli (those that precede a response) influence operant learning through stimulus generalization, discrimination, and stimulus control. Shaping, a form of operant conditioning, uses successive approximation to train animals to perform tricks.

Learning, even simple conditioning, is based on acquiring information. Higher-level cognitive learning involves memory, thinking, problem solving, and language. At a simpler level, cognitive maps, latent learning, and discovery learning show that learning is based on acquiring information. Learning also occurs through observation and imitating models. Observational learning imparts large amounts of information that would be hard to acquire in other ways.

Operant principles can be applied to manage one's own behavior and to break bad habits.

LEARNING OBJECTIVES

To demonstrate mastery of this chapter, you should be able to:

1. Define "learning."

2. Define "reinforcement" and explain its role in conditioning.

3. Differentiate between antecedents and consequences and explain how they are related to classical and operant conditioning.

4. Give a brief history of classical conditioning.

5. Describe the following terms as they apply to classical conditioning: a. neutral stimulus (NS) b. conditioned stimulus (CS) c. unconditioned stimulus (US) d. unconditioned response (UR) e. conditioned response (CR)

6. Describe and give an example of classical conditioning using the abbreviations US, UR, CS, and CR.

7. Explain how reinforcement occurs during the acquisition of a classically conditioned response. Include an explanation of higher-order conditioning.

8. Explain classical conditioning in terms of the informational view.

9. Describe and give examples of the following concepts as they relate to classical conditioning: a. extinction b. spontaneous recovery c. stimulus generalization d. stimulus discrimination

10. Describe the relationship between classical conditioning and reflex responses.

11. Explain what a conditioned emotional response (CER) is and how it is acquired. Include definitions of the terms "phobia" and "desensitization."

12. Explain the concept and importance of vicarious classical conditioning.

13. State the basic principle of operant conditioning. Include Thorndike's law of effect.

14. Contrast operant conditioning with classical conditioning. Include a brief comparison of the differences between what is meant by the terms "reward" and "reinforcement." Discuss the contributions of B. F. Skinner.

15. Explain operant conditioning in terms of the informational view. Explain what response contingent reinforcement is.

16. Describe how the delay of reinforcement can influence the effectiveness of the reinforcement.

17. Describe response chaining and explain how it can counteract the effects of delaying reinforcement.

18. Explain why superstitious behavior develops and why it persists.

19. Explain how shaping occurs. Include a definition of the term "successive approximations."

20. Explain how extinction and spontaneous recovery occur in operant conditioning.

21. Describe how negative attention seeking demonstrates reinforcement and extinction in operant conditioning.

22. Compare and contrast positive reinforcement, negative reinforcement, punishment and response cost punishment and give an example of each.

23. Differentiate primary reinforcers from secondary reinforcers and list four of each kind.

24. Discuss two ways in which a secondary reinforcer becomes reinforcing.

25. Discuss the major advantages and disadvantages of primary reinforcers and secondary reinforcers (tokens, for instance), and describe how tokens have been used to help "special" groups of people.

26. Define social reinforcers. Name two key elements that underlie learning and explain how they function together in learning situations.

27. Define feedback, indicate three factors that increase its effectiveness, and explain its importance in learning.

28. Briefly describe some ways in which conditioning techniques can be used to help people learn to conserve our energy resources.

29. Describe the following kinds of instruction and discuss their application in learning and teaching: programmed, computer-assisted, and interactive CD-ROM.

30. Compare and contrast the effects of continuous and partial reinforcement.

31. Describe, give an example of, and explain the effects of the following schedules of partial reinforcement: a. fixed ratio (FR) b. variable ratio (VR) c. fixed interval (FI) d. variable interval (VI)

32. Explain the concept of stimulus control.

33. Describe the processes of generalization and discrimination as they relate to operant conditioning.

34. Explain how punishers can be defined by their effects on behavior.

35. List and discuss three factors which influence the effectiveness of punishment.

36. Differentiate the effects of severe punishment from mild punishment.

37. List the three basic tools available to control simple learning.

38. Discuss how and why reinforcement should be used with punishment in order to change an undesirable behavior.

39. List seven guidelines that should be followed when using punishment.

40. List and discuss three problems associated with punishment.

41. Explain how using punishment can be habit forming and describe the behavior of children who are frequently punished.

42. Define "cognitive learning."

43. Describe the concepts of a cognitive map and latent learning.

44. Explain the difference between discovery learning and rote learning. Describe the behavior of the students who used each in the Wertheimer study.

45. Discuss the factors that determine whether observational learning (modeling) will occur.

46. Describe the experiment with children and the Bo-Bo doll that demonstrates the powerful effect of modeling on behavior.

47. Explain why what a parent does is more important than what a parent says.

48. Briefly describe the general conclusion that can be drawn from studies on the effects of TV violence and violent video games on children. Explain why it would be an exaggeration to say that TV violence causes aggression.

49. Describe the procedures and results of Williams' natural experiment with TV.

50. List and briefly describe the seven steps in a behavioral self-management program. Explain how the Premack principle may apply.

51. Describe how self-recording and behavioral contracting can aid a self-management program.

52. List four strategies for changing bad habits, and describe the use of a behavioral contract.

RECITE AND REVIEW

MODULE 7.1

Survey Question: What is learning? Pages 258-261

Learning is a relatively permanent change in [1] _____ due to experience. To understand learning we must study antecedents (events that [2] _____ responses) and consequences (events that [3] _____ responses).

Classical, or respondent, [4] _____ and operant, or instrumental, [5] _____ are two basic types of learning.

In classical conditioning, a previously neutral [6] _____ is associated with a stimulus that elicits a response. In operant conditioning, the pattern of voluntary [7] _____ is altered by consequences.

Both types of conditioning depend on reinforcement. In classical conditioning, learning is [8] _____ when a US follows the NS or CS. [9] _____ reinforcement is based on the consequences that follow a response.

Survey Question: How does classical conditioning occur? Pages 261-264

Classical conditioning, studied by Ivan Pavlov, occurs when a [10] _____ stimulus (NS) is associated with an unconditioned stimulus (US). The US triggers a reflex called the unconditioned [11] _____ (UR).

If the NS is consistently paired with the US, it becomes a conditioned [12] _____ (CS) capable of producing a response by itself. This response is a conditioned ([13] _____) response (CR).

During acquisition (training) of classical conditioning, the conditioned stimulus must be consistently followed by the unconditioned [14] _____ .

Higher-order conditioning occurs when a well-learned conditioned stimulus is used as if it were an unconditioned [15] _____ , bringing about further learning.

From an informational view, conditioning creates expectancies (or expectations about events), which alter [16] _____ patterns.

In classical conditioning, the CS creates an expectancy that the US will [17] _____ it.

When the CS is repeatedly presented alone, extinction takes place. That is, [18] _____ is weakened or inhibited.

After extinction seems to be complete, a rest period may lead to the temporary reappearance of a conditioned [19] _____ . This is called spontaneous recovery.

Through stimulus generalization, stimuli [20] _____ to the conditioned stimulus will also produce a response.

Generalization gives way to [21] _____ discrimination when an organism learns to respond to one stimulus, but not to similar stimuli.

Survey Question: Does conditioning affect emotions? Pages 264-266

Eye-blink conditioning can be used to detect [22] _____ (a mental disorder that affects a person's ability to read, think, and recognize family members).

Conditioning applies to visceral or emotional responses as well as simple [23] _____ . As a result, [24] _____ emotional responses (CERs) also occur.

Irrational fears called phobias may be CERs that are extended to a variety of situations by [25] _____ generalization.

The conditioning of emotional responses can occur vicariously ([26] _____) as well as directly.

Vicarious classical conditioning occurs when we [27] _____ another person's emotional responses to a stimulus.

MODULE 7.2

Survey Question: How does operant conditioning occur? Pages 268-272

Operant conditioning (or instrumental [28] _____) occurs when a voluntary action is followed by a reinforcer.

Reinforcement in operant conditioning [29] _____ the frequency or probability of a response.

This result is based on what Edward L. Thorndike called the law of [30] _____ .

An operant reinforcer is any event that follows a [31] _____ and [32] _____ its probability.

Learning in operant conditioning is based on the expectation that a response will have a specific

[33] _____ .

To be effective, operant [34] _____ must be [35] _____ contingent. Reinforcement is given after a desired response has occurred.

Delay of reinforcement reduces its effectiveness, but long [36] _____ of responses may be built up so that a [37] _____ reinforcer maintains many responses.

Superstitious behaviors (unnecessary responses) often become part of [38] _____ chains because they appear to be associated with reinforcement.

In a process called shaping, complex [39] _____ responses can be taught by reinforcing successive approximations (ever closer matches) to a final desired response.

If an operant response is not reinforced, it may extinguish (disappear). But after extinction seems complete, it may temporarily reappear (spontaneous [40] _____).

In positive reinforcement, [41] _____ or a pleasant event follows a response. In negative reinforcement, a response that [42] _____ discomfort becomes more likely to occur again.

Punishment [43] _____ responding. Punishment occurs when a response is followed by the onset of an aversive event or by the removal of a positive event (response [44] _____).

Survey Question: Are there different kinds of operant reinforcement? Pages 272-276

Primary reinforcers are "natural," physiologically based rewards. Intracranial stimulation of

"[45] _____ centers" in the [46] _____ can also serve as a primary reinforcer.

Secondary reinforcers are [47] _____ . They typically gain their reinforcing value by association with primary reinforcers or because they can be [48] _____ for primary reinforcers. Tokens and money gain their reinforcing value in this way.

Human behavior is often influenced by social reinforcers, which are based on learned desires for attention and [49] _____ from others.

Feedback, or knowledge of [50] _____ , aids learning and improves performance.

Programmed instruction breaks learning into a series of small steps and provides immediate [51] _____ .

Computer-assisted [52] _____ (CAI) does the same but has the added advantage of providing alternate exercises and information when needed. Variations of CAI are instructional games and educational simulations.

MODULE 7.3

Survey Question: How are we influenced by patterns of reward? Pages 278-281

Reward or reinforcement may be given continuously (after every [53] _____) or on a schedule of [54] _____ reinforcement. The study of schedules of reinforcement was begun by B. F. Skinner.

Partial reinforcement produces greater resistance to extinction. This is the partial reinforcement [55] _____ .

The four most basic schedules of reinforcement are [56] _____ ratio (FR), variable ratio (VR), [57] _____ interval (FI), and variable interval (VI).

FR and VR schedules produce [58] _____ rates of responding. An FI schedule produces moderate rates of responding with alternating periods of activity and inactivity. VI schedules produce [59] _____ , steady rates of responding and strong resistance to extinction.

Stimuli that [60] _____ a reinforced response tend to control the response on future occasions (stimulus control). Aspects of stimulus control are notice something, [61] _____ something, and get something.

Two aspects of stimulus control are generalization and [62] _____ .

In generalization, an operant response tends to occur when stimuli [63] _____ to those preceding reinforcement are present.

In discrimination, responses are given in the presence of discriminative stimuli associated with reinforcement ([64] _____) and withheld in the presence of stimuli associated with nonreinforcement ([65] _____).

MODULE 7.4

Survey Question: What does punishment do to behavior? Pages 283-285

A punisher is any consequence that [66] _____ the frequency of a target behavior.

Punishment is most effective when it is [67] _____ , consistent, and intense.

Mild punishment tends only to temporarily [68] _____ responses that are also reinforced or were acquired by reinforcement.

Three basic tools used by teachers and parents to control behaviors are reinforcement, [69] _____ , and punishment, which [70] _____ responses, causes responses to be extinguished, and [71] _____ responses, respectively.

The undesirable side effects of punishment include the conditioning of fear, the learning of [72] _____ and avoidance responses, and the encouragement of aggression.

Reinforcement and nonreinforcement are a better way to change behavior than punishment. When punishment is used, it should be [73] _____ and combined with reinforcement of alternate [74] _____ .

MODULE 7.5

Survey Question: What is cognitive learning? Pages 287-288

Cognitive learning involves higher mental processes, such as understanding, knowing, or anticipating.

Evidence of cognitive learning is provided by cognitive [75] _____ (internal representations of spatial relationships) and latent (hidden) [76] _____ .

Discovery learning emphasizes insight and [77] _____ in contrast to rote learning.

Guided [78] _____ refers to allowing students to actively think about problems and provide them with proper guidance to gain useful knowledge.

Survey Question: Does learning occur by imitation? Pages 288-291

Much human learning is achieved through [79] _____ , or modeling. Observational learning is influenced by the personal characteristics of the [80] _____ and the success or failure of the [81] _____ behavior.

Observational learning involves attention, remembering, [82] _____ , and outcome of reproduction.

Television characters can act as powerful [83] _____ for observational learning. Televised violence increases the likelihood of aggression by viewers.

People who play violent video games such as Mortal Kombat are prone to act [84] _____ toward others.

PSYCHOLOGY IN ACTION

Survey Question: How does conditioning apply to practical problems? Pages 293-294

Operant principles can be readily applied to manage behavior in everyday settings. Self-management of behavior is based on self-reinforcement, self-recording, [85] _____ , and behavioral contracting.

Prepotent, or frequent, high-probability [86] _____ can be used to reinforce low-frequency responses. This is known as the Premack [87] _____ .

Attempts to break bad habits are aided by reinforcing alternate [88] _____ , extinction, breaking [89] _____ chains, and [90] _____ cues or antecedents.

CONNECTIONS

MODULE 7.1

1. _____ respondent conditioning
2. _____ instrumental learning
3. _____ antecedents
4. _____ meat powder
5. _____ spontaneous recovery
6. _____ bell
7. _____ salivation
8. _____ consequences
9. _____ expectancies
10. _____ CS used as US
11. _____ desensitization
12. _____ extinction
13. _____ acquisition
14. _____ phobia

a. before responses
b. Pavlov's CS
c. after responses
d. higher-order conditioning
e. Pavlovian conditioning
f. US missing
g. reinforcement period
h. UR
i. Pavlov's US
j. operant conditioning
k. CER
l. extinction of fear
m. informational view
n. incomplete extinction

MODULE 7.2

1. _____ response cost
2. _____ negative reinforcement
3. _____ Skinner
4. _____ shaping
5. _____ primary reinforcer
6. _____ secondary reinforcer
7. _____ punishment
8. _____ law of effect
9. _____ tokens
10. _____ approval
11. _____ KR
12. _____ CAI

a. nonlearned reinforcer
b. increased responding
c. decreased responding
d. social reinforcer
e. Chimp-O-Mat
f. approximations
g. educational simulations
h. feedback
i. Edward Thorndike
j. losing privileges
k. learned reinforcer
l. conditioning chamber

MODULE 7.3

1. _____ fixed interval
2. _____ stimulus control
3. _____ continuous reinforcement
4. _____ partial reinforcement
5. _____ fixed ratio
6. _____ variable ratio
7. _____ variable interval
8. _____ discriminative stimuli

a. resistance to extinction
b. antecedent stimuli
c. paper due every two weeks
d. S+ and S-
e. high response rate
f. reinforcement schedule
g. steady response rate
h. reinforce all correct responses

MODULE 7.4

1. _____ punishment
2. _____ avoidance learning
3. _____ escape learning
4. _____ mild punishment
5. _____ fear and aggression

a. lying to prevent discomfort
b. side effects of punishment
c. escape and avoidance
d. running away
e. weak effect

MODULE 7.5

1. _____ cognitive map
2. _____ observational learning
3. _____ modeling
4. _____ discovery learning
5. _____ rote learning
6. _____ latent learning

a. insight
b. imitation
c. mental image of campus
d. learning through repetition
e. Albert Bandura
f. hidden learning

CHECK YOUR MEMORY

MODULE 7.1

Survey Question: What is learning? Pages 258-261

1. Learning to press the buttons on a vending machine is based on operant conditioning.
   TRUE or FALSE

2. In classical conditioning, the consequences that follow responses become associated with one another.
   TRUE or FALSE

3. Getting compliments from friends could serve as reinforcement for operant learning.
   TRUE or FALSE

Survey Question: How does classical conditioning occur? Pages 261-264

4. Ivan Pavlov studied digestion and operant conditioning in dogs.
    TRUE or FALSE

5. Pavlov used meat powder to reinforce conditioned salivation to the sound of a bell.
    TRUE or FALSE

6. During successful conditioning, the NS becomes a CS.
    TRUE or FALSE

7. During acquisition, the CS is presented repeatedly without the US.
    TRUE or FALSE

8. The optimal delay between the CS and the US is 5 to 15 seconds.
    TRUE or FALSE

9. Spontaneous recovery occurs when a CS becomes strong enough to be used like a US.
    TRUE or FALSE

10. Discriminations are learned when generalized responses to stimuli similar to the CS are extinguished.
    TRUE or FALSE

Survey Question: Does conditioning affect emotions? Pages 264-266

11. Narrowing of the pupils in response to bright lights is learned in early infancy.
    TRUE or FALSE

12. Emotional conditioning involves autonomic nervous system responses.
    TRUE or FALSE

13. Eye-blink conditioning, a form of operant conditioning, can be used to detect dementia.
    TRUE or FALSE

14. Stimulus generalization helps convert some CERs into phobias.
    TRUE or FALSE

15. Pleasant music can be used as a UR to create a CER.
    TRUE or FALSE

16. To learn a CER vicariously, you would observe the actions of another person and try to imitate them.
    TRUE or FALSE

MODULE 7.2

Survey Question: How does operant conditioning occur? Pages 268-272

17. In operant conditioning, learners actively emit responses.

    TRUE or FALSE

18. Rewards are the same as reinforcers.

    TRUE or FALSE

19. The Skinner box is primarily used to study classical conditioning.

    TRUE or FALSE

20. Reinforcement in operant conditioning alters how frequently involuntary responses are elicited.

    TRUE or FALSE

21. Operant reinforcers are most effective when they are response contingent.

    TRUE or FALSE

22. Operant learning is most effective if you wait a minute or two after the response is over before reinforcing it.

    TRUE or FALSE

23. Response chains allow delayed reinforcers to support learning.

    TRUE or FALSE

24. Superstitious responses appear to be associated with reinforcement, but they are not.

    TRUE or FALSE

25. Teaching a pigeon to play Ping-Pong would most likely make use of the principle of response cost.

    TRUE or FALSE

26. Children who misbehave may be reinforced by attention from parents.

    TRUE or FALSE

27. Negative reinforcement is a type of punishment that is used to strengthen learning.

    TRUE or FALSE

28. Pressing a button on the alarm clock to stop the annoying sound is an example of negative reinforcement.

    TRUE or FALSE

29. Avoiding eating hot sauce because it burns your mouth is an example of punishment.

    TRUE or FALSE

30. Both response cost and negative reinforcement decrease responding.

    TRUE or FALSE

Survey Question: Are there different kinds of operant reinforcement? Pages 272-276

31. Food, water, grades, and sex are primary reinforcers.
    TRUE or FALSE

32. ICS is a good example of a secondary reinforcer.
    TRUE or FALSE

33. Social reinforcers are secondary reinforcers.
    TRUE or FALSE

34. Attention and approval can be used to shape another person's behavior.
    TRUE or FALSE

35. The effects of primary reinforcers may quickly decline as the person becomes satiated.
    TRUE or FALSE

36. The Chimp-O-Mat accepted primary reinforcers and dispensed secondary reinforcers.
    TRUE or FALSE

37. People are more likely to recycle used materials if they receive weekly feedback about how much they have recycled.
    TRUE or FALSE

38. CAI is another term for informational feedback.
    TRUE or FALSE

39. In sports, feedback is most effective when a skilled coach directs attention to important details.
    TRUE or FALSE

40. The final level of skill and knowledge is almost always higher following CAI than it is with conventional methods.
    TRUE or FALSE

MODULE 7.3

Survey Question: How are we influenced by patterns of reward? Pages 278-281

41. Continuous reinforcement means that reinforcers are given continuously, regardless of whether or not responses are made.
    TRUE or FALSE

42. An FR-3 schedule means that each correct response produces three reinforcers.
    TRUE or FALSE

43. The time interval in FI schedules is measured from the last reinforced response.
    TRUE or FALSE

44. In business, commissions and profit sharing are examples of FI reinforcement.

    TRUE or FALSE

45. Antecedent stimuli tend to control when and where previously rewarded responses will occur.

    TRUE or FALSE

46. Stimulus control refers to noticing an event occurring, performing a behavior, then getting a reward for the behavior.

    TRUE or FALSE

47. Stimulus generalization is the primary method used to train dogs to detect contraband.

    TRUE or FALSE

48. S+ represents a discriminative stimulus that precedes a nonreinforced response.

    TRUE or FALSE

MODULE 7.4

Survey Question: What does punishment do to behavior? Pages 283-285

49. Like reinforcement, punishment should be response contingent.

    TRUE or FALSE

50. Punishment is most effective if it is unpredictable.

    TRUE or FALSE

51. Speeding tickets are an example of response cost.

    TRUE or FALSE

52. Mild punishment causes reinforced responses to extinguish more rapidly.

    TRUE or FALSE

53. Generally, punishment should be the last resort for altering behavior.

    TRUE or FALSE

54. Punishment does not have to be consistent to extinguish a behavior quickly as long as positive behaviors are reinforced.

    TRUE or FALSE

55. For humans, avoidance learning is reinforced by a sense of relief.

    TRUE or FALSE

56. Punishment frequently leads to increases in aggression by the person who is punished.

    TRUE or FALSE

MODULE 7.5

Survey Question: What is cognitive learning? Pages 287-288

57. Cognitive learning involves thinking, memory, and problem solving.
    TRUE or FALSE

58. Animals learning their way through a maze memorize the correct order of right and left turns to make.
    TRUE or FALSE

59. Typically, reinforcement must be provided in order to make latent learning visible.
    TRUE or FALSE

60. In many situations, discovery learning produces better understanding of problems.
    TRUE or FALSE

61. Rote learning produces skills through insight and understanding.
    TRUE or FALSE

Survey Question: Does learning occur by imitation? Pages 288-291

62. Modeling is another term for discovery learning.
    TRUE or FALSE

63. After a new response is acquired through modeling, normal reinforcement determines if it will be repeated.
    TRUE or FALSE

64. Successful observational learning requires two steps: observing and reproducing the behavior.
    TRUE or FALSE

65. Children imitate aggressive acts performed by other people, but they are not likely to imitate cartoon characters.
    TRUE or FALSE

66. Violence on television causes children to be more violent.
    TRUE or FALSE

67. Playing violent video games leads to an increase in aggression.
    TRUE or FALSE

PSYCHOLOGY IN ACTION

Survey Question: How does conditioning apply to practical problems? Pages 293-294

68. Choosing reinforcers is the first step in behavioral self-management.
    TRUE or FALSE

69. Self-recording can be an effective way to change behavior, even without using specific reinforcers.
TRUE or FALSE

70. A prepotent response is one that occurs frequently.
TRUE or FALSE

71. To use extinction to break a bad habit, you should remove, avoid, or delay the reinforcement that is supporting the habit.
TRUE or FALSE

72. It is necessary to use cues or antecedents when breaking a bad habit.
TRUE or FALSE

73. In a behavioral contract, you spell out what response chains you are going to extinguish.
TRUE or FALSE

74. Self-regulated learners actively seek feedback in both formal and informal ways.
TRUE or FALSE

FINAL SURVEY AND REVIEW

MODULE 7.1

Survey Question: What is learning? Pages 258-261

Learning is a relatively permanent change in behavior due to experience. To understand learning we must study [1] _____ (events that precede responses) and [2] _____ (events that follow responses).

Classical, or [3] _____ , conditioning and [4] _____ , or instrumental, conditioning are two basic types of learning.

In classical conditioning, a previously [5] _____ stimulus is associated with another stimulus that elicits a response. In operant conditioning, the pattern of voluntary responses is altered by [6] _____ .

Both types of conditioning depend on [7] _____ . In classical conditioning, learning is reinforced when a [8] _____ follows the NS or CS. Operant reinforcement is based on the consequences that follow a response.

Survey Question: How does classical conditioning occur? Pages 261-264

Classical conditioning, studied by [9] _____ [10] _____ , occurs when a neutral stimulus (NS) is associated with an [11] _____ stimulus (US). The US triggers a [12] _____ called the unconditioned response (UR).

If the NS is consistently paired with the US, it becomes a [13] _____ stimulus (CS) capable of producing a response by itself. This response is a [14] _____ (learned) response (CR).

During acquisition of classical conditioning, the conditioned stimulus must be consistently followed by the [15] _____ [16] _____ .

[17] _____ conditioning occurs when a well-learned conditioned stimulus is used as if it were an unconditioned stimulus, bringing about further learning.

From an [18] _____ view, conditioning creates expectancies (or expectations about events), which alter response patterns.

In classical conditioning, the [19] _____ creates an expectancy that the [20] _____ will follow it.

When the CS is repeatedly presented alone, [21] _____ takes place (learning is weakened or inhibited).

After extinction seems to be complete, a rest period may lead to the temporary reappearance of a conditioned response. This is called [22] _____ [23] _____ .

Through stimulus [24] _____ , stimuli similar to the conditioned stimulus will also produce a response.

Generalization gives way to stimulus [25] _____ when an organism learns to respond to one stimulus, but not to similar stimuli.

Survey Question: Does conditioning affect emotions? Pages 264-266

[26] _____ conditioning can be used to detect dementia (a mental disorder that affects a person's ability to read, think, and recognize family members).

Conditioning applies to visceral or emotional responses as well as simple reflexes. As a result, conditioned [27] _____ [28] _____ (CERs) also occur.

Irrational fears called [29] _____ may be CERs that are extended to a variety of situations by stimulus [30] _____ .

The conditioning of emotional responses can occur secondhand as well as directly. [31] _____ classical conditioning occurs when we observe another person's emotional responses to a stimulus.

MODULE 7.2

Survey Question: How does operant conditioning occur? Pages 268-272

Operant conditioning (or [32] _____ learning) occurs when a voluntary action is followed by a reinforcer.

Reinforcement in operant conditioning increases the frequency or [33] _____ of a response. This result is based on what Edward L. [34] _____ called the law of effect.

An operant reinforcer is any event that follows a [35] _____ and [36] _____ its probability.

Learning in operant conditioning is based on the [37] _____ that a response will have a specific effect.

To be effective, operant reinforcers must be response [38] _____ .

Delay of reinforcement [39] _____ its effectiveness, but long chains of responses may be built up so that a single [40] _____ maintains many responses.

[41] _____ behaviors (unnecessary responses) often become part of response chains because they appear to be associated with reinforcement.

In a process called [42] _____ , complex operant responses can be taught by reinforcing successive [43] _____ (ever closer matches) to a final desired response.

If an operant response is not reinforced, it may [44] _____ (disappear). But after extinction seems complete, it may temporarily reappear ([45] _____ recovery).

In [46] _____ reinforcement, reward or a pleasant event follows a response. In [47] _____ reinforcement, a response that ends discomfort becomes more likely to occur again.

Punishment decreases responding. Punishment occurs when a response is followed by the onset of an [48] _____ event or by the removal of a [49] _____ event (response cost).

Survey Question: Are there different kinds of operant reinforcement? Pages 272-276

[50] _____ reinforcers are "natural," physiologically based rewards. Intracranial

[51] _____ of "pleasure centers" in the brain can also serve as a reinforcer of this type.

[52] _____ reinforcers are learned. They typically gain their reinforcing value by association with

[53] _____ reinforcers or because they can be exchanged for [54] _____ reinforcers.

Tokens and money gain their reinforcing value in this way.

Human behavior is often influenced by [55] _____ reinforcers, which are based on learned

desires for attention and approval from others.

Feedback, or [56] _____ of results, aids learning and improves performance.

Programmed [57] _____ breaks learning into a series of small steps and provides immediate

feedback.

[58] _____ instruction (CAI) does the same but has the added advantage of providing alternate

exercises and information when needed. Variations of [59] _____ are instructional games

and educational simulations.

MODULE 7.3

Survey Question: How are we influenced by patterns of reward? Pages 278-281

Reward or reinforcement may be given continuously (after every response) or on a [60] _____ of

partial reinforcement like those studied by B. F. [61] _____ .

Partial reinforcement produces greater resistance to [62] _____ . This is the [63] _____

reinforcement effect.

The four most basic schedules of reinforcement are fixed and variable [64] _____ (FR and VR)

and fixed and variable [65] _____ (FI and VI).

[66] _____ and [67] _____ schedules produce high rates of responding. An

[68] _____ schedule produces moderate rates of responding with alternating periods of

activity and inactivity. VI schedules produce slow, steady rates of responding and strong resistance to

[69] _____ .

Stimuli that precede a reinforced response tend to control the response on future occasions. This is

called [70] _____ [71] _____ . Aspects of [72] _____ control are notice

something, do something, and get something.

Two aspects of stimulus control are [73] _____ and discrimination.

In [74] _____ , an operant response tends to occur when stimuli similar to those preceding reinforcement are present.

In [75] _____ , responses are given in the presence of stimuli associated with reinforcement (S+) and withheld in the presence of stimuli associated with nonreinforcement (S-).

MODULE 7.4

Survey Question: What does punishment do to behavior? Pages 283-285

A [76] _____ is any consequence that lowers the frequency of a target behavior.

Punishment is most effective when it is immediate, [77] _____ , and intense.

Mild punishment tends only to temporarily suppress responses that are also [78] _____ in some way.

Three basic tools used by teachers and parents to control behaviors are [79] _____ , nonreinforcement, and punishment, which [80] _____ responses, causes responses to be [81] _____ , and suppresses responses, respectively.

The undesirable side effects of punishment include the conditioning of fear, the learning of escape and [82] _____ responses, and the encouragement of [83] _____ against others.

[84] _____ and [85] _____ are a better way to change behavior than punishment.

MODULE 7.5

Survey Question: What is cognitive learning? Pages 287-288

Cognitive learning involves higher mental processes, such as understanding, knowing, or anticipating.

Evidence of cognitive learning is provided by [86] _____ [87] _____ (internal representations of spatial relationships) and [88] _____ (hidden) learning.

Discovery learning emphasizes insight and understanding in contrast to [89] _____ learning.

[90] _____ discovery refers to allowing students to actively think about problems and provide them with proper guidance to gain useful knowledge.

Survey Question: Does learning occur by imitation? Pages 288-291

Much human learning is achieved through observation, or [91] _____ . [92] _____ learning is influenced by the personal characteristics of the model and the success or failure of the model's behavior.

[93] _____ learning involves attention, remembering, reproduction, and outcome of reproduction.

Television characters can act as powerful models for [94] _____ learning. Televised violence increases the likelihood of aggression by viewers.

People who play violent video games such as Mortal Kombat are prone to act [95] _____ toward others.

PSYCHOLOGY IN ACTION

Survey Question: How does conditioning apply to practical problems? Pages 293-294

Operant principles can be readily applied to manage behavior in everyday settings. Self-management of behavior is based on self-reinforcement, self-recording, feedback, and behavioral [96] _____ .

Prepotent, or frequent, high-probability responses can be used to [97] _____ low-frequency responses. This is known as the [98] _____ principle.

Attempts to break bad habits are aided by reinforcing [99] _____ responses, extinction, breaking response [100] _____ , and removing cues or [101] _____ .

MASTERY TEST

1. Tokens are a good example of
   a. secondary reinforcers
   b. the effects of ICS on behavior
   c. noncontingent reinforcers
   d. generalized reinforcers

2. The principle of feedback is of particular importance to
   a. CERs
   b. ICS
   c. CAI
   d. higher-order conditioning

3. As a coffee lover, you have become very efficient at carrying out the steps necessary to make a cup of espresso. Your learning is an example of
    a. response chaining
    b. spontaneous recovery
    c. vicarious reinforcement
    d. secondary reinforcement

4. To teach a pet dog to use a new dog door, it would be helpful to use
    a. the Premack principle
    b. shaping
    c. respondent conditioning
    d. delayed reinforcement

5. To test for the presence of classical conditioning, you would omit the
    a. CS
    b. US
    c. CR
    d. S+

6. Which of the following does not belong with the others?
    a. Thorndike
    b. Skinner
    c. Pavlov
    d. instrumental learning

7. To teach a child to say "Please" when she asks for things, you should make getting the requested item
    a. the CS
    b. a token
    c. a negative reinforcer
    d. response contingent

8. Money is to secondary reinforcer as food is to
    a. ICS
    b. prepotent responses
    c. primary reinforcer
    d. negative reinforcer

9. Whether a model is reinforced has a great impact on
    a. discovery learning
    b. latent learning
    c. observational learning
    d. self-regulated learning

10. One thing that classical and operant conditioning have in common is that both
    a. were discovered by Pavlov
    b. depend on reinforcement
    c. are affected by the consequences of making a response
    d. permanently change behavior

11. To shape the behavior of a teacher in one of your classes, you would probably have to rely on
    a. tokens
    b. primary reinforcers
    c. negative attention seeking
    d. social reinforcers

12. The concept that best explains persistence at gambling is
    a. partial reinforcement
    b. continuous reinforcement
    c. fixed interval reinforcement
    d. fixed ratio reinforcement

13. Which of the following is NOT a common side effect of mild punishment?
    a. escape learning
    b. avoidance learning
    c. aggression
    d. accelerated extinction

14. With respect to televised violence it can be said that TV violence
    a. causes viewers to be more aggressive
    b. makes aggression more likely
    c. has no effect on the majority of viewers
    d. vicariously lowers aggressive urges

15. Which of the following types of learning is most related to the consequences of making a response?
    a. Pavlovian conditioning
    b. operant conditioning
    c. classical conditioning
    d. respondent conditioning

16. Which combination would most likely make a CER into a phobia?
    a. CER-discrimination
    b. CER-desensitization
    c. CER-response cost
    d. CER-generalization

17. A loud, unexpected sound causes a startle reflex; thus, a loud sound could be used as a _____ in conditioning.
    a. NS
    b. CR
    c. UR
    d. US

18. Antecedents are to _____ as consequences are to _____.
    a. discriminative stimuli, reinforcers
    b. shaping, response chaining
    c. conditioned stimuli, cognitive maps
    d. punishment, negative reinforcement

19. The use of self-recording to change personal behavior is closely related to the principle of
    a. response chaining
    b. feedback
    c. two-factor reinforcement
    d. stimulus control

20. _____ typically only temporarily suppresses reinforced responses.
    a. Negative reinforcement
    b. Extinction
    c. Mild punishment
    d. Stimulus generalization

21. In general, the highest rates of responding are associated with
    a. delayed reinforcement
    b. variable reinforcement
    c. interval reinforcement
    d. fixed ratio reinforcement

22. A child who has learned, through classical conditioning, to fear sitting in a dentist's chair becomes frightened when he is placed in a barber's chair. This illustrates the concept of
    a. stimulus generalization
    b. spontaneous recovery
    c. higher-order discrimination
    d. vicarious conditioning

23. The informational view of learning places emphasis on the creation of mental
    a. expectancies
    b. reinforcement schedules
    c. contracts
    d. antecedents

24. For some adults, blushing when embarrassed or ashamed is probably a _____ first formed in childhood.
    a. conditioned stimulus
    b. CAI
    c. discriminative stimulus
    d. CER

25. Learning to obey traffic signals is related to the phenomenon called
    a. stimulus control
    b. spontaneous recovery
    c. avoidance learning
    d. modeling

26. To be most effective, punishment should be combined with
    a. response costs
    b. aversive stimuli
    c. delayed feedback
    d. reinforcement

27. Involuntary responses are to _____ conditioning as voluntary responses are to _____ conditioning.
    a. classical, respondent
    b. classical, operant
    c. operant, classical
    d. operant, instrumental

28. Negative attention seeking by children demonstrates the impact of _____ on behavior.
    a. operant extinction
    b. social reinforcers
    c. response costs
    d. prepotent responses

29. Which consequence increases the probability that a response will be repeated?
    a. punishment
    b. response cost
    c. nonreinforcement
    d. negative reinforcement

30. Which method uses the principles of classical conditioning to detect early development of dementia?
    a. eye blinking
    b. memory task
    c. rote learning
    d. vocabulary test

31. Successive approximations are used in _____ to train animals to perform tricks.
    a. observational conditioning
    b. classical conditioning
    c. shaping
    d. latent learning

32. Putting on a pair of gloves to stop your hands from hurting while working in the cold weather demonstrates
    a. positive reinforcement
    b. negative reinforcement
    c. punishment
    d. response cost

33. Wanting to do some light reading while his roommate drove, Cody picked up a magazine, and after a few minutes, Cody felt nauseated and had to stop reading. To avoid getting sick in the future, Cody no longer read while riding in a car. This illustrates
    a. positive reinforcement
    b. negative reinforcement
    c. punishment
    d. response cost

34. Introducing an energy tax to reduce people's tendency to waste energy or polluting the environment utilizes _____, a form of operant conditioning.
    a. positive reinforcement
    b. negative reinforcement
    c. punishment
    d. response cost

35. _____ gives students enough freedom and guidance to actively think and gain knowledge.
    a. Guided discovery
    b. Latent discovery
    c. Observational learning
    d. Classical learning

36. Which of the following is the correct sequence when using observational learning?
    a. attention, remembering, reproduction, and rewards
    b. attention, rewards, reproduction, and remembering
    c. rewards, remembering, attention, and reproduction
    d. remembering, rewards, attention, and reproduction

37. Increased aggression and violence among children and adolescents has been attributed to
    a. watching violent TV programs
    b. playing violent video games
    c. imitating others' aggressive behaviors
    d. all the preceding

SOLUTIONS

RECITE AND REVIEW

MODULE 7.1

1. behavior
2. precede
3. follow

4. conditioning
5. conditioning
6. stimulus

7. responses
8. reinforced
9. Operant

10. neutral
11. response
12. stimulus
13. learned

14. stimulus
15. stimulus
16. response
17. follow

18. conditioning
19. response
20. similar
21. stimulus

22. dementia
23. reflexes

24. conditioned
25. stimulus

26. secondhand
27. observe

MODULE 7.2

28. learning
29. increases
30. effect
31. response
32. increases
33. effect
34. reinforcement

35. response
36. chains
37. single
38. response
39. operant
40. recovery
41. reward

42. ends
43. decreases
44. cost

45. pleasure
46. brain
47. learned

48. exchanged
49. approval
50. results

51. feedback
52. instruction

MODULE 7.3

53. response
54. partial
55. effect
56. fixed
57. fixed

58. high
59. slow
60. precede
61. do
62. discrimination

63. similar
64. S+
65. S-

MODULE 7.4

66. decreases
67. immediate
68. suppress

69. nonreinforcement
70. strengthens
71. suppresses

72. escape
73. mild
74. responses

Chapter 7

MODULE 7.5

75. maps
76. learning

77. understanding
78. discovery

79. imitation
80. model

81. model's
82. reproduction

83. models
84. aggressively

PSYCHOLOGY IN ACTION

85. feedback
86. responses

87. principle
88. responses

89. response
90. removing

CONNECTIONS

MODULE 7.1

1. e
2. j
3. a
4. i
5. n
6. b

7. h
8. c
9. m
10. d
11. l
12. f

13. g
14. k

MODULE 7.2

1. j
2. b
3. k
4. f

5. a
6. l
7. c
8. i

9. e
10. d
11. h
12. g

MODULE 7.3

1. f
2. b
3. h

4. a
5. e
6. c

7. g
8. d

MODULE 7.4

1. c
2. a

3. d
4. e

5. b

MODULE 7.5

1. c
2. e

3. b
4. a

5. d
6. f

CHECK YOUR MEMORY

MODULE 7.1

1. T	2. F	3. T

4. F	7. F	10. T
5. T	8. F	
6. T	9. F	

11. F	13. F	15. F
12. T	14. T	16. F

MODULE 7.2

17. T	23. T	29. T
18. F	24. T	30. F
19. F	25. F	
20. F	26. T	
21. T	27. F	
22. F	28. T	

31. F	35. T	39. T
32. F	36. F	40. F
33. T	37. T	
34. T	38. F	

MODULE 7.3

41. F	44. F	47. F
42. F	45. T	48. F
43. T	46. T	

MODULE 7.4

49. T	52. F	55. T
50. F	53. T	56. T
51. T	54. F	

MODULE 7.5

57. T	59. T	61. F
58. F	60. T	

62. F

63. T   65. F   67. T
64. F   66. F

PSYCHOLOGY IN ACTION

68. F   71. T   74. T
69. T   72. F
70. T   73. F

FINAL SURVEY AND REVIEW

MODULE 7.1

1. antecedents
2. consequences
3. respondent
4. operant
5. neutral
6. consequences
7. reinforcement
8. US

9. Ivan
10. Pavlov
11. unconditioned
12. reflex
13. conditioned
14. conditioned
15. unconditioned
16. stimulus
17. Higher-order
18. informational
19. CS
20. US
21. extinction
22. spontaneous
23. recovery
24. generalization
25. discrimination

26. Eye-blink
27. emotional
28. responses
29. phobias
30. generalization
31. Vicarious

MODULE 7.2

32. instrumental
33. probability
34. Thorndike
35. response
36. increases
37. expectation
38. contingent
39. decreases
40. reinforcer
41. Superstitious
42. shaping
43. approximations
44. extinguish
45. spontaneous
46. positive
47. negative
48. aversive
49. positive

50. Primary
51. stimulation
52. Secondary
53. primary
54. primary
55. social
56. knowledge
57. instruction
58. Computer-assisted
59. CAI

MODULE 7.3

60. schedule
61. Skinner
62. extinction

63. partial
64. ratio
65. interval
66. FR
67. VR

68. FI
69. extinction
70. stimulus
71. control
72. stimulus

73. generalization
74. generalization
75. discrimination

MODULE 7.4

76. punisher
77. consistent
78. reinforced
79. reinforcement

80. strengthens
81. extinguished
82. avoidance
83. aggression

84. Reinforcement
85. nonreinforcement

MODULE 7.5

86. cognitive
87. maps

88. latent
89. rote

90. Guided

91. modeling
92. Observational

93. Observational
94. observational

95. aggressively

PSYCHOLOGY IN ACTION

96. contracting
97. reinforce

98. Premack
99. alternate

100. chains
101. antecedents

MASTERY TEST

1. A, (p. 273)
2. C, (p. 275-276)
3. A, (p. 270)
4. B, (p. 271)
5. B, (p. 262)
6. C, (p. 268-269)
7. D, (p. 269-270)
8. C, (p. 272-273)
9. C, (p. 289)
10. B, (p. 260)
11. D, (p. 274)
12. A, (p. 278)
13. D, (p. 284)
14. B, (p. 290)

15. B, (p. 260)
16. D, (p. 265)
17. D, (p. 260)
18. A, (p. 260, 264)
19. B, (p. 293-294)
20. C, (p. 284)
21. D, (p. 279)
22. A, (p. 263)
23. A, (p. 263)
24. D, (p. 265)
25. A, (p. 280)
26. D, (p. 284)
27. B, (p. 268)
28. B, (p. 274)

29. D, (p. 271)
30. A, (p. 265)
31. C, (p. 271)
32. B, (p. 272)
33. C, (p. 272)
34. D, (p. 272)
35. A, (p. 288)
36. A, (p. 289)
37. D, (p. 289-291)

MEMORY

CHAPTER OVERVIEW

Memory systems encode and store information for later retrieval. A popular model divides memory into three systems: sensory memory, short-term memory (STM), and long-term memory (LTM). Sensory memory stores exact copies of sensory information for very brief periods. STM is limited to about seven bits of information, but chunking and recoding allow more information to be stored. Short-term memory lasts only a limited time; however, it can be extended through maintenance rehearsal. Long-term memory has nearly unlimited storage and is relatively permanent. It undergoes updating, revision, constructive processing, and forgetting. Elaborative rehearsal ensures information is encoded in LTM. Specific types of information that people store in LTM is influenced by the culture in which they live.

Long-term memory can be further divided into declarative memories (which may be semantic or episodic) and procedural memories. Explicit memories are revealed by recall, recognition, and relearning tasks. Implicit memories are revealed by priming. Eidetic imagery (photographic memory) is fairly common in children but rare among adults. Many people have internal memory images, and some have exceptional memory based on internal imagery. Exceptional memory capacity is based on both learned strategies and natural abilities.

Forgetting is most rapid immediately after learning. Some "forgetting" is based on a failure to encode information. Short-term forgetting is partly explained by the decay (weakening) of memory traces. Some long-term forgetting may also occur this way. Some forgetting is related to a lack of memory cues. Much forgetting is related to interference among memories. Clinical psychologists believe that memories are sometimes repressed (unconsciously held out of awareness). Some also believe that repressed childhood memories of abuse can be "recovered." However, there is often no way to separate true memories from fantasies.

In the brain, memory traces (engrams) must be consolidated before they become relatively permanent. The hippocampus is a structure involved in memory consolidation. Information appears to be stored in the brain through changes in nerve cells.

Memory can be improved by the use of mnemonic systems and by attention to factors that affect memory, such as overlearning, serial position, organization, and the like.

LEARNING OBJECTIVES

To demonstrate mastery of this chapter, you should be able to:

1. Explain how memory functions like a computer. Include definitions of "encoding," "storage," and "retrieval."

2. Describe sensory memory. Explain how icons and echoes function in this memory system.

3. Explain the function of selective attention in short-term memory. Describe this memory system in terms of capacity, permanence, how information is stored, and susceptibility to interference. Also explain how STM functions as a working memory.

4. Describe long-term memory in terms of permanence, capacity, and how information is stored.

5. Explain what dual memory is and how one's culture influences memory storage.

6. Explain what is meant by "the magic number seven (plus or minus two)."

7. Describe chunking (recoding), and rehearsal, and explain how they help memory. Describe the difference between maintenance and elaborative rehearsal.

8. Discuss the permanence of memory, including the work of Penfield.

9. Explain how memories are constructed. Include the concepts of constructive processing and pseudo-memories.

10. Discuss the effects of hypnosis on memory.

11. Briefly describe how long-term memories are organized including the network model and redintegrative memories.

12. Differentiate procedural (skill) memory from declarative (fact) memory. Differentiate the two kinds of declarative memory, semantic memory, and episodic memory.

13. Explain the tip-of-the-tongue phenomenon.

14. Describe and give an example of each of the following ways of measuring memory: a. recall (include the serial position effect) b. recognition (compare to recall and include the idea of distractors) c. relearning (include the concept of savings)

15. Distinguish between explicit and implicit memory. Describe how the concept of priming can demonstrate the existence of memories outside the realm of awareness.

16. Describe the concept of internal imagery and explain how it differs from eidetic imagery.

17. Describe eidetic imagery and its effects on long-term memory. Describe some examples of people with exceptional memories and the role of learned strategies in memory retrieval.

18. Characterize memory loss as demonstrated by Ebbinghaus' curve of forgetting. Discuss his findings as they relate to cramming versus spaced review.

The following objective is related to the material in the "Discovering Psychology" section of the text.

19. How does "Card Magic" work? What's the trick in this game?

20. Discuss the following explanations of forgetting: a. encoding failure b. decay of memory traces c. disuse (give three reasons to question this explanation) d. cue-dependent forgetting e. state-dependent forgetting f. interference (list and explain the two types of interference and how they are investigated in the laboratory) g. repression (and differentiate it from suppression)

21. Describe the false memory syndrome.

22. Describe flashbulb memories and explain how they may be formed.

23. Define "anterograde" and "retrograde amnesia." Describe the role of consolidation in memory.

24. Name the structure in the brain which is responsible for switching information from short-term memory (STM) to long-term (LTM).

25. Discuss how memories are recorded in the brain by describing how learning is related to engrams, transmitter chemicals, and brain circuits.

26. Describe each of the following in terms of how it can improve memory: a. memory strategies b. knowledge of results c. recitation d. rehearsal e. selection f. organization g. whole versus part learning h. serial position effect i. cues j. overlearning k. spaced practice l. sleep m. hunger n. extending how long you remember o. review p. using a strategy for recall

27. List and describe the four strategies of a cognitive interview.

28. Define mnemonics and explain the four basic principles of using mnemonics.

29. List and describe four techniques for using mnemonics to remember things in order.

RECITE AND REVIEW

MODULE 8.1

Survey Question: Is there more than one type of memory? Pages 298-300

Memory is an active [1] _____ . [2] _____ is first encoded (changed into the form in which it will be retained).

Next, it is [3] _____ in memory. Later, it must be retrieved to be put to use.

Humans appear to have [4] _____ interrelated memory systems. These are sensory memory, [5] _____ memory (STM), and [6] _____ memory (LTM).

Sensory memory holds an [7] _____ copy of what is seen or heard, in the form of an icon ([8] _____) or echo (sound sensation).

Short-term memories tend to be stored as [9] _____ . Long-term memories are stored on the basis of [10] _____ , or importance.

STM acts as a [11] _____ storehouse for small amounts of information. It provides a working memory where thinking, mental arithmetic, and the like take place. LTM acts as a [12] _____ storehouse for meaningful information.

Cultural values impact the types of [13] _____ we tend to store. American culture emphasizes the individual; therefore, American memories are [14] _____ -focused. The Chinese culture emphasizes group membership; therefore, Chinese memories are of social events, which include [15] _____ members, friends, and others.

MODULE 8.2

Survey Questions: What are the features of each type of memory? Is there more than one type of long-term memory? Pages 301-306

Sensory memory is exact but very brief, lasting only a few [16] _____ or less. Through selective attention, some information is transferred to [17] _____ .

The digit-span test reveals that STM has an average upper limit of about seven [18] _____ of information. However, this can be extended by chunking, or recoding information into [19] _____ units or groups.

The "[20] _____ number" 7 (plus or minus 2) refers to the limitation of [21] _____ memory discovered by George Miller. Nelson Cowan believes that the limitation of short-term memory is [22] _____ than the "magic number" 7.

Short-term memories are brief and very sensitive to [23] _____ , or interference; however, they can be prolonged by maintenance rehearsal (silent [24] _____).

Elaborative rehearsal, which emphasizes meaning, helps transfer information from [25] _____ to LTM. Elaborative rehearsal links new information with existing [26] _____ .

LTM seems to have an almost unlimited storage capacity. However, LTM is subject to constructive processing, or ongoing revision and [27] _____ . As a result, people often have pseudo-memories ([28] _____ memories) that they believe are true.

LTM is highly [29] _____ to allow retrieval of needed information. The pattern, or structure, of memory networks is the subject of current memory research. Network [30] _____ portray LTM as a system of linked ideas.

Redintegrative memories unfold as each added memory provides a cue for retrieving the next [31] _____ . Seemingly forgotten memories may be reconstructed in this way.

Within long-term memory, declarative memories for [32] _____ seem to differ from procedural memories for [33] _____ .

[34] _____ memories may be further categorized as semantic memories or episodic memories. Semantic memories consist of basic factual knowledge that is almost immune to [35] _____ . Episodic memories record [36] _____ experiences that are associated with specific times and places.

MODULE 8.3

Survey Question: How is memory measured? Pages 307-309

The tip-of-the-tongue [37] _____ shows that memory is not an all-or-nothing event. Memories may be revealed by [38] _____ , recognition, or relearning.

In recall, memory proceeds without specific cues, as in an [39] _____ exam. Recall of listed information often reveals a serial position effect ([40] _____ items on the list are most subject to errors).

A common test of [41] _____ is the multiple-choice question. [42] _____ is very sensitive to the kinds of distractors (wrong choices) used.

In relearning, "forgotten" material is learned again, and memory is indicated by a [43] _____ score.

Recall, recognition, and relearning mainly measure explicit [44] _____ that we are aware of having. Other techniques, such as priming, are necessary to reveal implicit [45] _____ , which are unconscious.

Survey Question: What are "photographic" memories? Pages 309-311

Eidetic imagery (photographic memory) occurs when a person is able to project an [46] _____ onto an external surface. Such images allow brief, nearly complete recall by some children.

Eidetic imagery is rarely found in [47] _____ . However, many adults have internal images, which can be very vivid and a basis for remembering.

Exceptional memory can be learned by finding ways to directly store information in [48] _____ .

Learning has no effect on the limits of [49] _____ . Some people may have naturally superior memory abilities that exceed what can be achieved through learning.

MODULE 8.4

Survey Questions: What causes forgetting? How accurate are everyday memories? Pages 313-319

Forgetting and memory were extensively studied by Herman Ebbinghaus, whose [50] _____ of forgetting shows that forgetting is typically most rapid immediately [51] _____ learning.

Ebbinghaus used nonsense syllables to study memory. The forgetting of [52] _____ material is much [53] _____ than shown by his curve of forgetting.

Failure to encode [54] _____ is a common cause of "forgetting."

Forgetting in sensory memory and STM probably reflects decay of memory [55] _____ in the nervous system. Decay or [56] _____ of memories may also account for some LTM loss, but most forgetting cannot be explained this way.

Often, forgetting is cue dependent. The power of cues to trigger memories is revealed by state-dependent [57] _____ , in which bodily [58] _____ at the time of learning and of retrieval affect memory.

Much [59] _____ in both STM and LTM can be attributed to interference of memories with one another.

When recent learning [60] _____ with retrieval of prior learning, retroactive interference has occurred. If old memories [61] _____ with new memories, proactive interference has occurred.

Repression is the [62] _____ of painful, embarrassing, or traumatic memories.

Repression is thought to be unconscious, in contrast to suppression, which is a [63] _____ attempt to avoid thinking about something.

Experts are currently debating the validity of childhood memories of [64] _____ that reappear after apparently being repressed for decades.

Independent evidence has verified that some recovered memories are [65] _____ . However, others have been shown to be [66] _____ .

In the absence of confirming or disconfirming [67] _____ , there is currently no way to separate true memories from fantasies. Caution is advised for all concerned with attempts to retrieve supposedly hidden memories.

Flashbulb memories, which seem especially vivid, are created at emotionally significant times. While such memories may not be accurate, we tend to place great [68] _____ in them.

Survey Question: What happens in the brain when memories are formed? Pages 319-321

Retrograde [69] _____ may be explained by the concept of consolidation.

Consolidation theory holds that engrams (permanent [70] _____ [71] _____) are formed

during a critical period after learning. Until they are consolidated, long-term memories are easily destroyed.

The hippocampus is a [72] _____ structure associated with the consolidation of memories.

The search within the brain for engrams has now settled on changes in individual [73] _____ cells.

The best-documented changes are alterations in the amounts of transmitter [74] _____ released by

nerve cells.

MODULE 8.5

Survey Question: How can I improve my memory? Pages 322-325

Memory can be improved by using feedback, recitation, and rehearsal, by selecting and [75] _____

information, and by using the progressive [76] _____ method, spaced practice, overlearning,

and active search strategies.

The effects of serial [77] _____ , sleep, review, cues, and elaboration should also be kept in

mind when studying or memorizing.

PSYCHOLOGY IN ACTION

Survey Question: How can I improve my memory? Pages 326-328

Mnemonic systems, such as the [78] _____ method, use mental images and unusual associations

to link new information with familiar memories already stored in [79] _____ . Such strategies

give information personal meaning and make it easier to recall.

Mnemonic techniques avoid rote learning and work best during the [80] _____ stages of learning.

CONNECTIONS

MODULE 8.1

1. _____ selective attention
2. _____ long-term memory
3. _____ incoming information
4. _____ encoding for LTM
5. _____ sensory memory
6. _____ short-term memory
7. _____ rehearsal buffer

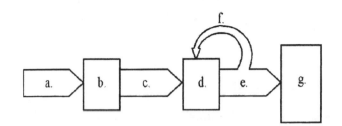

1. _____ storage
2. _____ encoding
3. _____ sensory memory
4. _____ echos and icons
5. _____ working memory

a. hard drive
b. STM
c. lasts for two to three seconds
d. keyboard
e. sensory memory

MODULE 8.2

1. _____ semantic memory
2. _____ long-term memory
3. _____ procedural memory
4. _____ sensory memory
5. _____ episodic memory
6. _____ short-term memory
7. _____ declarative memory

1. _____ chunking
2. _____ skill memory
3. _____ revised memories
4. _____ seven information bits
5. _____ memory structure

a. magic number
b. recoding
c. constructive processing
d. network model
e. procedures

MODULE 8.3

1. _____ relearning
2. _____ recall
3. _____ recognition memory
4. _____ implicit memory
5. _____ eidetic imagery
6. _____ serial position effect
7. _____ explicit memory

a. retrieval of facts
b. middle items are least recalled
c. multiple-choice questions
d. photographic memory
e. conscious memories
f. memories that are outside of awareness
g. memory test

MODULE 8.4

1. _____ memory trace
2. _____ amnesia
3. _____ suppression
4. _____ repression
5. _____ interference
6. _____ Ebbinghaus
7. _____ false memory
8. _____ hippocampus
9. _____ decay

a. disuse of memory
b. forgetting curve
c. pseudo memory
d. engram
e. memory loss
f. motivated forgetting
g. conscious forgetting
h. prevent retrieval of information
i. consolidation of memories

MODULE 8.5

1. _____ memory strategies
2. _____ recitation
3. _____ order of events
4. _____ rehearsal
5. _____ keyword method
6. _____ memory cue
7. _____ spaced practice

a. mnemonics
b. form a story
c. a stimulus linked with memory
d. mental review
e. study in short periods
f. summarize out loud
g. mandible: man dribbling

CHECK YOUR MEMORY

MODULE 8.1

Survey Question: Is there more than one type of memory? Pages 298-300

1. Incoming information must be encoded before it is stored in memory.
   TRUE or FALSE

2. Sensory memories last for a few minutes or less.
   TRUE or FALSE

3. A memory that cannot be retrieved has little value.
   TRUE or FALSE

4. Selective attention influences what information enters STM.
   TRUE or FALSE

5. Working memory is another name for sensory memory.
   TRUE or FALSE

6. Errors in long-term memory tend to focus on the sounds of words.
   TRUE or FALSE

7. Generally, the more you know, the more new information you can store in long-term memory.
   TRUE or FALSE

8. The type of memory people store is not affected by their cultural values.
   TRUE or FALSE

MODULE 8.2

Survey Questions: What are the features of each type of memory? Is there more than one type of long-term memory? Pages 301-306

9. For many kinds of information, STM can store an average of five bits of information.
   TRUE or FALSE

10. Nelson Cowan coined the term "magic number."
    TRUE or FALSE

11. Chunking recodes information into smaller units that are easier to fit into STM.
    TRUE or FALSE

12. The more times a short-term memory is rehearsed, the better its chance of being stored in LTM.
    TRUE or FALSE

13. On average, short-term memories last only about 18 minutes unless they are rehearsed.
    TRUE or FALSE

14. Maintenance rehearsal keeps memories active in sensory memory.

TRUE or FALSE

15. The surface of the brain records the past like a movie, complete with sound track.

TRUE or FALSE

16. Long-term memory is *relatively* permanent as we tend to update, change, lose, or revise our old memories.

TRUE or FALSE

17. Being confident about a memory tells little about the true accuracy of the memory.

TRUE or FALSE

18. False memory refers to having memories that never happened.

TRUE or FALSE

19. Eyewitnesses do not provide false testimonies as a result of false memories.

TRUE or FALSE

20. In combination with misleading questions, hypnosis increases false memories more than it does true ones.

TRUE or FALSE

21. Long-term memories appear to be organized alphabetically for speedy access.

TRUE or FALSE

22. Knowing how to swing a golf club is a type of declarative memory.

TRUE or FALSE

23. A person lacking declarative memory might still remember how to solve a mechanical puzzle.

TRUE or FALSE

24. Semantic memories are almost immune to forgetting.

TRUE or FALSE

25. Semantic memories are a type of declarative memory.

TRUE or FALSE

26. Episodic memories have no connection to particular times and places.

TRUE or FALSE

MODULE 8.3

Survey Question: How is memory measured? Pages 307-309

27. Remembering the first sound of a name you are trying to recall is an example of the tip-of-the-tongue state.

TRUE or FALSE

28. Tests of recognition require verbatim memory.
TRUE or FALSE

29. The serial position effect measures the strength of the feeling of knowing.
TRUE or FALSE

30. Recognition tends to be a more sensitive test of memory than recall.
TRUE or FALSE

31. False positives and distractors greatly affect the accuracy of relearning tests.
TRUE or FALSE

32. Recall, recognition, and relearning are used to measure explicit memories.
TRUE or FALSE

33. Priming is used to activate explicit (hidden) memories.
TRUE or FALSE

Survey Question: What are "photographic" memories? Pages 309-311

34. Eidetic images last for 30 seconds or more.
TRUE or FALSE

35. About 8 percent of all children have eidetic images.
TRUE or FALSE

36. Eidetic imagery becomes rare by adulthood.
TRUE or FALSE

37. Mr. S (the mnemonist) had virtually unlimited eidetic imagery.
TRUE or FALSE

38. Practice in remembering one type of information increases the capacity of STM to store other types of information too.
TRUE or FALSE

39. All contestants in the World Memory Championship performed poorly on tasks that prevented the use of learned strategies.
TRUE or FALSE

MODULE 8.4

Survey Questions: What causes forgetting? How accurate are everyday memories? Pages 313-319

40. Ebbinghaus chose to learn nonsense syllables so that they would all be the same length.
TRUE or FALSE

41. Ebbinghaus's curve of forgetting levels off after two days, showing little further memory loss after that.
TRUE or FALSE

42. Ebbinghaus's curve of forgetting only applies to memories of nonsense syllables.
TRUE or FALSE

43. The magic card trick demonstrates our ability to focus and pay attention.
TRUE or FALSE

44. Decay of memory traces clearly applies to information in STM.
TRUE or FALSE

45. Disuse theories of forgetting answer the question: Have I been storing the information in the first place?
TRUE or FALSE

46. The presence of memory cues almost always improves memory.
TRUE or FALSE

47. Information learned under the influence of a drug may be best remembered when the drugged state occurs again.
TRUE or FALSE

48. If you are in a bad mood, you are more likely to remember unpleasant events.
TRUE or FALSE

49. Categorizing a person as a member of a group tends to limit the accuracy of memories about the person's appearance.
TRUE or FALSE

50. Eyewitnesses are better at identifying members of other ethnic groups since they "look" different.
TRUE or FALSE

51. Sleeping tends to interfere with retaining new memories.
TRUE or FALSE

52. You learn information A and then information B. If your memory of B is lowered by having first learned A, you have experienced retroactive interference.
TRUE or FALSE

53. Interference only applies to the initial stage of learning. Learned information is permanent and can be easily retrieved.
TRUE or FALSE

54. Unconsciously forgetting painful memories is called negative transfer.
TRUE or FALSE

55. A conscious attempt to put a memory out of mind is called repression.
TRUE or FALSE

56. Suggestion and fantasy are elements of many techniques used in attempts to recover repressed memories.
TRUE or FALSE

57. Unless a memory can be independently confirmed, there is no way to tell if it is real or not.
TRUE or FALSE

58. Flashbulb memories tend to be formed when an event is surprising or emotional.
TRUE or FALSE

59. The confidence we have in flashbulb memories is well placed—they are much more accurate than most other memories.
TRUE or FALSE

Survey Question: What happens in the brain when memories are formed? Pages 319-321

60. Retrograde amnesia is a gap in memories of events preceding a head injury.
TRUE or FALSE

61. People with damage to the hippocampus typically cannot remember events that occurred before the damage.
TRUE or FALSE

62. In the early 1920s, Karl Lashley found the location of engrams in the brain.
TRUE or FALSE

63. Storing memories alters the activity, structure, and chemistry of the brain.
TRUE or FALSE

MODULE 8.5

Survey Question: How can I improve my memory? Pages 322-325

64. Recitation is a good way to generate feedback while studying.
TRUE or FALSE

65. Elaborative rehearsal involving "why" questions improves memory.
TRUE or FALSE

66. Overlearning is inefficient; you should stop studying at the point of initial mastery of new information.
TRUE or FALSE

67. Massed practice is almost always superior to spaced practice.
TRUE or FALSE

68. When learning, it helps to gradually extend how long you remember new information before reviewing it again.
TRUE or FALSE

69. Recalling events from different viewpoints is part of doing a cognitive interview.
    TRUE or FALSE

PSYCHOLOGY IN ACTION

Survey Question: How can I improve my memory? Pages 326-328

70. Roy G. Biv is a mnemonic for the notes on a musical staff.
    TRUE or FALSE

71. Many mnemonics make use of mental images or pictures.
    TRUE or FALSE

72. Mnemonics often link new information to familiar memories.
    TRUE or FALSE

73. The keyword method is superior to rote learning for memorizing vocabulary words in another language.
    TRUE or FALSE

FINAL SURVEY AND REVIEW

MODULE 8.1

Survey Question: Is there more than one type of memory? Pages 298-300

Memory is an active system. Information is first [1] _____ (changed into the form in which it will be retained).

Next, it is stored in memory. Later, it must be [2] _____ to be put to use.

Humans appear to have three interrelated memory systems. These are [3] _____ memory,

[4] _____ memory (STM), and long-term memory (LTM).

Sensory memory holds an exact copy of what is seen or heard, in the form of an [5] _____ (image) or [6] _____ (sound sensation).

[7] _____ memories tend to be stored as sounds. [8] _____ memories are stored on the basis of meaning, or importance.

[9] _____ acts as a temporary storehouse for small amounts of information. It provides a

[10] _____ memory where thinking, mental arithmetic, and the like take place. LTM acts as a permanent storehouse for [11] _____ information.

[12] _____ values impact the types of memories we tend to store. American culture emphasizes the individual; therefore, American memories are [13] _____ -focused. The Chinese culture

emphasizes [14] _____ membership; therefore, Chinese memories are of social events, which include family members, friends, and others.

MODULE 8.2

Survey Questions: What are the features of each type of memory? Is there more than one type of long-term memory? Pages 301-306

[15] _____ memory is exact but very brief, lasting only a few seconds or less. Through

[16] _____ [17] _____ , some information is transferred to STM.

The [18] _____ test reveals that STM has an average upper limit of about seven bits of information.

However, this can be extended by chunking, or [19] _____ information into larger units or groups.

The "[20] _____ " 7 (plus or minus 2) refers to the limitation of short-term memory discovered

by George [21] _____ . Nelson Cowan believes that the limitation of short-term memory is

[22] _____ than the "magic number" 7.

Short-term memories are brief and very sensitive to interruption, or [23] _____ ; however, they

can be prolonged by [24] _____ rehearsal (silent repetition).

[25] _____ rehearsal, which emphasizes meaning, helps transfer information from STM to LTM.

LTM seems to have an almost unlimited storage capacity. However, LTM is subject to [26] _____

processing, or ongoing revision and updating. As a result, people often have [27] _____ (false

memories) that they believe are true.

LTM is highly organized to allow retrieval of needed information. The pattern, or structure, of memory

[28] _____ is the subject of current memory research. [29] _____ models portray LTM

as a system of linked ideas.

[30] _____ memories unfold as each added memory provides a cue for retrieving the next

memory. Seemingly forgotten memories may be reconstructed in this way.

Within long-term memory, [31] _____ memories for facts seem to differ from [32] _____

memories for skills.

Declarative memories may be further categorized as [33] _____ memories or [34] _____

memories.

[35] _____ memories consist of basic factual knowledge that is almost immune to forgetting.

[36] _____ memories record personal experiences that are associated with specific times and

places.

MODULE 8.3

Survey Question: How is memory measured? Pages 307-309

The [37] _____ -of-the-[38] _____ state shows that memory is not an all-or-nothing event. Memories may be revealed by recall, [39] _____ , or relearning.

In [40] _____ , memory proceeds without specific cues, as in an essay exam. Remembering a list of information often reveals a [41] _____ [42] _____ effect (middle items on the list are most subject to errors).

A common test of recognition is the [43] _____ -choice question. Recognition is very sensitive to the kinds of [44] _____ (wrong choices) used.

In [45] _____ , "forgotten" material is learned again, and memory is indicated by a savings score. Recall, recognition, and relearning mainly measure [46] _____ memories that we are aware of having. Other techniques, such as priming, are necessary to reveal [47] _____ memories, which are unconscious.

Survey Question: What are "photographic" memories? Pages 309-311

[48] _____ [49] _____ (photographic memory) occurs when a person is able to project an image onto an external surface. Such images allow brief, nearly complete recall by some children.

[50] _____ [51] _____ is rarely found in adults. However, many adults have internal images, which can be very vivid and a basis for remembering.

[52] _____ memory can be learned by finding ways to directly store information in LTM. Learning has no effect on the [53] _____ of STM. Some people may have naturally superior memory abilities that exceed what can be achieved through learning.

MODULE 8.4

Survey Questions: What causes forgetting? How accurate are everyday memories? Pages 313-319

Forgetting and memory were extensively studied by Herman [54] _____ , whose curve of forgetting shows that forgetting is typically most rapid immediately after learning.

He used [55] _____ syllables to study memory. The forgetting of meaningful material is much slower than shown by his curve of forgetting.

Failure to [56] _____ information is a common cause of "forgetting."

Forgetting in [57] _____ memory and [58] _____ probably reflects decay of memory traces in the nervous system. Decay or disuse of memories may also account for some [59] _____ loss, but most forgetting cannot be explained this way.

Often, forgetting is [60] _____ dependent. The power of [61] _____ to trigger memories is revealed by [62] _____ learning, in which bodily states at the time of learning and of retrieval affect memory.

Much forgetting in both STM and LTM can be attributed to [63] _____ of memories with one another.

When recent learning interferes with retrieval of prior learning, [64] _____ interference has occurred. If old memories interfere with new memories, [65] _____ interference has occurred.

[66] _____ is the motivated forgetting of painful, embarrassing, or traumatic memories.

[67] _____ is thought to be unconscious, in contrast to [68] _____ , which is a conscious attempt to avoid thinking about something.

Experts are currently debating the validity of childhood memories of abuse that reappear after apparently being [69] _____ for decades.

Independent evidence has verified that some [70] _____ memories are true. However, others have been shown to be false.

In the absence of confirming or disconfirming evidence, there is currently no way to separate true memories from [71] _____ . Caution is advised for all concerned with attempts to retrieve supposedly hidden memories.

[72] _____ memories, which seem especially vivid, are created at emotionally significant times. While such memories may not be [73] _____ , we tend to place great confidence in them.

Survey Question: What happens in the brain when memories are formed? Pages 319-321

[74] _____ amnesia may be explained by the concept of consolidation.

Consolidation theory holds that [75] _____ (permanent memory traces) are formed during a critical period after learning. Until they are [76] _____ , long-term memories are easily destroyed.

The [77] _____ is a brain structure associated with the consolidation of memories.

The search within the brain for engrams has now settled on changes in individual [78] _____ [79] _____ .

The best-documented changes are alterations in the amounts of [80] _____ chemicals released by nerve cells.

MODULE 8.5

Survey Question: How can I improve my memory? Pages 322-325

Memory can be improved by using [81] _____ (knowledge of results), recitation, and rehearsal, by [82] _____ and organizing information, and by using the progressive part method, spaced practice, overlearning, and active [83] _____ strategies.

The effects of [84] _____ position, sleep, review, cues, and [85] _____ (connecting new information to existing knowledge) should also be kept in mind when studying or memorizing.

PSYCHOLOGY IN ACTION

Survey Question: How can I improve my memory? Pages 326-328

[86] _____ systems, such as the keyword method, use mental images and unusual associations to link new information with familiar memories already stored in LTM. Such strategies give information personal meaning and make it easier to recall.

Mnemonic techniques avoid [87] _____ learning and work best during the [88] _____ stages of learning.

MASTERY TEST

1. The meaning and importance of information has a strong impact on
   a. sensory memory
   b. eidetic memory
   c. long-term memory
   d. procedural memory

2. Pseudo-memories are closely related to the effects of
   a. repression
   b. suppression
   c. semantic forgetting
   d. constructive processing

3. The occurrence of _____ implies that consolidation has been prevented.
   a. retrograde amnesia
   b. hippocampal transfer
   c. suppression
   d. changes in the activities of individual nerve cells

4. Most of the techniques used to recover supposedly repressed memories involve
   a. redintegration and hypnosis
   b. suggestion and fantasy
   c. reconstruction and priming
   d. coercion and fabrication

5. Most daily memory chores are handled by
   a. sensory memory and LTM
   b. STM and working memory
   c. STM and LTM
   d. STM and declarative memory

6. Three key processes in memory systems are
   a. storage, organization, recovery
   b. encoding, attention, reprocessing
   c. storage, retrieval, encoding
   d. retrieval, reprocessing, reorganization

7. Procedural memories are to skills as _____ memories are to facts.
   a. declarative
   b. short-term
   c. redintegrative
   d. eidetic

8. An ability to answer questions about distances on a map you have seen only once implies that some memories are based on
   a. constructive processing
   b. redintegration
   c. internal images
   d. episodic processing

9. The first potential cause of forgetting that may occur is
   a. engram decay
   b. disuse
   c. cue-dependent forgetting
   d. encoding failure

10. The persistence of icons and echoes is the basis for
    a. sensory memory
    b. short-term memory
    c. long-term memory
    d. working memory

11. Priming is most often used to reveal
    a. semantic memories
    b. episodic memories
    c. implicit memories
    d. eidetic memories

12. "Projection" onto an external surface is most characteristic of
    a. sensory memories
    b. eidetic images
    c. flashbulb memories
    d. mnemonic images

13. Chunking helps especially to extend the capacity of
    a. sensory memory
    b. STM
    c. LTM
    d. declarative memory

14. There is presently no way to tell if a "recovered" memory is true or false unless independent _____ exists.
    a. evidence
    b. amnesia
    c. elaboration
    d. consolidation

15. Taking an essay test inevitably requires a person to use
    a. recall
    b. recognition
    c. relearning
    d. priming

16. A savings score is used in what memory task?
    a. recall
    b. recognition
    c. relearning
    d. priming

17. _____ rehearsal helps link new information to existing memories by concentrating on meaning.
    a. Redintegrative
    b. Constructive
    c. Maintenance
    d. Elaborative

18. Middle items are neither held in STM nor moved to LTM. This statement explains the
    a. feeling of knowing
    b. serial position effect
    c. tip-of-the-tongue state
    d. semantic forgetting curve

19. According to the curve of forgetting, the greatest decline in the amount recalled occurs during the _____ after learning.
    a. first hour
    b. second day
    c. third to sixth days
    d. retroactive period

20. Work with brain stimulation, truth serums, and hypnosis suggests that long-term memories are
    a. stored in the hippocampus
    b. relatively permanent
    c. unaffected by later input
    d. always redintegrative

21. Which of the following is most likely to improve the accuracy of memory?
    a. hypnosis
    b. constructive processing
    c. the serial position effect
    d. memory cues

22. To qualify as repression, forgetting must be
    a. retroactive
    b. proactive
    c. unconscious
    d. explicit

23. Which of the following typically is NOT a good way to improve memory?
    a. massed practice
    b. overlearning
    c. rehearsal
    d. recall strategies

24. A witness to a crime is questioned in ways that re-create the context of the crime and that provide many memory cues. It appears that she is undergoing
    a. retroactive priming
    b. the progressive part method
    c. retroactive consolidation
    d. a cognitive interview

25. One thing that is clearly true about flashbulb memories is that
    a. they are unusually accurate
    b. we place great confidence in them
    c. they apply primarily to public tragedies
    d. they are recovered by using visualization and hypnosis

26. One common mnemonic strategy is the
    a. serial position technique
    b. feeling of knowing tactic
    c. network procedure
    d. keyword method

27. A perspective that helps explain redintegrative memories is
    a. the feeling of knowing model
    b. recoding and chunking
    c. the network model
    d. mnemonic models

28. Which of the following is NOT considered a part of long-term memory?
    a. echoic memory
    b. semantic memory
    c. episodic memory
    d. declarative memory

29. You are very thirsty. Suddenly you remember a time years ago when you became very thirsty while hiking. This suggests that your memory is
    a. proactive
    b. state dependent
    c. still not consolidated
    d. eidetic

30. After memorizing five lists of words, you recall less of the last list than a person who only memorized list number five. This observation is explained by
    a. reactive processing
    b. reconstructive processing
    c. proactive interference
    d. retroactive interference

31. Who coined the term "magic number" 7 (plus or minus 2)?
    a. George Miller
    b. Nelson Cowan
    c. Herman Ebbinghaus
    d. Karl Lashley

32. When shown a picture of their third-grade class, a group of college students claimed to recall putting goo in the teacher's desk, an event that never took place, by simply filling in gaps with related childhood events. This is best explained by
    a. encoding failure
    b. retroactive interference
    c. retrograde amnesia
    d. constructive processing

33. People from the United States tend to recall memories that focus on what they did in a particular event while people from China tend to recall memories that focus on their interactions with family members and friends. Recalling different memories of similar events is the result of
    a. cultural influence
    b. effective use of mnemonic strategy
    c. highly developed cognition
    d. none of the above

34. False memory is likely to occur if hypnosis is used in conjunction with
    a. a medical doctor conducting the procedure
    b. the presence of a loved one
    c. misleading questions
    d. both a and b

35. To reduce false identification from eyewitnesses, police should
    a. have witnesses view all the pictures of people at one time
    b. have witnesses view pictures of people one at a time
    c. use hypnosis since it has proven to be a reliable source data gathering
    d. not use eyewitness testimonies since they are not reliable

36. The tendency for eyewitnesses to better identity members of their own ethnic group than other groups is best explained by
    a. eidetic memory
    b. serial position effect
    c. sensory memory
    d. categorization effect

37. A card dealer asks you to silently pick out a card from the six cards laid out in front of you and to memorize it. Without knowing the card you picked, he takes your card away and presents to you the other five cards. To perform this trick properly, the dealer hopes that
    a. you failed to encode the other five cards as you memorize the card you picked
    b. you do have eidetic memory
    c. you believe that he can read your mind
    d. the serial position effect does influence your memory

SOLUTIONS

RECITE AND REVIEW

MODULE 8.1

1. system
2. Information
3. stored
4. three
5. short-term
6. long-term
7. exact
8. image
9. sounds
10. meaning
11. temporary
12. permanent
13. memories
14. self
15. family

MODULE 8.2

16. seconds
17. STM
18. bits
19. larger
20. magic
21. short-term
22. lower
23. interruption
24. repetition
25. STM
26. memories
27. updating
28. false
29. organized
30. models
31. memory
32. facts
33. skills
34. Declarative
35. forgetting
36. personal

MODULE 8.3

37. state
38. recall
39. essay
40. middle
41. recognition
42. Recognition
43. savings
44. memories
45. memories

46. image
47. adults
48. LTM
49. STM

MODULE 8.4

50. curve
51. after
52. meaningful
53. slower
54. information
55. traces
56. disuse
57. learning
58. states
59. forgetting
60. interferes
61. interfere
62. forgetting
63. conscious
64. abuse
65. true
66. false
67. evidence
68. confidence

69. amnesia
70. memory
71. traces
72. brain
73. nerve
74. chemicals

MODULE 8.5

75. organizing

76. part   77. position

PSYCHOLOGY IN ACTION

78. keyword   79. LTM   80. initial

CONNECTIONS

MODULE 8.1

1. c   4. e   7. f
2. g   5. b
3. a   6. d

1. a   3. c   5. b
2. d   4. e

MODULE 8.2

1. f or g   4. a   7. e
2. c   5. f or g
3. d   6. b

1. b   3. c   5. d
2. e   4. a

MODULE 8.3

1. g   4. f   7. e
2. a   5. d
3. c   6. b

MODULE 8.4

1. d   4. f   7. c
2. e   5. h   8. i
3. g   6. b   9. a

MODULE 8.5

1. a   4. d   7. e
2. f   5. g
3. b   6. c

CHECK YOUR MEMORY

MODULE 8.1

1. T	4. T	7. T
2. F	5. F	8. F
3. T	6. F	

MODULE 8.2

9. T	15. F	21. F
10. F	16. T	22. F
11. F	17. T	23. T
12. T	18. T	24. T
13. F	19. F	25. T
14. F	20. T	26. F

MODULE 8.3

27. T	30. T	33. F
28. F	31. F	
29. F	32. T	

34. T	36. T	38. F
35. T	37. F	39. F

MODULE 8.4

40. F	48. T	56. T
41. T	49. T	57. T
42. F	50. F	58. T
43. F	51. F	59. F
44. T	52. F	
45. F	53. F	
46. T	54. F	
47. T	55. F	

60. T	62. F
61. F	63. T

MODULE 8.5

64. T	66. F	68. T
65. T	67. F	69. T

PSYCHOLOGY IN ACTION

70. F

71. T   72. T   73. T

FINAL SURVEY AND REVIEW

MODULE 8.1

1. encoded
2. retrieved
3. sensory
4. short term
5. icon
6. echo

7. Short-term
8. Long-term
9. STM
10. working
11. meaningful
12. Cultural

13. self
14. group

MODULE 8.2

15. Sensory
16. selective
17. attention
18. digit-span
19. recoding
20. magic number
21. Miller
22. lower

23. interference
24. maintenance
25. Elaborative
26. constructive
27. pseudo-memories
28. networks
29. Network
30. Redintegrative

31. declarative
32. procedural
33. semantic
34. episodic
35. Semantic
36. Episodic

MODULE 8.3

37. tip
38. tongue
39. recognition
40. recall

41. serial
42. position
43. multiple
44. distractors

45. relearning
46. explicit
47. implicit

48. Eidetic
49. imagery

50. Eidetic
51. imagery

52. Exceptional
53. limits

MODULE 8.4

54. Ebbinghaus
55. nonsense
56. encode
57. sensory
58. STM
59. LTM
60. cue
61. cues

62. state-dependent
63. interference
64. retroactive
65. proactive
66. Repression
67. Repression
68. suppression
69. repressed

70. recovered
71. fantasies
72. Flashbulb
73. accurate

74. Retrograde
75. engrams

76. consolidated
77. hippocampus

78. nerve
79. cells

80. transmitter

MODULE 8.5

81. feedback
82. selecting
83. search
84. serial
85. elaboration

PSYCHOLOGY IN ACTION

86. Mnemonic
87. rote
88. initial

MASTERY TEST

1. C, (p. 299)
2. D, (p. 303)
3. A, (p. 319)
4. B, (p. 318)
5. C, (p. 299)
6. C, (p. 298)
7. A, (p. 305)
8. C, (p. 309)
9. D, (p. 313)
10. A, (p. 298)
11. C, (p. 309)
12. B, (p. 310)
13. B, (p. 301)
14. A, (p. 318)
15. A, (p. 307)
16. C, (p. 308)
17. D, (p. 302)
18. B, (p. 307)
19. A, (p. 313)
20. B, (p. 302)
21. D, (p. 323)
22. C, (p. 318)
23. A, (p. 323)
24. D, (p. 324)
25. B, (p. 319)
26. D, (p. 327)
27. C, (p. 304)
28. A, (p. 305)
29. B, (p. 316)
30. C, (p. 317)
31. A, (p. 301)
32. D, (p. 303)
33. A, (p. 300)
34. C, (p. 304)
35. B, (p. 308)
36. D, (p. 315)
37. A, (p. 314)

COGNITION, INTELLIGENCE, AND CREATIVITY

CHAPTER OVERVIEW

Thinking is the mental manipulation of images, concepts, and language (or symbols). Most people use internal images (including kinesthetic images) for thinking. A concept is a generalized idea of a class of objects or events. We learn concepts from positive and negative instances and from rules. Three types of concepts are conjunctive, relational, and disjunctive. Prototypes are often used to identify concepts.

Semantics is the study of meaning in language. Research on semantics has shown that words and their meanings greatly influence our thought processes. Language translates events into symbols, which are combined using the rules of grammar and syntax. True languages are productive. Studies suggest that, with training, primates are capable of some language use.

The solution to a problem may be arrived at mechanically (by trial and error or by rote). An algorithm is used when a problem is solved using the rote method. Solutions by understanding usually begin with discovering the general properties of an answer. Next, functional solutions are proposed. Problem solving is frequently aided by heuristics, which narrow the search for solutions. When understanding leads to a rapid solution, insight has occurred. Three types of insights are selective encoding, selective combination, and selective comparison. Insight can be blocked by fixations. Work on artificial intelligence has focused on computer simulations and expert systems. Human expertise is based on organized knowledge and acquired strategies.

Intelligence refers to a general capacity to act purposefully, think rationally, and deal effectively with the environment. In practice, intelligence is operationally defined by creating tests. The first practical individual intelligence test was assembled by Alfred Binet. A modern version is the Stanford-Binet Intelligence Scale. A second major intelligence test is the Wechsler Adult Intelligence Scale. Culture-fair and group intelligence tests are also available. Intelligence is expressed as an intelligence quotient (IQ) or as a deviation IQ. The distribution of IQ scores approximates a normal curve. Intelligence reflects the combined effects of heredity and environment.

People with IQs in the gifted or "genius" range tend to be superior in many respects. In addition, many children are gifted or talented in other ways. The terms *mentally retarded* and *developmentally disabled* apply to persons who have an IQ below 70 or who lack various adaptive behaviors. About 50 percent of the cases of mental retardation are organic; the remaining cases are of undetermined cause (many are thought to be familial).

Creative solutions are practical, sensible, and original. Creative thinking requires divergent thought, characterized by fluency, flexibility, and originality. Tests of creativity measure these qualities. Five stages often seen in creative problem solving are orientation, preparation, incubation, illumination, and verification. There is only a small positive correlation between IQ and creativity. Most creative people are not mentally disturbed, and most mentally disturbed people are not creative.

Intuitive thinking often leads to errors. Wrong conclusions may be drawn when an answer seems highly representative of what we already believe is true. A second problem is allowing emotions to determine our decision making. A third problem is ignoring the base rate of an event. Clear thinking is usually aided by stating or framing a problem in broad terms. Major sources of thinking errors include rigid mental sets, faulty logic, and over simplifications. Various strategies, including brainstorming, tend to enhance creative problem solving.

LEARNING OBJECTIVES

To demonstrate mastery of this chapter, you should be able to:

1. Define the terms "cognition" and "cognitive psychology."

2. List the three basic units of thought.

3. Describe mental imagery (including the concept of mental rotation and a description of what happens in the brain during visual imaging). Explain how both stored and created images may be used to solve problems.

4. Explain how the size of a mental image can be important.

5. Explain how kinesthetic imagery aids thinking.

6. Define the terms "concept" and "concept formation," explain how they aid thought processes, and describe how they are learned. Define the term "conceptual rules."

7. Define the terms "conjunctive concept," "relational concept," and "disjunctive concept."

8. Explain the importance of prototypes.

9. Explain the difference between the denotative and connotative meaning of a word or concept and describe how the connotative meaning of a word is measured using the semantic differential.

10. Briefly discuss how using inaccurate concepts may lead to thinking errors. Include a discussion of social stereotypes and all-or-nothing thinking.

11. Define "semantics" and explain how semantic problems may arise.

The following objective is related to the material in the "Discovering Psychology" section of the text.

12. Describe the experiment conducted by Karylowski et al. in 2002 regarding faster or slower recognition of words as they are related to colors and explain how word meanings "color" our thoughts.

13. Briefly describe the following three requirements of a language and their related concepts: a. symbols i. phonemes ii. morphemes b. grammar i. syntax ii. transformation rules c. productivity

14. Briefly describe the concept of gestural languages, especially the role of ASL.

15. Describe the research involving attempts to teach primates (especially Viki, Washoe, Sarah, and Kanzi) to use language. Describe the criticisms and practical value of such attempts.

16. Compare and contrast mechanical solutions with solutions through understanding. Also include a discussion of general solutions and functional solutions to problem solving.

17. Define the term "heuristic" and contrast it with random search strategies.

18. Describe the process of insight as a problem solving technique.

19. List and describe the three abilities involved in insight.

20. Explain how fixation and functional fixedness block problem solving and give an example of each.

21. List and explain four common barriers to creative thinking.

22. Define the term "artificial intelligence" and state upon what fact it is based.

23. Explain how computer simulations and expert systems are used.

24. Explain the differences between experts and novices.

25. Define "intelligence."

26. Explain what an operational definition of intelligence is.

27. Describe Binet's role in intelligence testing.

28. Generally describe the construction of the Stanford-Binet Intelligence Scale.

29. Define "intelligence quotient," and use an example to show how it was computed. Define the terms "chronological age" and "mental age." Explain the purpose of deviation IQ scores.

30. Distinguish the Wechsler tests from the Stanford-Binet tests.

31. Define the term "culture-fair test," and explain how IQ tests may be unfair to certain groups.

32. Distinguish between group and individual intelligence tests.

33. Describe the pattern of distribution of IQ scores observed in the general population.

34. Discuss the relationship between IQ and achievement. Describe any differences between males and females with regard to IQ.

35. Briefly describe Terman's study of gifted children. State how successful subjects differed from the less successful ones.

36. List seven early signs of giftedness.

37. Describe Gardner's broader view of intelligence and list the eight different kinds of intelligence he discusses.

38. State the dividing line between normal intelligence and retardation (or developmental disability) and list the degrees of retardation.

39. Differentiate between organic and familial retardation.

40. Explain how the twin (identical and fraternal) studies can be used to support either side of the heredity/environment controversy.

41. Describe the evidence that strongly supports the environmental view of intelligence.

42. Describe the studies that indicate how much the environment can alter intelligence.

43. Discuss how the heredity/environment debate is currently viewed.

44. Describe the following four kinds of thought: a. inductive b. deductive c. logical d. illogical

45. Describe the following characteristics of creative thinking: a. fluency b. flexibility c. originality

46. Explain the relationship of creativity to divergent and convergent thinking. Describe how the ability to think divergently can be measured.

47. List and describe the five stages of creative thinking and relate them to a problem that you have solved.

48. List five conclusions about creative people.

49. Define "intuition."

50. Explain the following errors made when using intuition: a. representativeness b. underlying odds (base rate) c. emotion d. framing

51. Briefly describe the relationship between intelligence and wisdom.

52. Describe eight practical steps for encouraging creativity.

53. Describe the process of brainstorming, and explain how it can be used to solve problems.

54. Briefly list and describe the nine items on the "creativity checklist."

55. List eight ways that are suggested to become more creative.

RECITE AND REVIEW

MODULE 9.1

Survey Question: What is the nature of thought? Page 332

Cognition is the [1] _____ processing of information involving daydreaming, [2] _____ solving, and reasoning.

Thinking is the manipulation of [3] _____ representations of external problems or situations.

Three basic units of thought are images, concepts, and [4] _____ or symbols.

Survey Question: In what ways are images related to thinking? Pages 332-334

Many of the systems in the brain that are involved in processing [5] _____ images work in reverse to create mental images.

Most people have internal images of one kind or another. Images may be based on information stored in memory or they may be [6] _____ .

The size of images used in problem solving may [7] _____ . Images may be three-dimensional and they may be rotated in [8] _____ to answer questions.

Kinesthetic images are created from produced, remembered, or imagined [9] _____ sensations.

[10] _____ sensations and micromovements seem to help structure thinking for many people.

Survey Question: How do we learn concepts? Pages 334-336

A concept is a generalized idea of a [11] _____ of objects or events.

Forming concepts may be based on experiences with [12] _____ and negative instances.

Concepts may also be acquired by learning rules that define the [13] _____ .

Concepts may be classified as conjunctive ("[14] _____ " concepts), disjunctive ("[15] _____ " concepts), or relational concepts.

In practice, we frequently use prototypes (general [16] _____ of the concept class) to identify concepts.

The denotative meaning of a word or concept is its exact [17] _____ . Connotative meaning is [18] _____ or emotional.

Connotative meaning can be measured with the semantic differential. Most connotative meaning involves the dimensions [19] _____ , strong-weak, and active-passive.

The Stroop task demonstrates the effectiveness of [20] _____ influencing our thinking. The meaning of the word interferes with our ability to name the color of the word.

Survey Question: What is the role of language in thinking? Pages 336-340

Language allows events to be encoded into [21] _____ for easy mental manipulation.

Thinking in language is influenced by meaning. The study of [22] _____ is called semantics.

Language is built out of phonemes (basic speech [23] _____) and morphemes (speech sounds collected into [24] _____ units).

Language carries meaning by combining a set of symbols or signs according to a set of [25] _____ (grammar), which includes rules about word [26] _____ (syntax).

Various sentences are created by applying transformation [27] _____ to simple statements.

A true language is productive and can be used to generate new ideas or possibilities. American Sign Language (ASL) and other [28] _____ languages used by the deaf are true languages.

Animal communication is relatively limited because it lacks symbols that can be rearranged easily. As a result, it does not have the productive quality of [29] _____ language.

Attempts to teach chimpanzees ASL and other nonverbal systems suggest to some that primates are capable of language use. However, others believe that the chimps are merely using [30] _____ responses to get food and other reinforcers.

Studies that make use of lexigrams ([31] _____ word-symbols) provide the best evidence yet of animal language use.

MODULE 9.2

Survey Question: What do we know about problem solving? Pages 342-346

The solution to a problem may be found mechanically (by trial-and-error or by [32] _____ application of rules). However, mechanical solutions are frequently inefficient or ineffective, except where aided by [33] _____ .

Often a [34] _____ solution is achieved through an algorithm, a [35] _____ set of rules that always leads to a correct solution.

Solutions by understanding usually begin with discovery of the [36] _____ properties of an answer. Next comes proposal of a number of functional [37] _____ .

Problem solving is frequently aided by heuristics. These are strategies that typically [38] _____ the search for solutions.

When understanding leads to a rapid [39] _____ , insight has occurred. Three elements of insight are [40] _____ encoding, selective combination, and selective comparison.

The ability to apply [41] _____ comparison (comparing old solutions to new problems) effectively can be influenced by our culture.

Insights and other problem-solving attempts can be blocked by fixation (a tendency to repeat [42] _____ solutions).

Functional fixedness is a common [43] _____ , but emotional blocks, cultural values, learned conventions, and perceptual [44] _____ are also problems.

Survey Question. What Is artificial intelligence? Pages 346-347

Artificial intelligence refers to computer [45] _____ that can perform tasks that require [46] _____ when done by people.

Two principal areas of artificial intelligence research are [47] _____ simulations and expert systems.

Expert human problem solving is based on organized [48] _____ and acquired strategies rather than some general improvement in thinking ability.

MODULE 9.3

Survey Questions: How is human intelligence defined and measured? How do IQ scores relate to achievement and thinking abilities? Pages 349-358

The first practical [49] _____ [50] _____ was assembled in 1904, in Paris, by Alfred Binet.

Intelligence refers to one's general capacity to act purposefully, think [51] _____ , and deal effectively with the [52] _____ .

In practice, writing an intelligence test provides an operational [53] _____ of intelligence.

A modern version of Binet's test is the Stanford-Binet Intelligence [54] _____ , 5th Edition.

The Stanford-Binet measures [55] _____ reasoning, quantitative reasoning, visual-spatial processing, working [56] _____ , and knowledge.

Intelligence is expressed in terms of an intelligence [57] _____ (IQ). IQ is defined as mental age (MA) divided by chronological age (CA) and then multiplied by [58] _____ .

Modern IQ tests no longer calculate [59] _____ directly. Instead, the final score reported by the test is a deviation IQ, which gives a person's [60] _____ intellectual standing in his or her age group. An average IQ score of 100 would place a person at the [61] _____ percentile.

A second major intelligence test is the Wechsler [62] _____ Intelligence Scale, 3rd Edition (WAIS-III). The WAIS-III measures both verbal and performance ([63] _____) intelligence.

The Wechsler and Binet scales are designed to measure the IQ of people from middle-class [64] _____ cultures. To reduce the influence of verbal skills, cultural background, and [65] _____ level when measuring the IQ of people from another culture (e.g., China) or from a different background (e.g., poor community), culture-[66] _____ tests have been implemented. Intelligence tests have also been produced for use with [67] _____ of people. The Scholastic Assessment Test (SAT) measures a variety of [68] _____ aptitudes, and it can be used to estimate intelligence.

An "average" IQ of [69] _____ occurs when mental age [70] _____ chronological age. When graphed, the distribution (percentage of people receiving each score) of IQ scores approximates a normal ([71] _____ -shaped) [72] _____ .

There is no difference between men and women's [73] _____ level. The male-female performance gap is the result of certain opportunities provided to each sex.

People with IQs above 140 are considered to be in the [74] _____ or "genius" range.

Studies done by Lewis Terman showed that the gifted tend to be [75] _____ : They earned advanced degrees, held professional positions, and had written books.

The most successful gifted persons tend to be those who are persistent and [76] _____ to learn and succeed.

By criteria other than [77] _____ , a large proportion of children might be considered gifted or talented in one way or another.

Howard Gardner believes that [78] _____ IQ tests define intelligence too narrowly. According to Gardner, intelligence consists of abilities in language, logic and [79] _____ , [80] _____ and spatial thinking, music, kinesthetic skills, intrapersonal skills, interpersonal skills, and naturalist skills.

The terms *mentally* [81] _____ and *developmentally disabled* are applied to those whose IQ falls below [82] _____ or who lack various adaptive behaviors.

Further classifications of retardation are: [83] _____ (50-55 to 70), moderate (35-40 to 50-55), [84] _____ (20-25 to 35-40), and profound (below 20-25).

About [85] _____ percent of the cases of mental retardation are organic, being caused by [86] _____ injuries, fetal damage, metabolic disorders, or genetic abnormalities. The remaining cases are of undetermined cause.

Many cases of subnormal intelligence are thought to be the result of familial retardation (a low level of [87] _____ stimulation in the home, poverty, and poor nutrition).

Studies of family relationships in humans, especially comparisons between fraternal twins and identical twins (who have identical [88] _____), also suggest that intelligence is partly [89] _____ .

Environment is also important, as revealed by changes in tested intelligence, induced by [90] _____ environments and improved education.

[91] _____ therefore reflects the combined effects of heredity and environment.

Differences in the average IQ scores for various racial groups are based on environmental differences, not [92] _____ .

MODULE 9.4

Survey Question: What is creative thinking? Pages 360-363

[93] _____ may be deductive or inductive, logical or illogical.

Creative thinking requires divergent thought, characterized by fluency, flexibility, and [94] _____ .

Tests of [95] _____ , such as the Unusual Uses Test, the Consequences Test, and the Anagrams Test, measure the capacity for divergent thinking.

To be creative, a solution must be [96] _____ and sensible as well as original.

Five stages often seen in creative problem solving are orientation, [97] _____ , incubation, illumination, and verification.

Studies suggest that creative persons share a combination of thinking [98] _____ , personality characteristics, and a [99] _____ social environment. There is only a small correlation between IQ and creativity.

Most [100] _____ people do not suffer from mental disorders, and most [101] _____ disturbed people are not creative. However, there are a few exceptions in regard to [102] _____ disorders. The relation between creativity and mood disorders may be due to the level of productivity during the manic state.

Survey Question: How accurate is intuition? Pages 363-365

Intuitive thinking often leads to [103] _____ . Wrong conclusions may be drawn when an answer seems highly representative of what we already believe is [104] _____ , that is, when people apply the representativeness heuristic.

A second problem is allowing emotions such as [105] _____ , hope, [106] _____ , or disgust to guide [107] _____ in decision making.

The third problem is ignoring the base rate (or underlying [108] _____) of an event.

Clear thinking is usually aided by stating or framing a problem in [109] _____ terms.

PSYCHOLOGY IN ACTION

Survey Question: What can be done to improve thinking and promote creativity? Pages 367-370

[110] _____ sets can act as major barriers to creative [111] _____ .

Creativity can be enhanced by defining problems [112] _____ , by establishing a creative atmosphere by restating a problem in [113] _____ ways, by allowing [114] _____ for incubation, by seeking [115] _____ input, by taking sensible risks, and by looking for analogies.

Brainstorming, in which the production and criticism of ideas is kept [116] _____ , also tends to enhance creative problem solving.

CONNECTIONS

MODULE 9.1

1. _____ cognition	a.	3-D images
2. _____ language	b.	remembered perceptions
3. _____ social stereotypes	c.	images created by the brain
4. _____ mental rotation	d.	mental class
5. _____ reverse vision	e.	implicit actions
6. _____ stored images	f.	thinking
7. _____ kinesthetic imagery	g.	ideal or model
8. _____ concept	h.	semantic differential
9. _____ prototype	i.	faulty, oversimplified concepts
10. _____ connotative meaning	j.	symbols and rules

1. _____ word meanings	a.	meaningful unit
2. _____ morpheme	b.	ASL
3. _____ phoneme	c.	semantics
4. _____ "hidden" grammar	d.	lexigrams
5. _____ Washoe	e.	language sound
6. _____ if-then statement	f.	conditional relationship
7. _____ Kanzi	g.	transformation rules

MODULE 9.2

1. _____ expert versus novice
2. _____ AI
3. _____ insight
4. _____ trial-and-error
5. _____ random search strategy
6. _____ heuristic
7. _____ understanding
8. _____ selective comparison
9. _____ fixation
10. _____ expert system

a. mechanical solution
b. thinking strategy
c. element of insight
d. knowledge plus rules
e. a clear, sudden solution
f. trial-and-error
g. Deep Blue
h. acquired strategies
i. blind to alternatives
j. deep comprehension

MODULE 9.3

1. _____ Binet
2. _____ average intelligence
3. _____ identical twins
4. _____ IQ
5. _____ deviation IQ
6. _____ IQ of 115
7. _____ gifted people
8. _____ developmentally disabled
9. _____ group test
10. _____ WAIS
11. _____ normal curve
12. _____ multiple intelligence

a. same genes
b. relative standing
c. IQ of 140
d. Wechsler test
e. first intelligence test
f. "people smart" and "nature smart"
g. SAT
h. bell shape
i. 84th percentile
j. MA/CA x 100
k. IQ below 70
l. IQ of 100

MODULE 9.4

1. _____ fluency
2. _____ flexibility
3. _____ originality
4. _____ logical
5. _____ convergent thinking
6. _____ Anagrams Test
7. _____ mental set
8. _____ illumination
9. _____ base rate
10. _____ intuition

a. preconceived concept
b. many types of solutions
c. one correct answer
d. follow explicit rule
e. moment of insight
f. underlying odds
g. quick and impulsive thought
h. many solutions
i. measures divergent thinking
j. novelty of solutions

CHECK YOUR MEMORY

MODULE 9.1

Survey Question: What is the nature of thought? Page 332

1. Cognition refers to the process of encoding, storing, and retrieving information.
   TRUE or FALSE

2. Images, concepts, and language may be used to mentally represent problems.
   TRUE or FALSE

3. Images are generalized ideas of a class of related objects or events.
   TRUE or FALSE

4. Blindfolded chess players mainly use concepts to represent chess problems and solutions.
   TRUE or FALSE

Survey Question: In what ways are images related to thinking? Pages 332-334

5. Images are used to make decisions, change feelings, and to improve memory.
   TRUE or FALSE

6. Mental images may be used to improve memory and skilled actions.
   TRUE or FALSE

7. The visual cortex is activated when a person has a mental image.
   TRUE or FALSE

8. The more the image of a shape has to be rotated in space, the longer it takes to tell if it matches another view of the same shape.
   TRUE or FALSE

9. People who have good imaging abilities tend to score high on tests of creativity.
   TRUE or FALSE

10. The smaller a mental image is, the harder it is to identify its details.
    TRUE or FALSE

11. People with good kinesthetic imagery tend to learn sports skills faster than average.
    TRUE or FALSE

Survey Question: How do we learn concepts? Pages 334-336

12. Concept formation is typically based on examples and rules.
TRUE or FALSE

13. Prototypes are very strong negative instances of a concept.
TRUE or FALSE

14. "Greater than" and "lopsided" are relational concepts.
TRUE or FALSE

15. The semantic differential is used to rate the objective meanings of words and concepts.
TRUE or FALSE

16. Social stereotypes are accurate, oversimplified concepts people use to form mental images of groups of people.
TRUE or FALSE

Survey Question: What is the role of language in thinking? Pages 336-340

17. Encoding is the study of the meanings of language.
TRUE or FALSE

18. The Stroop interference test shows that thought is greatly influenced by language.
TRUE or FALSE

19. People can easily name the color of the word without the meaning of the word interfering with their thought processing.
TRUE or FALSE

20. Morphemes are the basic speech sounds of a language.
TRUE or FALSE

21. Syntax is a part of grammar.
TRUE or FALSE

22. Noam Chomsky believes that a child who says, "I drinked my juice," has applied the semantic differential to a simple, core sentence.
TRUE or FALSE

23. ASL has 600,000 root signs.
TRUE or FALSE

24. True languages are productive, thus ASL is not a true language.
TRUE or FALSE

25. If one is fluent in ASL, one can sign and understand other gestural languages such as Yiddish Sign.
TRUE or FALSE

26. Animal communication can be described as productive.
TRUE or FALSE

27. Chimpanzees have never learned to speak even a single word.
TRUE or FALSE

28. One of Sarah chimpanzee's outstanding achievements was mastery of sentences involving transformational rules.
TRUE or FALSE

29. Some "language" use by chimpanzees appears to be no more than simple operant responses.
TRUE or FALSE

30. Only a minority of the things that language-trained chimps "say" have anything to do with food.
TRUE or FALSE

31. Language-trained chimps have been known to hold conversations when no humans were present.
TRUE or FALSE

32. Kanzi's use of grammar is on a par with that of a two-year-old child.
TRUE or FALSE

MODULE 9.2

Survey Question: What do we know about problem solving? Pages 342-346

33. Except for the simplest problems, mechanical solutions are typically best left to computers.
TRUE or FALSE

34. An algorithm is a learned set of rules (grammar) for language.
TRUE or FALSE

35. Karl Duncker's famous tumor problem could only be solved by trial-and-error.
TRUE or FALSE

36. In solutions by understanding, functional solutions are usually discovered by use of a random search strategy.
TRUE or FALSE

37. Working backward from the desired goal to the starting point can be a useful heuristic.
TRUE or FALSE

38. In problem solving, rapid insights are more likely to be correct than those that develop slowly.
TRUE or FALSE

39. Selective encoding refers to bringing together seemingly unrelated bits of useful information.
TRUE or FALSE

40. An advantage of selective comparison is our ability to solve problems in all cultures.
TRUE or FALSE

41. Functional fixedness is an inability to see new uses for familiar objects.
TRUE or FALSE

42. Learned barriers in functional fixedness refer to our habits causing us to not identify other important elements of a problem.
TRUE or FALSE

Survey Question: What is artificial intelligence? Pages 346-347

43. AI is frequently based on a set of rules applied to a body of information.
TRUE or FALSE

44. Computer simulations are used to test models of human cognition.
TRUE or FALSE

45. Much human expertise is based on acquired strategies for solving problems.
TRUE or FALSE

46. Chess experts have an exceptional ability to remember the positions of chess pieces placed at random on a chessboard.
TRUE or FALSE

47. Deep Blue, an artificial computer program, has "fooled" people into believing that it is human; therefore, it is considered intelligent.
TRUE or FALSE

MODULE 9.3

Survey Questions: How is human intelligence defined and measured? How do IQ scores relate to achievement and thinking abilities? Pages 349-358

48. Alfred Binet's first test was designed to measure mechanical aptitude.
TRUE or FALSE

49. Lewis Terman helped write the Stanford-Binet intelligence test.
TRUE or FALSE

50. The Stanford-Binet intelligence test measures three intelligence factors: knowledge, quantitative reasoning, and visual-spatial processing.
TRUE or FALSE

51. The Stanford-Binet intelligence test does include a memory task (repeating a series of digits) to determine a person's ability to use his/her short-term memory.
TRUE or FALSE

52. Mental age refers to average mental ability for a person of a given age.
TRUE or FALSE

53. Mental age can't be higher than chronological age.
TRUE or FALSE

54. An IQ will be greater than 100 when CA is larger than MA.
TRUE or FALSE

55. Average intelligence is defined as an IQ from 90 to 109.
TRUE or FALSE

56. Modern IQ tests give scores as deviation IQs.
TRUE or FALSE

57. Being placed in the 84th percentile means that 16 percent of your peers received IQ scores higher than you and 84 percent have IQ scores lower than you.
TRUE or FALSE

58. The WISC is designed to test adult performance intelligence.
TRUE or FALSE

59. The Stanford-Binet, Wechsler's, and the SAT are all group intelligence tests.
TRUE or FALSE

60. In a normal curve, a majority of scores are found near the average.
TRUE or FALSE

61. The Stanford-Binet, Wechsler's, and the SAT are all culture-fair tests.
TRUE or FALSE

62. An IQ above 130 is described as "bright normal."
TRUE or FALSE

63. The correlation between IQ scores and school grades is .5.
TRUE or FALSE

64. Research has shown that men do score higher on the Stanford-Binet Intelligence Scale than women, which proves that men are smarter than women.
TRUE or FALSE

65. Only 12 people out of 100 score above 130 on IQ tests.
TRUE or FALSE

66. Gifted children tend to get average IQ scores by the time they reach adulthood.
    TRUE or FALSE

67. Gifted persons are more susceptible to mental illness.
    TRUE or FALSE

68. Talking in complete sentences at age two is regarded as a sign of giftedness.
    TRUE or FALSE

69. Howard Gardner suggests that each of us has eight different types of intelligence such as being "people smart," "word smart," etc.
    TRUE or FALSE

70. The moderately retarded can usually learn routine self-help skills.
    TRUE or FALSE

71. The IQs of identical twins are more alike than those of fraternal twins.
    TRUE or FALSE

72. Adult intelligence is approximately 50 percent hereditary.
    TRUE or FALSE

73. The environmental influence on twins does include development inside their mother's womb before birth.
    TRUE or FALSE

74. Herrnstein and Murray, in their book, *The Bell Curve*, suggested that racial group differences in IQ were due to environmental influences, not genes.
    TRUE or FALSE

MODULE 9.4

Survey Question: What is creative thinking? Pages 360-363

75. In inductive thinking, a general rule is inferred from specific examples.
    TRUE or FALSE

76. Fluency and flexibility are measures of convergent thinking.
    TRUE or FALSE

77. Creative thinkers typically apply reasoning and critical thinking to novel ideas after they produce them.
    TRUE or FALSE

78. Creative ideas combine originality with feasibility.
    TRUE or FALSE

79. Creative problem solving temporarily stops during the incubation period.
    TRUE or FALSE

80. Creative people have an openness to experience, and they have a wide range of knowledge and interests.
TRUE or FALSE

81. An IQ score of 120 or above means that a person is creative.
TRUE or FALSE

82. Most creative people like Vincent Van Gogh and Edgar Allan Poe tend to become insane later in life.
TRUE or FALSE

Survey Question: How accurate is intuition? Pages 363-365

83. Intuition is a quick, impulsive insight into the true nature of a problem and its solution.
TRUE or FALSE

84. The probability of two events occurring together is lower than the probability of either one occurring alone.
TRUE or FALSE

85. The representativeness heuristic is the strategy of stating problems in broad terms.
TRUE or FALSE

86. Being logical, most people do not let their emotions interfere when making important decisions.
TRUE or FALSE

87. Framing refers to the way in which a problem is stated or structured.
TRUE or FALSE

88. People who are intelligent are also wise because they live their lives with openness and tolerance.
TRUE or FALSE

PSYCHOLOGY IN ACTION

Survey Question: What can be done to improve thinking and promote creativity? Pages 367-370

89. Creative problem solving involves defining problems as narrowly as possible.
TRUE or FALSE

90. It is wise to allow time for incubation if you are seeking a creative solution to a problem.
TRUE or FALSE

91. Edward de Bono suggests that digging deeper with logic is a good way to increase your creativity.
TRUE or FALSE

92. People seeking creative solutions should avoid taking risks; doing so just leads to deadends.
TRUE or FALSE

93. Delaying evaluation during the early stages of creative problem solving tends to lead to poor thinking.
TRUE or FALSE

94. The cross-stimulation effect is an important part of brainstorming in groups.
TRUE or FALSE

FINAL SURVEY AND REVIEW

MODULE 9.1

Survey Question: What is the nature of thought? Page 332

[1] _____ is the mental processing of information involving daydreaming, problem solving, and reasoning.

Thinking is the manipulation of internal [2] _____ of external problems or situations.

Three basic units of thought are [3] _____ , [4] _____ , and language or

[5] _____ .

Survey Question: In what ways are images related to thinking? Pages 332-334

Many of the systems in the [6] _____ that are involved in processing [7] _____ images work in reverse to create [8] _____ images.

Most people have internal images of one kind or another. Images may be based on [9] _____

[10] _____ in memory or they may be created.

The [11] _____ of images used in problem solving may change. Images may be three-dimensional and they may be [12] _____ in space to answer questions.

Kinesthetic [13] _____ are created from produced, remembered, or imagined muscular sensations.

Kinesthetic sensations and [14] _____ seem to help structure thinking for many people.

Survey Question: How do we learn concepts? Pages 334-336

A concept is a [15] _____ idea of a class of objects or events.

Forming concepts may be based on experiences with positive and [16] _____ [17] _____ .

Concepts may also be acquired by learning [18] _____ that define the concept.

Concepts may be classified as [19] _____ ("and" concepts), [20] _____ ("either-or" concepts), or relational concepts.

In practice, we frequently use [21] _____ (general models of the concept class) to identify concepts.

The [22] _____ meaning of a word or concept is its exact definition. [23] _____ meaning is personal or emotional.

Connotative meaning can be measured with the [24] _____ differential. Most connotative meaning involves the dimensions good-bad, [25] _____ , and [26] _____ .

The Stroop task demonstrates the effectiveness of [27] _____ influencing our thoughts. The meaning of the word interferes with our ability to name the color of the word.

Survey Question: What is the role of language in thinking? Pages 336-340

Language allows events to be [28] _____ into symbols for easy mental manipulation.

Thinking in language is influenced by meaning. The study of meaning is called [29] _____ .

Language is built out of [30] _____ (basic speech sounds) and [31] _____ (speech sounds collected into meaningful units).

Language carries meaning by combining a set of symbols or signs according to a set of rules ([32] _____), which includes rules about word order ([33] _____).

Various sentences are created by applying [34] _____ rules to simple statements.

A true language is [35] _____ and can be used to generate new ideas or possibilities.

[36] _____ [37] _____ Language (ASL) and other gestural languages used by the deaf are true languages.

[38] _____ communication is relatively limited because it lacks symbols that can be rearranged easily. As a result, it does not have the [39] _____ quality of human language.

Attempts to teach chimpanzees ASL and other nonverbal systems suggest to some that [40] _____ are capable of language use. However, others believe that the chimps are merely using operant responses to get food and other [41] _____ .

Studies that make use of [42] _____ (geometric word-symbols) provide the best evidence yet of animal language use.

MODULE 9.2

Survey Question: What do we know about problem solving? Pages 342-346

The solution to a problem may be found [43] _____ (by trial and error or by rote application of rules). However, [44] _____ solutions are frequently inefficient or ineffective, except where aided by computer.

Often a rote solution is achieved through an [45] _____ , a learned set of rules that always leads to a correct solution.

Solutions by [46] _____ usually begin with discovery of the general properties of an answer.

Next comes proposal of a number of [47] _____ (workable) solutions.

Problem solving is frequently aided by [48] _____ . These are strategies that typically narrow the search for solutions.

When understanding leads to a rapid solution, [49] _____ has occurred. Three elements of [50] _____ are selective [51] _____ , selective combination, and selective comparison.

The ability to apply selective comparison (comparing [52] _____ solutions to new problems) effectively can be influenced by our [53] _____ .

Insights and other problem-solving attempts can be blocked by [54] _____ (a tendency to repeat wrong solutions).

[55] _____ fixedness is a common fixation, but emotional [56] _____ , cultural [57] _____ , learned conventions, and perceptual habits are also problems.

Survey Question: What is artificial intelligence? Pages 346-347

Artificial intelligence refers to [58] _____ [59] _____ that can perform tasks that require intelligence when done by [60] _____ .

Two principal areas of artificial intelligence research are computer simulations and [61] _____ [62] _____ .

Expert human problem solving is based on [63] _____ knowledge and acquired [64] _____ rather than some general improvement in thinking ability.

MODULE 9.3

Survey Questions: How is human intelligence defined and measured? How do IQ scores relate to achievement and thinking abilities? Pages 349-358

The first practical intelligence test was assembled in 1904, in Paris, by [65] _____ [66] _____ .

Intelligence refers to one's general capacity to act [67] _____ , [68] _____ rationally, and deal effectively with the environment.

In practice, writing an intelligence test provides an [69] _____ definition of intelligence.

A modern version of that test is the [70] _____ Intelligence Scale, 5th Edition.

The Stanford-Binet measures fluid reasoning, [71] _____ reasoning, [72] _____ -spatial processing, working [73] _____ , and knowledge.

Intelligence is expressed in terms of an intelligence quotient (IQ). IQ is defined as [74] _____ [75] _____ (MA) divided by [76] _____ [77] _____ (CA) and then multiplied by 100.

Modern IQ tests no longer calculate IQ directly. Instead, the final score reported by the test is a [78] _____ [79] _____ , which gives a person's relative intellectual standing in his or her age group. An average IQ score of 100 would place a person at the [80] _____ percentile.

A second major intelligence test is the [81] _____ Adult Intelligence Scale-III (WAIS-III). The WAIS-III measures both [82] _____ and [83] _____ (nonverbal) intelligence.

The Wechsler and Binet scales are designed to measure the IQ of people from middle-class [84] _____ cultures. To reduce the influence of verbal skills, cultural background, and educational level when measuring the IQ of people from another culture (e.g., China) or from a different background (e.g., poor community), [85] _____ tests have been implemented.

Intelligence tests have also been produced for use with groups of people. The [86] _____ [87] _____ Test (SAT) measures a variety of mental [88] _____ , and it can be used to estimate intelligence.

An "average" IQ of 100 occurs when [89] _____ age equals [90] _____ age.

When graphed, the [91] _____ (percentage of people receiving each score) of IQ scores approximates a [92] _____ (bell-shaped) curve.

There is [93] _____ difference between men and women's IQ level. The male-female performance gap is the result of certain [94] _____ provided to each sex.

People with IQs above [95] _____ are considered to be in the gifted or "genius" range.

Studies done by Lewis [96] _____ showed that the [97] _____ tend to be successful: They earned advanced degrees, held professional positions, and had written books.

The most [98] _____ gifted persons tend to be those who are [99] _____ and motivated to learn and succeed.

By criteria other than IQ, a large proportion of children might be considered [100] _____ or [101] _____ in one way or another.

Howard [102] _____ believes that traditional IQ tests define intelligence too narrowly. According to Gardner, intelligence consists of abilities in [103] _____ , logic and math, visual and spatial thinking, [104] _____ , kinesthetic skills, intrapersonal skills, interpersonal skills, and [105] _____ skills.

The terms *mentally retarded* and [106] _____ *disabled* are applied to those whose IQ falls below 70 or who lack various [107] _____ behaviors.

Further classifications of retardation are: mild (50-55 to 70), [108] _____ (35-40 to 50-55), severe (20-25 to 35-40), and [109] _____ (below 20-25).

About 50 percent of the cases of mental retardation are [110] _____ , being caused by birth injuries, fetal damage, metabolic disorders, or [111] _____ abnormalities. The remaining cases are of undetermined cause.

Many cases of subnormal intelligence are thought to be the result of [112] _____ retardation (a low level of intellectual stimulation in the home, poverty, and poor nutrition).

Studies of family relationships in humans, especially comparisons between [113] _____ twins and [114] _____ twins, suggest that intelligence is partly hereditary.

However, [115] _____ is also important, as revealed by changes in tested intelligence induced by stimulating [116] _____ and improved education.

Intelligence therefore reflects the combined effects of [117] _____ and [118] _____ .

Differences in the average IQ scores for various racial groups are based on [119] _____ differences, not heredity.

MODULE 9.4

Survey Question: What is creative thinking? Pages 360-363

Thinking may be deductive or [120] _____ , [121] _____ or illogical.

Creative thinking requires [122] _____ thought, characterized by [123] _____ , flexibility, and originality.

Tests of creativity, such as the Unusual [124] _____ Test, the Consequences Test, and the Anagrams Test, measure the capacity for [125] _____ thinking.

To be creative, a solution must be practical and sensible as well as [126] _____ .

Five stages often seen in creative problem solving are orientation, preparation, [127] _____ , [128] _____ , and verification.

Studies suggest that creative persons share a combination of thinking skills, [129] _____ characteristics, and a supportive social [130] _____ . There is only a small correlation between IQ and creativity.

Most creative people do not suffer from [131] _____ disorders, and most mentally disturbed people are not creative. However, there are a few exceptions in regard to [132] _____ disorders. The relation between creativity and mood disorders may be due to the level of productivity during the [133] _____ state.

Survey Question: How accurate is intuition? Pages 363-365

Intuitive thinking often leads to errors. Wrong conclusions may be drawn when an answer seems highly [134] _____ of what we already believe is true, that is, when people apply the representativeness [135] _____ .

A second problem is allowing [136] _____ such as fear, hope, anxiety, or disgust to guide thinking in [137] _____ making.

The third problem is ignoring the [138] _____ [139] _____ (or underlying probability) of an event.

Clear thinking is usually aided by stating or [140] _____ a problem in broad terms.

PSYCHOLOGY IN ACTION

Survey Question: What can be done to improve thinking and promote creativity? Pages 367-370

Mental [141] _____ can act as major barriers to [142] _____ thinking.

Creativity can be enhanced by defining problems broadly, by establishing a creative atmosphere, by allowing time for [143] _____ , by restating a problem in different ways, by seeking varied [144] _____ , by taking sensible [145] _____ , and by looking for analogies.

[146] _____ , in which the production and criticism of ideas is kept separate, also tends to enhance creative problem solving.

MASTERY TEST

1. The mark of a true language is that it must be
   a. spoken
   b. productive
   c. based on spatial grammar and syntax
   d. capable of encoding conditional relationships

2. Computer simulations and expert systems are two major applications of
   a. AI
   b. ASL
   c. brainstorming
   d. problem framing

3. Failure to wear automobile seat belts is an example of which intuitive thinking error?
   a. allowing too much time for incubation
   b. framing a problem broadly
   c. ignoring base rates
   d. recognition that two events occurring together are more likely than either one alone

4. One thing that images, concepts, and symbols all have in common is that they are
   a. morphemes
   b. internal representations
   c. based on reverse vision
   d. translated into micromovements

5. To decide if a container is a cup, bowl, or vase, most people compare it to
   a. a prototype
   b. its connotative meaning
   c. a series of negative instances
   d. a series of relevant phonemes

6. During problem solving, being "cold," "warm," or "very warm" is closely associated with
   a. insight
   b. fixation
   c. automatic processing
   d. rote problem solving

7. The Anagrams Test measures
   a. mental sets
   b. inductive thinking
   c. logical reasoning
   d. divergent thinking

8. "Either-or" concepts are
   a. conjunctive
   b. disjunctive
   c. relational
   d. prototypical

9. Which term does not belong with the others?
   a. selective comparison
   b. functional fixedness
   c. learned conventions
   d. emotional blocks

10. Separate collections of verbal and performance subtests are a feature of the
    a. WAIS
    b. Gardner-8
    c. CQT
    d. Stanford-Binet

11. Mental retardation is formally defined by deficiencies in
    a. aptitudes and self-help skills
    b. intelligence and scholastic aptitudes
    c. language and spatial thinking
    d. IQ and adaptive behaviors

12. A 12-year-old child, with an IQ of 100, must have an MA of
    a. 100
    b. 12
    c. 10
    d. 15

13. The difference between prime beef and dead cow is primarily a matter of
    a. syntax
    b. conjunctive meaning
    c. semantics
    d. the productive nature of language

14. Culture-fair tests attempt to measure intelligence without being affected by a person's
    a. verbal skills
    b. cultural background
    c. educational level
    d. all the preceding

15. Which of the listed terms does NOT correctly complete this sentence: Insight involves selective

    _____.
    a. encoding
    b. combination
    c. comparison
    d. fixation

16. Which of the following is LEAST likely to predict that a person is creative?
    a. high IQ
    b. a preference for complexity
    c. fluency in combining ideas
    d. use of mental images

17. "Try working backward from the desired goal to the starting point or current state." This advice describes a
    a. syllogism
    b. heuristic
    c. prototype
    d. dimension of the semantic differential

18. Language allows events to be _____ into _____.
    a. translated, concepts
    b. fixated, codes
    c. rearranged, lexigrams
    d. encoded, symbols

19. "A triangle must be a closed shape with three sides made of straight lines." This statement is an example of a
    a. prototype
    b. positive instance
    c. conceptual rule
    d. disjunctive concept

20. Fluency, flexibility, and originality are all measures of
    a. inductive thinking
    b. selective comparison
    c. intuitive framing
    d. divergent thinking

21. The form of imagery that is especially important in music, sports, dance, and martial arts is
    a. kinesthetic imagery
    b. semantic imagery
    c. prototypical imagery
    d. conjunctive imagery

22. Among animals trained to use language, Kanzi has been unusually accurate at
    a. using proper syntax
    b. substituting gestures for lexigrams
    c. expressing conditional relationships
    d. forming chains of operant responses

23. The largest number of people are found in which IQ range?
    a. 80-89
    b. 90-109
    c. 110-119
    d. below 70

24. Looking for analogies and delaying evaluation are helpful strategies for increasing
    a. divergent thinking
    b. convergent thinking
    c. functional fixedness
    d. concept formation

25. Comparing two three-dimensional shapes to see if they match is easiest if only a small amount of _____ is required.
    a. conceptual recoding
    b. mental rotation
    c. concept formation
    d. kinesthetic transformation

26. The good-bad dimension on the semantic differential is closely related to a concept's
    a. disjunctive meaning
    b. conjunctive meaning
    c. connotative meaning
    d. denotative meaning

27. The directions "modify, magnify, rearrange, and suspend judgment" could be expected to aid a group engaged in
    a. a means-ends analysis
    b. base rate framing
    c. brainstorming
    d. solving delayed response problems

28. According to Noam Chomsky, surface sentences are created by applying _____ to simple sentences.
    a. encoding grammars
    b. transformation rules
    c. conditional prototypes
    d. selective conjunctions

29. The occurrence of an insight corresponds to which stage of creative thinking?
    a. verification
    b. incubation
    c. illumination
    d. fixation

30. The _____ has demonstrated that people can quickly identify the color of a word if the word's meaning is similar to the word's color. This suggests that the meaning of words do influence our thoughts.
    a. memory task
    b. Stroop test
    c. Stanford-Binet Intelligence Scale
    d. American Sign Language

31. When one divides a number into another, step-by-step without the aid of a calculator, one is using a(an) _____ to find a solution.
    a. algorithm
    b. conceptual rule
    c. prototype
    d. Anagrams Test

32. Most American students were unable to solve a problem of how a chief can collect taxes without a scale to balance the right amount of gold coins each villager owes, whereas most Chinese students were able to since most Chinese students were familiar with a traditional story about weighing an elephant that is too big to be on a scale. This example illustrates which nature of insight?
    a. selective encoding
    b. selective combination
    c. selective comparison
    d. selective intuition

33. Which of the five Stanford-Binet Intelligence Scales measures how well people can imagine and correctly determine their location by following written instructions?
    a. fluid reasoning
    b. visual-spatial processing
    c. knowledge
    d. working memory

34. Winnie took an IQ test and she is ranked in the 97th percentile. Without knowing her actual IQ score, you can assume that
    a. she is smarter than 97 percent of the people who took the test
    b. she and 97 percent of the others who took the test have the same IQ scores
    c. she is smarter than 3 percent of the people who took the test
    d. 97 percent of the people who took the test are smarter than Winnie

35. The argument that people from different regions and cultures are taught to understand the world differently by using different kinds of knowledge and mental abilities suggests that a _____ is necessary to measure intelligence accurately.
    a. Stanford-Binet Intelligence Scale
    b. culture-fair test
    c. SAT
    d. WAIS

36. The performance gap on intelligence test scores between men and women can be traced back to
    a. heredity
    b. women being told they cannot outperform men
    c. women too busy taking care of their family to maintain their physical skills
    d. availability of resources allocated to men versus women

37. Most creative people do not suffer from mental disorders. However, an exception to this might include a few creative people who
    a. experience manic states
    b. express fantasy fulfillment
    c. seek attention
    d. both b and c

38. People who choose political candidates because they like them have fallen prey to which form of intuitive thinking error?
    a. representativeness
    b. emotions
    c. underlying odds
    d. framing

SOLUTIONS

RECITE AND REVIEW

MODULE 9.1

1. mental
2. problem
3. internal
4. language

5. visual
6. created
7. change
8. space
9. muscular
10. Kinesthetic

11. class
12. positive
13. concept
14. and
15. either-or
16. models
17. definition
18. personal
19. good-bad
20. words

21. symbols
22. meaning
23. sounds
24. meaningful
25. rules
26. order
27. rules
28. gestural
29. human
30. operant
31. geometric

MODULE 9.2

32. rote
33. computer
34. rote
35. learned
36. general
37. solutions
38. narrow
39. solution
40. selective
41. selective
42. wrong
43. fixation
44. habits

45. programs
46. intelligence
47. computer
48. knowledge

MODULE 9.3

49. intelligence
50. test
51. rationally
52. environment
53. definition
54. Scale
55. fluid
56. memory
57. quotient
58. 100
59. IQs
60. relative
61. 50th
62. Adult
63. nonverbal
64. Western
65. educational
66. fair
67. groups
68. mental
69. 100
70. equals
71. bell
72. curve

73. IQ
74. gifted
75. successful
76. motivated
77. IQ
78. traditional
79. math
80. visual

81. *retarded*
82. 70
83. mild
84. severe
85. 50
86. birth
87. intellectual
88. genes

89. hereditary
90. stimulating
91. Intelligence
92. genetics (or heredity)

MODULE 9.4

93. Thinking
94. originality
95. creativity
96. practical

97. preparation
98. skills
99. supportive
100. creative

101. mentally
102. mood

103. errors
104. true
105. fear

106. anxiety
107. thinking
108. probability

109. broad

PSYCHOLOGY IN ACTION

110. Mental
111. thinking
112. broadly

113. different
114. time
115. varied

116. separate

CONNECTIONS

MODULE 9.1

1. f
2. j
3. i
4. a

5. c
6. b
7. e
8. d

9. g
10. h

1. c
2. a
3. e

4. g
5. b
6. f

7. d

MODULE 9.2

1. h
2. g
3. e
4. a

5. f
6. b
7. j
8. c

9. i
10. d

MODULE 9.3

1.	e	5.	b	9.	g
2.	l	6.	i	10.	d
3.	a	7.	c	11.	h
4.	j	8.	k	12.	f

MODULE 9.4

1.	h	5.	c	9.	f
2.	b	6.	i	10.	g
3.	j	7.	a		
4.	d	8.	e		

CHECK YOUR MEMORY

MODULE 9.1

1.	F	3.	F		
2.	T	4.	F		

5.	T	8.	T	11.	T
6.	T	9.	T		
7.	T	10.	T		

12.	T	14.	T	16.	F
13.	F	15.	F		

17.	F	23.	F	29.	T
18.	T	24.	F	30.	T
19.	F	25.	F	31.	T
20.	F	26.	F	32.	T
21.	T	27.	F		
22.	F	28.	F		

MODULE 9.2

33.	T	37.	T	41.	T
34.	F	38.	T	42.	F
35.	F	39.	F		
36.	F	40.	F		

43.	T

44. T
45. T
46. F
47. F

MODULE 9.3

48. F
49. T
50. F
51. T
52. T
53. F
54. F
55. T
56. T
57. T
58. F
59. F
60. T
61. F
62. F
63. T
64. F
65. F
66. F
67. F
68. T
69. F
70. F
71. T
72. T
73. T
74. F

MODULE 9.4

75. T
76. F
77. T
78. T
79. F
80. T
81. F
82. F

83. F
84. T
85. F
86. F
87. T
88. F

PSYCHOLOGY IN ACTION

89. F
90. T
91. F
92. F
93. F
94. T

FINAL SURVEY AND REVIEW

MODULE 9.1

1. Cognition
2. representations
3. images
4. concepts
5. symbols

6. brain
7. visual
8. mental
9. information
10. stored
11. size
12. rotated
13. images
14. micromovements

15. generalized
16. negative
17. instances
18. rules
19. conjunctive
20. disjunctive
21. prototypes
22. denotative
23. Connotative
24. semantic
25. strong-weak
26. active-passive

27. words

28. encoded
29. semantics
30. phonemes
31. morphemes
32. grammar

33. syntax
34. transformation
35. productive
36. American
37. Sign

38. Animal
39. productive
40. primates
41. reinforcers
42. lexigrams

MODULE 9.2

43. mechanically
44. mechanical
45. algorithm
46. understanding
47. functional

48. heuristics
49. insight
50. insight
51. encoding
52. old

53. culture
54. fixation
55. Functional
56. blocks
57. values

58. computer
59. programs
60. people

61. expert
62. systems
63. organized

64. strategies

MODULE 9.3

65. Alfred
66. Binet
67. purposefully
68. think
69. operational
70. Stanford-Binet
71. quantitative
72. visual
73. memory
74. mental
75. age
76. chronological
77. age
78. deviation
79. IQ
80. 50th
81. Wechsler
82. verbal
83. performance

84. Western
85. culture-fair
86. Scholastic
87. Assessment
88. aptitudes
89. mental
90. chronological
91. distribution
92. normal
93. no
94. opportunities
95. 140
96. Terman
97. gifted
98. successful
99. persistent
100. gifted
101. talented
102. Gardner

103. language
104. music
105. naturalist
106. *developmentally*
107. adaptive
108. moderate
109. profound
110. organic
111. genetic
112. familial
113. fraternal
114. identical
115. environment
116. environments
117. heredity
118. environment
119. environmental

MODULE 9.4

120. inductive
121. logical
122. divergent

123. fluency
124. Uses
125. divergent

126. original
127. incubation
128. illumination

129. personality
130. environment

131. mental
132. mood

133. manic

134. representative
135. heuristic
136. emotions

137. decision
138. base
139. rate

140. framing

PSYCHOLOGY IN ACTION

141. sets
142. creative

143. incubation
144. input

145. risks
146. Brainstorming

MASTERY TEST

1. B, (p. 338)
2. A, (p. 346-347)
3. C, (p. 364-365)
4. B, (p. 332)
5. A, (p. 335)
6. A, (p. 344)
7. D, (p. 361)
8. B, (p. 335)
9. A, (p. 344)
10. A, (p. 352)
11. D, (p. 355-356)
12. B, (p. 351)
13. C, (p. 337)
14. D, (p. 353)

15. D, (p. 344)
16. A, (p. 363)
17. B, (p. 343)
18. D, (p. 336)
19. C, (p. 335)
20. D, (p. 360)
21. A, (p. 334)
22. A, (p. 340)
23. B, (p. 353)
24. A, (p. 368-369)
25. B, (p. 332-333)
26. C, (p. 336)
27. C, (p. 369)
28. B, (p. 337-338)

29. C, (p. 362)
30. B, (p. 337)
31. A, (p. 342)
32. C, (p. 345)
33. B, (p. 350)
34. A, (p. 352)
35. B, (p. 353)
36. D, (p. 354)
37. A, (p. 363)
38. B, (p. 364)

MOTIVATION AND EMOTION

CHAPTER OVERVIEW

Motivation typically involves needs, drives, goals, and goal attainment. Three types of motives are primary motives, stimulus motives, and secondary motives. Most primary motives maintain homeostasis.

Hunger is influenced by the stomach, blood sugar levels, metabolism in the liver, fat stores in the body, activity in the hypothalamus, diet, and other factors. Body Mass Index (BMI) measures one's body fat. A BMI value of 25 or more should be a cause for concern since obesity has been linked to heart disease, high blood pressure, stroke, diabetes, and premature death. External cues within our environment have increased the obesity problem and frequency of eating disorders in America. Anorexia and bulimia are serious, sometimes fatal, eating disorders. Behavioral dieting uses self-control techniques to change basic eating patterns and habits.

Thirst and other basic motives are affected by many factors, but they are primarily controlled by the hypothalamus. Pain avoidance is episodic and partially learned. The sex drive is nonhomeostatic. To some extent, it is influenced by hormone levels in the body.

The stimulus motives include drives for information, exploration, manipulation, and sensory input. Drives for stimulation are partially explained by arousal theory. The desired level of arousal or stimulation is measured by the Sensation-Seeking Scale. Optimal performance on a task usually occurs at moderate levels of arousal. Test anxiety is caused by a mixture of excessive worrying and heightened physiological arousal, which can be reduced through preparation, relaxation, rehearsal, and restructuring thoughts.

Social motives, which are learned, account for much of the diversity of human motivation. The need for achievement is a social motive correlated with success in many situations. Self-confidence also affects motivation by influencing the types of challenges that one takes.

Maslow's hierarchy of motives categorizes needs as basic or growth oriented. Self-actualization, the highest and most fragile need, is reflected in meta-needs. In many situations, extrinsic motivation can lower intrinsic motivation, enjoyment, and creativity.

Emotions are linked to basic adaptive behaviors. Other major elements of emotion are bodily changes, emotional expressions, and emotional feelings. Physiological changes during emotion are caused by adrenaline and the autonomic nervous system (ANS). The sympathetic branch of the ANS arouses the body, and the parasympathetic branch quiets it. A polygraph measures a person's general emotional arousal through changes in heart rate, blood pressure, breathing, and galvanic skin response.

Basic emotional expressions are unlearned. Facial expressions are central to emotion. Body gestures and movements (body language) also express feelings. A variety of theories and hypotheses have been proposed to explain emotion: the James-Lange theory, the Cannon-Bard theory, Schachter's Cognitive Theory of Emotion, attribution theory, and the facial feedback hypothesis.

Emotional intelligence involves a combination of skills, such as self-awareness, empathy, self-control, and an understanding of how to use emotions. For success in many situations, emotional intelligence is as important as IQ. Martin Seligman proposed that genuinely happy people are people who have cultivated their natural strengths into their lives to help to buffer against misfortunes.

LEARNING OBJECTIVES

To demonstrate mastery of this chapter, you should be able to:

1. Define "motivation."

2. Describe a motivational sequence using the need reduction model.

3. Explain how the incentive value of a goal can affect motivation and describe how incentive value is related to internal need.

4. List and describe the three types of motives and give an example of each.

5. Define "homeostasis."

6. Discuss why hunger cannot be fully explained by the contractions of an empty stomach.

7. Describe the relationship of each of the following to hunger: a. blood sugar b. liver c. hypothalamus i. feeding system (lateral hypothalamus) ii. satiety system (ventromedial hypothalamus) iii. blood sugar regulator (paraventricular nucleus) iv. neuropeptide Y (NPY) v. glucagon-like peptide 1 (GLP-1)

8. Explain how a person's set point is related to obesity in childhood and adulthood. Include the release of leptin by the fat cells.

The following objectives are related to the material in the "Discovering Psychology" section of the text.

9. What is the formula for one's body mass index (BMI)?

10. At what point should one get concerned about your BMI?

11. Explain the relationship between how much a person overeats and the person's obesity.

12. Describe the relationship between emotionality and overeating.

13. Explain the paradox of "yo-yo" dieting.

14. Explain what is meant by behavioral dieting, and describe the techniques which can enable you to control your weight.

15. Describe the impact of cultural factors and taste on hunger.

16. Explain how a taste aversion is acquired, give a practical example of the process, and briefly explain why psychologists believe these aversions exist.

17. Describe the essential features of the eating disorders anorexia nervosa and bulimia nervosa. Explain what causes them and what treatment is available for them.

18. Name the brain structure that appears to control thirst (as well as hunger). Differentiate extracellular and intracellular thirst.

19. Explain how the drive to avoid pain and the sex drive differ from other primary drives.

20. Briefly describe the impact of hormones and alcohol on the sex drive.

21. Describe the evidence for the existence of stimulus drives for exploration, manipulation, curiosity, and stimulation.

22. Explain the arousal theory of motivation including the inverted U function.

23. Relate arousal to the Yerkes-Dodson law and give an example of it.

24. Describe the two major components of test anxiety and describe four ways to reduce it.

25. Define "need for achievement (nAch)" and differentiate it from the need for power.

26. Describe people who are achievers and relate nAch to risk taking.

27. Describe the research of Russell, Rowe, and Smouse concerning the effectiveness of subliminal perception.

28. Explain the influences of drive and determination in the development of success for high achievers. Include a discussion of self-confidence and ways to enhance it.

29. List (in order) the needs found in Maslow's hierarchy of motives.

30. Explain why Maslow's lower (physiological) needs are considered prepotent. Define "growth needs."

31. Define "meta-need" and give an example of one.

32. Distinguish between intrinsic and extrinsic motivation, and explain how each type of motivation may affect a person's interest in work, leisure activities, and creativity.

33. Explain what is meant by the phrase "emotions aid survival."

34. List and describe the three major elements of emotions.

35. List the eight primary emotions proposed by Plutchik and explain his concept of mixing them.

36. Explain how a person may experience two opposite emotions simultaneously.

37. Describe, in general, the effects of the sympathetic and the parasympathetic branches of the ANS during and after emotion.

38. Define "parasympathetic rebound" and discuss its possible involvement in cases of sudden death.

39. Describe the cost of suppressing emotions.

40. Explain how the polygraph detects "lies."

41. Discuss the limitations and/or accuracy of lie detector devices.

42. Discuss Darwin's view of human emotion.

43. Briefly describe cultural and gender differences in emotion.

44. Describe the evidence that supports the conclusion that most emotional expressions are universal.

45. Define "kinesics."

46. List and describe the three emotional messages conveyed by facial expressions and the two most generally conveyed by body language.

47. Briefly describe the James-Lange theory of emotion.

48. Briefly describe the Cannon-Bard theory of emotion.

49. Briefly describe Schachter's cognitive theory of emotion and give experimental evidence to support his theory.

50. Describe and give an example of the effects of attribution on emotion.

51. Briefly describe the facial feedback hypothesis.

52. Discuss the role of appraisal in the contemporary model of emotion.

53. Describe the concept of emotional intelligence and how it may enhance one's life.

54. List five emotional intelligence skills.

55. Briefly describe the benefits of positive psychology and positive emotion.

RECITE AND REVIEW

MODULE 10.1

Survey Questions: What is motivation? Are there different types of motives? Pages 374-376

Motives [1] _____ (begin), sustain (perpetuate), and direct [2] _____ .

Motivation typically involves the sequence [3] _____ , drive, response, and [4] _____ attainment (need reduction).

Behavior can be activated either by needs ([5] _____) or by goals ([6] _____).

The attractiveness of a [7] _____ and its ability to initiate action are related to its incentive value (its value above and beyond its capacity to fill a [8] _____).

Three principal types of motives are primary motives, stimulus motives, and [9] _____ motives.

Most [10] _____ motives operate to maintain a [11] _____ state of bodily equilibrium called homeostasis.

MODULE 10.2

Survey Questions: What causes hunger? Overeating? Eating disorders? Pages 377-384

Hunger is influenced by a complex interplay between distention (fullness) of the [12] _____ ,

metabolism in the [13] _____ , and fat stores in the body.

The most direct control of eating is exerted by the hypothalamus, which has areas that act like feeding

([14] _____) and satiety ([15] _____) systems for hunger and eating.

The lateral hypothalamus acts as a [16] _____ system, the ventromedial hypothalamus is part of a

[17] _____ system; the paraventricular nucleus influences both hunger and satiety.

Other factors influencing hunger are the set point for the proportion of [18] _____ in the body,

external eating cues, and the attractiveness and variety of [19] _____ .

A body mass index is a measure of body fat that is calculated by dividing body [20] _____

squared over body [21] _____ multiplied by 703.

A BMI of [22] _____ or higher should be a cause for concern since obesity is linked to heart

disease, high blood pressure, stroke, diabetes, and premature death.

Hunger is also influenced by emotions, learned [23] _____ preferences and [24] _____

aversions, and cultural values.

A successful behavioral dieting approach begins with committing oneself to weight loss, [25] _____

, counting [26] _____ , developing techniques to control overeating, and charting one's progress.

Anorexia nervosa (self-inflicted [27] _____) and bulimia nervosa ([28] _____ and

purging) are two prominent eating disorders.

Treatments for anorexia begin with drug therapy then advance to [29] _____ .

Both eating disorders tend to involve conflicts about self-image, self-control, and [30] _____ .

Survey Questions: Is there more than one type of thirst? In what ways are pain avoidance and the sex
drive unusual? Pages 384-385

Like hunger, thirst and other basic motives are affected by a number of [31] _____ factors but are

primarily under the central control of the hypothalamus in the [32] _____ .

Thirst may be either intracellular (when [33] _____ is lost from inside [34] _____) or

extracellular (when [35] _____ is lost from the spaces between [36] _____).

Pain avoidance is unusual because it is episodic (associated with particular conditions) as opposed to cyclic (occurring in regular [37] _____).

Pain avoidance and pain tolerance are partially [38] _____ (influenced by training).

The sex drive in many lower animals is related to estrus (or "heat") in [39] _____ . The sex drive is unusual in that it is nonhomeostatic (both its [40] _____ and its reduction are sought).

Sex [41] _____ in both males and females may be related to bodily levels of androgens.

MODULE 10.3

Survey Question: How does arousal relate to motivation? Pages 387-389

The stimulus drives reflect needs for information, exploration, manipulation, and [42] _____ input.

Drives for stimulation are partially explained by arousal theory, which states that an ideal level of [43] _____ [44] _____ will be maintained if possible.

The desired level of [45] _____ or stimulation varies from person to person, as measured by the Sensation-Seeking Scale.

Optimal performance on a task usually occurs at [46] _____ levels of arousal. This relationship is described by an inverted U function.

The Yerkes-Dodson law further states that for [47] _____ tasks the ideal arousal level is higher, and for [48] _____ tasks it is lower.

Test anxiety is caused by a combination of [49] _____ worrying and heightened physiological arousal, which can be reduced with better [50] _____ , relaxation, [51] _____ , and restructuring thoughts.

Survey Questions: What are social motives? Why are they important? Pages 389-391

[52] _____ motives are learned through socialization and cultural conditioning.

One of the most prominent social motives is the [53] _____ for achievement (nAch).

High nAch is correlated with [54] _____ in many situations, with occupational choice, and with moderate [55] _____ taking.

Self-confidence affects [56] _____ because it influences the challenges you will undertake, the [57] _____ you will make, and how long you will [58] _____ when things don't go well.

To enhance self-confidence, one should do the following: Set goals that are specific, [59] _____ ,
and attainable, advance in [60] _____ steps, find a role model, get expert instructions, and get
[61] _____ support.

Survey Question: Are some motives more basic than others? Pages 391-393

Maslow's hierarchy (rank ordering) of motives categorizes needs as [62] _____ and growth
oriented.

[63] _____ needs in the hierarchy are assumed to be prepotent (dominant) over
[64] _____ needs.

[65] _____ -actualization, the highest and most fragile need, is reflected in
meta-[66] _____ .

In many situations, extrinsic motivation (that which is induced by obvious [67] _____ rewards)
can reduce intrinsic motivation, enjoyment, and creativity.

MODULE 10.4

Survey Questions: What happens during emotion? Can "lie detectors" really detect lies? Pages 395-399

Emotions are linked to many basic adaptive [68] _____ , such as attacking, retreating, feeding,
and reproducing.

Other major elements of emotion are physiological changes in the body, emotional expressions, and
emotional [69] _____ .

Physical changes associated with emotion are caused by the action of adrenaline, a [70] _____
released into the bloodstream, and by activity in the autonomic [71] _____ [72] _____
(ANS).

The following are considered to be primary emotions: fear, surprise, [73] _____ , disgust,
[74] _____ , anticipation, joy, and trust (acceptance). Other emotions seem to represent mixtures
of the primaries.

The sympathetic [75] _____ of the ANS is primarily responsible for arousing the body, the
parasympathetic [76] _____ for quieting it.

Sudden death due to prolonged and intense emotion is probably related to parasympathetic
[77] _____ (excess activity). Heart attacks caused by sudden intense emotion are more likely due
to sympathetic [78] _____ .

The polygraph, or "lie detector," measures [79] _____ [80] _____ by monitoring heart rate, blood pressure, breathing rate, and the galvanic skin response (GSR).

Asking a series of [81] _____ and irrelevant questions may allow the detection of

[82] _____ , but overall, the accuracy of the lie detector has been challenged by many researchers.

A polygraph makes use of such [83] _____ questions as "Have you ever stolen anything from your place of work?" to increase the person's anxiety level. Their answers will be compared to other

[84] _____ questions for which the police are seeking answers.

MODULE 10.5

Survey Question: How accurately are emotions expressed by "body language" and the face? Pages 400-402

Basic emotional expressions, such as smiling or baring one's teeth when angry, appear to be

[85] _____ .

Facial expressions of [86] _____ , anger, disgust, [87] _____ , and happiness are recognized by people of all cultures.

In Western culture, women are encouraged to express such emotions as [88] _____ , fear,

[89] _____ , and guilt, and men are expected to express [90] _____ and hostility.

The study of [91] _____ [92] _____ is known as kinesics.

Body gestures and movements (body language) also express [93] _____ , mainly by communicating emotional [94] _____ .

Three dimensions of [95] _____ expressions are pleasantness-unpleasantness, attention-rejection, and activation.

Survey Question: How do psychologists explain emotions? Pages 402-405

The James-Lange theory of emotion says that emotional experience [96] _____ an awareness of the bodily reactions of emotion.

In contrast, the Cannon-Bard theory says that bodily reactions and emotional experience occur

[97] _____ [98] _____ [99] _____ [100] _____ and that emotions are organized in the brain.

Schachter's cognitive theory of emotion emphasizes the importance of [101] _____ , or interpretations, applied to feelings of bodily arousal.

Also important is the process of attribution, in which bodily [102] _____ is attributed to a particular person, object, or situation.

Research on attribution theory has shown that physical arousal (e.g., an [103] _____ heart rate from exercise or fear) can be [104] _____ to different sources such as attraction or love for someone.

The facial feedback hypothesis holds that sensations and information from emotional [105] _____ help define what emotion a person is feeling.

Making faces does influence [106] _____ and bodily activities through the [107] _____ nervous system.

Contemporary views of emotion place greater emphasis on how [108] _____ are appraised. Also, all of the elements of emotion are seen as interrelated and interacting.

PSYCHOLOGY IN ACTION

Survey Question: What does it means to have "emotional intelligence"? Page 407-408

Emotional intelligence involves the following skills: [109] _____ -awareness, empathy, [110] _____ -control, and an understanding of how to use [111] _____ .

Emotionally intelligent people are good at reading facial expressions, tone of voice, and other signs of [112] _____ .

They also use their [113] _____ to enhance thinking and decision making.

[114] _____ emotions are not just a luxury. They tend to encourage personal growth and social connection.

Martin Seligman believes people can achieve genuine happiness by optimizing their natural [115] _____ , such as [116] _____ , originality, humor, [117] _____ , and generosity, to buffer them against misfortunes.

CONNECTIONS

MODULE 10.1

1. _____ incentive value
2. _____ motivational model
3. _____ need
4. _____ homeostasis
5. _____ secondary motives

a. internal deficiency
b. goal desirability
c. learned goals
d. need reduction
e. steady state

MODULE 10.2

1. _____ ventromedial hypothalamus
2. _____ lateral hypothalamus
3. _____ paraventricular nucleus

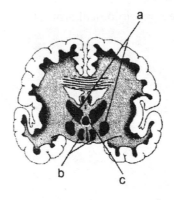

1. _____ extracellular thirst
2. _____ satiety system
3. _____ taste aversion
4. _____ set point
5. _____ hunger and satiety
6. _____ body mass index
7. _____ weight cycling
8. _____ changes eating habits
9. _____ feeding system
10. _____ estrus

a. weight/height^2 x 703
b. classical condition
c. result from diarrhea
d. thermostat for fat level
e. lateral hypothalamus
f. estrogen levels
g. yo-yo dieting
h. paraventricular nucleus
i. ventromedial hypothalamus
j. behavioral dieting

MODULE 10.3

1. _____ safety and security
2. _____ basic needs
3. _____ love and belonging
4. _____ self-actualization
5. _____ physiological needs
6. _____ esteem and self-esteem
7. _____ growth needs

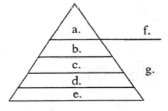

1. _____ safety and security
2. _____ heightened physiological arousal
3. _____ nAch
4. _____ SSS
5. _____ moderate risk takers
6. _____ meta-needs
7. _____ extrinsic motivation

a. standards of excellence
b. self-actualization
c. sensation seekers
d. impaired test performance
e. high in nAch
f. hierarchy of needs
g. external rewards

MODULE 10.4

1. _____ adrenaline
2. _____ parasympathetic rebound
3. _____ Robert Plutchik
4. _____ irrelevant questions
5. _____ polygraph
6. _____ sympathetic branch
7. _____ relevant questions
8. _____ mood

a. eight primary emotions
b. arousal-producing hormone
c. "Did you murder Hensley?"
d. nonemotional questions
e. prolonged mild emotion
f. fight or flight
g. intense emotional overreaction
h. lie detection

MODULE 10.5

1. _____ anxiety
2. _____ sadness
3. _____ authentic happiness
4. _____ James-Lange theory
5. _____ body language
6. _____ facial blend
7. _____ self-awareness
8. _____ Schachter's cognitive theory
9. _____ emotional intelligence

a. arousal + label then emotions
b. bodily arousal then emotions
c. mixing 2+ facial emotions
d. appraisal of loss
e. appraisal of threat
f. kinesics
g. emotional skills
h. in tune with own feelings
i. emphasize natural strengths

CHECK YOUR MEMORY

MODULE 10.1

Survey Questions: What is motivation? Are there different types of motives? Pages 374-376

1. The terms *need* and *drive* are used interchangeably to describe motivation.
   TRUE or FALSE

2. Incentive value refers to the "pull" of valued goals.
   TRUE or FALSE

3. Primary motives are based on needs that must be met for survival.
   TRUE or FALSE

4. Much of the time, homeostasis is maintained by automatic reactions within the body.
   TRUE or FALSE

MODULE 10.2

Survey Questions: What causes hunger? Overeating? Eating disorders? Pages 377-384

5. Cutting the sensory nerves from the stomach abolishes hunger.
   TRUE or FALSE

6. Lowered levels of glucose in the blood can cause hunger.
   TRUE or FALSE

7. The body's hunger center is found in the thalamus.
   TRUE or FALSE

8. The paraventricular nucleus is sensitive to neuropeptide Y.
   TRUE or FALSE

9. Both glucagon-like peptide 1 (GLP-1) and leptin act as stop signals that inhibit eating.
   TRUE or FALSE

10. BMI is an estimation of body fat.
    TRUE or FALSE

11. Dieting speeds up the body's metabolic rate.
    TRUE or FALSE

12. Exercise makes people hungry and tends to disrupt dieting and weight loss.
    TRUE or FALSE

13. External cues have little impact on one's tendency to overeat.
    TRUE or FALSE

14. The fast-food industry promotes healthy and tasty products that have contributed to the problem of obesity.
    TRUE or FALSE

15. "Yo-yo dieting" refers to repeatedly losing and gaining weight through the process of bingeing and purging.
    TRUE or FALSE

16. Behavioral dieting changes habits without reducing the number of calories consumed.
TRUE or FALSE

17. People who diet intensely every other day lose as much weight as those who diet moderately every day.
TRUE or FALSE

18. Charting daily progress is a basic behavioral dieting technique.
TRUE or FALSE

19. The incentive value of foods is largely determined by cultural values.
TRUE or FALSE

20. Taste aversions may be learned after longer time delays than in other forms of classical conditioning.
TRUE or FALSE

21. Taste aversions tend to promote nutritional imbalance.
TRUE or FALSE

22. Many victims of anorexia nervosa overestimate their body size.
TRUE or FALSE

23. Overtime anorexics lose their appetite and do not feel hungry.
TRUE or FALSE

24. Treatment for anorexia begins with counseling.
TRUE or FALSE

Survey Questions: Is there more than one type of thirst? In what ways are pain avoidance and the sex drive unusual? Pages 384-385

25. Bleeding, vomiting, or sweating can cause extracellular thirst.
TRUE or FALSE

26. Intracellular thirst is best satisfied by a slightly salty liquid.
TRUE or FALSE

27. Tolerance for pain is largely unaffected by learning.
TRUE or FALSE

28. Getting drunk decreases sexual desire, arousal, pleasure, and performance.
TRUE or FALSE

MODULE 10.3

Survey Question: How does arousal relate to motivation? Pages 387-389

29. It is uncomfortable to experience both very high and very low levels of arousal.
    TRUE or FALSE

30. Disinhibition and boredom susceptibility are characteristics of sensation-seeking persons.
    TRUE or FALSE

31. For nearly all activities, the best performance occurs at high levels of arousal.
    TRUE or FALSE

32. Test anxiety is a combination of arousal and excessive worry.
    TRUE or FALSE

33. Being overprepared is a common cause of test anxiety.
    TRUE or FALSE

Survey Questions: What are social motives? Why are they important? Pages 389-391

34. The need for achievement refers to a desire to have impact on other people.
    TRUE or FALSE

35. Subliminal self-help audiotapes such as "Improve Study Habits" and "Passing Exams" are effective. That is why each year consumers spend millions of dollars on them.
    TRUE or FALSE

36. People high in nAch generally prefer "long shots" or "sure things."
    TRUE or FALSE

37. Benjamin Bloom found that high achievement is based as much on hard work as it is on talent.
    TRUE or FALSE

38. Subliminal motivational tapes are no more effective than placebo tapes that lack any "hidden messages."
    TRUE or FALSE

39. For many activities, self-confidence is one of the most important sources of motivation.
    TRUE or FALSE

Survey Question: Are some motives more basic than others? Pages 391-393

40. Maslow's hierarchy of needs places self-esteem at the top of the pyramid.
    TRUE or FALSE

41. Maslow believed that needs for safety and security are more prepotent than needs for love and belonging.
    TRUE or FALSE

42. Meta-needs are the most basic needs in Maslow's hierarchy.
    TRUE or FALSE

43. Maslow believed that most people are motivated to seek esteem, love and security rather than self-actualization.
    TRUE or FALSE

44. Intrinsic motivation occurs when obvious external rewards are provided for engaging in an activity.
    TRUE or FALSE

45. People are more likely to be creative when they are intrinsically motivated.
    TRUE or FALSE

46. Happy, positive moods are as equally adaptive as negative moods in influencing creativity, efficiency, and helpfulness to others.
    TRUE or FALSE

MODULE 10.4

Survey Questions: What happens during emotion? Can "lie detectors" really detect lies? Pages 395-399

47. Emotions help people survive by bonding with each other as they socialize and work together.
    TRUE or FALSE

48. Most physiological changes during emotion are related to the release of adrenaline into the brain.
    TRUE or FALSE

49. Robert Plutchik's theory lists contempt as a primary emotion.
    TRUE or FALSE

50. For most students, elevated moods tend to occur on Saturdays and Tuesdays.
    TRUE or FALSE

51. Positive emotions are processed mainly in the left hemisphere of the brain.
    TRUE or FALSE

52. The sympathetic branch of the ANS is under voluntary controls and the parasympathetic branch is involuntary.
    TRUE or FALSE

53. The parasympathetic branch of the ANS slows the heart and lowers blood pressure.
    TRUE or FALSE

54. Most sudden deaths due to strong emotion are associated with the traumatic disruption of a close relationship.
    TRUE or FALSE

55. The polygraph measures the body's unique physical responses to lying.
    TRUE or FALSE

56. Only a guilty person should react emotionally to irrelevant questions.
    TRUE or FALSE

57. Control questions used in polygraph exams are designed to make almost everyone anxious.
    TRUE or FALSE

58. The lie detector's most common error is to label innocent persons guilty.
    TRUE or FALSE

59. Gestures such as rubbing hands, twisting hair, and biting lips are consistently related to lying.
    TRUE or FALSE

MODULE 10.5

Survey Question: How accurately are emotions expressed by "body language" and the face? Pages 400-402

60. Children born deaf and blind express emotions with their faces in about the same way as other people do.
    TRUE or FALSE

61. People from Asian cultures are more likely to express anger in public than people from Western cultures.
    TRUE or FALSE

62. In Western cultures, men tend to be more emotionally expressive than women.
    TRUE or FALSE

63. The "A-okay" hand gesture means "everything is fine" around the world.
    TRUE or FALSE

64. Facial blends mix two or more basic expressions.
    TRUE or FALSE

65. Liking is expressed in body language by leaning back and relaxing the extremities.
    TRUE or FALSE

Survey Question: How do psychologists explain emotions? Pages 402-405

66. The James-Lange theory of emotion says that we see a bear, feel fear, are aroused, and then run.
    TRUE or FALSE

67. The Cannon-Bard theory states that emotion and bodily arousal occur at the same time.
    TRUE or FALSE

68. According to Schachter's cognitive theory, arousal must be labeled in order to become an emotion.
    TRUE or FALSE

69. Attribution theory predicts that people are most likely to "love" someone who does not agitate, anger, and frustrate them.

TRUE or FALSE

70. Making facial expressions can actually cause emotions to occur and alter physiological activities in the body.

TRUE or FALSE

71. Emotional appraisal refers to deciding if your own facial expressions are appropriate for the situation you are in.

TRUE or FALSE

72. Moving toward a desired goal is associated with the emotion of happiness.

TRUE or FALSE

73. Emotional intelligence refers to the ability to use primarily the right cerebral hemisphere to process emotional events.

TRUE or FALSE

PSYCHOLOGY IN ACTION

Survey Question: What does it means to have "emotional intelligence"? Page 407-408

74. People who excel in life tend to be emotionally intelligent.

TRUE or FALSE

75. People who are empathetic are keenly tuned in to their own feelings.

TRUE or FALSE

76. People who are emotionally intelligent know what causes them to feel various emotions.

TRUE or FALSE

77. Negative emotions can be valuable because they impart useful information to us.

TRUE or FALSE

78. Positive emotions produce urges to be creative, to explore, and to seek new experiences.

TRUE or FALSE

79. Martin Seligman believes that to be genuinely happy, people must cultivate their own natural strengths.

TRUE or FALSE

80. A first step toward becoming emotionally intelligent is to pay attention to and value your feelings and emotional reactions.

TRUE or FALSE

FINAL SURVEY AND REVIEW

MODULE 10.1

Survey Questions: What is motivation? Are there different types of motives? Pages 374-376

Motives initiate (begin), [1] _____ (perpetuate), and [2] _____ activities.

Motivation typically involves the sequence need, [3] _____ , goal, and goal [4] _____ (need reduction).

Behavior can be activated either by [5] _____ (push) or by [6] _____ (pull).

The attractiveness of a goal and its ability to initiate action are related to its [7] _____

[8] _____ .

Three principal types of motives are [9] _____ motives, [10] _____ motives, and

[11] _____ motives.

Most primary motives operate to maintain a steady state of bodily equilibrium called [12] _____ .

MODULE 10.2

Survey Questions: What causes hunger? Overeating? Eating disorders? Pages 377-384

Hunger is influenced by a complex interplay between [13] _____ (fullness) of the stomach, metabolism in the liver, and fat stores in the body.

The most direct control of eating is exerted by the [14] _____ , which has areas that act like feeding (start) and [15] _____ (stop) systems for hunger and eating.

The [16] _____ hypothalamus acts as a feeding system; the [17] _____ hypothalamus is part of a satiety system; the paraventricular [18] _____ influences both hunger and satiety.

Other factors influencing hunger are the [19] _____ [20] _____ for the proportion of fat in the body, external eating [21] _____ , and that the attractiveness and variety of diet.

A [22] _____ (BMI) is a measure of body [23] _____ which is calculated by dividing body height squared over body weight multiplied by 703.

A BMI of [24] _____ or higher should be a cause for concern since obesity is linked to

[25] _____ disease, high blood pressure, [26] _____ , diabetes, and premature death.

Hunger is also influenced by emotions, learned taste preferences and taste [27] _____ (such as

[28] _____ [29] _____ in animals), and cultural values.

A successful behavioral dieting approach begins with committing oneself to weight loss, [30] _____ , counting [31] _____ , developing techniques to control overeating, and charting one's progress.

[32] _____ nervosa (self-inflicted starvation) and [33] _____ nervosa (gorging and purging) are two prominent eating disorders.

Treatments for anorexia begin with [34] _____ therapy then advance to counseling.

Both eating disorders tend to involve conflicts about [35] _____ , self-control, and anxiety.

Survey Questions: Is there more than one type of thirst? In what ways are pain avoidance and the sex drive unusual? Pages 384-385

Like hunger, thirst and other basic motives are affected by a number of bodily factors but are primarily under the central control of the [36] _____ in the brain.

Thirst may be either [37] _____ (when fluid is lost from inside cells) or [38] _____ (when fluid is lost from the spaces between cells).

Pain avoidance is unusual because it is [39] _____ (associated with particular conditions) as opposed to [40] _____ (occurring in regular cycles).

Pain [41] _____ and pain [42] _____ are partially learned.

The sex drive in many lower animals is related to [43] _____ (or "heat") in females. The sex drive is unusual in that it is [44] _____ (both its arousal and its reduction are sought).

Sex drive in both males and females may be related to bodily levels of [45] _____ .

MODULE 10.3

Survey Question: How does arousal relate to motivation? Pages 387-389

The [46] _____ drives reflect needs for information, [47] _____ , manipulation, and sensory input.

Drives for stimulation are partially explained by [48] _____ [49] _____ , which states that an ideal level of bodily arousal will be maintained if possible.

The desired level of arousal or stimulation varies from person to person, as measured by the [50] _____ Scale.

Optimal performance on a task usually occurs at moderate levels of arousal. This relationship is described by an [51] _____ [52] _____ function.

The [53] _____ law further states that for simple tasks the ideal arousal level is higher, and for complex tasks it is lower.

Test anxiety is caused by a combination of excessive [54] _____ and heightened physiological [55] _____ , which can be reduced with better preparation, relaxation, rehearsal, and restructuring thoughts.

Survey Questions: What are social motives? Why are they important? Pages 389-391

Social motives are learned through [56] _____ and cultural conditioning.

One of the most prominent social motives is the need for [57] _____ (nAch).

[58] _____ nAch is correlated with success in many situations, with occupational choice, and with [59] _____ risk taking.

[60] _____ affects motivation because it influences the challenges you will undertake, the effort you will make, and how long you will persist when things don't go well.

To enhance self-[61] _____ , one should do the following: Set goals that are specific, [62] _____ , and attainable, advance in small steps, find a role model, get expert instructions, and get [63] _____ support.

Survey Question: Are some motives more basic than others? Pages 391-393

Maslow's [64] _____ (rank ordering) of motives categorizes needs as basic and [65] _____ oriented.

Lower needs in the hierarchy are assumed to be [66] _____ (dominant) over higher needs.

Self-[67] _____ , the highest and most fragile need, is reflected in [68] _____ -needs.

In many situations, [69] _____ motivation (that which is induced by obvious external rewards) can reduce [70] _____ motivation, enjoyment, and creativity.

MODULE 10.4

Survey Questions: What happens during emotion? Can "lie detectors" really detect lies? Pages 395-399

Emotions are linked to many basic [71] _____ behaviors, such as attacking, retreating, feeding, and reproducing.

Other major elements of emotion are physiological changes in the body, emotional [72] _____ , and emotional feelings.

Physical changes associated with emotion are caused by the action of [73] _____ , a hormone released into the bloodstream, and by activity in the [74] _____ nervous system (ANS).

The following are considered to be [75] _____ emotions: fear, surprise, sadness, disgust, anger, anticipation, joy, and trust (acceptance).

The [76] _____ branch of the ANS is primarily responsible for arousing the body, the [77] _____ branch for quieting it.

Sudden death due to prolonged and intense emotion is probably related to [78] _____ rebound (excess activity). Heart attacks caused by sudden intense emotion are more likely due to [79] _____ arousal.

The [80] _____ , or "lie detector," measures emotional arousal by monitoring heart rate, blood pressure, breathing rate, and the [81] _____ skin response (GSR).

Asking a series of [82] _____ and [83] _____ questions may allow the detection of lies, but overall, the accuracy of the lie detector has been challenged by many researchers.

A [84] _____ makes use of such control questions as "Have you ever stolen anything from your place of work?" to increase the person's anxiety level. Their answers will be compared to other [85] _____ questions.

MODULE 10.5

Survey Question: How accurately are emotions expressed by "body language" and the face? Pages 400-402

Basic emotional [86] _____ , such as smiling or baring one's teeth when angry, appear to be unlearned.

[87] _____ expressions of fear, anger, disgust, sadness, and happiness are recognized by people of all cultures.

In Western culture, [88] _____ are encouraged to express such emotions as sadness, fear, shame, and guilt, and [89] _____ are expected to express anger and hostility.

The study of body language is known as [90] _____ .

Body [91] _____ and movements (body language) also express feelings, mainly by communicating emotional tone.

Three dimensions of emotional expressions are pleasantness-unpleasantness, attention-rejection, and [92] _____ .

Survey Question: How do psychologists explain emotions? Pages 402-405

The [93] _____ -Lange theory of emotion says that emotional experience follows an awareness of the bodily reactions of emotion.

In contrast, the [94] _____ -Bard theory says that bodily reactions and emotional experience occur at the same time and that emotions are organized in the brain.

Schachter's [95] _____ theory of emotion emphasizes the importance of labels, or interpretations, applied to feelings of bodily [96] _____ .

Also important is the process of [97] _____ , in which bodily arousal is attributed to a particular person, object, or situation.

Research on attribution theory has shown that [98] _____ [99] _____ (e.g., increased heart rate from exercise or fear) can be attributed to different sources such as attraction or love for someone.

The [100] _____ [101] _____ hypothesis holds that sensations and information from emotional expressions help define what emotion a person is feeling.

Making faces does influence [102] _____ and bodily activities through the [103] _____ nervous system.

Contemporary views of emotion place greater emphasis on how situations are [104] _____ (evaluated). Also, all of the elements of emotion are seen as interrelated and interacting.

PSYCHOLOGY IN ACTION

Survey Question: What does it means to have "emotional intelligence"? Page 407-408

Emotional [105] _____ involves the following skills: self-awareness, [106] _____ , self-control, and an understanding of how to use emotions.

Emotionally intelligent people are good at reading [107] _____ expressions, tone of [108] _____ , and other signs of emotion.

They also use their feelings to enhance [109] _____ and [110] _____ making.

Positive emotions are not just a luxury. They tend to encourage personal and [111] _____ connection.

Martin Seligman believes people can achieve genuine [112] _____ by optimizing their natural [113] _____ , such as kindness, originality, humor, optimism, and generosity, to buffer them against misfortunes.

MASTERY TEST

1. Which of the following is NOT one of the signs of emotional arousal recorded by a polygraph?
    a. heart rate
    b. pupil dilation
    c. blood pressure
    d. breathing rate

2. Plain water is most satisfying when a person has _____ thirst.
    a. intracellular
    b. hypothalamic
    c. extracellular
    d. homeostatic

3. We have a biological tendency to associate an upset stomach with foods eaten earlier. This is the basis for the development of
    a. taste aversions
    b. yo-yo dieting
    c. bulimia
    d. frequent weight cycling

4. Strong external rewards tend to undermine
    a. extrinsic motivation
    b. intrinsic motivation
    c. prepotent motivation
    d. stimulus motivation

5. Activity in the ANS is directly responsible for which element of emotion?
    a. emotional feelings
    b. emotional expressions
    c. physiological changes
    d. misattributions

6. Empathy is a major element of
    a. nAch
    b. intrinsic motivation
    c. emotional intelligence
    d. the sensation-seeking personality

7. Motivation refers to the ways in which activities are initiated, sustained, and
    a. acquired
    b. valued
    c. directed
    d. aroused

8. The psychological state or feeling we call thirst corresponds to which element of motivation?
   a. need
   b. drive
   c. deprivation
   d. incentive value

9. People who score high on the SSS generally prefer
   a. low levels of arousal
   b. moderate levels of arousal
   c. high levels of arousal
   d. the middle of the V function

10. Which facial expression is NOT recognized by people of all cultures?
    a. anger
    b. disgust
    c. optimism
    d. fear

11. Learning to weaken eating cues is useful in
    a. self-selection feeding
    b. yo-yo dieting
    c. rapid weight cycling
    d. behavioral dieting

12. People who score high on tests of the need for achievement tend to be
    a. motivated by power and prestige
    b. moderate risk takers
    c. sensation seekers
    d. attracted to long shots

13. Which theory holds that emotional feelings, arousal, and behavior are generated simultaneously in the brain?
    a. James-Lange
    b. Cannon-Bard
    c. cognitive
    d. attribution

14. Compared with people in North America, people in Asian cultures are less likely to express which emotion?
    a. anger
    b. jealousy
    c. curiosity
    d. fear

15. Binge eating is most associated with
    a. bulimia nervosa
    b. bait shyness
    c. low levels of NPY
    d. anorexia nervosa

16. Goals that are desirable are high in
    a. need reduction
    b. incentive value
    c. homeostatic valence
    d. motivational "push"

17. _____ is to pain avoidance as _____ is to the sex drive.
    a. Nonhomeostatic, episodic
    b. Episodic, nonhomeostatic
    c. Nonhomeostatic, cyclic
    d. Cyclic, nonhomeostatic

18. A specialist in kinesics could be expected to be most interested in
    a. facial blends
    b. circadian rhythms
    c. sensation seeking
    d. primary motives

19. Coping statements are a way to directly correct which part of test anxiety?
    a. overpreparation
    b. underarousal
    c. excessive worry
    d. compulsive rehearsal

20. Drives for exploration and activity are categorized as
    a. primary motives
    b. secondary motives
    c. stimulus motives
    d. extrinsic motives

21. Sudden death following a period of intense fear may occur when _____ slows the heart to a stop.
    a. a sympathetic overload
    b. adrenaline poisoning
    c. opponent-process feedback
    d. a parasympathetic rebound

22. People who enjoy skydiving and ski jumping are very likely high in
    a. parasympathetic arousal
    b. extrinsic motivation
    c. their desires to meet meta-needs
    d. the trait of sensation seeking

23. You could induce eating in a laboratory rat by activating the
    a. lateral hypothalamus
    b. corpus callosum
    c. rat's set point
    d. ventromedial hypothalamus

24. People think cartoons are funnier if they see them while holding a pen crosswise in their teeth. This observation supports
    a. the James-Lange theory
    b. the Cannon-Bard theory
    c. Schachter's cognitive theory
    d. the facial feedback hypothesis

25. Basic biological motives are closely related to
    a. nAch
    b. homeostasis
    c. activity in the thalamus
    d. levels of melatonin in the body

26. Self-actualization is to _____ needs as safety and security are to _____ needs.
    a. growth, basic
    b. basic, meta-
    c. prepotent, basic
    d. meta-, extrinsic

27. Which of the following is NOT a core element of emotion?
    a. physiological changes
    b. emotional expressions
    c. emotional feelings
    d. misattributions

28. The effects of a "supermarket diet" on eating are related to the effects of _____ on eating.
    a. anxiety
    b. metabolic rates
    c. incentive value
    d. stomach distention

29. According to the Yerkes-Dodson law, optimum performance occurs at _____ levels of arousal for simple tasks and _____ levels of arousal for complex tasks.
    a. higher, lower
    b. lower, higher
    c. minimum, high
    d. average, high

30. Contemporary models of emotion place greater emphasis on _____, or the way situations are evaluated.
    a. appraisal
    b. attribution
    c. feedback
    d. emotional tone

31. A _____ (BMI) measures one's body fat by applying the formula: weight/height^2 x 703.
    a. Body Magnitude Indicator
    b. Basic Magnitude Indicator
    c. Body Mass Index
    d. Basic Mass Index

32. Which statement correctly explains why there is an obesity problem in the United States?
    a. The all-you-can-eat dining halls and restaurants temp people to overeat.
    b. Although the food industry has made dinner easier to cook and buy, the food is high in fat and sugar.
    c. Overeating during large meals increases one's body set point.
    d. All the preceding

33. Although in some parts of the world, eating monkey eyes is considered a delicacy, to Americans it is not. This difference in preference is largely influenced by
    a. cultural values
    b. primary motives
    c. the availability of taste buds
    d. overdeveloped hypothalamus

34. Bev placed herself on a strict diet of eating no other fruits except for grapefruit. Eventually, she began to crave other fruits and could not stand seeing, smelling, or tasting another grapefruit. One explanation for Bev's strong dislike of grapefruit is her body was trying to avoid nutritional imbalance by producing
    a. positive reinforcement
    b. a taste aversion
    c. shaping
    d. purging

35. The causes of anorexia have been attributed to
    a. unrealistic comparison of body image to others
    b. seeking control
    c. distorted body image
    d. all the preceding

36. Variables that aid our survival include _____ moods, which help us make better decisions and be more helpful, efficient, and creative. The ability to understand and display _____ expressions such as anger helps us communicate with others.
    a. primary, universal
    b. negative, natural
    c. positive, facial
    d. natural, primary

37. The National Academy of Sciences has concluded that polygraph tests should not be used to screen _____ since the test tends to label honest people dishonest.
    a. immigrants
    b. employees
    c. government officials
    d. mentally disturbed people

38. According to Martin Seligman, to be genuinely happy, one must
    a. optimize one's natural strengths
    b. focus on fixing one's weaknesses
    c. strengthen negative emotions to better understand positive emotions
    d. balance both negative and positive emotions

Chapter 10

SOLUTIONS

RECITE AND REVIEW

MODULE 10.1

1. initiate
2. activities
3. need
4. goal
5. push
6. pull
7. goal
8. need
9. secondary
10. primary
11. steady

MODULE 10.2

12. stomach
13. liver
14. start
15. stop
16. feeding
17. satiety
18. fat
19. diet
20. height
21. weight
22. 25
23. taste
24. taste
25. exercise
26. calories
27. starvation
28. gorging
29. counseling
30. anxiety

31. bodily
32. brain
33. fluid
34. cells
35. fluid
36. cells
37. cycles
38. learned
39. females
40. arousal
41. drive

MODULE 10.3

42. sensory
43. physical
44. arousal
45. arousal
46. moderate
47. simple
48. complex
49. excessive
50. preparation
51. rehearsal

52. Social
53. need
54. success
55. risk
56. motivation
57. effort
58. persist
59. challenging
60. small
61. social

62. basic
63. Lower
64. higher
65. Self
66. needs
67. external

MODULE 10.4

68. behaviors
69. feelings
70. hormone
71. nervous
72. system
73. sadness

74. anger
75. branch
76. branch
77. rebound

78. arousal
79. emotional
80. arousal
81. relevant

82. lying
83. control
84. critical

MODULE 10.5

85. unlearned
86. fear
87. sadness
88. sadness

89. shame
90. anger
91. body
92. language

93. feelings
94. tone
95. facial

96. follows
97. at
98. the
99. same
100. time

101. labels
102. arousal
103. increased
104. attributed
105. expressions

106. emotions
107. autonomic
108. situations

PSYCHOLOGY IN ACTION

109. self
110. self
111. emotions

112. emotion
113. feelings (or emotions)
114. Positive

115. strengths
116. kindness
117. optimism

CONNECTIONS

MODULE 10.1

1. b
2. d

3. a
4. e

5. c

MODULE 10.2

1. b

2. a

3. c

1. c
2. i
3. b
4. d

5. h
6. a
7. g
8. j

9. e
10. f

MODULE 10.3
1. d

2. g	4. a	6. b
3. c	5. e	7. f

1. f	4. c	7. g
2. d	5. e	
3. a	6. b	

MODULE 10.4

1. b	4. d	7. c
2. g	5. h	8. e
3. a	6. f	

MODULE 10.5

1. e	4. b	7. h
2. d	5. f	8. a
3. i	6. c	9. g

CHECK YOUR MEMORY

MODULE 10.1

1. F	3. T
2. T	4. T

MODULE 10.2

5. F	13. F	21. F
6. T	14. F	22. T
7. F	15. F	23. F
8. T	16. F	24. F
9. T	17. T	
10. T	18. T	
11. F	19. T	
12. F	20. T	

25. T	27. F
26. F	28. T

MODULE 10.3

29. T	31. F	33. F
30. T	32. T	

34. F

35. F	37. T	39. T
36. F	38. T	

40. F	43. T	46. F
41. T	44. F	
42. F	45. T	

MODULE 10.4

47. T	52. F	57. T
48. F	53. T	58. T
49. F	54. T	59. F
50. F	55. F	
51. T	56. F	

MODULE 10.5

60. T	62. F	64. T
61. F	63. F	65. F

66. F	69. F	72. T
67. T	70. T	73. F
68. T	71. F	

PSYCHOLOGY IN ACTION

74. T	77. T	80. T
75. F	78. T	
76. T	79. T	

FINAL SURVEY AND REVIEW

MODULE 10.1

1. sustain	5. needs	9. primary
2. direct	6. goals	10. stimulus
3. drive	7. incentive	11. secondary
4. attainment	8. value	12. homeostasis

MODULE 10.2

13. distention	19. set	25. heart
14. hypothalamus	20. point	26. stroke
15. satiety	21. cues	27. aversions
16. lateral	22. body mass index	28. bait
17. ventromedial	23. fat	29. shyness
18. nucleus	24. 25	30. exercise

31. calories
32. Anorexia

33. bulimia
34. drug

35. self-image

36. hypothalamus
37. intracellular
38. extracellular
39. episodic

40. cyclic
41. avoidance
42. tolerance
43. estrus

44. nonhomeostatic
45. androgens

MODULE 10.3

46. stimulus
47. exploration
48. arousal
49. theory

50. Sensation-Seeking
51. inverted
52. U
53. Yerkes-Dodson

54. worrying
55. arousal

56. socialization
57. achievement
58. High

59. moderate
60. Self-confidence
61. confidence

62. challenging
63. social

64. hierarchy
65. growth
66. prepotent

67. actualization
68. meta
69. extrinsic

70. intrinsic

MODULE 10.4

71. adaptive
72. expressions
73. adrenaline
74. autonomic
75. primary

76. sympathetic
77. parasympathetic
78. parasympathetic
79. sympathetic
80. polygraph

81. galvanic
82. relevant
83. irrelevant
84. polygraph
85. critical

MODULE 10.5

86. expressions
87. Facial
88. women

89. men
90. kinesics
91. gestures

92. activation

93. James
94. Cannon
95. cognitive
96. arousal

97. attribution
98. physical
99. arousal
100. facial

101. feedback
102. emotions
103. autonomic
104. appraised

PSYCHOLOGY IN ACTION
105. intelligence

106. empathy
107. facial
108. voice

109. thinking
110. decision
111. social

112. happiness
113. strengths

MASTERY TEST

1. B, (p. 398)
2. A, (p. 384)
3. A, (p. 381)
4. B, (p. 393)
5. C, (p. 395-396)
6. C, (p. 407)
7. C, (p. 374)
8. B, (p. 374)
9. C, (p. 388)
10. C, (p. 400)
11. D, (p. 382)
12. B, (p. 390)
13. B, (p. 402)

14. A, (p. 401)
15. A, (p. 383)
16. B, (p. 374)
17. B, (p. 384-385)
18. A, (p. 401-402)
19. C, (p. 389)
20. C, (p. 374)
21. D, (p. 397)
22. D, (p. 387)
23. A, (p. 377-378)
24. D, (p. 404)
25. B, (p. 375)
26. A, (p. 391)

27. D, (p. 395)
28. C, (p. 374, 380)
29. A, (p. 388)
30. A, (p. 404-405)
31. C, (p. 379)
32. D, (p. 379-380)
33. A, (p. 381)
34. B, (p. 381)
35. D, (p. 383)
36. C, (p. 395-396)
37. B, (p. 399)
38. A, (p. 408)

PERSONALITY

CHAPTER OVERVIEW

Personality refers to unique and enduring behavior patterns. Character is personality evaluated. Temperament refers to the hereditary and physiological aspects of one's emotional nature. Personality traits are lasting personal qualities. Personality types are categories defined by groups of shared traits. Behavior is also influenced by self-concept. Personality theories combine various ideas and principles to explain personality.

Allport's trait theory classifies traits as common, individual, cardinal, central, or secondary. Cattell's trait theory attributes visible surface traits to the existence of 16 underlying source traits. The five-factor model reduces traits to five dimensions. Traits appear to interact with situations to determine behavior. Behavioral genetics suggests that heredity influences personality traits. Twin studies suggest that heredity accounts for 25 percent -50 percent of the variability in personality traits. The other 50 percent is attributed to the environment.

Like other psychodynamic approaches, Sigmund Freud's psychoanalytic theory emphasizes unconscious forces and conflicts within the personality. Behavioral theories of personality emphasize learning, conditioning, and the immediate effects of the environment. Social learning theory adds cognitive elements such as perception, thinking, and understanding to the behavioral view. Many differences between males and females are based on social learning. Humanistic theory emphasizes subjective experiences and needs for self-actualization. Positivistic theory focuses on characteristics that contribute to a person's well-being and life satisfaction.

Techniques typically used for personality assessment are interviews, direct observation, questionnaires, and projective tests.

Shyness is a mixture of social inhibition and social anxiety. It is marked by heightened public self-consciousness and a tendency to regard one's shyness as a lasting trait. Shyness can be lessened by changing self-defeating beliefs and by improving social skills.

LEARNING OBJECTIVES

To demonstrate mastery of this chapter, you should be able to:

1. Define the term "personality" and explain how personality differs from character and temperament.

2. Define the term "trait."

3. Discuss the stability of personality traits from one situation to another.

4. Briefly describe at what age personality traits are firmly established.

5. Describe the trait approach and the type approach to personality, and explain the shortcoming of the type approach. Define the terms "introvert" and "extrovert."

6. Explain the concepts self-concept and self-esteem and how they affect behavior and personal adjustment.

7. Briefly describe cultural differences in self-esteem.

8. Define the term "personality theory."

9. List and describe the five broad perspectives of personality included in this chapter.

10. Characterize the general approach to the study of personality taken by a trait theorist.

The following objective is related to the material in the "Discovering Psychology" section of the text.

11. Describe the four types of personalities that are related to musical tastes.

12. Distinguish common traits from individual traits.

13. Define and give examples of Allport's cardinal traits, central traits, and secondary traits.

14. Distinguish between surface traits and source traits, and state how Cattell measures source traits.

15. Explain how Cattell's approach to personality traits differed from Allport's approach.

16. Discuss the five-factor model of personality.

17. Explain what a trait-situation interaction is.

18. Explain how twin studies are used to assess the relative contributions of heredity and environment to personality.

19. Discuss how the similarities in the personalities of twins can be explained.

20. Discuss relative contributions of heredity and environment to the makeup of personality.

21. Briefly discuss the development of psychoanalytical theory and its founder. List and describe the three parts of the personality according to Freud and discuss the principle that each operates on.

22. Describe the dynamic conflict between the three parts of the personality and relate neurotic and moral anxiety to the conflict.

23. Describe the three levels of awareness and their relationship to the three parts of the personality.

24. List and describe Freud's four psychosexual stages. In your answer, include an explanation of fixation and the corresponding age range for each stage.

25. Discuss the positive and negative aspects of Freud's developmental theory.

26. Explain how behaviorists view personality and traits. Include a definition of the term "situational determinants."

27. Explain how learning theorists view the structure of personality. Include in your discussion the terms "habit," "drive," "cue," "response," and "reward."

28. Explain how learning theory and social learning theory differ. Include in your discussion a description of the terms "psychological situation," "expectancy," "reinforcement value," "self-reinforcement," and "self-efficacy."

29. Explain how self-reinforcement is related to self-esteem and depression.

30. Using the behavioristic view of development, explain why feeding, toilet training, sex training, and learning to express anger or aggression may be particularly important to personality formation.

31. Describe the role of identification, imitation, and social reinforcement in the development of sex-appropriate behavior.

32. Briefly explain how the humanists set themselves apart from the Freudian and behaviorist viewpoints of personality.

33. Describe the development of Maslow's interest in self-actualization.

34. Using at least five of the characteristics of self-actualizers listed in your text, describe a self-actualizing person. From the original list of 11, evaluate yourself and explain what may be helping or hindering your self-actualization.

35. List and briefly explain or describe (where applicable) eight steps to promote self-actualization.

36. List and briefly describe the six human strengths that contribute to well-being and life satisfaction.

37. Describe Rogers' view of a fully functioning individual.

38. Discuss Rogers' view of an incongruent person. Include a description of the terms "self," "self-image," "symbolization," and the "ideal self."

39. Explain how "possible selves" help translate our hopes, dreams, and fears and ultimately direct our future behavior.

40. Explain how "conditions of worth," "positive self-regard," "organismic valuing," and "unconditional positive regard" may affect personality formation.

41. Discuss the following assessment techniques in terms of purpose, method, advantages, and limitations: a. unstructured and structured interviews (include halo effect.) b. direct observation (include rating scales, behavioral assessment, and situational testing) c. personality questionnaires (include validity, reliability, and a description of the MMPI-2) d. honesty tests e. projective tests (include descriptions of Rorschach, TAT)

42. Describe the personality characteristics of sudden murderers and explain how their characteristics are related to the nature of their homicidal actions.

43. List and describe the three elements of shyness.

44. State what situations usually cause shyness.

45. Compare the personality of the shy and the non-shy. Include the concepts labeling and self-esteem.

46. List and discuss the changes that can be made to three major areas of a shy person's life that can help reduce shyness.

RECITE AND REVIEW

MODULE 11.1

Survey Questions: How do psychologists use the term *personality*? What core concepts make up the psychology of personality? Pages 412-415

Personality is made up of one's unique and relatively stable [1] _____ patterns.

Character is personality that has been judged or [2] _____ . That is, it is the possession of desirable qualities.

Temperament refers to the [3] _____ and physiological aspects of one's emotional nature.

Personality traits are lasting personal qualities that are inferred from [4] _____ .

A personality type is a style of personality defined by having a group of related [5] _____ or similar characteristics.

Two widely recognized personality [6] _____ are an introvert (shy, self-centered person) and an extrovert (bold, outgoing person).

Behavior is influenced by self-concept, which is a person's perception of his or her own [7] _____ traits.

Culture determines how people go about developing and maintaining [8] _____ (self-evaluation):

People with high self-esteem are confident, [9] _____ , and self-respecting, and people with low self-esteem are insecure, [10] _____ , and lack confidence.

[11] _____ theories combine interrelated assumptions, ideas, and principles to explain personality.

Five major types of personality theories are: [12] _____ , psychodynamic, behavioristic, social learning, and humanistic.

Survey Question: Are some personality traits more basic or important than others? Pages 415-420

Research has found a link between personality characteristics and [13] _____ . For example, people who value aesthetic experiences, have good [14] _____ skills, and are liberal and tolerant of others tend to prefer jazz, [15] _____ , classical, and folk music.

Trait [16] _____ attempt to specify qualities of personality that are most lasting or characteristic of a person.

Gordon Allport made useful distinctions between common traits (which are shared by most members of a culture) and [17] _____ traits (characteristics of a single person).

Allport also identified cardinal traits (a trait that influences nearly all of a person's activities), central traits (core traits of personality), and [18] _____ traits (superficial traits).

The theory of Raymond Cattell attributes visible [19] _____ traits to the existence of 16 underlying source traits (which he identified using factor [20] _____).

Source traits are measured by the Sixteen [21] _____ Questionnaire (16 PF).

The outcome of the 16 PF and other personality tests may be graphically presented as a [22] _____ profile.

The five-factor model of personality reduces traits to five [23] _____ dimensions of personality.

The five factors are: extroversion, [24] _____ , conscientiousness, neuroticism, and openness to [25] _____ .

[26] _____ interact with situations to determine behavior.

Heredity is responsible for 25 to 50 percent of the variation in personality [27] _____ .

Studies of separated [28] _____ twins suggest that heredity contributes significantly to adult personality traits. Overall, however, personality is shaped as much, or more, by differences in environment.

MODULE 11.2

Survey Question: How do psychodynamic theories explain personality? Pages 422-425

Psychodynamic theories focus on the inner workings of personality, especially hidden or [29] _____ forces and internal conflicts.

According to Sigmund Freud's psychoanalytic theory, personality is made up of the id, [30] _____ , and superego.

The id operates on the pleasure [31] _____ . The ego is guided by the reality [32] _____ .

Libido, derived from the [33] _____ instincts, is the primary [34] _____ running the personality.

The [35] _____ is made up of the conscience and the ego ideal.

Conflicts within the personality may cause neurotic [36] _____ or moral [37] _____ and motivate use of ego-defense mechanisms.

The personality operates on three levels, the [38] _____ , preconscious, and unconscious.

The id is completely [39] _____ ; the ego and superego can operate at all three levels of awareness.

The Freudian view of personality development is based on a series of psychosexual [40] _____ :

the [41] _____ anal, phallic, and genital.

Fixations (unresolved emotional conflicts) at any stage can leave a lasting imprint on [42] _____ .

Freud's theory pioneered the idea that feeding, toilet training, and early sexual experiences leave an

imprint on [43] _____ .

During the phallic stage of Freud's [44] _____ stages of development, boys must confront and

resolve the [45] _____ complex and girls must confront and resolve the Electra complex.

Freud's theory has been influential toward the understanding of personality development for several

reasons: He suggested that adult personality is formed during the [46] _____ years of a person's

life; he identified feeding, [47] _____ training, and early sexual experiences as critical events;

and he indicated that development proceeds in [48] _____ .

MODULE 11.3

Survey Question: What do behaviorists and social learning theorists emphasize in personality? Pages
427-431

Behavioral theories of personality emphasize [49] _____ , conditioning, and immediate effects of

the environment.

Learning theorists generally stress the effects of prior learning and [50] _____ determinants

of behavior.

Learning theorists John Dollard and Neal Miller consider [51] _____ the basic core of personality.

[52] _____ express the combined effects of drive, cue, response, and [53] _____ .

[54] _____ learning theory adds cognitive elements, such as perception, thinking, and

understanding, to the behavioral view of personality.

Examples of social learning concepts are the [55] _____ situation (the situation as it is perceived),

expectancies (expectations about what effects a response will have), and reinforcement [56] _____

(the subjective value of a reinforcer or activity).

Bandura believes one's self-efficacy (belief in our [57] _____ to produce a desired outcome)

is an important aspect of expectancy.

Some social learning theorists treat "conscience" as a case of [58] _____ -reinforcement.

The behavioristic view of personality development holds that social reinforcement in four situations is critical. The critical situations are [59] _____ , toilet or cleanliness training, sex training, and [60] _____ or aggression training.

Identification (feeling emotionally connected to a person) and [61] _____ (mimicking another person's behavior) are of particular importance in sex (or gender) training.

MODULE 11.4

Survey Question: How do humanistic theories differ from other perspectives? Pages 432-436

Humanistic theory views human nature as [62] _____ and emphasizes subjective experience, [63] _____ choice, and needs for self-actualization.

Abraham Maslow's study of self-actualizers identified characteristics they share, ranging from efficient perceptions of reality to frequent [64] _____ (temporary moments of self-actualization).

The process of self-actualization involves multiple steps, some of which include being willing to change, taking [65] _____ , examining one's motives, getting involved, and making use of [66] _____ experiences.

A person's well-being and life [67] _____ are linked to six human strengths: wisdom and knowledge, [68] _____ , humanity, justice, [69] _____ , and transcendence.

The congruent or [70] _____ functioning person is flexible and open to experiences and feelings.

Carl Rogers's theory views the [71] _____ as an entity that emerges when experiences that match the self-[72] _____ are symbolized (admitted to consciousness) while those that are incongruent are excluded.

The incongruent person has a highly unrealistic [73] _____ and/or a mismatch between the [74] _____ and the ideal self.

In the development of personality, humanists are primarily interested in the emergence of a [75] _____ and in self-evaluations.

As parents apply conditions of [76] _____ (standards used to judge thoughts, feelings, and actions) to a child, the child begins to do the same.

Internalized conditions of worth contribute to incongruence, they damage [77] _____ self-regard, and they disrupt the organismic [78] _____ process.

MODULE 11.5

Survey Question: How do psychologists measure personality? Pages 438-444

Techniques typically used for personality assessment are [79] _____ , observation, questionnaires, and projective [80] _____ .

Structured and unstructured [81] _____ provide much information, but they are subject to [82] _____ bias and misperceptions. The halo effect may also [83] _____ accuracy.

Direct observation, sometimes involving situational tests, behavioral assessment, or the use of [84] _____ scales, allows evaluation of a person's actual [85] _____ .

Personality questionnaires, such as the [86] _____ Personality Inventory-2 (MMPI-2), are objective and [87] _____ , but their validity is open to question.

Honesty tests, which are essentially personality [88] _____ , are widely used by businesses to make hiring decisions. Their validity is hotly debated.

Projective tests ask a subject to project thoughts or feelings onto an ambiguous [89] _____ or unstructured situation.

The Rorschach, or [90] _____ test, is a well-known projective technique. A second is the [91] _____ Apperception Test (TAT).

The validity and objectivity of projective tests are quite [92] _____ . Nevertheless, projective techniques are considered useful by many clinicians, particularly as part of a [93] _____ battery.

PSYCHOLOGY IN ACTION

Survey Questions: What causes shyness? What can be done about it? Pages 446-448

Shyness is a mixture of [94] _____ inhibition and [95] _____ anxiety.

Shy persons tend to lack social skills and they feel social anxiety (because they believe they are being [96] _____ by others).

Shy persons also have a self-defeating bias in their [97] _____ (they tend to blame [98] _____ for social failures).

Shyness is marked by heightened [99] _____ self-consciousness (awareness of oneself as a [100] _____ object) and a tendency to regard shyness as a lasting trait.

Shyness can be lessened by changing self-defeating [101] _____ and by improving [102] _____ skills.

CONNECTIONS

MODULE 11.1

1. _____ character
2. _____ trait
3. _____ Type A
4. _____ melancholic
5. _____ choleric
6. _____ phlegmatic
7. _____ behavior genetics
8. _____ sanguine
9. _____ trait situation
10. _____ 16 PF
11. _____ common traits
12. _____ Big Five

a. heart attack risk
b. hot-tempered
c. personality judged
d. cheerful
e. source traits
f. culturally typical
g. sluggish
h. universal dimensions
i. sad, gloomy
j. lasting personal quality
k. twin studies
l. interaction

MODULE 11.2

1. _____ Thanatos
2. _____ Eros
3. _____ conscience
4. _____ ego ideal
5. _____ oral stage
6. _____ anal stage
7. _____ phallic stage
8. _____ id
9. _____ Oedipus complex
10. _____ Electra complex

a. mouth
b. pride
c. genitals
d. female conflict
e. male conflict
f. death instinct
g. elimination
h. life instinct
i. guilt
j. pleasure principle

MODULE 11.3

1. _____ self-efficacy
2. _____ reward
3. _____ expectancy
4. _____ situational determinants
5. _____ habits
6. _____ social learning

a. anticipation
b. belief in one's capability
c. learned behavior pattern
d. positive reinforcer
e. external causes
f. cognitive behaviorism

MODULE 11.4

1. _____ unconditional positive regards
2. _____ Rogers
3. _____ Maslow
4. _____ congruence
5. _____ subjective experience

a. self-image = ideal self
b. unshakable love
c. private perceptions of reality
d. fully functioning person
e. self-actualization

MODULE 11.5

1. _____ validity scale
2. _____ social anxiety
3. _____ MMPI
4. _____ inkblot
5. _____ private self-consciousness
6. _____ situational test
7. _____ public self-consciousness
8. _____ honesty test
9. _____ self-defeating bias
10. _____ halo effect

a. Rorschach
b. integrity at work
c. interview problem
d. personality questionnaire
e. faking good
f. Shoot Don't Shoot
g. view self as social object
h. focus on inner feelings
i. distortion in thinking
j. evaluation fears

CHECK YOUR MEMORY

MODULE 11.1

Survey Questions: How do psychologists use the term *personality*? What core concepts make up the psychology of personality? Pages 412-415

1. The term *personality* refers to charisma or personal style.
   TRUE or FALSE

2. Personality is a person's relatively stable pattern of attitudes.
   TRUE or FALSE

3. Character refers to the inherited "raw material" from which personality is formed.
   TRUE or FALSE

4. A person with genuine high self-esteem has a tendency to accurately appraise his/her own strengths and weaknesses.
   TRUE or FALSE

5. In Asian cultures, self-esteem is strongly tied to personal achievement rather than group success.
   TRUE or FALSE

6. Traits are stable or lasting qualities of personality, displayed in most situations.
   TRUE or FALSE

7. Personality traits typically become quite stable by age 30 with the exception of conscientiousness and agreeability.
   TRUE or FALSE

8. Paranoid, dependent, and antisocial personalities are regarded as personality types.
   TRUE or FALSE

9. Two major dimensions of Eysenck's personality theory are stable-unstable and calm-moody.
   TRUE or FALSE

10. Trait theories of personality stress subjective experience and personal growth.
    TRUE or FALSE

Survey Question: Are some personality traits more basic or important than others? Pages 415-420

11. Extroverted students tend to study in noisy areas of the library.
    TRUE or FALSE

12. Peter Rentfrow and Samuel Gosling found that one's preference to music is linked to personality characteristics.
    TRUE or FALSE

13. People who are cheerful, conventional, extroverted, and reliable tend to prefer blues, jazz, and classical music.
    TRUE or FALSE

14. Nearly all of a person's activities can be traced to one or two common traits.
    TRUE or FALSE

15. Roughly seven central traits are needed, on the average, to describe an individual's personality.
    TRUE or FALSE

16. Allport used factor analysis to identify central traits.
    TRUE or FALSE

17. The 16 PF is designed to measure surface traits.
    TRUE or FALSE

18. Judging from scores on the 16 PF, airline pilots have traits that are similar to creative artists.
    TRUE or FALSE

19. As one of the Big Five factors, neuroticism refers to having negative, upsetting emotions.
    TRUE or FALSE

20. The expression of personality traits tends to be influenced by external situations.
TRUE or FALSE

21. Similarities between reunited identical twins show that personality is mostly shaped by genetics.
TRUE or FALSE

22. Studies of identical twins show that personality traits are approximately 70 percent hereditary.
TRUE or FALSE

23. Some of the coincidences shared by identical twins appear to be based on the fallacy of positive instances.
TRUE or FALSE

24. Unrelated people can share amazingly similar personality characteristics due to their age, gender, and living conditions.
TRUE or FALSE

MODULE 11.2

Survey Question: How do psychodynamic theories explain personality? Pages 422-425

25. Freud described the id, ego, and superego as "little people" that manage the human psyche.
TRUE or FALSE

26. The id is totally unconscious.
TRUE or FALSE

27. The ego is guided by the pleasure principle.
TRUE or FALSE

28. The superego is the source of feelings of guilt and pride.
TRUE or FALSE

29. Threats of punishment from the Thanatos cause moral anxiety.
TRUE or FALSE

30. Oral-dependent persons are gullible.
TRUE or FALSE

31. Vanity and narcissism are traits of the anal-retentive personality.
TRUE or FALSE

32. According to Freud, boys experience the Oedipus complex and girls experience the Electra complex.
TRUE or FALSE

33. The genital stage occurs between the ages of three and six, just before latency.
TRUE or FALSE

34. Boys are more likely to develop a strong conscience if their fathers are affectionate and accepting.
TRUE or FALSE

35. Freud regarded latency as the most important stage of psychosexual development.
   TRUE or FALSE

36. Erik Erikson's psychosocial stages were derived, in part, from Freud's psychosexual stages.
   TRUE or FALSE

MODULE 11.3

Survey Question: What do behaviorists and social learning theorists emphasize in personality? Pages 427-431

37. Behaviorists view personality as a collection of learned behavior patterns.
   TRUE or FALSE

38. Behaviorists attribute our actions to prior learning and specific situations.
   TRUE or FALSE

39. Behaviors are influenced by an interaction between the situation and previously gained knowledge.
   TRUE or FALSE

40. Knowing the consistent ways people respond to certain situations allows us to predict their personality characteristics.
   TRUE or FALSE

41. According to Dollard and Miller, habits are acquired through observational learning.
   TRUE or FALSE

42. Cues are signals from the environment that guide responses.
   TRUE or FALSE

43. An expectancy refers to the anticipation that making a response will lead to reinforcement.
   TRUE or FALSE

44. Self-reinforcement is highly related to one's self-esteem.
   TRUE or FALSE

45. People who are depressed tend to engage in a high rate of self-reinforcement to make themselves feel better.
   TRUE or FALSE

46. Social reinforcement is based on attention and approval from others.
   TRUE or FALSE

47. In elementary school, misbehaving boys typically get more attention from teachers than girls.
   TRUE or FALSE

MODULE 11.4

Survey Question: How do humanistic theories differ from other perspectives? Pages 432-436

48. Humanists believe that humans are capable of free choice.
    TRUE or FALSE

49. To investigate self-actualization, Maslow studied eminent men and women exclusively.
    TRUE or FALSE

50. Self-actualizers usually try to avoid task centering.
    TRUE or FALSE

51. Personal autonomy is a characteristic of the self-actualizing person.
    TRUE or FALSE

52. People who live happy and meaningful lives are people who possess the traits characteristic of a self-actualizer and express such human strengths as courage, justice, and temperance.
    TRUE or FALSE

53. Information inconsistent with one's self-image is described as incongruent.
    TRUE or FALSE

54. Images of our possible selves are derived from our hopes, fears, fantasies, and goals.
    TRUE or FALSE

55. Poor self-knowledge is associated with high self-esteem because people do not have to think about their own faults.
    TRUE or FALSE

56. Congruence represents a close correspondence between self-image, the ideal self, and the true self.
    TRUE or FALSE

57. Images of possible selves typically cause feelings of incongruence.
    TRUE or FALSE

58. Rogers believed that organismic valuing is healthier than trying to meet someone else's conditions of worth.
    TRUE or FALSE

MODULE 11.5

Survey Question: How do psychologists measure personality? Pages 438-444

59. Planned questions are used in a structured interview.
    TRUE or FALSE

60. The halo effect may involve either a positive or a negative impression.
    TRUE or FALSE

61. Personality questionnaires are used to do behavioral assessments.
    TRUE or FALSE

62. Judgmental firearms training is a type of honesty test.
    TRUE or FALSE

63. Items on the MMPI-2 were selected for their ability to identify persons with psychiatric problems.
    TRUE or FALSE

64. The validity scale of the MMPI-2 is used to rate Type A behavior.
    TRUE or FALSE

65. The psychasthenia scale of the MMPI-2 detects the presence of phobias and compulsive actions.
    TRUE or FALSE

66. It is very easy to fake responses to a projective test.
    TRUE or FALSE

67. The TAT is a situational test.
    TRUE or FALSE

68. Habitually violent prison inmates are aggressive and overcontrolled.
    TRUE or FALSE

PSYCHOLOGY IN ACTION

Survey Questions: What causes shyness? What can be done about it? Pages 446-448

69. Shyness is closely related to private self-consciousness.
    TRUE or FALSE

70. Nonshy persons believe that external situations cause their occasional feelings of shyness.
    TRUE or FALSE

71. The odds of meeting someone interested in socializing are about the same wherever you are.
    TRUE or FALSE

72. Open-ended questions help keep conversations going.
    TRUE or FALSE

FINAL SURVEY AND REVIEW

MODULE 11.1

Survey Questions: How do psychologists use the term *personality*? What core concepts make up the psychology of personality? Pages 412-415

[1] _____ is made up of one's unique and relatively stable behavior [2] _____ .

[3] _____ is personality that has been judged or evaluated. That is, it is the possession of desirable qualities.

[4] _____ refers to the hereditary and physiological aspects of one's emotional nature.

Personality [5] _____ are lasting personal qualities that are inferred from behavior.

A personality [6] _____ is a style of personality defined by having a group of related traits or similar characteristics.

Two widely recognized personality types are an [7] _____ (shy, self-centered person) and an [8] _____ (bold, outgoing person).

Behavior is influenced by [9] _____ , which is a person's perception of his or her own personality traits.

[10] _____ determines how people go about developing and maintaining self-esteem (self-evaluation): People with [11] _____ self-esteem are confident, proud, and self-respecting, and people with [12] _____ self-esteem are insecure, self-critical, and lack confidence.

Personality [13] _____ combine interrelated assumptions, ideas, and principles to explain personality.

Five major types of personality theories are: trait, [14] _____ , behavioristic, social learning, and [15] _____ .

Survey Question: Are some personality traits more basic or important than others? Pages 415-420

Research has found a link between [16] _____ characteristics and music. For example, people who value [17] _____ experiences, have good [18] _____ skills, and are liberal and tolerant of others tend to prefer jazz, blues, classical, and folk music.

[19] _____ theories attempt to specify qualities of personality that are most lasting or characteristic of a person.

Gordon [20] _____ made useful distinctions between [21] _____ traits (which are shared by most members of a culture) and individual traits (characteristics of a single person).

He also identified [22] _____ traits (a trait that influences nearly all of a person's activities), [23] _____ traits (core traits of personality), and secondary traits (superficial traits).

The theory of Raymond [24] _____ attributes visible surface traits to the existence of 16 underlying [25] _____ traits (which he identified using [26] _____ analysis).

[27] _____ [28] _____ are measured by the Sixteen Personality Factor Questionnaire (16 PF).

The outcome of the 16 PF and other personality tests may be graphically presented as a trait [29] _____ .

The [30] _____ model of personality reduces traits to five universal dimensions of personality.

They are: [31] _____ , agreeableness, conscientiousness, [32] _____ , and openness to experience.

Traits [33] _____ with [34] _____ to determine behavior.

Heredity is responsible for [35] _____ to [36] _____ percent of the variation in personality traits.

Studies of separated identical twins suggest that [37] _____ contributes significantly to adult personality traits. Overall, however, personality is shaped as much, or more, by differences in [38] _____ .

MODULE 11.2

Survey Question: How do psychodynamic theories explain personality? Pages 422-425

Psychodynamic theories focus on the inner workings of [39] _____ , especially hidden or unconscious forces and internal [40] _____ .

According to Sigmund Freud's [41] _____ theory, personality is made up of the [42] _____ , ego, and [43] _____ .

The id operates on the [44] _____ principle. The ego is guided by the [45] _____ principle.

[46] _____ , derived from the life [47] _____ , is the primary energy running the personality.

The superego is made up of the [48] _____ and the [49] _____ ideal.

Conflicts within the personality may cause [50] _____ anxiety or [51] _____ anxiety and motivate use of ego-defense mechanisms.

The personality operates on three levels, the conscious, [52] _____ , and [53] _____ .

The [54] _____ is completely unconscious; the [55] _____ and [56] _____ can operate at all three levels of awareness.

The Freudian view of personality development is based on a series of [57] _____ stages: the oral, anal, [58] _____ , and genital.

[59] _____ (unresolved emotional conflicts) at any stage can leave a lasting imprint on personality.

Freud's theory pioneered the idea that [60] _____ , [61] _____ training, and early sexual experiences leave an imprint on personality.

During the [62] _____ stage of Freud's psychosexual stages of development, [63] _____ must confront and resolve the Oedipus complex and [64] _____ must confront and resolve the Electra complex.

Freud's theory has been influential toward the understanding of personality development for several reasons: He suggested that [65] _____ personality is formed during the first few years of a person's life; he identified feeding, toilet training, and early sexual experiences as [66] _____ events; and he indicated that development proceeds in [67] _____ .

MODULE 11.3

Survey Question: What do behaviorists and social learning theorists emphasize in personality? Pages 427-431

[68] _____ theories of personality emphasize learning, conditioning, and immediate effects of the environment.

Learning theorists generally stress the effects of prior learning and situational [69] _____ of behavior.

Learning theorists John Dollard and Neal Miller consider habits the basic core of personality. Habits express the combined effects of [70] _____ , [71] _____ , response, and reward.

Social learning theory adds [72] _____ elements, such as perception, thinking, and understanding, to the behavioral view of personality.

Examples of social learning concepts are the psychological situation (the situation as it is perceived), [73] _____ (expectations about what effects a response will have), and [74] _____ value (the subjective value of a reinforcer or activity).

Bandura believes one's self-[75] _____ (belief in our ability to produce a desired outcome) is an important aspect of [76] _____ .

Some social learning theorists treat "conscience" as a case of self-[77] _____ .

The behavioristic view of personality development holds that social reinforcement in four situations is critical. The critical situations are feeding[78] _____ sex training, and anger or

[79] _____ training.

[80] _____ (feeling emotionally connected to a person) and imitation (mimicking another person's behavior) are of particular importance in sex (or gender) training.

MODULE 11.4

Survey Question: How do humanistic theories differ from other perspectives? Pages 432-436

Humanistic theory views human nature as good and emphasizes [81] _____ experience, free choice, and needs for self-[82] _____ .

Abraham [83] _____ study of [84] _____ identified characteristics they share, ranging from efficient perceptions of reality to frequent peak experiences.

The process of self-[85] _____ involves multiple steps, some of which include being willing to change, taking responsibility, examining one's motives, getting involved, and making use of positive experiences.

A person's well-[86] _____ and life satisfaction are linked to six human [87] _____ : wisdom and knowledge, courage, humanity, justice, temperance, and transcendence.

The [88] _____ or fully functioning person is flexible and open to experiences and feelings.

Carl Rogers's theory views the self as an entity that emerges when experiences that match the self-image are [89] _____ (admitted to consciousness) while those that are [90] _____ are excluded.

The [91] _____ person has a highly unrealistic self-image and/or a mismatch between the self-image and the [92] _____ self.

In the development of personality, humanists are primarily interested in the emergence of a self-image and in [93] _____ .

As parents apply [94] _____ of worth (standards used to judge thoughts, feelings, and actions) to a child, the child begins to do the same.

Internalized [95] _____ contribute to incongruence, they damage positive self-regard, and they disrupt the [96] _____ valuing process.

MODULE 11.5

Survey Question: How do psychologists measure personality? Pages 438-444

Techniques typically used for personality assessment are interviews, direct [97] _____ ,

questionnaires, and [98] _____ tests.

Structured and [99] _____ interviews provide much information, but they are subject to interviewer

[100] _____ and misperceptions. The halo effect may also lower the accuracy of an interview.

Direct observation, sometimes involving [101] _____ tests, behavioral assessment, or the use of

rating scales, allows evaluation of a person's actual [102] _____ .

Personality questionnaires, such as the Minnesota Multiphasic [103] _____ [104] _____

-2 (MMPI-2), are objective and reliable, but their [105] _____ is open to question.

[106] _____ tests, which are essentially personality questionnaires, are widely used by businesses

to measure integrity and make hiring decisions.

[107] _____ tests ask subjects to react to an ambiguous stimulus or unstructured situation.

The [108] _____ , or inkblot test, is a well-known projective technique. A second is the Thematic

[109] _____ Test (TAT).

The [110] _____ and objectivity of projective tests are quite low. Nevertheless, projective

techniques are considered useful by many clinicians, particularly as part of a test [111] _____ .

PSYCHOLOGY IN ACTION

Survey Questions: What causes shyness? What can be done about it? Pages 446-448

Shyness is a mixture of social [112] _____ and social anxiety.

Shy persons tend to lack social [113] _____ and they feel social anxiety (because they believe

they are being evaluated by others).

Shy persons also have a [114] _____ bias in their thinking (they tend to blame themselves for

social failures).

Shyness is marked by heightened public self-[115] _____ (awareness of oneself as a

[116] _____ object) and a tendency to regard shyness as a lasting [117] _____ .

Shyness can be lessened by changing [118] _____ beliefs and by improving social

[119] _____ .

MASTERY TEST

1. The hereditary aspects of a person's emotional nature define his or her
   a. character
   b. personality
   c. cardinal traits
   d. temperament

2. Two parts of the psyche that operate on all three levels of awareness are the
   a. id and ego
   b. ego and superego
   c. id and superego
   d. id and ego ideal

3. The four critical situations Miller and Dollard consider important in the development of personality are feeding, toilet training,
   a. sex, and aggression
   b. cleanliness, and language
   c. attachment, and imitation
   d. and social learning

4. Scales that rate a person's tendencies for depression, hysteria, paranoia, and mania are found on the
   a. MMPI-2
   b. Rorschach
   c. TAT
   d. 16 PF

5. In the five-factor model, people who score high on openness to experience are
   a. intelligent
   b. extroverted
   c. choleric
   d. a personality type

6. Maslow used the term _____ to describe the tendency to make full use of personal potentials.
   a. full functionality
   b. self-potentiation
   c. ego-idealization
   d. self-actualization

7. Studies of reunited identical twins support the idea that
   a. personality traits are 70 percent hereditary
   b. fixations influence the expression of personality traits
   c. personality traits are altered by selective mating and placement in families of comparable status
   d. personality is shaped as much or more by environment as by heredity

8. A person's perception of his or her own personality is the core of
   a. temperament
   b. source traits
   c. self-concept
   d. trait-situation interactions

9. Which of the following concepts is NOT part of Dollard and Miller's behavioral model of personality?
   a. drive
   b. expectancy
   c. cue
   d. reward

10. The terms *structured* and *unstructured* apply most to
    a. the halo effect
    b. interviews
    c. questionnaires
    d. honesty tests

11. Behavioral theorists account for the existence of a conscience with the concept of
    a. traits of honesty and integrity
    b. the superego
    c. self-reinforcement
    d. conditions of worth

12. Feelings of pride come from the _____, a part of the _____.
    a. libido, conscience
    b. ego ideal, superego
    c. reality principle, superego
    d. superego, ego

13. Four types of temperament recognized by the early Greeks are: melancholic, choleric, phlegmatic, and
    a. sanguine
    b. sardonic
    c. sagittarian
    d. sagacious

14. Freud believed that boys identify with their fathers in order to resolve the _____ complex.
    a. Animus
    b. Electra
    c. Oedipus
    d. Persona

15. Maslow regarded peak experiences as temporary moments of
    a. task centering
    b. congruent selfhood
    c. self-actualization
    d. organismic valuing

16. Ambiguous stimuli are used primarily in the
    a. MMPI-2
    b. Shoot Don't Shoot Test
    c. Rorschach
    d. 16 PF

17. A person who is generally extroverted is more outgoing in some situations than in others. This observation supports the concept of
    a. trait-situation interactions
    b. behavioral genetic determinants
    c. situational fixations
    d. possible selves

18. Allport's concept of central traits is most closely related to Cattell's
    a. surface traits
    b. source traits
    c. secondary traits
    d. cardinal traits

19. According to Freud, tendencies to be orderly, obstinate, and stingy are formed during the _____ stage.
    a. genital
    b. anal
    c. oral
    d. phallic

20. Which of the following is NOT part of Carl Rogers's view of personality?
    a. possible selves
    b. organismic valuing
    c. conditions of worth
    d. congruence

21. Rating scales are primarily used in which approach to personality assessment?
    a. projective testing
    b. direct observation
    c. questionnaires
    d. the TAT technique

22. Which theory of personality places the greatest emphasis on the effects of the environment?
    a. trait
    b. psychodynamic
    c. behavioristic
    d. humanistic

23. Freudian psychosexual stages occur in the order
    a. oral, anal, genital, phallic
    b. oral, phallic, anal, genital
    c. genital, oral, anal, phallic
    d. oral, anal, phallic, genital

24. Rogers described mismatches between one's self-image and reality as a state of
    a. moral anxiety
    b. incongruence
    c. basic anxiety
    d. negative symbolization

25. All but one of the following are major elements of shyness; which does not apply?
    a. private self-consciousness
    b. social anxiety
    c. self-defeating thoughts
    d. belief that shyness is a lasting trait

26. People who all grew up in the same culture would be most likely to have the same _____ traits.
    a. cardinal
    b. common
    c. secondary
    d. source

27. A trait profile is used to report the results of
    a. the 16 PF
    b. situational tests
    c. the TAT
    d. the inkblot test

28. Expectancies and the psychological situation are concepts important to
    a. the five-factor model
    b. development of the superego
    c. social learning theory
    d. Maslow

29. In Asian cultures, _____ tends to be more strongly related to group membership and the success of the group.
    a. temperament
    b. character
    c. self-esteem
    d. moral anxiety

30. An emphasis on the situational determinants of actions is a key feature of _____ theories of personality.
    a. psychodynamic
    b. projective
    c. learning
    d. humanist

31. Which two personality characteristics continue to increase as people age?
    a. creativity and organization
    b. conscientiousness and agreeability
    c. affection and trust
    d. irritability and disorganization

32. People who prefer hip-hop, soul, and electronic music tend to
    a. be talkative and forgiving
    b. value aesthetic experiences
    c. be conservative
    d. enjoy taking risks

33. Jill was invited to go snowboarding, an activity she has not done before. Jill believes she has the ability to learn snowboarding and keep up with her friends because she is a fast learner. Bandura would say that Jill is high in
    a. self-actualizing
    b. organismic valuing
    c. congruence
    d. self-efficacy

34. _____ psychologists believe that one's well-being and life satisfaction are influenced by six personality traits, including courage, temperance, and transcendence.
    a. Behavioral
    b. Positive
    c. Psychodynamic
    d. Learning

SOLUTIONS

RECITE AND REVIEW

MODULE 11.1

1. behavior
2. evaluated
3. hereditary
4. behavior

5. traits
6. types
7. personality
8. self-esteem

9. proud
10. self-critical
11. Personality
12. trait

13. music
14. verbal
15. blues
16. theories
17. individual
18. secondary

19. surface
20. analysis
21. Personality Factor
22. trait
23. universal
24. agreeableness

25. experience
26. Traits
27. traits
28. identical

MODULE 11.2

29. unconscious
30. ego
31. principle
32. principle
33. life
34. energy
35. superego
36. anxiety

37. anxiety
38. conscious
39. unconscious
40. stages
41. oral
42. personality
43. personality
44. psychosexual

45. Oedipus
46. first few
47. toilet
48. stages

MODULE 11.3

49. learning
50. situational
51. habits
52. Habits
53. reward

54. Social
55. psychological
56. value
57. ability
58. self

59. feeding
60. anger
61. imitation

MODULE 11.4

62. good
63. free
64. peak experiences
65. responsibility
66. positive
67. satisfaction
68. courage

69. temperance
70. fully
71. self
72. image
73. self-image
74. self-image
75. self-image

76. worth
77. positive
78. valuing

MODULE 11.5

79. interviews
80. tests
81. interviews
82. interviewer
83. lower

84. rating
85. behavior
86. Minnesota Multiphasic
87. reliable
88. questionnaires

89. stimulus
90. inkblot
91. Thematic
92. low
93. test

PSYCHOLOGY IN ACTION

94. social
95. social
96. evaluated

97. thinking
98. themselves
99. public

100. social
101. beliefs
102. social

CONNECTIONS

MODULE 11.1

1. c
2. j
3. a
4. i

5. b
6. g
7. k
8. d

9. l
10. e
11. f
12. h

MODULE 11.2

1. f
2. h
3. i
4. b

5. a
6. g
7. c
8. j

9. e
10. d

MODULE 11.3

1. b
2. d

3. a
4. e

5. c
6. f

MODULE 11.4

1. b
2. d

3. e
4. a

5. c

MODULE 11.5

1. e
2. j
3. d
4. a

5. h
6. f
7. a
8. b

9. i
10. c

CHECK YOUR MEMORY

MODULE 11.1

1. F

2. F	5. F	8. T
3. F	6. T	9. F
4. T	7. T	10. F

11. T	17. F	23. T
12. T	18. F	24. T
13. F	19. T	
14. F	20. T	
15. T	21. F	
16. F	22. F	

MODULE 11.2

25. F	29. F	33. F
26. T	30. T	34. T
27. F	31. F	35. F
28. T	32. T	36. T

MODULE 11.3

37. T	41. F	45. F
38. T	42. T	46. T
39. T	43. T	47. T
40. T	44. T	

MODULE 11.4

48. T	52. T	56. T
49. F	53. T	57. F
50. F	54. T	58. T
51. T	55. F	

MODULE 11.5

59. T	63. T	67. F
60. T	64. F	68. F
61. F	65. T	
62. F	66. F	

PSYCHOLOGY IN ACTION

| 69. F | 71. F |
| 70. T | 72. T |

FINAL SURVEY AND REVIEW

MODULE 11.1

| 1. Personality | 2. patterns | 3. Character |

Chapter 11

4. Temperament
5. traits
6. type
7. introvert

8. extrovert
9. self-concept
10. Culture
11. high

12. low
13. theories
14. psychodynamic
15. humanistic

16. personality
17. aesthetic
18. verbal
19. Trait
20. Allport
21. common
22. cardinal
23. central
24. Cattell

25. source
26. factor
27. Source
28. traits
29. profile
30. five-factor
31. extroversion
32. neuroticism
33. interact

34. situations
35. 25
36. 50
37. heredity
38. environment

MODULE 11.2

39. personality
40. conflicts
41. psychoanalytic
42. id
43. superego
44. pleasure
45. reality
46. Libido
47. instincts
48. conscience

49. ego
50. neurotic
51. moral
52. preconscious
53. unconscious
54. id
55. ego
56. superego
57. psychosexual
58. phallic

59. Fixations
60. feeding
61. toilet
62. phallic
63. boys
64. girls
65. adult
66. critical
67. stages

MODULE 11.3

68. Behavioral
69. determinants
70. drive
71. cue
72. cognitive

73. expectancies
74. reinforcement
75. efficacy
76. expectancy
77. reinforcement

78. , toilet training,
79. aggression
80. Identification

MODULE 11.4

81. subjective
82. actualization
83. Maslow's
84. self-actualizers
85. actualization
86. being

87. strengths
88. congruent
89. symbolized
90. incongruent
91. incongruent
92. ideal

93. self-evaluations
94. conditions
95. conditions of worth
96. organismic

MODULE 11.5

97. observation
98. projective

99. unstructured
100. bias

101. situational
102. behavioral

103. Personality
104. Inventory
105. validity

106. Honesty
107. Projective
108. Rorschach

109. Apperception
110. validity
111. battery

PSYCHOLOGY IN ACTION

112. inhibition
113. skills
114. self-defeating

115. consciousness
116. social
117. trait

118. self-defeating
119. skills

MASTERY TEST

1. D, (p. 412)
2. B, (p. 424)
3. A, (p. 429)
4. A, (p. 441)
5. A, (p. 418)
6. D, (p. 432)
7. D, (p. 420)
8. C, (p. 414)
9. B, (p. 428)
10. B, (p. 438)
11. C, (p. 427)
12. B, (p. 422)

13. A, (p. 414)
14. C, (p. 425)
15. C, (p. 433)
16. C, (p. 422)
17. A, (p. 419)
18. B, (p. 417)
19. B, (p. 425)
20. A, (p. 434-436)
21. B, (p. 438-439)
22. C, (p. 436)
23. D, (p. 424)
24. B, (p. 434)

25. A, (p. 446)
26. B, (p. 416)
27. A, (p. 417)
28. C, (p. 428)
29. C, (p. 415)
30. C, (p. 427)
31. B, (p. 413)
32. A, (p. 416)
33. D, (p. 428-429)
34. B, (p. 434)

HEALTH, STRESS, AND COPING

CHAPTER OVERVIEW

Health psychologists study behavioral risk factors and health-promoting behaviors. Various "lifestyle" diseases are directly related to unhealthy personal habits. To reduce lifestyle diseases, people are encouraged to adopt health-promoting behaviors, such as getting regular exercise, controlling smoking and alcohol use, maintaining a balanced diet, getting good medical care, and managing stress. In addition to health-promoting behaviors, early prevention programs and community health campaigns have been implemented. Stress is also a major risk factor. At work, prolonged stress can lead to burnout. Emotional appraisals greatly affect our stress reactions and coping attempts. Traumatic stressors, such as violence, torture, or natural disasters, tend to produce severe stress reactions.

Frustration and conflict are common sources of stress. Major behavioral reactions to frustration include persistence, more vigorous responding, circumvention, direct aggression, displaced aggression, and escape or withdrawal. Five major types of conflict are approach-approach, avoidance-avoidance, approach-avoidance, double approach-avoidance, and multiple approach-avoidance.

Anxiety, threat, or feelings of inadequacy frequently lead to the use of defense mechanisms. Common defense mechanisms include compensation, denial, fantasy, intellectualization, isolation, projection, rationalization, reaction formation, regression, repression, and sublimation. Learned helplessness explains some depression and some failures to cope with threat. Mastery training acts as an antidote to helplessness.

A large number of life changes can increase susceptibility to illness. However, immediate health is more closely related to the severity of daily hassles or microstressors. Intense or prolonged stress may cause psychosomatic problems. Biofeedback may be used to combat stress and psychosomatic illnesses. People with Type A personalities run a heightened risk of suffering a heart attack. People with hardy personality traits are resistant to stress and tend to maintain positive emotions that promote creativity, the seeking of new experiences, and an appreciation of life. Direct or imagined social support from family, friends, and pets can also reduce stress. The body reacts to stress in a pattern called the general adaptation syndrome (G.A.S.). In addition, stress may lower the body's immunity to disease.

The College Life Stress Inventory, which is similar to the SRRS, can be used to rate the amount of stress an undergraduate student has experienced. A number of coping skills can be applied to manage stress. Most focus on bodily effects, ineffective behaviors, and upsetting thoughts.

LEARNING OBJECTIVES

To demonstrate mastery of this chapter, you should be able to:

1. Describe health psychology including its focus.

2. Define the terms" behavioral medicine" and "lifestyle diseases."

3. List 11 behavioral risk factors that can adversely affect one's health.

4. Define the term "disease-prone personality."

5. Briefly describe the research demonstrating the relationship of health-promoting behaviors and longevity.

6. Describe the impact of refusal skills training, life skills training, and community health campaigns on illness prevention.

7. Define the term "wellness" by listing the characteristics of wellness.

8. Explain the similarity between your body's stress reaction and emotion.

9. List four aspects of stress that make it more intense and damaging.

10. Describe burnout. List and describe the three aspects of the problem.

11. Describe three things that can be done to help reduce burnout.

12. Give an example of how primary and secondary appraisal is used in coping with a threatening situation.

13. Explain how the perception of control of a stressor influences the amount of threat felt.

14. Differentiate problem-focused coping from emotion-focused coping and explain how they may help or hinder each other.

15. Describe the impact of traumatic stress and list five ways to cope with reactions to traumatic stress.

16. Briefly describe what happens when traumatic stresses are severe or repeated.

17. List and describe the two different kinds of frustration.

18. List four factors that increase frustration.

19. List and describe five common reactions to frustration. Include the term "scapegoating" in your discussion of displaced aggression as a reaction to frustration.

20. Define stereotyped response and give an example of it.

21. Discuss three effective ways to avoid frustration.

22. Describe and give an example of each of the following five types of conflict: a. approach-approach b. avoidance-avoidance c. approach-avoidance (include the terms ambivalence and partial approach in your response) d. double approach-avoidance (include the term vacillate in your response e. multiple approach-avoidance conflicts

23. Describe four techniques to manage conflicts more effectively.

24. Define the term "defense mechanism". Discuss the positive value of defense mechanisms.

25. Describe the following defense mechanisms and give an example of each: a. denial b. repression c. reaction formation d. regression e. projection f. rationalization g. compensation h. sublimation

26. Describe the development of learned helplessness and relate this concept to attribution and depression.

27. Explain how learned helplessness may be prevented from spreading.

28. List three similarities between learned helplessness and depression.

29. Discuss the concept of hope and its relationship to mastery training.

30. Describe the six problems that typically contribute to depression among college students.

31. List the five conditions of depression and describe how it can be combated.

32. Discuss the relationship between life changes and long-term health.

33. Describe the SRRS. Explain how hassles are related to immediate health.

34. List the causes of psychosomatic disorders.

35. Distinguish between psychosomatic disorders and hypochondria.

36. Name several of the most common types of psychosomatic problems.

37. Discuss biofeedback in terms of the process involved and its possible applications.

38. Differentiate between Type A and Type B personalities. Students should note the 12 strategies for reducing hostility and be able to apply them.

39. Describe what a hardy personality is and list the three ways such people view the world.

40. Discuss how hardiness, optimism, happiness, and social support contribute to individual well-being.

The following objective is related to material in the "Discovering Psychology" section of the text.

41. List the four questions to ask yourself about someone who is supportive of you.

42. Describe how thinking about his person (or one's pet) can reduce stress.

43. Discuss the General Adaptation Syndrome and its three stages.

44. Explain how stress affects the immune system. Include the term "psychoneuroimmunology."

45. Define the term "stress management" and list the three responses that are triggered by stress.

46. Briefly discuss the College Life Stress Inventory.

47. List four ways to manage bodily reactions to stress.

48. List and briefly discuss four ways to modify ineffective behavior.

49. Define the terms "stress inoculation" and "negative self-statements."

50. Discuss how humor is worth cultivating as a way to reduce stress.

RECITE AND REVIEW

MODULE 12.1

Survey Questions: What is health psychology? How does behavior affect health? Pages 452-455

Health psychologists are interested in [1] _____ that helps maintain and promote health. The related field of behavioral medicine applies psychology to [2] _____ treatment and problems.

Most people today die from lifestyle diseases caused by unhealthy personal [3] _____ .

Studies have identified a number of behavioral risk factors such as smoking, poor diet, or alcohol abuse that increase the chances of [4] _____ or injury.

A general disease-prone personality pattern also raises the risk of [5] _____ .

Health-promoting [6] _____ tend to maintain good health. They include practices such as getting regular exercise, controlling [7] _____ and alcohol use, maintaining a balanced [8] _____ , getting good medical care, avoiding sleep deprivation, and managing stress.

Health psychologists attempt to promote wellness (a positive state of [9] _____) through community health [10] _____ that educate people about risk factors and healthful behaviors.

MODULE 12.2

Survey Questions: What is stress? What factors determine its severity? Pages 456-459

Stress occurs when we are forced to [11] _____ or adapt to external demands.

Stress is more damaging in situations involving pressure (responding at full capacity for long periods), a lack of [12] _____ , unpredictability of the stressor, and [13] _____ or repeated emotional shocks.

In [14] _____ settings, prolonged stress can lead to burnout, marked by emotional [15] _____ , depersonalization (detachment from others), and reduced personal accomplishment.

The [16] _____ (initial) appraisal of a situation greatly affects our emotional response to it. Stress reactions, in particular, are related to an appraisal of [17] _____ .

During a [18] _____ appraisal, some means of coping with a situation are selected. Coping may be either problem focused (managing the situation) or emotion focused (managing one's emotional reactions) or both.

[19] _____ is intensified when a situation is perceived as a threat and when a person does not feel competent to cope with it.

Traumatic [20] _____ , such as violence, torture, or natural disasters, tend to produce severe [21] _____ reactions.

Traumatic [22] _____ leave people feeling threatened, vulnerable, and with the sense that they are losing control over their [23] _____ .

Severe or [24] _____ traumatic [25] _____ can leave people with lasting emotional handicaps called stress disorders.

Survey Question: What causes frustration and what are typical reactions to it? Pages 459-462

Frustration is the negative emotional state that occurs when progress toward a [26] _____ is [27] _____ . Sources of frustration may be external or personal.

External frustrations are based on delay, failure, rejection, loss, and other direct blocking of motives.

Personal frustration is related to [28] _____ characteristics over which one has little control.

Frustrations of all types become more [29] _____ as the strength, urgency, or importance of the blocked motive increases.

Major behavioral reactions to frustration include persistence, more [30] _____ responding, and circumvention of barriers.

Other reactions to frustration are [31] _____ aggression, displaced aggression (including scapegoating), and escape or [32] _____ .

Ways of [33] _____ with frustration include identifying its source, determining if the source is manageable, and deciding if [34] _____ the source is worth the effort.

Survey Questions: Are there different types of conflict? How do people react to conflict? Pages 462-464

[35] _____ occurs when we must choose between contradictory alternatives.

Three basic types of conflict are approach-approach (choice between two [36] _____ alternatives), avoidance-avoidance (both alternatives are [37] _____), and approach-avoidance (a goal or activity has both positive and negative aspects).

Approach-approach conflicts are usually the [38] _____ to resolve.

Avoidance conflicts are [39] _____ to resolve and are characterized by inaction, indecision, freezing, and a desire to escape (called [40] _____ the field).

People usually remain in approach-avoidance conflicts but fail to fully resolve them. Approach-avoidance conflicts are associated with ambivalence (mixed feelings) and [41] _____ approach.

More complex conflicts are: double approach-avoidance (both alternatives have [42] _____ and [43] _____ qualities) and multiple approach-avoidance (several alternatives each have good and bad qualities).

Vacillation (wavering between choices) is the most common reaction to double [44] _____ conflicts.

Managing conflicts effectively involves not making hasty decisions, trying out a few [45] _____ at a time, looking for [46] _____ , and sticking with the choice.

MODULE 12.3

Survey Question: What are defense mechanisms? Pages 466-468

Anxiety, threat, or feelings of [47] _____ frequently lead to the use of psychological defense mechanisms. These are habitual strategies used to avoid or reduce anxiety.

A number of defense mechanisms have been identified, including denial, fantasy, intellectualization, isolation, projection, rationalization, [48] _____ formation, regression, and [49] _____ (motivated forgetting).

Two defense mechanisms that have some [50] _____ qualities are compensation and sublimation.

Survey Question: What do we know about coping with feelings of helplessness and depression? Pages 468-471

Learned helplessness is a learned inability to overcome obstacles or to [51] _____ punishment.

Learned helplessness explains the failure to cope with some threatening situations. The symptoms of learned helplessness and depression are nearly [52] _____ .

Mastery [53] _____ and hope act as antidotes to helplessness.

Nearly [54] _____ percent of all college students suffer from depression due to being [55] _____ from their families, lacking the basic skills necessary for [56] _____ success, abusing alcohol, and feeling they are missing out on life.

Depression (a state of deep sadness or despondency) is a serious emotional problem. Actions and thoughts that counter feelings of helplessness tend to [57] _____ depression.

MODULE 12.4

Survey Question: How is stress related to health and disease? Pages 472-480

Work with the Social Readjustment Rating Scale (SRRS) indicates that a large number of life

[58] _____ units (LCUs) can increase susceptibility to [59] _____ or illness.

Immediate health is more closely related to the intensity and severity of daily annoyances, known as

[60] _____ or microstressors.

Intense or prolonged stress may damage the body in the form of psychosomatic disorders (illnesses in

which [61] _____ factors play a part).

Psychosomatic (mind-body) disorders have no connection to hypochondria, the tendency to imagine

that one has a [62] _____ .

During biofeedback training, bodily processes are [63] _____ and converted to a signal that

indicates what the body is doing.

Biofeedback allows alteration of many bodily activities. It shows promise for promoting

[64] _____ , self-regulation, and for treating some psychosomatic illnesses.

People with Type A ([65] _____ attack-prone) personalities are competitive, striving, and

frequently angry or hostile, and they have a chronic sense of [66] _____ urgency.

[67] _____ and hostility are especially likely to increase the chances of heart attack.

People who have traits of the hardy personality seem to be resistant to [68] _____ even if

they also have Type A traits.

People who have a hardy personality tend to be [69] _____ and have [70] _____

emotions such as joy, interest, and contentment. These factors reduce bodily arousal and help people find

[71] _____ solutions when they are stressed.

Unlike pessimists, optimists tend to deal with their problems head on, are less likely to be

[72] _____ and anxious, believe they will [73] _____ , and take better care of themselves.

Stress can be reduced through the mechanism of [74] _____ support by allowing people to seek

assistance and to share [75] _____ events with friends and families.

Thinking about a person who provides [76] _____ or having a [77] _____ present can

reduce one's level of stress.

The body reacts to stress in a series of stages called the [78] _____ adaptation syndrome (G.A.S.).

The stages of the G.A.S. are alarm, resistance, and exhaustion. The G.A.S. contributes to the development

of [79] _____ disorders.

Stress weakens the immune system and lowers the body's resistance to [80] _____ .

PSYCHOLOGY IN ACTION

Survey Question: What are the best strategies for managing stress? Pages 481-484

Most stress management skills focus on one of three areas: bodily effects, ineffective [81] _____ ,

and upsetting [82] _____ .

Bodily effects can be managed with exercise, meditation, progressive [83] _____ , and guided

imagery.

The impact of ineffective behavior can be remedied by slowing down, getting organized, striking a balance

between "good stress" and [84] _____ , accepting your limits, and seeking social support.

A good way to control upsetting thoughts is to replace negative self-statements with [85] _____

coping statements.

CONNECTIONS

MODULE 12.1

1.	_____ wellness	a.	well-being
2.	_____ tobacco	b.	people who are depressed
3.	_____ refusal skills	c.	health-promoting behavior
4.	_____ managing stress	d.	leading cause of death
5.	_____ risk factors	e.	lifestyle diseases
6.	_____ disease-prone personality	f.	smoking prevention

MODULE 12.2

1.	_____ problem-focused coping	a.	ANS arousal
2.	_____ stress reaction	b.	blocked motive
3.	_____ burnout	c.	plans to reduce stress
4.	_____ primary appraisal	d.	psychological escape
5.	_____ frustration	e.	scapegoat
6.	_____ displaced aggression	f.	approach-avoidance
7.	_____ apathy	g.	"Am I in trouble?"
8.	_____ ambivalence	h.	job stress

MODULE 12.3

1. _____ compensation
2. _____ denial
3. _____ fantasy
4. _____ intellectualization
5. _____ isolation
6. _____ projection
7. _____ rationalization
8. _____ reaction formation
9. _____ regression
10. _____ repression
11. _____ sublimation

a. fulfilling unmet desires in imagined activities
b. separating contradictory thoughts into "logic-tight" mental compartments
c. preventing actions by exaggerating opposite behavior
d. justifying your behavior by giving reasonable but false reasons for it
e. unconsciously preventing painful thoughts from entering awareness
f. counteracting a real or imagined weakness by seeking to excel
g. retreating to an earlier level of development
h. attributing one's own shortcomings or unacceptable impulses to others
i. protecting oneself from an unpleasant reality by refusing to perceive it
j. working off unacceptable impulses in constructive activities
k. thinking about threatening situations in impersonal terms

1. _____ defense mechanism
2. _____ feeling despondent
3. _____ learned helplessness
4. _____ mastery training

a. depression
b. Sigmund Freud
c. hope
d. shuttle box

MODULE 12.4

1. _____ College Life Stress Inventory
2. _____ SRRS
3. _____ hassle
4. _____ hardy personality
5. _____ psychosomatic
6. _____ modifying ineffective behavior
7. _____ Type A
8. _____ biofeedback
9. _____ coping statements
10. _____ G.A.S.

a. LCU
b. mind-body
c. self-regulation
d. cardiac personality
e. alarm reaction
f. stress resistant
g. microstressor
h. stress rating scale
i. Keep It Simple (K.I.S.)
j. stress inoculation

CHECK YOUR MEMORY

MODULE 12.1

Survey Questions: What is health psychology? How does behavior affect health? Pages 452-455

1. Heart disease, lung cancer, and stroke are typical lifestyle diseases.
   TRUE or FALSE

2. A person who is overweight doubles the chance of dying from cancer or heart disease.
   TRUE or FALSE

3. One can expect to lose up to 20 years of life expectancy if he/she is overweight by the age of 20.
   TRUE or FALSE

4. Illicit use of drugs is the second most common cause of death in the United States after smoking.
   TRUE or FALSE

5. Behavioral risk factors such as smoking, poor diet, or alcohol abuse are linked to infectious diseases.
   TRUE or FALSE

6. People with disease-prone personalities are depressed, anxious, and hostile.
   TRUE or FALSE

7. Maintaining a healthy diet means a person must live on a high-protein diet consisting of tofu and wheat grain.
   TRUE or FALSE

8. Moderation in drinking refers to having three to five drinks per day.
   TRUE or FALSE

9. Community health campaigns provide refusal skills training to large numbers of people.
   TRUE or FALSE

10. School-based prevention programs have successfully increased teens' negative attitudes toward smoking.
    TRUE or FALSE

11. Wellness can be described as an absence of disease.
    TRUE or FALSE

MODULE 12.2

Survey Questions: What is stress? What factors determine its severity? Pages 456-459

12. Unpleasant activities produce stress, whereas pleasant activities do not.
    TRUE or FALSE

13. Initial reactions to stressors are similar to those that occur during strong emotion.
TRUE or FALSE

14. Short-term stresses rarely do any damage to the body.
TRUE or FALSE

15. Unpredictable demands increase stress.
TRUE or FALSE

16. Pressure occurs when we are faced with a stressor we can control.
TRUE or FALSE

17. Burnout is especially a problem in helping professions.
TRUE or FALSE

18. The opposite of burnout is positive job engagement.
TRUE or FALSE

19. Stress is often related to the meaning a person places on events.
TRUE or FALSE

20. The same situation can be a challenge or a threat, depending on how it is appraised.
TRUE or FALSE

21. In a secondary appraisal, we decide if a situation is relevant or irrelevant, positive or threatening.
TRUE or FALSE

22. When confronted by a stressor, it is best to choose one type of coping—problem focused or emotion focused.
TRUE or FALSE

23. A distressed person may distract herself by listening to music, taking a walk to relax, or seeking emotional support from others. Such strategies illustrate problem-focused coping.
TRUE or FALSE

24. Emotion-focused coping is best suited to managing stressors you cannot control.
TRUE or FALSE

25. Nightmares, grief, flashbacks, nervousness, and depression are common reactions to traumatic stress.
TRUE or FALSE

26. It is possible to have stress symptoms from merely witnessing traumatically stressful events on television.
TRUE or FALSE

27. An excellent way to cope with traumatic stress is to stop all of your daily routines and isolate yourself from others.
TRUE or FALSE

Survey Question: What causes frustration and what are typical reactions to it? Pages 459-462

28. Delays, rejections, and losses are good examples of personal frustrations.
TRUE or FALSE

29. Varied responses and circumvention attempt to directly destroy or remove barriers that cause frustration.
TRUE or FALSE

30. Scapegoating is a good example of escape or withdrawal.
TRUE or FALSE

31. Abuse of drugs can be a way of psychologically escaping frustration.
TRUE or TRUE

32. Persistence must be flexible before it is likely to aid a person trying to cope with frustration.
TRUE or FALSE

Survey Questions: Are there different types of conflict? How do people react to conflict? Pages 462-464

33. Approach-approach conflicts are fairly easy to resolve.
TRUE or FALSE

34. Indecision, inaction, and freezing are typical reactions to approach-approach conflicts.
TRUE or FALSE

35. People find it difficult to escape approach-avoidance conflicts.
TRUE or FALSE

36. Wanting to eat but not wanting to be overweight creates an approach-approach conflict.
TRUE or FALSE

37. People are very likely to vacillate when faced with a double approach-avoidance conflict.
TRUE or FALSE

MODULE 12.3

Survey Question: What are defense mechanisms? Pages 466-468

38. Defense mechanisms are used to avoid or distort sources of threat or anxiety.
TRUE or FALSE

39. Denial is a common reaction to bad news, such as learning that a friend has died.
TRUE or FALSE

40. In reaction formation, a person fulfills unmet desires in imagined achievements.
TRUE or FALSE

41. A child who becomes homesick while visiting relatives may be experiencing a mild regression.
    TRUE or FALSE

42. Denial and repression are the two most positive of the defense mechanisms.
    TRUE or FALSE

Survey Question: What do we know about coping with feelings of helplessness and depression? Pages 468-471

43. The deep depression experienced by prisoners of war appears to be related to learned helplessness.
    TRUE or FALSE

44. Learned helplessness occurs when events appear to be uncontrollable.
    TRUE or FALSE

45. Attributing failure to lasting, general factors, such as personal characteristics, tends to create the most damaging feelings of helplessness.
    TRUE or FALSE

46. Mastery training restores feelings of control over the environment.
    TRUE or FALSE

47. At any given time, 52 to 61 percent of all college students are experiencing the symptoms of depression.
    TRUE or FALSE

48. Making a daily schedule will only emphasize the goals that a person cannot accomplish and will push him/her deeper into depression.
    TRUE or FALSE

49. Depression is more likely when students find it difficult to live up to idealized images of themselves.
    TRUE or FALSE

50. Writing rational answers to self-critical thoughts can help counteract feelings of depression.
    TRUE or FALSE

MODULE 12.4

Survey Question: How is stress related to health and disease? Pages 472-480

51. Scores on the SRRS are expressed as life control units.
    TRUE or FALSE

52. A score of 300 LCUs on the SRRS is categorized as a major life crisis.
    TRUE or FALSE

53. According to the SRRS, being fired at work involves more LCUs than divorce does.
    TRUE or FALSE

54. Microstressors tend to predict changes in health one to two years after the stressful events took place.
TRUE or FALSE

55. Psychosomatic disorders involve actual damage to the body or damaging changes in bodily functioning.
TRUE or FALSE

56. A person undergoing biofeedback can sleep if he or she desires—the machine does all the work.
TRUE or FALSE

57. Type B personalities are more than twice as likely to suffer heart attacks as Type A personalities.
TRUE or FALSE

58. People with the hardy personality type tend to see life as a series of challenges.
TRUE or FALSE

59. People with a hardy personality have had to cope with many adversities and therefore have a negative view of life.
TRUE or FALSE

60. Both men and women will seek social support when they are stressed.
TRUE or FALSE

61. Thinking about a supportive person or having a pet present can help lower one's stress level.
TRUE or FALSE

62. In the stage of resistance of the G.A.S., people have symptoms of headache, fever, fatigue, upset stomach, and the like.
TRUE or FALSE

63. Serious health problems tend to occur when a person reaches the stage of exhaustion in the G.A.S.
TRUE or FALSE

64. Stress management training can actually boost immune system functioning.
TRUE or FALSE

65. Happiness and high levels of arousal due to stress have been shown to strengthen the immune system's response.
TRUE or FALSE

PSYCHOLOGY IN ACTION

Survey Question: What are the best strategies for managing stress? Pages 481-484

66. Concern about being pregnant is the most stressful item listed on the College Life Stress Inventory.
TRUE or FALSE

67. Exercising for stress management is most effective when it is done daily.
TRUE or FALSE

68. Guided imagery is used to reduce anxiety and promote relaxation.
   TRUE or FALSE

69. Merely writing down thoughts and feelings about daily events can provide some of the benefits of social support.
   TRUE or FALSE

70. To get the maximum benefits, coping statements should be practiced in actual stressful situations.
   TRUE or FALSE

71. Humor increases anxiety and emotional distress because it put problems into perspective for individuals.
   TRUE or FALSE

FINAL SURVEY AND REVIEW

MODULE 12.1

Survey Questions: What is health psychology? How does behavior affect health? Pages 452-455

Health psychologists are interested in behavior that helps maintain and promote health. The related field of

[1] _____ applies psychology to medical treatment and problems.

Most people today die from [2] _____ diseases caused by unhealthy personal habits.

Studies have identified a number of behavioral [3] _____ [4] _____ (e.g., smoking, poor

diet, or alcohol abuse) that increase the chances of disease or injury.

A general [5] _____ personality pattern also raises the risk of illness.

Health-[6] _____ behaviors tend to maintain good health. They include practices such as getting

regular exercise, controlling smoking and alcohol use, maintaining a balanced diet, getting good medical

care, avoiding sleep [7] _____ , and managing [8] _____ .

Health psychologists attempt to promote [9] _____ (a positive state of health) through

[10] _____ campaigns that educate people about risk factors and healthful behaviors.

MODULE 12.2

Survey Questions: What is stress? What factors determine its severity? Pages 456-459

Stress occurs when we are forced to adjust or [11] _____ to external [12] _____ .

Stress is more damaging in situations involving [13] _____ (responding at full capacity for

long periods), a lack of control, unpredictability of the [14] _____ , and intense or repeated

emotional shocks.

In work settings, prolonged stress can lead to [15] _____ , marked by emotional exhaustion,

[16] _____ (detachment from others), and reduced personal accomplishment.

The primary [17] _____ of a situation greatly affects our emotional response to it. Stress

reactions, in particular, are related to an [18] _____ of threat.

During a secondary appraisal, some means of coping with a situation are selected. Coping may be either

[19] _____ focused (managing the situation) or [20] _____ focused (managing one's

emotional reactions) or both.

Stress is intensified when a situation is perceived as a [21] _____ and when a person does not feel

[22] _____ to cope with it.

[23] _____ stressors, such as violence, torture, or natural disasters, tend to produce severe

stress reactions.

Traumatic stresses leave people feeling threatened, vulnerable, and with the sense that they are losing

[24] _____ over their lives.

Severe or repeated traumatic stress can leave people with lasting emotional handicaps called

[25] _____ .

Survey Question: What causes frustration and what are typical reactions to it? Pages 459-462

[26] _____ is the negative emotional state that occurs when progress toward a goal is blocked.

Sources of frustration may be external or [27] _____ .

[28] _____ frustrations are based on delay, failure, rejection, loss, and other direct blocking

of motives. [29] _____ frustration is related to personal characteristics over which one has

little control.

Frustrations of all types become more intense as the strength, urgency, or importance of the

[30] _____ increases.

Major behavioral reactions to frustration include [31] _____ , more vigorous responding,

and [32] _____ of barriers.

Other reactions to frustration are direct aggression, [33] _____ aggression (including

[34] _____), and escape or withdrawal.

Ways of coping with [35] _____ include identifying its source, determining if the source is

[36] _____ , and deciding if changing the source is worth the effort.

Survey Questions: Are there different types of conflict? How do people react to conflict? Pages 462-464

Conflict occurs when we must choose between [37] _____ alternatives.

Three basic types of conflict are [38] _____ (choice between two positive alternatives),

[39] _____ (both alternatives are negative), and approach-avoidance (a goal or activity has both positive and negative aspects).

[40] _____ conflicts are usually the easiest to resolve.

[41] _____ conflicts are difficult to resolve and are characterized by inaction, indecision, freezing, and a desire to escape (called leaving the field).

People usually remain in approach-avoidance conflicts but fail to fully resolve them. Approach-avoidance conflicts are associated with [42] _____ (mixed feelings) and partial approach.

More complex conflicts are: [43] _____ approach-avoidance (both alternatives have positive and negative qualities) and [44] _____ approach-avoidance (several alternatives each have good and bad qualities).

[45] _____ (wavering between choices) is the most common reaction to double approach-avoidance conflicts.

Managing [46] _____ effectively involves not making [47] _____ decisions, trying out a few possibilities at a time, looking for compromises, and sticking with the choice.

MODULE 12.3

Survey Question: What are defense mechanisms? Pages 466-468

Anxiety, threat, or feelings of inadequacy frequently lead to the use of psychological [48] _____ .

These are habitual strategies used to avoid or reduce [49] _____ .

A number of defense mechanisms have been identified, including [50] _____ (refusing to perceive an unpleasant reality), fantasy, intellectualization, isolation, projection, [51] _____ (justifying one's behavior), reaction formation, regression, and repression.

Two defense mechanisms that have some positive qualities are [52] _____ and [53] _____ .

Survey Question: What do we know about coping with feelings of helplessness and depression? Pages 468-471

Learned [54] _____ is a learned inability to overcome obstacles or to avoid [55] _____ .

The symptoms of learned helplessness and [56] _____ are nearly identical.

[57] _____ training and hope act as antidotes to helplessness.

Nearly 80 percent of all [58] _____ students suffer from [59] _____ due to being isolated from their families, lacking basic skills necessary for academic success, abusing alcohol, and feeling they are missing out on life.

[60] _____ (a state of deep sadness or despondency) is a serious emotional problem. Actions and thoughts that counter feelings of [61] _____ tend to reduce depression.

MODULE 12.4

Survey Question: How is stress related to health and disease? Pages 472-480

Work with the [62] _____ Scale (SRRS) indicates that a large number of life change units (LCUs) can increase susceptibility to accident or illness.

Immediate health is more closely related to the intensity and severity of daily annoyances, known as hassles or [63] _____ .

Intense or prolonged stress may damage the body in the form of [64] _____ disorders (illnesses in which psychological factors play a part).

[65] _____ (mind-body) disorders have no connection to [66] _____ , the tendency to imagine that one has a disease.

During [67] _____ training, bodily processes are monitored and converted to a [68] _____ that indicates what the body is doing.

Biofeedback allows alteration of many bodily activities. It shows promise for promoting relaxation, self-[69] _____ , and for treating some psychosomatic illnesses.

People with [70] _____ (heart attack-prone) personalities are competitive, striving, and frequently [71] _____ or hostile, and they have a chronic sense of time urgency.

Anger and hostility are especially likely to increase the chances of [72] _____ .

People who have traits of the [73] _____ personality seem to be resistant to stress, even if they also have Type A traits.

People who have a [74] _____ personality tend to be optimists and have [75] _____ emotions such as joy, interest, and contentment. These factors [76] _____ bodily arousal and help people find creative solutions when they are stressed.

Unlike pessimists, [77] _____ tend to deal with their problems head on, are [78] _____ likely to be stressed and anxious, believe they [79] _____ succeed, and take better care of themselves.

Stress can be [80] _____ through the mechanism of social support by allowing people to seek assistance and to share positive [81] _____ with friends and families.

Thinking about a [82] _____ who provides support or having a pet present can [83] _____ one's level of stress.

The body reacts to stress in a series of stages called the general [84] _____ [85] _____ (G.A.S.).

The stages of the G.A.S. are [86] _____ , resistance, and [87] _____ . The G.A.S. contributes to the development of psychosomatic disorders.

Stress weakens the [88] _____ system and lowers the body's resistance to illness.

PSYCHOLOGY IN ACTION

Survey Question: What are the best strategies for managing stress? Pages 481-484

Most stress management skills focus on one of three areas: bodily effects, [89] _____ behavior, and [90] _____ thoughts.

Bodily effects can be managed with exercise, meditation, [91] _____ relaxation, and [92] _____ imagery.

The impact of ineffective behavior can be remedied by slowing down, getting organized, striking a balance between "good stress" and relaxation, accepting your [93] _____ , and seeking [94] _____ support.

A good way to control upsetting thoughts is to replace [95] _____ self-statements with positive [96] _____ statements.

MASTERY TEST

1. When stressful events appear to be uncontrollable, two common reactions are
   a. apathy and double-approach conflict
   b. helplessness and depression
   c. assimilation and marginalization
   d. psychosomatic disorders and hypochondria

2. The College Life Stress Inventory is most closely related to the
   a. SRRS
   b. A.S.
   c. I.S.
   d. Disease-Prone Personality Scale

3. We answer the question "Am I okay or in trouble" when making
   a. negative self-statements
   b. coping statements
   c. a primary appraisal
   d. a secondary appraisal

4. Which of the following is NOT a major symptom of burnout?
   a. emotional exhaustion
   b. depersonalization
   c. reduced accomplishment
   d. dependence on coworkers

5. A child who displays childish speech and infantile play after his parents bring home a new baby shows signs of
   a. compensation
   b. reaction formation
   c. regression
   d. sublimation

6. Persistent but inflexible responses to frustration can become
   a. stereotyped behaviors
   b. imagined barriers
   c. negative self-statements
   d. sublimated and depersonalized

7. The leading cause of death in the United States is
   a. tobacco
   b. diet/inactivity
   c. alcohol
   d. infection

8. Both mountain climbing and marital strife
   a. are behavioral risk factors
   b. are appraised as secondary threats
   c. cause stress reactions
   d. produce the condition known as pressure

9. LCUs are used to assess
   a. burnout
   b. social readjustments
   c. microstressors
   d. what stage of the G.A.S. a person is in

10. Sujata is often ridiculed by her boss, who also frequently takes advantage of her. Deep inside, Sujata has come to hate her boss, yet on the surface she acts as if she likes him very much. It is likely that Sujata is using the defense mechanism called
    a. reaction formation
    b. Type B appraisal
    c. problem-focused coping
    d. sublimation

11. Lifestyle diseases are of special interest to _____ psychologists.
    a. health
    b. community
    c. wellness
    d. psychosomatic

12. Which of the following is NOT characteristic of the hardy personality?
    a. commitment
    b. a sense of control
    c. accepting challenge
    d. repression

13. Unhealthy lifestyles are marked by the presence of a number of
    a. health refusal factors
    b. behavioral risk factors
    c. cultural stressors
    d. Type B personality traits

14. The most effective response to a controllable stressor is
    a. problem-focused coping
    b. emotion-focused coping
    c. leaving the field
    d. depersonalization

15. Delay, rejection, failure, and loss are all major causes of
    a. pressure
    b. frustration
    c. conflict
    d. helplessness

16. There is evidence that the core lethal factor of Type A behavior is
    a. time urgency
    b. anger and hostility
    c. competitiveness and ambition
    d. accepting too many responsibilities

17. What stress, smoking, and overeating all have in common is that they are behavioral
    a. hassles
    b. risk factors
    c. sources of burnout
    d. causes of depersonalization

18. A person is caught between "the frying pan and the fire" in an _____ conflict.
    a. approach-approach
    b. avoidance-avoidance
    c. approach-avoidance
    d. double appraisal

19. Which of the following is NOT one of the major health-promoting behaviors listed in the text?
    a. do not smoke
    b. get adequate sleep
    c. get regular exercise
    d. avoid eating between meals

20. Ambivalence and partial approach are very common reactions to what type of conflict?
    a. approach-approach
    b. avoidance-avoidance
    c. approach-avoidance
    d. multiple avoidance

21. Which of the following terms does not belong with the others?
    a. Type A personality
    b. stage of exhaustion
    c. displaced aggression
    d. psychosomatic disorder

22. Coping statements are a key element in
    a. stress inoculation
    b. the K.I.S. technique
    c. guided imagery
    d. refusal skills training

23. Which of the following factors typically minimizes the amount of stress experienced?
    a. predictable stressors
    b. repeated stressors
    c. uncontrollable stressors
    d. intense stressors

24. Scapegoating is closely related to which response to frustration?
    a. leaving the field
    b. displaced aggression
    c. circumvention
    d. reaction formation

25. The study of the ways in which stress and the immune system affect susceptibility to disease is called
    a. neuropsychosymptomology
    b. immunohypochondrology
    c. psychosomatoneurology
    d. psychoneuroimmunology

26. Refusal skills training is typically used to teach young people how to
    a. avoid drug use
    b. cope with burnout
    c. resist stressors at home and at school
    d. avoid forming habits that lead to heart disease

27. Which combination is most relevant to managing bodily reactions to stress?
    a. social support, self-pacing
    b. exercise, social support
    c. exercise, negative self-statements
    d. progressive relaxation, guided imagery

28. Stress reactions are most likely to occur when a stressor is viewed as a _____ during the _____.
    a. pressure, primary appraisal
    b. pressure, secondary appraisal
    c. threat, primary appraisal
    d. threat, secondary appraisal

29. External symptoms of the body's adjustment to stress are least visible in which stage of the G.A.S.?
    a. alarm
    b. regulation
    c. resistance
    d. exhaustion

30. A perceived lack of control creates a stressful sense of threat when combined with a perceived
    a. sense of time urgency
    b. state of sublimation
    c. need to change secondary risk factors
    d. lack of competence

31. Behavioral risk factors such as smoking cigarettes, drinking alcohol, and overeating have been linked to
    a. Type B personality
    b. infectious diseases
    c. high life expectancy
    d. hardy personality

32. Consuming no more than one to two alcoholic drinks per day, exercising three to four times a week, and eating a healthy diet are
    a. stress-induced behaviors
    b. behavioral risk factors
    c. health-promoting behaviors
    d. factors that increase heart disorders

33. Shane likes to listen to his favorite music and taking long walks in the park to relax when he is distressed or stressed. Shane's method involves
    a. defense mechanism
    b. reaction formation
    c. problem focused coping
    d. emotion focused coping

34. People with a _____ personality tend to be optimistic and have positive emotions that help them reduce and find creative solutions to stress.
    a. realistic
    b. Type A
    c. hardy
    d. high-strung

35. Real or imagined social support and encouragement from _____ can reduce one's level of stress.
    a. family members
    b. friends
    c. pets
    d. all the preceding

36. Which factor reduces one's stress or emotional distress?
    a. humor
    b. smoking
    c. high blood pressure
    d. approach-avoidance

SOLUTIONS

RECITE AND REVIEW

MODULE 12.1

1. behavior
2. medical
3. habits
4. disease (or illness)
5. illness (or disease)
6. behaviors
7. smoking
8. diet
9. health
10. campaigns

MODULE 12.2

11. adjust
12. control
13. intense
14. work
15. exhaustion
16. primary
17. threat
18. secondary
19. Stress
20. stressors
21. stress
22. stresses
23. lives
24. repeated
25. stress

26. goal
27. blocked
28. personal
29. intense
30. vigorous
31. direct
32. withdrawal
33. coping
34. changing

35. Conflict
36. positive
37. negative
38. easiest
39. difficult
40. leaving
41. partial
42. positive
43. negative
44. approach-avoidance
45. possibilities
46. compromises

MODULE 12.3

47. inadequacy
48. reaction
49. repression
50. positive

51. avoid
52. identical
53. training
54. 80
55. isolated
56. academic
57. reduce

MODULE 12.4

58. change
59. accident
60. hassles
61. psychological
62. disease
63. monitored
64. relaxation
65. heart
66. time
67. Anger
68. stress
69. optimists
70. positive
71. creative
72. stressed
73. succeed
74. social
75. positive

76. support
77. pet

78. general
79. psychosomatic

80. disease (or illness)

PSYCHOLOGY IN ACTION

81. behavior
82. thoughts

83. relaxation
84. relaxation

85. positive

CONNECTIONS

MODULE 12.1

1. a
2. d

3. f
4. c

5. e
6. b

MODULE 12.2

1. c
2. a
3. h

4. g
5. b
6. e

7. d
8. f

MODULE 12.3

1. f
2. i
3. a
4. k

5. b
6. h
7. d
8. c

9. g
10. e
11. j

1. b
2. a

3. d
4. c

MODULE 12.4

1. h
2. a
3. g
4. f

5. b
6. i
7. d
8. c

9. j
10. e

CHECK YOUR MEMORY

MODULE 12.1

1. T
2. T
3. T
4. F

5. T
6. T
7. F
8. F

9. F
10. T
11. F

MODULE 12.2

12. F

13. T	18. T	23. F
14. T	19. T	24. T
15. T	20. T	25. T
16. F	21. F	26. T
17. T	22. F	27. F

28. F	30. F	32. T
29. F	31. T	

33. T	35. T	37. T
34. F	36. F	

MODULE 12.3

38. T	40. F	42. F
39. T	41. T	

43. T	46. T	49. T
44. T	47. F	50. T
45. T	48. F	

MODULE 12.4

51. F	56. F	61. T
52. T	57. F	62. F
53. F	58. T	63. T
54. F	59. F	64. T
55. T	60. F	65. F

PSYCHOLOGY IN ACTION

66. F	68. T	70. T
67. T	69. T	71. F

FINAL SURVEY AND REVIEW

MODULE 12.1

1. behavioral medicine	5. disease-prone	9. wellness
2. lifestyle	6. promoting	10. community health
3. risk	7. deprivation	
4. factors	8. stress	

MODULE 12.2
11. adapt

12. demands
13. pressure
14. stressor
15. burnout
16. depersonalization
17. appraisal

18. appraisal
19. problem
20. emotion
21. threat
22. competent
23. Traumatic

24. control
25. stress disorders

26. Frustration
27. personal
28. External
29. Personal

30. blocked motive
31. persistence
32. circumvention
33. displaced

34. scapegoating
35. frustration
36. manageable

37. contradictory
38. approach-approach
39. avoidance-avoidance
40. Approach-approach

41. Avoidance
42. ambivalence
43. double
44. multiple

45. Vacillation
46. conflicts
47. hasty

MODULE 12.3

48. defense mechanisms
49. anxiety

50. denial
51. rationalization

52. compensation
53. sublimation

54. helplessness
55. punishment
56. depression

57. Mastery
58. college
59. depression

60. Depression
61. helplessness

MODULE 12.4

62. Social Readjustment Rating
63. microstressors
64. psychosomatic
65. Psychosomatic
66. hypochondria
67. biofeedback
68. signal
69. regulation
70. Type A
71. angry

72. heart attack
73. hardy
74. hardy
75. positive
76. reduce
77. optimists
78. less
79. will
80. reduced
81. events

82. person
83. reduce
84. adaptation
85. syndrome
86. alarm
87. exhaustion
88. immune

PSYCHOLOGY IN ACTION

89. ineffective

90. upsetting
91. progressive
92. guided

93. limits
94. social
95. negative

96. coping

MASTERY TEST

1. B, (p. 469)
2. A, (p. 472)
3. C, (p. 458)
4. D, (p. 457)
5. C, (p. 466)
6. A, (p. 462)
7. A, (p. 452)
8. C, (p. 456)
9. B, (p. 472)
10. A, (p. 466)
11. A, (p. 452)
12. D, (p. 476)

13. B, (p. 452)
14. A, (p. 459)
15. B, (p. 459)
16. B, (p. 475)
17. B, (p. 452)
18. B, (p. 463)
19. D, (p. 453-454)
20. C, (p. 463-464)
21. C, (p. 461, 474, 475, 479)
22. A, (p. 484)
23. A, (p.456)
24. B, (p. 461)

25. D, (p. 479)
26. A, (p. 454)
27. D, (p. 481)
28. C, (p. 458)
29. C, (p. 479)
30. D, (p. 458)
31. B, (p. 453)
32. C, (p. 454)
33. D, (p. 458)
34. C, (p. 477)
35. D, (p. 478)
36. A, (p. 484)

PSYCHOLOGICAL DISORDERS

CHAPTER OVERVIEW

Abnormal behavior is defined by subjective discomfort, deviation from statistical norms, social nonconformity, and cultural or situational contexts. Disordered behavior is also maladaptive. Major types of psychopathology are described by DSM-IV-TR. Risk factors contributing to psychopathology include social, family, psychological, and biological factors. Psychopathology is not isolated to Western societies. Every culture recognizes the existence of psychological disorders. In the United States, insanity is a legal term, not a mental disorder.

Personality disorders are deeply ingrained, maladaptive personality patterns, such as the antisocial personality. In addition to maladaptive patterns of behaviors, personality disorders are diagnosed and differentiated based on the degree of impairment. Ranging from moderate to severe impairment, some personality disorders are narcissistic, histrionic, borderline, and schizotypal.

Anxiety disorders, dissociative disorders, and somatoform disorders are characterized by high levels of anxiety, rigid defense mechanisms, and self-defeating behavior patterns. Anxiety disorders include generalized anxiety disorder, panic disorder (with or without agoraphobia), agoraphobia, specific phobia, social phobia, obsessive-compulsive disorders, post-traumatic stress disorder, and acute stress disorders. Dissociative disorders may take the form of amnesia, fugue, or identity disorder (multiple personality). Somatoform disorders center on physical complaints that mimic disease or disability.

Psychodynamic explanations of anxiety disorders emphasize unconscious conflicts. The humanistic approach emphasizes faulty self-images. The behavioral approach emphasizes the effects of learning, particularly avoidance learning. The cognitive approach stresses maladaptive thinking patterns.

Psychosis is a break in contact with reality. Persons suffering from delusional disorders have delusions of grandeur, persecution, infidelity, romantic attraction, or physical disease. The most common delusional disorder is paranoid psychosis.

Schizophrenia is the most common psychosis. Four types of schizophrenia are disorganized, catatonic, paranoid, and undifferentiated. Explanations of schizophrenia emphasize environmental stress, inherited susceptibility, and biochemical abnormalities.

Mood disorders involve disturbances of emotion. Two moderate mood disorders are dysthymic disorder and cyclothymic disorder. Major mood disorders include bipolar disorders and major depressive disorder. Seasonal affective disorder is another common form of depression. Biological, psychoanalytic, cognitive, and behavioral theories of depression have been proposed. Heredity is clearly a factor in susceptibility to mood disorders. Labeling someone with a disorder rather than the problems that people experience can dramatically influence how people with mental disorders are treated. They often are faced with prejudice and discrimination, denied jobs and housing, and accused of crimes they did not commit.

Two basic approaches to treating major disorders are psychotherapy and medical therapies. Suicide is statistically related to such factors as age, sex, and marital status. However, in individual cases the potential for suicide is best identified by a desire to escape, unbearable psychological pain, frustrated psychological needs, and a constriction of options. Suicide can sometimes be prevented by the efforts of family, friends, and mental health professionals.

LEARNING OBJECTIVES

To demonstrate mastery of this chapter, you should be able to:

1. Present information to indicate the magnitude of mental health problems in this country and define "psychopathology."

2. Describe the following ways of viewing normality including the shortcoming(s) of each: subjective discomfort statistical abnormality social nonconformity situational context cultural relativity

The following objective is related to the material in the "Discovering Psychology" section of the text.

3. List five exercises that people could do to understand how it felt to be "crazy for a day" and describe which facet of abnormal behavior the exercises demonstrate.

4. Discuss gender bias in judging abnormality.

5. State conditions under which a person is usually judged to need help; include the term "maladaptive."

6. Describe what the DSM-IV is, what it is used for, and define the term "mental disorder."

7. Generally describe each of the following categories of mental disorders found in the DSM IV: a. psychotic disorders b. organic mental disorders c. substance-related disorders d. mood disorders e. anxiety disorders f. somatoform disorders g. dissociative disorders h. personality disorders i. sexual and gender identity disorders

8. List the four general risk factors that may contribute to mental disorders. Describe the term "neurosis" and list several folk names for mental disorders found in various cultures.

9. Distinguish the term "insanity" from true mental disorder.

10. Define "personality disorder" and describe ten different types of personality disorders.

11. Describe the distinctive characteristics, causes, and treatment of the antisocial personality.

12. Define "anxiety."

13. Outline the three features of anxiety-related problems.

14. State what is usually meant when the term "nervous breakdown" is used.

15. Differentiate an adjustment disorder from an anxiety disorder.

16. Define the key element of most anxiety disorders.

17. Differentiate generalized anxiety disorders from the two types of panic disorders.

18. Describe the following conditions: a. agoraphobia b. specific phobia c. social phobia d. obsessive-compulsive disorder e. stress disorders i. post-traumatic stress disorder ii. acute stress disorder f. dissociative disorders i. dissociative amnesia ii. dissociative fugue iii. dissociative identity disorder g. somatoform disorders i. hypochondriasis ii. somatization pain disorder iii. conversion disorder

19. Discuss how each of the four major perspectives in psychology views anxiety disorders. a. psychodynamic b.. humanistic-existential (include the concepts of self-image and existential anxiety) c. behavioral (include the terms "self-defeating," "paradox," "avoidance learning," and "anxiety reduction hypothesis") d. cognitive

20. Define what is meant by the term "psychosis."

21. Define "delusion."

22. Define "hallucination" and name the most common type.

23. Describe the emotion, communication, and personality changes that may occur in someone with a psychosis. Include an explanation of the frequency of occurrence for these changes.

24. Differentiate an organic from a functional psychosis.

25. Describe "dementia."

26. Describe Alzheimer's disease, including its incidence, symptoms, and neurological concomitants.

27. Describe the characteristics of delusional disorders, including each of the five delusional types.

28. Describe a paranoid psychosis. Explain why treatment of this condition is difficult.

29. Generally describe schizophrenia.

30. List and describe the four major types of schizophrenia.

31. Explain how paranoid delusional disorder and paranoid schizophrenia differ.

32. Describe the general relationship between violence and mental illness.

33. Describe the roles of the following three areas as causes of schizophrenia: a. Environment i. prenatal problems and birth complications ii. psychological trauma iii. disturbed family environment iv. deviant communication patterns b. Heredity c. Brain chemistry i. dopamine ii. CT, MRI, PET scans

34. Discuss the stress-vulnerability model of psychosis

35. Describe the characteristics of depressive disorders. Include a description of dysthymia and cyclothymia.

36. List and describe the three major mood disorders.

37. Explain the difference between major mood disorders and dysthymia and cyclothymia.

38. Generally describe the likely causes of mood disorders, including biological causes (brain chemicals and genetic) and psychological explanations (psychoanalytical, behavioral, cognitive, and social and environmental).

39. Define and briefly discuss the symptoms of maternity blues and postpartum depression.

40. Define "seasonal affective disorder (SAD)," list five major symptoms, and briefly describe the treatment of SAD.

41. Explain the dangers of social stigma when using psychiatric labels.

42. Discuss how each of the following factors affects suicide rates: season, sex, age, income, and marital status.

43. List the nine major risk factors that typically precede suicide. Discuss why people try to kill themselves.

44. Briefly list the twelve warning signals to potential suicide.

45. List four common characteristics of suicidal thoughts and feelings.

46. Explain how you can help prevent suicide.

RECITE AND REVIEW

MODULE 13.1

Survey Questions: How is normality defined, and what are the major psychological disorders? Pages 488-494

Psychopathology refers to mental [1] _____ themselves or to psychologically [2] _____ behavior.

Formal definitions of abnormality usually take into account subjective [3] _____ (private feelings of suffering or unhappiness).

Statistical definitions define abnormality as an extremely [4] _____ or [5] _____ score on some dimension or measure.

Social nonconformity is a failure to follow societal [6] _____ for acceptable conduct.

Frequently, the [7] _____ or situational context in which a behavior takes place affects judgments of normality and abnormality.

[8] _____ of the preceding definitions are relative standards.

A key element in judgments of disorder is that a person's [9] _____ must be maladaptive (it makes it difficult for the person to [10] _____ to the demands of daily life).

Major disorders and categories of psychopathology are described in the *Diagnostic and Statistical*
[11] _____ *of* [12] _____ *Disorders* (DSM-IV-TR).

A [13] _____ disorder is a significant impairment in psychological functioning.

Psychotic disorders are characterized by a retreat from [14] _____ , by hallucinations and
delusions, and by [15] _____ withdrawal.

Organic mental disorders are problems caused by [16] _____ injuries and [17] _____ .

Substance-related disorders are defined as abuse of or dependence on [18] _____ or
behavior-altering [19] _____ .

Mood disorders involve disturbances in affect, or [20] _____ .

[21] _____ disorders involve high levels of fear or [22] _____ and distortions in
behavior that are anxiety related.

Somatoform disorders involve physical symptoms that mimic physical [23] _____ or injury for
which there is no identifiable [24] _____ .

Dissociative disorders include cases of sudden amnesia, multiple [25] _____ , or episodes
of depersonalization.

Personality disorders are deeply ingrained, unhealthy [26] _____ patterns.

Sexual and [27] _____ disorders include gender identity disorders, paraphilias, and
[28] _____ dysfunctions.

In the past, the term "neurosis" was used to describe milder, [29] _____ -related disorders.
However, the term is fading from use.

Psychological disorders are [30] _____ in every culture. For example, Native Americans
who are preoccupied with death and the deceased have [31] _____ sickness, and East Asians
who experience intense anxiety that their penis, vulva, or nipples are receding into their bodies have
[32] _____ disorder.

Insanity is a [33] _____ term defining whether a person may be held responsible for his or her
actions. Sanity is determined in [34] _____ on the basis of testimony by expert witnesses.

MODULE 13.2

Survey Question: What is personality disorder? Pages 496-497

People with borderline [35] _____ disorder tend to react to ordinary criticisms by feeling rejected and [36] _____ , which then causes them to respond with anger, self-hatred, and [37] _____ .

Personality disorders are deeply ingrained, [38] _____ personality patterns.

The personality disorders are antisocial, avoidant, [39] _____ , dependent, histrionic, narcissistic, obsessive-[40] _____ , paranoid, schizoid, and schizotypal.

Antisocial persons (sociopaths) seem to lack a [41] _____ . They are [42] _____ shallow and manipulative.

Possible causes attributed to people with antisocial [43] _____ disorder include emotional deprivation, neglect, [44] _____ abuse as children, and boredom due to receiving little stimulation from the environment.

People with [45] _____ -compulsive disorder are plagued with images or thoughts that they cannot force out of [46] _____ . To reduce anxiety caused by these constantly occurring images and thoughts, they are compelled to [47] _____ irrational acts.

Survey Question: What problems result when a person suffers high levels of anxiety? Pages 498-502

The term "nervous breakdown" has no formal meaning. However, "emotional breakdowns" do correspond somewhat to adjustment disorders, in which the person is overwhelmed by ongoing [48] _____ .

Anxiety disorders include generalized anxiety disorder (chronic [49] _____ and worry) and panic disorder (anxiety attack and [50] _____ panic).

Panic disorder may occur with or without agoraphobia (fear of [51] _____ places, unfamiliar situations, or leaving the [52] _____).

Other anxiety disorders are agoraphobia and [53] _____ phobia (irrational fears of specific objects or situations).

In the anxiety disorder called social phobia, the person fears being [54] _____ , evaluated, embarrassed, or humiliated by others in [55] _____ situations.

Obsessive-compulsive disorders (obsessions and compulsions) and post-traumatic stress disorder or acute stress disorder (emotional disturbances triggered by severe [56] _____) are also classified as [57] _____ disorders.

Dissociative disorders may take the form of dissociative amnesia (loss of [58] _____ and personal identity) or [59] _____ fugue (flight from familiar surroundings).

A more dramatic problem is dissociative identity disorder, in which a person develops [60] _____ personalities.

Somatoform disorders center on physical complaints that mimic [61] _____ or disability.

In hypochondriasis, persons think that they have specific diseases when they are, in fact, [62] _____ .

In a somatization disorder, the person has numerous [63] _____ complaints. The person repeatedly seeks medical [64] _____ for these complaints, but no organic problems can be found.

Somatoform pain refers to discomfort for which there is no identifiable [65] _____ cause.

In conversion disorders, actual symptoms of disease or disability develop, but their causes are really [66] _____ .

Anxiety disorders, dissociative disorders, and somatoform disorders involve high levels of [67] _____ , rigid [68] _____ mechanisms, and self-defeating behavior patterns.

Survey Question: How do psychologists explain anxiety-based disorders? Pages 502-504

The behavioral approach emphasizes the effects of previous [69] _____ , particularly avoidance [70] _____ .

Some patterns in anxiety disorders can be explained by the [71] _____ reduction hypothesis, which states that immediate [72] _____ from anxiety rewards self-defeating behaviors.

According to the cognitive view, distorted [73] _____ patterns cause anxiety disorders.

MODULE 13.3

Survey Question: What are the general characteristics of psychotic disorders? Pages 506-508

Psychosis is a [74] _____ in contact with reality.

Some common types of delusions are depressive, [75] _____ , grandeur, [76] _____ , persecution, and reference.

Psychosis is marked by delusions, [77] _____ (false sensations), and sensory changes.

Other symptoms of psychosis are disturbed emotions, disturbed communication, and [78] _____ disintegration.

An organic psychosis is based on known injuries or [79] _____ of the brain.

The most common [80] _____ problem is dementia, a serious mental impairment in old age caused by deterioration of the [81] _____ .

One of the common causes of [82] _____ is Alzheimer's disease.

Survey Question: What is the nature of delusional disorder? Pages 508-509

A diagnosis of delusional disorder is based primarily on the presence of [83] _____ .

Delusions may concern grandeur, [84] _____ (harassment or threat), infidelity, [85] _____ attraction, or physical disease.

The most common delusional disorder is paranoid psychosis. Because they often have intense and irrational delusions of [86] _____ , paranoids may be violent if they believe they are threatened.

Survey Questions: What forms does schizophrenia take? What causes it? Pages 509-514

Schizophrenia is distinguished by a [87] _____ between [88] _____ and emotion and by delusions, hallucinations, and communication difficulties.

Disorganized schizophrenia is marked by extreme [89] _____ disintegration and silly, bizarre, or obscene behavior. [90] _____ impairment is usually extreme.

Catatonic schizophrenia is associated with stupor, [91] _____ (inability to speak), [92] _____ flexibility, and odd postures. Sometimes violent and agitated behavior also occurs.

In paranoid schizophrenia (the most common type), outlandish delusions of grandeur and [93] _____ are coupled with psychotic symptoms and personality breakdown.

Undifferentiated schizophrenia is the term used to indicate a [94] _____ of clear-cut patterns of disturbance.

A number of environmental factors appear to increase the risk of developing schizophrenia. These include viral [95] _____ during the mother's pregnancy and [96] _____ complications.

Early psychological [97] _____ (psychological injury or shock) and a disturbed [98] _____ environment, especially one marked by deviant communication, also increase the risk of schizophrenia.

Studies of [99] _____ and other close relatives strongly support heredity as a major factor in schizophrenia.

Recent biochemical studies have focused on abnormalities in brain [100] _____ substances, especially dopamine and glutamate and their receptor sites.

Current explanations of schizophrenia emphasize a combination of environmental [101] _____ , inherited susceptibility, and biochemical [102] _____ in the body or brain.

Other known causes that induce schizophrenic symptoms are the hallucinogenic drug [103] _____ and stress, which affect [104] _____ and dopamine levels in the brain.

Additional abnormalities in brain structure or [105] _____ have been detected in schizophrenic brains by the use of CT scans, MRI scans, and PET scans.

The dominant explanation of schizophrenia is the [106] _____ -vulnerability model.

MODULE 13.4

Survey Questions: What are mood disorders? What causes depression? Pages 516-519

Mood disorders primarily involve disturbances of mood or [107] _____ .

Long-lasting, though relatively moderate [108] _____ is called a dysthymic disorder.

Chronic, though moderate swings in mood between [109] _____ and [110] _____ are called a cyclothymic disorder.

In a bipolar I disorder the person alternates between extreme mania and [111] _____ .

In a bipolar II disorder the person is mostly [112] _____ but has had at least one episode of hypomania (mild [113] _____).

The problem known as major depressive disorder involves extreme sadness and despondency but no evidence of [114] _____ .

Major mood disorders more often appear to be endogenous (produced from [115] _____) rather than reactions to [116] _____ events.

Postpartum depression is a mild to moderate depressive disorder that affects many women after they give birth. Postpartum depression is more serious than the more common [117] _____ .

[118] _____ affective disorder (SAD), which occurs during the [119] _____ months, is another common form of depression. SAD is typically treated with phototherapy.

Biological, psychoanalytic, cognitive, and [120] _____ theories of depression have been proposed. Heredity is clearly a factor in susceptibility to mood disorders.

Factors that influence the development of depression include being a woman, [121] _____ , not being married, having limited [122] _____ , high levels of [123] _____ , and feelings of hopelessness.

David Rosenhan demonstrated the damaging effects of [124] _____ a person with a disorder in our society. They are stigmatized, [125] _____ jobs and housing, and accused of [126] _____ that they did not commit.

PSYCHOLOGY IN ACTION

Survey Questions: Why do people commit suicide? Can suicide be prevented? Pages 521-523

[127] _____ is statistically related to such factors as age, sex, and marital status.

Major risk factors for suicide include [128] _____ or [129] _____ abuse, a prior attempt, depression, hopelessness, antisocial behavior, suicide by relatives, shame, failure, or rejection, and the availability of a [130] _____ .

In individual cases the potential for suicide is best identified by a desire to [131] _____ , unbearable psychological pain, frustrated psychological needs, and a constriction of [132] _____ .

Suicidal [133] _____ usually precede suicide threats, which progress to suicide attempts.

Suicide can often be prevented by the efforts of family, friends, and mental health professionals to establish [134] _____ and rapport with the person and by gaining day-by-day commitments from her or him.

CONNECTIONS

MODULE 13.1

1. _____ DSM-IV-TR
2. _____ drapetomania
3. _____ mood disorder
4. _____ somatoform disorder
5. _____ insanity
6. _____ organic disorder
7. _____ neurosis
8. _____ paraphilia
9. _____ amok

a. culturally recognized disorder
b. physical symptoms
c. legal problem
d. outdated term
e. sexual deviation
f. diagnostic manual
g. fear of germs
h. brain pathology
i. mania or depression

MODULE 13.2

1. _____ dependent personality	a. self-importance
2. _____ histrionic personality	b. rigid routines
3. _____ narcissistic personality	c. submissiveness
4. _____ antisocial personality	d. little emotion
5. _____ obsessive-compulsive	e. attention seeking
6. _____ schizoid personality	f. unstable self-image
7. _____ avoidant personality	g. odd, disturbed thinking
8. _____ borderline personality	h. suspiciousness
9. _____ paranoid personality	i. fear of social situations
10. _____ schizotypal personality	j. no conscience

1. _____ adjustment disorder	a. afraid to leave the house
2. _____ generalized anxiety	b. fears being observed
3. _____ panic disorder	c. conversion disorder
4. _____ agoraphobia	d. one month after extreme stress
5. _____ specific phobia	e. dissociation
6. _____ social phobia	f. within weeks after extreme stress
7. _____ PTSD	g. sudden attacks of fear
8. _____ acute stress disorder	h. normal life stress
9. _____ glove anesthesia	i. chronic worry
10. _____ fugue	j. fears objects or activities

MODULE 13.3

1. _____ psychosis	a. retreat from reality
2. _____ catatonic type	b. incoherence, bizarre thinking
3. _____ paranoid type	c. false belief
4. _____ disorganized type	d. genetics of schizophrenia
5. _____ psychological trauma	e. grandeur or persecution
6. _____ twin studies	f. chemical messenger
7. _____ hallucinations	g. risk factor for schizophrenia
8. _____ dopamine	h. dementia
9. _____ delusion	i. imaginary sensations
10. _____ Alzheimer's disease	j. stuporous or agitated

MODULE 13.4

1.	_____ bipolar I	a.	produced from within
2.	_____ social stigma	b.	winter depression
3.	_____ bipolar II	c.	depression after childbirth
4.	_____ endogenous	d.	light treatment
5.	_____ suicide	e.	leads to prejudice
6.	_____ postpartum depression	f.	desire to end all pains
7.	_____ phototherapy	g.	depression and hypomania
8.	_____ SAD	h.	severe mania and depression

CHECK YOUR MEMORY

MODULE 13.1

Survey Questions: How is normality defined, and what are the major psychological disorders? Pages 488-494

1. Psychopathology refers to the study of mental disorders and to disorders themselves.

   TRUE or FALSE

2. One out of every 10 persons will require mental hospitalization during his or her lifetime.

   TRUE or FALSE

3. Statistical definitions do not automatically tell us where to draw the line between normality and abnormality.

   TRUE or FALSE

4. To understand how social norms define normality, a person could perform a mild abnormal behavior in public to observe the public's reaction.

   TRUE or FALSE

5. Cultural relativity refers to making personal judgments about another culture's practices.

   TRUE or FALSE

6. All cultures classify people as abnormal if they fail to communicate with others.

   TRUE or FALSE

7. Drapetomania, childhood masturbation, and nymphomania are considered mental disorders listed in the DSM-IV-TR.

   TRUE or FALSE

8. Gender is a common source of bias in judging normality.

   TRUE or FALSE

9. Being a persistent danger to oneself or others is regarded as a clear sign of disturbed psychological functioning.

   TRUE or FALSE

10. Poverty, abusive parents, low intelligence, and head injuries are risk factors for mental disorder.

    TRUE or FALSE

11. "Organic mental disorders" is one of the major categories in DSM-IV-TR.

    TRUE or FALSE

12. Koro, locura, and zar are brain diseases that cause psychosis.

    TRUE or FALSE

13. Neurosis is a legal term, not a type of mental disorder.

    TRUE or FALSE

MODULE 13.2

Survey Question: What is personality disorder? Pages 496-497

14. The "emotional storms" experienced by people with borderline personality disorder is a normal process about which they and their friends have a clear understanding.

    TRUE or FALSE

15. Histrionic persons are preoccupied with their own self-importance.

    TRUE or FALSE

16. Personality disorders usually appear suddenly in early adulthood.

    TRUE or FALSE

17. The schizoid person shows little emotion and is uninterested in relationships with others.

    TRUE or FALSE

18. "Psychopath" is another term for the borderline personality.

    TRUE or FALSE

19. Sociopaths usually have a childhood history of emotional deprivation, neglect, and abuse.

    TRUE or FALSE

20. Antisocial behavior typically declines somewhat after age.

    TRUE or FALSE

21. Antisocial personality disorders are often treated successfully with drugs.

    TRUE or FALSE

Survey Question: What problems result when a person suffers high levels of anxiety? Pages 498-502

22. Anxiety is an emotional response to an ambiguous threat.
    TRUE or FALSE

23. Adjustment disorders occur when severe stresses outside the normal range of human experience push people to their breaking points.
    TRUE or FALSE

24. Sudden, unexpected episodes of intense panic are a key feature of generalized anxiety disorder.
    TRUE or FALSE

25. A person who fears he or she will have a panic attack in public places or unfamiliar situations suffers from acrophobia.
    TRUE or FALSE

26. Arachnophobia, claustrophobia, and pathophobia are all specific phobias.
    TRUE or FALSE

27. Many people who have an obsessive-compulsive disorder are checkers or cleaners.
    TRUE or FALSE

28. PTSD is a psychological disturbance lasting more than one month after exposure to severe stress.
    TRUE or FALSE

29. Multiple personality is a dissociative disorder.
    TRUE or FALSE

30. Multiple personality is the most common form of schizophrenia.
    TRUE or FALSE

31. Depersonalization and fusion are the goals of therapy for dissociative identity disorders.
    TRUE or FALSE

32. The word "somatoform" means "body form."
    TRUE or FALSE

33. An unusual lack of concern about the appearance of a sudden disability is a sign of a conversion reaction.
    TRUE or FALSE

Survey Question: How do psychologists explain anxiety-based disorders? Pages 502-504

34. Anxiety disorders appear to be partly hereditary.
    TRUE or FALSE

35. The psychodynamic approach characterizes anxiety disorders as a product of id impulses that threaten a loss of control.
TRUE or FALSE

36. Carl Rogers interpreted emotional disorders as the result of a loss of meaning in one's life.
TRUE or FALSE

37. Disordered behavior is paradoxical because it makes the person more anxious and unhappy in the long run.
TRUE or FALSE

38. The cognitive view attributes anxiety disorders to distorted thinking that leads to avoidance learning.
TRUE or FALSE

MODULE 13.3

Survey Question: What are the general characteristics of psychotic disorders? Pages 506-508

39. The most common psychotic delusion is hearing voices.
TRUE or FALSE

40. People with depressive delusions believe that they are depressed but that they do not need therapy.
TRUE or FALSE

41. Even a person who displays flat affect may continue to privately feel strong emotion.
TRUE or FALSE

42. Severe brain injuries or diseases sometimes cause psychoses.
TRUE or FALSE

43. Children must eat leaded paint flakes before they are at risk for lead poisoning.
TRUE or FALSE

44. Roughly 80 percent of all cases of Alzheimer's disease are genetic.
TRUE or FALSE

Survey Question: What is the nature of delusional disorder? Pages 508-509

45. In delusional disorders, people have auditory hallucinations of grandeur or persecution.
TRUE or FALSE

46. Delusions of persecution are a key symptom of paranoid psychosis.
TRUE or FALSE

47. A person who believes that his body is diseased and rotting has an erotomanic type of delusional disorder.
TRUE or FALSE

48. Delusional disorders are common and are easily treated with drugs.
    TRUE or FALSE

Survey Questions: What forms does schizophrenia take? What causes it? Pages 509-514

49. One person out of 100 will become schizophrenic.
    TRUE or FALSE

50. Schizophrenia is the most common dissociative psychosis.
    TRUE or FALSE

51. Silliness, laughter, and bizarre behavior are common in disorganized schizophrenia.
    TRUE or FALSE

52. Periods of immobility and odd posturing are characteristic of paranoid schizophrenia.
    TRUE or FALSE

53. At various times, patients may shift from one type of schizophrenia to another.
    TRUE or FALSE

54. Exposure to influenza during pregnancy produces children who are more likely to become schizophrenic later in life.
    TRUE or FALSE

55. If one identical twin is schizophrenic, the other twin has a 46 percent chance of also becoming schizophrenic.
    TRUE or FALSE

56. Excess amounts of the neurotransmitter substance PCP are suspected as a cause of schizophrenia.
    TRUE or FALSE

57. The brains of schizophrenics tend to be more responsive to dopamine and glutamate than the brains of normal persons.
    TRUE or FALSE

58. PET scans show that activity in the frontal lobes of schizophrenics tends to be abnormally low.
    TRUE or FALSE

59. At least three schizophrenic patients out of four are completely recovered 10 years after being diagnosed.
    TRUE or FALSE

60. The stress-vulnerability model suggests that psychotic disorders are caused by a combination of environment and heredity.
    TRUE or FALSE

MODULE 13.4

Survey Questions: What are mood disorders? What causes depression? Pages 516-519

61. The two most basic types of mood disorder are bipolar I and bipolar II.
    TRUE or FALSE

62. In bipolar disorders, people experience both mania and depression.
    TRUE or FALSE

63. If a person is moderately depressed for at least two weeks, a dysthymic disorder exists.
    TRUE or FALSE

64. A cyclothymic disorder is characterized by moderate levels of depression and manic behavior.
    TRUE or FALSE

65. Endogenous depression appears to be generated from within, with little connection to external events.
    TRUE or FALSE

66. Behavioral theories of depression emphasize the concept of learned helplessness.
    TRUE or FALSE

67. Overall, women are twice as likely as men to become depressed.
    TRUE or FALSE

68. Having limited education, experiencing high levels of stress, not being married, and feeling hopeless are some characteristics that increase a woman's chance of being depressed.
    TRUE or FALSE

69. Research indicates that heredity does not play a role in major mood disorder.
    TRUE or FALSE

70. Postpartum depression typically lasts from about two months to a year after giving birth.
    TRUE or FALSE

71. SAD is most likely to occur during the winter in countries lying near the equator.
    TRUE or FALSE

72. Phototherapy is used to treat SAD successfully 80 percent of the time.
    TRUE or FALSE

73. Labeling a person with a disorder when they do not have it does not harm them in any way.
    TRUE or FALSE

74. People who have been successfully treated for a mental disorder are no longer a threat to society and, therefore, are not stigmatized like criminals.
    TRUE or FALSE

PSYCHOLOGY IN ACTION

Survey Questions: Why do people commit suicide? Can suicide be prevented? Pages 521-523

75. The greatest number of suicides during a single day takes place at New Year's.
    TRUE or FALSE

76. More men than women complete suicide.
    TRUE or FALSE

77. Suicide rates steadily decline after young adulthood.
    TRUE or FALSE

78. Most suicides involve despair, anger, and guilt.
    TRUE or FALSE

79. People who threaten suicide rarely actually attempt it—they're just crying wolf.
    TRUE or FALSE

80. Only a minority of people who attempt suicide really want to die.
    TRUE or FALSE

81. The risk of attempted suicide is high if a person has a concrete, workable plan for doing it.
    TRUE or FALSE

FINAL SURVEY AND REVIEW

MODULE 13.1

Survey Questions: How is normality defined, and what are the major psychological disorders? Pages 488-494

[1] _____ refers to mental disorders themselves or to psychologically unhealthy behavior.

Formal definitions of abnormality usually take into account [2] _____ discomfort (private feelings of suffering or unhappiness).

[3] _____ definitions define abnormality as an extremely high or low score on some dimension or measure.

[4] _____ is a failure to follow societal standards for acceptable conduct.

Frequently, the cultural or situational [5] _____ in which a behavior takes place affects judgments of normality and abnormality.

All of the preceding definitions are [6] _____ standards.

A key element in judgments of disorder is that a person's behavior must be [7] _____ (it makes it difficult for the person to adapt to the environment).

Major disorders and categories of psychopathology are described in the [8] _____ *and*

[9] _____ *Manual of Mental Disorders* (DSM-IV-TR).

A mental disorder is a significant impairment in [10] _____ functioning.

[11] _____ disorders are characterized by a retreat from reality, by [12] _____ and delusions, and by social withdrawal.

[13] _____ mental disorders are problems caused by brain injuries and diseases.

[14] _____ disorders are defined as abuse of or dependence on mood- or behavior-altering drugs.

[15] _____ disorders involve disturbances in [16] _____ , or emotion.

[17] _____ disorders involve high levels of fear or anxiety and distortions in behavior that are anxiety related.

[18] _____ disorders involve physical symptoms that mimic physical disease or injury for which there is no identifiable cause.

[19] _____ disorders include cases of sudden [20] _____ , multiple personality, or episodes of depersonalization.

[21] _____ disorders are deeply ingrained, unhealthy personality patterns.

Sexual and gender disorders include gender [22] _____ disorders, paraphilias, and sexual

[23] _____ .

In the past, the term [24] _____ was used to describe milder, anxiety-related disorders. However, the term is fading from use.

Psychological disorders are recognized in every culture. For example, Native Americans who are preoccupied with death and the deceased have [25] _____ , and [26] _____ who experience intense anxiety that their penis, vulva, or nipples are receding into their bodies have Koro disorder.

[27] _____ is a legal term defining whether a person may be held responsible for his or her actions. Sanity is determined in court on the basis of testimony by expert witnesses.

MODULE 13.2

Survey Question: What is personality disorder? Pages 496-497

People with [28] _____ personality disorder tend to react to ordinary criticisms by feeling rejected and abandoned, which then causes them to respond with anger, self-hatred, and [29] _____ .

Personality disorders are deeply [30] _____ , maladaptive personality patterns.

The personality disorders are antisocial, avoidant, borderline, [31] _____ , histrionic, narcissistic, obsessive-compulsive, [32] _____ , schizoid, and [33] _____ .

[34] _____ persons (sociopaths) seem to lack a conscience. They are emotionally shallow and [35] _____ .

Possible causes attributed to people with [36] _____ personality disorder include [37] _____ deprivation, neglect, physical abuse as [38] _____ , and boredom due to receiving little stimulation from the environment.

People with [39] _____ disorder are plagued with images or thoughts that they cannot force out of awareness. To reduce [40] _____ caused by these constant occurring images and thoughts, they are compelled to repeat irrational acts.

Survey Question: What problems result when a person suffers high levels of anxiety? Pages 498-502

The term nervous [41] _____ has no formal meaning. However, people do experience[42] _____ disorders, in which the person is overwhelmed by ongoing life stresses.

Anxiety disorders include [43] _____ anxiety disorder (chronic anxiety and worry) and [44] _____ disorder (anxiety attack and sudden panic).

Panic disorder may occur with or without [45] _____ (fear of public places or leaving the home).

Other anxiety disorders are [46] _____ (fear of public places, [47] _____ situations, or leaving the home) and specific phobia (irrational fears of specific objects or situations).

In the anxiety disorder called [48] _____ [49] _____ , the person fears being observed[50] _____ , embarrassed, or humiliated by others in social situations.

[51] _____ -compulsive disorders and [52] _____ stress disorder (PTSD) or [53] _____ stress disorder (emotional disturbances triggered by severe stress) are also classified as anxiety disorders.

Dissociative disorders may take the form of dissociative [54] _____ (loss of memory and personal identity) or dissociative [55] _____ (confused identity and flight from familiar surroundings).

A more dramatic problem is dissociative [56] _____ , in which a person develops multiple personalities.

[57] _____ disorders center on physical complaints that mimic disease or disability.

In [58] _____ , persons think that they have specific diseases when they are, in fact, healthy.

In a [59] _____ disorder, the person has numerous physical complaints. The person repeatedly seeks medical treatment for these complaints, but no organic problems can be found.

[60] _____ refers to discomfort for which there is no identifiable physical cause.

In [61] _____ disorders, actual symptoms of disease or disability develop, but their causes are actually psychological.

Anxiety disorders, [62] _____ disorders, and [63] _____ disorders are characterized by high levels of anxiety, rigid defense mechanisms, and self-defeating behavior patterns.

Survey Question: How do psychologists explain anxiety-based disorders? Pages 502-504

The [64] _____ approach emphasizes unconscious conflicts within the personality as the cause of disabling anxiety.

The [65] _____ approach emphasizes the effects of a faulty self-image.

The [66] _____ approach emphasizes the effects of previous learning, particularly [67] _____ learning.

Some patterns in anxiety disorders can be explained by the anxiety [68] _____ hypothesis, which states that immediate relief from anxiety rewards [69] _____ behaviors.

According to the [70] _____ view, distorted thinking patterns cause anxiety disorders.

MODULE 13.3

Survey Question: What are the general characteristics of psychotic disorders? Pages 506-508

[71] _____ is a break in contact with [72] _____ .

Some common types of [73] _____ are depressive, somatic, grandeur, influence, persecution, and reference.

Psychosis is marked by [74] _____ (false beliefs), hallucinations, and [75] _____ changes.

Other symptoms of psychosis are disturbed emotions, disturbed [76] _____ , and personality
[77] _____ .

An [78] _____ psychosis is based on known injuries or diseases of the brain.

The most common organic problem is [79] _____ , a serious mental impairment in old age
caused by deterioration of the brain.

One of most common causes of dementia is [80] _____ disease.

Survey Question: What is the nature of delusional disorder? Pages 508-509

A [81] _____ of [82] _____ disorder is based primarily on the presence of delusions.

Delusions may concern [83] _____ (personal importance), persecution, infidelity, romantic
attraction, or physical [84] _____ .

The most common delusional disorder is [85] _____ psychosis. Because they often have
intense and irrational delusions of persecution, afflicted persons may be [86] _____ if they
believe they are threatened.

Survey Questions: What forms does schizophrenia take? What causes it? Pages 509-514

Schizophrenia is distinguished by a split between thought and [87] _____ and by delusions,
hallucinations, and [88] _____ difficulties.

[89] _____ schizophrenia is marked by extreme personality [90] _____ and silly,
bizarre, or obscene behavior. Social impairment is usually extreme.

[91] _____ schizophrenia is associated with stupor, mutism, waxy [92] _____ , and
odd postures. Sometimes violent and agitated behavior also occurs.

In [93] _____ schizophrenia (the most common type), outlandish delusions of [94] _____
and persecution are coupled with psychotic symptoms and personality breakdown.

[95] _____ schizophrenia is the term used to indicate a lack of clear-cut patterns of disturbance.

A number of [96] _____ factors appear to increase the risk of developing schizophrenia. These
include viral infection during the mother's pregnancy and birth complications.

Early [97] _____ trauma and a disturbed family environment, especially one marked by
[98] _____ communication, also increase the risk of schizophrenia.

Studies of twins and other close relatives strongly support [99] _____ as a major factor in schizophrenia.

Recent biochemical studies have focused on abnormalities in brain transmitter substances, especially [100] _____ and glutamate and their [101] _____ sites.

Current explanations of schizophrenia emphasize a combination of [102] _____ stress, inherited susceptibility, and [103] _____ abnormalities in the body or brain.

Other known causes that induce [104] _____ symptoms are the [105] _____ drug PCP and stress, which affect glutamate and dopamine levels in the brain.

Additional abnormalities in brain structure or function have been detected in schizophrenic brains by the use of [106] _____ scans, [107] _____ scans, and [108] _____ scans.

The dominant explanation of schizophrenia is the stress-[109] _____ model.

MODULE 13.4

Survey Questions: What are mood disorders? What causes depression? Pages 516-519

Mood disorders primarily involve disturbances of [110] _____ or emotion.

Long-lasting, though relatively moderate depression is called a [111] _____ disorder.

Chronic, though moderate swings in mood between depression and elation are called a [112] _____ disorder.

In a [113] _____ disorder the person alternates between extreme [114] _____ and depression.

In a [115] _____ [116] _____ disorder the person is mostly depressed but has had at least one episode of [117] _____ (mild mania).

The problem known as [118] _____ disorder involves extreme sadness and despondency but no evidence of mania.

Major mood disorders more often appear to be [119] _____ (produced from within) rather than reactions to external events.

[120] _____ depression is a mild to moderate depressive disorder that affects many women after they give birth. It is more serious than the more common maternity blues.

Seasonal [121] _____ disorder (SAD), which occurs during the winter months, is another common form of depression. SAD is typically treated with [122] _____ (exposure to bright light).

[123] _____ , psychoanalytic, [124] _____ , and behavioral theories of depression have been proposed. Heredity is clearly a factor in susceptibility to mood disorders.

Factors that influence the development of [125] _____ include being a woman, Latina, not being married, having limited education, high levels of stress, and feelings of [126] _____ .

David Rosenhan demonstrated the damaging effects of [127] _____ a person with a disorder in our society. They are [128] _____ , denied jobs and housing, and accused of crimes that they did not commit.

PSYCHOLOGY IN ACTION

Survey Questions: Why do people commit suicide? Can suicide be prevented? Pages 521-523

Suicide is [129] _____ related to such factors as age, sex, and marital status.

Major [130] _____ for suicide include drug or alcohol abuse, a prior attempt, depression, hopelessness, [131] _____ behavior, suicide by relatives, shame, failure, rejection, and the availability of a firearm.

In individual cases the potential for suicide is best identified by a desire to escape, unbearable psychological [132] _____ , frustrated psychological needs, and a constriction of options.

Suicidal thoughts usually precede suicide [133] _____ , which progress to suicide [134] _____ .

Suicide can often be prevented by the efforts of family, friends, and mental health professionals to establish communication and [135] _____ with the person and by gaining day-by-day [136] _____ from her or him.

MASTERY TEST

1. The difference between an acute stress disorder and PTSD is
   a. how long the disturbance lasts
   b. the severity of the stress
   c. whether the anxiety is free-floating
   d. whether dissociative behavior is observed

2. A person is at greatest risk of becoming schizophrenic if he or she has
   a. schizophrenic parents
   b. a schizophrenic fraternal twin
   c. a schizophrenic mother
   d. a schizophrenic sibling

3. A core feature of all abnormal behavior is that it is
   a. statistically extreme
   b. associated with subjective discomfort
   c. ultimately maladaptive
   d. marked by a loss of contact with reality

4. Excess amounts of dopamine in the brain, or high sensitivity to dopamine, provide one major explantion for the problem known as
   a. PTSD
   b. schizophrenia
   c. major depression
   d. SAD

5. The descriptions acro, and claustro, and pyro refer to
   a. common obsessions
   b. specific phobias
   c. free-floating anxieties
   d. hypochondriasis

6. Glove anesthesia strongly implies the existence of a(an)_____ disorder.
   a. organic
   b. depersonalization
   c. somatization
   d. conversion

7. In the stress-vulnerability model of psychosis, vulnerability is primarily attributed to
   a. heredity
   b. exposure to influenza
   c. psychological trauma
   d. disturbed family life

8. A patient believes that she has a mysterious disease that is causing her body to rot away. What type of symptom is she suffering from?
   a. bipolar
   b. delusion
   c. neurosis
   d. cyclothymic

9. Phototherapy is used primarily to treat
   a. postseasonal depression
   b. SAD
   c. catatonic depression
   d. affective psychoses

10. Psychopathology is defined as an inability to behave in ways that
    a. foster personal growth and happiness
    b. match social norms
    c. lead to personal achievement
    d. do not cause anxiety

11. Which of the following is NOT characteristic of suicidal thinking?
    a. desires to escape
    b. psychological pain
    c. frustrated needs
    d. too many options

12. Fear of using the restroom in public is
    a. a social phobia
    b. an acute stress disorder
    c. a panic disorder
    d. an adjustment disorder

13. A person who displays personality disintegration, waxy flexibility, and delusions of persecution suffers from_____ schizophrenia.
    a. disorganized
    b. catatonic
    c. paranoid
    d. undifferentiated

14. You find yourself in an unfamiliar town and you can't remember your name or address. It is likely that you are suffering from
    a. paraphilia
    b. Alzherimer's disease
    c. a borderline personality disorder
    d. a dissociative disorder

15. A major problem with statistical definitions of abnormality is
    a. calculating the normal curve
    b. choosing dividing lines
    c. that they do not apply to groups of people
    d. that they do not take norms into account

16. DSM-IV-TR primarily describes and classifies_____ disorders.
    a. mental
    b. organic
    c. psychotic
    d. cognitive

17. A person who is a frequent checker may have which disorder?
    a. agoraphobia
    b. somatization
    c. free-floating fugue
    d. obsessive-compulsive

18. The most direct explanation for the anxiety-reducing properties of self-defeating behavior is found in
    a. an overwhelmed ego
    b. avoidance learning
    c. the loss of meaning in one's life
    d. the concept of existential anxiety

19. A person with a(an) _____ personality disorder might be described as charming by people who don't know the person well.
    a. avoidant
    b. schizoid
    c. antisocial
    d. dependent

20. One of the most powerful situational contexts for judging the normality of behavior is
    a. culture
    b. gender
    c. statistical norms
    d. private discomfort

21. A person who is manic most likely suffers from a(an) _____ disorder.
    a. anxiety
    b. somatoform
    c. organic
    d. mood

22. The principal problem in paranoid psychosis is
    a. delusions
    b. hallucinations
    c. disturbed emotions
    d. personality disintegration

23. A problem that may occur with or without agoraphobia is
    a. dissociative disorder
    b. somatoform disorder
    c. panic disorder
    d. obsessive-compulsive disorder

24. Hearing voices that do not exist is an almost sure sign of a_____ disorder.
    a. psychotic
    b. dissociative
    c. personality
    d. delusional

25. A conversion reaction is a type of_____ disorder.
    a. somatoform
    b. dissociative
    c. obsessive-compulsive
    d. postpartum

26. The existence, in the past, of disorders such as drapetomania and nymphomania suggests that judging normality is greatly affected by
    a. gender
    b. cultural disapproval
    c. levels of functioning
    d. subjective discomfort

27. Which of the following terms does NOT belong with the others?
    a. neurosis
    b. somatoform disorder
    c. personality disorder
    d. dissociative disorder

28. Threats to one's self-image are a key element in the_____ approach to understanding anxiety and disordered functioning.
    a. Freudian
    b. humanistic
    c. existential
    d. behavioral

29. Which of the following is NOT classified as an anxiety disorder?
    a. adjustment disorder
    b. panic disorder
    c. agoraphobia
    d. obsessive-compulsive disorder

30. Cyclothymic disorder is most closely related to
    a. reactive depression
    b. major depressive disorder
    c. bipolar disorder
    d. SAD

31. Pretending to possess a delusional disorder (schizophrenia) by walking around campus on a sunny day with a raincoat on and holding an open umbrella over one's head and, when inside, continuing to hold the open umbrella over one's head is a way to
    a. understand how social norms define normality
    b. determine how normality is defined
    c. test cultural relativism
    d. all the preceding

32. A person who sometimes is friendly, charming, impulsive, moody, extremely sensitive to ordinary criticisms, and suicidal has the _____ personality disorder.
    a. dependent
    b. borderline
    c. dissociative
    d. narcissistic

33. A person who is "blind" to signs that would disgust others, charming, lacks a conscience, and feels no guilt, shame, fear, loyalty, or love has the _____ personality disorder.
    a. histrionic
    b. schizoid
    c. avoidant
    d. antisocial

34. Which of the following is NOT a type of delusion?
    a. avoidant
    b. depressive
    c. reference
    d. influence

35. Which of the following statement is true of delusional disorders?
    a. The disorders are common and easily treated.
    b. The main feature is a deeply held false belief.
    c. Symptoms include perceiving sensations that do not exist (e.g., seeing insects crawling under their skin).
    d. The disorder is genetically linked.

36. Which of the following is NOT a cause of schizophrenia?
    a. Malnutrition during pregnancy and exposure to influenza.
    b. Females are more vulnerable to developing schizophrenic disorder.
    c. Psychological trauma during childhood increases the risk.
    d. Sensitivity to neurotransmitters dopamine and glutamate.

37. Knowing that Lloyd is suffering from bipolar disorder and currently is undergoing treatment, Joan assumes that he will relapse sooner or later and, therefore, refuses to hire him as a delivery person. Joan's reaction and response to Lloyd's application reflects the impact of
    a. labeling a person with a disorder rather than the problem
    b. prejudice and discrimination
    c. stigmatism
    d. all the preceding

SOLUTIONS

RECITE AND REVIEW

MODULE 13.1

1. disorders
2. unhealthy
3. discomfort
4. high
5. low
6. standards
7. cultural
8. All
9. behavior
10. adapt
11. *Manual*
12. *Manual*
13. mental
14. reality
15. social
16. brain
17. diseases
18. mood
19. drugs
20. emotion
21. Anxiety
22. anxiety
23. disease
24. cause
25. personality
26. personality
27. gender
28. sexual
29. anxiety
30. recognized
31. Ghost
32. Koro
33. legal
34. court

MODULE 13.2

35. personality
36. abandoned
37. impulsiveness
38. maladaptive
39. borderline
40. compulsive
41. conscience
42. emotionally
43. personality
44. physical
45. obsessive
46. awareness
47. repeat

48. life stresses
49. anxiety
50. sudden
51. public
52. home
53. specific
54. observed
55. social
56. stress
57. anxiety
58. memory
59. dissociative
60. multiple
61. disease
62. healthy
63. physical
64. treatment
65. physical
66. psychological
67. anxiety
68. defense

69. learning
70. learning
71. anxiety
72. relief
73. thinking

MODULE 13.3

74. break
75. somatic
76. influence
77. hallucinations
78. personality
79. diseases
80. organic
81. brain
82. dementia

83. delusions
84. persecution
85. romantic
86. persecution

87. split
88. thought
89. personality
90. Social
91. mutism
92. waxy
93. persecution
94. lack

95. infection
96. birth
97. trauma
98. family
99. twins
100. transmitter
101. stress
102. abnormalities

103. PCP
104. glutamate
105. activity
106. stress

MODULE 13.4

107. emotion
108. depression
109. depression
110. elation
111. depression
112. depressed
113. mania
114. mania

115. within
116. external
117. maternity blues
118. Seasonal
119. winter
120. behavioral
121. Latina
122. education

123. stress
124. labeling
125. denied
126. crimes

PSYCHOLOGY IN ACTION

127. Suicide
128. alcohol
129. drug

130. firearm
131. escape
132. options

133. thoughts
134. communication

CONNECTIONS

MODULE 13.1

1. f
2. a
3. i

4. b
5. c
6. h

7. d
8. e
9. g

MODULE 13.2

1. c
2. e
3. a
4. j

5. b
6. d
7. i
8. f

9. h
10. g

1. h
2. i

3. g
4. a

5. j
6. b

7. d	9. c
8. f	10. e

MODULE 13.3

1. a	5. g	9. c
2. j	6. d	10. h
3. e	7. i	
4. b	8. f	

MODULE 13.4

1. h	4. a	7. d
2. e	5. f	8. b
3. g	6. c	

CHECK YOUR MEMORY

MODULE 13.1

1. T	6. T	11. F
2. F	7. F	12. F
3. T	8. T	13. F
4. T	9. T	
5. F	10. T	

MODULE 13.2

14. F	17. T	20. F
15. F	18. F	21. F
16. F	19. T	

22. T	26. T	30. F
23. F	27. T	31. F
24. F	28. T	32. T
25. F	29. T	33. T

34. T	36. F	38. F
35. T	37. T	

MODULE 13.3

39. F	41. T	43. F
40. F	42. T	44. F

45. F

46. T	47. F	48. F

49. T	53. T	57. T
50. F	54. T	58. T
51. T	55. T	59. F
52. F	56. F	60. T

MODULE 13.4

61. F	67. T	73. F
62. T	68. T	74. F
63. F	69. F	
64. T	70. T	
65. T	71. F	
66. T	72. T	

PSYCHOLOGY IN ACTION

75. T	78. T	81. T
76. T	79. F	
77. F	80. T	

FINAL SURVEY AND REVIEW

MODULE 13.1

1. Psychopathology	11. Psychotic	21. Personality
2. subjective	12. hallucinations	22. identity
3. Statistical	13. Organic	23. dysfunctions
4. Social nonconformity	14. Substance-related	24. neurosis
5. context	15. Mood	25. Ghost sickness
6. relative	16. affect	26. East Asians
7. maladaptive	17. Anxiety	27. Insanity
8. *Diagnostic*	18. Somatoform	
9. *Diagnostic*	19. Dissociative	
10. psychological	20. amnesia	

MODULE 13.2

28. borderline	33. schizotypal	38. children
29. impulsiveness	34. Antisocial	39. obsessive-compulsive
30. ingrained	35. manipulative	40. anxiety
31. dependent	36. antisocial	
32. paranoid	37. emotional	

41. breakdown	43. generalized	45. agoraphobia
42. adjustment	44. panic	46. agoraphobia

47. unfamiliar
48. social
49. phobia
50. evaluated
51. Obsessive
52. post-traumatic
53. acute

54. amnesia
55. fugue
56. identity disorder
57. Somatoform
58. hypochondriasis
59. somatization
60. Somatoform pain

61. conversion
62. dissociative
63. somatoform

64. psychodynamic
65. humanistic
66. behavioral

67. avoidance
68. reduction
69. self-defeating

70. cognitive

MODULE 13.3

71. Psychosis
72. reality
73. delusions
74. delusions

75. sensory
76. communication
77. disintegration
78. organic

79. dementia
80. Alzheimer's

81. diagnosis
82. delusional

83. grandeur
84. disease

85. paranoid
86. violent

87. emotion
88. communication
89. Disorganized
90. disintegration
91. Catatonic
92. flexibility
93. paranoid
94. grandeur
95. Undifferentiated

96. environmental
97. psychological
98. deviant
99. heredity
100. dopamine
101. receptor
102. environmental
103. biochemical
104. schizophrenic

105. hallucinogenic
106. CT,
107. MRI,
108. PET
109. vulnerability

MODULE 13.4

110. mood
111. dysthymic
112. cyclothymic
113. bipolar I
114. mania
115. bipolar
116. II

117. hypomania
118. major depressive
119. endogenous
120. Postpartum
121. affective
122. phototherapy
123. Biological

124. cognitive
125. depression
126. hopelessness
127. labeling
128. stigmatized

PSYCHOLOGY IN ACTION

129. statistically

130. risk factors
131. antisocial
132. pain

133. threats
134. attempts
135. rapport

136. commitments

MASTERY TEST

1. A, (p. 501)
2. A, (p. 511-512)
3. C, (p. 489)
4. B, (p. 512)
5. B, (p. 499)
6. D, (p. 502)
7. A, (p. 514)
8. B, (p. 506)
9. B, (p. 519)
10. A, (p. 488)
11. D, (p. 523)
12. A, (p. 500)
13. D, (p. 509, 511)

14. D, (p. 501)
15. B, (p. 488)
16. A, (p. 490)
17. D, (p. 500)
18. B, (p. 504)
19. C, (p. 497)
20. A, (p. 489)
21. D, (p. 493)
22. A, (p. 508)
23. C, (p. 499)
24. A, (p. 506)
25. A, (p. 502)
26. B, (p. 490)

27. A, (p. 493)
28. B, (p. 503)
29. A, (p. 498)
30. C, (p. 516)
31. D, (p. 489)
32. B, (p. 496)
33. D, (p. 497)
34. A, (p. 506)
35. B, (p. 506)
36. B, (p. 511-512)
37. D, (p. 519)

THERAPIES

CHAPTER OVERVIEW

Psychotherapies may be classified as individual, group, insight, action, directive, nondirective, time-limited, positive, supportive, and combinations of these. Primitive and superstitious approaches to mental illness have included trepanning and demonology. More humane treatment began in 1793 with the work of Philippe Pinel in Paris.

Freudian psychoanalysis seeks to release repressed thoughts and emotions from the unconscious. Brief psychodynamic therapy has largely replaced traditional psychoanalysis.

Client-centered (or person-centered) therapy is a nondirective humanistic technique dedicated to creating an atmosphere of growth. Existential therapies focus on the meaning of life choices. Gestalt therapy attempts to rebuild thinking, feeling, and acting into connected wholes.

Behavior therapists use behavior modification techniques such as aversion therapy, systematic desensitization, operant shaping, extinction, and token economies. The tension-release method teaches people to recognize tensed muscles and learn to relax them. Of the various behavioral techniques, desensitization has been the most successful form of treatment to reduce fears, anxiety, and psychological pain.

Cognitive therapists attempt to change troublesome thought patterns. Major distortions in thinking include selective perception, overgeneralization, and all-or-nothing thinking. In rational-emotive behavior therapy, clients learn to recognize and challenge their own irrational beliefs.

Group therapies, such as psychodrama and family therapy, may be based on individual therapy methods or special group techniques. Sensitivity groups, encounter groups, and large group awareness trainings also try to promote constructive changes.

All psychotherapies offer a caring relationship, emotional rapport, a protected setting, catharsis, explanations for one's problems, a new perspective, and a chance to practice new behaviors. Many basic counseling skills underlie the success of therapies. Successful therapists may also need to overcome cultural barriers to be effective with people from diverse backgrounds. Because of the high cost of mental health services, future therapy may include short-term therapy; solution-focused; problem-solving approaches; master's-level practitioners; Internet services; telephone counseling; and self-help groups.

Three medical approaches to the treatment of psychological disorders are pharmacotherapy, electroconvulsive therapy, and psychosurgery. When using drugs as a form of treatment, patients must be aware of the trade-offs between the benefits and risks of drug use. Most professionals recommend using limited amounts of ECT with drug therapy to treat depression. When other therapeutic techniques are not effective at reducing mental illness symptoms, deep lesioning is considered.

Mental hospitalization can serve as a treatment for psychological disorders. Prolonged hospitalization has been discouraged by deinstitutionalization and by partial-hospitalization policies. Community mental health centers attempt to prevent mental health problems before they become serious.

Cognitive and behavioral techniques such as covert sensitization, thought stopping, covert reinforcement, and desensitization can aid self-management. In most communities, competent therapists can be located through public sources or by referrals.

LEARNING OBJECTIVES

To demonstrate mastery of this chapter, you should be able to:

1. Define "psychotherapy."

2. Describe each of the following approaches to therapy: a. individual therapy b. group therapy c. insight therapy d. action therapy e. directive therapy f. non-directive therapy g. time-limited therapy h. supportive therapy i. positive therapy

3. Evaluate what a person can expect as possible outcomes from psychotherapy.

4. Briefly describe the history of the treatment of psychological problems. Include in your description trepanning, demonology, exorcism, ergotism, and Philippe Pinel.

5. Explain why the first psychotherapy was developed.

6. List the four basic techniques used in psychoanalysis and explain their purpose.

7. Name and describe the therapy that is frequently used today instead of psychoanalysis.

8. Describe the criticism that helped prompt the switch, including the concept of spontaneous remission.

9. Contrast client-centered (humanistic) therapy and psychoanalysis.

10. Describe client-centered therapy, including the four conditions that should be maintained for successful therapy.

11. Explain the approach of existential therapy and compare and contrast it with client-centered therapy.

12. Name a key aspect of existential therapy.

13. Briefly describe Gestalt therapy, including its main emphasis.

14. Discuss the limitations of media and phone psychologists and describe what the APA recommends should be the extent of their activities.

15. Briefly describe the advantages and disadvantages of cybertherapy and describe how videoconferencing can avoid many of the limitations of nontraditional therapy.

16. Contrast the goal of behavior therapy with the goal of insight therapies.

17. Define "behavior modification" and state its basic assumption.

18. Explain the relationship of aversion therapy to classical conditioning.

19. Describe aversion therapy and explain how it can be used to stop smoking and drinking.

20. Explain how relaxation, reciprocal inhibition, and use of a hierarchy are combined to produce desensitization.

21. State what desensitization is used for and give an example of desensitization therapy or vicarious desensitization therapy.

The following objective is related to material in the "Discovering Psychology" section of the text.

22. Describe the tension-release method and how it is related to desensitization techniques.

23. Explain how virtual reality exposure may be used to treat phobias.

24. Very briefly describe eye-movement desensitization and reprocessing.

25. List and briefly describe the seven operant principles most frequently used by behavior therapists.

26. Explain how nonreinforcement and time out can be used to bring about extinction of a maladaptive behavior.

27. Describe a token economy, including its advantages and possible disadvantages. Include the terms "token" and "target behavior" in your description.

28. Describe what sets a cognitive therapist apart from a behavior therapist.

29. List and describe three thinking errors that underlie depression and explain what can be done to correct such thinking.

30. Describe rational-emotive behavior therapy.

31. List the three core ideas that serve as the basis of most irrational beliefs.

32. Describe the advantages of group therapy.

33. Briefly describe each of the following group therapies: a. psychodrama (include the terms "role-playing," "role reversal," and "mirror technique") b. family therapy c. group awareness training (include sensitivity groups, encounter groups, and large group awareness training)

34. Evaluate the effectiveness of encounter groups and sensitivity groups. Include the concept of the therapy placebo effect.

35. Discuss the effectiveness of psychotherapy.

36. Describe the rate at which typical doses of therapy help people improve.

37. List the eight goals of psychotherapy, state the four means used to accomplish the goals, briefly compare the strengths of the different psychotherapies, and describe future changes that will most likely occur in psychotherapy.

38. List and briefly describe the nine points or tips that can help a person when counseling a friend.

39. List and explain the seven characteristics of culturally skilled counselors.

40. Define "pharmacotherapy."

41. List and describe the three classes of drugs used to treat psychopathology.

42. Discuss the advantages and disadvantages of the use of pharmacotherapy in the treatment of psychosis.

43. Describe the risk-benefit controversy for drugs such as Clozaril and Risperdal.

44. Describe what is known about the uses and effectiveness of the following techniques in the treatment of psychosis: a. electroconvulsive therapy b. psychosurgery (include the term "deep lesioning")

45. Describe the role of hospitalization and partial hospitalization in the treatment of psychological disorders.

46. Explain what deinstitutionalization is and how halfway houses have attempted to help in the treatment of mental health.

47. Discuss the role of community mental health centers in mental health. Define the terms "crisis intervention" and "paraprofessionals."

48. Describe how covert sensitization, thought stopping, and covert reinforcement can be used to reduce unwanted behavior.

49. Give an example of how you can overcome a common fear or break a bad habit using the steps given for desensitization.

50. Describe four indicators that may signal the need for professional psychological help.

51. List six methods a person can use for finding a therapist. Describe how one can choose a psychotherapist.

52. Distinguish among paraprofessionals, peer counselors, and self-help groups.

53. Summarize what is known about the importance of the personal qualities of the therapist and the client for successful therapy.

54. List six psychotherapy danger signals.

RECITE AND REVIEW

MODULE 14.1

Survey Questions: How do psychotherapies differ? How did psychotherapy originate? Pages 528-530

Psychotherapy is any psychological technique used to facilitate [1] _____ changes in a person's personality, [2] _____ , or adjustment.

[3] _____ therapies seek to produce personal understanding. Action therapies try to directly change troublesome thoughts, feelings, or behaviors.

Directive therapists provide strong [4] _____ . Nondirective therapists assist but do not [5] _____ their clients.

Supportive therapies provide ongoing support rather than actively promoting personal [6] _____ .

Positive therapists seek to enhance [7] _____ growth by nurturing [8] _____ traits in individuals rather than trying to "fix" weakness.

Therapies may be conducted either individually or in groups, and they may be [9] _____ limited (restricted to a set number of sessions).

Primitive approaches to mental illness were often based on [10] _____ .

Trepanning involved boring a hole in the [11] _____ .

Demonology attributed mental disturbance to supernatural forces and prescribed [12] _____ as the cure.

In some instances, the actual cause of bizarre behavior may have been ergotism or [13] _____ fungus [14] _____ .

More humane treatment began in 1793 with the work of Philippe Pinel who created the first [15] _____ in Paris.

Sigmund Freud's psychoanalysis was the first formal [16] _____ .

Psychoanalysis was designed to treat cases of hysteria (physical symptoms without known [17] _____ causes).

Survey Question: Is Freudian psychoanalysis still used? Pages 530-531

Psychoanalysis seeks to release repressed thoughts, memories, and emotions from the [18] _____ and resolve [19] _____ conflicts.

The psychoanalyst uses [20] _____ association, [21] _____ analysis, and analysis of resistance and transference to reveal health-producing insights.

Freud believed that in order to uncover the individual's unconscious [22] _____ and feelings, a psychoanalyst must conduct [23] _____ analysis to discover the [24] _____ content that is expressed through the manifest content of a person's dream.

[25] _____ psychodynamic therapy (which relies on psychoanalytic theory but is brief and focused) is as effective as other major therapies.

Some critics have argued that traditional psychoanalysis may frequently receive credit for [26] _____ remissions of symptoms. However, psychoanalysis has been shown to be better than no treatment at all.

MODULE 14.2

Survey Question: What are the major humanistic therapies? Pages 533-536

[27] _____ therapies try to help people live up to their potential and to give tendencies for mental health to emerge.

Carl Rogers's client-centered (or [28] _____ -centered) therapy is nondirective and is dedicated to creating an atmosphere of [29] _____ .

In client-centered therapy, unconditional [30] _____ regard, [31] _____ (feeling what another is feeling), authenticity, and reflection are combined to give the client a chance to solve his or her own problems.

Existential therapies focus on the end result of the [32] _____ one makes in life.

Clients in existential therapy are encouraged through confrontation and encounter to exercise free [33] _____ , to take responsibility for their [34] _____ , and to find [35] _____ in their lives.

The goal of Gestalt therapy is to rebuild thinking, feeling, and acting into connected [36] _____ and to help clients break through emotional blocks.

Frederick Perls's Gestalt therapy emphasizes immediate [37] _____ of thoughts and feelings and discourages people from dwelling on what they ought to do.

Media psychologists, such as those found on the radio, are supposed to restrict themselves to [38] _____ listeners rather than actually doing [39] _____ .

Telephone therapists and cybertherapists working on the [40] _____ may or may not be competent. Even if they are, their effectiveness may be severely limited.

In an emerging approach called telehealth, [41] _____ is being done at a distance through the use of videoconferencing (two-way [42] _____ links).

MODULE 14.3

Survey Questions: What is behavior therapy? How is behavior therapy used to treat phobias, fears, and anxieties? Pages 537-541

Behavior therapists use various behavior modification techniques that apply [43] _____ principles to change human behavior.

Classical conditioning is a basic form of [44] _____ in which existing reflex responses are [45] _____ with new conditioned stimuli.

In aversion therapy, classical conditioning is used to associate maladaptive behavior with

[46] _____ or other aversive events in order to inhibit undesirable responses.

To be most effective, aversive [47] _____ must be response contingent (closely connected

with responses).

In desensitization, gradual [48] _____ and reciprocal inhibition break the link between fear

and particular situations.

Classical conditioning also underlies [49] _____ desensitization, a technique used to reduce

fears, phobias, and anxieties.

Typical steps in desensitization are construct a fear hierarchy, learn to produce total [50] _____ ,

and perform items on the hierarchy (from least to most disturbing).

Desensitization may be carried out in real settings or it may be done by vividly [51] _____

scenes from the fear hierarchy.

The tension-release method allows individuals, through practice, to [52] _____ their bodies'

tensed muscles and to learn to [53] _____ them on command.

Desensitization is also effective when it is administered vicariously, that is, when clients watch

[54] _____ perform the feared responses.

In a newly developed technique, virtual [55] _____ exposure is used to present

[56] _____ stimuli to patients undergoing desensitization.

Another new technique called eye-movement desensitization shows promise as a treatment for traumatic

[57] _____ and [58] _____ disorders.

MODULE 14.4

Survey Question: What role does reinforcement play in behavior therapy? Pages 543-545

Behavior modification also makes use of operant principles, such as positive reinforcement,

nonreinforcement, extinction, punishment, shaping, stimulus [59] _____ , and [60] _____

-out.

Nonreward can extinguish troublesome behaviors. Often this is done by simply identifying and eliminating

[61] _____ .

Time-out is an extinction technique in which attention and approval are withheld following undesirable

[62] _____ .

Time-out can also be done by [63] _____ a person from the setting in which misbehavior occurs so that it will not be reinforced.

Attention, approval, and concern are subtle [64] _____ that are effective at [65] _____ human behaviors.

To apply positive reinforcement and operant shaping, symbolic rewards known as tokens are often used.

Tokens allow [66] _____ reinforcement of selected target [67] _____ .

Full-scale use of [68] _____ in an institutional setting produces a token economy.

Toward the end of a token economy program, patients are shifted to social rewards such as recognition and [69] _____ .

Survey Question: Can therapy change thoughts and emotions? Pages 545-547

Cognitive therapy emphasizes changing [70] _____ patterns that underlie emotional or behavioral problems.

Aaron Beck's cognitive therapy for depression corrects major distortions in thinking, including [71] _____ perception, overgeneralization, and all-or-nothing [72] _____ .

The goals of cognitive therapy are to correct distorted thinking and/or teach improved coping [73] _____ .

In a variation of cognitive therapy called rational-emotive behavior therapy (REBT), clients learn to recognize and challenge their own irrational [74] _____ that lead to upsetting consequences.

Some [75] _____ beliefs that lead to conflicts are: I am worthless if I am not loved, I should be [76] _____ competent, I should [77] _____ on others who are stronger than I am, and it is easier for me to avoid difficulties than to face them.

MODULE 14.5

Survey Question: Can psychotherapy be done with groups of people? Pages 548-549

Group therapy may be a simple extension of [78] _____ methods or it may be based on techniques developed specifically for groups.

In psychodrama, individuals use [79] _____ -playing, [80] _____ reversals, and the mirror technique to gain insight into incidents resembling their real-life problems.

In family therapy, the family group is treated as a [81] _____ so that the entire [82] _____ system is changed for the better.

Although they are not literally [83] _____ , sensitivity groups and encounter groups attempt to encourage positive personality change.

In recent years, commercially offered large group awareness [84] _____ have become popular.

The therapeutic benefits of large group techniques are questionable and may reflect nothing more than a [85] _____ placebo effect.

Survey Question: What do various therapies have in common? Pages 549-553

After eight therapy sessions, [86] _____ percent of all patients showed an improvement, and after [87] _____ therapy sessions, 75 percent of all patients improved.

To alleviate personal problems, all psychotherapies offer a caring relationship and [88] _____ rapport in a protected [89] _____ .

All therapies encourage catharsis, and they provide explanations for the client's [90] _____ .

In addition, psychotherapy provides a new perspective and a chance to practice new [91] _____ .

Psychotherapy in the future may include short-term therapy, [92] _____ -focused approaches, [93] _____ -help groups, Internet services, [94] _____ counseling, paraprofessional, and master's-level practitioners.

Many basic [95] _____ skills are used in therapy. These include listening actively and helping to clarify the problem.

Effective therapists also focus on feelings and avoid giving unwanted [96] _____ .

It helps to accept the person's perspective, to reflect thoughts and feelings, and to be patient during [97] _____ .

Culturally skilled [98] _____ have the knowledge and skills needed to intervene successfully in the lives of clients from diverse cultural backgrounds.

In counseling it is important to use [99] _____ questions when possible and to maintain confidentiality.

Many [100] _____ barriers to effective counseling and therapy exist.

The culturally skilled counselor must be able to establish rapport with a person from a [101] _____ cultural background and adapt traditional theories and techniques to meet the needs of clients from non-European ethnic or racial groups.

Survey Question: How do psychiatrists treat psychological disorders? Pages 553-556

Three [102] _____ (bodily) approaches to treatment of psychosis are pharmacotherapy (use of

[103] _____), electroconvulsive therapy (ECT—brain shock for the treatment of depression), and

psychosurgery (surgical alteration of the [104] _____).

Pharmacotherapy is done with [105] _____ tranquilizers (antianxiety drugs), antipsychotics

(which reduce delusions and [106] _____), and antidepressants ([107] _____ elevators).

All psychiatric drugs involve a trade-off between [108] _____ and benefits.

Electroconvulsive therapy (ECT) and [109] _____ , especially prefrontal lobotomy, once received

great acclaim for their effectiveness but recently have [110] _____ support from professionals.

If psychosurgery is necessary, deep [111] _____ , where a small targeted area in the brain is

[112] _____ , is the preferred alternative to a lobotomy.

[113] _____ hospitalization is considered a form of treatment for mental disorders.

Prolonged hospitalization has been discouraged by deinstitutionalization (reduced use of commitment to

treat mental disorders) and by [114] _____ -hospitalization policies.

Halfway [115] _____ within the community can help people make the transition from a hospital

or institution to [116] _____ living.

Community mental health centers were created to help avoid or minimize [117] _____ .

Community mental health centers also have as their goal the prevention of mental health problems through

education, consultation, and [118] _____ intervention.

PSYCHOLOGY IN ACTION

Survey Question: How are behavioral principles applied to everyday problems? Pages 558-560

In covert sensitization, aversive [119] _____ are used to discourage unwanted behavior.

Thought stopping uses mild [120] _____ to prevent upsetting thoughts.

Covert reinforcement is a way to encourage desired [121] _____ by mental rehearsal.

Desensitization pairs [122] _____ with a hierarchy of upsetting images in order to lessen fears.

Survey Question: How could a person find professional help? Pages 560-562

In most communities, a competent and reputable therapist can usually be located through public sources of information or by a [123] _____ .

Practical considerations such as [124] _____ and qualifications enter into choosing a therapist. However, the therapist's personal characteristics are of equal importance.

Self-help [125] _____ , made up of people who share similar problems, can sometimes add valuable support to professional treatment.

CONNECTIONS

MODULE 14.1

1. _____ positive therapy
2. _____ trepanning
3. _____ exorcism
4. _____ ergotism
5. _____ Pinel
6. _____ free association
7. _____ Freud
8. _____ dream analysis
9. _____ transference
10. _____ spontaneous remission

a. tainted rye
b. old relationships
c. hysteria
d. waiting list control
e. Bicêtre
f. latent content
g. possession
h. enhanced personal strength
i. release of evil spirits
j. saying anything on mind

MODULE 14.2

1. _____ telephone therapy
2. _____ authenticity
3. _____ unconditional positive regards
4. _____ rephrasing
5. _____ distance therapy
6. _____ existentialist
7. _____ Rogers
8. _____ Gestalt therapy

a. reflection
b. client centered
c. no facades
d. being in the world
e. lack visual cues
f. telehealth
g. whole experiences
h. unshakable personal acceptance

MODULE 14.3

1. _____ behavior modification		a.	unlearned reaction
2. _____ unconditional response		b.	easing post-traumatic stress
3. _____ vicarious desensitization		c.	secondhand learning
4. _____ desensitization		d.	applied behavior analysis
5. _____ EMDR		e.	aversion therapy
6. _____ rapid smoking		f.	fear hierarchy

MODULE 14.4

1. _____ overgeneralization		a.	operant extinction
2. _____ cognitive therapy		b.	token economy
3. _____ time-out		c.	Aaron Beck
4. _____ REBT		d.	thinking error
5. _____ target behaviors		e.	irrational beliefs

MODULE 14.5

1. _____ psychodrama		a.	public education
2. _____ family therapy		b.	enhanced self-awareness
3. _____ sensitivity group		c.	emotional release
4. _____ encounter group		d.	positive imagery
5. _____ media psychologist		e.	shared problems
6. _____ therapeutic alliance		f.	systems approach
7. _____ catharsis		g.	aversive imagery
8. _____ covert sensitization		h.	role reversals
9. _____ covert reinforcement		i.	caring relationship
10. _____ self-help group		j.	intense interactions

CHECK YOUR MEMORY

MODULE 14.1

Survey Questions: How do psychotherapies differ? How did psychotherapy originate? Pages 528-530

1. A goal of positive therapy is to "fix" a person's weaknesses to enhance their personal strength.
   TRUE or FALSE

2. A particular psychotherapy could be both insight and action oriented.
   TRUE or FALSE

3. With the help of psychotherapy, chances of improvement are fairly good for phobias and low self-esteem.
   TRUE or FALSE

4 Psychotherapy is sometimes used to encourage personal growth for people who are already functioning well.
   TRUE or FALSE

5. Personal autonomy, a sense of identity, and feelings of personal worth are elements of mental health.
   TRUE or FALSE

6. Trepanning was really an excuse to kill people since none of the patients survived.
   TRUE or FALSE

7. Exorcism sometimes took the form of physical torture.
   TRUE or FALSE

8. Trepanning was the most common treatment for ergotism.
   TRUE or FALSE

9. Pinel was the first person to successfully treat ergotism.
   TRUE or FALSE

10. The problem Freud called hysteria is now called a somatoform disorder.
    TRUE or FALSE

Survey Question: Is Freudian psychoanalysis still used? Pages 530-531

11. During free association, patients try to remember the earliest events in their lives.
    TRUE or FALSE

12. Freud called transference the royal road to the unconscious.
    TRUE or FALSE

13. Using dream analysis, a therapist seeks to uncover the latent content or symbolic meaning of a person's dreams.
    TRUE or FALSE

14. The manifest content of a dream is its surface or visible meaning.
    TRUE or FALSE

15. In an analysis of resistance, the psychoanalyst tries to understand a client's resistance to forming satisfying relationships.
    TRUE or FALSE

16. Therapists use direct interviewing as part of brief psychodynamic therapy.
    TRUE or FALSE

17. If members of a waiting list control group improve at the same rate as people in therapy, it demonstrates that the therapy is effective.

    TRUE or FALSE

MODULE 14.2

Survey Question: What are the major humanistic therapies? Pages 533-536

18. Through client-centered therapy, Carl Rogers sought to explore unconscious thoughts and feelings.

    TRUE or FALSE

19. The client-centered therapist does not hesitate to react with shock, dismay, or disapproval to a client's inappropriate thoughts or feelings.

    TRUE or FALSE

20. In a sense, the person-centered therapist acts as a psychological mirror for clients.

    TRUE or FALSE

21. Existential therapy emphasizes our ability to freely make choices.

    TRUE or FALSE

22. According to the existentialists, our choices must be courageous.

    TRUE or FALSE

23. Existential therapy emphasizes the integration of fragmented experiences into connected wholes.

    TRUE or FALSE

24. Fritz Perls was an originator of telehealth.

    TRUE or FALSE

25. Gestalt therapy may be done individually or in a group.

    TRUE or FALSE

26. Gestalt therapists urge clients to intellectualize their feelings.

    TRUE or FALSE

27. The APA suggests that media psychologists should discuss only problems of a general nature.

    TRUE or FALSE

28. Under certain conditions, telephone therapy can be as successful as face-to-face therapy.

    TRUE or FALSE

29. The problem with doing therapy by videoconferencing is that facial expressions are not available to the therapist or the client.

    TRUE or FALSE

MODULE 14.3

Survey Questions: What is behavior therapy? How is behavior therapy used to treat phobias, fears, and anxieties? Pages 537-541

30. Behavior modification, or applied behavior analysis, uses classical and operant conditioning to directly alter human behavior.

TRUE or FALSE

31. Aversion therapy is based primarily on operant conditioning.

TRUE or FALSE

32. For many children, the sight of a hypodermic needle becomes a conditioned stimulus for fear because it is often followed by pain.

TRUE or FALSE

33. Rapid smoking creates an aversion because people must hyperventilate to smoke at the prescribed rate.

TRUE or FALSE

34. About one-half of all people who quit smoking begin again.

TRUE or FALSE

35. In aversion therapy for alcohol abuse, the delivery of shock must appear to be response-contingent to be most effective.

TRUE or FALSE

36. Poor generalization of conditioned aversions to situations outside of therapy can be a problem.

TRUE or FALSE

37. During desensitization, the steps of a hierarchy are used to produce deep relaxation.

TRUE or FALSE

38. Relaxation is the key ingredient of reciprocal inhibition.

TRUE or FALSE

39. Clients typically begin with the most disturbing item in a desensitization hierarchy.

TRUE or FALSE

40. Desensitization is most effective when people are directly exposed to feared stimuli.

TRUE or FALSE

41. The tension-release method is used to produce deep relaxation.

TRUE or FALSE

42. Live or filmed models are used in vicarious desensitization.

TRUE or FALSE

43. During eye-movement desensitization, clients concentrate on pleasant, calming images.

TRUE or FALSE

44. According to REBT, you would hold an irrational belief if you believe that you should depend on others who are stronger than you.
TRUE or FALSE

MODULE 14.4

Survey Question: What role does reinforcement play in behavior therapy? Pages 543-545

45. Operant punishment is basically the same thing as nonreinforcement.
TRUE or FALSE

46. Shaping involves reinforcing ever closer approximations to a desired response.
TRUE or FALSE

47. An undesirable response can be extinguished by reversing stimulus control.
TRUE or FALSE

48. Misbehavior tends to decrease when others ignore it.
TRUE or FALSE

49. To be effective, tokens must be tangible rewards, such as slips of paper or poker chips.
TRUE or FALSE

50. The value of tokens is based on the fact that they can be exchanged for other reinforcers.
TRUE or FALSE

51. A goal of token economies is to eventually switch patients to social reinforcers.
TRUE or FALSE

Survey Question: Can therapy change thoughts and emotions? Pages 545-547

52. Cognitive therapy is especially successful in treating depression.
TRUE or FALSE

53. Depressed persons tend to magnify the importance of events.
TRUE or FALSE

54. Cognitive therapy is as effective as drugs for treating many cases of depression.
TRUE or FALSE

55. Stress inoculation is a form of rational-emotive behavior therapy.
TRUE or FALSE

56. The A in the ABC analysis of REBT stands for anticipation.
TRUE or FALSE

57. The C in the ABC analysis of REBT stands for consequence.
TRUE or FALSE

MODULE 14.5

Survey Question: Can psychotherapy be done with groups of people? Pages 548-549

58. The mirror technique is the principal method used in family therapy.
TRUE or FALSE

59. Family therapists try to meet with the entire family unit during each session of therapy.
TRUE or FALSE

60. A trust walk is a typical sensitivity group exercise.
TRUE or FALSE

61. Large group awareness training has been known to create emotional crises where none existed before.
TRUE or FALSE

Survey Question: What do various therapies have in common? Pages 549-553

62. Half of all people who begin psychotherapy feel better after eight sessions.
TRUE or FALSE

63. Emotional rapport is a key feature of the therapeutic alliance.
TRUE or FALSE

64. Therapy gives clients a chance to practice new behaviors.
TRUE or FALSE

65. An increase in short-term therapy, telephone counseling, and self-help groups in the future is likely the result of the high cost of mental health services.
TRUE or FALSE

66. Competent counselors do not hesitate to criticize clients, place blame when it is deserved, and probe painful topics.
TRUE or FALSE

67. Why don't you . . . Yes, but . . . is a common game used to avoid taking responsibility in therapy.
TRUE or FALSE

68. Closed questions tend to be most helpful in counseling another person.
TRUE or FALSE

69. Cultural barriers to effective counseling include differences in language, social class, and nonverbal communication.
TRUE or FALSE

70. A necessary step toward becoming a culturally skilled counselor is to adopt the culture of your clients as your own.
TRUE or FALSE

Survey Question: How do psychiatrists treat psychological disorders? Pages 553-556

71. Major mental disorders are primarily treated with psychotherapy.
TRUE or FALSE

72. When used for long periods of time, major tranquilizers can cause a neurological disorder.
TRUE or FALSE

73. Two percent of all patients taking Clozaril suffer from a serious blood disease.
TRUE or FALSE

74. ECT treatments are usually given in a series of 20 to 30 sessions, occurring once a day.
TRUE or FALSE

75. ECT is most effective when used to treat depression.
TRUE or FALSE

76. To reduce a relapse, antidepressant drugs are recommended for patients with depression following ECT treatment.
TRUE or FALSE

77. The prefrontal lobotomy is the most commonly performed type of psychosurgery today.
TRUE or FALSE

78. In the approach known as partial hospitalization, patients live at home.
TRUE or FALSE

79. Admitting a person to a mental institution is the first step to treating the disorder.
TRUE or FALSE

80. Deinstitutionalization increased the number of homeless persons living in many communities.
TRUE or FALSE

81. Most halfway houses are located on the grounds of mental hospitals.
TRUE or FALSE

82. Crisis intervention is typically one of the services provided by community mental health centers.
TRUE or FALSE

83. Most people prefer to seek help from a professional doctor over a paraprofessional because of their approachability.
TRUE or FALSE

PSYCHOLOGY IN ACTION

Survey Question: How are behavioral principles applied to everyday problems? Pages 558-560

84. To do covert sensitization, you must first learn relaxation exercises.
    TRUE or FALSE

85. Disgusting images are used in thought stopping.
    TRUE or FALSE

86. Covert reinforcement should be visualized before performing steps in a four hierarchy.
    TRUE or FALSE

Survey Question: How could a person find professional help? Pages 560-562

87. Approximately 50 percent of all American households had someone who received mental health treatment.
    TRUE or FALSE

88. Significant changes in your work, relationships, or use of drugs or alcohol can be signs that you should seek professional help.
    TRUE or FALSE

89. Marital problems are the most common reason for seeing a mental health professional.
    TRUE or FALSE

90. For some problems, paraprofessional counselors and self-help groups are as effective as professional psychotherapy.
    TRUE or FALSE

91. All major types of psychotherapy are about equally successful.
    TRUE or FALSE

92. All therapists are equally qualified and successful at treating mental disorders.
    TRUE or FALSE

FINAL SURVEY AND REVIEW

MODULE 14.1

Survey Questions: How do psychotherapies differ? How did psychotherapy originate? Pages 528-530

[1] _____ is any psychological technique used to facilitate positive changes in a person's

[2] _____ , behavior, or adjustment.

Insight therapies seek to produce personal understanding. [3] _____ _____ therapies try to directly change troublesome thoughts, feelings, or behaviors.

[4] _____ therapists provide strong guidance. [5] _____ therapists assist but do not guide their clients.

[6] _____ therapies provide ongoing assistance rather than actively promoting personal change.

[7] _____ therapists seek to enhance personal growth by nurturing positive traits in individuals rather than trying to [8] _____ weakness.

Therapies may be conducted either [9] _____ or in [10] _____ , and they may be time [11] _____ (restricted to a set number of sessions).

[12] _____ approaches to mental illness were often based on superstition.

[13] _____ involved boring a hole in the skull.

[14] _____ attributed mental disturbance to supernatural forces and prescribed exorcism as the cure.

In some instances, the actual cause of bizarre behavior may have been [15] _____ , a type of [16] _____ poisoning.

More humane treatment began in 1793 with the work of Philippe [17] _____ who created the first mental hospital in [18] _____ .

Sigmund [19] _____ [20] _____ was the first formal psychotherapy.

Psychoanalysis was designed to treat cases of [21] _____ (physical symptoms without known physical causes).

Survey Question: Is Freudian psychoanalysis still used? Pages 530-531

Psychoanalysis seeks to release [22] _____ thoughts, memories, and emotions from the unconscious and resolve unconscious conflicts.

The psychoanalyst uses free [23] _____ , dream analysis, and analysis of [24] _____ and transference to reveal health-producing insights.

Freud believed that in order to uncover the individual's [25] _____ desires and feelings, a psychoanalyst must conduct [26] _____ analysis to discover the latent content of a person's dream.

Brief [27] _____ therapy (which relies on [28] _____ theory but is brief and focused) is as effective as other major therapies.

Some critics have argued that traditional psychoanalysis may frequently receive credit for spontaneous [29] _____ of symptoms. However, psychoanalysis has been shown to be better than no treatment at all.

MODULE 14.2

Survey Question: What are the major humanistic therapies? Pages 533-536

Humanistic therapies try to help people live up to their [30] _____ and to give tendencies for mental health to emerge.

Carl [31] _____ client-centered (or person-centered) therapy is [32] _____ and is dedicated to creating an atmosphere of growth.

In client-centered therapy, [33] _____ positive regard, empathy, authenticity, and [34] _____ (restating thoughts and feelings) are combined to give the client a chance to solve his or her own problems.

[35] _____ therapies focus on the end result of the choices one makes in life.

Clients in existential therapy are encouraged through [36] _____ and [37] _____ to exercise free will, to take responsibility for their choices, and to find meaning in their lives.

The goal of Perls's approach is to rebuild thinking, feeling, and acting into connected wholes and to help clients break through [38] _____ .

Frederick Perls's [39] _____ therapy emphasizes immediate awareness of thoughts and feelings and discourages people from dwelling on what they ought to do.

[40] _____ psychologists, such as those found on the radio, are supposed to restrict themselves to educating listeners rather than actually doing therapy.

Telephone therapists and [41] _____ working on the Internet may or may not be competent. Even if they are, their effectiveness may be severely limited.

In an emerging approach called [42] _____ , therapy is being done at a distance through the use of [43] _____ (two-way audio-video links).

MODULE 14.3

Survey Questions: What is behavior therapy? How is behavior therapy used to treat phobias, fears, and anxieties? Pages 537-541

[44] _____ therapists use various behavior [45] _____ techniques that apply learning principles to change human behavior.

[46] _____ conditioning is a basic form of learning in which existing [47] _____
responses are associated with new conditioned stimuli.

In [48] _____ therapy, classical conditioning is used to associate maladaptive behavior with pain
or other unpleasant events in order to inhibit undesirable responses.

To be most effective, aversive stimuli must be [49] _____ (closely connected with responses).

In this approach, gradual adaptation and reciprocal [50] _____ break the link between fear
and particular situations.

Classical conditioning also underlies systematic [51] _____ , a technique used to reduce fears,
phobias, and anxieties.

Typical steps are construct a fear [52] _____ , learn to produce total relaxation, and perform
items on the [53] _____ (from least to most disturbing).

Desensitization may be carried out in real settings or it may be done by vividly imagining scenes from the
[54] _____ .

The [55] _____ -release method allows individuals, through practice, to recognize their bodies'
tensed [56] _____ and to learn to relax them on command.

Desensitization is also effective when it is administered [57] _____ , that is, when clients watch
models perform the feared responses.

In a newly developed technique, [58] _____ reality [59] _____ is used to present
fear stimuli to patients undergoing desensitization.

Another new technique called [60] _____ desensitization shows promise as a treatment for
traumatic memories and stress disorders.

MODULE 14.4

Survey Question: What role does reinforcement play in behavior therapy? Pages 543-545

Behavior modification also makes use of [61] _____ principles, such as positive reinforcement,
non-reinforcement, [62] _____ (eliminating responses), punishment, [63] _____
(molding responses), stimulus control, and time-out.

[64] _____ [65] _____ can extinguish troublesome behaviors. Often this is done by
simply identifying and eliminating reinforcers.

Time-out is an [66] _____ technique in which attention and approval are withheld following
undesirable responses.

Time-out can also be done by removing a person from the [67] _____ in which misbehavior occurs so that it will not be [68] _____ .

Attention, approval, and concern are subtle [69] _____ that are effective at maintaining human [70] _____ .

To apply positive reinforcement and operant shaping, symbolic rewards known as [71] _____ are often used. These allow immediate reinforcement of selected [72] _____ behaviors.

Full-scale use of symbolic rewards in an institutional setting produces a [73] _____ .

Toward the end of such programs, patients are shifted to [74] _____ rewards such as recognition and approval.

Survey Question: Can therapy change thoughts and emotions? Pages 545-547

[75] _____ therapy emphasizes changing thinking patterns that underlie emotional or behavioral problems.

Its goals are to correct distorted thinking and/or teach improved [76] _____ skills.

Aaron [77] _____ therapy for depression corrects major distortions in thinking, including selective perception, [78] _____ , and all-or-nothing thinking.

In a variation called [79] _____ therapy (REBT), clients learn to recognize and challenge their own irrational beliefs that lead to upsetting consequences.

Some irrational [80] _____ that lead to conflicts are: I am [81] _____ if I am not loved, I should be completely competent, I should [82] _____ on others who are stronger than I am, and it is easier for me to avoid difficulties than to face them.

MODULE 14.5

Survey Question: Can psychotherapy be done with groups of people? Pages 548-549

[83] _____ therapy may be a simple extension of individual methods or it may be based on techniques developed specifically for [84] _____ .

In [85] _____ , individuals use role-playing, role [86] _____ , and the mirror technique to gain insight into incidents resembling real-life problems.

In [87] _____ therapy, the [88] _____ group is treated as a unit so that the entire family system is changed for the better.

Although they are not literally psychotherapies, sensitivity groups and [89] _____ groups attempt to encourage positive personality change.

In recent years, commercially offered large group [90] _____ trainings have become popular.

The therapeutic benefits of large group techniques are questionable and may reflect nothing more than a therapy [91] _____ effect.

Survey Question: What do various therapies have in common? Pages 549-553

After [92] _____ therapy sessions, 50 percent of all patients showed an improvement, and after 26 therapy sessions, [93] _____ percent of all patients improved.

To alleviate personal problems, all psychotherapies offer a caring relationship and emotional [94] _____ in a [95] _____ setting.

All therapies encourage [96] _____ (emotional release) and they provide explanations for the client's problems.

In addition, psychotherapy provides a new [97] _____ and a chance to practice new behaviors.

[98] _____ in the future may include [99] _____ -term therapy, solution-focused approaches, self-help groups, [100] _____ services, telephone counseling, paraprofessional, and [101] _____ -level practitioners.

Many basic counseling skills are used in therapy. These include listening [102] _____ and helping to [103] _____ the problem.

Effective therapists also focus on [104] _____ and avoid giving unwanted advice.

It helps to accept the person's [105] _____ , to [106] _____ thoughts and feelings, and to be patient during silences.

In counseling it is important to use open questions when possible and to maintain [107] _____ .

Many cultural [108] _____ to effective counseling and therapy exist.

[109] _____ counselors have the knowledge and skills needed to intervene successfully in the lives of clients from diverse cultural backgrounds.

The aware counselor must be able to establish [110] _____ with a person from a different cultural background and [111] _____ traditional theories and techniques to meet the needs of clients from non-European ethnic or racial groups.

Survey Question: How do psychiatrists treat psychological disorders? Pages 553-556

Three somatic approaches to treatment of psychosis are [112] _____ (use of drugs),

[113] _____ therapy (ECT), and psychosurgery.

Pharmacotherapy is done with minor tranquilizers (antianxiety drugs), [114] _____ (which control

delusions and hallucinations), and [115] _____ (mood elevators).

All psychiatric drugs involve a trade-off between risks and [116] _____ .

[117] _____ therapy (ECT) and psychosurgery, especially prefrontal lobotomy, once received

great acclaim for their [118] _____ but recently have lost support from professionals.

If psychosurgery is necessary, [119] _____ , where a small targeted area in the brain is destroyed,

is the preferred alternative to a lobotomy.

Psychiatric [120] _____ is considered a form of treatment for mental [121] _____ .

Prolonged hospitalization has been discouraged by [122] _____ (reduced use of commitment to

treat mental disorders) and by partial-hospitalization policies.

[123] _____ houses within the community can help people make the transition from a hospital or

institution to independent living.

[124] _____ health centers were created to help avoid or minimize hospitalization.

These centers also have as their goal the [125] _____ of mental health problems through

education, consultation, and crisis [126] _____ .

PSYCHOLOGY IN ACTION

Survey Question: How are behavioral principles applied to everyday problems? Pages 558-560

In [127] _____ sensitization, aversive images are used to discourage unwanted behavior.

[128] _____ uses mild punishment to prevent upsetting thoughts.

Covert [129] _____ is a way to encourage desired responses by mental rehearsal.

[130] _____ pairs relaxation with a hierarchy of upsetting images in order to lessen fears.

Survey Question: How could a person find professional help? Pages 560-562

In most communities, a [131] _____ and reputable therapist can usually be located through public

sources of information or by a referral.

Practical considerations such as cost and qualifications enter into choosing a therapist. However, the therapist's [132] _____ are of equal importance.

[133] _____ groups, made up of people who share similar [134] _____ , can sometimes add valuable support to professional treatment.

MASTERY TEST

1. To demonstrate that spontaneous remissions are occurring, you could use a
   a. patient-defined hierarchy
   b. waiting list control group
   c. target behavior group
   d. short-term dynamic correlation

2. In desensitization, relaxation is induced to block fear, a process known as
   a. systematic adaptation
   b. vicarious opposition
   c. stimulus control
   d. reciprocal inhibition

3. Role reversals and the mirror technique are methods of
   a. psychodrama
   b. person-centered therapy
   c. family therapy
   d. brief psychodynamic therapy

4. One thing that both trepanning and exorcism have in common is that both were used
   a. to treat ergotism
   b. by Pinel in the Bicêtre Asylum
   c. to remove spirits
   d. to treat cases of hysteria

5. Unconditional positive regard is a concept particularly associated with
   a. Beck
   b. Frankl
   c. Perls
   d. Rogers

6. Many of the claimed benefits of large group awareness trainings appear to represent a therapy
   a. remission
   b. education
   c. placebo
   d. transference

7. Personal change is LEAST likely to be the goal of
   a. supportive therapy
   b. action therapy
   c. desensitization
   d. humanistic therapy

8. Inducing seizures is a standard part of using
   a. Gestalt therapy
   b. antidepressants
   c. ECT
   d. cybertherapy

9. Which counseling behavior does not belong with the others listed here?
   a. paraphrasing
   b. judging
   c. reflecting
   d. active listening

10. In psychoanalysis, the process most directly opposite to free association is
    a. resistance
    b. transference
    c. symbolization
    d. remission

11. Identification of target behaviors is an important step in designing
    a. a desensitization hierarchy
    b. activating stimuli
    c. token economies
    d. encounter groups

12. A person who wants to lose weight looks at a dessert and visualizes maggots crawling all over it. The person is obviously using
    a. systematic adaptation
    b. covert sensitization
    c. stress inoculation
    d. systematic desensitization

13. Which of the following is NOT a humanistic therapy?
    a. client-centered
    b. Gestalt
    c. existential
    d. cognitive

14. Not many emergency room doctors drive without using their seat belts. This observation helps explain the effectiveness of
    a. systematic desensitization
    b. aversion therapy
    c. covert reinforcement
    d. the mirror technique

15. Telephone counselors have little chance of using which element of effective psychotherapy?
    a. empathy
    b. nondirective reflection
    c. the therapeutic alliance
    d. accepting the person's frame of reference

16. Which of the following is a self-management technique?
    a. thought stopping
    b. vicarious reality exposure
    c. REBT
    d. EMDR

17. A good example of a nondirective insight therapy is _____ therapy.
    a. client-centered
    b. Gestalt
    c. psychoanalytic
    d. brief psychodynamic

18. Which statement about psychotherapy is true?
    a. Most therapists are equally successful.
    b. Most techniques are equally successful.
    c. Therapists and clients need not agree about the goals of therapy.
    d. Effective therapists instruct their clients not to discuss their therapy with anyone else.

19. Analysis of resistances and transferences is a standard feature of
    a. client-centered therapy
    b. Gestalt therapy
    c. REBT
    d. psychoanalysis

20. Both classical and operant conditioning are the basis for
    a. desensitization
    b. token economies
    c. behavior therapy
    d. aversion therapy

21. Rational-emotive behavior therapy is best described as
    a. insight, nondirective, individual
    b. insight, supportive, individual
    c. action, supportive, group
    d. action, directive, individual

22. Deep lesioning is a form of
    a. ECT
    b. psychosurgery
    c. pharmacotherapy
    d. PET

23. Identifying and removing rewards is a behavioral technique designed to bring about
    a. operant shaping
    b. extinction
    c. respondent aversion
    d. token inhibition

24. Culturally skilled counselors must be aware of their own cultural backgrounds as well as
    a. the percentage of ethnic populations in the community
    b. that of their clients
    c. the importance of maintaining confidentiality
    d. the life goals of minorities

25. A behavioral therapist would treat acrophobia with
    a. desensitization
    b. aversion therapy
    c. covert sensitization
    d. cybertherapy

26. Which technique most closely relates to the idea of nondirective therapy?
    a. confrontation
    b. dream analysis
    c. role reversal
    d. reflection

27. Fifty percent of psychotherapy patients say they feel better after the first _____ sessions.
    a. 4
    b. 8
    c. 12
    d. 20

28. Overgeneralization is a thinking error that contributes to
    a. depression
    b. somatization
    c. phobias
    d. emotional reprocessing

29. Death, freedom, and meaning are special concerns of
    a. REBT
    b. cognitive therapy
    c. existential therapy
    d. psychodrama

30. An intense awareness of present experience and breaking through emotional impasses is the heart of
    a. action therapy
    b. Gestalt therapy
    c. time-limited therapy
    d. REBT

31. The ABCs of REBT stand for
    a. anticipation, behavior, conduct
    b. action, behavior, conflict
    c. activating experience, belief, consequence
    d. anticipation, belief, congruent experience

32. Which of the following in NOT a "distance therapy"?
    a. REBT
    b. telephone therapy
    c. cybertherapy
    d. telehealth

33. Virtual reality exposure is a type of
    a. psychodrama
    b. ECT therapy
    c. cognitive therapy
    d. desensitization

34. ECT is most often used to treat
    a. psychosis
    b. anxiety
    c. hysteria
    d. depression

35. Which of the following is most often associated with community mental health programs?
    a. pharmacotherapy
    h. covert reinforcement
    c. crisis intervention
    d. REBT

36. Which therapy's main purpose is to enhance people's personal strengths rather than try to fix their weakness?
    a. supportive
    b. positive
    c. insight
    d. directive

37. An element of positive mental health that therapists seek to promote is
    a. dependency on therapist
    b. a sense of identity
    c. personal autonomy and independence
    d. both b and c

38. Which theory relies on dream analysis to uncover the unconscious roots of neurosis?
    a. existential
    b. psychoanalytic
    c. client-centered
    d. telehealth

39. _____ has been one of the most successful behavioral therapies for reducing fears, anxieties, and psychological pains.
    a. Vicarious desensitization
    b. Virtual reality exposure
    c. Eye-movement desensitization
    d. Desensitization

40. Research suggests that, as a solution to handling people with mental illness, mental hospitals in our society are being replaced by
    a. a full-time live-in nurse
    b. placing them in jail
    c. medicating the mentally ill until they reach 65 years old
    d. allowing the mentally ill to take care of themselves

41. "There is always a perfect solution to human problems and it is awful if this solution is not found" is a typical _____ statement.
    a. irrational belief
    b. self-awareness
    c. health-promoting
    d. response-contingent

42. Experts predict that, in the near future, traditional forms of psychotherapy will be replaced by short-term, solution-focused, telephone, and self-help group therapy is a reflection of
    a. the lack of time available in people's busy life to seek mental health services
    b. fewer people needing mental health services
    c. societal pressures to reduce costs in mental health services
    d. people being afraid to reveal their mental illness

SOLUTIONS

RECITE AND REVIEW

MODULE 14.1

1. positive
2. behavior
3. Insight
4. guidance
5. guide
6. change
7. personal

8. positive
9. time
10. superstition
11. skull
12. exorcism
13. ergot
14. poisoning

15. mental hospital
16. psychotherapy
17. physical

18. unconscious
19. unconscious
20. free

21. dream
22. desires
23. dream

24. latent
25. Brief
26. spontaneous

MODULE 14.2

27. Humanistic
28. person
29. growth
30. positive
31. empathy
32. choices

33. will
34. choices
35. meaning
36. wholes
37. awareness
38. educating

39. therapy
40. Internet
41. therapy
42. audio-video

MODULE 14.3

43. learning
44. learning
45. associated
46. pain
47. stimuli
48. adaptation

49. systematic
50. relaxation
51. imagining
52. recognize
53. relax
54. models

55. reality
56. fear
57. memories
58. stress

MODULE 14.4

59. control
60. time
61. reinforcers
62. responses

63. removing
64. reinforcers
65. maintaining
66. immediate

67. behaviors
68. tokens
69. approval

70. thinking
71. selective
72. thinking

73. skills
74. beliefs
75. irrational

76. completely
77. depend

MODULE 14.5

78. individual
79. role
80. role

81. unit
82. family
83. psychotherapies

84. trainings
85. therapy

86. 50
87. 26
88. emotional
89. setting
90. problems
91. behaviors

92. solution
93. self
94. telephone
95. counseling
96. advice
97. silences

98. counselors
99. open
100. cultural
101. different

102. somatic
103. drugs
104. brain
105. minor
106. hallucinations
107. mood
108. risks

109. psychosurgery
110. lost
111. lesioning
112. destroyed
113. Mental or (Psychiatric)
114. partial
115. houses

116. independent
117. hospitalization
118. crisis

PSYCHOLOGY IN ACTION

119. images
120. punishment

121. responses
122. relaxation

123. referral

124. cost (or fees)

125. groups

CONNECTIONS

MODULE 14.1

1. h
2. i
3. g
4. a

5. e
6. j
7. c
8. f

9. b
10. d

MODULE 14.2

1. e
2. c
3. h

4. a
5. f
6. d

7. b
8. g

MODULE 14.3

1. d

2. a   4. f   6. e
3. c   5. b

MODULE 14.4

1. d   3. a   5. b
2. c   4. e

MODULE 14.5

1. h   5. a   9. d
2. f   6. i   10. e
3. b   7. c
4. j   8. g

CHECK YOUR MEMORY

MODULE 14.1

1. F   5. T   9. F
2. T   6. F   10. T
3. T   7. T
4. T   8. F

11. F   14. F   17. F
12. F   15. F
13. T   16. T

MODULE 14.2

18. F   22. T   26. F
19. F   23. F   27. T
20. T   24. F   28. T
21. T   25. T   29. F

MODULE 14.3

30. T   35. T   40. T
31. F   36. T   41. T
32. T   37. F   42. T
33. F   38. T   43. F
34. T   39. F   44. T

MODULE 14.4

45. F   48. T   51. T
46. T   49. F
47. F   50. T

| 52. T | 54. T | 56. F |
| 53. T | 55. F | 57. T |

MODULE 14.5

| 58. F | 60. T | |
| 59. F | 61. T | |

62. T	65. T	68. F
63. T	66. F	69. T
64. T	67. T	70. F

71. F	76. T	81. F
72. T	77. F	82. T
73. T	78. T	83. F
74. F	79. F	
75. T	80. T	

PSYCHOLOGY IN ACTION

| 84. F | 85. F | 86. F |

| 87. T | 89. F | 91. T |
| 88. T | 90. T | 92. F |

FINAL SURVEY AND REVIEW

MODULE 14.1

1. Psychotherapy	9. individually	17. Pinel
2. personality	10. groups	18. Paris
3. Action	11. limited	19. Freud's
4. Directive	12. Primitive	20. psychoanalysis
5. Nondirective	13. Trepanning	21. hysteria
6. Supportive	14. Demonology	
7. Positive	15. ergotism	
8. "fix"	16. fungus	

22. repressed

23. association
24. resistance
25. unconscious

26. dream
27. psychodynamic
28. psychoanalytic

29. remissions

MODULE 14.2

30. potential
31. Rogers's
32. nondirective
33. unconditional
34. reflection
35. Existential

36. confrontation
37. encounter
38. emotional blocks
39. Gestalt
40. Media
41. cybertherapists

42. telehealth
43. videoconferencing

MODULE 14.3

44. Behavior
45. modification
46. Classical
47. reflex
48. aversion
49. response contingent
50. inhibition

51. desensitization
52. hierarchy
53. hierarchy
54. fear hierarchy
55. tension
56. muscles
57. vicariously

58. virtual
59. exposure
60. eye-movement

MODULE 14.4

61. operant
62. extinction
63. shaping
64. Nonreward
65. (or nonreinforcement)
66. extinction

67. setting
68. reinforced
69. reinforcers
70. behaviors
71. tokens
72. target

73. token economy
74. social

75. Cognitive
76. coping
77. Beck's

78. overgeneralization
79. rational-emotive behavior
80. beliefs

81. worthless
82. depend

MODULE 14.5

83. Group
84. groups
85. psychodrama

86. reversals
87. family
88. family

89. encounter
90. awareness
91. placebo

92. eight
93. 75
94. rapport
95. protected
96. catharsis

97. perspective
98. Psychotherapy
99. short
100. Internet
101. master's

102. actively
103. clarify
104. feelings
105. perspective
106. reflect

107. confidentiality
108. barriers
109. Culturally skilled
110. rapport
111. adapt

112. pharmacotherapy
113. electroconvulsive
114. antipsychotics
115. antidepressants
116. benefits
117. Electroconvulsive
118. effectiveness
119. deep lesioning
120. hospitalization
121. disorders
122. deinstitutionalization
123. Halfway
124. Community mental
125. prevention
126. intervention

PSYCHOLOGY IN ACTION

127. covert
128. Thought stopping
129. reinforcement
130. Desensitization

131. competent
132. personal characteristics
133. Self-help
134. problems

MASTERY TEST

1. B, (p. 531)
2. D, (p. 539)
3. A, (p. 548)
4. C, (p. 529)
5. D, (p. 533)
6. C, (p. 549)
7. A, (p. 528)
8. C, (p. 554)
9. B, (p. 551-553)
10. A, (p. 530)
11. C, (p. 544)
12. B, (p. 558)
13. D, (p. 545)
14. B, (p. 537)
15. C, (p. 550)

16. A, (p. 559)
17. A, (p. 528, 533, 550)
18. B, (p. 562)
19. D, (p. 530-531)
20. C, (p. 537)
21. D, (p. 528, 546, 550)
22. B, (p. 555)
23. B, (p. 543)
24. B, (p. 552)
25. A, (p. 539)
26. D, (p. 528, 533)
27. B, (p. 549-550)
28. A, (p. 545)
29. C, (p. 534)
30. B, (p. 534)

31. C, (p. 546)
32. A, (p. 534-536)
33. D, (p. 539-540)
34. D, (p. 554)
35. C, (p. 556)
36. B, (p. 528)
37. D, (p. 528)
38. B, (p. 530)
39. D, (p. 540)
40. B, (p. 556)
41. A, (p. 546)
42. C, (p. 551)

GENDER AND SEXUALITY

CHAPTER OVERVIEW

A person's sex is determined by a combination of genetic sex, gonadal sex, hormonal sex, genital sex, and gender identity. The development of primary and secondary sexual characteristics is influenced by androgens and estrogens. Hormonal imbalance before birth may cause a person to develop ambiguous sexual anatomy or become an intersexual. Corrective surgery can be performed to give the genitals a male or female appearance. Prenatal hormones may also exert a biological biasing effect that combines with social factors to influence psychosexual development.

On most psychological dimensions, men and women are more alike than they are different. Social factors are especially apparent in learned gender identity and the effects of gender roles. Gender roles often lead to gender role stereotypes that can be seen in the amount of money males and females earn. When females violate gender norms by performing tasks that are traditionally male, they are less liked. Gender role socialization accounts for most observed male/female differences beginning at the age of three when children participate in sex-segregated play. Psychological androgyny as defined by BSRI is related to greater personal adaptability.

"Normal" sexual behavior is defined differently by various cultures. There is little difference in male and female sexual responsiveness. The difference lies in the subjective feelings of arousal in which females tend to focus more on their emotional responses to erotic cues. Contrary to belief, high amounts of alcohol consumption and many drugs actually decrease sexual desire, arousal, pleasure, and performance.

Sexual orientation refers to whether a person is heterosexual, homosexual, or bisexual. A combination of heredity, biological, social, and psychological influences combine to produce one's sexual orientation. Some theorists believe that evolutionarily, homosexuality may have developed to reduce competition among men for female mates.

Human sexual response can be divided into four phases: (1) excitement, (2) plateau, (3) orgasm, and (4) resolution, which apply to both males and females.

Atypical sexual behavior can produce troubling sexual disorders such as pedophilia and fetishism. Such disorders are called paraphilias.

Attitudes toward sexual behavior have grown more liberal, but actual changes in behavior have been more gradual. People who are sexually active, even with one person, may increase their risk of getting STDs, including the HIV virus, if they do not practice safe sex and have indirect sex with others through their partner's indiscretion.

The principal problems in sexual adjustment are desire disorders, arousal disorders, orgasm disorders, and sexual pain disorders. Behavioral methods and counseling techniques can alleviate each problem. However, communication skills that foster and maintain intimacy are the real key to successful relationships.

LEARNING OBJECTIVES

To demonstrate mastery of this chapter, you should be able to:

1. Distinguish between the terms "sex" and "gender."

2. Differentiate primary from secondary sex characteristics and state (in general) what causes them.

3. Define or describe the following terms or concepts: a. menarche b. ovulation c. menopause d. gonads e. estrogen f. androgens g. testosterone

4. List and describe the five dimensions of sex.

5. Explain how a person's sex develops. Include in your discussion a description of these conditions: a. androgen insensitivity b. intersexual person c. androgenital syndrome d. biological biasing effect e. X chromosomes and Y chromosomes

6. Differentiate gender identity from gender role and explain how gender identity is formed.

7. Describe the relationship between sex and intelligence.

8. Discuss whether there are universal psychological differences between males and females.

9. Define "gender role stereotypes."

10. Discuss how these stereotypes ignore the "diversity of humanity."

The following objective is related to the material in the "Discovering Psychology" section of the text.

11. Discuss why women who are successful at "men's work" are considered less likable.

12. Describe the effects of socialization on gender roles and include a discussion of instru-mental and expressive behaviors.

13. Discuss the concept of androgyny and its relationship to masculinity, femininity, and adaptability.

14. Describe the development of sexual behavior in humans and show how cultural norms influence that development. Define the term "erogenous zones."

15. Explain the concept of a sexual script.

16. Discuss the differences between males and females and their degree of arousal to erotic stimuli.

17. Explain what causes increases in sex drives in males and females.

18. Describe the effects of castration, sterilization, and aging on the sex drive.

19. Discuss the frequency, importance, normality, and acceptability of masturbation.

20. Describe the factors that determine one's sexual orientation.

21. Describe the effect of heredity and hormones on one's sexual orientation.

22. Discuss homosexuality in terms of incidence, acceptability, psychological normality, and when homosexuals develop their sexual orientation.

23. Define the terms "homophobia" and "heterosexism" and describe their significance to homosexuals.

24. List in order and briefly describe the four phases of sexual response in women and men.

25. Discuss the debate concerning possible differences between vaginal and clitoral orgasms and how the issue has been resolved

26. Describe what is known concerning gender differences in sexual response styles in these two areas: rate of passage through the sexual phases and sexual responsiveness.

27. Explain the difference between public and private standards of sexual behavior.

28. Explain what sets true sexual deviations apart from other sexual activity.

29. Define "paraphilia" and list and define eight paraphilias.

30. Describe exhibitionism, including who the offenders are, why they do it, and how one's reactions may encourage them.

31. Describe child molestation, including who does it, what the offenders are like, and the factors that affect the seriousness of the molestation.

32. List seven signs that indicate possible child molestation.

32. Briefly describe ways that children can be taught to protect themselves against molestation.

33. List six tactics of child molesters.

34. Briefly discuss the damaging effects of child molestation on the victim.

35. List the two characteristics that emerge in the picture of sexual deviance.

36. List or describe four changes that have taken place in sexual attitudes or behavior that lead some people to label the differences a sexual revolution.

37. Summarize the current status of the sexual revolution. Explain how your answer reflects on the position of the double standard in our society.

38. Describe how the changing sexual attitudes and values of the society interact with one's personal freedom. Include the term "acquaintance rape."

39. Describe the research demonstrating the relationship between gender role stereotyping and rape.

40. List and discuss five rape myths.

41. Explain why rape is not viewed by experts as primarily a sexual act.

42. Briefly describe what is currently known about the factors affecting the spread of AIDS. Include in your answer a discussion of "at risk" groups, risky behaviors, and the impact that AIDS has on sexual practices.

43. Describe the following sexual problems, including the nature, cause, and treatment of each: a. desire disorders i. hypoactive sexual desire ii. sexual aversion b. arousal disorders i. male erectile disorder (include the term psychogenic) ii. female sexual arousal disorder c. orgasm disorders i. female orgasmic disorder ii. male orgasmic disorder iii. premature ejaculation d. sexual pain disorders i. dyspareunia ii. vaginismus

44. Explain what is meant by referring to sex as a form of communication within a relationship.

45. List the four elements of a healthy sexual relationship.

46. List seven techniques that can be used to facilitate healthy communication in a relationship.

RECITE AND REVIEW

MODULE 15.1

Survey Questions: What are the basic dimensions of sex? How does one's sense of maleness or femaleness develop? Pages 566-572

Physical differences between males and females can be divided into [1] _____ and

[2] _____ sexual characteristics.

Primary sexual characteristics are the [3] _____ and internal reproductive organs.

Secondary sexual characteristics are bodily features such as breast development, body [4] _____

, and facial hair.

Reproductive maturity in females is signaled by menarche (the onset of [5] _____). Soon after,

ovulation (the release of [6] _____ , or eggs) begins.

The development of sexual characteristics is influenced by androgens ([7] _____ sex hormones)

and estrogens ([8] _____ sex hormones) secreted by the gonads (sex [9] _____).

A person's sex can be broken down into genetic sex, gonadal sex, [10] _____ , sex, genital

sex, and [11] _____ identity.

Sexual development begins with [12] _____ sex (XX or XY chromosomes). Two X chromosomes

normally produce a [13] _____ ; an X plus a Y produces a [14] _____ .

During prenatal sexual development, the presence of testosterone produces [15] _____ genitals;

an absence of testosterone produces [16] _____ genitals.

Androgen insensitivity, exposure to progestin, and the androgenital [17] _____ result in

[18] _____ ambiguities called hermaphroditism.

Corrective [19] _____ with hormone therapy can alter the genital [20] _____ and secondary sex characteristics for intersexuals (children with [21] _____ sexual anatomy) to either male or female. However, these factors alone do not determine gender identity; socialization is also important.

Social factors are especially apparent in learned gender identity (a private sense of [22] _____ or [23] _____) and the effect of gender roles (patterns of behavior defined as male or female within a particular culture).

Gender identity, which is based to a large extent on labeling, usually becomes stable by age [24] _____ or [25] _____ years.

Many researchers believe that prenatal [26] _____ can exert a biological biasing [27] _____ that combines with social factors present after birth to influence psychosexual development.

On most psychological dimensions, men and women are more [28] _____ than they are [29] _____ .

Gender roles contribute to the development of [30] _____ stereotypes (oversimplified beliefs about the nature of men and women) that often distort perceptions about the kinds of occupations for which men and women are suited.

As a result of gender role [31] _____ , for every $1.00 men earn in business, academia, medicine, law, sports, and politics, white [32] _____ earn $.75, black [33] _____ earn $.67, and Latino women earn $.54.

Another effect of gender role [34] _____ is that women are [35] _____ liked by their peers for violating [36] _____ norms, such as holding a job that as been defined as traditionally "male."

Culture determines the gender [37] _____ of males and females in each society.

[38] _____ socialization (learning gender roles) seems to account for most observed male/female differences.

Parents tend to encourage [39] _____ in instrumental behaviors and [40] _____ in expressive behaviors.

By age [41] _____ , [42] _____ -segregated playing can be seen in boys and girls: Boys play [43] _____ games that focus on superheroes, and girls play [44] _____ games that focus on house-related activities.

Survey Questions: What is psychological androgyny (and is it contagious)? Pages 572-573

Androgyny is measured with the *Bem* [45] _____ *Inventory* (BSRI).

Research conducted by Sandra Bem indicates that roughly one-third of all persons are androgynous (they possess both [46] _____ and [47] _____ traits).

Being [48] _____ means that a person is independent and assertive.

Being [49] _____ means that a person is nurturant and interpersonally oriented.

Psychological [50] _____ appears related to greater adaptability or flexibility in behavior.

MODULE 15.2

Survey Question: What are the most typical patterns of human sexual behavior? Pages 575-579

Sexual behavior, including orgasm (sexual [51] _____), is apparent soon after birth and expressed in various ways throughout life.

Sexual arousal is related to stimulation of the body's erogenous zones (areas that produce erotic [52] _____), but cognitive elements such as [53] _____ and images are equally important.

"Normal" sexual behavior is defined differently by various [54] _____ . Also, each person uses learned sexual scripts (plots or mental plans) to guide sexual behavior.

There is little difference in sexual [55] _____ between males and females.

Research suggests that both women and men are equal in physiological sexual [56] _____ but differ in the [57] _____ feelings of arousal. Women's sexual arousal is linked to their [58] _____ responses to cues and acknowledgment from their partners of their needs and preferences.

Evidence suggests that sexual activity peaks at a [59] _____ age for females than it does males, although this difference is diminishing.

Sex [60] _____ in both males and females may be related to bodily levels of androgens. As testosterone levels decline with [61] _____ , so does [62] _____ drive; both males and females can take testosterone supplements to restore it.

The belief that alcohol and other drugs enhance sex drive is a [63] _____ . Alcohol is a depressant, which in large doses tends to [64] _____ sexual desire, arousal, pleasure, and performance. Other drugs like [65] _____ , amyl nitrite, barbiturates, cocaine, Ecstasy, LSD, and marijuana tend to

[66] _____ sexual responses.

[67] _____ (removal of the gonads) may or may not influence sex drive in humans, depending on

how sexually experienced a person is. Sterilization (a vasectomy or tubal ligation) does not alter sex drive.

There is a gradual [68] _____ in the frequency of sexual intercourse with increasing age.

Masturbation is a normal, harmless behavior practiced by a large percentage of the population. For many,

masturbation is an important part of sexual self [69] _____ .

Sexual orientation refers to one's degree of emotional and erotic attraction to members of the same

[70] _____ , opposite [71] _____ , or both [72] _____ .

A person may be heterosexual, [73] _____ , or bisexual.

A combination of heredity, biological, social, and psychological influences combine to produce one's

[74] _____ .

Research conducted on [75] _____ orientation or behavior by neurobiologist Simon LeVay

suggests a [76] _____ link between mothers and children. Other theorists believe that

homosexuality may have developed to [77] _____ the male and female competition for sexual

partners.

A national survey suggests that of every 100 people, [78] _____ identify themselves as

homosexual or [79] _____ .

However, gay men and lesbians are frequently affected by homophobia (fear of [80] _____) and

heterosexism (the belief that heterosexuality is more natural than homosexuality).

As a group, homosexual men and women do not differ psychologically from [81] _____ .

MODULE 15.3

Survey Question: To what extent do females and males differ in sexual response? Pages 581-583

In a series of landmark studies, William [82] _____ and Virginia Johnson directly observed sexual

response in a large number of adults.

Human sexual response can be divided into four phases: (1) [83] _____ , (2) plateau, (3)

[84] _____ , and (4) resolution.

There do not appear to be any differences between vaginal [85] _____ and clitoral

[86] _____ in the female.

Males experience a refractory period after [87] _____ and ejaculation. Only five percent of men are [88] _____ orgasmic.

Both males and females may go through all four stages in [89] _____ or [90] _____ minutes. But during lovemaking, most females typically take longer than this, averaging from 10 to 20 minutes.

Mutual [91] _____ has been abandoned by most sex counselors as the ideal in lovemaking.

Fifteen percent of women are consistently [92] _____ orgasmic, and at least 48 percent are capable of [93] _____ orgasm.

Survey Question: What are the most common sexual disorders? Pages 583-584

Definitions of sexual deviance are highly [94] _____ . Many sexually deviant behaviors are acceptable in private or in some [95] _____ .

Sexual [96] _____ that often cause difficulty are called paraphilias.

Some paraphilias include pedophilia (sex with children), [97] _____ (sexual arousal associated with inanimate objects), voyeurism (viewing the genitals of others without their permission), and [98] _____ (displaying the genitals to unwilling viewers).

Other paraphilias are transvestic fetishism (achieving sexual arousal by wearing clothing of the opposite sex), sexual [99] _____ (deriving sexual pleasure from inflicting pain), sexual [100] _____ (desiring pain as part of the sex act), and frotteurism (sexually touching or rubbing against a nonconsenting person).

Exhibitionists are rarely dangerous and can best be characterized as sexually [101] _____ and immature.

The effects of child molestation vary greatly, depending on the [102] _____ of the molestation and the child's relationship to the molester.

Children who have been [103] _____ may display such signs as fear of being seen [104] _____ , anxiety, [105] _____ , or discomfort to references of [106] _____ behaviors and express low self-esteem or self-worth.

Child molesters tend to gain access to children through caretaking [107] _____ and bring them to their homes. Some tactics molesters use to lull children are bribing them with [108] _____ , encouraging them to talk about sex, and using threats to gain [109] _____ .

Survey Question: Have recent changes in attitudes affected sexual behavior? Pages 584-587

Attitudes toward sexual behavior, especially the behavior of others, have become more liberal, but actual changes in sexual [110] _____ have been more gradual.

Another change has been [111] _____ and more frequent sexual activity among adolescents and young adults, including larger percentages of people who have premarital [112] _____ .

Also evident are a greater acceptance of [113] _____ sexuality and a narrowing of differences in male and female patterns of sexual [114] _____ . In other words, the double standard is fading.

Acquaintance ([115] _____) rape and [116] _____ -supportive myths and attitudes remain major problems.

[117] _____ is primarily a violent crime of aggression rather than a sex crime.

Survey Question: What impacts have sexually transmitted diseases had on sexual behavior? Pages 587-590

Based on a recent study, approximately [118] _____ percent of sexually active teenage [119] _____ reported that they do not believe they will get [120] _____ transmitted diseases (STDs) because their partners [121] _____ show symptoms of STDs.

People who are sexually [122] _____ , even with only one person, may still be engaging in risky sex from [123] _____ contact with others through their partner's indiscretion.

The emergence of [124] _____ deficiency syndrome (AIDS) is caused by the human immunodeficiency [125] _____ (HIV).

STDs have had a sizable impact on patterns of sexual behavior, including increased awareness of high-[126] _____ behaviors and some curtailment of [127] _____ taking.

It is predicted that over the next 20 to 30 years, the dominant group of individuals that will spread the [128] _____ virus are heterosexuals, and unless preventions are taken, [129] _____ million people will die of AIDS.

PSYCHOLOGY IN ACTION

Survey Questions: What are the most common sexual adjustment problems? How are they treated? Pages 592-597

The principal problems in sexual adjustment are [130] _____ disorders, arousal disorders, orgasm disorders, and sexual [131] _____ disorders.

Desire disorders include hypoactive [132] _____ (a loss of sexual desire) and [133] _____ aversion (fear or disgust about engaging in sex).

Arousal disorders include [134] _____ erectile disorder and [135] _____ sexual arousal disorder.

Approximately 40 percent of [136] _____ disorders result from psychogenic causes (having [137] _____ or emotional origin) rather than physical illnesses, diseases, or [138] _____ to the penis.

Both males and females have similar causes for sexual [139] _____ disorder, which include anxiety, [140] _____ toward their partner, depression, stress, [141] _____ experiences, having a strict religious background, and distrust of men or women.

To [142] _____ a healthy relationship through communication, people should [143] _____ gunnysacking each other, be open about their feelings, not [144] _____ each other's characteristics, not be mind readers, and try to understand the other's perspectives.

Orgasm disorders are male orgasmic disorder (retarded [145] _____), premature [146] _____ , and female orgasm disorder (an inability to reach orgasm during lovemaking).

Sexual pain disorders are dyspareunia ([147] _____ intercourse) and vaginismus ([148] _____ of the vagina).

Behavioral methods such as sensate [149] _____ and the squeeze technique have been developed to alleviate each problem. In addition, counseling can be quite helpful.

However, most sexual adjustment problems are closely linked to the general health of a couple's [150] _____ .

For this reason, communication skills that foster and maintain [151] _____ are the key to successful relationships.

CONNECTIONS

MODULE 15.1

1. _____ pelvic bone
2. _____ urethra
3. _____ labia minora
4. _____ ovary
5. _____ vagina
6. _____ uterus
7. _____ rectum
8. _____ fallopian tube
9. _____ clitoris
10. _____ labia majora
11. _____ urinary bladder
12. _____ cervix

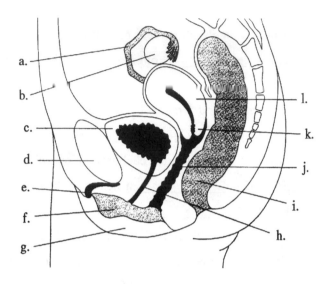

1. _____ Cowper's gland
2. _____ glans penis
3. _____ urethra
4. _____ seminal vesicle
5. _____ vas deferens
6. _____ pelvic bone
7. _____ urinary bladder
8. _____ testis
9. _____ rectum
10. _____ urethral orifice
11. _____ epididymis
12. _____ prostate

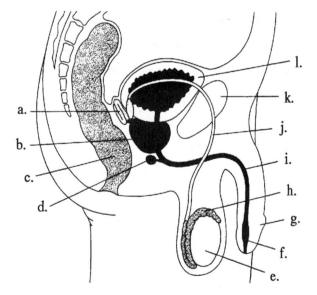

1. _____ androgen
2. _____ estrogen
3. _____ genetic sex
4. _____ gonadal sex
5. _____ hermaphroditism
6. _____ gender identity
7. _____ gender role
8. _____ androgyny

a. ovaries or testes
b. cultural pattern
c. self-perception
d. female hormone
e. man-woman
f. XX or XY
g. androgenital syndrome
h. testosterone

MODULE 15.2

1. _____ masturbation
2. _____ homophobia
3. _____ heterosexual
4. _____ homosexual
5. _____ bisexual
6. _____ sex drive
7. _____ sterilization
8. _____ erogenous zone
9. _____ castration
10. _____ sexual script

a. attracted to both sexes
b. attracted to opposite sex
c. attracted to same sex
d. safest sex
e. infertility
f. testical removal
g. fear of homosexuality
h. motivation for intercourse
i. dialogue for sexual behavior
j. productive of pleasure

MODULE 15.3

1. _____ orgasmic disorder
2. _____ STD
3. _____ voyeurism
4. _____ psychogenic
5. _____ excitement phase
6. _____ gunnysacking
7. _____ pedophilia
8. _____ exhibitionism
9. _____ safer sex practices
10. _____ dyspareunia
11. _____ acquaintance rape
12. _____ orgasm

a. expressing saved-up complaints
b. genital pain from intercourse
c. inability to reach orgasm
d. psychological origin
e. date rape
f. "flashing"
g. "peeping"
h. child molesting
i. sexual climax
j. signs of sexual arousal
k. using a condom
l. AIDS

CHECK YOUR MEMORY

MODULE 15.1

Survey Questions: What are the basic dimensions of sex? How does one's sense of maleness or femaleness develop? Pages 566-572

1. Primary sexual characteristics involve differences in the reproductive organs and the breasts.
    TRUE or FALSE

2. The term "menarche" refers to the ending of regular monthly fertility cycles in females.
    TRUE or FALSE

3. The female gonads are the ovaries.
    TRUE or FALSE

4. Cowper's glands are female reproductive structures.
    TRUE or FALSE

5. All individuals normally produce both androgens and testosterones.
    TRUE or FALSE

6. Transsexuals are persons who have had their genetic sex altered medically.
    TRUE or FALSE

7. Without testosterone, a human embryo will develop into a female.
    TRUE or FALSE

8. Androgen insensitivity results in the development of female genitals.
    TRUE or FALSE

9. Corrective surgery determines intersexuals' gender identity by altering their ambiguous genital appearance to be either male or female.
    TRUE or FALSE

10. Differences in male and female scores on the SAT have narrowed in recent years.
    TRUE or FALSE

11. Observed differences in the abilities of males and females are based on averages; they tell nothing about a particular person.
    TRUE or FALSE

12. Gender identity refers to all the behaviors that are defined as male or female by one's culture.
    TRUE or FALSE

13. Babies are perceived differently and treated differently when they are labeled as males than when they are labeled as females.
    TRUE or FALSE

14. Due to gender role stereotyping, women today are liked more by their peers for successfully holding a job that has been defined as traditionally "male."
    TRUE or FALSE

15. Women continue to receive unequal pay for work comparable to that of men.
    TRUE or FALSE

16. Women of all ethnic groups receive the same unequal pay of $.75 for every $1.00 men earn.
    TRUE or FALSE

17. Even though their culture is quite different, the sex roles of Tchambuli men and women are almost identical to those in North America.
    TRUE or FALSE

18. Boys are allowed to roam over wider areas than girls.
    TRUE or FALSE

19. Expressive behaviors are those that directly express a person's desire to attain a goal.
    TRUE or FALSE

20. Sex-segregated play means that boys and girls do not play with each other.
    TRUE or FALSE

Survey Questions: What is psychological androgyny (and is it contagious)? Pages 572-573

21. The BSRI consists of 20 masculine traits and 20 feminine traits.
    TRUE or FALSE

22. About 50 percent of all people who take the BSRI are scored as androgynous.
    TRUE or FALSE

23. Masculine men and feminine women consistently choose to engage in sex-appropriate activities.
    TRUE or FALSE

24. Masculine men find it difficult to accept support from others.
    TRUE or FALSE

25. Androgynous persons tend to be more satisfied with their lives than nonandrogynous persons are.
    TRUE or FALSE

MODULE 15.2

Survey Question: What are the most typical patterns of human sexual behavior? Pages 575-579

26. Sexual scripts determine when, where, and with whom we are likely to express sexual feelings.
    TRUE or FALSE

27. Women are less physically aroused by erotic stimuli than men.
    TRUE or FALSE

28. Research suggests that women and men are equal in the level of physiological sexual arousal but differ in the subjective feelings of arousal.
    TRUE or FALSE

29. Differences between male and female sexuality are accurately perceived by the general public.
    TRUE or FALSE

30. More women than men have sexual dreams that result in orgasm.
    TRUE or FALSE

31. As testosterone levels decline with age, females can take testosterone supplements to restore their sex drive.
    TRUE or FALSE

32. Alcohol and other drugs enhance sexual desire, arousal, and pleasure.
    TRUE or FALSE

33. Drunkenness lowers sexual arousal and performance.
    TRUE or FALSE

34. Sterilization tends to abolish the sex drive in the sexually inexperienced.
    TRUE or FALSE

35. Masturbation typically ends soon after people get married.
    TRUE or FALSE

36. The average frequency of sexual intercourse declines dramatically between the ages of 30 and 39.
    TRUE or FALSE

37. Your sexual orientation is revealed, in part, by who you have erotic fantasies about.
    TRUE or FALSE

38. Gay males are converted to homosexuality during adolescence by other homosexuals.
    TRUE or FALSE

39. Sexual orientation is a very stable personal characteristic.
    TRUE or FALSE

40. Sexual orientation is influenced by heredity.
    TRUE or FALSE

41. Hormone imbalances cause most instances of homosexuality and bisexuality.
    TRUE or FALSE

42. Fifteen percent of men and 13 percent of women identify themselves as homosexual.
    TRUE or FALSE

43. A national survey suggests that of every 100 people, seven identify themselves as homosexual or bisexual.
TRUE or FALSE

44. Evolutionists suggested that homosexuality may have developed to reduce male competition for female mates.
TRUE or FALSE

45. Homosexual persons tend to discover their sexual orientation at a later age than heterosexual persons.
TRUE or FALSE

MODULE 15.3

Survey Question: To what extent do females and males differ in sexual response? Pages 581-583

46. Masters and Johnson's data on human sexuality was restricted to questionnaires and interviews.
TRUE or FALSE

47. During the excitement phase of sexual response, the nipples become erect in both males and females.
TRUE or FALSE

48. In males, orgasm is always accompanied by ejaculation.
TRUE or FALSE

49. Almost all women experience a short refractory period after ejaculation.
TRUE or FALSE

50. Both orgasm and resolution tend to last longer in females than they do in males.
TRUE or FALSE

51. Contemporary research has confirmed that clitoral orgasms are an inferior form of sexual response.
TRUE or FALSE

52. Women tend to go through the phases of sexual response more slowly than men.
TRUE or FALSE

53. One woman in three does not experience orgasm during the first year of marriage.
TRUE or FALSE

Survey Question: What are the most common sexual disorders? Pages 583-584

54. Oral sex and masturbation are formally classified as paraphilias.
TRUE or FALSE

55. Frotteurism refers to sex with children.
TRUE or FALSE

56. Most exhibitionists are male and married.
    TRUE or FALSE

57. An exhibitionist who approaches closer than arm's length may be dangerous.
    TRUE or FALSE

58. In the majority of cases of child molesting, the offender is an acquaintance or relative of the child.
    TRUE or FALSE

59. Child molesting is especially likely to be harmful if the molester is someone the child deeply trusts
    TRUE or FALSE

60. Child molesters tend to kidnap children on playgrounds in parks when caretakers are not looking.
    TRUE or FALSE

Survey Question: Have recent changes in attitudes affected sexual behavior? Pages 584-587

61. In recent decades the gap between sexual values and actual behavior has narrowed.
    TRUE or FALSE

62. A majority of young adults continue to believe that premarital sex is unacceptable.
    TRUE or FALSE

63. The incidence of extramarital sex has not changed much in the last 40 years.
    TRUE or FALSE

64. The majority of men and women have sexual experiences before marriage.
    TRUE or FALSE

65. About 12 percent of all adult Americans are sexually abstinent.
    TRUE or FALSE

66. Women who are raped usually asked for trouble by wearing sexy clothes.
    TRUE or FALSE

67. One woman in 70 will be raped in her lifetime.
    TRUE or FALSE

68. The majority of rapists are friends or acquaintances of the victim.
    TRUE or FALSE

69. Males high in sex role stereotyping are more aroused by stories about rape than males low in sex role stereotyping.
    TRUE or FALSE

Survey Question: What impacts have sexually transmitted diseases had on sexual behavior? Pages 587-590

70. Many people suffering from STDs are asymptomatic.

    TRUE or FALSE

71. People who are sexually active with one partner do not have to worry about STDs or indirect sexual contact with others.

    TRUE or FALSE

72. Teenage girls today are well educated about STDs and understand that they may get STDs if they are sexually active.

    TRUE or FALSE

73. The first symptoms of AIDS may not appear for up to 10 years.

    TRUE or FALSE

74. HIV infections are spread by direct contact with body fluids.

    TRUE or FALSE

75. The AIDS epidemic has dramatically altered the sexual behavior of college students.

    TRUE or FALSE

76. Most women who contract the HIV virus today do so through intravenous drug use.

    TRUE or FALSE

77. It is unwise to count on a partner for protection from HIV infection.

    TRUE or FALSE

78. Gonorrhea can be prevented by vaccination.

    TRUE or FALSE

79. Hepatitis B can be prevented by vaccination.

    TRUE or FALSE

80. Chlamydia is now the most common STD among men.

    TRUE or FALSE

81. Heterosexuals are predicted to be the main group of people to spread the HIV virus in the next 20 years.

    TRUE or FALSE

82. In America, three million people die each year from AIDS, and worldwide five million people die each year.

    TRUE or FALSE

PSYCHOLOGY IN ACTION

Survey Questions: What are the most common sexual adjustment problems? How are they treated?
Pages 592-597

83. In a desire disorder the person desires sex but does not become sexually aroused.

TRUE or FALSE

84. A person who is repelled by sex and seeks to avoid it suffers from a sexual aversion.

TRUE or FALSE

85. Men suffering from primary erectile dysfunction have never had an erection.

TRUE or FALSE

86. The squeeze technique is the most commonly recommended treatment for erectile disorders.

TRUE or FALSE

87. The majority of erectile dysfunctions are psychogenic.

TRUE or FALSE

88. The causes of erectile disorders include physical illnesses, diseases, and damage to the penis.

TRUE or FALSE

89. Males' sexual arousal disorder is caused by physical illnesses, and females' sexual arousal disorder is caused by traumatic childhood experiences.

TRUE or FALSE

90. Treatment for female sexual arousal disorder usually involves sensate focus.

TRUE or FALSE

91. Female orgasmic disorder is the female equivalent of premature ejaculation in the male.

TRUE or FALSE

92. Both males and females can experience dyspareunia.

TRUE or FALSE

93. Masters and Johnson regard all sexual problems as mutual, or shared by both parties.

TRUE or FALSE

94. Gunnysacking is an important communication skill that all couples should master.

TRUE or FALSE

95. Rather than telling your partner what he or she thinks, you should ask her or him.

TRUE or FALSE

FINAL SURVEY AND REVIEW

MODULE 15.1

Survey Questions: What are the basic dimensions of sex? How does one's sense of maleness or femaleness develop? Pages 566-572

Physical differences between males and females can be divided into primary and secondary [1] _____ .

[2] _____ refers to the genitals and internal [3] _____ organs.

[4] _____ refers to bodily features such as [5] _____ development in females, body shape, and facial [6] _____ .

Reproductive maturity in females is signaled by [7] _____ (the onset of menstruation). Soon after, [8] _____ (the release of eggs) begins.

The development of sexual characteristics is influenced by [9] _____ (male sex hormones) and [10] _____ (female sex hormones) secreted by the [11] _____ (sex glands).

A person's sex can be broken down into [12] _____ sex, [13] _____ sex, hormonal, sex, [14] _____ sex, and gender identity.

Sexual development begins with genetic sex (XX or XY [15] _____). Two [16] _____ normally produce a female; [17] _____ plus a [18] _____ produces a male.

During prenatal sexual development, the presence of [19] _____ produces male [20] _____ ; an absence of testosterone produces female [21] _____ .

[22] _____ insensitivity, exposure to progestin, and the androgenital syndrome result in sexual ambiguities called [23] _____ .

[24] _____ with hormone therapy can alter the genital appearance and secondary sexual characteristics for [25] _____ (children with ambiguous sexual anatomy) to either male or female.

However, these factors alone do not determine gender identity; [26] _____ is also important.

Social factors are especially apparent in learned [27] _____ (a private sense of maleness or femaleness) and the effect of [28] _____ (patterns of behavior defined as male or female within a particular culture).

Gender identity, which is based to a large extent on [29] _____ , usually becomes stable by age three or four years.

Many researchers believe that [30] _____ hormones can exert a biological [31] _____ effect that combines with social factors present after birth to influence psychosexual development.

On most [32] _____ dimensions, men and women are more alike than they are different.

Gender roles contribute to the development of gender role [33] _____ (oversimplified beliefs about the nature of men and women) that often distort perceptions about the kinds of occupations for which men and women are suited.

As a result of gender role [34] _____ , for every $1.00 men earn in business, academia, medicine, law, sports, and politics, white women earn $.[35] _____ , black women earn $.[36] _____ , and Latino women earn $.[37] _____ .

Another effect of gender role [38] _____ is that [39] _____ are less liked by their peers for violating gender norms when they hold a job that as been defined as traditionally "male."

[40] _____ determines gender roles of males and females in each society.

Gender role [41] _____ (learning gender roles) seems to account for most observed male/female differences.

Parents tend to encourage boys in [42] _____ behaviors (goal-directed actions) and girls in [43] _____ (emotional) behaviors.

By age three, [44] _____ play can be seen in boys and girls: Boys play outdoor games that focus on superheroes, and girls play indoor games that focus on house-related activities.

Survey Questions: What is psychological androgyny (and is it contagious)? Pages 572-573

Androgyny is measured with the [45] _____ *Sex Role* [46] _____ (BSRI).

Research conducted by Sandra Bem indicates that roughly one-[47] _____ of all persons are [48] _____ (they possess both masculine and feminine traits).

Being masculine means that a person is [49] _____ and assertive.

Being feminine means that a person is [50] _____ (helpful and comforting) and interpersonally oriented.

Psychological androgyny appears related to greater [51] _____ or flexibility in behavior.

MODULE 15.2

Survey Question: What are the most typical patterns of human sexual behavior? Pages 575-579

Sexual behavior, including [52] _____ (sexual climax), is apparent soon after birth and expressed in various ways throughout life.

Sexual arousal is related to stimulation of the body's [53] _____ zones (areas that produce erotic pleasure), but [54] _____ elements such as thoughts and images are equally important.

"Normal" sexual behavior is defined differently by various cultures. Also, each person uses learned sexual [55] _____ (plots or mental [56] _____) to guide sexual behavior.

There is little [57] _____ in sexual behavior between males and females.

Research suggests that [58] _____ women and men are [59] _____ in physiological sexual arousal but [60] _____ in the subjective feelings of arousal. Women's sexual arousal is linked to their emotional responses to cues and acknowledgment from their partners of their needs and preferences.

Evidence suggests that the sexual activity peaks at a later age for [61] _____ than it does [62] _____ , although this difference is diminishing.

Sex drive in both males and females may be related to bodily levels of [63] _____ . As testosterone levels decline with age, so does [64] _____ drive; both males and females can take [65] _____ supplements to restore it.

The belief that alcohol and other drugs [66] _____ sex drive is a myth. Alcohol is a depressant, which in large doses tends to [67] _____ sexual desire, arousal, pleasure, and performance. Other drugs like amphetamines, amyl nitrite, barbiturates, cocaine, Ecstasy, LSD, and marijuana tend to impair sexual responses.

Castration (removal of the gonads) may or may not influence sex drive in humans, depending on how sexually experienced a person is. [68] _____ (a vasectomy or tubal ligation) does not alter sex drive.

There is a gradual decline in the [69] _____ of sexual intercourse with increasing [70] _____ . However, many elderly persons remain sexually active, and great variations exist at all ages.

[71] _____ (sexual self-stimulation) is a normal, harmless behavior practiced by a large percentage of the population. For many, it is an important part of sexual self-discovery.

Sexual [72] _____ refers to one's degree of emotional and erotic attraction to members of the same sex, opposite sex, or both sexes.

A person may be [73] _____ , homosexual, or [74] _____ .

A combination of [75] _____ , biological, [76] _____ , and psychological influences combine to produce one's sexual orientation.

Research conducted on sexual [77] _____ or behavior by neurobiologist Simon LeVay suggests a genetic link between [78] _____ and children. Other theorists believe that homosexuality may have developed to [79] _____ the male and female competition for sexual partners.

A national survey suggests that of every 100 people, 7 identify themselves as [80] _____ or bisexual.

However, gay men and lesbians are frequently affected by [81] _____ (fear of homosexuality) and [82] _____ (the belief that heterosexuality is better than homosexuality).

As a group, [83] _____ men and women do not differ psychologically from [84] _____ .

MODULE 15.3

Survey Question: To what extent do females and males differ in sexual response? Pages 581-583

In a series of landmark studies, William Masters and Virginia [85] _____ directly observed sexual response in a large number of adults.

Human sexual response can be divided into four phases: (1) excitement, (2) [86] _____ , (3) orgasm, and (4) [87] _____ .

There do not appear to be any differences between [88] _____ orgasms and [89] _____ orgasms in the female.

Males experience a [90] _____ period after orgasm and ejaculation. Only 5 percent of men are multi[91] _____ .

Both males and females may go through all four stages in four or five minutes. But during lovemaking, most [92] _____ typically take longer than this, averaging from 10 to 20 minutes.

[93] _____ orgasm has been abandoned by most sex counselors as the ideal in lovemaking.

[94] _____ percent of women are consistently [95] _____ , and at least 48 percent are capable of multiple orgasm.

Survey Question: What are the most common sexual disorders? Pages 583-584

Definitions of [96] _____ are highly subjective. Many publicly disapproved sexual behaviors are acceptable in private or in some cultures.

Sexual deviations that often cause difficulty are called [97] _____ (destructive deviations in sexual preferences or behavior).

Some of these problems include [98] _____ (sex with children), fetishism (sexual arousal associated with inanimate objects), [99] _____ (viewing the genitals of others without their permission), and exhibitionism (displaying the genitals to unwilling viewers).

Others are [100] _____ fetishism (achieving sexual arousal by wearing clothing of the opposite sex), sexual sadism (deriving sexual pleasure from inflicting pain), sexual masochism (desiring pain as part of the sex act), and [101] _____ (sexually touching or rubbing against a nonconsenting person).

[102] _____ ("flashers") are rarely dangerous and can best be characterized as sexually inhibited and immature.

The effects of child molestation vary greatly, depending on the severity of the [103] _____ and the child's [104] _____ to the molester.

[105] _____ who have been molested may display such signs as fear of being seen [106] _____ , anxiety, shame, or discomfort to references of [107] _____ behaviors and express low self-esteem or self-worth.

Child molesters tend to gain access to children through [108] _____ opportunities and bring them to their homes. Some tactics molesters use to lull children are [109] _____ them with gifts, encouraging them to [110] _____ about sex, and using threats to gain compliance.

Survey Question: Have recent changes in attitudes affected sexual behavior? Pages 584-587

[111] _____ toward sexual behavior, especially the behavior of others, have become more [112] _____ , but actual changes in sexual behavior have been more gradual.

Another change has been earlier and more frequent sexual activity among adolescents and young adults, including larger percentages of people who have [113] _____ intercourse.

Also evident are a greater acceptance of female sexuality and a narrowing of differences in male and female patterns of sexual behavior. In other words, the [114] _____ is fading.

[115] _____ (date) rape and rape-supportive [116] _____ (false beliefs) and attitudes remain major problems.

Rape is primarily a violent crime of [117] _____ rather than a sex crime.

Survey Question: What impacts have sexually transmitted diseases had on sexual behavior? Pages 587-590

Based on a recent study, approximately 90 percent of [118] _____ teenage girls reported that they do not believe they will get [119] _____ diseases (STDs) because their partners did not show symptoms of STDs.

People who are sexually active, even with only one person, may still be engaging in [120] _____ sex from indirect [121] _____ with others through their partner's indiscretion.

The emergence of acquired immune [122] _____ syndrome (AIDS) is caused by the human [123] _____ virus (HIV).

[124] _____ have had a sizable impact on patterns of sexual behavior, including increased awareness of high-risk behaviors and some curtailment of risk taking.

It is predicted that over the next 20 to 30 years, the dominant group of individuals that will spread the HIV virus are [125] _____ , and unless preventions are taken, 65 million people will die of [126] _____ .

PSYCHOLOGY IN ACTION

Survey Questions: What are the most common sexual adjustment problems? How are they treated? Pages 592-597

The principal problems in sexual adjustment are desire disorders, [127] _____ disorders, [128] _____ disorders, and sexual pain disorders.

Desire disorders include [129] _____ sexual desire (a loss of sexual desire) and sexual [130] _____ (fear or disgust about engaging in sex).

Arousal disorders include male [131] _____ disorder and female sexual [132] _____ disorder.

Approximately 40 percent of [133] _____ disorders result from [134] _____ causes (having psychological or emotional origin) rather than physical illnesses, diseases, or damage to the penis.

Both males and females have similar causes for sexual [135] _____ disorder, which include

[136] _____ , hostility toward their partner, depression, stress, childhood experiences, having a

[137] _____ religious background, and distrust of men or women.

To maintain a [138] _____ relationship through communication, people should

[139] _____ gunnysacking each other, be open about their [140] _____ , not attack each

other's [141] _____ , not be mind readers, and try to understand the other's perspectives.

Orgasm disorders are male orgasmic disorder ([142] _____ ejaculation), [143] _____

ejaculation, and female [144] _____ disorder (an inability to reach orgasm during lovemaking).

Sexual pain disorders are [145] _____ (painful intercourse) and [146] _____ (muscle

spasms of the vagina).

Behavioral methods such as [147] _____ focus and the [148] _____ technique

for premature ejaculation have been developed to alleviate each problem. In addition, counseling can

be quite helpful.

However, most sexual [149] _____ problems are closely linked to the general health of a

couple's relationship.

For this reason, [150] _____ skills that foster and maintain intimacy are the key to successful

relationships.

MASTERY TEST

1. The strength of the sex drive in both men and women increases when _____ levels
   are higher in the body.
   a. androgen
   b. progestin
   c. ovulin
   d. androgenin

2. Worldwide, the main source of HIV infection is
   a. heterosexual sex
   b. homosexual sex
   c. intravenous drug use
   d. blood transfusions

3. Boys are encouraged to be strong, aggressive, dominant, and achieving through the process of
   a. biological biasing
   b. sexual orienting
   c. gender adaptation
   d. gender role socialization

4. Before birth, a genetic male will develop as a female if which condition exists?
   a. excessive progestin
   b. an androgen insensitivity
   c. the androgenital syndrome
   d. the testes produce testosterone

5. Concerning masturbation, it can be concluded that
   a. masturbation typically ceases after marriage
   b. after age 30, women masturbate more than men do
   c. those who are most sexually active masturbate the most
   d. masturbation slows psychosexual development

6. One of the greatest changes in attitudes toward sex in North America is a greater tolerance for
   a. teenage pregnancies
   b. the sexual behavior of others
   c. the double standard
   d. STDs

7. The squeeze technique is typically used to treat
   a. dyspareunia
   b. vaginismus
   c. female sexual arousal disorder
   d. premature ejaculation

8. In a female, gonadal sex is determined by the presence of
   a. estrogens
   b. androgens
   c. ovaries
   d. a vagina and uterus

9. A policeman who accepts emotional support from others, especially from women, would most likely be scored as _____ on the BSRI.
   a. masculine
   b. feminine
   c. androgynous
   d. expressive-nurturant

10. Which of the following is POOR advice for couples who want to communicate effectively and maintain intimacy?
    a. Avoid gunnysacking.
    b. Avoid expressing anger.
    c. Don't try to win.
    d. Don't be a mind reader.

11. The aspect of sex that is essentially formed by age four is
    a. gender identity
    b. gender roles
    c. sexual scripting
    d. psychological androgyny

12. In a female, broadening of the hips and breast development are
    a. primary sexual characteristics
    b. secondary sexual characteristics
    c. caused by the release of androgens
    d. associated with the presence of a Y chromosome

13. The first two phases of the sexual response cycle are
    a. excitement, arousal
    b. arousal, orgasm
    c. excitement, plateau
    d. stimulation, arousal

14. A special danger in the transmission of STDs is that many people are _____ at first.
    a. noninfectious
    b. androgynous
    c. androgenital
    d. asymptomatic

15. The presence of a Y chromosome is associated with
    a. intersexuals
    b. prenatal testosterone
    c. menarche
    d. the presence of progestin

16. With respect to the behaviors parents encourage in their children, which is a correct match?
    a. controlling-female
    b. goal oriented-female
    c. expressive-male
    d. instrumental-male

17. Which condition is LEAST likely to lower sexual performance?
    a. sterilization
    b. castration
    c. extreme alcohol intoxication
    d. sexual aversion

18. Prenatally masculinized females tend to be tomboys during childhood and observation that supports the
    a. biological biasing effect
    b. estrogen paradox
    c. view that gender is genetically determined
    d. idea that gender role socialization is dominant

19. Which of the following increases the likelihood that a man will commit rape?
    a. drinking alcohol
    b. being high in gender role stereotyping
    c. belief in rape myths
    d. all the preceding

20. Gender role _____ treat learned gender role differences as if they were real gender differences.
    a. labels
    b. behavior patterns
    c. stereotypes
    d. templates

21. Regarding sexual response, it can be said that
    a. orgasm and resolution tend to last longer in women
    b. a short refractory period occurs just before orgasm in males
    c. some women skip the arousal phase of the cycle
    d. men are incapable of having second orgasms

22. The decline of the double standard refers to abandoning different standards for
    a. risky sex and "safe" sex
    b. heterosexual relationships and homosexual relationships
    c. sexuality before and after marriage
    d. male and female sexual behavior

23. Declines in the differences in male and female scores on the SAT call into question which concept?
    a. the androgenital syndrome
    b. the biological biasing effect
    c. gender role socialization
    d. gender identity

24. When expectations of a friendly first date clash with an attempted seduction, the problem can be attributed to differences in
    a. gender roles
    b. erogenous confrontation
    c. gender myths
    d. sexual scripts

25. Which statement concerning sexual orientation is TRUE?
    a. Sexual orientation is partly hereditary.
    b. Homosexuality is caused by a hormone imbalance.
    c. Sexual orientation can be changed fairly easily.
    d. Heterosexual persons tend to discover their sexual orientation at a later date than homosexual persons.

26. Which of the following is NOT one of the basic dimensions of sex?
    a. genetic sex
    b. gonadal sex
    c. hormonal sex
    d. androgenital sex

27. Pedophilia, fetishism, and sadism are classified as
    a. the three basic forms of child molestation
    b. STDs
    c. paraphilias
    d. hormonal disorders

28. All but one of the following is a rape myth. Which is NOT a myth?
    a. Women who get raped ask for it in one way or another.
    b. A majority of rapes are committed by a friend or acquaintance of the victim.
    c. Women who are sexually active are usually lying if they say they were raped.
    d. Many women who are raped secretly enjoy it.

29. Which of the following diseases is currently untreatable?
    a. gonorrhea
    b. chlamydia
    c. syphilis
    d. hepatitis B

30. The male sexual disorder that corresponds most closely to female sexual arousal disorder is
    a. sexual aversion
    b. erectile disorder
    c. premature ejaculation
    d. dyspareunia

31. Corrective surgery can alter genital appearances to either male or female for _____ or children with ambiguous sexual anatomy.
    a. pedophilia
    b. sexual masochism
    c. sexual sadism
    d. intersexuals

32. Women earning approximately $.54 to $.75 for every $1.00 men earn is the result of
    a. gender identity
    b. gender role stereotyping
    c. sexual orientation
    d. androgen insensitivity

33. Research suggests that women who have violated _____ are _____ by their peers when they hold a job that has been defined as traditionally "male."
    a. gender norms; less liked
    b. sexual scripts; well liked
    c. cultural norms; supported
    d. biological biasing; harassed

34. At an early age, boys play outdoor games with other boys that focus on who's the boss, and girls play indoor games with other girls that focus on house-related activities and cooperation. This difference is the result of
    a. gender role socialization
    b. sex-segregated play
    c. instrumental versus expressive behaviors
    d. all the preceding

35. Research suggests that physiological sexual arousal for men and women is _____, but their subjective feelings of arousal are
    a. equal; different
    b. different; equal
    c. culturally defined; biologically defined
    d. easily measured; not measurable

36. To restore sex drive due to aging, both men and women can
    a. increase their sexual activities
    b. take estrogen supplements
    c. take testosterone supplements
    d. eat oysters and drink wine

37. Cocaine and large doses of alcohol _____ sexual desire, arousal, pleasure, and performance.
    a. increase
    b. decrease
    c. do not affect
    d. enhance men's

38. Evolution theorists believe that homosexuality was developed
    a. to reduce male competition for female sexual partners
    b. to explain why certain men not physically capable of performing "manly" duties
    c. as a result of hormonal imbalance
    d. as a result of survival of the fittest

39. Which of the following is NOT a tactic used by child molesters?
    a. use the chat room on the Internet to encourage children to talk about sex
    b. bribe children with gifts
    c. use threats to gain children's compliance
    d. have partners to help lull children to their homes

40. A recent study found that as high as _____ of teenage girls who are sexually active do not believe that they will get STDs because their partners did not exhibit any symptoms of STDs.
    a. 90 percent
    b. 75 percent
    c. 45 percent
    d. 35 percent

SOLUTIONS

RECITE AND REVIEW

MODULE 15.1

1. primary
2. secondary
3. genitals
4. shape
5. menstruation
6. ova
7. male
8. female
9. glands
10. hormonal
11. gender
12. genetic
13. female
14. male
15. male
16. female
17. syndrome
18. sexual
19. surgery
20. appearance
21. ambiguous
22. maleness
23. femaleness
24. three
25. four
26. hormones
27. effect
28. alike
29. different
30. gender role
31. stereotypes
32. women
33. women
34. stereotyping
35. less
36. gender
37. roles
38. Gender role
39. boys
40. girls
41. three
42. sex
43. outdoor
44. indoor

45. *Sex Role*
46. masculine
47. feminine
48. masculine
49. feminine
50. androgyny

MODULE 15.2

51. climax
52. pleasure
53. thoughts
54. cultures
55. responsiveness
56. arousal
57. subjective
58. emotional
59. later
60. drive
61. age
62. sex
63. myth
64. decrease
65. amphetamines
66. impair
67. Castration
68. decline (or decrease)
69. discovery
70. sex
71. sex
72. sexes
73. homosexual
74. sexual orientation
75. sexual
76. genetic
77. reduce
78. seven
79. bisexual
80. homosexuality
81. heterosexuals

MODULE 15.3

82. Masters
83. excitement
84. orgasm
85. orgasms
86. orgasms
87. orgasm
88. multi
89. four
90. five
91. orgasm
92. multi
93. multiple

94. subjective

95. cultures
96. deviations
97. fetishism
98. exhibitionism
99. sadism

100. masochism
101. inhibited
102. severity
103. molested
104. nude

105. shame
106. sexual
107. opportunities
108. gifts
109. compliance

110. behavior
111. earlier
112. intercourse

113. female
114. behavior
115. date

116. rape
117. Rape

118. 90
119. girls
120. sexually
121. did not

122. active
123. indirect
124. acquired immune
125. virus

126. risk
127. risk
128. HIV
129. 65

PSYCHOLOGY IN ACTION

130. desire
131. pain
132. sexual desire
133. sexual
134. male
135. female
136. erectile
137. psychological

138. damage
139. arousal
140. hostility
141. childhood
142. maintain
143. avoid
144. attack
145. ejaculation

146. ejaculation
147. painful
148. muscle spasms
149. focus
150. relationship
151. intimacy

CONNECTIONS

MODULE 15.1

1. d
2. h
3. f
4. b

5. j
6. l
7. i
8. a

9. e
10. g
11. c
12. k

1. d
2. g
3. i
4. a

5. j
6. k
7. l
8. e

9. c
10. f
11. h
12. b

1. h

2. d	5. g	8. e
3. f	6. c	
4. a	7. b	

MODULE 15.2

1. d	5. a	9. f
2. g	6. h	10. i
3. b	7. e	
4. c	8. j	

MODULE 15.3

1. c	5. j	9. k
2. l	6. a	10. b
3. g	7. h	11. e
4. d	8. f	12. i

CHECK YOUR MEMORY

MODULE 15.1

1. F	9. F	17. F
2. F	10. T	18. T
3. T	11. T	19. F
4. F	12. F	20. T
5. F	13. T	
6. F	14. F	
7. T	15. T	
8. T	16. F	

21. F	23. T	25. T
22. F	24. T	

MODULE 15.2

26. T	34. F	42. F
27. F	35. F	43. T
28. T	36. F	44. T
29. F	37. T	45. T
30. F	38. F	
31. T	39. T	
32. F	40. T	
33. T	41. F	

MODULE 15.3

46. F	48. F	50. T
47. T	49. F	51. F

52. T	53. T	

54. F	57. T	60. T
55. F	58. T	
56. T	59. T	

61. T	64. T	67. F
62. F	65. T	68. T
63. T	66. F	69. T

70. T	75. F	80. F
71. F	76. F	81. T
72. F	77. T	82. F
73. T	78. F	
74. T	79. T	

PSYCHOLOGY IN ACTION

83. F	88. F	93. T
84. T	89. F	94. F
85. T	90. T	95. T
86. F	91. F	
87. T	92. T	

FINAL SURVEY AND REVIEW

MODULE 15.1

1. sexual characteristics	16. Xs	31. biasing
2. Primary	17. X	32. psychological
3. reproductive	18. Y	33. stereotypes
4. Secondary	19. testosterone	34. stereotypes
5. breast	20. genitals	35. 75
6. hair	21. genitals	36. 67
7. menarche	22. Androgen	37. 54
8. ovulation	23. hermaphroditism	38. stereotyping
9. androgens	24. Corrective surgery	39. women
10. estrogens	25. intersexuals	40. Culture
11. gonads	26. socialization	41. socialization
12. genetic	27. gender identity	42. instrumental
13. gonadal	28. gender roles	43. expressive
14. genital	29. labeling	44. sex-segregated
15. chromosomes	30. prenatal	

45. *Bem*
46. *Bem*

47. third
48. androgynous
49. independent

50. nurturant
51. adaptability

MODULE 15.2

52. orgasm
53. erogenous
54. cognitive
55. scripts
56. plans
57. difference
58. both
59. equal
60. differ
61. females
62. males
63. androgens

64. sex
65. testosterone
66. enhance
67. decrease
68. Sterilization
69. frequency
70. age
71. Masturbation
72. orientation
73. heterosexual
74. bisexual
75. heredity

76. social
77. orientation
78. mothers
79. reduce
80. homosexual
81. homophobia
82. heterosexism
83. homosexual
84. heterosexuals

MODULE 15.3

85. Johnson
86. plateau
87. resolution
88. vaginal

89. clitoral
90. refractory
91. orgasmic
92. females

93. Mutual
94. Fifteen
95. multiorgasmic

96. sexual deviance
97. paraphilias
98. pedophilia
99. voyeurism
100. transvestic

101. frotteurism
102. Exhibitionists
103. molestation
104. relationship
105. Children

106. nude
107. sexual
108. caretaking
109. bribing
110. talk

111. Attitudes
112. liberal
113. premarital

114. double standard
115. Acquaintance
116. myths

117. aggression

118. sexually active
119. sexually transmitted
120. risky

121. contact
122. deficiency
123. immunodeficiency

124. STDs
125. heterosexuals
126. AIDS

PSYCHOLOGY IN ACTION

127. arousal
128. orgasm
129. hypoactive

130. aversion
131. erectile
132. arousal

133. erectile
134. psychogenic
135. arousal

136. anxiety
137. strict
138. healthy
139. avoid
140. feelings

141. characteristics
142. retarded
143. premature
144. orgasm
145. dyspareunia

146. vaginismus
147. sensate
148. squeeze
149. adjustment
150. communication

MASTERY TEST

1. A, (p. 576)
2. A, (p. 588)
3. D, (p. 570)
4. B, (p. 568)
5. C, (p. 577)
6. B, (p. 585)
7. D, (p. 594-595)
8. C, (p. 566)
9. C, (p. 572)
10. B, (p. 596-597)
11. A, (p. 568)
12. B, (p. 566)
13. C, (p. 581)
14. D, (p. 587)

15. B, (p. 567)
16. D, (p. 572)
17. A, (p. 577)
18. A, (p. 569)
19. D, (p. 586-587)
20. C, (p. 570)
21. A, (p. 582)
22. D, (p. 586)
23. B, (p. 569-570)
24. D, (p. 575)
25. B, (p. 579)
26. D, (p. 567)
27. C, (p. 583)
28. B, (p. 586-587)

29. D, (p. 588)
30. B, (p. 592-593)
31. D, (p. 569)
32. B, (p. 570)
33. A, (p. 571)
34. D, (p. 572)
35. A, (p. 576)
36. C, (p. 576)
37. B, (p. 576-577)
38. A, (p. 579)
39. D, (p. 584)
40. A, (p. 587)

SOCIAL BEHAVIOR

CHAPTER OVERVIEW

Social psychology is the study of behavior in social situations. Affiliating with others is related to needs for approval, support, friendship, information, and reassurance. Social comparison theory holds that we affiliate to evaluate our actions, feelings, and abilities.

Interpersonal attraction is increased by physical proximity, frequent contact, physical attractiveness, competence, similarity, and self-disclosure. Romantic love is marked by mutual absorption between lovers who also like one another. Evolutionary psychology attributes human mating patterns to the reproductive challenges faced by men and women since the dawn of time.

Social groups that we belong to and the roles we take on greatly influence our behaviors. The dimensions of any group include group structure and cohesion. Group cohesiveness is strong for in-group members who tend to attribute positive traits to members of the group. Negative qualities tend to be attributed to out-group members. Attribution theory summarizes how we make inferences about behavior. The fundamental attributional error is to think that the actions of others are the result of internal causes. Because of an actor-observer bias, we tend to attribute our own behavior to external causes.

Social influence refers to how our behavior is changed by the behavior of others. Examples are conformity, groupthink, obedience, and complying with direct requests. Three main types of compliance techniques used by salespeople to encourage customers to buy their products are foot-in-the-door, door-in-the-face, and low-ball. To even the odds, customers should conduct a background search on the product and compare prices to other stores before making a commitment. Self-assertion is another method to reduce the pressure to conform, obey, and comply to others' suggestions. Self-assertion involves clearly stating your wants and needs to others. Learning to be assertive can be aided by role-playing.

Attitudes have belief, emotional, and action components. Attitudes are formed through direct contact, interacting with others, childrearing, group pressures, peergroup influences, the mass media, and chance conditioning. Attitude change is related to reference group membership, to deliberate persuasion, and to personal experiences. Effective persuasion occurs when characteristics of the communicator, the message, and the audience are well matched. Cognitive dissonance theory explains how attitudes are maintained and changed. Brainwashing is forced attitude change. Some cults recruit new members with high-pressure techniques similar to brainwashing. Members are expected to give their loyalty and be obedient to a leader of the cult.

Prejudice is a negative attitude held toward out-group members. Prejudice can be attributed to scapegoating, personal prejudice, group norms, and authoritarian personality traits. Intergroup conflict leads to hostility and stereotyping. Status inequalities tend to build prejudices. Equal-status contact and superordinate goals tend to reduce these problems.

Ethologists blame aggression on instincts. Biological explanations emphasize brain mechanisms and physical factors. Aggression tends to follow frustration, especially when aggression cues are present. Social learning theory relates aggressive behavior to the influence of aggressive models. Students who plan to commit violence in school might disrupt classes, fight, join gangs, destroy property, get frustrated easily, react with extreme anger to criticism, blame others for their troubles, and use drugs.

Four decision points that must be passed before we give help to others are: noticing, defining an emergency, taking responsibility, and selecting a course of action. Helping is less likely at each point when other potential helpers are present. Giving help tends to encourage others to help too.

Multiculturalism is an attempt to give equal status to different ethnic, racial, and cultural groups. To reduce conflict and misunderstanding between members of different ethnic groups, one can do the following: Be aware of stereotyping, seek individuating information, beware of just-world beliefs, understand that race is a social construction, look for commonalities, and set examples for others. Cultural awareness is a key element in promoting greater social harmony.

LEARNING OBJECTIVES

To demonstrate mastery of this chapter, you should be able to:

1. Define "social psychology."

2. Describe the research that indicates that humans have a need to affiliate.

3. Describe the social comparison theory.

4. List and describe four factors that affect interpersonal attraction.

5. Define "homogamy."

6. Explain how self-disclosure is important in the process of getting to know someone. Explain how overdisclosure can affect the same process.

7. Describe Rubin's studies of romantic love.

8. Discuss the differences between loving and liking. Include the term "mutual absorption" in your discussion.

9. Define "evolutionary psychology."

10. Discuss the possible evolution of male and female mate selection.

11. Define the following terms and describe the studies related to these terms: a. social role b. ascribed role c. achieved role d. role conflict e. group structure f. group cohesiveness g. in-groups h. out-groups i. status

12. Explain what attribution theory is and the difference between internal and external causes of behavior.

13. Explain the fundamental attributional error and define the term "actor-observer bias."

14. Briefly discuss the research on the double standard in attribution of male and female success.

15. Define the term "social influence."

16. Describe Asch's experiment on conformity and information in the text about factors that influence conformity in any situation, not just the experiment.

17. Define "groupthink" and explain how it may contribute to poor decision-making. Describe six ways to prevent groupthink.

18. Explain how group sanctions and unanimity affect conformity.

19. Describe Milgram's study of obedience and identify the factors that affect the degree of obedience.

The following objective is related to material in the "Discovering Psychology" section of the text.

20. According to Halonen, 1986, people tend to obey legitimate authority long after that person's demands have become unreasonable. If one person in a group begins to resist orders, would that help others to disobey? Support your answer from Milgram's study.

21. Describe the following methods of compliance: a. foot-in-the-door b. door-in-the-face c. low-ball technique

22. What is one of the main benefits of knowing these strategies for gaining compliance?

23. Describe the process of assertiveness training, including the term "self-assertion."

24. Describe how a person can learn to be more assertive using rehearsal, role-playing, overlearning, and the broken record technique.

25. Define "attitude."

26. Describe the belief, emotional, and action components of an attitude.

27. List, describe, and give examples of six ways in which attitudes are acquired.

28. Explain why people may exhibit discrepancies between attitudes and behavior.

29. Differentiate between reference groups and membership groups.

30. Define "persuasion" and list nine conditions of persuasion that can be applied to bring about attitude change.

31. Present an overview of cognitive dissonance theory, indicate its influence on attitude formation, and describe the effect of justification on dissonance.

32. List two types of forced attitude change.

33. Describe the three techniques used in brainwashing.

34. Explain how beliefs may unfreeze, change, and refreeze and indicate how permanent the attitude changes brought about by brainwashing are.

35. Describe how cults are able to recruit, convert, and retain their members.

36. Define and differentiate "prejudice" and "discrimination" and describe the development of prejudice. Include the terms "scapegoating," "personal prejudice," and "group prejudice" in your discussion.

37. What are the characteristics of the prejudice-prone personality?

38. Describe the characteristic beliefs (including egocentrism and dogmatism) and childhood experiences of the authoritarian personality. Include how these beliefs are measured.

39. Present the major characteristics of social stereotypes and indicate how they may lead to intergroup conflicts.

40. Define "symbolic prejudice."

41. Briefly describe the role of dehumanization in promoting violent conflicts.

42. Explain how status inequalities may lead to the development of stereotypes and how equal-status contact may reduce intergroup tension. Give an example of each situation.

43. Explain how superordinate goals can reduce conflict and hostility.

44. Explain how a "jigsaw" classroom utilizes superordinate goals and helps reduce prejudice.

45. Define the term "mutual interdependence."

46. Describe the relationship between aggression and each of the following: a. instincts b. biology c. frustration (include frustration-aggression hypothesis and aversive stimuli) d. aggression cues (include the weapons effect) e. social learning

47. With respect to the effects of violence on television: a. summarize the relationship between television violence and real life b. explain how television violence may teach antisocial actions, disinhibit dangerous impulses, and desensitize a person to violence

48. List eleven characteristics of students who are violence prone.

49. Explain how parents can buffer the impact of television violence on their children and ways to minimize anger, aggression, and violence in their children.

50. Define "prosocial behavior."

51. Trace the progress of an individual through the four decision points that must be passed before helping behavior is given.

52. Describe what is meant by bystander apathy and diffusion of responsibility, describe the bystander apathy/intervention studies, and indicate how the presence of other people can influence this apathy.

53. Define the terms "empathic arousal" and "empathy-helping relationship" and how they are related to bystander intervention.

54. Briefly note how a person can "de-victimize" oneself.

55. Briefly discuss the impact of positive psychology on prosocial behaviors along with some examples of heroic acts.

56. Define "multiculturalism."

57. List nine ways to "break the prejudice habit."

RECITE AND REVIEW

MODULE 16.1

Survey Questions: Why do people affiliate? What factors influence interpersonal attraction? Pages 602-606

[1] _____ psychology studies how individuals behave, think, and feel in social situations.

The need to affiliate is tied to needs for [2] _____ , support, friendship, and [3] _____ .

Additionally, research indicates that we sometimes affiliate to [4] _____ anxiety and uncertainty.

Social comparison theory holds that we affiliate to [5] _____ our actions, feelings, and abilities.

Interpersonal attraction is increased by physical proximity ([6] _____) and frequent

[7] _____ .

Initial acquaintance and [8] _____ are influenced by physical attractiveness (beauty), competence (high ability), and similarity (being alike).

A large degree of [9] _____ on many dimensions is characteristic of [10] _____ selection, a pattern called homogamy.

Self-disclosure ([11] _____ oneself to others) occurs to a greater degree if two people like one another.

Self-disclosure follows a reciprocity [12] _____ : Moderate self-disclosure elicits personal replies, and overdisclosure tends to inhibit [13] _____ by others.

Romantic love can be distinguished from liking by the use of attitude scales. Dating couples

[14] _____ and [15] _____ their partners but only [16] _____ their friends.

Romantic love is also associated with greater [17] _____ absorption between people.

Evolutionary psychology attributes human [18] _____ patterns to the differing reproductive challenges faced by men and women since the dawn of time.

MODULE 16.2

Survey Question: How does group membership affect our behavior? Pages 608-610

One's position in [19] _____ defines a variety of roles to be played.

[20] _____ , which may be achieved or ascribed, are particular behavior patterns associated with social positions.

When two or more [21] _____ roles are held, role conflict may occur.

Two dimensions of a group are group structure (network of [22] _____ , communication pathways, and power) and group cohesiveness (members' desire to [23] _____ in the group). Group cohesion is strong for [24] _____ members.

Members of the [25] _____ identify themselves based on a combination of dimensions such as nationality, [26] _____ , age, [27] _____ , income, etc. People tend to attribute [28] _____ traits to members of their in-group and negative traits to members of the [29] _____ .

Positions within [30] _____ typically carry higher or lower levels of status. High status is associated with special privileges and respect.

Norms are [31] _____ of conduct enforced (formally or informally) by [32] _____ .

Attribution theory is concerned with how we make inferences about the [33] _____ of behavior.

Behavior can be attributed to internal [34] _____ or external [35] _____ .

The fundamental attributional [36] _____ is to ascribe the actions of others to [37] _____ causes. This is part of the actor-observer bias in which we ascribe the behavior of others to [38] _____ causes and our own behavior to [39] _____ causes.

Survey Question: What factors influence our willingness to conform to a majority? Pages 610-612

Social influence refers to alterations in [40] _____ brought about by the behavior of [41] _____ .

Conformity to group pressure is a familiar example of social influence. Virtually everyone [42] _____ to a variety of broad social and cultural [43] _____ .

Conformity pressures also exist within small [44] _____ . The famous Asch experiments demonstrated that various [45] _____ sanctions encourage conformity.

Groupthink refers to compulsive conformity in group [46] _____ . Victims of groupthink seek to maintain each other's approval, even at the cost of critical thinking.

MODULE 16.3

Survey Question: What have psychologists learned about obedience, compliance, and self-assertion? Pages 613-618

Obedience to [47] _____ has been investigated in a variety of experiments, particularly those by Stanley Milgram.

[48] _____ in Milgram's studies decreased when the victim was in the same room, when the victim and subject were face-to-face, when the authority figure was absent, and when others refused to obey.

Compliance with direct [49] _____ by a person who has little or no social [50] _____ is another means by which behavior is influenced.

Three strategies for inducing compliance are the [51] _____ -in-the-door technique, the door-in-the-[52] _____ approach, and the low-ball technique.

To [53] _____ the odds with salespeople, one should know a rough [54] _____ of the product, get the negotiated price in [55] _____ , and compare the negotiated price with other stores to get the best deal.

Self-assertion involves clearly stating one's [56] _____ and [57] _____ to others.

Aggression expresses one's feelings and desires, but it [58] _____ others.

Learning to be [59] _____ is accomplished by role-playing and rehearsing assertive actions.

MODULE 16.4

Survey Questions: How do we acquire attitudes, and how are they changed? Pages 619-621

Attitudes are learned tendencies to respond in a [60] _____ or [61] _____ way.

Attitudes are made up of a belief component, an emotional component, and an [62] _____ component.

Attitudes may be formed by [63] _____ contact, interaction with others, the effects of [64] _____ -rearing practices, and social pressures from group membership.

Peer group influences, the mass [65] _____ , and [66] _____ conditioning (accidental learning) also appear to be important in attitude formation.

The [67] _____ consequences of actions, how we think others will [68] _____ our actions, and habits all influence whether attitudes are converted to actions.

Attitudes held with conviction are most likely to be [69] _____ in behavior.

Survey Question: Under what conditions is persuasion most effective? Pages 621-623

People tend to change their attitudes to match those of their reference group (a group the person [70] _____ with and refers to for guidance).

Effective persuasion occurs when characteristics of the communicator, the [71] _____ , and the audience are well matched.

In general, a likable and believable communicator who repeats a credible message that arouses [72] _____ in the audience and states clear-cut [73] _____ will be persuasive.

Maintaining and changing attitudes is closely related to needs for [74] _____ in thoughts and actions. Cognitive dissonance theory explains the dynamics of such needs.

Cognitive dissonance occurs when there is a [75] _____ between thoughts or between thoughts and actions.

The amount of reward or justification (reasons) for one's actions influences whether [76] _____ occurs.

We are motivated to [77] _____ dissonance when it occurs, often by changing beliefs or attitudes.

Survey Questions: Is brainwashing actually possible? How are people converted to cult membership? Pages 623-625

Brainwashing is a form of [78] _____ attitude change. It depends on control of the target person's total environment.

Three steps in brainwashing are unfreezing (loosening) old attitudes and beliefs, [79] _____ , and refreezing (rewarding and strengthening) new attitudes and beliefs.

Many cults recruit new members with high-pressure indoctrination techniques resembling [80] _____ .

Cults attempt to catch people when they are vulnerable. Then they combine isolation, displays of [81] _____ , discipline and rituals, intimidation, and escalating commitment to bring about [82] _____ .

MODULE 16.5

Survey Question: What causes prejudice and intergroup conflict? Pages 626-631

Prejudice is a [83] _____ attitude held toward members of various out-groups.

Racism, ageism, and sexism are specific types of prejudice based on race, age, and [84] _____ .

One theory attributes prejudice to scapegoating, which is a type of displaced [85] _____ .

A second account says that prejudices may be held for personal reasons such as direct threats to a person's well-being (personal prejudice) or simply through adherence to group [86] _____ (group prejudice).

Prejudiced individuals tend to have an authoritarian [87] _____ , characterized by rigidity, inhibition, intolerance, and [88] _____ .

Authoritarians tend to be very ethnocentric (they use their own [89] _____ as a basis for judging all others).

Intergroup [90] _____ gives rise to hostility and the formation of social stereotypes (oversimplified images of members of various groups).

Symbolic prejudice, or prejudice expressed in [91] _____ ways, is common today.

[92] _____ inequalities (differences in power, prestige, or privileges) tend to build prejudices.

In-group beliefs of superiority, [93] _____ , vulnerability, and distrust are common variables that promote [94] _____ between groups.

Equal-status contact (social interaction on an equal footing) tends to [95] _____ prejudice.

Superordinate [96] _____ (those that rise above all others) usually reduce intergroup conflict.

On a small scale, jigsaw [97] _____ (which encourage cooperation through [98] _____ interdependence) have been shown to be an effective way of combating prejudice.

MODULE 16.6

Survey Question: How do psychologists explain human aggression? Pages 632-635

Ethologists explain aggression as a natural expression of inherited [99] _____ .

Biological explanations emphasize brain mechanisms and physical factors that [100] _____ the threshold (trigger point) for aggression.

According to the frustration-[101] _____ hypothesis, frustration and [102] _____ are closely linked.

Frustration is only one of many aversive [103] _____ that can arouse a person and make aggression more likely. Aggression is especially likely to occur when [104] _____ cues (stimuli associated with aggression) are present.

Social learning theory has focused attention on the role of aggressive [105] _____ in the development of aggressive behavior.

Aggressive [106] _____ on television encourage aggression because they desensitize (lower the sensitivity of) [107] _____ to violence and disinhibit (remove restraints against) aggressive impulses.

Students who plan to [108] _____ violence in school might disrupt classes, fight, join gangs, [109] _____ property, get [110] _____ easily, react with [111] _____ anger to criticism, blame others for their troubles, and use drugs.

To [112] _____ anger, aggression, and violence, parents should [113] _____ children, avoid hitting children, be consistent in disciplining children, and teach children [114] _____ ways to solve problems.

Survey Question: Why are bystanders so often unwilling to help in an emergency? Pages 635-638

Prosocial behavior is [115] _____ , constructive, or altruistic toward others.

Bystander apathy is the unwillingness of bystanders to offer [116] _____ to others during emergencies.

Four decision points that must be passed before a person gives help are: [117] _____ , defining an emergency, taking responsibility, and selecting a course of action.

Helping is [118] _____ likely at each point when other potential helpers are present.

Helping is encouraged by general arousal, empathic [119] _____ , being in a good mood, low effort or [120] _____ , and perceived similarity between the victim and the helper.

Altruistic behaviors can be seen in people who perform acts of [121] _____ by saving people from various disasters, [122] _____ their kidneys and blood, volunteering for the Peace Corps, and [123] _____ children's games.

A method to [124] _____ negative stereotypes is to use individuating information, which requires getting to know someone on an [125] _____ and personal level.

PSYCHOLOGY IN ACTION

Survey Question: What can be done to avoid prejudice and promote social harmony? Pages 640-642

Multiculturalism is an attempt to give [126] _____ status to different ethnic, racial, and cultural groups.

To [127] _____ prejudice, one can do the following: Be [128] _____ of stereotyping, seek individuating information, beware of [129] _____ -world beliefs, understand that race is a [130] _____ construction, look for commonalities, and set examples for others.

[131] _____ awareness is a key element in promoting greater social harmony.

Greater tolerance can be encouraged by neutralizing stereotypes with individuating information (which helps see others as [132] _____).

Tolerance comes from looking for commonalties with others and by avoiding the effects of just-world [133] _____ , self-fulfilling prophecies, and [134] _____ competition.

Cultural awareness refers to [135] _____ one's understanding of how people from different cultures and religious backgrounds practice their [136] _____ and traditions to [137] _____ misunderstanding, stereotyping, and prejudice.

CONNECTIONS

MODULE 16.1

1. _____ competency
2. _____ reciprocity
3. _____ proximity
4. _____ interpersonal attraction
5. _____ social comparison
6. _____ need to affiliate

a. comparing ourselves to others
b. return in kind
c. a person's proficiency
d. affinity to others
e. desire to associate
f. nearness

MODULE 16.2

1. _____ achieved role
2. _____ ascribed role
3. _____ attribution
4. _____ norm
5. _____ social comparison
6. _____ conformity
7. _____ status
8. _____ group sanctions

a. privilege and importance
b. rule or standard
c. assigned role
d. matching behavior
e. relating self to others
f. rewards and punishments
g. voluntary role
h. social inference

MODULE 16.3

1. _____ assertiveness
2. _____ broken record
3. _____ obedience
4. _____ compliance
5. _____ foot-in-the-door

a. self-assertion technique
b. salesperson's tactic
c. honest expression
d. following authority
e. yielding to requests

MODULE 16.4

1. _____ brainwashing
2. _____ attitude
3. _____ reference group
4. _____ chance conditioning
5. _____ persuasion
6. _____ dissonance

a. change attitude with arguments
b. coincidence
c. belief + emotion + action
d. uncomfortable clash
e. standard for social comparison
f. thought reform

MODULE 16.5

1. _____ scapegoat
2. _____ stereotype
3. _____ superordinate
4. _____ symbolic prejudice
5. _____ discrimination
6. _____ authoritarianism
7. _____ ethnocentric

a. aggression target
b. above all others
c. group centered
d. unequal treatment
e. oversimplified image
f. F Scale
g. modern bias

MODULE 16.6

1. _____ bystander apathy
2. _____ desensitization
3. _____ prosocial
4. _____ disinhibition
5. _____ weapons effect
6. _____ empathic arousal
7. _____ aggression
8. _____ multiculturalism

a. "tossed salad"
b. reduced emotional sensitivity
c. remove inhibition
d. feeling someone's anguish
e. aggression cue
f. Kitty Genovese
g. intent to harm
h. altruistic behavior

CHECK YOUR MEMORY

MODULE 16.1

Survey Questions: Why do people affiliate? What factors influence interpersonal attraction? Pages 602-606

1. The Stanford prison experiment investigated the impact of the roles of prisoner and guard.
   TRUE or FALSE

2. The need to affiliate is a basic human characteristic.
   TRUE or FALSE

3. People who are frightened prefer to be with others who are in similar circumstances.
TRUE or FALSE

4. Interpersonal attraction to someone takes weeks to develop.
TRUE or FALSE

5. Social comparisons are used to confirm objective evaluations and measurements.
TRUE or FALSE

6. Useful social comparisons are usually made with persons similar to ourselves.
TRUE or FALSE

7. Nearness has a powerful impact on forming friendships.
TRUE or FALSE

8. Homogamy, marrying someone who is like oneself, does not apply to unmarried couples.
TRUE or FALSE

9. Physical proximity leads us to think of people as competent and therefore worth knowing.
TRUE or FALSE

10. The halo effect is the tendency to generalize a positive or negative first impression to other personal characteristics.
TRUE or FALSE

11. Physical attractiveness is closely associated with intelligence, talents, and abilities.
TRUE or FALSE

12. The risk of divorce is higher than average for couples who have large differences in age and education.
TRUE or FALSE

13. In choosing mates, women rank physical attractiveness as the most important feature.
TRUE or FALSE

14. Self-disclosure is a major step toward friendship.
TRUE or FALSE

15. Overdisclosure tends to elicit maximum self-disclosure from others.
TRUE or FALSE

16. Self-disclosure through an Internet chat room can lead to genuine, face-to-face friendship.
TRUE or FALSE

17. The statement "I find it easy to ignore _____'s faults" is an item on the Liking Scale.
TRUE or FALSE

18. Where their mates are concerned, men tend to be more jealous over a loss of emotional commitment than they are over sexual infidelities.
TRUE or FALSE

MODULE 16.2

Survey Question: How does group membership affect our behavior? Pages 608-610

19. Son, husband, and teacher are achieved roles.
    TRUE or FALSE

20. Persons of higher status tend to receive special treatment and privileges.
    TRUE or FALSE

21. A group could have a high degree of structure but low cohesiveness.
    TRUE or FALSE

22. Group cohesion refers to the dimensions that define a group such as ethnicity, age, or religion.
    TRUE or FALSE

23. "Us and them" refers to members of the in-group perceiving themselves as one unit and everyone else as the out-group.
    TRUE or FALSE

24. The more trash that is visible in public places, the more likely people are to litter.
    TRUE or FALSE

25. If someone always salts her food before eating, it implies that her behavior has an external cause.
    TRUE or FALSE

26. Attributing the actions of others to external causes is the most common attributional error.
    TRUE or FALSE

27. Good performances by women are more often attributed to luck than skill.
    TRUE or FALSE

Survey Question: What factors influence our willingness to conform to a majority? Pages 610-612

28. Conformity situations occur when a person becomes aware of differences between his or her own behavior and that of a group.
    TRUE or FALSE

29. Most subjects in the Asch conformity experiments suspected that they were being deceived in some way.
    TRUE or FALSE

30. Seventy-five percent of Asch's subjects yielded to the group at least once.
    TRUE or FALSE

31. People who are anxious are more likely to conform to group pressure.
    TRUE or FALSE

32. Groupthink is more likely to occur when people emphasize the task at hand rather than the bonds between group members.
    TRUE or FALSE

33. Rejection, ridicule, and disapproval are group norms that tend to enforce conformity.
    TRUE or FALSE

34. A unanimous majority of three is more powerful than a majority of eight with one person dissenting.
    TRUE or FALSE

MODULE 16.3

Survey Question: What have psychologists learned about obedience, compliance, and self-assertion?
Pages 613-618

35. Milgram's famous shock experiment was done to study compliance and conformity.
    TRUE or FALSE

36. Over half of Milgram's "teachers" went all the way to the maximum shock level.
    TRUE or FALSE

37. Being face-to-face with the learner had no effect on the number of subjects who obeyed in the Milgram experiments.
    TRUE or FALSE

38. People are less likely to obey an unjust authority if they have seen others disobey.
    TRUE or FALSE

39. The foot-in-the-door effect is a way to gain compliance from another person.
    TRUE or FALSE

40. The low-ball technique involves changing the terms that a person has agreed to so that they are less desirable from the person's point of view.
    TRUE or FALSE

41. Using the door-in-the-face strategy is an effective way to even the odds with salespeople for using the low-ball technique.
    TRUE or FALSE

42. Many people have difficulty asserting themselves because they have learned to be obedient and good.
    TRUE or FALSE

43. Self-assertion involves the rights to request, reject, and retaliate.
    TRUE or FALSE

44. In order to be assertive, you should never admit that you were wrong.
    TRUE or FALSE

MODULE 16.4

Survey Questions: How do we acquire attitudes, and how are they changed? Pages 619-621

45. Attitudes predict and direct future actions.
TRUE or FALSE

46. What you think about the object of an attitude makes up its belief component.
TRUE or FALSE

47. Attitudes are only composed of our positive or negative opinions of others. They do not include a behavioral component.
TRUE or FALSE

48. If both parents belong to the same political party, their child probably will too.
TRUE or FALSE

49. A person who deviates from the majority opinion in a group tends to be excluded from conversation.
TRUE or FALSE

50. Heavy TV viewers feel safer than average because they spend so much time in security at home.
TRUE or FALSE

51. An attitude held with conviction is more likely to be acted upon.
TRUE or FALSE

Survey Question: Under what conditions is persuasion most effective? Pages 621-623

52. Our attitudes are more likely to match those held by members of our reference groups than our membership groups.
TRUE or FALSE

53. Persuasion refers to a deliberate attempt to change a person's reference groups.
TRUE or FALSE

54. Persuasion is less effective if the message appeals to the emotions.
TRUE or FALSE

55. For a poorly informed audience, persuasion is more effective if only one side of the argument is presented.
TRUE or FALSE

56. A persuasive message should not be repeated; doing so just weakens its impact.
TRUE or FALSE

57. Acting contrary to one's attitudes or self-image causes cognitive dissonance.
TRUE or FALSE

58. Public commitment to an attitude or belief makes it more difficult to change.

    TRUE or FALSE

59. The greater the reward or justification for acting contrary to one's beliefs, the greater the cognitive dissonance felt.

    TRUE or FALSE

60. Dissonance is especially likely to be felt when a person causes an undesired event to occur.

    TRUE or FALSE

Survey Questions: Is brainwashing actually possible? How are people converted to cult membership? Pages 623-625

61. Roughly 16 percent of American POWs in the Korean War signed false confessions.

    TRUE or FALSE

62. True brainwashing requires a captive audience.

    TRUE or FALSE

63. In brainwashing, the target person is housed with other people who hold the same attitudes and beliefs that he or she does.

    TRUE or FALSE

64. In most cases, the effects of brainwashing are very resistant to further change.

    TRUE or FALSE

65. Cult leaders, like David Koresh, use brainwashing as a technique to persuade people to conform.

    TRUE or FALSE

66. A cult is a group in which the belief system is more important than the leader who espouses it.

    TRUE or FALSE

67. Cults play on emotions and discourage critical thinking.

    TRUE or FALSE

68. Cult members are typically isolated from former reference groups.

    TRUE or FALSE

MODULE 16.5

Survey Question: What causes prejudice and intergroup conflict? Pages 626-631

69. Sexism is a type of prejudice.

    TRUE or FALSE

70. The term "racial profiling" refers to giving preferential treatment to some students seeking admission to college.

    TRUE or FALSE

71. Scapegoating is a prime example of discrimination.

    TRUE or FALSE

72. A person who views members of another group as competitors for jobs displays group prejudice.

    TRUE or FALSE

73. Authoritarian persons tend to be prejudiced against all out-groups.

    TRUE or FALSE

74. The F in F Scale stands for fanatic.

    TRUE or FALSE

75. An authoritarian would agree that people can be divided into the weak and the strong.

    TRUE or FALSE

76. Social stereotypes can be positive as well as negative.

    TRUE or FALSE

77. Symbolic prejudice is the most obvious and socially unacceptable form of bigotry.

    TRUE or FALSE

78. Children as young as age three have begun to show signs of racial bias.

    TRUE or FALSE

79. Beliefs on superiority, injustice, and distrust are common variables that tend to promote conflict among members of the in-group.

    TRUE or FALSE

80. Symbolic prejudice occurs when people understand the causes of prejudice and do not discriminate against minorities.

    TRUE or FALSE

81. The key to creating prejudice in Jane Elliot's experiment was her use of scapegoating to cause group conflict.

    TRUE or FALSE

82. Equal-status contact tends to reduce prejudice and stereotypes.

    TRUE or FALSE

83. Superordinate groups help people of opposing groups to see themselves as members of a single larger group.

    TRUE or FALSE

MODULE 16.6

Survey Question: How do psychologists explain human aggression? Pages 632-635

84. Ethologists argue that humans learn to be aggressive by observing aggressive behavior in lower animals.
TRUE or FALSE

85. Specific areas of the brain are capable of initiating or ending aggression.
TRUE or FALSE

86. Intoxication tends to raise the threshold for aggression, making it more likely.
TRUE or FALSE

87. Higher levels of the hormone testosterone are associated with more aggressive behavior by both men and women.
TRUE or FALSE

88. The frustration-aggression hypothesis says that being aggressive is frustrating.
TRUE or FALSE

89. People exposed to aversive stimuli tend to become less sensitive to aggression cues.
TRUE or FALSE

90. Murders are less likely to occur in homes where guns are kept.
TRUE or FALSE

91. Social learning theorists assume that instinctive patterns of human aggression are modified by learning.
TRUE or FALSE

92. American Quakers have adopted a nonviolent way of life as a way to inhibit aggression.
TRUE or FALSE

93. According to Eron, children learn aggression from direct contact with other children and not from indirect contact from TV programs.
TRUE or FALSE

94. To discourage violence, parents should get themselves and their children involved in community-related activities.
TRUE or FALSE

95. Aggressive crimes in TV dramas occur at a much higher rate than they do in real life.
TRUE or FALSE

Survey Question: Why are bystanders so often unwilling to help in an emergency? Pages 635-638

96. In the Kitty Genovese murder, no one called the police until after the attack was over.
TRUE or FALSE

97. In an emergency, the more potential helpers present, the more likely a person is to get help.
TRUE or FALSE

98. The first step in giving help is to define the situation as an emergency.
TRUE or FALSE

99. Emotional arousal, especially empathic arousal, lowers the likelihood that one person will help another.
TRUE or FALSE

100. You are more likely to help a person who seems similar to yourself.
TRUE or FALSE

101. In many emergency situations it can be more effective to shout "Fire!" rather than "Help!"
TRUE or FALSE

PSYCHOLOGY IN ACTION

Survey Question: What can be done to avoid prejudice and promote social harmony? Pages 640-642

102. Multiculturalism is an attempt to blend multiple ethnic backgrounds into one universal culture.
TRUE or FALSE

103. A study conducted in Canada found that increasing interaction among different groups only increases negative stereotypes of both groups.
TRUE or FALSE

104. Members of major groups in the United States rated themselves better than other groups to enhance their self-esteem.
TRUE or FALSE

105. The emotional component of prejudicial attitudes may remain even after a person intellectually renounces prejudice.
TRUE or FALSE

106. Both prejudiced and nonprejudiced people are equally aware of social stereotypes.
TRUE or FALSE

107. Individuating information forces us to focus mainly on the labels attached to a person.
TRUE or FALSE

108. From a scientific point of view, race is a matter of social labeling, not a biological reality.
TRUE or FALSE

109. People who hold just-world beliefs assume that people generally get what they deserve.
TRUE or FALSE

110. Each ethnic group has strengths that members of other groups could benefit from emulating.
TRUE or FALSE

111. The statement "Don't judge somebody until you know them. The color of their skin doesn't matter" is an example of a way to promote understanding in an ethnically diverse group of people. TRUE or FALSE

FINAL SURVEY AND REVIEW

MODULE 16.1

Survey Questions: Why do people affiliate? What factors influence interpersonal attraction? Pages 602-606

[1] _____ studies how individuals behave, think, and feel in social situations.

The [2] _____ to [3] _____ is tied to additional needs for approval, support, friendship, and information.

Additionally, research indicates that we sometimes affiliate to reduce [4] _____ and uncertainty.

Social [5] _____ theory holds that we affiliate to evaluate our actions, feelings, and abilities.

Interpersonal attraction is increased by physical [6] _____ (nearness) and frequent contact.

Initial acquaintance and attraction are influenced by [7] _____ attractiveness (beauty),

[8] _____ (high ability), and similarity.

A large degree of similarity on many dimensions is characteristic of mate selection, a pattern called

[9] _____ .

[10] _____ (revealing oneself to others) occurs to a greater degree if two people like one another.

Self-disclosure follows a [11] _____ norm: Moderate self-disclosure elicits more personal replies, and [12] _____ (excessive) tends to inhibit self-disclosure by others.

Romantic love can be distinguished from liking by the use of [13] _____ [14] _____ .

Dating couples love and like their partners but only like their friends.

Romantic love is also associated with greater mutual [15] _____ between people.

[16] _____ psychology attributes human mating patterns to the differing [17] _____ challenges faced by men and women since the dawn of time.

MODULE 16.2

Survey Question: How does group membership affect our behavior? Pages 608-610

One's position in groups defines a variety of [18] _____ to be played.

Social roles, which may be [19] _____ or [20] _____ , are particular behavior patterns associated with social positions.

When two or more contradictory roles are held, role [21] _____ may occur.

Two dimensions of a group are group [22] _____ (network of roles, communication pathways, and power) and group [23] _____ (members' desire to remain in the group). Group cohesion is strong for [24] _____ members.

Members of the [25] _____ identify themselves based on a combination of dimensions such as nationality, ethnicity, age, religion, income, etc. People tend to attribute [26] _____ traits to members of their in-group and [27] _____ traits to members of the out-group.

Positions within groups typically carry higher or lower levels of [28] _____ . [29] _____ [30] _____ is associated with special privileges and respect.

[31] _____ are standards of conduct enforced (formally or informally) by groups.

[32] _____ theory is concerned with how we make inferences about the causes of behavior.

Behavior can be attributed to [33] _____ causes or [34] _____ causes.

The [35] _____ error is to ascribe the actions of others to internal causes. This is part of an [36] _____ bias in which we ascribe the behavior of others to internal causes and our own behavior to external causes.

Survey Question: What factors influence our willingness to conform to a majority? Pages 610-612

[37] _____ refers to alterations in behavior brought about by the behavior of others.

[38] _____ to group pressure is a familiar example of social influence. Virtually everyone conforms to a variety of broad social and [39] _____ norms.

Conformity pressures also exist within small groups. The famous [40] _____ experiments demonstrated that various group [41] _____ encourage conformity.

[42] _____ refers to compulsive conformity in group decision making. Its victims seek to maintain each other's [43] _____ , even at the cost of critical thinking.

MODULE 16.3

Survey Question: What have psychologists learned about obedience, compliance, and self-assertion? Pages 613-618

[44] _____ to authority has been investigated in a variety of experiments, particularly those by Stanley [45] _____ .

Obedience in his studies [46] _____ when the victim was in the same room, when the victim and subject were face-to-face, when the [47] _____ figure was absent, and when others refused to obey.

[48] _____ with direct requests by a person who has little or no social power is another means by which behavior is influenced.

Three strategies for getting people to comply are the foot-in-the-[49] _____ technique, the [50] _____ -in-the-face approach, and the [51] _____ technique.

[52] _____ involves clearly stating one's wants and needs to others.

To [53] _____ the odds with salespeople, one should know a rough [54] _____ of the product, get the negotiated price in [55] _____ , and compare the negotiated price with other stores to get the best deal.

[56] _____ expresses one's feelings and desires, but it hurts others.

Learning to be assertive is accomplished by [57] _____ and rehearsing assertive actions.

MODULE 16.4

Survey Questions: How do we acquire attitudes, and how are they changed? Pages 619-621

Attitudes are [58] _____ to respond in a positive or negative way.

Attitudes are made up of a [59] _____ component, an [60] _____ component, and an action component.

Attitudes may be formed by direct [61] _____ interaction with others, the effects of child-rearing practices, and social pressures from [62] _____ .

[63] _____ group influences, the mass media, and chance [64] _____ (accidental learning) also appear to be important in attitude formation.

The immediate [65] _____ of actions, how we think others will evaluate our actions, and [66] _____ all influence whether attitudes are converted to actions.

Attitudes held with [67] _____ are most likely to be expressed in behavior.

Survey Question: Under what conditions is persuasion most effective? Pages 621-623

People tend to change their attitudes to match those of their [68] _____ group (a group the person identifies with and refers to for guidance).

Effective persuasion occurs when characteristics of the [69] _____ , the message, and the [70] _____ are well matched.

In general, a likable and believable [71] _____ who repeats a credible message that arouses emotion in the [72] _____ and states clear-cut conclusions will be persuasive.

Maintaining and changing attitudes is closely related to needs for consistency in thoughts and actions. Cognitive [73] _____ theory explains the dynamics of such needs.

Cognitive [74] _____ occurs when there is a clash between [75] _____ or between thoughts and actions.

The amount of [76] _____ or [77] _____ (reasons) for one's actions influences whether dissonance occurs.

We are motivated to reduce dissonance when it occurs, often by changing [78] _____ or [79] _____ rather than behavior.

Survey Questions: Is brainwashing actually possible? How are people converted to cult membership? Pages 623-625

Brainwashing is a form of forced attitude change. It depends on [80] _____ of the target person's total [81] _____ .

Three steps in brainwashing are [82] _____ (loosening) old attitudes and beliefs, change, and [83] _____ (rewarding and strengthening) new attitudes and beliefs.

Many cults recruit new members with high-pressure [84] _____ techniques resembling brainwashing.

Cults attempt to catch people when they are vulnerable. Then they combine isolation, displays of affection, discipline and [85] _____ , intimidation, and escalating [86] _____ to bring about conversion.

MODULE 16.5

Survey Question: What causes prejudice and intergroup conflict? Pages 626-631

Prejudice is a negative attitude held toward members of various [87] _____ .

[88] _____ , [89] _____ , and [90] _____ are specific types of prejudice based on race, age, and gender.

One theory attributes prejudice to [91] _____ , which is a type of [92] _____ aggression.

A second account says that prejudices may be held for personal reasons such as direct threats to a person's well-being ([93] _____ prejudice) or simply through adherence to group norms ([94] _____ prejudice).

Prejudiced individuals tend to have an [95] _____ personality characterized by rigidity, inhibition, intolerance, and oversimplification.

Authoritarians tend to be very [96] _____ (they use their own group as a basis for judging all others).

Intergroup conflict gives rise to hostility and the formation of [97] _____ [98] _____ (oversimplified images of members of various groups).

[99] _____ prejudice, or prejudice expressed in disguised ways, is common today.

Status [100] _____ (differences in power, prestige, or privileges) tend to build prejudices.

[101] _____ beliefs of superiority, injustice, vulnerability, and distrust are common variables that promote [102] _____ between groups.

[103] _____ contact (social interaction on an equal footing) tends to reduce prejudice.

[104] _____ goals (those that rise above all others) usually reduce intergroup conflict.

On a small scale, [105] _____ classrooms (which encourage cooperation through mutual [106] _____) have been shown to be an effective way of combating prejudice.

MODULE 16.6

Survey Question: How do psychologists explain human aggression? Pages 632-635

[107] _____ explain aggression as a natural expression of inherited instincts.

Biological explanations emphasize brain mechanisms and physical factors that lower the [108] _____ (trigger point) for aggression.

According to the [109] _____ -aggression hypothesis, [110] _____ and aggression are closely linked.

Frustration is only one of many [111] _____ stimuli that can arouse a person and make aggression more likely. Aggression is especially likely to occur when aggression [112] _____ (stimuli associated with aggression) are present.

[113] _____ theory has focused attention on the role of aggressive models in the development of aggressive behavior.

Aggressive models on television encourage aggression because they [114] _____ (lower the sensitivity of) viewers to violence and [115] _____ (remove restraints against) aggressive impulses.

Students who plan to commit [116] _____ in school might disrupt classes, fight, join gangs, destroy property, get [117] _____ easily, react with [118] _____ anger to criticism, blame others for their troubles, and use drugs.

To [119] _____ anger, aggression, and violence, parents should supervise children, [120] _____ hitting children, be consistent in disciplining children, and teach children [121] _____ ways to solve problems.

Survey Question: Why are bystanders so often unwilling to help in an emergency? Pages 635-638

Prosocial behavior is helpful, constructive, or [122] _____ toward others.

Bystander [123] _____ is the unwillingness of bystanders to offer help to others during emergencies.

Four decision points that must be passed before a person gives help are: noticing, defining an [124] _____ , taking [125] _____ , and selecting a course of action.

Helping is less likely at each point when other [126] _____ are present.

Helping is encouraged by general arousal, [127] _____ arousal, being in a good mood, low effort or risk, and perceived [128] _____ between the victim and the helper.

[129] _____ behaviors can be seen in people who perform acts of heroism by [130] _____ people from various disasters, [131] _____ their kidneys and blood, volunteering for the Peace Corps, and coaching children's games.

A method to reduce negative stereotypes is to use [132] _____ information, which requires getting to know someone on an individual and personal level.

PSYCHOLOGY IN ACTION

Survey Question: What can be done to avoid prejudice and promote social harmony? Pages 640-642

[133] _____ is an attempt to give equal status to different ethnic, racial, and cultural groups.

To reduce prejudice, one can do the following: Be [134] _____ of stereotyping, seek individuating information, beware of [135] _____ -world beliefs, understand that race is a [136] _____ construction, look for commonalities, and set examples for others.

Cultural [137] _____ is a key element in promoting greater social harmony.

Greater tolerance can be encouraged by neutralizing stereotypes with [138] _____ information (which helps see others as individuals).

Tolerance comes from looking for commonalties with others and by avoiding the effects of [139] _____ beliefs, [140] _____ prophecies, and social competition.

[141] _____ awareness refers to increasing one's [142] _____ of how people from different cultures and religious backgrounds practice their beliefs and traditions to prevent misunderstanding, [143] _____ , and prejudice.

MASTERY TEST

1. Homogamy is directly related to which element of interpersonal attraction?
    a. competence
    b. similarity
    c. beauty
    d. proximity

2. The weapons effect refers to the fact that weapons can serve as aggression
    a. thresholds
    b. cues
    c. models
    d. inhibitors

3. Suspicion and reduced attraction are associated with
    a. reciprocity
    b. self-disclosure
    c. competence and proximity
    d. overdisclosure

4. The Seekers's renewed conviction and interest in persuading others after the world failed to end can be explained by the
    a. social competition hypothesis
    b. frustration-persuasion hypothesis
    c. group's just-world beliefs
    d. theory of cognitive dissonance

5. One thing that REDUCES the chances that a bystander will give help in an emergency is
    a. heightened arousal
    b. empathic arousal
    c. others who could help
    d. similarity to the victim

6. One consequence of seeing aggression portrayed on TV is a loss of emotional response, called
   a. disinhibition
   b. disassociation
   c. deconditioning
   d. desensitization

7. If you are speaking to a well-informed audience, it is important to _____ if you want to persuade them.
   a. repeat your message
   b. give both sides of the argument
   c. be likable
   d. appeal to their emotions

8. "President of the United States" is
   a. an ascribed role
   b. an achieved role
   c. a structural norm
   d. a cohesive role

9. Where attribution is concerned, wants, needs, motives, or personal characteristics are perceived as
   a. external causes
   b. situational attributions
   c. discounted causes
   d. internal causes

10. Asch is to _____ experiments as Milgram is to _____ experiments.
    a. compliance, assertion
    b. conformity, obedience
    c. autokinetic, social power
    d. groupthink, authority

11. Social psychology is the scientific study of how people
    a. behave in the presence of others
    b. form into groups and organizations
    c. form and maintain interpersonal relationships
    d. make inferences about the behavior of others

12. "A person who first agrees with a small request is later more likely to comply with a larger demand." This statement summarizes the
    a. low-ball technique
    b. set-the-hook technique
    c. door-in-the-face effect
    d. foot-in-the-door effect

13. Which view of human aggression is most directly opposed to that of the ethologists?
    a. social learning
    b. brain mechanisms
    c. attributional
    d. innate releaser

14. Creating superordinate goals is an important way to
    a. reduce group conflict
    b. break the frustration-aggression link
    c. promote bystander intervention
    d. reverse self-fulfilling prophecies

15. A key element in the effectiveness of jigsaw classrooms is
    a. deindividuation
    b. the promotion of self-fulfilling prophecies
    c. mutual interdependence
    d. selecting competent student leaders

16. Which of the following factors tends to REDUCE prejudice and stereotyping?
    a. just-world beliefs
    b. social competition
    c. self-fulfilling prophecies
    d. individuating information

17. A guard in the Stanford prison experiment who discovers that one of the prisoners is a friend would very likely experience
    a. role conflict
    b. a change in status
    c. groupthink
    d. a shift to coercive power

18. Groupthink is a type of _____ that applies to decision making in groups.
    a. conformity
    b. social comparison
    c. social power
    d. obedience

19. A good antidote for social stereotyping is
    a. adopting just-world beliefs
    b. creating self-fulfilling prophecies
    c. accepting status inequalities
    d. seeking individuating information

20. An important difference between brainwashing and other types of persuasion is that brainwashing
    a. requires a captive audience
    b. is almost always permanent
    c. changes actions, not attitudes and beliefs
    d. is reversed during the refreezing phase

21. In Milgram's studies, the smallest percentage of subjects followed orders when
    a. the teacher and learner were in the same room
    b. the teacher received orders by phone
    c. the teacher and learner were face-to-face
    d. the experiment was conducted off campus

22. The most basic attributional error is to attribute the behavior of others to _____ causes, even when they are caused by _____ causes.
    a. inconsistent, consistent
    b. internal, external
    c. random, distinctive
    d. situational, personal

23. In an experiment, most women waiting to receive a shock preferred to wait with others who
    a. were about to be shocked
    b. did not share their fears
    c. were trained to calm them
    d. had been shocked the day before

24. Evolutionary theories attribute mate selection, in part, to the _____ of past generations.
    a. food-gathering habits
    b. tribal customs
    c. maternal instincts
    d. reproductive success

25. People tend to act like what is beautiful is good. However, beauty has little connection to
    a. talents
    b. intelligence
    c. ability
    d. all the preceding traits

26. Which of the following gives special privileges to a member of a group?
    a. convergent norms
    b. high cohesiveness
    c. actor-observer bias
    d. high status

27. Your actions are most likely to agree with one of your attitudes when
    a. the actions reverse an old habit
    b. the attitude is held with conviction
    c. you know that others disagree with your position
    d. you score high on an attitude scale

28. When we are subjected to conformity pressures, the _____ of a majority is more important than the number of people in it.
    a. unanimity
    b. cohesion
    c. proximity
    d. comparison level

29. If it is easier for Anglo-Americans to get automobile insurance than it is for African Americans, then African Americans have experienced
    a. discrimination
    b. scapegoating
    c. ethnocentrism
    d. personal prejudice

30. The Bennington College study showed that attitudes are not affected very much by
    a. membership groups
    b. childrearing
    c. reference groups
    d. chance conditioning

31. _____ consists of a network of roles, communication pathways, and power in a group.
    a. Group cohesiveness
    b. Group structure
    c. Group norm
    d. Group goal

32. Members of the _____ are people who share similar values, goals, interest, and identify themselves as belonging to a same group.
    a. in-group
    b. out-group
    c. pepgroup
    d. essential group

33. Which tactic should one use to get someone to voluntarily comply with a request?
    a. foot-in-the-door
    b. door-in-the-face
    c. high-ball
    d. both a and b

34. Kyle has taken a psychology class and is aware of the tactics that salespeople use to hook customers into buying their products. He reviewed the cost of a car model that he is interested in from a consumer's reports guide. Having a general idea of a price, Kyle can negotiate with the salesperson, and after getting a quote from a salesperson, Kyle should
    a. buy the car immediately because the salesperson is offering him a good deal
    b. tell the salesperson he has changed his mind and does not need a new car
    c. tell the salesperson he cannot afford it
    d. leave the store and compare the quoted price to other car dealers

35. In April 1993 in Waco, Texas, David Koresh used a mixture of manipulation, isolation, deception, and fear to gain absolute loyalty and obedience from a group of followers who ultimately committed suicide at his request. This is an example of
    a. brainwashing
    b. scapegoating
    c. desensitization
    d. discrimination

36. Beliefs concerning superiority, injustice, vulnerability, and distrust are common variables that promote
    a. cooperation from out-group members
    b. cooperation from in-group members
    c. hostilities between out-group members
    d. hostilities within in-group members

37. When a white candidate is given "the benefit of the doubt" on his/her abilities to perform a task and is hired for a position for which other black candidates are qualified, is an example of
    a. symbolic prejudice
    b. modern racism
    c. justice
    d. both a and b

38. Which theory combines learning principles with cognitive processes, socialization, and modeling to explain human behavior?
    a. social learning
    b. individuating information
    c. existential
    d. multiculturalism

39. Students who are disruptive, get into fights, destroy property, react with extreme anger to criticism, blame others for their troubles, and use drugs are exhibiting signs that they might
    a. commit violent acts toward others
    b. commit suicide
    c. join the Peace Corps
    d. none of the above

40. Billy's new neighbor is from Pakistan. Because Billy wants to avoid misunderstandings and conflict when he meets and talks to his neighbor, he attends a cultural event sponsored by the Pakistani student club at his university. Billy is attempting to
    a. set an example for others in his neighborhood
    b. increase his cultural awareness of other's culture
    c. reduce stereotypes and prejudicial views of others
    d. all the preceding

SOLUTIONS

RECITE AND REVIEW

MODULE 16.1

1. Social
2. approval
3. information
4. reduce
5. evaluate
6. nearness
7. contact
8. attraction
9. similarity
10. mate
11. revealing
12. norm
13. self-disclosure
14. like
15. love
16. like
17. mutual
18. mating

MODULE 16.2

19. groups
20. Social roles
21. contradictory
22. roles
23. remain
24. in-group
25. in-group
26. ethnicity
27. religion
28. positive
29. out-group
30. groups
31. standards
32. groups
33. causes
34. causes
35. causes
36. error
37. internal
38. internal
39. external

40. behavior
41. others
42. conforms
43. norms
44. groups
45. group
46. decision making

MODULE 16.3

47. authority
48. Obedience
49. requests
50. power
51. foot
52. face
53. even
54. price
55. writing
56. wants
57. needs
58. hurts
59. assertive

MODULE 16.4

60. positive
61. negative
62. action
63. direct
64. child
65. media
66. chance
67. immediate
68. evaluate
69. expressed

70. identifies
71. message
72. emotion
73. conclusions
74. consistency
75. clash
76. dissonance
77. reduce

78. forced

79. changing
80. brainwashing

81. affection
82. conversion

MODULE 16.5

83. negative
84. gender (or sex)
85. aggression
86. norms
87. personality
88. oversimplification

89. group
90. conflict
91. disguised
92. Status
93. injustice
94. hostilities

95. reduce
96. goals
97. classrooms
98. mutual

MODULE 16.6

99. instincts
100. lower
101. aggression
102. aggression
103. stimuli
104. aggression

105. models
106. models
107. viewers
108. commit
109. destroy
110. frustrated

111. extreme
112. minimize
113. supervise
114. nonaggressive

115. helpful
116. help
117. noticing
118. less

119. arousal
120. risk
121. heroism
122. donating

123. coaching
124. reduce
125. individual

PSYCHOLOGY IN ACTION

126. equal
127. reduce
128. aware
129. just

130. social
131. Cultural
132. individuals
133. beliefs

134. social
135. increasing
136. beliefs
137. prevent

CONNECTIONS

MODULE 16.1

1. c
2. b

3. f
4. d

5. a
6. e

MODULE 16.2

1. g
2. c
3. h

4. b
5. e
6. d

7. a
8. f

MODULE 16.3

1. c

2. a

3. d

4. e	5. b	

MODULE 16.4

1. f	3. e	5. a
2. c	4. b	6. d

MODULE 16.5

1. a	4. g	7. c
2. e	5. d	
3. b	6. f	

MODULE 16.6

1. f	4. c	7. g
2. b	5. e	8. a
3. h	6. d	

CHECK YOUR MEMORY

MODULE 16.1

1. T	7. T	13. F
2. T	8. F	14. T
3. T	9. F	15. F
4. F	10. T	16. T
5. F	11. F	17. F
6. T	12. T	18. F

MODULE 16.2

19. F	22. F	25. F
20. T	23. T	26. F
21. T	24. T	27. T
28. T	31. T	34. T
29. F	32. F	
30. T	33. F	

MODULE 16.3

35. F	39. T	43. F
36. T	40. T	44. F
37. F	41. F	
38. T	42. T	

MODULE 16.4
45. T

46. T	48. T	50. F
47. F	49. T	51. T

52. T	55. T	58. T
53. F	56. F	59. F
54. F	57. T	60. T

61. T	64. F	67. T
62. T	65. T	68. T
63. F	66. F	

MODULE 16.5

69. T	74. F	79. F
70. F	75. T	80. F
71. F	76. T	81. F
72. F	77. F	82. T
73. T	78. T	83. T

MODULE 16.6

84. F	88. F	92. T
85. T	89. F	93. F
86. F	90. F	94. T
87. T	91. F	95. T

96. T	98. F	100. T
97. F	99. F	101. T

PSYCHOLOGY IN ACTION

102. F	106. T	110. T
103. F	107. F	111. T
104. T	108. T	
105. T	109. T	

FINAL SURVEY AND REVIEW

MODULE 16.1

1. Social psychology	6. proximity	11. reciprocity
2. need	7. physical	12. overdisclosure
3. affiliate	8. competence	13. attitude
4. anxiety	9. homogamy	14. scales
5. comparison	10. Self-disclosure	15. absorption

16. Evolutionary   17. reproductive

MODULE 16.2

18. roles   25. in-group   32. Attribution
19. achieved   26. positive   33. internal
20. ascribed   27. negative   34. external
21. conflict   28. status   35. fundamental attributional
22. structure   29. High   36. actor-observer
23. cohesiveness   30. status
24. in-group   31. Norms

37. Social influence   40. Asch   43. approval
38. Conformity   41. sanctions
39. cultural   42. Groupthink

MODULE 16.3

44. Obedience   50. door   56. Aggression
45. Milgram   51. low-ball   57. role-playing
46. decreased   52. Self-assertion
47. authority   53. even
48. Compliance   54. price
49. door   55. writing

MODULE 16.4

58. learned tendencies   62. group membership   66. habits
59. belief   63. Peer   67. conviction
60. emotional   64. conditioning
61. contact   65. consequences

68. reference   72. audience   76. reward
69. communicator   73. dissonance   77. justification
70. audience   74. dissonance   78. beliefs
71. communicator   75. thoughts   79. attitudes

80. control   83. refreezing   86. commitment
81. environment   84. indoctrination
82. unfreezing   85. rituals

MODULE 16.5

87. out-groups   89. ageism   91. scapegoating
88. Racism   90. sexism   92. displaced

93. personal
94. group
95. authoritarian
96. ethnocentric
97. social
98. stereotypes

99. Symbolic
100. inequalities
101. In-group
102. hostilities
103. Equal-status
104. Superordinate

105. jigsaw
106. interdependence

MODULE 16.6

107. Ethologists
108. threshold
109. frustration
110. frustration
111. aversive

112. cues
113. Social learning
114. desensitize
115. disinhibit
116. violence

117. frustrated
118. extreme
119. minimize
120. avoid
121. nonaggressive

122. altruistic
123. apathy
124. emergency
125. responsibility

126. potential helpers
127. empathic
128. similarity
129. Altruistic

130. saving
131. donating
132. individuating

PSYCHOLOGY IN ACTION

133. Multiculturalism
134. aware
135. just
136. social

137. awareness
138. individuating
139. just-world
140. self-fulfilling

141. Cultural
142. understanding
143. stereotyping

MASTERY TEST

1. B, (p. 604)
2. B, (p. 633)
3. D, (p. 604)
4. D, (p. 619, 622)
5. C, (p. 636, 637)
6. D, (p. 634)
7. B, (p. 622)
8. B, (p. 608)
9. D, (p. 609)
10. B, (p. 610, 613)
11. A, (p. 602)
12. D, (p. 615)
13. A, (p. 634)
14. A, (p. 630)
15. C, (p. 630)

16. D, (p. 640)
17. A, (p. 608)
18. A, (p. 611)
19. D, (p. 640)
20. A, (p. 623)
21. B, (p. 614)
22. B, (p. 609)
23. A, (p. 602)
24. D, (p. 606)
25. D, (p. 603)
26. D, (p. 608)
27. B, (p. 620)
28. A, (p. 612)
29. A, (p. 626)
30. C, (p. 621)

31. B, (p. 608)
32. A, (p. 608)
33. D, (p. 615)
34. D, (p. 617)
35. A, (p. 623)
36. C, (p. 627)
37. D, (p. 629)
38. A, (p. 634)
39. A, (p. 636)
40. D, (p. 641-642)

APPLIED PSYCHOLOGY

CHAPTER OVERVIEW

Applied psychologists attempt to solve practical problems. Some major applied specialties are: clinical and counseling, industrial/organizational, environmental, educational, legal, and sports psychology.

Industrial/organizational psychologists are interested in the problems people face at work. They specialize in personnel psychology and human relations at work. Personnel psychologists try to match people with jobs by combining job analysis with various tests and selection procedures. Two basic approaches to business and industrial management are scientific management (Theory X) and human relations (Theory Y) approaches. Healthy organizations express concern for the well-being of their employees by promoting trust, promoting open confrontation to avoid "desk rage," empowering their employees, and encouraging cooperation. Communication at work can be improved by following a few simple guidelines for effective speaking and listening.

Environmental psychologists study the effects of behavioral settings, physical or social environments, and human territoriality, among many other major topics. Overpopulation is a major world problem, often reflected at an individual level in crowding. Environmental psychologists are solving many practical problems—from noise pollution to architectural design. The question of whether human activities cause harm to the environment is being debated by two worldviews: the traditional Western view and the ecological worldview.

The psychology of law includes courtroom behavior and other topics that pertain to the legal system. Psychologists serve various consulting and counseling roles in legal, law enforcement, and criminal justice settings.

Sports psychologists seek to enhance sports performance and the benefits of sports participation. A careful task analysis of sports skills is a major tool for improving coaching and performance. The psychological dimension contributes greatly to peak performance.

Space psychologists study the behavioral challenges that accompany space flight, space habitats, and life in restricted environments.

LEARNING OBJECTIVES

To demonstrate mastery of this chapter, you should be able to:

1. Define the term "applied psychology."

2. Describe the typical activities of an industrial/organizational psychologist.

3. Describe the activities of personnel psychologists by defining or describing the following areas: a. job analysis (include the term "critical incidents") b. biodata c. personal interview (include the term "halo effect") d. vocational interest text e. aptitude test f. multimedia computerized tests g. assessment center i. situational judgment tests ii. in-basket test iii. leaderless group discussion

4. Differentiate scientific management styles (Theory X) from human relations approaches (Theory Y) to management.

5. Contrast work efficiency versus psychological efficiency.

6. Define the terms "participative management," "management by objectives," "self-managed teams," and "quality circles."

7. List eight factors that seem to contribute the most to job satisfaction.

8. Explain the concept of flextime.

9. Discuss the four basic coping styles in making career decisions.

10. Explain how jobs may be enriched and what should be increased as a result.

11. Define "organizational culture," "organizational citizenship," and "desk rage."

12. List and describe six ways to improve communication skills.

13. List and describe six ways to be a good listener.

14. Explain the main focus of environmental psychology, including three types of environments or settings of particular interest.

15. Define the term "personal space."

16. Define "proxemics, "and describe the four basic spatial norms and the nature of the interactions that occur in each.

17. Define the terms "territoriality" and give examples of territorial markers.

18. Discuss the results of animal experiments on the effects of overcrowding and state the possible implications for humans.

19. Differentiate between crowding and density.

20. Define the term "attentional overload," and describe the possible effects of noise pollution.

The following objective is related to the material in the "Discovering Psychology" section of your text.

21. What is the traditional Western view regarding living things and natural resources? How seriously do human activities impact the environment?

22. Explain the concepts social trap and the tragedy of the commons. Explain how they can be avoided or escaped.

23. List eight strategies to promote recycling.

24. Explain how environmental assessment, architectural psychology, or even simple feedback can be used to solve environmental problems.

25. Discuss the psychology of law and identify topics of special interest.

26. Discuss the use of mock juries to examine the ways in which jurors reach decisions. Include four major problems in jury behavior discovered by jury research.

27. Define the term "scientific jury selection" and describe four techniques commonly used to assess the potential usefulness of prospective jurors.

28. Describe what is meant by the term "death-qualified jury."

29. Explain the ways in which a sports psychologist might contribute to peak performance by an athlete.

30. Define the term "task analysis."

31. Define the terms "motor skill" and "motor program."

32. List and explain six rules that can aid skill learning. Include the concept of mental practice.

33. Discuss the concept of peak performance.

34. List seven ways for athletes to mentally improve performance.

35. Describe the main focus of a space psychologist.

36. Describe some human factors that space station design must take into account, for example privacy, sensory restriction, cultural differences, and social isolation.

37. Briefly describe some of the mental health concerns associated with space psychology.

RECITE AND REVIEW

MODULE 17.1

Survey Question: How is psychology applied in business and industry? Pages 646-652

Applied psychology refers to the use of psychological principles and research methods to solve

[1] _____ .

Major applied specialties include clinical and [2] _____ psychology.

Psychology is also applied to problems that arise in the environment, in education, in law, and in

[3] _____ .

Other applied areas are related to business, such as [4] _____ /organizational psychology.

Industrial/organizational psychologists are interested in the problems people face at [5] _____ and within organizations.

Typically they specialize in personnel psychology and human [6] _____ at work.

Personnel psychologists try to match people with [7] _____ by combining [8] _____ analysis with a variety of selection procedures.

To effectively match people with jobs, it is important to identify critical incidents (situations with which [9] _____ employees must be able to cope).

Personnel selection is often based on gathering biodata (detailed [10] _____ information about an applicant).

The traditional [11] _____ interview is still widely used to select people for jobs. However, interviewers must be aware of the halo effect and other sources of [12] _____ .

Standardized psychological [13] _____ , such as vocational interest tests, aptitude tests, and multi-media [14] _____ tests, are mainstays of personnel selection.

In the assessment center approach, in-depth [15] _____ of job candidates are done by observing them in simulated [16] _____ situations.

Two popular assessment center techniques are the in-basket test, and leaderless [17] _____ discussions.

Two basic approaches to business and industrial management are scientific management (Theory [18] _____) and human relations approaches (Theory [19] _____).

Theory [20] _____ is most concerned with work efficiency (productivity), whereas, Theory [21] _____ emphasizes psychological efficiency (good human relations).

Two common Theory [22] _____ methods are participative management and [23] _____ by objectives.

Recently, many companies have given employees more autonomy and responsibility by creating self-managed [24] _____ .

Below the management level, employees may be encouraged to become more involved in their work by participating in [25] _____ circles.

Job satisfaction is related to [26] _____ , and it usually affects absenteeism, morale, employee turnover, and other factors that affect overall business efficiency.

Job satisfaction is usually enhanced by [27] _____ [28] _____ oriented job enrichment.

When making career decisions, people tend to adopt a [29] _____ that is [30] _____ (effective and active), complacent (passive), defensive-avoidant (evasive and indecisive), or hypervigilant (frantic).

Businesses and other [31] _____ , tend to develop unique cultures. The most [32] _____ members of an organization typically display good organizational citizenship.

"Desk rage" (workplace [33] _____) occurs from job-related [34] _____ , work-related conflicts, people feeling that they have been treated [35] _____ , and people perceiving that their self-esteem is threatened.

[36] _____ organizations express concerns for the well-being of their employees by promoting trust, open [37] _____ of problems, employee [38] _____ and participation, cooperation, and full use of human potential.

Survey Question: What can be done to improve communication at work? Pages 652-654

To improve communication at work you should state your message [39] _____ and precisely.

Try to avoid overuse of obscure vocabulary, jargon, [40] _____ , and loaded words.

Learn and use people's [41] _____ . Be polite, but not servile.

To be a good listener, you should [42] _____ pay attention.

Try to identify the speaker's purpose and core [43] _____ .

Suspend evaluation while listening but check your [44] _____ frequently and note non-verbal information.

Be expressive when you [45] _____ . Pay attention to non-verbal cues and the messages they send.

MODULE 17.2

Survey Question: What have psychologists learned about the effects of our physical and social environments? Pages 656-666

Environmental psychologists are interested in the effects of behavioral [46] _____ , physical or [47] _____ environments, and human territoriality, among many other major topics.

The study of [48] _____ is called proxemics.

Four basic spatial zones around each person's body are intimate distance (0-18 inches), [49] _____ distance (1.5-4 feet), [50] _____ distance (4-12 feet), and public distance (12 feet or more).

Norms for the use of personal space vary considerably in various [51] _____ .

Territorial behavior involves defining a space as one's own, frequently by placing [52] _____ markers (signals of ownership) in it.

Over-population is a major world problem, often reflected at an individual level in [53] _____ .

Animal experiments indicate that excessive crowding can be unhealthy and lead to [54] _____ and pathological behaviors.

However, human research shows that psychological feelings of [55] _____ do not always correspond to density (the number of people in a given space).

One major consequence of [56] _____ is attentional overload (stress caused when too many demands are placed on a person's attention).

Toxic or poisoned environments, pollution, excess consumption of natural resources, and other types of environmental [57] _____ , pose serious threats to future [58] _____ .

Human activities greatly impact the environment by [59] _____ its resources, producing global warming, and introducing [60] _____ concentrations of [61] _____ pollutants.

The traditional [62] _____ view holds that [63] _____ are superior to all living creatures, that the environment has [64] _____ resources, and that advanced technology can solve any problem. In contrast, the [65] _____ worldview holds that humans are [66] _____ with other living creatures and the environment has limited resources.

Recycling can be encouraged by monetary [67] _____ , removing barriers, persuasion, obtaining public commitment, [68] _____ setting, and giving feedback.

A social trap is a social situation in which immediately rewarded actions have [69] _____ effects in the long run.

One prominent social trap occurs when limited public [70] _____ are overused, a problem called the tragedy of the commons.

In many cases, solutions to environmental problems are the result of doing a careful [71] _____ assessment (an analysis of the effects environments have on behavior).

Architectural psychology is the study of the effects [72] _____ have on behavior and the design of [73] _____ using [74] _____ principles.

MODULE 17.3

Survey Question: What does psychology reveal about juries and court verdicts? Pages 667-669

The psychology of law includes studies of courtroom behavior and other topics that pertain to the [75] _____ system.

Studies of mock juries ([76] _____ , juries) show that jury decisions are often far from [77] _____ .

Psychologists are sometimes involved in jury [78] _____ . Demographic information, a community survey, non-verbal behavior, and looking for authoritarian [79] _____ traits may be used to select jurors.

Survey Question: Can psychology enhance athletic performance? Pages 669-672

Sports psychologists seek to enhance sports performance and the benefits of sports [80] _____ .

A careful task analysis breaks [81] _____ into their subparts.

Motor skills are the core of many sports performances. Motor skills are non-verbal [82] _____ chains assembled into a smooth sequence.

Motor skills are guided by internal [83] _____ plans or models called motor programs.

[84] _____ performances are associated with the flow experience, an unusual mental state.

Top athletes typically [85] _____ their arousal level so that it is appropriate for the task. They also focus [86] _____ on the task and mentally rehearse it beforehand.

Most top athletes use various self-regulation strategies to [87] _____ their performances and make necessary adjustments.

PSYCHOLOGY IN ACTION

Survey Question: How is psychology being applied in space missions? Pages 673-675

Space psychologists study the many behavioral challenges that accompany space flight and life in restricted [88] _____ .

Space habitats (living areas) must be designed with special attention to environmental stressors, such as noise, control of the environment, [89] _____ cycles, and [90] _____ restriction.

Psychological issues, such as [91] _____ isolation, [92] _____ resolution, privacy, cultural differences, and maintaining mental health are equally important.

CONNECTIONS

MODULE 17.1

1. _____ defensive-avoidant style
2. _____ I/O psychology
3. _____ Flexitime
4. _____ Biodata
5. _____ Jargon
6. _____ critical incident
7. _____ Kuder
8. _____ in-basket test
9. _____ Theory X
10. _____ quality circle
11. _____ loaded word
12. _____ Theory Y

a. poor career decisions
b. communication barrier
c. vocational interests
d. essential work problem
e. variable schedule
f. work efficiency
g. personal history
h. work and organizations
i. psychological efficiency
j. discussion group
k. strong emotional meaning
l. typical work problems

MODULE 17.2

1. _____ spatial norm
2. _____ territorial marker
3. _____ density
4. _____ social traps
5. _____ noise pollution
6. _____ architectural psychology
7. _____ environmental psychology
8. _____ proxemics

a. intrusive sounds
b. pollution
c. persons in area
d. study of personal space norms
e. public distance
f. ownership signal
g. tragedy of the commons
h. solution for overcrowded buildings

MODULE 17.3

1. _____ mental practice
2. _____ jury selection
3. _____ sports psychology
4. _____ death-qualified jury
5. _____ mock jury
6. _____ motor program
7. _____ peak performance
8. _____ space habitat

a. coaching styles
b. favoring death penalty
c. imagined performance
d. simulated trial
e. movement plan
f. flow
g. avoid authoritarian personality
h. micro-society

CHECK YOUR MEMORY

MODULE 17.1

Survey Question: How is psychology applied in business and industry? Pages 646-652

1. Applied psychology can be defined as the use of learning principles to change undesirable human behavior.

   TRUE or FALSE

2. Psychological research has shown that the best fire alarm is a recorded voice.

   TRUE or FALSE

3. During a fire in a high-rise building, you should use the elevators, rather than the stairwell, so that you can leave as quickly as possible.

   TRUE or FALSE

4. Personnel psychology is a specialty of I/O psychologists.

   TRUE or FALSE

5. The basic idea of flexitime is that employees can work as many or as few hours a week as they choose.

   TRUE or FALSE

6. One way of doing a job analysis is to interview expert workers.

   TRUE or FALSE

7. Critical incidents are serious employee mistakes identified by doing a job analysis.

   TRUE or FALSE

8. Use of biodata is based on the idea that past behavior predicts future behavior.

   TRUE or FALSE

9. Because of their many shortcomings, personal interviews are fading from use as a way of selecting job applicants.

   TRUE or FALSE

10. The halo effect is a major problem in aptitude testing.

    TRUE or FALSE

11. Excessive self-promotion tends to lower the ratings candidates receive in job interviews.

    TRUE or FALSE

12. "I would prefer to read a good book," is the kind of statement typically found on aptitude tests.

    TRUE or FALSE

13. Multi-media computerized tests seek to present realistic work situations to job candidates.

    TRUE or FALSE

14. Leaderless quality circles are a typical task applicants face in assessment centers.
    TRUE or FALSE

15. Theory X assumes that workers enjoy autonomy and accept responsibility.
    TRUE or FALSE

16. The main benefit of a Theory X management style is a high level of psychological efficiency among workers.
    TRUE or FALSE

17. Participative management aims to make work a cooperative effort.
    TRUE or FALSE

18. Quality circles are typically allowed to choose their own methods of achieving results as long as the group is effective.
    TRUE or FALSE

19. Job satisfaction comes from a good fit between work and a person's interests, needs, and abilities.
    TRUE or FALSE

20. Job enrichment involves assigning workers a large number of new tasks.
    TRUE or FALSE

21. A hypervigilant style usually leads to the best career decsions.
    TRUE or FALSE

22. People who display organizational citizenship tend to contribute in ways that are not part of their job description.
    TRUE or FALSE

23. "Desk rage" refers to the unique arrangement of each employee's belongings on the desk.
    TRUE or FALSE

24. A healthy organization encourages their employees to openly confront their problems.
    TRUE or FALSE

Survey Question: What can be done to improve communication at work? Pages 652-654

25. Effective communication addresses the who, what, when, where, how, and why of events.
    TRUE or FALSE

26. Ambiguous messages are desirable because they leave others room to disagree.
    TRUE or FALSE

27. Jargon is an acceptable means of communication as long as you are sure that listeners are familiar with it.
    TRUE or FALSE

28. True politeness puts others at ease.
    TRUE or FALSE

29. To add credibility to your message, you should learn to speak very slowly and deliberately.
    TRUE or FALSE

30. Arriving late for meetings is a form of communication.
    TRUE or FALSE

31. To be a good listener, learn to evaluate each sentence as it is completed.
    TRUE or FALSE

32. Good listening improves communication as much as effective speaking does.
    TRUE or FALSE

MODULE 17.2

Survey Question: What have psychologists learned about the effects of our physical and social environments? Pages 656-666

33. A study of the pace of life found that the three fastest cities in the U.S. are Boston, New York, and Los Angeles.
    TRUE or FALSE

34. Environmental psychologists study physical environments rather than social environments.
    TRUE or FALSE

35. The traditional Western view holds that people are depleting earth's resources and destroying the environment.
    TRUE or FALSE

36. The ecological worldview holds that humans should not waste the limited resources available on earth.
    TRUE or FALSE

37. A dance is a behavioral setting.
    TRUE or FALSE

38. Most people show signs of discomfort when someone else enters their personal space without permission.
    TRUE or FALSE

39. The Dutch sit closer together when talking than the English do.
    TRUE or FALSE

40. Social distance basically keeps people within arm's reach.
    TRUE or FALSE

41. Formal interactions tend to take place in the 4 to 12 foot range.
    TRUE or FALSE

42. Saving a place at a theater is a type of territorial behavior.
TRUE or FALSE

43. Burglars tend to choose houses to break into that have visible territorial markers.
TRUE or FALSE

44. World population doubled between 1950 and 1987. By 2050, nine billion people will populate the earth.
TRUE or FALSE

45. In Calhoun's study of overcrowding in a rat colony, food and water rapidly ran out as the population increased.
TRUE or FALSE

46. High densities invariably lead to subjective feelings of crowding.
TRUE or FALSE

47. Stress is most likely to result when crowding causes a loss of control over a person's immediate social environment.
TRUE or FALSE

48. People suffering from attentional overload tend to ignore non-essential events and their social contacts are superficial.
TRUE or FALSE

49. Exposure to toxic hazards increases the risk of mental disease, as well as physical problems.
TRUE or FALSE

50. Long-corridor dormitories reduce feelings of crowding and encourage friendships.
TRUE or FALSE

51. Providing feedback about energy consumption tends to promote conservation of resources.
TRUE or FALSE

52. Direct monetary rewards have little or no effect on whether or not people recycle.
TRUE or FALSE

MODULE 17.3

Survey Question: What does psychology reveal about juries and court verdicts? Pages 667-669

53. In court, attractive defendants are less likely to be found guilty than unattractive persons.
TRUE or FALSE

54. Jurors are supposed to take into account the severity of the punishment that a defendant faces, but many don't.
TRUE or FALSE

55. Scientific jury selection is only used in laboratory studies-the practice isn't allowed in real jury trials.
TRUE or FALSE

56. Demographic information consists of the most prominent personality traits a person displays.
TRUE or FALSE

57. All members of a death-qualified jury must be opposed to the death penalty.
TRUE or FALSE

Survey Question: Can psychology enhance athletic performance? Pages 669-672

58. Peak performances in sports require both mental and physical training.
TRUE or FALSE

59. Distance running tends to reduce anxiety, tension, and depression.
TRUE or FALSE

60. The most accurate marksmen are those who learn to pull the trigger just as their heart beats.
TRUE or FALSE

61. Motor programs adapt complex movements to changing conditions.
TRUE or FALSE

62. Verbal rules add little to learning a sports skill; you should concentrate on lifelike practice.
TRUE or FALSE

63. To enhance motor skill learning, feedback should call attention to correct responses.
TRUE or FALSE

64. Mental practice refines motor programs.
TRUE or FALSE

65. The top athletes in most sports are the ones who have learned how to force the flow experience to occur.
TRUE or FALSE

66. Better athletes often use imagery, relaxation techniques, and fixed routines to control their arousal levels.
TRUE or FALSE

PSYCHOLOGY IN ACTION

Survey Question: How is psychology being applied in space missions? Pages 673-675

67. Many of the social and psychological problems of space flight can be prevented by carefully selecting astronauts before they leave Earth.
TRUE or FALSE

68. In space, astronauts have no preference for rooms with an obvious top or bottom.
TRUE or FALSE

69. Sleep cycles are best allowed to run freely in space since there are no real light and dark cycles.

    TRUE or FALSE

70. The need for privacy in space habitats can be met, in part, by defining private territories for each astronaut.

    TRUE or FALSE

71. Most people in restricted environments prefer games and other interactive pastimes as a way to break the monotony.

    TRUE or FALSE

72. In the specialized environment of a space station, differences in culture no longer seem important.

    TRUE or FALSE

73. Fifteen percent of space inhabitants are expected to experience a serious psychological disturbance.

    TRUE or FALSE

74. Most major problems facing the world day are behavioral.

    TRUE or FALSE

FINAL SURVEY AND REVIEW

MODULE 17.1

Survey Question: How is psychology applied in business and industry? Pages 646-652

Applied psychology refers to the use of psychological [1] _____ and [2] _____ methods to solve practical problems.

Major applied specialties include [3] _____ and counseling psychology.

Psychology is also applied to problems that arise in the natural and social [4] _____ , in [5] _____ , in law, and in sports.

Other applied areas are related to business, such as industrial/[6] _____ psychology.

[7] _____ psychologists are interested in the problems people face at work and within organizations.

Typically they specialize in [8] _____ psychology (testing, selecting, and promoting employees) and human relations at work.

[9] _____ psychologists try to match people with jobs by combining job [10] _____ with a variety of selection procedures.

To effectively match people with jobs, it is important to identify [11] _____ incidents (situations with which competent employees must be able to cope).

Personnel selection is often based on gathering [12] _____ (detailed biographical information about an applicant).

The traditional personal [13] _____ is still widely used to select people for jobs. However, interviewers must be aware of the [14] _____ effect and other sources of bias.

Standardized psychological tests, such as [15] _____ interest tests, [16] _____ tests, and multimedia computerized tests, are mainstays of personnel selection.

In the [17] _____ approach, in-depth evaluations of job candidates are done by observing them in simulated work situations.

Two popular assessment center techniques are the in-[18] _____ test and [19] _____ group discussions.

Two basic approaches to business and industrial management are [20] _____ management (Theory X) and [21] _____ [22] _____ approaches (Theory Y).

Theory X is most concerned with work [23] _____ (productivity), whereas Theory Y emphasizes [24] _____ efficiency (good human relations).

Two common Theory Y methods are [25] _____ management and management by [26] _____ .

Recently, many companies have given employees more autonomy and responsibility by creating [27] _____ teams.

Below the management level, employees may be encouraged to become more involved in their work by participating in [28] _____ .

Job [29] _____ is related to productivity, and it usually affects absenteeism, [30] _____ , employee turnover, and other factors that affect overall business efficiency.

Comfort with one's work is usually enhanced by Theory Y-oriented job [31] _____ .

When making career decisions, people tend to adopt a style that is vigilant (effective and active), [32] _____ (passive), defensive-avoidant (evasive and indecisive), or [33] _____ (frantic).

Businesses and other organizations tend to develop unique cultures. The most successful members of an organization typically display good [34] _____ .

"[35] _____ " (workplace anger) occurs from [36] _____ -related stresses, work-related conflicts, people feeling that they have been treated unfairly, and people perceiving that their self-esteem is threatened.

[37] _____ organizations express concerns for the well-being of their employees by promoting trust, [38] _____ confrontation of problems, employee empowerment and [39] _____ , cooperation, and full use of human potential.

Survey Question: What can be done to improve communication at work? Pages 652-654

To improve communication at work you should state your [40] _____ clearly and precisely.

Try to avoid overuse of obscure [41] _____ , [42] _____ (inside lingo), slang, and loaded words.

Learn and use people's names. Be [43] _____ but not servile.

To be a good [44] _____ , you should actively [45] _____ .

Try to identify the speaker's [46] _____ and core message.

Suspend [47] _____ while listening but check your understanding frequently and note non-verbal information.

Be [48] _____ when you speak. Pay attention to [49] _____ cues and the messages they send.

MODULE 17.2

Survey Question: What have psychologists learned about the effects of our physical and social environments? Pages 656-666

[50] _____ psychologists are interested in the effects of [51] _____ settings, physical or social environments, and human territoriality, among many other major topics.

The study of personal space is called [52] _____ .

Four basic spatial zones around each person's body are [53] _____ distance (0-18 inches), personal distance (1.5-4 feet), social distance (4-12 feet), and [54] _____ distance (12 feet or more).

[55] _____ for the use of personal space vary considerably in various cultures.

Territorial behavior involves defining a space as one's own, frequently by placing territorial

[56] _____ (signals of ownership) in it.

[57] _____ is a major world problem, often reflected at an individual level in crowding.

Animal experiments indicate that excessive [58] _____ can be unhealthy and lead to abnormal and pathological behaviors.

However, human research shows that psychological feelings of crowding do not always correspond to [59] _____ (the number of people in a given space).

One major consequence of crowding is [60] _____ (stress caused when too many demands are placed on a person's attention).

Toxic or poisoned environments, [61] _____ , excess consumption of natural [62] _____ , and other types of environmental damage pose serious threats to future generations.

Human [63] _____ greatly impact the environment by [64] _____ its resources, producing global warming, and introducing unhealthy concentrations of [65] _____ pollutants.

The [66] _____ view holds that humans are superior to all living creatures, that the environment has unlimited resources, and that advance technology can solve any problem. In contrast, the [67] _____ holds that humans arc interdependent with other living creatures and the environment has limited resources.

Recycling can be encouraged by [68] _____ rewards, removing barriers, persuasion, obtaining public [69] _____ , goal setting, and giving feedback.

A social trap is a social situation in which [70] _____ actions have undesired effects in the long run.

One prominent social trap occurs when limited public resources are [71] _____ , a problem called the [72] _____ of the [73] _____ .

In many cases, solutions to environmental problems are the result of doing a careful environmental [74] _____ (an analysis of the effects environments have on behavior).

[75] _____ psychology is the study of the effects buildings have on behavior and the design of buildings using psychological principles.

MODULE 17.3

Survey Question: What does psychology reveal about juries and court verdicts? Pages 667-669

The psychology of [76] _____ includes studies of courtroom behavior and other topics that pertain to the legal system.

Studies of [77] _____ juries (simulated juries) show that jury decisions are often far from objective.

Psychologists are sometimes involved in jury selection. [78] _____ information (population data), a community survey, nonverbal behavior, and looking for [79] _____ personality traits may be used to select jurors.

Survey Question: Can psychology enhance athletic performance? Pages 669-672

Sports psychologists seek to enhance sports [80] _____ and the benefits of sports participation.

A careful [81] _____ breaks sports skills into their subparts.

[82] _____ skills are the core of many sports performances. Such skills are [83] _____ response [84] _____ assembled into a smooth sequence.

Motor skills are guided by internal mental plans or models called [85] _____ .

Peak performances are associated with the [86] _____ experience, an unusual [87] _____ state.

Top athletes typically adjust their [88] _____ level so that it is appropriate for the task. They also focus attention on the task and mentally [89] _____ it beforehand.

Most top athletes use various [90] _____ strategies to evaluate their performances and make necessary adjustments.

PSYCHOLOGY IN ACTION

Survey Question: How is psychology being applied in space missions? Pages 673-675

[91] _____ psychologists study the many behavioral challenges that accompany space flight and life in [92] _____ environments.

Space [93] _____ (living areas) must be designed with special attention to environmental [94] _____ , such as noise, control of the environment, sleep cycles, and sensory restriction.

Psychological issues, such as social [95] _____ , conflict [96] _____ , privacy, cultural [97] _____ , and maintaining mental health are equally important.

MASTERY TEST

1. Procrastination, inaction, and indecision are most characteristic of the _____ style of career decision making.
   a. vigilant
   b. complacent
   c. defensive-avoidant
   d. hypervigilant

2. Which is POOR advice for learning motor skills?
   a. Observe a skilled model.
   b. Learn only nonverbal information.
   c. Get feedback.
   d. Avoid learning artificial parts of a task.

3. Which of the following would be a question for applied psychology?
   a. How does conditioning occur?
   b. How can eyewitness memory be improved?
   c. What are the most basic personality traits?
   d. Do athletes have unusual personality profiles?

4. Signs are placed on a recycling container each week showing how many aluminum cans were deposited during the previous week. This practice dramatically increases recycling, showing the benefits of using _____ to promote recycling.
   a. feedback
   b. public commitment
   c. consumer symbolization
   d. persuasion

5. Psychological efficiency is promoted by
   a. scientific management
   b. Theory Y
   c. time-and-motion studies
   d. progressive pay schedules

6. In court, being attractive does NOT help a defendant avoid being found guilty when
   a. a majority of jurors are also attractive
   b. the defendant is a man
   c. the defendant is over age 30
   d. being attractive helped the person commit a crime

7. The best antidote for social isolation on extended space missions is expected to be
   a. defining private social territories for crew members
   b. coordinated sleep schedules
   c. radio contact with earth
   d. making conflict resolution teams part of all missions

8. Which of the following is NOT a specialty of I/O psychologists?
   a. personnel psychology
   b. theories of management
   c. human relations
   d. architectural psychology

9. Dividing long-corridor dormitories into two areas separated by a lounge
   a. makes residents feel more crowded, not less
   b. decreases social contacts
   c. increases energy consumption
   d. decreases stress

10. You leave a book on a table in the library to save your place. The book is a territorial
    a. display
    b. marker
    c. strategy
    d. control

11. When professional golfer Jack Nicklaus talks about "watching a movie" in his head before each shot, he is referring to the value of _____ for enhancing sports performance.
    a. mental practice
    b. self-regulation
    c. skilled modeling
    d. task analysis

12. What cognitive maps, behavioral settings, and crowding have in common is that all
    a. are studied by community psychologists
    b. produce attentional overload
    c. are studied by environmental psychologists
    d. are characteristics of Type A cities

13. Potentials for learning the skills used in various occupations are measured by
    a. interest tests
    b. aptitude tests
    c. in-basket tests
    d. cognitive mapping

14. Looking at past behavior is a good way to predict future behavior. This is the principle behind using _____ to select people for employment.
    a. biodata
    b. the halo effect
    c. Theory Y
    d. spaced interviewing

15. A good job analysis should identify
    a. critical incidents
    b. compatible controls
    c. motor programs
    d. essential biodata

16. High _____ is experienced as crowding when it leads to a loss of _____ one's immediate environment.
    a. overload, attention to
    b. density, control over
    c. stimulation, interest in
    d. arousal, contact with

17. Studies of flextime would most likely be done by a _____ psychologist.
    a. community
    b. environmental
    c. I/O
    d. consumer

18. The halo effect is a problem in
    a. collecting biodata
    b. scoring interest inventories
    c. conducting interviews
    d. aptitude testing

19. Mental practice is one way to improve
    a. motor programs
    h the flow experience
    c. the accuracy of cognitive maps
    d. job satisfaction

20. Joan has been given a specific sales total to meet for the month, suggesting that she works for a company that uses
    a. quality circles
    b. job enrichment
    c. flexi-quotas
    d. management by objectives

21. Which of the following is NOT recommended for people who want to be effective listeners in the workplace?
    a. Identify the speaker's purpose.
    b. Evaluate as you listen.
    c. Check your understanding.
    d. Attend to nonverbal messages.

22. Planning, control, and orderliness are typical of _____ management.
    a. Theory X
    b. participative
    c. Theory Y
    d. enriched

23. A psychologist who checks demographic information, does a community survey, and looks for authoritarian traits is most likely
    a. a personnel psychologist
    b. doing a community mental health assessment
    c. a consumer welfare advocate
    d. a legal consultant

24. A very important element of job enrichment is
    a. switching to indirect feedback
    b. increasing worker knowledge
    c. use of bonuses and pay incentives
    d. providing closer supervision and guidance

25. Large desks in business offices almost ensure that interactions with others take place at
    a. ascribed distance
    b. social distance
    c. personal distance
    d. public distance

26. An I/O psychologist hears someone make such claims as "He was really stressed out, and because of that he was often angry" and can predict that the individual may be experiencing
    a. "road rage"
    b. "desk rage"
    c. "private rage"
    d. "postal rage"

27. Which of the following is a method to increase employees' well-being?
    a. open confrontation of problems
    b. adhered to structured schedules
    c. employee empowerment
    d. both a and c

28. Which view holds that with advanced technology, humans can solve any problem presented to them?
    a. ecological worldview
    b. traditional Western view
    c. psychological view
    d. historical view

SOLUTIONS

RECITE AND REVIEW

MODULE 17.1

1. practical problems
2. counseling
3. sports
4. industrial
5. work
6. relations
7. jobs
8. job
9. competent
10. biographical
11. personal
12. bias
13. tests
14. computerized
15. evaluations
16. work
17. group
18. X
19. Y
20. X
21. Y
22. Y
23. management
24. teams
25. quality
26. productivity
27. Theory
28. Y
29. style
30. vigilant
31. organizations
32. successful
33. anger
34. stresses
35. unfairly
36. Healthy
37. confrontation
38. empowerment

39. clearly
40. slang
41. names
42. actively
43. message
44. understanding
45. speak

MODULE 17.2

46. settings
47. social
48. personal space
49. personal
50. social
51. cultures
52. territorial
53. crowding
54. abnormal
55. crowding
56. crowding
57. damage
58. generations
59. depleting
60. unhealthy
61. air
62. Western
63. humans
64. unlimited
65. ecological
66. interdependent
67. rewards
68. goal
69. undesired
70. resources
71. environmental
72. buildings
73. buildings
74. behavioral

MODULE 17.3

75. legal
76. simulated
77. objective
78. selection
79. personality

80. participation
81. sports skills
82. response
83. mental
84. Peak
85. adjust
86. attention
87. evaluate

PSYCHOLOGY IN ACTION

88. environments
89. sleep

90. sensory
91. social

92. conflict

CONNECTIONS

MODULE 17.1

1. a
2. h
3. e
4. g

5. b
6. d
7. c
8. l

9. f
10. j
11. k
12. i

MODULE 17.2

1. e
2. f
3. c

4. g
5. a
6. h

7. b
8. d

MODULE 17.3

1. c
2. g
3. a

4. b
5. d
6. e

7. f
8. h

CHECK YOUR MEMORY

MODULE 17.1

1. F
2. T
3. F
4. T
5. F
6. T
7. F
8. T
9. F

10. F
11. T
12. F
13. T
14. F
15. F
16. F
17. T
18. F

19. T
20. F
21. F
22. T
23. F
24. T

25. T
26. F
27. T

28. T
29. F
30. T

31. F
32. T

MODULE 17.2

33. F
34. F
35. F

36. T
37. F
38. T

39. F
40. F
41. F

42. T	46. F	50. F
43. F	47. T	51. T
44. T	48. T	52. F
45. F	49. T	

MODULE 17.3

53. T	55. F	57. F
54. F	56. F	

58. T	61. T	64. T
59. T	62. F	65. F
60. F	63. T	66. T

PSYCHOLOGY IN ACTION

67. T	70. T	73. F
68. F	71. F	74. T
69. F	72. F	

FINAL SURVEY AND REVIEW

MODULE 17.1

1. principles	15. vocational	29. satisfaction
2. research	16. aptitude	30. morale
3. clinical	17. assessment center	31. enrichment
4. environment	18. basket	32. complacent
5. education	19. leaderless	33. hypervigilant
6. organizational	20. scientific	34. organizational citizenship
7. Industrial/organizational	21. human	35. Desk rage
8. personnel	22. relations	36. job
9. Personnel	23. efficiency	37. Healthy
10. analysis	24. psychological	38. open
11. critical	25. participative	39. participation
12. biodata	26. objectives	
13. interview	27. self-managed	
14. halo	28. quality circles	

40. message	44. listener	48. expressive
41. vocabulary	45. pay attention	49. nonverbal
42. jargon	46. purpose	
43. polite	47. evaluation	

MODULE 17.2
50. Environmental

51. behavioral
52. proxemics
53. intimate
54. public
55. Norms
56. markers
57. Overpopulation
58. crowding
59. density

60. attentional overload
61. pollution
62. resources
63. activities
64. depleting
65. air
66. traditional Western
67. ecological worldview
68. monetary

69. commitment
70. immediately rewarded
71. overused
72. tragedy
73. commons
74. assessment
75. Architectural

MODULE 17.3

76. law
77. mock

78. Demographic
79. authoritarian

80. performance
81. task analysis
82. Motor
83. nonverbal

84. chains
85. motor programs
86. flow
87. mental

88. arousal
89. rehearse
90. self-regulation

PSYCHOLOGY IN ACTION

91. Space
92. restricted
93. habitats

94. stressors
95. isolation
96. resolution

97. differences

MASTERY TEST

1. B, (p. 651)
2. B, (p. 670-671)
3. B, (p. 644)
4. A, (p. 662)
5. B, (p. 649)
6. D, (p. 667)
7. C, (p. 674)
8. D, (p. 646)
9. D, (p. 665)
10. B, (p. 658)
11. A, (p. 671)

12. C, (p. 656)
13. B, (p. 648)
14. A, (p. 647)
15. A, (p. 646)
16. B, (p. 660)
17. C, (p. 651)
18. C, (p. 647)
19. A, (p. 670-671)
20. D, (p. 650)
21. B, (p. 654)
22. A, (p. 649)

23. D, (p. 668)
24. B, (p. 652)
25. B, (p. 658)
26. B, (p. 653)
27. D, (p. 653)
28. B, (p. 662)

BEHAVIORAL STATISTICS

OVERVIEW

Descriptive statistics are used to summarize data. Inferential statistics are used to make decisions and generalizations or to draw conclusions. Graphical statistics, such as histograms and frequency polygons, provide pictures (graphs) of groups of numbers. Measures of central tendency, such as the mean, median, and mode, supply a number describing an "average" or "typical" score in a group of scores. The range and standard deviation are measures of variability, or the spread of scores. Standard scores (z-scores) combine the mean and standard deviation in a way that tells how far above or below the mean a particular score lies. The normal curve is a bell-shaped distribution of scores that has useful and well known properties.

While psychologists are ultimately interested in entire populations, they must usually observe only a representative sample. Nevertheless, it is possible to tell if the results of an experiment are statistically significant (unlikely to be due to chance alone).

When measurements, scores, or observations come in pairs, it is possible to determine if they are correlated. The correlation coefficient tells if the relationship between two measures is positive or negative and how strong it is. While correlations are quite useful, correlation does not demonstrate causation.

LEARNING OBJECTIVES

To demonstrate mastery of this chapter, you should be able to:

1. Define and distinguish between the two major types of statistics, descriptive and inferential statistics.

2. List the three types of descriptive statistics.

3. Describe graphical statistics, including the terms frequency distribution, histogram, and frequency polygon.

4. Describe the three measures of central tendency. Explain why the mean is not always the best measure for central tendency.

5. Describe the use of the range and standard deviation as measures of the variability of scores around the mean.

6. Explain what a z-score is.

7. Describe the use of the normal curve and its relationship to standard deviations and z-scores.

8. Distinguish between a population and a sample, and include the concepts of representative samples and random samples.

9. Explain the concept of statistical significance.

10. Describe the concept of correlation, including scatter diagrams.

11. Distinguish among positive relationships, negative relationships, and zero correlations.

12. Define the coefficient of correlation, including the value of a perfect positive or perfect negative correlation.

13. Briefly discuss the value of correlations for making predictions. Include the concept of percent of variance.

14. Describe the limitations of correlation as it relates to causation.

RECITE AND REVIEW

MODULE A.1

Survey Questions: What are descriptive statistics? How are statistics used to identify an average score? What statistics do psychologists use to measure how much scores differ from one another? Pages 680-684

Descriptive statistics are used to [1] _____ data. Inferential statistics are used to make decisions and generalizations or to draw [2] _____ .

Three basic types of [3] _____ statistics are graphical statistics, measures of central tendency, and measures of variability.

A frequency distribution organizes data by breaking an entire range of scores into [4] _____ of equal size. Then, the number of scores falling in each [5] _____ is recorded.

Graphical statistics provide [6] _____ (graphs) of collections of numbers.

A histogram is drawn by placing class intervals on the abscissa ([7] _____ line) and frequencies on the ordinate ([8] _____ line) of a graph.

Next, vertical bars are drawn for each class interval with the [9] _____ of the bars being determined by the number of scores in each class.

A frequency polygon (line graph) results when points are plotted at the [10] _____ of each class interval and connected by lines.

Measures of central tendency are numbers describing an "[11] _____" or "typical" score in a group of scores.

The mean is calculated by [12] _____ all the scores for a group and then dividing by the total number of scores.

The median is found by arranging scores from the highest to the lowest and then selecting the [13] _____ score.

The mode is the [14] _____ occurring score in a group of scores.

Measures of variability tell how varied or widely [15] _____ scores are.

The range is the [16] _____ score minus the [17] _____ score.

The standard deviation is calculated by finding the difference between each score and the [18] _____ . These differences are then [19] _____ . Then the squared deviations are totaled and their mean is found.

Standard scores ([20] _____ -scores) are found by subtracting the [21] _____ from a score. The resulting number is then divided by the standard deviation.

Standard scores tell how far above or below the [22] _____ a particular score lies.

When they are collected from large groups of people, many psychological measures form a normal [23] _____ .

In a normal curve, 68 percent of all scores fall between plus and minus 1 standard deviation from the [24] _____ .

Ninety-five percent of all cases fall between plus and minus [25] _____ standard deviations from the mean.

Ninety-nine percent of all cases fall between plus and minus [26] _____ standard deviations from the mean.

MODULE A.2

Survey Question: What are inferential statistics? Page 686

The [27] _____ of subjects, objects, or events of interest in a scientific investigation is called a population.

When an entire population cannot be observed, a sample (smaller cross section) of the [28] _____ is selected.

Samples must be representative (they must truly reflect the characteristics of the [29] _____).

[30] _____ drawn from representative samples are assumed to apply to the entire population.

Tests of statistical significance tell how often the results of an experiment could have occurred by [31] _____ alone.

An experimental result that could have occurred only five times out of 100 (or less) by chance alone is considered [32] _____ .

Survey Question: How are correlations used in psychology? Pages 686-689

When measurements, scores, variables, or observations come in pairs, it is possible to determine if they are co-related (varying together in an [33] _____ fashion).

The coefficient of correlation tells if the relationship between two measures is [34] _____ or [35] _____ and how strong it is.

The percent of variance (amount of [36] _____ in scores) is accounted for by the correlation and can be derived by multiplying the [37] _____ by itself.

While correlations are quite useful for making predictions, correlation does not [38] _____ causation.

CONNECTIONS

MODULE A.1

1. _____ histogram
2. _____ standard deviation
3. _____ frequency distribution
4. _____ normal curve
5. _____ range
6. _____ standard score
7. _____ mean

a. grouped scores
b. picture of frequencies
c. central tendency
d. spread of scores
e. average squared difference
f. z-score
g. model distribution

MODULE A.2

1.	_____ population	a.	subset
2.	_____ sample	b.	graphed correlation
3.	_____ representative	c.	randomly selected
4.	_____ zero correlation	d.	correlation coefficient
5.	_____ scatter diagram	e.	no relationship
6.	_____ Pearson *r*	f.	entire set
7.	_____ *r* squared	g.	percent of variance

CHECK YOUR MEMORY

MODULE A.1

Survey Questions: What are descriptive statistics? How are statistics used to identify an average score? What statistics do psychologists use to measure how much scores differ from one another? Pages 680-684

1. Descriptive statistics extract and summarize information.
   TRUE or FALSE

2. Inferential statistics are used to make pictures (graphs) out of data.
   TRUE or FALSE

3. Measures of variability are descriptive statistics.
   TRUE or FALSE

4. A frequency distribution is made by recording the most frequently occurring score.
   TRUE or FALSE

5. A frequency polygon is a graphical representation of a frequency distribution.
   TRUE or FALSE

6. On a graph, the ordinate is the line that shows the frequency of scores at the center of each class interval.
   TRUE or FALSE

7. The mean, median, and mode are all averages.
   TRUE or FALSE

8. The median is the most frequently occurring score in a group of scores.
   TRUE or FALSE

9. To find the mode, you would have to know how many people obtained each possible score.
   TRUE or FALSE

10. The standard deviations can be different in two groups of scores even if their means are the same.
    TRUE or FALSE

11. To find the range, you would have to know what the highest and lowest scores are.
    TRUE or FALSE

12. To find a z-score, you must know the median and the standard deviation.
    TRUE or FALSE

13. A z-score of one means a person scored exactly at the mean.
    TRUE or FALSE

14. The majority of scores are found near the middle of a normal curve.
    TRUE or FALSE

15. Fifty percent of all scores are found below the mean in a normal curve.
    TRUE or FALSE

MODULE A.2

Survey Question: What are inferential statistics? Page 686

16. Psychologists prefer to study entire populations whenever it is practical to do so.
    TRUE or FALSE

17. Random selection of subjects usually makes a sample representative.
    TRUE or FALSE

18. A result that could have occurred by chance alone 25 times out of 100 is considered statistically significant.
    TRUE or FALSE

19. A probability of .05 or less is statistically significant.
    TRUE or FALSE

Survey Question: How are correlations used in psychology? Pages 686–689

20. A scatter diagram is a plot of two sets of unrelated measurements on the same graph.
    TRUE or FALSE

21. In a positive relationship, increase in measure X is matched by increase in measure Y.
    TRUE or FALSE

22. A correlation coefficient of .100 indicates a perfect positive relationship.
    TRUE or FALSE

23. The Pearson r ranges from $-.100$ to $+.100$.
    TRUE or FALSE

24. Correlations allow psychologists to make predictions.
    TRUE or FALSE

25. Two correlated measures may be related through the influence of a third variable.
    TRUE or FALSE

26. Correlation proves that one variable causes another if the correlation coefficient is significant.
    TRUE or FALSE

FINAL SURVEY AND REVIEW

MODULE A.1

Survey Questions: What are descriptive statistics? How are statistics used to identify an average score? What statistics do psychologists use to measure how much scores differ from one another? Pages 680-684

[1] _____ statistics are used to summarize data. [2] _____ statistics are used to make decisions and generalizations or to draw conclusions.

Three basic types of descriptive statistics are graphical statistics, measures of [3] _____ tendency, and measures of [4] _____ .

A [5] _____ organizes data by breaking an entire range of scores into classes of equal size. Then, the number of scores falling in each class is recorded.

[6] _____ statistics provide pictures of collections of numbers.

A [7] _____ is drawn by placing class intervals on the [8] _____ (horizontal line) and frequencies on the [9] _____ (vertical line) of a graph.

Next, vertical bars are drawn for each [10] _____ , with the height of the bars being determined by the number of scores in each class.

A [11] _____ (line graph) results when points are plotted at the center of each class interval and connected by lines.

Measures of [12] _____ are numbers describing an "average" or "typical" score in a group of scores.

The [13] _____ is calculated by adding all the scores for a group and then [14] _____ by the total number of scores.

The [15] _____ is found by arranging scores from the highest to the lowest and then selecting the middle score.

The [16] _____ is the most frequently occurring score in a group of scores.

Measures of [17] _____ tell how varied or widely spread scores are.

The [18] _____ is the highest score minus the lowest score.

The [19] _____ is calculated by finding the difference between each score and the mean. These differences are then squared. Then the squared deviations are totaled and their mean is found.

[20] _____ scores (z-scores) are found by subtracting the mean from a score. The resulting number is then divided by the [21] _____ .

[22] _____ tell how far above or below the mean a particular score lies.

When they are collected from large groups of people, many psychological measures form a [23] _____ curve.

In such curves, [24] _____ percent of all scores fall between plus and minus 1 standard deviation from the mean.

[25] _____ percent of all cases fall between plus and minus two standard deviations from the mean.

[26] _____ percent of all cases fall between plus and minus three standard deviations from the mean.

MODULE A.2

Survey Question: What are inferential statistics? Page 686

The entire set of subjects, objects, or events of interest in a scientific investigation is called a [27] _____ .

When an entire set cannot be observed, a [28] _____ (smaller cross section) is selected.

Samples must be [29] _____ (they must truly reflect the characteristics of the population).

Conclusions drawn from [30] _____ are assumed to apply to the entire population.

Tests of statistical [31] _____ tell how often the results of an experiment could have occurred by chance alone.

An experimental result that could have occurred only [32] _____ times out of [33] _____ (or less) by chance alone is considered significant.

Survey Question: How are correlations used in psychology? Pages 686-689

When measurements, scores, variables, or observations come in pairs, it is possible to determine if they are [34] _____ (varying together in an orderly fashion).

The [35] _____ of correlation tells if the relationship between two measures is positive or negative and how [36] _____ it is.

The percent of [37] _____ (amount of variation in scores) that is accounted for by the correlation and can be derived by multiplying the *r* by itself.

While correlations are quite useful for making predictions, correlation does not demonstrate [38] _____ .

MASTERY TEST

1. _____ statistics are especially valuable for decision making and drawing conclusions.
   a. Graphical
   b. Descriptive
   c. Inferential
   d. Significant

2. Measures of central tendency are _____ statistics.
   a. graphical
   b. descriptive
   c. inferential
   d. significant

3. Sorting scores into classes is a necessary step in creating a
   a. frequency distribution
   b. correlation
   c. scatter diagram
   d. variability plot

4. Vertical bars are used to indicate frequencies in a
   a. frequency polygon
   b. scatter diagram
   c. normal distribution
   d. histogram

5. Which is NOT a measure of central tendency?
   a. mean
   b. midst
   c. mode
   d. median

6. A group of scores must be arranged from the lowest to the highest in order to find the
   a. mean
   b. midst
   c. mode
   d. median

7. The _____ is sensitive to extremely high or low scores in a distribution.
   a. mean
   b. midst
   c. mode
   d. median

8. Which is a measure of variability?
   a. Pearson *r*
   b. z-score
   c. midst
   d. range

9. What two statistics are needed to calculate a standard score?
   a. range and midst
   b. mean and standard deviation
   c. range and mode
   d. standard deviation and z-score

10. If the mean on a test is 90 and the standard deviation is 10, a person with a z-score of −1 scored _____ on the test.
    a. 70
    b. 80
    c. 100
    d. 110

11. The largest percentage of scores falls between _____ SD in a normal curve.
    a. 0 and +1
    b. +1 and −1
    c. +2 and +3
    d. −3 and −2

12. What percent of all cases are found between +3 SD and −3 SD in a normal curve?
    a. 50
    b. 86
    c. 95
    d. 99

13. An effective way to make sure that a sample is representative is to
    a. use random selection
    b. calculate the correlation coefficient
    c. make sure that the standard deviation is low
    d. use a scatter diagram

14. Results of an experiment that have a chance probability of _____ are usually regarded as statistically significant.
    a. .5
    b. .05
    c. 1.5
    d. 1.05

15. A good way to visualize a correlation is to plot a
    a. frequency histogram
    b. polygon coefficient
    c. scatter diagram
    d. normal ordinate

16. When measure X gets larger, measure Y gets smaller in a
    a. zero correlation
    b. positive relationship
    c. variable relationship
    d. negative relationship

17. When plotted as a graph, a zero correlation forms a cluster of points in the shape of a
    a. diagonal oval to the right
    b. diagonal oval to the left
    c. horizontal line
    d. circle

18. The largest possible correlation coefficient is
    a. 1
    b. .001
    c. 100
    d. 10

19. To find the percent of variance in one measure accounted for by knowing another measure, you should square the
    a. mean
    b. z-score
    c. Pearson *r*
    d. standard deviation

20. Correlations do not demonstrate whether
    a. a relationship is positive or negative
    b. a cause-and-effect connection exists
    c. knowing one measure allows prediction of another
    d. two events are really co-relating public distance

SOLUTIONS

RECITE AND REVIEW

MODULE A.1

1. summarize
2. conclusions
3. descriptive
4. classes
5. class
6. pictures
7. horizontal
8. vertical
9. height
10. center

11. average
12. adding
13. middle
14. most frequently
15. spread
16. highest
17. lowest
18. mean
19. squared
20. z

21. mean
22. mean
23. curve
24. mean
25. two
26. three

MODULE A.2

27. entire set
28. population

29. population
30. Conclusions

31. chance
32. significant

33. orderly
34. positive

35. negative
36. variation

37. *r*
38. demonstrate

CONNECTIONS

MODULE A.1

1. b
2. e
3. a

4. g
5. d
6. f

7. c

MODULE A.2

1. f
2. a
3. c

4. e
5. b
6. d

7. g

CHECK YOUR MEMORY

MODULE A.1

1. T
2. F
3. T
4. F
5. T

6. F
7. T
8. F
9. T
10. T

11. T
12. F
13. F
14. T
15. T

MODULE A.2

16. T	18. F
17. T	19. T

20. F	23. F	26. F
21. T	24. T	
22. F	25. T	

FINAL SURVEY AND REVIEW

MODULE A.1

1. Descriptive	11. frequency polygon	21. standard deviation
2. Inferential	12. central tendency	22. Z-scores (or standard scores)
3. central	13. mean	23. normal
4. variability	14. dividing	24. 68
5. frequency distribution	15. median	25. Ninety-five
6. Graphical	16. mode	26. Ninety-nine
7. histogram	17. variability	
8. abscissa	18. range	
9. ordinate	19. standard deviation	
10. class interval	20. Standard	

MODULE A.2

27. population	30. representative samples	33. 100
28. sample	31. significance	
29. representative	32. five	

34. co-related	36. strong	38. causation
35. coefficient	37. variance	

MASTERY TEST

1. C, (p. 678)	9. B, (p. 683)	17. D, (p. 687)
2. B, (p. 680)	10. B, (p. 683)	18. A, (p. 687)
3. A, (p. 680)	11. B, (p. 684)	19. C, (p. 688)
4. D, (p. 680)	12. D, (p. 684)	20. B, (p. 689)
5. B, (p. 681)	13. A, (p. 686)	
6. D, (p. 681)	14. B, (p. 686)	
7. A, (p. 681)	15. C, (p. 687)	
8. D, (p. 681-682)	16. D, (p. 687)	

PART II:

Language Development Guide

CHAPTER 1

Introducing Psychology and Research Methods

The number of the page in the text where the idiom, word, phrase, or name can be found is shown in parentheses. The term or phrase is shown *in italics*. Where necessary for clarity, the phrase or sentence containing the term is given in parentheses. The meaning of the selected term or phrase follows the colon.

The Mysteries of Human Behavior (p. 12)
   (12) *riddle*: puzzling question
   (12) *panorama*: wide-ranging view
   (12) *envy*: be jealous of

Module 1.1 The Science of Psychology (pp. 14-18)
   (14) *X-rays:* process to "see" through one's skin to view underlying body structures
   (14) *"You can't teach an old dog new tricks"*: it is difficult for people (as well as dogs) to learn new ways of doing things
   (14) *blazing hot*: very hot (*blazing* suggests fire)
   (14) *frazzled:* impatient and irritated
   (14) *stalled*: stopped, engine won't start
   (14) *leaning on the horn*: blowing the horn in an automobile
   (15) *sluggish*: drowsy; lacking energy
   (15) *Mozart:* a renowned classical music composer
   (15) *conception*: the moment when egg and sperm meet and a new being is created
   (16) *child rearing:* the process of raising children
   (16) *endangered species:* animals at risk of becoming extinct
   (17) *bystander apathy*: lack of interest or concern among witnesses to an accident or
      crime
   (17) *"diffusion of responsibility"*: responsibility for action is spread out and lessened;
      it is not clear who should act
   (17) *to pitch in* (…so no one feels required *to pitch in.*): to get involved
   (17) *perplexing*: very hard to understand
   (17) *stranded*: left without means to depart or leave
   (17) *boil down* (…the goals *boil down* to asking: What is the nature of this
      behavior?): are reduced to this question

Module 1.2 History and Major Perspectives (pp. 19-26)

(19) *probe*: examine in detail

(19) *heft*: to get the feel of, to lift something up

(20) *Charles Darwin*: the scientist who proposed the theory of evolution

(20) *spurred*: to incite to action or increased growth or development

(20) *overstatement*: exaggeration

(21) *Freud believed that mental life is like an iceberg...* : the unknown of the unconscious mind is hidden below consciousness like the large part of the submerged iceberg is below the surface of the water

(22) *slips of the tongue*: The tongue speaks before the mind realizes all the consequences.

(22) *"Freudian slips"*: While the mind is thinking about the obvious, the tongue speaks about hidden, unrevealed thoughts.

(24) *"hot topics"*: popular, highly interesting ideas

(24) *mechanistic* (somewhat *mechanistic* view of human nature): can be explained by mechanical laws; no free will

(24) *reductionistic* (neutral, *reductionistic*, mechanistic view of human nature): simplifying human nature to its basic units

Module 1.3 Psychologists and Their Specialties (pp. 27-30)

(27) *"About $30 an hour. (And going up.)"*: You need to pay $30 more to visit a psychiatrist, than if you visit a psychologist.

(27) *"shrinks"*: a slang term for psychiatrists or head doctors

(27) *postgraduate*: training or education beyond the bachelor's degree

(28) *mustache and goatee:* facial hair above the lip (mustache) and a small, usually pointed beard (goatee)

(28) *"hang out a shingle"*: start up a business by hanging up a sign

(28) *rebirther*: a guide who takes you through the birth experience again

(28) *primal feeling facilitator*: a guide who tries to help you understand your most basic feelings

(28) *cosmic aura balancer*: a guide who tries to help you balance unseen forces around the body

(28) *rolfer*: a person who gives deep massage for therapy

(30) *odds are*: it is likely

Module 1.4 Research Methods, Naturalistic Observation, and Correlation (pp. 31-36)

(33) *implications*: possible results

(33) *Jane Goodall*: well-known anthropologist who spent years studying chimpanzee behavior

(34) *recorders*: devices used to make audio or video reproductions

(34) *IQs*: intelligent quotients; measures of intelligence

(35) *TV zombie effect*: watching television for so long that a person doesn't appear to be affected by the world around them; hypnotic effect

(36) *Frosted Flakes*: a breakfast cereal with a high sugar content

Module 1.5 The Psychology Experiment (pp. 37-41)

(38) *dunces*: a slang term for someone who isn't intelligent

(38) *hung-over*: the effects a person feels hours after drinking too much alcohol

Module 1.6 Critical and Survey Methods, Critical Thinking (pp. 42-48)

(42) *rampage*: wild, uncontrolled activity

(43) *blue-collar workers*: non-professional employees, such as, laborers, factory workers, and service workers

(43) *paint a false picture*: yield inaccurate results

(44) *to "buy" outrageous claims*: to believe claims that are too extraordinary to be true

(44) *dowsing*: to use a special stick called a divining rod to find underground water

(44) *occult*: beyond the range of ordinary knowledge; mysterious

(44) *Bermuda Triangle*: an area of the ocean where some people claim that ships are mysteriously lost

(44) *UFOs*: Unidentified Flying Objects. Typically refers to alien space craft visiting earth.

(45) *transcend*: to rise above or go beyond the limits

(45) *guru*: personal religious teacher and spiritual guide

(45) *gullible*: believe everything you hear

(45) *provisional*: until more information can be found

(46) *"ring of truth"*: sounds like it could be true

(46) *nitpicking*: unjustified criticism

(46) *vague*: very general, not specific

(46) *zodiac*: an imaginary belt in the nighttime sky that contains the apparent paths of the planets

(47) *hemmed in*: held back from doing something

(47) *fads*: short-lived, very popular ideas, clothing, activities, and events

Module 1.7 Psychology in the News—Separating Fact from Fiction (pp. 49-51)

(49) *biofeedback machines*: measuring devices to monitor physiological responses, such as heart rate and blood pressure, to allow individuals to involuntarily control such responses

(49) *subliminal tapes*: audio tapes that are advertised to help persons lose weight, stop smoking, improve their love life, and similar behaviors; such tapes have "messages" that persons cannot hear directly but are supposedly imbedded below the detection level

(49) *ESP*: extra-sensory perception; the supposed ability to "see" into the future or to receive signals and messages unavailable through normal channels of sensation, such as vision, hearing, touch, smell, and taste

(49) *hyperactivity:* excessively active behavior

CHAPTER 2

Brain and Behavior

The number of the page in the text where the idiom, word, phrase, or name can be found is shown in parentheses. The term or phrase is shown *in italics*. Where necessary for clarity, the phrase or sentence containing the term is given in parentheses. The meaning of the selected term or phrase follows the colon.

Finding Music in Tofu (p. 52)
>   (52) *glandular system*: groups of cells that secrete chemical substances into the blood

Module 2.1 Neurons, the Nervous System, and Brain Research (pp. 54-65)
>   (54) *spidery*: composed of thin threads like a spider's web
>   (55) *metaphor*: a word or phrase that links one idea or object to another
>   (55) *trigger point:* the point at which the nerve impulse occurs
>   (56) *a wave of falling blocks will zip rapidly to the end of the line*: when one block (domino) is pushed, it will push over the one next to it, and this will continue down the row of dominoes
>   (57) *sites*: areas
>   (57) *squirt gun*: toy gun that shoots water
>   (58) *ablaze with activity:* extremely active
>   (58) *playing catch with a frisbee:* a game in which a round plastic disk (a frisbee) is thrown back and forth
>   (58) *wired for action*: set up and ready to go
>   (60) *"vegetative"*: involuntary
>   (60) *grafting techniques*: ways to unite disconnected living tissue
>   (60) *to raise false hopes*: to believe in something that will not likely come true
>   (61) *reflex:* an action occurring without being consciously willed
>   (61) *tumors*: mass of new tissue growth
>   (62) *epilepsy:* disease due to disturbed electrical rhythms of the central nervous system and which may cause convulsions
>   (62) *grandstand catch:* in baseball, to catch the ball so as to impress the fans
>   (62) *realm*: kingdom, area
>   (63) *stroke:* a sudden loss of consciousness, sensation and voluntary movement caused usually by a blood clot in the brain

(64) *It is just a matter of time until even brighter beacons are flashed into the shadowy inner world of thought*: soon there will be new discoveries about the human brain

(64) *peripheral:* the part found away from the center; at the edges

(65) *creatures*: beings or objects of uncertain nature

(66) *folklore:* traditional beliefs held by a people

Module 2.2 Cerebral Cortex and Lobes of the Brain (pp. 66-73)

(66) *puny:* small and weak

(67) *brighter subjects*: more intelligent

(67) *burned more glucose than the man on the right*: used up more glucose

(67) *consumption*: usage

(68) "*the right hand not knowing what the left hand is doing*": In the Bible, Jesus told those giving money to the poor not to brag about their good deeds. His advice, "Do not let your right hand know what your left hand does."

(68) *overrides*: takes control over

(70) *impaired:* showing loss of function

(71) *bulk*: majority

(71) *utter*: to speak

Module 2.3 Subcortex and Endocrine System (pp. 74-80)

(74) "*switching station*": place where railroad cars are changed from one track to another, in this case the meaning is that the thalamus is the area of the brain where information from the senses is routed to the correct part of the cortex

(74) *karate chop*: hitting with the hand

(74) *like hidden gemstones:* the author is comparing the thalamus and hypothalamus to precious stones inside the earth—like diamonds in a mine

(74) *snaps to attention*: quickly awakens out of a semi-conscious state

(75) *posture*: the position of the body

(78) *dwarf*: person of abnormally small size

(78) *giant*: person of abnormally large size

(78) *retardation:* less than normal intelligence

(79) *ebb and flow:* decreasing and increasing

Module 2.4 Handedness—If Your Brain is Right, What's Left (pp. 81-85)

(81) *"right-hand man":* most helpful or reliable assistant

(81) *ambidextrous:* able to use either the right or left hand equally well

(81) *dexterity:* skill in using one's hands

(81) *left out:* not invited, not included

(81) *left-handed compliment:* one that is insincere or unflattering

(81) *people with "two left feet":* clumsy, uncoordinated people

(82) *anesthetizing:* causing loss of sensation by the use of a drug

(82) *foolproof:* absolute, true

(82) *leap to any conclusions:* make a decision before looking at all the facts

(82) *traumas:* bodily injury or shock

(83) *breech birth:* the delivery of a baby rear end first, rather than head first

(83) *lopsided:* not symmetrical or balanced in shape

(83) *ultrasound:* ultrasonic (above the range that can be heard by the human ear) waves used in medical diagnosis

(84) *gifted:* talented

CHAPTER 3

Child Development

The number of the page in the text where the idiom, word, phrase, or name can be found is shown in parentheses. The term or phrase is shown *in italics*. Where necessary for clarity, the phrase or sentence containing the term is given in parentheses. The meaning of the selected term or phrase follows the colon.

A Star is Born—Here's Amy (p. 86)
   (86) *prune*: a small, wrinkled fruit

Module 3.1 Heredity and Environment (pp. 88-94)
   (88) "*the womb to the tomb*": from birth to death
   (88) *distractibility*: ability to have one's attention divided in different directions
   (88) *irritability*: easily angered or annoyed
   (88) *score one for those who favor heredity*: those people who favor heredity as the most important factor are correct in this case
   (88) *susceptibility*: lack of ability to resist
   (89) *nurture*: training, upbringing
   (89) *Upper Paleolithic*: late Stone Age (30,000 years ago) characterized by use of rough stone tools
   (90) *alter*: change
   (90) *optimal*: ideal or most desirable
   (90) *reared*: raised
   (91) *albinism*: hereditary condition that causes a lack of pigment (color) in skin and hair, and pink eyes
   (91) *cystic fibrosis*: hereditary disease that is characterized by poor digestion and by difficulty in breathing
   (91) *hemophilia*: sex-linked hereditary blood defect characterized by delayed clotting of the blood (a tendency to bleed very easily)
   (91) *muscular dystrophy*: hereditary disease characterized by wasting away of the muscles
   (91) *sickle-cell anemia*: chronic inherited condition involving a defect in the red blood cells
   (92) *deprivation*: lack of healthful environmental influences

(92) *enriched environment*: a situation in which there are many opportunities for learning

(92) *mute*: unable to speak

(93) *dazzling speed*: very fast

Module 3.2 The Neonate and Early Maturation (pp. 95-100)

(95) *imitate*: to try to do something the same way

(95) *trapeze artists*: performers on the trapeze, a bar suspended in the air by two ropes

(97) *extremities*: hands and feet

(98) *"hard-wired"*: initial state not subject to change

(98) *abundant*: more than enough

(98) *milestones*: key points in development

(98) *say goodbye to diapers*: to become toilet trained

(99) *haphazard*: random

Module 3.3 Social Development (pp. 101-104)

(101) *I'm stuck on you*: I'm attracted to you

(102) *drowsy*: sleepy

(102) *intrusive*: entering where one is not welcome

(103) *coordinate*: to bring together or unite

(103) *menagerie*: collection of wild animals kept for exhibition

(103) *stockade*: a place where prisoners are kept

(103) *trivial*: of little or no importance

(104) *parallels*: similar situations

Module 3.4 Parental Influences (pp. 105-110)

(105) *caregivers*: the persons primarily responsible for a child

(106) *conventional*: standard

(106) *pudding*: a sweet, creamy dessert

(106) *run amok*: run around in a wild, uncontrolled way

Module 3.5 Language Development (pp. 111-114)

(111) *mischief*: action that annoys or tricks

(111) *stubborn*: unwilling to change

(111) *temper tantrums*: anger expressed with uncontrolled behavior such as screaming, hitting, crying, etc.

(112) *linguist*: one who specializes in the study of language

(112) *predisposition*: natural inclination or ability

(113) *distinct*: unlike other things of the same type

Module 3.6 Cognitive Development (pp. 115-121)

(116) *panty-girdle*: a woman's elasticized underwear

(117) *deductive reasoning*: to reason from the general to the specific; from a known idea

(117) *inductive reasoning*: to reason from the specific to the general; from specific instances or facts to a general conclusion

(118) *mortgages*: method of buying property by which a loan is obtained (for example, from a bank)

(118) *pacts*: deals, arrangements

Module 3.7 Effective Parenting—Raising Healthy Children (pp. 122-127)

CHAPTER 4

From Birth to Death: Life-Span Development

The number of the page in the text where the idiom, word, phrase, or name can be found is shown in parentheses. The term or phrase is shown *in italics*. Where necessary for clarity, the phrase or sentence containing the term is given in parentheses. The meaning of the selected term or phrase follows the colon.

The Story of a Lifetime (p. 128)

(128) *Jennifer Lopez:* popular American actress

(128) *Michael Jordan:* former National Basketball Association star basketball player

(128) *Hillary Clinton*: wife of former American president Bill Clinton

(128) *Bill Gates:* billionaire computer industry executive

(128) *Whoopi Goldberg*: popular American actress

(128) *Maya Angelou:* well-known American poet

(128) *Amy Tan*: popular American novel writer

(128) *scan*: examine

Module 4.1 The Life Cycle (pp. 130-133)

(130) *rocky road* or *garden path*: a rocky road symbolizes difficulties in life; a garden path means an easy and pleasant life

(131) *autonomy*: self-sufficiency, self-reliance

(131) *turbulent*: characterized by unrest, disturbance

(132) *integrity*: quality of being complete, honest to oneself

(132) *stagnation*: not advancing or developing

(132) *whirlwind*: very brief

Module 4.2 Problems of Childhood (pp. 134-139)

(134) *bullied*: abused, forced

(134) *his adult interest in plumbing the depths of the psyche might have gone down the drain*: his adult interest in examining the psyche might have totally disappeared

(134) *parents can help keep such conflicts within bounds by not "playing favorites"*: preferring one child over the other

(135) *autistic*: absorbed in self-centered mental activity and withdrawn from reality

(135) *frothing*: foaming

(135) *temper tantrums*: fits of bad temper, characterized by crying, kicking the heels on the floor, etc.

(136) *amphetamine-like*: similar in effects to drugs that stimulate the nervous system

(136) *diagnosis*: an analysis of the cause or nature of a problem or situation

(136) *potent*: powerful

(136) *side effects*: unintended, generally negative reactions resulting from the use of a drug

(137) *ingenuity*: cleverness

(137) *parrot back*: repeat

(138) *condoning*: allowing

Module 4.3 Adolescence and Moral Development (pp. 140-146)

(140) *exuberance*: unrestrained joy and enthusiasm

(141) *poised*: socially mature

(141) *X-rated movies*: of such a nature (usually pornographic) that admission is denied to those under a specified age (usually 17)

(142) "*on stage*": standing out, being deliberately different from other people

(142) *outlandish*: unusual, weird

(143) *cliques*: circle or group held together by common interests or views

(143) *jock, preppy, brain, hacker, surfer, etc.*: slang words used to characterize types of students

aardvark: a large, burrowing nocturnal (night) animal

brain: very intelligent, "A" student

cowboy: a student who dresses in western-style clothes

criminal: one who has committed an illegal act

dervish: a creature who dances wildly; whirling

druggy: a student who obviously uses drugs

gargoyle: a grotesquely carved figure; often on rooftop as spouts to carry water runoff

hacker: one interested in computers

jock: athlete

mod: originally short for modern; one who is bold or trendy in dress, style, behavior

nerd: a person who does not fit in with the rest of the crowd; often associated with interest in math, computers, science, etc.

preppy: one who dresses or behaves like a student at a preparatory school (neatly and classically)

punk: one who dresses or behaves like a punk rocker (for example, with hair dyed purple)

rapper: one who dresses or behaves like a rap music performer

surfer: one who likes to surf

warthog: a wild African hog

(144) *classified*: described in broad terms

Module 4.4 Adulthood and Aging (pp. 147-156)

(147) *mellowing*: being made gentle and accepting by age or experience

(147) *the die is cast*: decisions made cannot now be changed, one's fate is now set

(148) *corresponds*: in agreement with

(148) *steward*: manager

(150) *discord*: lack of agreement

(150) *mastery*: command of

(150) *run the gauntlet of modern life*: deal with the problems and difficulties of daily living

(151) *senile*: forgetful and childlike as a result of old age

(153) *desirable*: worthy of pursuing or having

(154) *ageism*: prejudice against the elderly

(154) *meddling*: interfering

(155) *desolate*: abandoned, sorrowful

(156) *witnessed*: seen

Module 4.5 Death and Dying (pp. 157-161)

(157) *apparent*: easily seen

(157) *artificial*: not natural

(158) *come to terms with*: accept

(159) *unleashes tears and bottled-up feelings of despair*: cries and releases emotions

(160) *apathy*: lack of feeling or emotion

(161) *contradict*: prove false

(161) *impending*: about to happen

(161) *preceding*: coming before

Module 4.6 Well-Being and Happiness—What Makes a Good Life (pp. 162-165)

(162) *subjective well-being*: feeling good about one's self

(163) *lotteries*: large games of chance where people win money by buying tickets for drawings

(163) *tied the knot*: got married

(163) *crotchety*: irritable

(163) *Ferrari*: expensive sports car

CHAPTER 5

Sensation and Perception

The number of the page in the text where the idiom, word, phrase, or name can be found is shown in parentheses. The term or phrase is shown *in italics*. Where necessary for clarity, the phrase or sentence containing the term is given in parentheses. The meaning of the selected term or phrase follows the colon.

Murder on Aisle Nine (p. 166)
- (166) *drink in the beauty of a sunset*: to appreciate or enjoy the beauty of a sunset
- (166) *passed out:* became unconscious

Module 5.1 Sensory Systems and Vision (pp. 168-176)
- (168) *"squash"*: to apply a slight amount of pressure
- (168) *"tuned" to detect*: able to sense or perceive
- (168) *light-years away*: a unit of length used equal to the distance that light travels in one year (about 5.88 trillion miles)
- (168) *peer*: see
- (169) *catching some rays*: slang for sun-tanning; the author is making a joke because in vision the eye actually does "catch" light rays
- (169) *crude*: not exact; unfinished
- (169) *drab*: dull or difficult to see
- (170) *accommodate*: to provide for or to make fit
- (170) *concave*: rounded inward
- (170) *convex*: rounded outward
- (170) *fuzzy*: out of focus
- (170) *sharp*: in focus
- (170) *symmetrical*: evenly distributed on two sides
- (171) *defects*: imperfections or mistakes
- (172) *diminishing*: gradually getting smaller
- (172) *holds*: believes
- (173) *anyone who regularly draws hoots of laughter*: anyone who is very funny
- (173) *clashing*: not matching
- (173) *fire*: release
- (173) *pigments*: coloring matter in cells

(173) *sheepishly*: in an ashamed manner

(174) *replica*: an exact copy

(175) *airplane cockpits*: the area where the pilots control the plane

(175) *ready rooms*: rooms where the pilots wait before they board the plane

(175) *threshold*: limit

(176) *beam of light*: a narrow stream of light rays

(176) *land on the retina*: make contact with the retina

(176) *misshapen*: deformed, not in the normal shape

Module 5.2 Hearing, Smell and Taste (pp. 177-182)

(177) *good vibrations*: the title of a well-known pop music song; implies feeling good

(177) *"shades"*: sunglasses

(177) *pitch*: level (high or low musical note) of a sound

(177) *transduce*: to convert or process

(177) *triggers*: stimulates

(177) *tuning fork*: a metal device that gives a fixed musical tone when it is struck

(177) *vacuum*: empty space

(179) *"like a radio that isn't quite tuned in"*: like a radio that is not receiving a station clearly

(179) *artificial*: not natural; made by humans

(179) *cobweb*: spider web

(179) *intact*: in one piece; unbroken

(179) *spurred*: started

(180) *airborne*: traveling in the air

(180) *foraged*: searched for

(180) *inedible*: unable to eat due to poison

(180) *molecules*: the smallest particle of a substance that contains one or more atoms

(180) *musky*: having an odor like musk, a substance with a long lasting odor obtained from the male musk deer and used in perfume

(180) *wine taster*: a person whose job it is to sample wines in order to judge their quality

(181) *gourmet*: a person very knowledgeable about good food and drink

(181) *intricately*: delicately

(182) *aroma*: typical smell

(182) *convert*: change

(182) *mentally trace*: imagine

Module 5.3 Somesthetic Senses, Adaptation, Attention, and Gating (pp. 183-188)

- (183) *plight*: unfortunate situation
- (183) *routine*: skilled procedure in gymnastics or dance
- (183) *uneven bars*: a piece of equipment used in gymnastics
- (184) *agony*: pain
- (184) *carried away*: over-enthusiastic
- (184) *chronic*: constant
- (184) *dramatic*: large or significant
- (184) *endure*: to survive, tolerate
- (184) *iPod*: portable digital audio player where one can listen to music one has downloaded from a computer
- (184) *jab*: to poke quickly or abruptly
- (184) *motion sickness*: nausea and sometimes vomiting caused by the motion of a car or boat
- (184) *nagging*: unpleasantly reminding
- (184) *take the edge off*: decrease the pain
- (184) *tattooing*: making designs on the body by inserting color under the skin or by producing scars
- (184) *terminal*: not curable and leading ultimately to death
- (184) *the roar of the surf*: the sound of the waves crashing on the beach
- (184) *the whirr of a dentist's drill*: the drilling sound
- (184) *Walkman*: small headphones one can walk around with and listen to music
- (185 *tug of gravity*: pull of gravity
- (185) *"green" and miserable with motion sickness*: feeling nauseated, sick to the stomach
- (185) *disorientation*: confusion about location
- (185) *heaving, pitching boat*: moving in a rocking or bumpy motion
- (185) *nausea*: feeling of sickness
- (186) *"tune in on"*: concentrate
- (186) *encompass*: take in all of
- (186) *head cheese*: sausage made from the head, feet, and sometimes tongue and heart of a pig
- (186) *tuning in and tuning out*: slang for "paying attention" and the opposite
- (186) *you would probably pass out at the door*: you would faint because of the overpowering bad smell
- (187) *debatable*: arguable; not proven
- (188) *clairvoyance*: the supposed ability to perceive things that are not in sight or that cannot be seen

(188) *jumbled*: unorganized or not in the correct order

(188) *put the puzzle together*: to make sense of

Module 5.4 Perceptual Constancies and Perceptual Grouping (pp. 189-193)

(189) *cataract*: clouding of the lens of the eye

(189) *constancy*: free from change

(189) *Madonna*: popular singer who sometimes resembles Marilyn Monroe

(189) *Marilyn Monroe*: famous blonde movie actress (1926-1962)

(190) *hurdles*: problems to overcome

(190) *neon lamps*: type of electric lighting characterized by bright colors that glow

(191) "*Birds of a feather flock together*": just as birds of one type tend to stay together, so do people or things with similar characteristics group together

(191) *Gestalt psychologists:* psychologists who attempted to study experiences as wholes, rather that analyzing them into separate parts

(192) *"three-pronged widget"*: impossible figure used to illustrate perceptual organization problems

(192) *camouflaged*: disguised, hidden

Module 5.5 Depth Perception (pp. 194-199)

(194) "*skydiving*": the sport of jumping out of an airplane with a parachute; here referring to the baby jumping off the table

(194) *3-D*: giving the illusion of depth, stands for 3-dimensional

(194) *goggles*: large glasses or lenses

(194) *shoot baskets*: to play basketball

(194) *to zap flies*: to kill flies

(195) *stereogram*: a picture that creates a sense of depth

(195) *superimposing*: placing over

(196) "*sensational*": as used here, "sensational" has two meanings: excellent or great, and of or relating to the senses

(196) *Star Wars*: futuristic adventure movie noted for its imagery and special effects technology.

(197) *lithograph*: a print made by inking one surface and applying it to another

(198) *dime*: a coin that is approximately 1/2" in diameter

(198) *silver dollar*: a coin that is approximately 1 1/2" in diameter

(199) *rush of excitement*: thrill

Module 5.6 Perception and Objectivity (pp. 200-206)

(201) *doctored* face: altered, changed

(204) *assemble*: put together

(204) *infatuated*: highly attracted with

(204) *swastika*: symbol used by Adolf Hitler in Nazi Germany, and so perceived as an anti-Semitic (anti-Jewish) symbol

(205) "*bitch*": slang term for a cold, mean female

(205) "*punk*": a juvenile delinquent, a young person who has been in trouble with the law

(205) "*queer*": slang term for a homosexual person

(205) *runners at a track meet may jump the gun*: start before the signal (often a gunshot) is given

(206) *habitually*: over and over

(206) *ingrained*: innate, firmly fixed

Module 5.7 Extrasensory Perception (pp. 207-210)

(207) *die*: singular of dice; a small cube used in games

(207) *hunch*: guess

(207) *psi*: concerned with, or relating to psychic events or powers

(208) *accounts*: stories

(208) *fraud*: deception, cheating

(208) *marking cards with a fingernail*: using your fingernail to bend or scratch a particular card

(208) *telepathy*: supposed communication between minds by some means

(209) "*psychic*": a person who claims to be sensitive to nonphysical or supernatural forces and influences

(209) *"die in the box" tests:* the person being tested is asked to guess which number is showing on a die (singular of dice) that is hidden in a box

(209) *a quick trip to a casino would allow the person to retire for life*: if a person really had ESP he or she could gamble and be sure of winning lots of money

(209) *paranormal*: not explainable by science

(209) *Stage ESP (like stage magic) is based on patented gadgets*: tricks done by magicians and by those who practice ESP on stage use devices that can be bought in magic supply stores, such as trick playing cards or dice

Module 5.8 Psychology in Action: Becoming a Better Eyewitness to Life (pp. 211-215)

    (211) *carries a lot of weight*: is very influential

    (211) *to put it bluntly*: to say plainly

    (211) *victims fall prey to*: are deceived by

    (213) *channels*: a path of information

    (213) *in a haze*: not paying attention to detail

    (213) *maxims*: statements or truth or rules of conduct

    (213) *pigeonhole*: to place something in a small category

CHAPTER 6

States of Consciousness

The number of the page in the text where the idiom, word, phrase, or name can be found is shown in parentheses. The term or phrase is shown *in italics*. Where necessary for clarity, the phrase or sentence containing the term is given in parentheses. The meaning of the selected term or phrase follows the colon.

A Visit to Several States (of Consciousness) (p. 216)
   (216) *mythical*: not based on fact; exisiting in the imagination

Module 6.1 Altered States and Sleep (pp. 218-225)
   (218) "*highway hypnotism*": refers to the fact that drivers on long distance trips sometimes lose concentration due to the sameness of the road and scenery
   (218) "*possession*" *by spirits*: the belief that an evil spirit (the devil) or the spirit of a dead person can inhabit the body of a living being
   (218) *"rave" parties*: all-night parties that involve music, dancing, and sometimes drug use
   (218) *chant*: to say the same words repeatedly
   (218) *dehydration*: abnormal loss of body fluids
   (218) *enlightenment*: understanding yourself
   (218) *hyperventilation*: excessive rate of respiration (breathing)
   (218) *Mardi Gras*: a very large, crowded street party celebrated forty days before Easter (in the spring) in New Orleans
   (218) *monotonous*: unchanging
   (218) *mosh pit*: a large group of young people at a music concert who aggressively push and shove each other
   (219) "*the lion and the lamb shall lie down together*": according to the Bible, at the end of the world enemies will become friends, even in the animal world
   (219) *give way*: bring an end to
   (219) *hallucinations*: imaginary perception of objects that do not exist in reality
   (219) *macro*: large
   (219) *snooze*: nap, short sleep
   (219) *stupor*: a condition when your senses are greatly slowed down

(220) *bounding*: jumping or moving quickly

(220) *jarring crash*: very low point

(220) *to spell disaster*: to ensure that a disaster will happen

(221) *siesta*: nap

(221) *whims*: a sudden or unplanned idea or event

(222) "*burned the midnight oil*": before electricity, lamps filled with kerosene oil were used to light a room; today this refers to staying up late at night studying

(222) *agility*: easy and quick movements

(222) *the nightly roller coaster ride*: a roller coaster is an amusement park ride that causes the rider to go up and then quickly down steep inclines; here referring to the fact that sleep is characterized by stages, from the lightest (stage one) to the deepest (stage four)

(223) *inhibit*: prevent

(223) *see-saw back and forth*: to alternately move to opposite sides

(223) *skeptics*: nonbelievers

(224) a *feature movie*: a movie that you would see on television or in the theater

(224) *a state of oblivion*: the act or state of forgetting

(224) *emotionally charged events*: a highly emotional event

(224) *escapades*: adventures

(224) *exertion*: activity or exercise

(224) *hilarious*: very amusing or funny

(224) *iguana*: large tropical American lizard

(224) *paralyzed*: unable to move

(224) *thrash*: to move or toss about

Module 6.2 Sleep Disturbances and Dreaming (pp. 226-231)

(226) "*rebound insomnia*": inability to sleep after one has stopped taking sleeping pills

(226) "*sleeping-pill junkies*": people who are addicted to sleeping pills

(226) *irony*: a result that is different, or the opposite, from what is expected

(226) *muscle twitches*: a sudden movement of a muscle

(226) *pastimes*: activities

(228) *banished*: to force out or remove

(229) *age-old questions*: questions that are difficult to answer without further testing

(229) *Golden Era*: period of great happiness, prosperity, and achievement

(229) *sensory deprivation*: being cut off from information normally received through the five senses

(229) *speaking very loosely*: speaking very casually, or rewording something so that it is easier to understand

(229) *What's in the Pot?*: slang term for marijuana

(230) *the brain does not shut down during sleep*: turning off, being inactive

(231) *immobilized*: incapable of movement

Module 6.3 Hypnosis, Meditation, and Sensory Deprivation (pp. 232-237)

(232) *"animal magnetism"*: a mysterious force that Mesmer claimed enabled him to hypnotize patients

(232) *coined*: created

(232) *fraud*: intentionally lying or deceiving

(232) *myths*: unconfirmed stories

(232) *role-playing*: pretending to be someone else

(232) *susceptibility*: lack of ability to resist

(234) *ammonia*: a liquid used for cleaning that has a very strong odor

(234) *amputees*: one that has had an arm or a leg amputated

(234) *antics*: playful or funny acts

(234) *bar*: prevent

(234) *brings out the "ham" in many people*: actor; a person who overacts

(234) *disinhibits*: takes away inhibitions, or restraints on behavior

(234) *disrobing*: undressing

(234) *immoral*: going against the general beliefs of right and wrong

(234) *suggestibility*: easily influenced

(234) *yield*: follow

(235) *"Suspend judgment until you have something solid to stand on."*: don't make a decision until you hear all of the facts

(236) *clamor*: continuous noise

(236) *Epsom salts*: salts that are supposed to purify one's emotions and bring one back to full awareness.

Module 6.4 Psychoactive Drugs (pp. 238-252)

(238) *barbiturates*: derivatives of barbituric acid used as sedatives or hypnotics

(238) *illicit*: illegal

(239) *"crashes"*: sudden, greatly reduced functioning following a prolonged period of stimulant use

(239) *binges*: unrestrained use of drugs

(239) *paranoid delusions*: irrational belief that one is being persecuted; distrustfulness

(239) *someone is out to get them*: trying to harm them

(239) *speed freaks*: persons addicted to stimulant drugs

(240) *convulsions*: abnormal violent and involuntary contractions of the muscles

(240) *the "real thing"*: this used to be the slogan for Coca-Cola

(242) *adulterated with other substances*: made impure by the addition of other

(242) *arrhythmias*: irregularities in heart beat

(242) *potential*: possibility, something that can develop or become actual

(242) *rush of energy*: a sudden, intense feeling of energy or activity

(243) *cysts*: closed sacs developing abnormally in a structure of the body

(243) *modest amounts*: small amounts

(243) *tremors*: uncontrollable shaking

(244) *AIDS*: acquired immunodeficiency syndrome; a disease that attacks the immune system making the body unable to fight off life-threatening conditions such as pneumonia

(244) *quit cold turkey*: stop smoking completely and suddenly instead of gradually

(244) *relapse*: to fall back into former habits

(244) *sobering*: unpleasant

(244) *staggering*: astonishing or overwhelming

(244) *Taxpayers pick up the bill*: taxpayers end up paying for the costs associated with smoking

(245) *sedative drugs (sedatives):* drugs that calm nervousness or excitement

(246) *aphrodisiac*: a substance that increases sexual performance or desire

(246) *delirium*: a mental disturbance characterized by confusion, disordered speech, and hallucinations

(246) *distilled*: a purified liquid

(246) *downing five or more drinks*: drinking a lot very quickly

(246) *ER*: emergency room in a hospital

(246) *fermented*: a chemical change that turns fruit into alcohol

(246) *get completely wasted*: get veru drunk

(246) *to spike drinks*: add alcohol

(246) *unwary*: people who do not know what is happening

(248) *"dry"*: stopped drinking

(248) *blackouts*: periods of loss of consciousness or memory

(248) *deteriorate*: become worse

(248) *premise*: belief or understanding

(249) "*hit rock bottom*": reached the lowest point personally and emotionally

(250) "*joints*": marijuana cigarettes

(250) *clean bill of health*: free from guilt or fault

(250) *miscarriages*: failure to continue a pregnancy (loss of the fetus)

(250) more dangerous than the *black plague*: contagious and deadly disease that killed many people in Europe and Asia 600 years ago

(250) *ovulation*: the release of the egg cell by the ovaries in a female's body

(250) *pharmacologist*: one who studies drugs and their effects

(250) *suppress*: to stop or prohibit

(251) *alienated*: alone or unaccepted

(251) *delinquency*: behavior that is not accepted socially or by the law

(251) *ebb and flow*: decrease and increase

(252) *contradiction*: a statement that implies both truth and falsity

(252) *subsidize*: to pay for or provide finances for

Module 6.5 Psychology in Action: Exploring and Using Dreams (pp. 253-256)

(253) *exhibitionist:* a person who displays himself or herself indecently in public

(253) *literal*: actual, obvious

(253) *vulnerable*: open to attack

(254) *insights*: self-knowledge

(254) *intuitions*: gaining knowledge without evident rational thought

(254) *puns*: the humorous use of words in such a way as to suggest two or more of its meanings

(254) *recurrent*: repeating

(254) *someone is "twisting your arm"*: making you do something that you would rather not do

(255) *a novel solution*: a unique or unusual solution

(255) *lucid*: clear, understandable

(255) *steep yourself in the problem*: immerse yourself, concentrate very hard

(256) *Freud*: Sigmund Freud, founder of psychoanalysis

CHAPTER 7

Conditioning and Learning

The number of the page in the text where the idiom, word, phrase, or name can be found is shown in parentheses. The term or phrase is shown *in italics*. Where necessary for clarity, the phrase or sentence containing the term is given in parentheses. The meaning of the selected term or phrase follows the colon.

What Did You Learn in School Today? (p. 258)
(258) *"starving to death"*: so hungry a person feels he or she will die
(258) *flock*: a large group; usually applied to birds or other fowl, here used to mean a large group of college students

Module 7.1 Learning and Classical Conditioning (pp. 260-267)
(260) *bassoon*: a musical instrument
(260) *incapacitated*: incapable of functioning normally
(261) *Does the name Pavlov Ring a Bell?*: Is it familiar to you?
(261) *drooled*: salivated
(261) *eliciting*: bringing forth
(261) *evoke*: to call up, suggest, or produce
(261) *innately*: existing from the beginning, as opposed to learned from experience
(261) *snicker*: laugh in an unkind way
(262) *this little trick could be a real hit*: very popular
(264) *"fight-or-flight" reflexes*: instinctive response to danger is either to stay and fight or to run away
(267) *provoke*: to bring about, often by anger
(267) *withdrawal*: the act of stopping the use of a drug; often very physically and mentally painful

Module 7.2 Operant Conditioning (pp. 268-277)
(268) *rule of thumb*: guideline, practical method
(269) *Mickey Rat "shapes up"*: improves
(270) *better safe than sorry*: it's better to do everything possible to bring about a desired result than to fail
(270) *get the large half of a wishbone*: refers to the practice in which two people pull on opposite sides of a chicken or turkey breastbone; the person

who has the larger piece when the bone breaks is considered to be the one who will get what he or she wished for

(270) *golfer*: a person who plays golf

(270) *superstitions*: beliefs or practices resulting from trust in magic or chance

(270) *walk under a ladder*: considered by some people to bring bad luck

(271) *Ping-Pong*: table tennis

(271) *show off*: try to attract attention by one's behavior

(271) *throw tantrums*: yell, scream or throw things in order to get what one wants

(272) *parents who "ground" their teenage children*: parents who punish teenagers by forbidding them to go out

(273) *Microsoft*: a large American computer software company

(273) *Playboy*: a well-known magazine for men

(273) *poker chips*: tokens used in a card game that take the place of money

(273) *tangible*: something that can be touched

(273) *tokens*: something that can be exchanged for goods

(274) *amenities*: things that provide material comfort

(274) *check out their split ends*: examine the ends of one's hair (especially girls); a sign of boredom

(274) *toying with*: playing with, fingering aimlessly

Module 7.3 Partial Reinforcement and Stimulus Control (pp. 278-282)

(278) *Bingo!*: I won!; Bingo is a board game where the winner yells Bingo!

(278) *Even psychologists visiting Las Vegas often get cleaned out*: lose their money

(278) *Las Vegas or a similar "gambling mecca"*: Las Vegas is a city where gambling is legal, so people who like to gamble (play for money) are attracted there; Mecca is a Moslem holy city to which Moslems make pilgrimages (a religious trip); therefore, a mecca is a place visited by many people

(278) *payoff*: money won

(278) *persistent*: stubborn, determined

(278) *slot machine*: a coin-operated gambling machine

(279) *fanatic*: enthusiast

(279) *grooms*: cleans, licks itself

(279) *saunters*: walks slowly

(279) *spurts*: brief periods of time

(280) *anglers*: fishermen

(280) *bulldog tenacity*: bulldogs were bred to hold on to a bull's nose and not let go; therefore this means extreme stubbornness, refusal to give up

(280) *doggedly*: in a determined or persistent manner

(280) *frenzy*: intense activity

(280) *Thanksgiving turkey*: the customary meal on the American holiday of Thanksgiving, celebrated in November

(280) *the presence of a police car brings about rapid reductions in driving speed...and, in Los Angeles, gun battles*: refers to the fact that some drivers on the freeways in Los Angeles have shot at other drivers with guns

(281) *baited*: containing

(281) *contraband*: illegal items

(281) *feat*: accomplishment

(282) *everyday*: ordinary or commonplace

(282) *persistently*: lasting in spite of opposition

Module 7.4 Punishment (pp. 283-286)

(283) *haphazardly*: marked by lack of plan, order, or direction

(283) *Putting the Brakes on Behavior*: stopping behavior

(283) *reprimand*: scolding, expression of disapproval

(284) *drawbacks*: negative effects

(284) *obnoxious*: unpleasant, disagreeable person

(285) *"sparing the rod"*: part of a common saying that suggests that if a child is not punished physically, he or she will behave badly and have a bad character

(285) *silence may be "golden"*: the common saying "silence is golden" means that quiet moments are rare and should be enjoyed

Module 7.5 Cognitive Learning and Imitation (pp. 287-292)

(289) *a large blowup "Bo-Bo the Clown" doll*: an inflatable (gas-filled) life-sized plastic doll

(289) *tune-up*: general adjustment of a car to improve performance

(290) *penchant*: strong desire

(290) *tube*: television

Module 7.6 PSYCHOLOGY IN ACTION: Behavioral Self-Management—A Rewarding Project (pp. 293-295)

(293) *fall short*: fail to reach your goal

(294) *American Nazi Party*: racist political group opposed to minorities, especially Jews

(294) *forfeit*: give up, lose

(294) *Ku Klux Klan*: a racist secret society in the U.S.; its members are opposed to minorities

CHAPTER 8

Memory

The number of the page in the text where the idiom, word, phrase, or name can be found is shown in parentheses. The term or phrase is shown *in italics*. Where necessary for clarity, the phrase or sentence containing the term is given in parentheses. The meaning of the selected term or phrase follows the colon.

"What the Hell's Going On Here?" (p. 296)
   (296) *Put yourself in Steven's shoes.*: imagine you are Steven

Module 8.1: Memory Systems (pp. 298-300)
   (299) *"dumped" from STM*: removed
   (300) *persists*: lasts in the face of opposition
   (300) *retain*: to keep
   (300) *transparent*: easily seen through

Module 8.2: STM and LTM (pp. 301-306)
   (301) *IBM:* International Business Machines, a very large, U.S.-based computer company
   (301) *TV*: television
   (301) *USN*: United States Navy
   (301) *YMCA*: Young Men's Christian Association, an international organization that promotes the spiritual, social, and physical welfare of young men
   (302) *appreciate*: to be grateful for
   (303) *colored by emotions*: affected by our feelings
   (303) *impression*: an effect on the intellect or emotions
   (303) *in a lineup*: a line of people to be viewed and possibly identified by the victim or witness of a crime
   (303) *lashed together*: bound to another with rope or cord
   (303) *notoriously*: famous in an unfavorable way
   (303) *quirks*: peculiar actions or behavior
   (304) *abducted*: kidnapped, taken against one's will
   (304) *break the case*: solve the crime, find the criminals
   (304) *hypothetical*: assumed as an example
   (304) *ransom*: money demanded by kidnappers for the return of the victim

(305) *autobiographical*: related to one's own experiences or history

(305) *encyclopedia*: a work in several volumes that contains information on all branches of knowledge

Module 8.3: Measuring Memory and Exceptional Memory (pp. 307-312)

(307) "*drew a blank*": could not remember

(307) *World Series*: a series of baseball games played each fall to decide the professional championship of the U.S.

(308) "*It's all Greek to me!*": I don't understand

(309) "*prime*" *his memory*: activate, stimulate

(309) *nutritionists*: those who specialize in the study of the way food is used in the body

(310) *mnemonist*: a person who uses special techniques (mnemonics) to improve the memory

(311) *digits*: any of the Arabic numbers 0 to 9

(311*) matrix*: a pattern of items set into a rectangular arrangement of rows and columns

(311) *phenomenal*: outstanding

Module 8.4: Forgetting (pp. 313-321)

(313) *cramming*: studying hastily just before an examination

(313) *swayed*: influenced

(315) *scrapbook*: a blank book in which items such as newspaper articles or pictures are collected and kept

(315) *trivial*: unimportant

(315) *unleashes*: releases

(315) *Vietnam Veterans Memorial*: a memorial in Washington, D.C. that consists of a black marble wall containing the names of all Americans who died in the Vietnam War

(316) *farfetched*: exaggerated or unbelievable

(318) *truth drug*: drug that causes a person being questioned to talk freely

(318) *traumatic*: very disturbing or upsetting

(319) *John F. Kennedy*: President of the U.S. from 1960 until his assassination in 1963

(319) *Pearl Harbor attack*: the Japanese attack on American ships in Pearl Harbor (Hawaii) caused the U.S. to enter World War II

(319) *the Challenger space shuttle disaster*: the spaceship named *Challenger* exploded shortly after take-off, killing the six astronauts on board (January, 1986)

(321) *hard time*: difficulty

Module 8.5: Improving Memory (pp. 322-325)

(322) *if you boil down the material*: summarize

(323) *clear to the back of the stack*: all the way to the bottom of the stack

(323) *elaborate*: to expand with details

(323) *repeatedly*: happening over and over

(324) *eluded*: escaped

(324) *jogging*: making alert

Module 8.6: PSYCHOLOGY IN ACTION: Mnemonics—Memory Magic (pp. 326-329)

(326) *port* and *starboard*: terms used for the left and right sides of a boat

(326) *the budding sailor*: inexperienced but learning

(326) *vivid*: very intense or clear

(327) *exaggerated*: increased in size beyond normal

(327) *Van Gogh*: Vincent Van Gogh (1853-1890), well-known Dutch painter

(328) *associated*: connected with or brought into relation with

(328) *ick*: a slang term used to express disgust

(328) *imp*: a little devil or child prone to mischief or annoying behaviors

(328) *skeptical*: unbelieving

CHAPTER 9

Cognition, Intelligence, and Creativity

The number of the page in the text where the idiom, word, phrase, or name can be found is shown in parentheses. The term or phrase is shown *in italics*. Where necessary for clarity, the phrase or sentence containing the term is given in parentheses. The meaning of the selected term or phrase follows the colon.

Gizmos and Doohickeys (p. 330)
(330) *contraptions*: devices, usually not simple or ordinary
(330) *Darwin*: Charles Darwin, a naturalist (1809-1882)
(330) *Edison*: Thomas Edison: an inventor, famous for inventing the light bulb (1847-1931)
(330) *Einstein*: Albert Einstein, a brilliant physicist and mathematician (1879-1955)
(330) *gadget*: small mechanical device
(330) *Galileo*: an Italian astronomer and physicist (1564-1642)
(330) *gizmos and doohickeys*: small items whose common name is unknown or forgotten
(330) *hilarious*: very amusing or funny
(330) *how many engineering students does it take to screw in a light bulb*: refers to the common opening of a joke-- "engineering students" can be replaced by any number of professions or groups
(330) *Madame Curie*: Marie Curie, a French chemist (1867-1934)
(330) *Martha Graham*: an American dancer, associated with the beginning of modern dance as a style (1893-1991)
(330) *Michelangelo*: an Italian painter and sculptor (1475-1564)
(330) *mind-boggling*: amazing or incredible
(330) *Mozart*: Wolfgang Mozart, an Austrian composer (1756-1791)
(330) *Newton*: Sir Isaac Newton, an English mathematician and philosopher (1642-1727)
(330) *novelty*: a new thing or creation
(330) *pulleys*: wheels that transfer power through a cord, rope, belt, etc. passing over its rim
(330) *teeing up a golf ball*: putting a golf ball on a small wooden holder called a tee
(330) *wacky*: unrealistic or impractical

(330) *zany*: crazy or silly

Module 9.1: Imagery, Concepts, and Language (pp. 332-341)

(334) *whatchamacallit*: what you may call it; used when the exact name for something cannot be remembered

(335) *daze*: state of confusion

(335) *fusion*: music that blends jazz elements and the heavy repetitive rhythms of rock. Also called *jazz-fusion, jazz-rock*

(335) *grunge rock*: (sometimes also referred to as the Seattle Sound) that was an offshoot of punk music and alternative rock in the late 1980s and early 1990s

(335) *heavy metal*: energetic and highly amplified rock music with a hard beat

(335) *hip-hop*: a popular urban youth culture, closely associated with rap music and with the style and fashions of African-American inner-city residents.

(335) *punk*: music marked by extreme and often offensive expressions of social discontent

(335) *rap*: characterized by lyrics that are spoken rather than sung

(335) *salsa*: popular music of Latin American origin combining rhythm and blues, jazz, and rock

(336) *connoisseurs*: experts

(336) *conscientious*: extremely careful and attentive to details

(336) *movie censor*: person who gives ratings to movies depending on their sexual content and amount of violence

(336) *nuances*: not obvious qualities

(336) *nudist*: person who wears no clothes in groups and special places (nudist camps)

(336) *pop-tart*: a brand name for a ready-made turnover or tart that you can heat up in the toaster

(336) *tannins*: a product of the wine-making process

(337) *circumcised*: having the foreskin of the penis removed

(338) *declarative sentence*: a sentence that makes a statement, as opposed to one that asks a question

(338) *mime*: to imitate actions without using words

(338) *spatial*: relating to space

(339) "*That sucker I saw yesterday*": used as a general term to refer to something or someone (slang)

(339) *belch*: burp

(340) *apes have made monkeys out of their trainers*: made fools of

(340) *plagued*: bothered, caused difficulties

(340) *Washoe once "wet" on*: urinated

(341) *gestural*: using motions of the hands or body as a means of expression

(341) *morph*: to change

(341) *true sports car has… excellent handling*: drives very well

(341) *unicycle*: a single-wheel machine which one rides and pedals with the feet; similar to a bicycle but with only one wheel

Module 9.2: Problem Solving and Artificial Intelligence (pp. 342-348)

(342) *insightful*: with awareness and careful observation

(342) *rote*: use of memory, usually with little intelligence

(344) *hourglass*: an instrument for measuring time consisting of a glass container having two sections, one above the other; sand, water, or mercury runs from the upper section to the lower in one hour

(344) *the tendency to get "hung up" on wrong solutions*: delayed, detained by

(346) *taboos*: restrictions imposed by social custom

(347) *eclipsed*: reduced in importance or reputation

(347) *novices*: beginners, amateurs

(347) *stymied*: confused

Module 9.3: Intelligence (pp. 349-359)

(350) *yields*: gives or shows

(355) *intricate*: complicated

(355) *persevere*: to be persistent in spite of opposition

(355) *shortchange*: cheat

(356) *siblings*: brothers and sisters

Module 9.4: Creative Thinking and Intuition (pp. 360-366)

(360) *novel*: new

(362) *"harebrained scheme"*: foolish idea

(362) *"stroke of genius"*: clever idea

(362) *eccentric*: odd, strange

(362) *futile*: useless

(362) *incubation*: period during which ideas are developed

(362) *inept*: unskilled

(362) *introverted*: being primarily concerned with and interested in one's own mental life

(362) *neurotic:* emotionally unstable or troubled by anxiety

(363) *outlandish*: very out of the ordinary, strange

(364) *flawed*: containing defects or errors

(364) *pitfall*: a hidden danger or difficulty

(365) *custody*: legal care

(365) *disqualify*: not considered

(365) *drawbacks*: things or actions not in one's favor

(365) *rapport*: how well one communicates with others

Module 9.5: PSYCHOLOGY IN ACTION: Enhancing Creativity— Brainstorms (pp. 367-371)

(368) *analogies*: similarities

(368) *extract*: get or understand

(368) *jog yourself out of ruts and habitual modes of thought*: to get yourself out of your normal and usual ways of thinking

(369) *defer*: put off, postpone

(369) *elaborate*: add to

(369) *Let your imagination "run amok"*: go wild

(369) *suspend*: postpone in order to wait for further information

CHAPTER 10

Motivation and Emotion

The number of the page in the text where the idiom, word, phrase, or name can be found is shown in parentheses. The term or phrase is shown *in italics*. Where necessary for clarity, the phrase or sentence containing the term is given in parentheses. The meaning of the selected term or phrase follows the colon.

The Sun Sets Twice in Utah (p. 372)
- (372) *mosquitoes*: small flying, biting insects
- (372) *detect*: to discover or find out
- (372) *vistas*: views
- (372) *twilight*: the brief period of time just as the sun is sinking below the horizon

Module 10.1 Overview of Motivation (pp. 374-376)
- (374) *depletion*: lessening or loss
- (374) *incentives*: motivating factors
- (376) *mentally list*: think about but do not write down

Module 10.2 Hunger, Thirst, Pain, and Sex (pp. 377-386)
- (377) "*hunger pangs*": extreme feeling of hunger
- (378) *obesity*: extreme overweight
- (378) *stigma*: mark or sign of shame
- (382) "*threshold*": a set point or amount; a dividing line
- (383) *atypically*: out of the ordinary
- (383) *gorge*: eat to excess
- (383) *relentless parade*: a series seemingly without end
- (384) *Gatorade*: a drink taken especially after exercise to help restore minerals lost through perspiration
- (385) *reputation*: the general opinion of others about a person or thing
- (385) *suppresses*: to hold back or stop

Module 10.3 Arousal, Achievement, and Growth Needs (pp. 387-394)

(387) *skydiving*: the sport of jumping from an airplane with a parachute

(391) *eminent*: prominent, famous

(391) *prodigies*: highly talented people, especially children

(392) *drudgery*: dull and fatiguing work

(394) *impaired*: weakened or negatively affected

Module 10.4 Emotion and Physiological Arousal (pp. 395-399)

(395) *choking up*: fail to perform effectively because of fear

(394) *occupy most of your time and energy*: are the most important things or concerns in your life

(395) *stage fright*: nervousness felt when appearing before an audience

(395) *"butterflies" in the stomach*: feeling of nervousness

(396) *"Blue Monday"*: because Monday is the beginning of the work and school week, it is a "blue," or sad, day

(396) *prowler*: a person moving about secretly, as in search of things to steal

(398) *irrelevant*: not important to the matter being considered

(3398) *Monica*: Monica Lewinsky, a White House intern who was involved in a sexual relationship with President Bill Clinton

(398) *O. J.*: O. J. Simpson, a star football player of the 1960s and 1970s, who was acquitted of the murder of his ex-wife in a highly publicized 1995 trial.

(398) *the polygraph may be thrown off*: give inaccurate readings

Module 10.5 Emotional Expression and Theories of Emotion (pp. 400-406)

(400) *Halloween*: celebrated on October 31; children wear masks and costumes and go to neighbors' houses asking for candy

(401) *"You're an ass!"*: meaning: you're a stupid person (usually considered vulgar)

(401) *detriment*: harm or loss

(403) *added an interesting wrinkle*: contributed something new

(403) *chasm*: deep hole in the earth

(403) *element of truth*: partially but not completely correct

(403) *seeing each other "on the sly"*: secretly

(403) *slapstick*: type of comedy

(403) *suspension bridge*: a bridge that has its roadway hanging from cables anchored on each side

(404) *billboard*: a large panel that contains outdoor advertising

(405) *lunges*: rushes forward suddenly

(405) *snarling*: growling

(406) *predictions*: ideas about what might happen in the future, usually based on supporting evidence

Module 10.6 PSYCHOLOGY IN ACTION: Emotional Intelligence—The Fine Art of Self-control (pp. 407-409)

(407) *empathy*: the ability to put oneself in another person's place

(407) *mend*: fix

(407) *roast*: good-humored public teasing of a well-liked individual

(407) *sabotage*: block progress toward a goal

(407) *toast*: wishing an individual, couple, or group well by raising a glass in admiration

(407) *toll*: burden

(408) *altruism*: giving to others without recognition for oneself

(408) *save their skins*: survive

(408) *savor*: enjoy to the fullest

CHAPTER 11

Personality

The number of the page in the text where the idiom, word, phrase, or name can be found is shown in parentheses. The term or phrase is shown *in italics*. Where necessary for clarity, the phrase or sentence containing the term is given in parentheses. The meaning of the selected term or phrase follows the colon.

The Essence of Annette (p. 410)
(410) *hooting and whooping*: yelling with pleasure and excitement
(410) *lumberjack*: logger; one who cuts trees for lumber

Module 11.1 Overview of Personality, Trait Theories (pp. 412-421)
(412) *charisma*: special magnetic charm or appeal
(412) *inferred*: resulted from
(412) *these ideas should help you keep your bearings*: understand the text
(413) *oversimplify*: to explain without a lot of details or information
(413) *paranoid*: having irrational feelings of being persecuted
(414) *arrogance*: a feeling of being better than others that is shown in one's behavior
(415) *uninhibited*: not restrained by social norms, informal
(416) *"Monicagate" scandal*: the White House sex scandal involving President Bill Clinton and intern Monica Lewinsky that occurred in 1998-1999. The "gate" in the name refers to an earlier White House scandal, known as Watergate, which happened during President Nixon's term in the 1970s.
(416) *the Hopi of Northern Arizona*: a Native American tribe
(418) *consistent*: happen on a regular basis
(418) *knowing where a person stands*: how one is perceived or judged in relation to certain issues
(418) *obvious*: clearly seen
(418) *spiteful*: malicious, nasty
(419) *boisterous*: marked by high spirits
(419) *excels*: is good at, or performs well at
(419) *nervous tics*: nervous habits or actions
(419) *reared apart*: raised in separate homes
(420) *"wired in"*: unchangeable

(420) *astute*: observant

(420) *rival*: be competitive with

(420) *similarities blaze brightly*: more attention is paid to the similarities than to the differences

(421) *prominent*: standing out so as to be easily seen

Module 11.2 Psychoanalytic Theory (pp. 422-426)

(422) *chaotic*: confused, totally disorganized

(423) "*Go for it!*": go after what you want; do it

(423) *censor*: one who represses unacceptable notions or ideas

(423) *sublimate*: to redirect an urge toward a more socially accepted activity

(424) *a fixation is an unresolved conflict or emotional hang-up*: problem, barrier

(424) *latency*: period of inactivity

(425) *Electra*: character in a Greek tragedy that kills her mother

(425) *embrace*: believe in; hold to be true

(425) *forte:* originally a musical term meaning loud or strong, it is also used to mean strength or specialty

(425) *Oedipus*: character in a Greek tragedy that unknowingly married his mother and killed his father

(425) *offshoot*: development, derivation

(425) *psychosexual development is "on hold"*: postponed, put off until a later time

(426) *the workings*: the actions or operations in a process

Module 11.3 Behavioral and Social Learning Theories (pp. 427-431)

(427) *R2D2 of Star Wars*: R2D2 was a robot character in the popular futuristic movie Star Wars

(428) *goad*: something that urges or stimulates into action

(430) *aghast*: horrified

(430) *arbitrary*: selected at random or without reason

(430) *assault*: physical confrontation

(430) *imitate*: to try to do something exactly the way it was done when first seen

(430) *passive*: inactive and not showing feeling or interest

(430) *rebukes*: disapproves

(430) *scoldings*: harsh verbal discipline

(430) *submissive*: allowing oneself to be governed by another

(430) *unwittingly*: not intentionally

(430) *vicariously*: experienced indirectly

(431) *"shop 'til you drop"*: describes the strong urge that some people have to shop until they are too tired to shop anymore

Module 11.4 Humanistic Theories (pp. 432-437)

(432) *engaged*: actively involved

(432) *inherently*: involved in the framework or essential character of something

(432) *mission*: purpose or goal

(433) *gauge*: measure

(433) *gleaned*: to gather information from

(433) *solitude*: the state of being alone

(433) *wry*: ironically humorous

(434) *seething*: boiling

(435) *harbors*: contains

(435) *obese*: extremely overweight

(436) *fared*: succeeded

(436) *gut-level response*: arising from one's innermost self, instinctual

(436) *they are "prized" as worthwhile human beings*: valued, thought of as important

Module 11.5 Personality Assessment (pp. 438-445)

(438) *accentuate*: make more obvious

(438) *swayed*: persuaded

(438) *you have probably "sized up" a potential date*: evaluated, measured

(439) *make split-second decisions*: very fast

(441) *pessimism*: the tendency to emphasize the worst possible outcome

(442) *ambiguous*: able to be interpreted in more than one way

(442) *brushes with the law*: illegal actions

(443) *predispose*: influence

(444) *"someone you could easily push around"*: someone who is easily bullied or influenced by others

(444) *amnesia*: temporary loss of memory

(444) *belittlement*: causing to seem little or less

(445) *informally*: in a manner that is not exactly defined

Module 11.6 PSYCHOLOGY IN ACTION: Barriers and Bridges— Understanding Shyness (pp. 446-449)

(447) *"stage fright"*: fear such as an actor feels when standing before the audience

(448) *broken the ice*: concluded an introduction, became acquainted

CHAPTER 12

Health, Stress, and Coping

The number of the page in the text where the idiom, word, phrase, or name can be found is shown in parentheses. The term or phrase is shown *in italics*. Where necessary for clarity, the phrase or sentence containing the term is given in parentheses. The meaning of the selected term or phrase follows the colon.

Taylor's (Not So Very Fine) Adventure (p. 450)

(450) *bronchitis*: an illness that affects the passages that move air to and from the lungs

(450) *colossal*: huge

(450) *cramming*: fitting much into a short period of time

(450) *frustration*: defeated in achieving one's goals

(450) *kick back*: to reduce or stop work after a period of activity

(450) *make-or-break*: essential to success

(450) *one-finger salute*: an indecent hand gesture

(450) *stress*: to place added importance on

Module 12.1 Health Psychology (pp. 452-455)

(453) *plaque*: fatty substances deposited in the inner layers of the arteries

(453) *sermon*: lecture or talk by minister or priest

(454) *abstain*: to not take part in

(454) *aerobic*: using or increasing the use of oxygen

(454) *forgo*: to give up or not do something

(455) *laying the foundation*: an early action that later actions can build on

Modure 12.2 Stress, Frustration, and Conflict (pp. 456-465)

(456) *The threat of injury or death..."takes a toll"*: has a negative, or harmful effect

(457) *apathetic*: showing little or no feeling or concern

(457) *detachment*: state of being uninvolved, uninterested

(458) *interchange*: the placement of objects, persons, or ideas in contact with other objects, persons, or ideas, usually resulting in some new effect or behavior

(459) *"getting stuck"* with a flat tire: stopped and unable to proceed

(459) "*the straw that broke the camel's back*": the last negative event in a series of negative events

(459) *blind alleys and lead balloons*: blind alleys lead nowhere; balloons made of lead would not fly, therefore both are symbols of frustration

(459) *impede*: slow, make difficult

(459) *T-bone*: a beef steak

(461) *vigorous*: very strong or active

(463) *tampered*: interfered

Modure 12.3 Defenses, Helplessness, and Depression (pp. 466-471)

(466) *put up with*: tolerate, endure

(466) *throws a temper tantrum*: has an emotional display of anger or frustration

(466) *tightwad*: a person unwilling to spend money

(466) *X-rays*: shadow pictures showing the inside of the body

(467) *go belly-up*: stop working

(467) *the last straw*: the final event in a series of difficulties

(469) *"immunize"*: protect, provide a way to resist

(469) *transatlantic*: across the Atlantic Ocean

(470) *episodes*: incidents that occur in the course of a person's life

(471) *blind to our own reliance*: not aware of how much we need something

(471) *impairment*: damage, injury

Modure 12.4 Stress and Health (pp. 472-480)

(472) *hassles*: difficulties, problems

(473) *take it easy*: relax

(474) *deteriorating*: becoming worse

(474) *hives*: an allergic disorder that causes the skin to itch and break out in bumps

(474) *paperwork*: written reports or records needed as part of a job or task

(474) *quarreling*: having disagreements with another person

(474) *rheumatoid arthritis*: disease characterized by pain, stiffness, and swelling of the joints

(476) *lethal*: deadly

(477) *cynical*: distrusting of human nature

(477) *setbacks*: defeats or problems, often temporary

(479) *bereavement*: death of a loved one

(479) *lymph nodes*: rounded masses of lymph tissue (lymph is a fluid that bathes the tissues and contains white blood cells)

(479) *melodramatic*: exaggerated, overly dramatic

(479) *spleen*: organ that destroys red blood cells, stores blood, and produces white blood cells

(479) *the "double whammy" of getting sick when you are trying to cope with stress*: being attacked by two things at once

(480) *acquaintance*: a person whom one knows but is not a close friend

Modure 12.5 PSYCHOLOGY IN ACTION: Stress Management (pp. 481-485)

(481) *"uptight"*: tense, nervous

(482) *cheat on you*: to have your boyfriend or girlfriend go out or have sex with another person and not tell you

(482) *flunking*: not successfully completing something, such as a class or test

(482) *fraternity or sorority rush*: a period during the beginning of a school year in which campus social groups made up of the same sex--called fraternities for men and sororities for women--invite new students to join

(482) *HIV-positive*: a test result that shows that one has been exposed to the AIDS virus

(482) *housing situation*: any arrangement that involves where or with whom one lives

(482) *straight A's*: getting the highest grade possible for all of one's courses

(483) *browsing*: looking over casually

(483) *get blown out of proportion*: become exaggerated in importance

(483) *loafing*: resting, relaxing

(483) *puttering*: moving or acting aimlessly or idly

(484) *cultivating*: developing

(484) *I'm "psyched up" to do my best*: ready, prepared

(484) *life's ups and downs*: the good and bad things that happen over a lifetime

CHAPTER 13

Psychological Disorders

The number of the page in the text where the idiom, word, phrase, or name can be found is shown in parentheses. The term or phrase is shown *in italics*. Where necessary for clarity, the phrase or sentence containing the term is given in parentheses. The meaning of the selected term or phrase follows the colon.

Beware the Helicopters (p. 486)
(486) *plagued*: consistently bothered
(486) *incapacitated*: left unable to function at normal levels
(486) *"crazy," "insane," "cracked,"* and *"lunatic"*: terms used in the past to describe severe psychological disorders
(486) *weigh*: judge

Module 13.1 Normality and Psychopathology (pp. 488-495)
(488) *"on top of the world"*: great, wonderful
(488) *"That guy is really wacko. His porch lights are dimming." "Yeah, the butter's sliding off his waffle. I think he's ready to go postal"*: slang expressions for crazy, insane
(488) *snap judgments*: hurried decisions
(490) *histrionic*: very emotional; displaying emotion to gain attention
(493) *amphetamines*: drugs that are used as stimulants for the central nervous system
(493) *distortions*: significant changes from what is real or normal
(493) *fetishism*: erotic fixation on an object or bodily part
(493) *voyeurism*: practice of seeking sexual stimulation by visual means
(494) *commitment*: the sending of someone involuntarily to a mental institution
(495) *bad mood*: a period of unhappiness and/or anger

Module 13.2 Personality Disorders and Anxiety-Based Disorders (pp. 496-505)
(496) *bizarre*: extremely unusual or strange
(496) *flamboyant*: elaborate or colorful behavior; showy
(497) *emotion-laden*: filled with memories or meanings that produce strong feelings

(497) *maggot*: the wormlike young of various insects, often associated with decay

(498) *"just around the corner"*: about to happen soon

(499) *clammy*: damp

(500) contaminated: made impure or poisonous

(500) *jingle*: short verse or song

(500) *recluse*: hermit, one who prefers to be alone

(502) *atypical*: not the usual

(502) *uncontrollable*: impossible to stop

(504) *excessively*: to an unnecessary extent, beyond what is needed

(504) *intensifies*: increases and strengthens in effect

(504) *magnify*: to increase greatly the importance or size of something

(505) *key difference*: the one particular quality or feature that makes one or more things distinctly unlike each other

Module 13.3 Psychosis, Delusional Disorders, and Schizophrenia (pp. 506-515)

(506) *psychoses*: basic mental derangements characterized by loss of contact with reality

(507) *defy*: refuse to give in to or obey

(507) *paving*: covering soil with material that makes the surface hard and smooth

(507) *persistently despondent*: a feeling of extreme unhappiness that continues over time

(507) *soldered*: joined together by melting metal alloys and then allowing them to re-cool and harden

(508) *"the Mafia"*: organized crime group

(508) *atrophy*: wasting away, decrease in size

(508) *crank letter*: crazy, eccentric letter

(509) *stupor*: mental apathy and dullness

(511) *enigma*: puzzle

(512) *"angel dust"*: a psychedelic drug that causes vivid mental imagery

(512) *laden*: full of

(512) *prying*: to look

(513) *agitation*: a state of emotional unrest or excitement

(513) *bind to*: connect with strongly

(515) *exposure*: the condition of being unprotected

Module 13.4 Mood Disorders (pp. 516-520)

(516) *down and out:* physically weakened or incapable; depressed

(518) *"cabin fever":* extreme irritability and restlessness resulting from living in isolation or within a confined indoor area for a long period

Module 13.5 PSYCHOLOGY IN ACTION: Suicide—Lives on the Brink (pp. 521-525)

(523) *on the verge:* on the edge of danger

(523) *tip the scales:* have a deciding influence

(524) *anguish:* extreme pain or suffering

(524) *suicide hotline:* a phone-in counseling service to which individuals having suicidal thoughts can call for help

CHAPTER 14

Therapies

The number of the page in the text where the idiom, word, phrase, or name can be found is shown in parentheses. The term or phrase is shown *in italics*. Where necessary for clarity, the phrase or sentence containing the term is given in parentheses. The meaning of the selected term or phrase follows the colon.

Cold Terror on a Warm Afternoon (p. 526)
(526) *alleviate*: reduce, lessen
(526) *come to grips*: to understand and accept

Module 14.1 Psychotherapy and Psychoanalysis (pp. 528-532)
(528) *"major overhaul"* of the psyche or personality: complete repair
(529) *squalid*: dirty, filthy
(529) *witchcraft*: use of sorcery or magic
(530) *impotence*: inability to perform sexually
(530) *Since it is the "granddaddy" of more modern psychotherapies*: psychoanalysis is the first and oldest form of psychotherapy from which others are descended
(531) *"heart"*: center
(532) *"cursed"*: exposed to misfortune beyond one's control that is believed to be caused by an outside force

Module 14.2 Insight Therapies (pp. 533-536)
(533) *picture*: imagine
(534) *"psych jockeys"*: radio psychologists; because music announcers on the radio are called disc jockeys, the author calls psychologists *"psych jockeys"*
(535) *overstep this boundary*: go beyond what has been decided as acceptable
(536) *pros and cons*: the positive and negative aspects of something
(536) *two-way audio-video link*: a form of electronic communication in which both parties can see and hear each other, though they are separated by distance

Module 14.3 Behavior Therapy (pp. 537-542)

(537) *aversion*: intense dislike

(537) *covert*: hidden

(538) *"evil weed"*: tobacco in cigarettes

(538) *nicotine*: the active, habit-forming ingredient in cigarette smoke

(540) *clench*: tighten

(540) *flashbacks*: remembered images of events from the past

(541) *break the link*: break the relationship

(542) *goes berserk*: becomes very upset and nervous

Module 14.4 Operant Therapies and Cognitive Therapies (pp. 543-547)

(544) *subsided*: lessened

(544) *subsided*: lessened

(545) *disrobing*: removing one's clothes

(545) *disrobing*: removing one's clothes

(545) *incentive*: urge

(545) *incentive*: urge

(546) *"I must be a total zero"*: I must be worthless

(546) *"I must be a total zero"*: I must be worthless

(546) *dumped*: broke a relationship with

(546) *dumped*: broke a relationship with

(547) *inconvenient*: not happening at a good time

(547) *inconvenient*: not happening at a good time

(547) *loser*: one who is unable to succeed

(547) *loser*: one who is unable to succeed

Module 14.5 Group Therapy, Helping Skills, and Medical Therapies (pp. 548-557)

(549) *placebo effect*: a placebo is a fake medicine; a placebo effect is a response to treatment that is not directly due to the treatment

(550) *catharsis*: a purification of emotions that brings about spiritual renewal

(550) *sanctuary*: a safe place

(551) *distilled*: extracted or taken from

(552) *down about school*: unmotivated or depressed

(552) *hassling*: annoying, bothering

(553) *gossip*: to share personal information with someone about other people

(553) *my boss has it in for me*: is against me, doesn't like me

(553) *valid*: appropriate or logical

(556) *half-way houses*: centers for formerly institutionalized people (mental patients or drug addicts) to help them readjust to private life

Module 14.6 PSYCHOLOGY IN ACTION: Self-Management and Seeking Professional Help (pp. 537-542)

(558) *"Throw out the snake oil..."*: in the past traveling salesmen sold "tonics," or fake medicine, supposedly made from a variety of ingredients (such as snake oil) to cure illnesses

(558) *curb*: to control or restrain

(559) *grossed out*: disgusted

(559) *put yourself down*: criticize yourself harshly

(559) *maggots*: fly larvae

(560) *dismayed*: upset

(561) *outreach clinics*: clinics that are usually set up in neighborhoods to make it easier for people to use them

(562) *integrity*: honesty

(562) *terminate*: end, stop

CHAPTER 15

Gender and Sexuality

The number of the page in the text where the idiom, word, phrase, or name can be found is shown in parentheses. The term or phrase is shown *in italics*. Where necessary for clarity, the phrase or sentence containing the term is given in parentheses. The meaning of the selected term or phrase follows the colon.

That Magic Word (p. 564)
   (564) *ambiguities*: uncertainties
   (564) *reproduction*: sexual activity in order to have children
   (564) *transsexuals*: persons who undergo surgery to modify their sex organs to mimic those of the opposite sex

Module 15.1 Sex, Gender, and Androgyny (pp. 564-574)
   (566) *puberty*: the period of time when a person matures sexually and becomes capable of reproduction
   (567) *coiled*: formed into loops or rings
   (567) *embryos*: fertilized eggs; fetuses
   (568) *tomboys*: females who prefer to play with males and participate in typically male activities
   (568) *reared*: raised
   (569) *battle of the sexes*: various points of argument between men and women
   (569) *rote*: from memory
   (570) *adorning*: decorating
   (570) *Are women suited to be fighter pilots*: are women qualified to be fighter pilots
   (570) *courting*: dating
   (570) *obstacle*: problem to be solved
   (570) *pokes fun*: finds humor in
   (570) *theatrics*: staged shows or events
   (571) *segregated*: separated
   (572) *effeminate*: having female characteristics
   (572) *gullible*: easily tricked
   (572) *rigid*: clearly defined
   (573) *as the dust begins to settle*: as the argument dies down; as time passes
   (573) *instrumental*: important; to play a large part in

(573) *nurturant*: nurturing; giving affectionate care and attention

(574) *ambiguous*: uncertain or having several different meanings

Module 15.2 Sexual Behavior and Sexual Orientation (pp. 575-580)

(575) *agendas*: plans of things to be done

(575) *consenting*: giving permission

(575) *erotic*: showing sexual desire

(575) *exhibit*: show

(575) *explicit*: showing great detail

(575) *extramarital sex*: a married person having sex with someone who is not their spouse

(575) *norms*: socially accepted behavior

(575) *spontaneously*: proceeding from natural feeling or momentary impulse

(576) *macho*: a strong sense of masculine pride

(577) *abstinent*: not participating in sexual activities

(577) *cynics*: people who predict the worst possible outcome of an event

(577) *enlightened*: free from ignorance and misinformation

(577) *widowed*: one whose spouse has died

(578) *nil*: none; zero

(578) *people are being urged to practice "safer sex"*: people are being urged to avoid having sex, to have a monogamous relationship, or to always use a condom when participating in sexual activities; this is a result of the outbreak of the AIDS virus

(579) *in all walks of life*: in various different cultures and environments; all different kinds of people

(579) *monogamous*: having only one partner

(579) *myths*: unproven stories

Module 15.3 Sexual Response, Attitudes, and Behavior (pp. 581-591)

(582) *jock itch*: ringworm, or itching in the crotch area

(582) *flaccid*: not erect, limp

(582) *flushed*: red

(582) *potency*: ability to engage in sexual intercourse

(582) *spontaneity*: making a decision instantly

(582) *Victorian era*: the time period when Queen Victoria reigned in England (1837-1901), characterized by excessive modesty regarding sexual matters

(583) *at odds*: in conflict with

(585) *cohabitation*: living together as if married

(585) *preludes*: introductions, preparations

(586) *mores*: moral attitudes

(586) *tacitly*: implied or indicated indirectly

(587) *ambivalence*: an inability to make a decision

(587) *plot*: story

(588) *commemorate*: to honor the memory of a person or event

(588) *incubation*: period between the infection of an individual and the appearance of symptoms of disease

(589) *hemophiliacs*: those who have a blood disease characterized by delayed clotting of the blood and resulting tendency to bleed easily

(589) *prior*: happening in an earlier time

(590) *curtailment*: decrease

(590) *Russian roulette*: the practice of spinning the cylinder of a gun loaded with one bullet, pointing the gun at one's head, and pulling the trigger; here it means taking extreme risks with one's health

Module 15.4 Sexual Problems—When Pleasure Fades (pp. 592-599)

(592) *dysfunction*: an inability to function

(593) *dejection*: having low emotion; depression

(593) *harsh*: strong or strict

(595) *inevitable*: incapable of being avoided

(595) *take their toll*: have a negative effect

(596) *bridges to sexual satisfaction*: methods or ways to reach a healthy sexual relationship

(596) *spontaneous*: happening without a plan

(597) *hitting below the belt*: being unfair and hurtful

(597) *equitable*: fair

(597) *foster*: encourage

(597) *haven*: a safe hiding place

(598) *to do it*: to have sex

CHAPTER 16

Social Behavior

The number of the page in the text where the idiom, word, phrase, or name can be found is shown in parentheses. The term or phrase is shown *in italics*. Where necessary for clarity, the phrase or sentence containing the term is given in parentheses. The meaning of the selected term or phrase follows the colon.

We Are Social Animals (p. 600)
>   (600) *demeaning*: degrading

Module 16.1 Affiliation, Friendship, and Love (pp. 602-607)
>   (602) *misery loves company*: those in an unpleasant situation like to be with others in the same situation
>   (602) *ominously*: in a threatening or alarming way
>   (603) *birds of a feather flock together*: those with similar characteristics or personalities will seek one another
>   (603) *familiarity breeds contempt*: the more one knows about a person, the less one likes that person
>   (603) *affiliate*: associate, connect
>   (603) *folklore*: traditional customs, stories, or sayings of a people
>   (603) *proximity*: closeness in space
>   (604) *back off*: become more reserved, less friendly
>   (606) *potential*: possible
>   (607) *contemporary*: modern

Module 16.2 Groups, Social Influence, and Conformity (pp. 608-612)
>   (608) *flunk*: fail
>   (608) *parties*: persons involved
>   (608) *streamline*: simplify
>   (609) *inferences*: guesses
>   (609) *littering*: scattering trash, wastepaper, or garbage around
>   (610) *cheapskates*: stingy, miserly people
>   (610) *dog the heels*: pursue, harass, annoy
>   (610) *Ye Old Double Standard*: the old double standard; the idea that there is one set of rules to be applied to women, and a different set of rules for men

(611) *rock the boat*: disturbing the situation, making any changes

(611) *Columbia space shuttle disaster*: the space shuttle that exploded over Texas 73 seconds after lift-off in February, 2003, killing all seven astronauts on board

(611) *devil's advocate*: to argue in support of the less accepted or approved alternative

(611) *fall prey*: give in to, become influenced by

(611) *fiascoes*: complete failures

(611) *ridicule*: to tease someone or make them the object of laughter

(611) *sanctions*: rules or laws

(612) *in your corner*: on your side, supportive of you

(612) *prominent*: standing out in a way that is easily seen

(612) *yielded*: conformed

Module 16.3 Obedience and Compliance (pp.613-618)

(613) *compliance*: conformity, agreeing to a demand or proposal

(613) *electrocute*: to kill by electric shock

(614) *simulated*: pretended, faked

(614) *to knuckle under*: to submit or to give in

(616) *"low-ball" prices*: prices that are deceptively low, but not in reality

(616) *"making a scene"*: exhibiting anger or improper behavior

(616) *bump the price up*: increase the price

(617) *broken record*: repetition of one phrase over and over

(617) *flustered*: confused, agitated

(618) *charity*: an organization that helps others in need

(618) *defective*: faulty, lacking in some essential ingredient

Module 16.4 Attitudes an Persuasion (pp. 619-625)

(619) *doomsday group*: groups who believe that the end of the world is coming soon

(619) *orient*: make familiar

(619) *persuade*: to convince or influence

(620) *intentions*: determination to do some action

(622) *lure*: to draw someone away from their normal path

(623) *POW*: prisoner of war

(623) *rigid*: stiff, inflexible

(625) *components*: parts of a whole

Module 16.5 Prejudice and Intergroup Conflict (pp. 626-631)

    (626) *anti-Semitism*: prejudice against Jews

    (626) *fascism*: tendency toward strong autocratic or dictatorial control

    (627) *bigotry*: prejudice

    (627) *covet*: to wish for, to desire

    (627) *distort*: to create false ideas that affect how something or someone is perceived

    (627) *perpetuate*: to help an event or action continue

    (627) *redneck*: white working class member usually living in the country

    (630) *we're all in the same boat*: we are all in the same situation, facing the same kinds of problems

    (630) *baited*: teased, harassed

    (630) *free-for-all*: brawl, fight

    (630) *gang colors*: particular colors, usually of clothing, that identify members of particular groups, or gangs, of youths

    (630) *in-group/out-group distinctions*: ways in which people identify the positive or negative status of others

    (630) *jigsaw puzzle*: a puzzle consisting of small irregularly cut pieces that are to be fitted together to form a picture

    (630) *vandalism*: the destruction of others' property without care

    (630) *violations*: the disobeying of laws or rules

    (631) *accessories*: people who contribute as assistants to the committing of an offense

    (631) *breaks down the walls of prejudice*: helps stop the thought processes that people use to form judgments about others or things without a basis in knowledge

    (631) *mentally scan*: quickly think about a list of items or events

Module 16.6 Aggression and Prosocial Behavior (pp. 632-639)

    (632) *Eskimo*: native people of northern Canada, Greenland, Alaska, and eastern Siberia

    (632) *road rage*: angry and aggressive behavior while driving

    (632) *the Arapesh, the Senoi, the Navajo*: the Arapesh and Senoi are tribes in Malaysia; the Navajo refers to a Native American tribe

    (635) *altruistic*: characterized by unselfish regard for the welfare of others

    (636) *alienation*: feelings of isolation and aloneness

Module 16.7 PSYCHOLOGY IN ACTION: Multiculturalism—Living with Diversity (pp. 640-643)

(640) *melting pot*: a container of blended materials, usually metals

(640) *tossed salad*: a salad into which are tossed a variety of ingredients

(640) *forsake*: give up

(641) *fabled*: made up

CHAPTER 17

Applied Psychology

The number of the page in the text where the idiom, word, phrase, or name can be found is shown in parentheses. The term or phrase is shown *in italics*. Where necessary for clarity, the phrase or sentence containing the term is given in parentheses. The meaning of the selected term or phrase follows the colon.

The Towering Inferno (p. 644)
> (644) *The Towering Inferno*: the title of a well-known movie about a devastating fire in a high-rise building

Module 17.1 Industrial-Organizational Psychology (pp. 646-655)
> (646) *better to wear out than to rust out*: it is better to be active and productive than to be idle
> (646) *at stake*: at risk
> (646) *flight simulators*: mechanical devices that imitate or act and react like real jet fighters
> (647) *flagrant*: obviously offensive
> (649) *assembly line*: an arrangement of machines, equipment, and workers in which work passes from operation to operation in direct line until the product is assembled (put together)
> (649) *autonomy*: self-directing freedom
> (649) *goaded*: urged into action
> (649) *reads like a corporate Who's Who*: a listing of brief biographical sketches of famous people in a particular field
> (649) *simulated*: pretend, not real
> (650) *absenteeism*: not being at work or school when expected to be
> (650) *meshed*: combined
> (650) *sabotage*: destruction of an employer's property, or the hindering (slowing down) of manufacturing by discontented workers
> (651) *intrinsically*: belonging to the essential nature of a thing
> (652) *feedback*: evaluation, corrective information
> (652) *muddled*: confused
> (653) *"buzz words"*: important-sounding, usually technical words often of little meaning used chiefly to impress
> (653) *give me a hand*: help me

(653) *trendy*: fashionable

(654) *digressing*: talking about subjects not related to the current topic

(654) *dispute*: disagreement

(654) *impersonal*: without an emotional connection

(654) *jargon*: technical language of a special activity or group

(654) *lingo*: special vocabulary of a particular field of interest

(654) *servile*: submissive

(654) *stilted*: artificial, stiff or unnatural

Module 17.2 Environmental Psychology (pp. 656-666)

(656) *proxemics*: study of the spatial separation that individuals maintain around themselves

(658) *saving a place at a theater or beach*: keeping a place available for someone who will be coming at a later time

(658) *graffiti*: writings or drawings made on some public surface

(658) *vandalism*: willful or malicious destruction of public or private property

(659) *callousness*: feeling no sympathy for others

(659) *ghettos*: areas of a city where members of a minority group live

(659) *pathological*: abnormal, unhealthy

(659) *rampant*: widespread

(660) *fending off*: keeping away, repelling

(662) *squandered*: wasted

(663) *hunger for*: desire for

(663) *sustainable*: able to be used, such as a resource, but not used up completely

(665) *a dorm hall can be quite a "zoo"*: place characterized by crowding, confusion, or unrestrained behavior

(665) *they "vahnted to be alone"*: Greta Garbo, a famous Swedish film star, was known for valuing her privacy; in her accented English, "want" sounded like "vahnt"

(665) *truancy*: staying out of school without permission

Module 17.3 The Psychology of Law and Sports (pp. 667-672)

(667) *arbitration*: the hearing of a case by an arbiter, or person who has the power to decide

(667) *inadmissible evidence*: not allowable in court

(667) *quirks*: strange or peculiar traits

(667) *suspend*: withhold

(667) *swindling*: stealing from an unsuspecting person

(668) *indifferent*: without interest or caring

(668) *O.J. Simpson*: former professional football player accused and acquitted of his ex-wife's murder

(669) *conditioning*: preparation

(669) *one-winner mentality*: the idea that there is only one winner in any competition and everyone else is a loser

(669) *enhance*: improving in quality

(669) *Menendez brothers*: two brothers of a wealthy family accused of murdering their parents

(669) *net effect*: result

(669) *personality profiles*: types

(669) *William Kennedy Smith*: a nephew of President John Kennedy who was accused and later acquitted of rape

(670) *homespun coaching methods*: self-taught

(670) *astray*: off target

(670) *bull's-eye*: the center of a target

(670) *marksmanship*: skilled shooting at a target

(670) *optimal*: best

(670) *prone*: lying down

(670) *set their sights on*: focus on

(671) *choking*: losing concentration that affects performance at a critical moment

(671) *personal best*: an individual's best performance, usually athletic

(671) *trance*: a hypnotic or deeply meditative state

(672) *impartial*: without prior judgment or bias

Module 17.4 PSYCHOLOGY IN ACTION: Space Psychology: Life on the High Frontier (pp. 673-677)

(673) *aloft*: above, in space

(673) *monotony*: sameness

(674) *alleviate*: reduce

(674) *antidote*: remedy or cure

(674) *apathetic*: having little or no interest

(674) *gagged*: choked

(674) *repulsed*: disgusted or sickened

(675) *dazzling*: very bright and beautiful

APPENDIX

Behavioral Statistics

The number of the page in the text where the idiom, word, phrase, or name can be found is shown in parentheses. The term or phrase is shown *in italics*. Where necessary for clarity, the phrase or sentence containing the term is given in parentheses. The meaning of the selected term or phrase follows the colon.

Statistics from "Heads" to "Tails" (p. 678)
(678) *game of chance*: gambling
(678) *recoup*: gain back, recover
(678) *skinned*: lose all of one's money
(678) *hypothetical*: made up, not real

Module A.1 Descriptive Statistics (pp. 680-685)
Module A.2 Inferential Statistics (pp. 686-690)

(680) *jumble*: random collection
(680) *hypnotic susceptibility*: easy to hypnotize
(680) *overall "picture"*: a large view of a situation
(681) *agitated*: nervous, excited
(683) *midterms*: college exams given half-way through a term
(686) *fluctuations*: movements up and down
(686) *detecting*: observing
(686) *socioeconomic*: one's level of income, education, and occupational status
(681) *agitated*: nervous, excited